Understanding Creativity

by

Jane Piirto, Ph.D.

Scottsdale, Arizona
Great Potential Press, Inc.
2004

Understanding Creativity

Copy Editor: Jen Ault Rosso
Indexer: Lisa Rivero
Cover Design/Layout: ATG Productions, Phoenix, AZ
Interior Design/Layout: The Printed Page, Phoenix, AZ

Published by
Gifted Unlimited, LLC
12340 U.S. Hwy. 42 #453
Goshen, KY 40026
502-715-6306
www.giftedunlimitedllc.com

Printed and bound in the United States of America
08 07 06 05 04   6 5 4 3 2 1

Library of Congress Cataloging-in-Publication Data

Piirto, Jane, 1941-
  Understanding creativity / by Jane Piirto.
      p. cm.
Rev. ed. of: Understanding those who create. 2nd ed. 1998.
Includes bibliographical references and index.
  ISBN 0-910707-58-8
  ISBN 0-910707-59-6 (pbk.)
1. Creative ability. I. Piirto, Jane, 1941- Understanding those who create. II. Title.
  BF408.P87 2004
  153.3'5—dc22
                              2003019982

To my granddaughter Danielle
whose creative spirit and laughter guide me

Contents

List of Tables and Figures

Acknowledgments

First and foremost, I would like to acknowledge F. Christopher Reynolds, with whom I talked over most of these changes and who advised me, patiently listening to me read from the new stuff. He knew more than anyone what needed to be done, as he has been teaching from the book for the past eight years. He is my book friend. I responded to his suggestions not only with my intellectual soul, but also with my poetic soul. Thank you, cher ami. Thank you also to Diane Montgomery, Jennifer Allen, and Michael Piechowski, who also discussed the changes with me.

Thank you to reviewers of the second edition who were uniformly kind and positive: Dean Keith Simonton, Warren Brodsky, Sandra Warren, and Francis Cartier. Thank you to Igor Kusyszyn and his Canadian students, who were helpful in their suggestions and comments over the years. Thank you to those who sent me e-mails, letters, and cards telling me how this book has changed your life and your way of looking at things.

Thank you to the reference librarians at Ashland University and to my students here and at workshops I have conducted. Thank you to editors Janet Gore, Lisa Rivero, and Jen Ault Rosso, whose comments and suggestions were helpful. Thanks to Great Potential Press for encouraging me to write an update. Thank you to my creative mother, to my sisters and their families, and to my creative children.

Preface

They're a mystery, those creative kids. We want to understand them. They might not do their homework. They might not obey. They might get so involved in their projects outside of school that the school calls them underachievers. The family might be in turmoil, and they have to raise themselves—and do, somehow, but with lifelong scars that are subsumed to their struggle to achieve in the domain they have chosen. They seem smart but won't conform. They might wear odd clothes, read odd books, stick around with odd people, hang around at the corner or the roller rink. How do we figure them out? Why won't they do what we tell them to? This book is dedicated to them, and to the adults they become.

This book, formerly called *Understanding Those Who Create,* has been retitled, *Understanding Creativity,* as the revisions have been substantial.

For this version I collected about 500 articles and books published since the last edition, sifted through them, read them, and distilled them into a synthesis.

I've reorganized the book at the suggestion of readers. I've included the course taught here at Ashland University as I and my colleagues have developed it over the years. Perhaps there are some exercises you might want to try with a class or alone.

I've reorganized the creativity domain chapters in the middle section, using my Piirto Pyramid of Talent Development as an organizational frame. I've added a short chapter with the Piirto Pyramid, as an introduction to Section III.

My findings about the paths of creative people by domain are not often referenced but certainly bear looking at. My desk, couch, tables, have piled up again and again, with biographies and studies. I look for themes. I read and read. I try to illustrate with anecdotes from real creative lives. By now, the patterns that I intuited back in 1992 are not so intuitive, but rather somewhat predictable. To confirm what I've found, my undergraduate and graduate students have done about a thousand biographical studies in these years, and they have found that, for the most part, the patterns in the lives of people in domains are rather credible.

I've tried to make the book accessible, but still full of information you might want to know. Enjoy!

Jane Piirto, Ph.D.
www.ashland.edu/~jpiirto
September 2003

Katherine Miller had just been hired to teach in a special program for gifted, talented, and creative children in fourth, fifth, and sixth grade. Her new superintendent had received an announcement for the state convention for teachers of the talented, and he told Katherine that he would pay her way to go so she could learn what she was supposed to teach.

Katherine hadn't learned anything about talented children in her under-graduate education courses, though she had taken one course in the education of other special education children, so she had gone to the state university library in a town nearby to do some reading for her interview. She memorized the catego-ries of the talented children that her state served. Among these were "creative" children. Katherine was not sure what creativity was, and she was even less sure who "creative" children were. Were they the ones who colored outside the lines? Were they the ones who looked a little weird? She stepped into the large ballroom of the hotel where the convention was being held, took a cup of coffee, and sat down at a table with others to hear the first keynote speaker.

The conference organizer introduced the speaker as one of the leading experts on creativity. "Oh good," Katherine thought as she settled in to listen. The speaker told a joke or two—he was a little mussed, his hair caught into a fashionable ponytail, his cowboy boots and jeans in sharp contrast to his blazer and striped tie. He spoke with a microphone snapped to that tie, and his voice reverberated throughout the ballroom. Katherine had not expected so many people to be here. There were almost a thousand people! Were all of them educa-tors of the gifted and talented?

Words and images bloomed behind him on the giant screen. There were diagrams and curves and arrows and dots and lists. He illustrated his points with cartoons. There was a list of tests, also, but Katherine couldn't imagine how you could have a test for creativity.

Well, he must know. She scanned the program as he spoke, and she under-lined all of the sessions that were about creativity. If he was a keynote speaker and the topic was creativity, obviously she was supposed to know something about creativity. This would be her main emphasis at this convention. She col-lected the handouts of the dots and diagrams and psychological terms and hurried down the hallway of the hotel convention wing to a small room where the next workshop session was being held.

There, with a pitcher of ice water and two glasses, behind a table with a podium, a microphone, a smaller screen, were two middle-aged women. They were local gifted education coordinators in a faraway corner of the state, and they were going to talk about how to enhance creativity in elementary school

*children. They also had many visual aids, blooming like flowers on the confer-
ence room wall, and in addition, they asked the group to play some simple
creativity games. It was fun, and everyone relaxed. But Katherine was getting
worried. The coordinators were very good speakers, and they were using words
like "fluency" and "flexibility" and "elaboration," and they talked about creativity as if it were "problem-solving."*

*Well, they must know, Katharine thought, for they have been in this field
a lot longer than I have. In the back of her mind, however, she thought that creativity was a little bit more than games and generating alternative solutions to a
sample problem. But Katherine followed her plan, and that day and the next
she attended seven more sessions in which "creativity" was part of the title of the
session. By Friday evening, she was exhausted, and she had a briefcase full of sta-
pled handouts with dots and arrows and curves and diagrams and key words
highlighted with bullets. She had played games and had practiced techniques.
She had packets of ideas for lessons. But she still didn't know what creativity
was. Oh well, she'd think about it next week.*

*On Saturday, she and her fiancé, Brad, a computer consultant who had
been an infamous hacker during his high school and college years, were going to
spend the weekend at a retreat at a camp in the woods about 50 miles away.
They were going to attend a workshop in transformational empowerment. Brad
was really into nature and preserving the environment, as well as the New Age,
and he wanted Katherine to appreciate the mystery and beauty of inner contemplation. This was the third session they had been to. The sessions were held once
a month.*

*Katherine had been raised in her family's traditional Protestant church,
and her mother was not very pleased that she was attending these workshops. "I
don't want you to be influenced by a cult," her mother said.*

*"Mother!" Katherine responded. "We just do meditation and visualiza-
tion and relaxation, and we probe our inner selves. Brad wants us to take our
place to save the earth, and in order to save the earth, we first have to understand our inner selves. Why don't you come sometime? I feel very creative when I
visualize and meditate. You will, too. We do that, and then we write for a
while, or draw, or share. We want to be the best that we can be. It's like when
you went to that church retreat for a weekend and took that intensive journal-
writing workshop a few years ago. Remember?" Katherine realized she'd used
that word—"creative"—again.*

*As she and Brad drove to the camp, she sat silently, thinking about the
teachers' conference and thinking about how wonderful she always felt when she*

3

and Brad sat with the group and meditated. Then she remembered her high school track coach who had asked the girls to visualize themselves running the track before they went into competition. Was this "creativity," too, just as much as the black-line lessons she'd collected at the conference to use with her students at her new job?

She knew she had a lot to learn, but she felt good about it, and though she was a little confused, she knew she would sort it all out sooner or later.

Chapter 1
Making Sense of Creativity

The secret at the heart of all creative activity has something to do with our desire to complete a work, to impose perfection upon it, so that, hammered out of profane materials, it becomes sacred: Which is to say, no longer merely personal.
—Joyce Carol Oates

Creativity is fashionable these days. Everyone uses the word. Yet creativity is confusing. By late 2002, the term was used in more than 15,500 references to titles of scholarly books and articles. The ERIC Clearinghouse showed 5,281 references on creativity and education from 1966 to 2002. The Psych Info database had 8,500 references, including 1,900 doctoral dissertations in the arts, psychology, business, and education, as well as 320 books. The Modern Language Association database had 1,500 references; Applied Science and Technology had 450; Art and Architecture had 1,250; Humanities Abstracts had 850.

Amazon.com listed 1,885 books with "creativity" in the title. There were books on creativity in business, creativity in psychology, creativity for parents, creativity and spirituality, creativity and teaching, creativity and aging, creativity and the arts, creativity and the sciences, creativity and mathematics, creativity and problem solving, creativity and problem finding, creativity and...and...and...100 hints, 200 activities, 400 ideas, 12 steps. Everyone claims to be an expert. How does one make sense of it all?

This interest in creativity is a truly postmodern perplexity, for little is tangible, all is one, one is many, everything is true, and nothing is true. However, few can get an authoritative and comprehensive handle on creativity. The terms *chaos*, *fracture*, and *split* fit the creativity enterprise well.

As musician Matt Callahan said, "Something as porous as creativity defies definition, resists quantification and refuses access to those who seek to possess it like a Thing."

The purpose of this book is to help you, the reader, begin to appreciate creativity's complexity. Let's start at the beginning.

The Term "Creativity"

The root of the words "create" and "creativity" comes from the Latin *creâtus* and *creâre*, meaning "to make or produce," or literally, "to grow." The word also comes from the Old French base *kere*, and the Latin *crescere* and *creber*. The Roman goddess of the earth, Ceres, is an example, as is the Italian corn goddess, Cereris. Creativity as a word has roots in the earth. Other words with these same roots are *cereal, crescent, creature, concrete, crescendo, decrease, increase,* and *recruit*.

"Creativity," a relatively new noun, came into parlance much as have the verbs "prioritize" and "network" and the noun, "infrastructure"— words invented because there was a need for them. The word does not appear in the 1971 *Oxford English Dictionary,* the standard for the English language. It does appear in the 1964 *Funk and Wagnalls Standard Dictionary, International Edition,* published in the United States, but not in the 1964 College Edition of the *American Heritage Dictionary of the American Language.* By 1988, Webster's Dictionary stated that creativity is "creative ability; artistic or intellectual inventiveness." That creativity is an *ability* has been an assumption made by educators since the early 1950s. The noun "creativity" seems to have origins in psychology. The first two mentions I could find were these: (1) J. P. Guilford used the word as the title of a speech to the American Psychological Association in 1950, and (2) in 1953, Morris L. Stein published an article in the *Journal of Psychology* called "Creativity and Culture."

The Dictionary of Developmental and Educational Psychology in 1986 defines creativity as "man's capacity to produce new ideas, insights, inventions or artistic objects, which are accepted of being of social, spiritual, aesthetic, scientific, or technological value." The inclusion of an aspect of *social utility* for the product of the creator's imagination is vital here.

To be "creative" is to be "originative." *Originative* implies making something new. *To be creative, then, is to make something new or novel.* The word "novelty" appears and reappears in numerous definitions of creativity. By 1999, creativity had been so imbued into the culture that a two-volume

Encyclopedia of Creativity (1999) was published. Topics ranged from the esoteric to the idiosyncratic. Each was written by a scholar in the field. I myself wrote two entries, one on Poetry, and one on Synchronicity. Table 1.1 contains the complete list of the topics.

Table 1.1: Topics in the 1999 *Encyclopedia of Creativity*
(Eds. Mark Runco and Steven Pritzker)

Acting, Adaptation and Creativity, Advertising, Affective Disorders, Aging, Alcohol and Creativity, Altered and Transitional States, Analogies, Architecture, Modern Western, Archival Investigation, Art and Aesthetics, Art and Artists, Articulation, Artificial Intelligence, Associative Theory, Attention, Attribution and Creativity, Autonomy and Independence, Barriers to Creativity and Creative Attitudes, Behavioral Approaches to Creativity, Alexander Graham Bell, Birth Order, Brain Biology and Brain Functioning, Brain and the Creative Act, Brainstorming, Brontë Sisters, Business Strategy, Lewis Carroll, Paul Cézanne, Chaos Theory and Creativity, Cognitive Style and Creativity, Collaboration and Competition, Componential Models, Computer Programs, Concepts of Creativity: A History, Conditions and Settings/ Environment, Conformity, Consensual Assessment, Consistency of Creativity across the Life Span, Contrarianism, Conventionality, Corporate Culture, Counseling, Creative Climate, Creative Products, Creativity in the Future, Creativity in the Moral Domain, Creatology, Crime and Creativity, Critical Thinking, Cross-Cultural Differences, Marie Curie, Dance and Creativity, Dark Side of Creativity, Charles Darwin, Leonardo da Vinci, Definitions of Creativity, Design, Developmental Trends in Creative Abilities and Potentials, Deviance, Dialectical Thinking: Implications for Creative Thinking, Isak Dinesen, Discovery, Distribution of Creativity, Divergent Thinking, Diversity, Cultural, Domains of Creativity, Dreams and Creativity, Drugs and Creativity, Eccentricity, Economic Perspective on Creativity, Education, Albert Einstein, Eminence, Emotion/Affect, Enhancement of Creativity, Ensemble of Metaphor, Everyday Creativity, Evolving Systems Approach, Expertise, Families and Creativity, Five-Part Typology, Fixation, Flexibility, Four Ps of Creativity, Fourth Grade Slump, Sigmund Freud, Gender Differences, Generativity Theory, Genetics, Giftedness and Creativity, Group Creativity, Guilford's View, Handwriting and Creativity, Heuristics, Historiometry, History and Creativity, Homospatial Process, Humane Creativity, Humor, Imagery, Imagination, Implicit Theories, Improvisation, Incubation, Innovation, Insight, Institute of Personality Assessment and Research, Intelligence, Intuition, Invention, Janusian Process, Jungian Theory, Knowledge, Hans Adolf Krebs, Leadership, Learning Styles, Logic and Reasoning, Longitudinal Studies, Mad Genius Controversy, Marginality, Matthew Effects, Memory and Creativity, Metacognition, Metaphors, Mindfulness, Misjudgment, Mood, Motivation/Drive, Multiple Discovery, Multiple Intelligences, Music, Novelty, Georgia O'Keeffe, Old Age Style, Organizations Interested in Creativity, Overexcitabilities, Paradigm Shifts, Perceptgenesis, Perception and Creativity, Personality, Perspectives, Fernando Pessoa, Jean Piaget, Sylvia Plath, Play, Poetry, Political Science and Creativity, Postmodernism and Creativity, Proactive Creativity, Problem Finding, Problem Solving, Prodigies, Productivity and Age, Programs and Courses in Creativity, Psycholinguistics, Quantum Theory of Creativity, Schizophrenia, Robert Schumann, Science, Self-Actualization, Self Processes and Creativity, Serendipity, Anne Sexton, William Shakespeare, George Bernard Shaw, Split Brains: Interhemispheric Exchange in Creativity, Sports and Creativity, Suicide, Synchronicity, Synesthesia, Systems Approach, Tactics and Strategies for Creativity, Rbindranath Tagore, Talent and Creativity, Teaching Creativity, Teams, Television and Creativity, Time, Henri de Toulouse-Lautrec, Unconscious, Vincent van Gogh, Lev Semenovich Vygotsky, Women and Creativity, Virginia Woolf, William Wordsworth, Orville and Wilbur Wright, Writing and Creativity, Zeitgeist

---

The encyclopedia's two volumes are the latest and most comprehensive summary of creativity research and thought. An eminent panel of advisers formed its editorial board, including Howard Gardner, Ravenna Helson, Ruth Richards, Tudor Rickards, Dean Keith Simonton, and Robert J. Sternberg. The encyclopedia should stand for quite a while as a picture of creativity and creativity research at the end of the twentieth century, and it is available in the reference shelves of university libraries.

Psychological, Psychoanalytic, Philosophic, and Religious Overtones

Psychologists, in fact, seem to have cornered the market in the study of creativity, and when one searches for the word "creativity" at dot.com booksellers, psychologist Robert Sternberg's *Handbook of Creativity* pops up first. But it seems that the philosophers, the psychoanalysts, and even the theologians also have vested interests. Freud, founder of psychoanalysis, said that the source of creativity is "the sublimation of energy into acceptable and fruitful channels." Note his use of the agricultural word "fruitful" and the word "channels," a word with roots in water, the source of life. Several philosophers have held that creativity is what is common to both man and God. Creativity is what is good in humans, and this is what brings humans into communion with God.

The linking of creativity to divinity is truly an ancient notion that goes back even farther than the Greeks, who called poetry "divine madness." To relate "creativity" to "creation" expands the term. To Judeao Christians, God created the world in seven days. He filled the void. As we shall see, this identification of creativity with spiritual oneness with God is quite common in considering the creative process. In *Creative Mythology*, Joseph Campbell traced the history of the focus of creative thought within the world's religions, which was always the search for the elemental, the true, the archetypal.

The original connections of creativity with divinity, and with agricultural growth, with newness, and with intuition, still resonate today. For example, the metaphor of the seed is often used by educators when they speak of enhancing creativity in children. Allow them to grow, we say. Nurture them. Don't stifle them. The natural child is popularly thought to be very creative. The school, the family, and the society "ruin" the natural child's creativity by civilizing the child. Thus, creativity dies. This common metaphor is part of American folklore.

Creativity and Psychology

Creativity has been a topic of discussion and of research in the domain of psychology for approximately 50 years. Psychology, the scientific study of mental operations and behavior, asks: *What makes people creative? How can creativity be measured? How can creativity be enhanced? What can we learn from creative adults that will help us raise more creative children? Is creativity an aptitude? Is creativity an ability? Is creativity a domain? Is creativity acquired? Is creativity innate? What happens in the mind while a person is creating? What are the conditions for creative production? What inhibits creative production? What does the social setting contribute to creativity? Is creativity a solitary or community activity?* All of these and more are questions that psychologists have sought to study with regard to creativity.

Psychology has several threads of research into creativity. Sternberg and Lubart in the *Handbook of Creativity* in 1999 divided these threads into: (1) mystical approaches (such as those of Jung, Plato, and the anecdotes of various creators); (2) pragmatic approaches (such as those of de Bono, Osborn, and von Oech); (3) psychodynamic approaches (such as those of Freud, Kris, Rothenberg, and Weisberg); (4) psychometric approaches (such as those of Guilford and Torrance); (5) cognitive approaches (such as those of Gardner, Ward, and Perkins); (6) social-personality approaches (such as those of Barron, MacKinnon and Gough); and (7) confluence approaches (such as those of Sternberg, Csikszentmihalyi, Amabile, and Lubart).

This next section divides the psychological approaches into psychometric, developmental, cognitive, educational, humanistic, and positive.

Psychometric Approaches

In 1950, J. P. Guilford, who was then President of the American Psychological Association (APA), gave a speech that is often called the beginning of the modern interest in creativity as a measurable phenomenon. Guilford is the developer of a theory called The Structure of Intellect, sometimes called the SI, in which he theorized that there are 120 kinds of measurable intelligence. (Later, a student of his, Mary Meeker, in the mid-1970s, took 26 of his tests and called them the SOI.) In *The Nature of Human Intelligence*, Guilford "proved" that one could measure divergent production. In his 1950 speech to the APA, Guilford called for research on two questions: (1) how to find the promise of creativity in our children; and

(2) how to enhance the development of the creative personality. In this address, he called for the analysis of several factors of what is called divergent production.

Here are Guilford's original terms that have gained such currency in the world of creativity enhancement: (1) Fluency; (2) Novelty; (3) Flexibility; (4) Synthesizing ability; (5) Analyzing ability; (6) Reorganization or redefinition of already existing ideas; (7) Degree of complexity; and (8) Evaluation. The trouble that has come from this, in my opinion, is that divergent production has been confused with creativity. Divergent production can be measured easily, but is it creativity?

J. P. Guilford differentiated between "convergent" intellect and "divergent" intellect. "Convergent" intellect is a way of thinking that emphasizes remembering what is known, being able to learn what exists, and being able to save that information in one's brain. "Divergent" intellect is a mode of cognition that emphasizes the revision of what is already known, of exploring what would be known, and of building new information. People who prefer the "convergent" mode of intellect supposedly tend to do what is expected of them, while those who prefer the "divergent" mode of intellect supposedly tend to take risks and to speculate.

Among the most frequently cited studies that took divergent and convergent intellect into account were one by Getzels and Jackson, and one by Wallach and Kogan. These individuals were trying to quantify creativity, to make tests of creativity by studying sixth through twelfth graders in a private school in Illinois. The Getzels and Jackson study was widely interpreted to mean that those with high creative potential need a certain *threshold of intelligence*, but not necessarily the highest intelligence. By 1971, Wallach said that the most fruitful researches would probably be into the areas of creativity within domains. This comment has resonance today, as many researchers are studying creativity with reference to domains of talent, knowledge, and practice. James Kaufman and John Baer have recently edited a book on creativity within domains, *Faces of the Muse* (in which I wrote a chapter on the creative process in poets).

Torrance's Tests

E. P. Torrance took Guilford seriously and set out to create and validate tests that would identify creative potential. By the 1970s, his *Torrance Tests of Creative Thinking* (TTCT) began to be widely used in schools. These tests were similar to the Guilford tests of divergent production, and they tested fluency, flexibility, and the like. The higher the score, the more potentially creative the child was. In 2001, Millar published a book of case studies following up on the students who were studied in 1958, calling those who had creative accomplishments "beyonders." In 2002, Torrance published *The Manifesto*, a summary of his life's work—the implications of creativity for career planning.

In attempting to show that creative potential can be identified with paper and pencil tests of divergent thinking, these researchers began a controversial practice that still continues today. Mainstream educators have continued to attempt to identify creative potential by calling creative potential a *type* of giftedness, rather than a necessary aspect of *all* giftedness. This separation of creativity and intelligence has led to much confusion, which I describe next.

The Federal Definitions

Current U.S. and Canadian school definitions of creative potential are variations of the 1972 Marland Report, in which giftedness takes—or can be found in—six forms. These are: (1) superior cognitive ability; (2) specific academic ability; (3) creativity; (4) leadership ability; (5) visual and performing arts ability; and (6) psychomotor ability. Divergent production was operationalized and carried into the public schools in the form of various tests, especially the *Torrance Tests of Creative Thinking*. The wider definitions of creativity discussed at the beginning of the chapter became narrower definitions emphasizing a cognitive view, a view that was able to be tested with paper and pencil tests so that students could enter into gifted programs as "creatively gifted."

The Tangling of Giftedness and Creativity

Education is an important factor in the development of creativity. When Marland postulated that one of the forms of giftedness is "creativity," schools were presented with a quandary. How would they find and serve people who have so-called *creative* giftedness? Taking the research on the threshold effect—that people who score highest on divergent production tests often have above-average IQs—schools began to define creativity operationally. First the child had to score above average on an IQ test. Second, the child had to score high on some other test that purportedly "measured" creativity. Most popular of these were checklists and divergent production tests. (Note: These tests and checklists are discussed in Chapter 12.)

In 1978, Joseph Renzulli came up with a definition of giftedness which said that a gifted person had three characteristics: above average intelligence, creativity, and task commitment. He pictured these components as overlapping circles, a Venn diagram. If one of the components is missing, the person is presumably not gifted. Renzulli, the only current theorist whose work has been adopted by the public schools to any great degree, insists that the gifted person must have "creativity" and not simply a high IQ. Gardner's theory of multiple intelligences says that creativity is possible within each intelligence. Practicality suggests that creativity should be codified into numbers, percentiles, or ranks, but this is difficult, for the working definition of creativity is not standardized. For schools to say that "creative potential" is *measurably* separate from having academic ability or high academic achievement is the tough part. What does that mean?

Marland's 1972 federal definition also separated out the visual and performing arts and the athletic as being separate kinds of giftedness. That visual and performing arts and athletic giftedness—being gifted in painting, drawing, acting, music, dance, sculpture, sports, and the like, and intellectual giftedness—are different from creative giftedness is sometimes difficult to understand. Aren't brainy scientists creative? Aren't verbal writers creative? Aren't visual artists creative? Aren't actors creative? Aren't dancers creative? Aren't musicians creative? Aren't athletes creative?

The inclusion of creativity as a separate *type* of giftedness in Marland's definition, rather than *as* giftedness has posed many problems for contemporary educators, as they have struggled to make the distinctions between high IQ and creative potential, as they have wrestled with thresholds of test scores and measures of ability, as they have tried to meet demands that they be accountable, when accountability is defined as numerical outcomes. Psychologist R. Hoge said that educators have misused the tests used to identify giftedness and that, instead, the tests have become in themselves the definitions of giftedness. This could also be said to be true for creativity, at least in some states, where the students with so-called "creative potential" have scored high on paper and pencil tests and checklists in order to be called *creative*.

In 1992, a new federal report, called *National Excellence: A Case for Developing America's Talent*, was published. The new definition proposed that giftedness—or talent—occurs in all groups across all cultures and is not necessarily in the test scores, but in a person's "high performance capability" in the intellectual, in the *creative*, and in the artistic realms [italics

12

added]. The importance of environmental influence upon a person is apparent in this definition. Here, in this 1992 attempt to define the role of schools in nurturing talent, we see again that the intellectual, the creative, and the artistic are separated. This seems to imply that the intellectual is not creative, the creative is not intellectual, the artistic is not intellectual or creative. Common sense says that both the intellectual and the artistically talented are creative, and that creative people can be both intellectual and artistic. People disparage the psychometric or testing approach, but it is still alive and well in America's schools.

Developmental Psychology

Developmental psychologists seek to understand the stages in the development of the creative person. Creativity is realized in the process of a lifetime in various stages, through a network of enterprises by a predictable developmental path. Stage theory assumes that one must pass through a lower stage in order to reach a higher stage, and thus it is hierarchical. One way to figure out what the stages are is to do a developmental case study.

Gruber's "Darwin"

One of the notable case studies is Gruber's 1974 study of Darwin. Gruber has attempted to relate the psychological and personal development of various creative people with their milieu—the surroundings in which they find themselves. Gruber called this "the evolving systems theory." Over the years, he has elaborated on this, discussing facets such as networks of enterprise, uniqueness, pluralism, insight, and evolving belief systems. Especially important to the systems that creators create are the "ensembles of metaphors" they make to describe their discoveries. Through metaphor, they symbolize their thoughts, making the abstract visual or literary. Examples are William James' "*stream* of consciousness"; Stephen Tolman's "mind as *maze* and mind as *map*"; or Charles Darwin's "*tree* of life." Creative people often, during their youth, make initial sketches of their later works as a type of foreshadowing. Creativity is the work of a lifetime, and not a moment of "Aha!" It is a process of insight and motivation and not a flash of lightning.

The case study method yields knowledge of the moments of insight creators have had. Highly creative people may have as many as two insights a day while working on a creative project. This would lead to about 5,000 insights during a project that takes 10 years. Gruber and his colleagues (1999) studied Benjamin Franklin, Charles Darwin, William James, John Locke,

Dorothy Richardson, and others in attempting to discover how these thinkers reached their insights.

For example, researchers have found that creative people repeat their discoveries in different varieties that reveal minute differences. Gruber and his colleagues have found that creative people have a "network of enterprises"—that is, they work on many related things at once. Writers, for example, often write poems, stories, novels, articles, and scholarly books simultaneously.

Feldman's "Gambit"

Feldman and Goldsmith (1986) provided another developmental approach to understanding creativity. They studied extreme cases, prodigies—children who had adult achievement in a domain before the age of 10—in order to understand how ability develops. By studying extraordinary talent in young people, Feldman and Goldsmith said that the existence of such prodigies helps us understand rapid human development as well as to understand Gruber's assertion that the development of creativity has evolutionary implications.

Feldman called creativity "a special form of development that yields a product that is new and valuable not only to an individual but also to a field." He used the word "transformations" to describe these products. The creative person works within a domain within a field, and stretches the knowledge of that domain within that field. For example, a poet works within the poetry domain within the literature field; a painter works within the visual arts field in a domain called painting.

Changing the World, by Feldman, Csikszentmihalyi, and Gardner, diagrammed a developmental theory of creativity, emphasizing that the *truly* creative contribution is made only when the field is transformed. For example, the invention of penicillin transformed the field of medicine. They proposed a framework for studying creativity that takes into account the individual, the field, and the domain. Feldman called creativity the "transformational imperative," meaning that the person is innately impelled to "change reality outside the bounds of stable, ordered experience." Creative achievement is on a continuum from the universal to the specific, and the products of the person who creates are also on this continuum. But first, the person who is creating must master the domain, must acquire expertise.

Expertise

Expertise is defined by Eriksson and Lehmann as "reliable superior performance in a domain." Every field and domain of knowledge in which creativity can be demonstrated has novice levels, apprenticeship levels, expert levels, and special jargons. People at the expert levels use special methods distinct to the field in which the creativity is demonstrated. Empirical research is characteristic of the sciences; practical work is characteristic of the arts. Those who become experts transform the field or domain and then extend its boundaries. They do this with the help of master teachers. Few reach expert levels without having been taught. Often, families relocate in order that their young potential star can work with a proven master. This is especially true in music, chess, and in certain sports such as gymnastics, tennis, and ice-skating. Even drum and bugle corps attract students willing to move to perform. The Cavaliers of Illinois are an example; at their annual auditions, 500 teenage snare drummers from all over the world compete for fewer than five positions. The master coaches and teachers have codified the knowledge necessary for mastering the domain. The students then incrementally spend more and more time in deliberate practice.

High intelligence is not necessary for many fields of expertise; rather, practice and experience are. A 10 year rule has been proposed—that is, any person must have been working in a domain for a minimum of 10 years in order to achieve international levels of recognition. The reason that one gets bored at professional sports events is that the performances are so alike—those who have reached the stage of professional excellence have modified, codified, and intensified their games to the point where the only variation comes from mistakes. The more mistakes, the less expert the performance is. Thus, accident reaches a state of low occurrence.

What is the relationship of creativity to the acquisition of expertise? Isn't creativity free, free-form, spontaneous, improvisational, and without rules? Well, yes, and no. In expertise theory, creativity comes from redefining the field through knowing where the holes are in any domain. People don't make genuine contributions to a domain unless they have mastered the domain. Extensive study and practice are necessary. What differentiates experts who don't move the domain from those who do?

Erikson's "Stages"

Joan Erikson worked with her husband Erik, who described the psychosocial stages of life that every education or developmental psychology major has memorized: (1) Trust vs. Mistrust; (2) Autonomy vs. Shame; (3) Initiative vs. Guilt; (4) Industry vs. Inferiority; (5) Identity vs. Role Diffusion; (6) Intimacy vs. Isolation; (7) Generativity vs. Stagnation; (8) Integrity vs. Despair. Joan subsequently described "generativity" and "integrity" in the final two stages as being enhanced by a person's creative endeavors. She said that wisdom, wonder, awe, and reverence are gained through being creative. Her elaboration of her husband's stage theory provided needed amplification of the last stages, the adult stages of life.

Evolutionary Creativity

For the past several years, we have seen the trend, in all psychological research, toward evolutionary explanations for many phenomena. Developmental theory methodology explores the relationship between development and evolution. Another thread of developmentalism and cognition is the current biological/operant conditioning research. Researchers are no longer working within one specific field of psychology, but the behaviorists, the developmentalists, cognitive psychologists, and social psychologists all cross boundaries in their research.

Morgan, Morgan, and Toth noted, "many cognitive scientists, particularly those studying creativity and problem solving, embrace an evolutionary model of cognition that, minus some organismic language, bears a striking resemblance to operant accounts of complex human behavior." These authors assert that Skinnerism—i.e., behavioral conditioning—is not dead, only reframed. Many theorists note that truly innovative contributions to creativity theory by psychologists are by those who venture outside of the domains into which they have been socialized through their scientific education.

Domain experts such as Pfeiffer have traced the evolutionary paths of the arts and religions. Ornstein has traced the sources of human consciousness and thus human creativity through a synthesis of evolutionary theory and historical events. Studying creativity with a historical evolutionary view of the interaction of biology and culture yields insights that take into account the totality of human experience, according to Csikszentmihalyi in his 1993 work on evolution and creativity, *The Evolving Self.* Evolutionary creativity theory considers the Darwinian notions of natural selection, survival of the fittest, and the chance creation of anomalies.

Simonton in 1999 wrote *Origins of Genius: Darwinian Perspective on Creativity,* in which he proposed that "creative genius is Darwinian to its very core." He explicated the surprising connections between Darwinism and genius, with reference to cognition (how the brain creates), variation (the relationship between psychopathology and creativity), development (Is the genius more influenced by genes or environment?), products (the implications of productivity), and the presence of group phenomena such as kinship, birth order, race, gender, culture, niches, and social learning.

Social Psychology

Creative people have intrinsic motivation and are often aggressive in pursuing their creativity as they interact with the Zeitgeist, or milieu. The social psychologist looks at environmental influences on the creative person and studies such phenomena as motivation. A social psychological approach to creativity has been that of Albert, who focused on genius, continuing in the wake of Galton, Lombroso, Hollingworth, Terman, and Oden. Albert (1983) asserted that creative people begin the creative production early in life, are productive throughout life, and have certain experiences such as parental warmth. Theresa Amabile (1989) has made important contributions with her experiments utilizing practicing artists. She made a Venn diagram similar to Renzulli's, in which she described creativity as occurring when intrinsic motivation intersects with two kinds of skills: the skills required to master the domain, and the skills of creative production. In the late 1990s, she revised her intrinsic motivation theory to include certain kinds of extrinsic motivation as being important as well.

Csikszentmihalyi's "Big C" and "little c"

Mihalyi Csikszentmihalyi's own developmental path as a psychologist has taken him from collaboration with Getzels in a study of visual artists, to a study of talented teenagers, to interviews of several hundred persons known for transforming their domains. The "Big C" creative person is eminent, a person whose work is well known by people within the field and domain. The "little c" creative person is not. "Big C" Creativity is that which leads to a domain being changed. "Little c" creativity is that by which human beings lead their everyday lives, figuring out ways to prevent raccoons from tipping over the garbage can or ways to get to work in a shorter amount of time. In *Creativity* (1996), Csikszentmihalyi said, "creativity is any act, idea, or product that changes an existing domain, or that transforms an existing domain into a new one." Csikszentmihalyi is adamant in his insistence that creativity operates within a system that encompasses more than the cognitive, and that includes the milieu and the context.

17

Csikszentmihalyi and his colleagues have conducted several other studies investigating the notion of " flow," or a sense of timelessness while creating—using beepers on talented teenagers to interrupt them and ask what they are doing and when they create. This approach bleeds into the realm of cognitive psychology. They have also interviewed creative producers in the arts and the sciences, inquiring about their creative processes. Csikszentmihalyi's book *Creativity* details these studies.

Simonton's Work

Following upon Albert and the Goertzels, the social psychologist Dean Keith Simonton—beginning in the 1970s and continuing with an astonishing rate of books, studies, and chapters in handbooks—has shown also that creativity is the result of the work of a life. This lifetime has to encompass certain aspects of environment, depending on the type of creative product that the creator is making, including the social factors that impinge on the genius during the lifespan, from birth to grave.

Simonton built upon the work of Campbell (1960), who said that creativity can be measured by the total number of variations in quantity and quality that an individual can produce. Simonton quantified this by using a statistical technique he calls historiometry, which considers rates of information processing, age at career onset, developmental antecedents, and other phenomena such as lifetime productivity, the sheer quantity of output as compared to the quality of output, and what Simonton calls "the swan song phenomenon," which is an odd but notable increase in the quality and nature of a creator's output five years before death.

His deductions from the statistics generated by projections from these historiometric features of geniuses' lives are described throughout this book. In Simonton's view, creativity is a form of leadership—that is, the creator is a persuader. Creativity has often been viewed through the lens of process, product, or person; however, chance intervenes and makes the true creator a persuader. There are two types of genius—the intuitive and the analytical. Both are characterized by extreme productivity. The more works, the more the chance of influencing the domain and of assuming leadership in the domain. Some have accused Simonton of elitism in concentrating on eminent creators. He replied:

> *Identify the 10% who have contributed the most to some endeavor, whether it be songs, poems, paintings, patents, articles, items of legislation, battles, films, designs, or anything else. Count*

*up all the accomplishments that they have to their credit. Now
tally the contributions of the remaining 90% who struggled in the
same area of achievement. The first tally will equal or surpass the
second. Period.* (1995, pp. 419-420)

In 1999, Simonton proposed seven qualitative levels of creative attainment: (1) those whose creativity has impacted a domain and also the general culture—e.g., those whose "images grace t-shirts"—Einstein, Michelangelo, Mozart; (2) those whose creativity has impacted a domain but who are not known by people in the general culture—e.g., Juan Gris or Joseph Priestley; (3) those who tried to change a domain but who had only a minimal impact, or those with Warhol's "15 minutes of fame"; (4) those who tried to change a domain but who had no impact—e.g., scientists whose articles are never cited, poets who publish in many smaller magazines but who are never anthologized or who never win the big prizes; (5) those who created, but only for personal use—e.g., amateur inventors or poets; (6) those who did not create but who appreciated creative works—e.g., connoisseurs and critics; and (7) those who do not like anything new or different. Simonton's work continues to lead current thought in creativity studies.

Cognitive Psychology

The cognitive psychologist seeks to find out what happens in the mind while a person is creating. Creativity is insight, intuition, a process of selection, and the ability to adapt to novelty. Creative people who are successful find problems that enhance the domain. In their 1976 groundbreaking study of problem finding in visual artists, Getzels and Csikszentmihalyi thought that creativity was an attempt to reduce tension that may or may not be perceived consciously. The way artists did this was to seek problems that could be symbolically solved through human imagination. When an artist works, the conflict that the artist feels is changed within him- or herself into a problem. The artist "finds" a problem that will lead to a work of art. The work of art is the symbolic solution to that problem. This happens over and over again as the artist works. This study will be discussed in greater detail in Chapter 6.

Creative Cognition

"Creative cognition" is a term used by cognitive psychologists such as Thomas Ward, the editor of the *Journal of Creative Behavior.* These researchers seek to use psychological research methods in order to study the underlying cognitive means by which humans (and other animals) produce creative thought. They affirm the generativity of the human mind and assume that "the capacity for creative thought is the rule rather than the exception in human cognitive functioning." Although these researchers acknowledge the importance of factors such as "intrinsic motivation, situational contingencies, the timeliness of the idea, and the values that different cultures place on innovation" in creativity, they concentrate on the cognitive because "many non-cognitive factors achieve their impacts by way of their influence on cognitive functioning."

Cognitive psychologists have done controlled experiments on people's exploratory processes, pre-inventive structures, insight, extending concepts, recently activated knowledge, creative imagery, mental blocks, and conceptual combination. These researchers believe that studying creative cognition can resolve the quintessential conflicts about the complex construct of creativity such as whether creativity is goal-oriented or exploratory, whether creativity skills are domain-specific or universal, or whether creative insights are structured or unstructured. In 2001, Ward used a case study approach to illustrate these points in his explication of the writing process of fantasy writer Stephen Donaldson.

Gardner's "Frames"

Howard Gardner, in *Frames of Mind,* said that there are seven different intelligences. The intelligences are these: (1) Linguistic Intelligence; (2) Musical Intelligence; (3) Logical-Mathematical Intelligence; (4) Spatial Intelligence; (5) Bodily-Kinesthetic Intelligence; (6) Interpersonal Intelligence; and (7) Intrapersonal Intelligence. In late 1996, Gardner added another intelligence, that of the naturalist (such as John James Audubon, Charles Darwin, and others). In Gardner's theory, creativity is an aspect of each of these intelligences as they are perfected and developed, and not a separate intelligence or ability. Gardner asserted that creativity cannot take place without the odd interaction, or "asynchrony" of place, time, talent, and morality. There is tautness or strain "between intellectual and personality styles, and by a striking lack of fit between personality and domain, intelligence and field, and biological constitution and choice of career." He said that this pressure may be the impetus that causes a person to go off and make something new and creative.

Gardner has been exploring these "intelligences" domain by domain. He published case studies of geniuses in each of the seven intelligences under the title *Creating Minds*. Every one of his books has the word "mind" in the title to emphasize that he is speaking of the cognitive, that he is interested in what happens in the brain. His theories had great impact on public and private schools in the mid-1990s as teachers began to teach using the multiple intelligences. Gardner's definition of creativity is that a creative person "solves problems, fashions products, or poses new questions within a domain in a way that is initially considered to be unusual but is eventually accepted within a least one cultural group."

In *Creating Minds*, Gardner illustrated his theory of development by using the lives of seven creators—six men and one woman. Simply stated, Gardner's complex theory of the development of creative individuals takes into account three relationships: (1) between the creative child and the adult he or she becomes; (2) between the creative person and others; and (3) between the creative person and the work he or she does.

Gardner took a lifespan perspective emphasizing these interactions throughout the course of the eminent people's lives in the areas of cognition, personality, motivation, and interaction with the Zeitgeist. Each of the creators worked with the domain's unique symbol system in a way that changed the domain. Gardner also studied how the creators interacted with others in their field. One necessity in each of these cases was that there was some "fruitful asynchrony"—that is, something was not quite plumb, but rather askew, and this gave the creator a way to make something never before seen by the domain. In these studies, Gardner noticed that each creator had to make a Faustian bargain with the devil—all was not rosy between them and the world.

Feldman (2002), in a developmental case study, conjectured that Gardner himself is one of the most creative psychologists around. Feldman noted that, ironically, the domain Gardner changed was education and the field of psychometrics within psychology, and not his own major field of developmental psychology. Feldman theorized that Gardner was able to do this because he won the MacArthur "genius" award early in his work, in 1980, and this freed him from economic dependence, and from dependence upon not offending the big names in his field. Gardner also had powerful mentors and an outstanding ability to synthesize various fields' premises in order to come up with the eight criteria for each intelligence, a departure from the previous factor analysis method by which intelligence was defined.

Sternberg's Triarchies and Hierarchies, Investments, Propulsions, and Wisdom

Another contemporary psychologist cum cognitive scientist, Robert Sternberg, in *The Triarchic Mind*, named three types of intelligence: the creative, the analytic, and the practical. The creative includes the ability to adapt to what is novel or the ability to make something new. He called his theory "triarchic," insisting that each intelligent act incorporates creativity in insight, planning, research, and finally, doing the act. Like many contemporary psychologists and educators, Sternberg suggested that having a high IQ is not the main requirement for a successful life, but that other components are necessary. Again we are seeing the evolving idea that creativity is necessary for the development of talent. Sternberg focused on the everyday creativity that is exhibited when one leads an intelligent life. The six facets of creativity are these: (1) having creative intelligence; (2) having specific knowledge within the domain; (3) having a certain style of mind and (4) certain aspects of personality; (5) having motivation; and (6) having a nurturing environment. None of these is earth shaking or new.

By 1995, Sternberg and his colleague Lubart had published several variations on a theory of creativity called the "investment" theory, on which Lubart elaborated at a 1996 international conference in Vienna. Using the somewhat cute metaphor of the stock market, these two psychologists stated that the truly creative risk taker "invests" by trying to buy low and sell high—that is, "creatively insightful people need to invest themselves in their projects to yield the value added to the initial idea." In 2002, Sternberg, in an interview by Keane and Shaughnessy, said, "After working on the investment theory, I realized it did not tell the whole story," because the investment theory did not deal enough with the evolution of creative thinking.

By 2001, Sternberg, Kaufman, and Pretz had revised the investment theory to include a propulsion theory; they delineated eight different types of creative contributions that are possible within any given field of a domain. Four of these accept the current paradigms and attempt to extend them. These are (1) Replication, (2) Redefinition, (3) Forward incrementation, and (4) Advance forward incrementation. Three kinds of creative contributions reject current paradigms and attempt to replace them. These are (5) Redirection, (6) Reconstruction/redirection, and (7) Reinitiation.

The eighth kind of creativity is one that synthesizes the paradigms, and this is (8) Integration. Space does not permit further explanation of these ideas.

Educational Psychology

A popular 1960s song by Harry Chapin spoke about a child learning to make a flower just like everyone else's flower, meaning that as the child was socialized, forced to lose his innate creativity. Enhancing creativity and not just describing it or researching its cognitive or personality factors is the task of educational psychologists. The oldest creativity enhancement programs were general, talking about enhancing fluency, flexibility, and the like. A recent emphasis has been on creativity in domains. The first edition of this book, in 1992, had, like this edition, chapters on creativity in domains. Baer called creativity in domains task-specific and idiosyncratic to the domain, calling for creativity enhancement programs to modify their tasks to be specific to the domain. For example, brainstorming is a common creativity enhancement technique, but people in business can brainstorm about business-related problems; people writing a comedy show can brainstorm about ideas for the next episode; people in creative writing classes can brainstorm about ideas specific to the domain of creative writing. All general techniques of creativity should be made specific to the domain in which they are practiced.

How to educate creators is also a matter for discussion. For educational psychologists, successful creators have similar patterns of education and familial influence, depending on the *domain* in which the creativity is practiced. Studies done by Bloom and his colleagues explored the patterns in the lives of research neurologists, pianists, sculptors, mathematicians, and tennis players. These studies will be discussed in more detail in Part II. Likewise, a multitude of studies done at the Study for Mathematically Precocious Youth (SMPY) by Benbow, Brody, and Stanley have studied the paths that lead to high mathematical creativity and its cousin, scientific creativity.

Educational psychology researchers such as these have devoted their research efforts to studying persons by domain of achievement rather than by general creativity aptitude, with a view to how their life paths can inform the educational process. Studies of creative people within domains of achievement have led to some of the best evidence of what behaviors and situations predict the likelihood of creative productivity in adulthood. For example, Subotnik has interviewed masters in the sciences, mathematics, medicine, music, chess, theater, biology, and the like. She noted, "The masters…devoted years of creative energy and disciplined practice to the perfection of their skills and productive ideas." Each domain has its own rules of accomplishment and paths to achievement.

Humanistic Psychology

The humanistic psychologists are "little c" creativity advocates. Humanistic psychologists such as Carl Rogers, Clark Moustakas, and Rollo May say that the creative life is a healthy life. Rogers wrote that "there is no fundamental difference in the creative process as it is evidenced in painting a picture, composing a symphony, devising new instruments of killing, developing a scientific theory, discovering new procedures in human relationships, or creating new formings of one's own personality." Maslow also contributed to confusion about creativity when he insisted that no product of creativity is necessary but the product of a healthy life.

Do many "little c" creativity acts amount to a "Big C" Creative life? Such discussions verge on the spiritual, which brings us back to the original meaning of creativity, as having a connection with the divine: "God created the Heaven and the Earth." Maslow, in discussing creativeness, said that he had to revise his whole definition of creativity when he considered the lives of truly self-actualized people. He said that self-actualized (SA) creativeness "stresses first the personality rather than its achievements" and may even be "synonymous with health itself." Maslow also differentiated between big-picture creativity and everyday creativity. He thought that everyone is creative, that creativity comes in small ways, and that public recognition is not necessary, or as Csikszentmihalyi put it in 1999, "a person who reinvents Einstein's formula for relativity is as creative as Einstein was."

Dabrowski: Overexcitabilities and Developmental Levels

In the theory of psychoanalyst Kazmierz Dabrowksi, and among adherents to the New Age spiritual movement that has arisen out of the humanistic psychology movement, one's *life* is the creative product, and a person labors to become a vibrant, alive, and transcendent being as the ultimate manifestation of creativity. In the Dabrowski theory, there are five levels of development. One grows from level to level through conflict, and one's propensity for growth is termed "developmental potential." The levels are not fixed in time—they do not occur at certain ages—but they may occur simultaneously as a person is in a conflict of growth and development. The transition occurs and the higher level dominates. Not all can reach the highest levels. Positive disintegration and reintegration are necessary. Level V is beyond Maslow's self-actualization. When a person reaches Level V, selflessness and a sense of universal unity prevail.

A theory of overexcitabilities, or intensities, accompanies Dabrowski's conjecture. Five overexcitabilities exist: psychomotor, sensual, imaginational, emotional, and intellectual. Dabrowski and his translator and co-researcher, counseling psychologist Michael Piechowski, studied creative producers and found that they possessed high overexcitabilities in the emotional, intellectual, and imaginational areas. The emotional and intellectual are mediated by the imaginational, and that is why many creative people, who supposedly possess imaginational overexcitability, are able to reach these levels. However, "little c" creativity is possible at any level.

If one regards one's life and manner of living as creativity, then one can be creative without a tangible product in a domain. One's life thus can be one's work of art. Personal creativity is the creativity all persons have, and it is the type of creativity that many creativity enhancement and training programs and classes seek to address.

Humanistic psychology has always paid attention to the spiritual nature of creativity, expanding its boundaries rather than narrowing them in a reductivist scientific psychological study mode. Creativity research has been diminished by computer simulations that, under the rubric of "cognitive science," have studied creativity as a step by step process no different from problem solving.

Transpersonal psychology and depth psychology are forging new horizons for creativity research. Jungian research psychologists have advocated a consideration of dream imagery in order to cast illumination on the path that the creative life is taking. Others look into the role of psychedelic drugs, meditation, chanting, trance dancing, exercise, and prayer in enhancing personal creativity, the creativity of a person's way of living. This may also include the making of creative products such as books, music, art, and household comforts. Psychologists such as Thomas Moore have written best-selling books celebrating the small graces that one encounters in daily life. Poets such as Robert Bly and Sam Keen have joined forces with psychologists like Michael Meade to reconfigure the role of males in society. Gilligan, Pipher, and other women psychologists have begun to consider the adolescent passage in girls. The implied outcome is that people will be able to lead creative lives if they consider a holistic approach to living.

Positive Psychology

In the late 1990s, the term "positive psychology" became current. Martin Seligman, then President of the American Psychological Association, reminded psychologists that "psychology is not just the study of disease, weakness and damage; it also is the study of strength and virtue." In 2002, he published his *Handbook of Positive Psychology*. It covered such topics as resilience, flow, coping, spirituality, hope, self-efficacy, setting goals, wisdom, authenticity, humility, compassion, forgiveness, gratitude, and creativity. Simonton wrote about the positive nature of creativity, noting that most societies value their creators by encouraging them through special means such as education and special recognition. In keeping with this emphasis, the new DSM IV (*Diagnostic and Statistical Manual*) has a category called "spiritual emergency," as well as the classic psychiatric diagnoses, implying that creativity might be a result of a spiritual rather than a psychotic crisis in those who create.

Psychoanalysis, Psychiatry, and Creativity

Psychoanalysts have always been interested in the creative person in terms of psychopathology—in other words, the relationship of creativity to certain mental illnesses such as schizophrenia, depression, psychosis, and bipolar diseases. The psychoanalytic encounter is the therapeutic couch. The primary method for studying these relationships has been the case study. Recently, psychoanalyst Barry Panter published an edited book called *Creativity and Madness*, and he leads a medical education group that sponsors seminars featuring case studies of famous creators, mostly in the arts.

The original psychoanalyst, Freud (1856-1939), thought that creativity had links to the unconscious, to dreams, to sublimation of sexual energy, and to defense mechanisms, and he thought that creators resolved conflicts through making creative products. He focused on childhood experiences as unconscious motivation for creativity. Ernst Kris, a contemporary of Freud who extended ego psychology, thought creativity was "regression in service of the ego," and it happened when the ego was weak—"in sleep, in falling asleep, in fantasy, in intoxication, and in the psychoses—but also during many types of creative processes." Others with Freudian orientation were Lawrence Kubie, Phyllis Greenacre, and Philip Weissman.

Freud's colleague, Carl Jung (1875-1961), broke with him about the issues of sexual sublimation, ego, and spirituality. Jung stated, "Freud's is not a psychology of the healthy mind." Jung believed that "man's advance towards a spiritual life, which began with the primitive rites of initiation, must not be denied." Jung thought that creativity included archetypes, or ancient coded messages. In *Modern Man in Search of a Soul* (1955), Jung said that the creative act "finds its clearest expression in art," but is mysterious, "baffles all attempts at rational formulation," and "will forever elude the human understanding."

He stated, "Ideas spring from a source that is not contained within one man's personal life. We do not create them; they create us." Further, he went on to say, "The psychotherapist must not allow his vision to be colored by the glasses of pathology." Jung said that "the ailing mind is a human mind, and that, for all its ailments, it shares in the whole of the psychic life of man." If the ego is ill, it is because "it is cut off from the whole, and has lost its connection with mankind as well as with the spirit." He said, "All too easily does self-criticism poison one's naiveté, that priceless possession or rather gift which no creative man can be without." The list of artistic creators who sought therapy in the Jungian style includes Jackson Pollock and Graham Greene.

Psychiatrist Albert Rothenberg studied creative writers such as Sylvia Plath, August Strindberg, Emily Dickinson, Eugene O'Neill, and William Faulkner. He also conducted experiments with control groups of normal people, showing that the creators operated with a Janusian two-faced process of creativity (in which he used case material from his psychiatric patients who were writers). In 1990, Rothenberg said, "Only one characteristic of personality and orientation to life and work is absolutely, *across the board*, present in *all* creative people: motivation." He speculated whether this motivation was externally or internally formed, whether it came from environmental or genetic factors, and he reached no conclusions.

Psychiatrist Sylvano Arieti focused on creativity as a "magical synthesis," and in 1976 wrote about a system theory of creativity. An Italian psychiatrist, Cesare Lombroso, stated in 1891 that many, if not most, creative geniuses had neuroses or psychoses. However, the definitions of such and the biographical evidence were and still are in flux. In summary, then, the psychiatric or psychoanalytic approach focuses on the creative person as unhealthy, needing to be fixed, needing to be normalized—whatever that is.

Creativity and Business and Technology

Those who try to enhance creativity in business and technology value creativity for developing products that customers will buy. They are interested in linear, step-by-step processes such as Creative Problem Solving (CPS), Creativity Support Systems (CSS), or Computerized Creativity Support Systems (CSSS). Programs have acronyms: PAIR, PARC, COSTART. "Directed creative thinking," as Plsek said, uses three basic mental processes—attention, escape, and movement—and four tools to analyze customers' needs—defining, examining where creativity can be applied, noting what concepts are beneath these needs, and understanding what concepts drive the customers' needs.

Choosing the appropriate technique in solving problems is important. McFadzean categorized CPS techniques in a continuum ranging from paradigm-preserving to paradigm-breaking. Brainstorming, brainwriting, and force field analysis were paradigm-preserving; drawing, role-playing, fantasizing, and visioning were paradigm-transformational; object stimulation and metaphors were paradigm-stretching, and wishful thinking and rich pictures were paradigm-stretching. One can see that the techniques used in business and industry are similar to those used in several school-targeted creativity enhancement programs. However, the purpose is different. In the business world, individual personal growth is not as important as company success.

As Kletke noted, "Organizational support of employees' creative problem-solving outputs is critical for maintaining a competitive advantage and for institutionalizing creativity." Managers are encouraged to nurture creativity on multidisciplinary teams, according to Elliott. Bruce Buchanan, President of the American Association for Artificial Intelligence, advocated taking what some people call creativity's inexplicableness and putting it into steps and into computer programs.

Philosophy and Creativity: Why Are We So Interested in Creativity, Anyway?

Philosophers also weigh in. Philosophers trust in logic and reason. Why *are* we so interested in creativity? Jarvie said that the current literature on creativity is impoverished and irrational for these reasons: (1) the problem to be solved by the study of creativity is not clearly stated; (2) researchers and thinkers treat creativity as an issue of psychological import and not logical import; (3) when one explains creativity, one explains it away; and (4) "when we create an explanation that explains creativity, it, also, paradoxically, must explain itself."

Reasons of Quantity

The aim of people who attempt to discover and promote creativity is, presumably, not to increase the flood of papers, inventions, works of art that already inundate publishers, galleries, critics. Every day in the United States, 5,000 books are published. Who wants more? The educated consumer of literature cannot even keep up with what is now being published.

Too many creative people are struggling for recognition, acceptance, and financial reward right now, another argument goes. Let me use myself as an example. I am a published poet, novelist, and short story writer. One year I totaled more than 40 rejections. One rejection letter from an agent said, "I am not representing any new fiction right now, but if I were, I would consider your novel. Keep it circulating." An agent who read the nonfiction book said, "although extremely well written and easily read, it would be a difficult sell in today's commercial publishing world." Is there a glut? Are there too many novels, poems, and nonfiction books being written and too few being read? The people who ask me to do public readings of my work, and even pay me for doing so, consider me a talented writer. But at the moment, my talent is not wanted or needed by the world of commercial publishing.

Art schools turn out artists. Yet most of these artists' work will not see the track lights of a one-person show in a gallery. Music schools turn out musicians, composers, and teachers. Yet most composers, from even the most elite schools, will never see their work performed, especially if their work is orchestral. Even that most brutal of performing arts, dance, has hopefuls studying, dancing seven days a week for a chance to get into the corps de ballet. New York City has the most handsome and beautiful waiters and waitresses in the world, most of them struggling actors and actresses, auditioning like crazy, studying like crazy, waiting for their big break. Athletes have "hoop dreams" and turn out in droves for tryouts with minor league teams in hopes that their creative talent in their sport will be recognized.

The United States Patent Office receives thousands of applications annually. Do we need more creative production?

Quality as Creativity

A particularly complex reason alleged to underlie the interest in creativity is the drive to produce quality creative works. Given the plethora of production noted above, an underlying implication is that much of the creative output nowadays is substandard. What is art to some is trash to others, as we saw in the controversy over the funding of the 1990 Robert Mapplethorpe exhibit, which included several homoerotic photographs. The fallout from this brouhaha almost left the National Endowment for the Arts without funding, and it created guidelines verging on censorship for works of art. The NEA is always in a precarious position as the debate continues unabated over whether the government should even be in the business of funding the arts. The work of performance artists such as Cindy Sherman is trash to some and art to others. Mayor Rudolph Giuliani of New York City led the outrage against a cross painted in urine and a portrait done in elephant dung at an exhibit of outsider art at the Brooklyn Museum of Art a few years ago. How do we decide what is art?

The often-heard comment about abstract art, that a child or a monkey could do it, also illustrates the argument about quality. The subject matter chosen by the artist, the use of materials, the very genetically inherited body—for who can be a ballet dancer without the right turn of instep?—all point to the necessity for quality. But whose idea of quality? The creator's or the public's? When Andy Warhol first painted a Campbell's soup can, the public screamed about lack of quality. When Elvis first sang "Hound Dog," the public bemoaned the passing of an era. Each artist, however, started a new era. Now Warhol is ensconced in museums as important in the history of art and culture, and the era of rock and roll was born with Elvis. When Stravinsky's *Rites of Spring* premiered in the early 1900s, the audience rioted. The suggestion that a bomb could be built from nuclear fusion prompted the world to shake its head with disbelief, and then with horror.

Quality is most often defined by the domain itself, by expert peers, *connoisseurs* and *critics,* in Eisner's terms, who, with expert eyes, see the merits of a person's creative work. This is not necessarily the judgment of the marketplace or of popular taste, however, and people buy art to match their couches rather than because the artist has won peer recognition. Censorship often results when the popular taste is pitted against the judgment of qualified peers. That is why we have two Vietnam memorials—one judged as art by the Congressmen and one commissioned by a committee made up of connoisseurs of contemporary sculpture.

That Van Gogh was a great painter was ultimately decided not by the public but by the connoisseurs of the domain. That such and such a restaurant rates four or five stars is decided by the experts, fellow chefs and food critics. That Suzanne Farrell was a great ballerina is ultimately decided by the dance critics, professional dancers, and connoisseurs. The book on the top of the bestseller list may make its writer a lot of money, but it is the serious literary writers and the connoisseurs of literature who will ultimately put any book into the literature classroom or the few copies of the under-appreciated and under-printed first edition, with dust jacket, into the ranks of the rare and desirable. Jonathan Franzen, in 2001, didn't want the Oprah Book Club logo on his novel, *The Corrections*, as he thought it popularized his work too much; yet he made millions from that logo's placement, and he also won the National Book Award, an indication that his book was both popular and judged by the experts to be fine art as well.

Creativity and Nationalism

Others have said that we should develop our creativity for nationalistic reasons. In the late 1950s and throughout the Cold War, a nationalistic spirit prevailed in the U.S., especially after the Russians put Sputnik into orbit. Creativity was deemed necessary to keep the U.S. ahead of Russia. Mid-century psychologists saw creativity as necessary for combating the Soviet threat. In recent years, the popular culture has shown people using the same nationalistic argument with reference to competition with the Japanese and with the Europeans. A common assertion among patriotic educators is that the U.S. leads the world in patent applications, and that the U.S. inventors design, while the Japanese and Germans can only improve on the basic designs. These patriotic people then go on to repeat the call for an emphasis on creativity training in the schools. The call for creativity in finding and dealing with terrorism after the bombings of September 11 also resonated in political speeches and pundit opining.

Creativity and Equity

A fourth reason for emphasizing creativity has racist and classist overtones, usually implicit rather than stated explicitly. It goes like this. People in the middle and upper socioeconomic classes do perform better at school-related creativity such as creative writing, higher mathematics, and science.

31

These domains require a lot of formal education. My 2002 study of contemporary creative writers showed that all of them except one had at least a bachelor's degree in English literature. One cannot be a scientist without a Ph.D. One cannot do mathematical theorizing without a Ph.D. One cannot be a classical musician without having had formal training in music. All of these take money, family support, and some financial wherewithal.

Poor people don't score particularly well on the tests that are required to move along in the educational world. Socioeconomic status (SES) is a confounding variable that educators, policy makers, and thinkers have wrestled with, with limited success, for years. Poor people are discriminated against by paper and pencil tests, no matter how well designed they are. Poor people have had to make their contributions in domains that are not dependent on getting a higher education. Racecar drivers with quick reaction time are not known for their intellectuality. Young athletes clamor to quit college and join the NBA or the NHL.

African-Americans have been stereotyped as having musical creativity and superior physical giftedness. Many African-Americans who came from poverty have significantly shaped American popular music, rhythm and blues, and jazz, and they have also revolutionized most sports they have been exposed to. Even the "rich" sports of golf and tennis now have top performers of color.

Latinos have had a great influence on popular dance and music. Hip-hop music and hip-hop fashion have had an impact, and not only on the poor—they are now favorites among White suburban kids. These creative achievements have taken place in the real world outside of the school world. Who is creative here? What is equitable here?

Creativity as Human Freedom

We seek to unmask the mystery of creativity precisely because it is so unexplainable. We write so much and think so much about creativity because we simply want to explain the creative achievement, to find out the truth about what makes a creative product. However, as soon as we think we discover the process, it eludes us.

The philosopher's reason for studying creativity is that creativity implies a kind of human freedom. Despite what Calvinists and astrologers may say, life is not pre-determined, and people thus demonstrate creativity in how they make their life productive. Psychologists have set out to identify the creative personality. What happens in the mind while a person is being creative? That is another question. Professionals set out to make up tests; they design experiments that will be able to ferret out people who will be able to produce creative products. But will they ever succeed?

Domain specialists, creative people such as artists, writers, mathematicians, and dancers, are not very interested in what happens in the mind while a person creates, nor about what the personalities of various creators show. Practitioners of the various creative disciplines are more interested in the product that the creator makes. Is it new? Is it valuable? Does it extend the field? The fascination with personality, process, and product continues.

Can a Person Be Creative Without a Product?

A major concern is whether one can be a creative person without a creative product. Logic suggests that without judging the creativeness of the product, we cannot conclude that a person is creative. But that is essentially what we do when we talk about creativity or creative potential as a type of giftedness. We often identify children with what is called *creative potential* without any reference to the products they have produced or will produce. However, if the creative product is a person's life, then no concrete thing is necessary—a composition, a poem, a pot, or a theorem.

The education establishment wonders how to judge objectively whether or not a product is creative—that is, whether or not it is a valuable novelty. Recent educational practices have emphasized the development of portfolios—the assessment of authentic work rather than abstract test scores. We have begun to look at creativity in children as demonstrated by what they can do. Some object and say that, in young children, the creative product is still in the emergent stage, and who knows whether future products will turn into the gold spun from the straw of the initial effort? Runco, in 1997, cautioned against looking at student products as indicators of creative giftedness, though he admitted that creative people should produce products.

Precocity as Predictive

Others note that there are developmental paths in each talent domain and that experts know these paths and know which children are exceptional. Such children are often precocious, in that they display work that is similar to that of much older children. People familiar with the developmental path of music, for instance, can tell when a student is precocious, just as can people familiar with the developmental paths of athletics, writing, mathematics, science, visual arts, and other domains. The precocity is often shown in *predictive behaviors*. However, all adult creative producers did not demonstrate or show precocious childhood behaviors in their domains. For children who are precocious, special efforts need to be made, and for those children who are not, they can be allowed to develop in due time.

The pushing of children into careers in tennis, say, or in ice-skating, acting, or gymnastics has led to widespread manipulation, commercialization, and loss of childhood for many young stars. Tofler and DeGeronimo named a syndrome after these pushy parents and selfish teachers—the Achievement by Proxy Distortion Syndrome. They said, "Some parents risk their children's health and well-being by abusing their authority to dominate simply because they themselves are narcissistic, egomaniacal, greedy, or autocratic." Tofler and DeGeronimo give several suggestions for parents and coaches.

Creativity of the Moment and for the Ages

What is judged creative at any one time depends on the Zeitgeist, or temperature of the times. For example, take the recent soaring prices of Van Gogh's work. Van Gogh himself made nary a farthing from his work. His paintings were not valued by the art galleries, art critics, or the auction houses of his day, but only by a few of his artist peers. Yet the auction houses and rich buyers of today have parlayed some of his paintings into a net worth of upwards of 50 million dollars. Was Van Gogh creative then, or is he only creative now? Are his paintings examples of creativity?

If we had been Van Gogh's teachers, we probably would not have rated his products creative in comparison to others because of the violent emotion and raging anger and blinding color that his paintings showed. Even his art teachers didn't think he had much potential. Van Gogh was probably a very scary boy, as well as a difficult, scary man. He mailed his ear to a woman who spurned him, and then he did a self-portrait. Yet less than a hundred years later, his creativity is the most valued—in monetary terms—in the entire art world. This could be called the creativity theory of value accruing after death, or posthumous creativity. Yet it is often the creator of the moment whom we praise, and not the creator of the future.

Creators of the moment are probably those who extend the knowledge of the field just a little bit, enough so that we can understand it, just as leaders of the moment are people with whom we can identify as just a little smarter than we are, but not so much smarter that we can't relate to them. In the past, creators have had their works destroyed because their contemporaries didn't value them—a loss to future generations. In particular, the creative works of many women, poor people, and minorities weren't valued during their time and so were lost. Historical re-examination may help some of these works to surface for future generations, if they haven't been destroyed.

Creativity Can Take Place Without Mastery

Though those who argue that eminence is a criterion for creativity would disagree, a person can be creative, can have creativity, while learning the discipline. In fact, many disciplines are never truly mastered—for example, music, dance, creative writing, and the rest of the arts. The pianist who has practiced and prepared himself for years in order to interpret a master work achieves a novel interpretation—he transforms what he has done before and even transforms, to an extent, the individual work. This person is creative, even though he hasn't extended the discipline for the record books, but only in the temporal and ephemeral memories of his audience. The work may not be recorded, and thus the people in the field do not know whether or not that person has extended the discipline, but the judges know whether or not he has been momentarily creative. This "momentary" creativity comes as the result of years and years of preparation.

Much dance, because it is physical movement, has not been notated. The dancer achieves certain moves that the choreographer has just sketched out. The collaborative nature of the medium recognizes the choreographer as the one who is the more creative. But isn't the dancer also? The dancer achieves mastery within the domain, and in performance, extends the field. But if the dance is not videotaped, the only record is in the memories of the audience. The trained dancer or choreographer watching the performance can observe and be able to replicate steps, but nuances of stretch and gesture are still unique to the interpreter.

The visual artist with the mute lump of clay or the empty white canvas is also creative, for she, like the writer with the blank page, is finding a problem, not solving a problem. Her problem is not defined. She defines it as she works with her medium. She defines the problem as she creates. She is choosing the problem, finding it, and in doing so is being creative. Often, the choice of the problem is motivated by personal reasons, personal need, personal pathology. The execution of the solution of the problem uses the media provided by the field's constraints. The odds of her creating something that will move the domain to new heights without her having studied and practiced for about 10 years are slim.

Suffice it to say, for the purposes of this book, that *creativity is having gained respectable mastery and recognition by peers in the field to make something momentarily new.* One extends one's own limits, one works on one's own edge, until, perhaps, that edge is the edge of the domain, and it extends the discipline.

In performance creativity, one may also extend the domain. James Sloan Allen differentiated between two types of artists: the creators, and the performers. Creators invent works of art, and performers interpret works of art. Both are creative. "Performers...share with creative artists the gift of an unteachable talent for artistic expression, and like all artists, are afflicted with ambivalence over displaying that talent in public, relishing acclaim, apprehensive of rejection." The performer (singer, instrumentalist, actor, dancer, athlete, speaker) interprets the written symbols of the creator through bodily and physical skill, and through an intuitive understanding of the symbols, changing them for the purposes of the moment, interacting with the electricity in the air and with the audience in an intangible communicative moment of wholeness. (Physical performers are discussed in Chapter 11.)

Special schools and separate classes for those who want to be performers or athletes owe their existence to the need for training. There is a distance between the composer and the choreographer, the playwright or screenwriter and the actor, and that distance is marked by the necessity for performers such as actors, athletes, and dancers to combine bodily intelligence and emotional intelligence in synergy with the work and with the audience.

The Existence and Development of Talent

The creatively productive person must have what is called "talent." Here we come upon the problem of heredity and environment. Is a person born with talent, or can a person acquire talent? In American English, "talent" is considered innate. I concur with what Simonton stated in 1999, that talent is "any innate capacity that enables an individual to display exceptionally high performance in a domain that requires special skills and training." The aspects of talent are physiological and psychological, of course. A musician needs dexterity. A visual artist needs visual acuity. A scientist needs curiosity. A writer needs verbal facility. An actor and a dancer need physical suppleness.

Talent is a natural proclivity. Developed talent is what is necessary for creativity, "Big C" Creativity for sure, but even for "little c" creativity. In studies of eminence, such as Galton's, talent was thought to be inherited or evolved in certain families. The immigrant experience in the United States has shown that even children from very poor families, when given the proper nurturing and environment, often have outstanding talent, and that the propensity and the ability to create is more common than classist evolutionary hereditists have thought. This process usually takes at least three generations from the poverty of steerage to the promise of potential.

I have formulated a pyramid framework to discuss talent development, presented in Chapter 5, which illustrates various influences on creativity.

Creativity Is Natural

So, dear reader, listen up. Here is what I have come to think after all my reading and talking and dreaming:

> *Creativity is in the personality, the process, and the product within a domain in interaction with genetic influences and with optimal environmental influences of home, school, community and culture, gender, and chance. Creativity is a basic human need to make new.*

—Jane Piirto

While creativity is the natural propensity of human being-ness, creativity can be enhanced and also stifled. The creative personality can be developed and also thwarted.

Creativity takes certain habits of mind. Creativity is not separate from intelligence or from artistry, but part of the whole. What is unnatural and sad is for it to be repressed, suppressed, and stymied through the process of growing up and being educated. What happens to most of us is that somewhere along the way, and often necessarily, we begin to distrust our creative self. Survival dictates that we subordinate our creative poetic self to a more practical, prosaic self. We go along and forget who we are or who we were. Oftentimes the creative poetic self is recaptured in a creativity class, or in therapy, or at a retreat, or in alone time in a cabin in the woods. The creative poetic self is close to our spiritual, personal self, and when we express our creativity, we express our personal side. This is often dangerous and leaves us vulnerable, and so we snap back to the practical and the prosaic out of defense.

Barron, in 1995, described the underlying necessity for the creator to be transformed. He said that the will to create is built deeply within God's creatures. The creative person is a "transformed transformer." Even the smallest act of making new, of transforming, is viewed with a sense of awe when one engages in it. "All of us are potentially and actually creative in our lives. This is a part of the gift of personality."

Further, *creativity is the underpinning, the basement, the foundation that permits talent to be realized.* To be creative is necessary in the realization of a fulfilling life, but with all due respect to Mensa, having scored high on an intelligence test is not necessary. We are all creative. Those who are more creative than others have learned to take risks, to value complexity, to see the world, or their own surroundings with naiveté. They have learned to be creative, or their creativity has not been pushed down, stifled, and diminished by sarcasm and abuse. The rest of this book discusses motivation for creativity, how creativity can be enhanced, how people in certain domains are creative, how creativity has been assessed, and how creativity can be taught.

Summary

1. Many fields have a proprietary interest in creativity. Among these are psychology, psychoanalysis, philosophy, the arts, business, and the sciences.

2. The term "creativity" is a relatively new term.

3. Creativity has come to be considered either a form of giftedness or to be synonymous with giftedness, or to be a form of genius or to be synonymous with genius.

4. The psychologists, both the psychometricians (the testers) and the cognitive psychologists, have had a great impact on the field of education in its definitions of creativity and giftedness.

5. Some people believe that a person can be creative without a product, and some people believe that such creativity is not creativity at all.

6. There are many reasons for the emphasis on creativity. Some of these are reasons of quantity, quality, equity, national competition and pride, and reasons of freedom.

7. Talent is probably genetic, but who knows?

8. Developing a talent requires both genetic and environmental factors, certain attributes of personality, enough intelligence to function in the domain, and the will to persist.

9. Everyone is creative. Those who are more creative have learned to be so.

Chapter 2
The Creative Process

The artistic experience, at its highest, was actually a natural analogue of mystical experience. It produced a kind of intuitive perception.
—Thomas Merton

I called the Muse/she pleaded a headache.
—Derek Walcott

The daimon of creativity has ruthlessly had its way with me.
—Carl Jung

There is much that is mystical, magical, and phenomenological about what goes on before and while a person is creating. The creative process engages many thinkers because they feel that if the process can be duplicated, more people will be creative. This chapter discusses some of the most cogent theories.

Current Psychological Theories of the Creative Process

The most popular theory of the creative process is that there are four steps. This is the theory propounded by Wallas in 1926. Wallas said that there are four stages in the creative process: (1) Preparation, (2) Incubation, (3) Illumination, and (4) Verification. In the first stage, the person does both formal and informal work—she gets herself ready for the act of creation by studying, thinking, searching for answers, asking people, and so forth. In the second stage, the process rests, is in gestation, the person is pregnant with the creative product. The unconscious is working on the problem. In the third stage, a solution arises, and light is thrown on the problem. Then the person works to complete the problem.

Cognitive Psychology: Selection

Psychologists, especially cognitive psychologists, wonder and theorize about what happens in the brain while a creator is thinking. David Perkins debunked much of the given wisdom about the creative process. How creative people come to formulate synonyms, how creative people recognize patterns, and how creative people solve problems were some of the things he studied. Among the techniques he used was the observation of working artists—interrupting them while they were working and asking them what they were thinking. Ultimately, according to Perkins, the creative process is one of *selection*. There is not much that is mysterious about it.

Zoologist Edward Wilson, in Findlay and Lumsden's *The Creative Mind*, called the creative process the "grandmother of problems in the human sciences." The creative process is intractable. Thus, the work of demystification, like that of Perkins and the other cognitive scientists, is important in understanding the human process called creativity, even though many of us would like to retain the mystery.

Industrial Psychology: The CPS Model

Another very common explanation of the creative process is the Creative Problem-Solving Model (CPS). This is a model whereby individuals, most often working in teams, go through five steps on the way to formulating and solving a problem. Step 1 is "Mess-Finding"; Step 2 is "Problem-Finding"; Step 3 is "Data-Finding"; Step 4 is "Solution-Finding"; and Step 5 is "Acceptance-Finding." This group-oriented model is very popular in business, education, and industry. Thousands of people from all over the world attend the yearly CPS creativity conferences at Buffalo, New York, seeking to enhance the creative processes of teams. But solitary creators approach the creative process from a more interior point of view.

Psychoanalytic Theory: Janusian and Homospatial

Psychoanalysts have a great opportunity to study the creative process in their creative patients. Albert Rothenberg formulated a theory of the creative process which he called the Janusian process after the Roman god Janus, the two-faced god. Rothenberg said, "In the Janusian process, multiple opposites or antitheses are conceived simultaneously, either as existing side by side, or as equally operative, valid, or true."

Creative scientists, writers, and artists are able to hold opposites in their minds while creating and to see the possibilities of working with these opposites. Thesis becomes antithesis, and both are integrated into the theme of the work. Irony, metaphor, ambiguity, and creative tension are hallmarks of the Janusian process. These are organic and are seen by the creator as crucial to the meaning of the work.

The Janusian process is used in the beginning during the generation of ideas, and then later, a *homospatial* process is used by creators. The homospatial part of the process is where metaphors are created by superimposing unlike elements upon the same space. Thus the creator combines what is seen in the mind's eye, the mind's ear, the mind's touch. Sounds have color and sights have sound. Tastes have texture and movement. Rothenberg thought that artists, writers, and scientists consciously develop this metaphorization process, but that it also rises spontaneously.

Social Psychological Theories: The Power of Suggestion and Motivation

In researching the creative process, Amabile, in the 1980s, focused on how intrinsic motivation is developed. She and her team of researchers did many experiments with various types of creators. For example, they gave a writing task to one group of writers and told them to write the best poem they could; then they gave the same writing task to another group of writers and told them that the poem they wrote would be published by a major publisher. Independent analysis of the finished poems indicated that when the writers knew they would be judged by editors, their work became much more tentative and conservative. Amabile concluded that extrinsic motivation might stifle creativity. Later, in 1996, she revised her theory to show that certain extrinsic motivation, such as deadlines and contracts, are also helpful.

On the one hand, we have cognitive psychologists saying that anecdotal accounts of what happens during the process of creating are not reliable, and on the other hand, we have those who say critical thinking and creative problem solving teach certain step-by-step processes which cause creativity to flower. But the people who are themselves the creators—scientists, mathematicians, visual artists, musicians, writers, and theater people—never seem to refer to any of these psychologists' theories when they talk about the creative process.

The Work of Brewster Ghiselin

A most useful source of anecdotal information about the creative process is Brewster Ghiselin, who, in 1952, collected the accounts of many creators in an anthology called *The Creative Process*. His book is a classic. In his introduction, he describes the organic process that most creators seem to go through. Ghiselin says that a creator gives in to a feeling of vague unrest and then surrenders the self to some internal necessity. He called this surrender "oceanic consciousness." Then the creator, previously prepared through study and practice, works with automaticity, using expertise wrought through long practice. The part of the creative process most often underplayed is the enormous preparation that creators have to do within their fields. Viewers see a finished work and forget the hard work and sweat that led up to the final product.

Ghiselin also noted that the process is characterized by restlessness and that creative people often move on to other projects just when the rest of the world is beginning to catch on to what they have done. The word "movement"—as in "Romantic Movement," "Neoclassical Movement," and "Abstract Expressionist Movement"—illustrates this restlessness. It was said of Picasso that he was not in any movements; he started them. Willem de Kooning said that when you can see the bandwagon, it's already gone. Ghiselin noted that whatever the domain, the creator feels great emotion—a feeling for the *aesthetic*s, for the *beauty* unique to the field.

Ghiselin then described the physical manifestations of the creative process, the *massive concentration* that the creator exhibits. One could say that the person is in a kind of a trance, concentrating so much that he seems to be hypnotized or sleepwalking. But this state differs from actual hypnotism or trance, for the person is collected, autonomous, and watchful. An example of this trancelike state is found in a comment from an interview John Hersey gave to George Plimpton's 1988 "Writers at Work" series. John Hersey, the writer who changed the world with his portrait of Hiroshima's devastation, described his creative dreamlike state thus: "When the writing is really working, I think there is something like dreaming going on. I don't know how to draw the line between the conscious management of what you're doing and this state." Hersey said that this dreamlike mood happens during the first stages, the drafts of his work. He said, "When I feel really engaged with a passage, I become so lost in it that I'm unaware of my real surroundings, totally involved in the pictures and sounds that that passage evokes." He went on to say that "this mysterious feeling may be one of the things that attract those of us who write."

Flow

What Ghiselin, Hersey, and many other creative people describe as this trancelike state is now called "flow." This word was coined in 1990 by psychologist Mihalyi Csikszentmihalyi. He said that this feeling occurs "when a person's body or mind is stretched to its limits in a voluntary effort to accomplish something difficult and worthwhile." Csikszentmihalyi subsequently interviewed 91 eminent creators in the sciences, business, government, and the arts. He noted nine elements that make up "flow":

(1) There are clear goals every step of the way.

(2) There is immediate feedback to one's actions.

(3) There is a balance between challenges and skills.

(4) Actions and awareness are merged.

(5) Distractions are excluded from consciousness.

(6) There is no worry of failure.

(7) Self-consciousness disappears.

(8) The sense of time becomes distorted.

(9) The activity becomes an end in itself, or autotelic.

Ghiselin continued describing the creative process. In the creative process, a willingness to sit down and concentrate is not enough. The work often disregards the structure imposed on it. For example, Virginia Woolf wrote in her diary that she had planned and organized the structure of her novel, *Mrs. Dalloway*, but had to abandon that organization when it didn't work. She then proceeded blindly, without a plan. Clearly, the previous plan had not been what she needed in order to express her impulse in writing the book. Therefore, the plan must be organic.

Finally, inspiration must be realized by good hard work. After the work is completed, the process is not finished, for the creator must determine whether her excitement over the work has created something new, fresh, and useful. Often, she may find that the value of the work has been in its intrinsic benefit to her development. When she submits it to critical review, it may be found wanting. Then she may work on it some more or reject it and begin again.

Ghiselin's "Introduction" still remains one of the best summaries of what happens during the creative process.

Core Attitudes in the Creative Process

Core Attitude of Naiveté

The Institute for Personality Assessment and Research, in its studies more than 50 years ago at Berkeley, said that creators have "naiveté." Naiveté means openness and refers to the fact that creative people pay attention to the small things and are able to see the old in their fields and domains as if it were new. Psychoanalyst Carl Jung pointed out that naiveté is easily poisoned: "All too easily does self-criticism poison one's naiveté, that priceless possession or rather gift which no creative man can be without" (1933, p. 167). Julian Green went so far as to say that this naiveté is a component of what we call talent: "One of the secrets of real talent is to see everything for the first time, to look at a leaf as though one had never seen one before, for then only can it appear to us in all its newness" (p. 105).

Another example of naiveté in creators is Vincent Van Gogh, who said that he saw drawings and pictures everywhere, even in peasant huts and in dusty rooms. He felt irresistibly drawn to these potential portraits. Of his early painting, *The Potato Eaters*, done in 1885 while living in Nuenen with his parents, he wrote his brother Theo:

> *I think you will see what I mean in the picture of the potato eaters. It is very dark, however, and in the white, for instance, hardly any white has been used, but simply the neutral color, which is made by mixing red, blue, yellow, for instance, vermilion, Paris blue and Naples yellow. Therefore that color is in itself a pretty dark gray, but in the picture it looks white. I'll tell you why I do it that way. Here the subject is a gray interior, lit by a little lamp. The dirty linen tablecloth, the smoky wall, the dirty caps in which the women have worked in the field—when seen through the eyelashes in the light of the lamp, all this proves to be a very dark gray; and the lamp, though a yellow-reddish glow, is even lighter—even a great deal—than the white in question. When I went to the cottage tonight, I found the people at supper in the light of the small window instead of under the lamp—oh, it was splendid! The color was extraordinary, too; you remember those heads painted against the window—the effect was like that, but even darker.*

This is a basic personality characteristic of creative people—the attitude of naiveté, of acceptance and curiosity about the odd and strange. It includes the ability to notice and to remark differences in details. Igor Stravinsky called it "the gift of observation." He said, "the true creator may be recognized by his ability always to find about him, in the commonest and humblest thing, items worthy of note" (p. 192).

Core Attitude of Self-Discipline

Work, work, work, for the night is coming. When people ask me how I can get so much writing done, I say I have a simple secret. It's called "Put your bum on the chair. Every day." Some people have self-discipline for diet, some for exercise, but creators in the arts and sciences have self-discipline for their creative work.

When one studies the lives of creators, one often finds that they have created many, many works, even though they are only known for one, two, or a few. This self-discipline leads to the great productivity of creators. Van Gogh wrote to Theo, "I am daily working on drawing figures. I shall make a hundred of them before I paint them" (p. 294). Choreographer Agnes de Mille, in her biography of Martha Graham, noted that "all artists—indeed all great careerists—submit themselves, as well as their friends, to lifelong, relentless discipline, largely self-imposed and never for any reason relinquished" (p. 158).

Core Attitude of Risk-Taking

Risk-taking in creative people has been noticed since creativity began to be studied. Risk-taking enables one to try new things. Risk-taking does not mean climbing onto a high bridge and bungee jumping off. While introverted and shy creators may eschew physical risk-taking, professional risk-taking in creators may be manifested in trying new forms, styles, or subjects. As Simonton said, "Great creators are great risk-takers besides" (1995, p. 255). The kind of courage they have is the courage to stumble, to fail, and after rejection, to try, try again.

The psychiatrist Rollo May differentiated among physical courage, moral courage, social courage, and creative courage. Creative courage is finding the new, providing the vanguard's warning of what is about to happen in the culture, showing in image and symbol through their imaginations what is possible. In their work, artists show what the culture values spiritually if only the people could see it. This takes courage in the presence of censure and rejection, because in this struggle, the artists—the poets, painters and sculptors, musicians, dramatists—threaten what is. That is why, in repressive societies, those who speak out in image and in symbol are jailed or exiled.

The risk-taking is often like symbolically cutting one's own jugular in order to tell the truth. Poet Anne Sexton, known for her frank, confessional writing, was asked by interviewer Barbara Kevles why she dug so deeply into her own painful experiences.

> *There was a part of me that was horrified, but the gutsy part of me drove on. Still, part of me was appalled by what I was doing. On the one hand, I was digging up shit, with the other hand, I was covering it with sand. Nevertheless, I went on ahead. I didn't know any better. Sometimes, I felt like a reporter researching himself. Yes, it took a certain courage, but as a writer one has to take the chance on being a fool...yes, to be a fool, that perhaps requires the greatest courage.* (p. 281)

Core Attitude of Group Trust

In collaborative creativity, which is the kind used in team efforts, the group must have some modicum of trust. The comedy writing team or the business innovation team needs to create in a climate where the unorthodox, the unusual, the zany, the unconventional, are valued and not put down or ridiculed. Elliott urged that teams seeking to innovate must have managers who encourage creativity, and she noted that multidisciplinary teams in business seem to have more success, as they are able to bring different kinds of knowledge to the problems.

Group trust is also important in dance and in the theater. Viola Spolin, the actor and acting teacher, wrote that working in a group creates an interdependency, as each member has a role to play and a job to do and cannot be egotistical or selfish or the whole project will suffer. One person cannot dominate; everyone must play and experience together. Trust is necessary among the members of the group. In creativity class also, developing group trust is imperative if people are to take risks, exhibit naiveté, and be transformed. One of the most important things in establishing group trust is in offering feedback to people in a way that will let them know that they were heard. Group leaders and group members need to gain skills in how to do this in a useful way.

The Seven I's

At this point, I would like to present what I call the Seven I's of the creative process. They are Inspiration, Imagery, Imagination, Intuition, Insight, Incubation, and Improvisation. I will discuss Inspiration first.

Inspiration

There are six major kinds of inspiration: the visitation of the muse; the inspiration of nature; inspiration through substances; inspiration by works of art and music; inspiration from dreams; and the inspiration of novel surroundings—travel.

All creators talk about inspiration. Literally, inspiration is a taking in of breath. The *Oxford English Dictionary* says inspiration is a breathing or infusion into the mind or soul of an exaltation. In terms of creativity, inspiration provides the motivation to create. When one takes in breath, one fills the lungs with air, with environment, with the stuff of life—and after the intake, there must be a release.

The Visitation of the Muse

The 1999 comedy movie *The Muse* featured Albert Brooks as a screenwriter with writer's block who sought inspiration from a goddess-like Sharon Stone. Actually, the mythology of the muse—of being inspired by another, has been with us for eons and is still alive and well. The Greeks created nine Muses who were the daughters of Memory (Mnemosyne) and of Zeus. Together with the Graces, the muses lived on the "hallowed slopes of Olympus." They caused the soul of the creator of various arts to remember the divine and to seek help from the divine in creating the arts.

Muse originally meant "reminder." Muses had to do with life, with water, with babbling springs that spoke prophecy and provided imagination with inspiration. If you visit the back galleries of a large museum, you will find, no doubt, a painting by someone such as Tura or Poussin of a muse inspiring a poet, musician, or artist, or paintings like the 1890 *Pygmalion and Galatea* by Jean Léon Gérome, or Marc Chagall's 1917 *Apparition (Self Portrait with Muse)*. The quintessential homage to and historical explanation of the power of the muse is Robert Graves' long, complicated, and fascinating tome called *The White Goddess,* who is the moon, or muse.

Each muse had her own province in music, literature, art, and science. The muse of epic poetry was Calliope; of history, Clio; of lyric poetry, Euterpe; of tragedy, Melpomene; of choral dance and song, Terpsichore.

Erato was the muse of love poetry, and Polyhymnia was the muse of sacred poetry. Urania was the muse of astronomy, and Thalia the muse of comedy. Ingres painted *The Composer Cherubini with the Muse of Lyric Poetry* in 1842, with the muse holding her hand over the musician's head as if she were about to pat him. Vermeer's *The Allegory of Painting* portrayed the muse Clio. In Herodotus' 450 B.C. *History*, each of the nine books was named for a muse. The muses came to symbolize the feminine principle, while the male principle was symbolized by the Seven Spheres.

Thus, "The Music of the Spheres" symbolized the union of the male and female principles, the male being the animus, and the female being the anima. The male creator unites with his anima, or female side, and the female creator unites with her animus, her male side, according to Jungian thought. Dante had his Beatrice, Lancelot his Guinevere, Tristan his Isolde, Ilmarainen his Maid of North Farm. Dante had as his guide through hell, Virgil, who could be called a general muse or a desired mentor. At the beginning of Homer's *Iliad*, the blind poet invokes the muses in order to help him tell his story. The muses were inspirations to creative men. Do creative women have muses? "Yes," says Carolyn Kizer in her essay "A Muse." This muse was her mother, but women's muses are not always mothers. I think all creative women could name their muses. I have had several.

Today, the other muses seem to be sleeping, and when we speak of the muse, we speak of the inspiration of love, or Erato, the muse of love. Inspiration often comes in response to a feeling for someone, quite possibly a sexual feeling, certainly an emotional identification. Everyone has written a secret love poem, whether the love is requited or unrequited. The longing lyrics of the Brownings show that the place of erotic desire and longing for sexual union cannot be underestimated in considering the products of any artists. Poets write love poems, as Elizabeth Barrett Browning did with her sonnet "How Do I Love Thee? Let Me Count the Ways."

Choreographers make ballets for their muses, as Balanchine did for Suzanne Farrell. Visual artists paint nudes, as Picasso did for each of his many muses (and then he painted them as monsters after the relationships ended). Many of these works are efforts to express eroticism within the boundaries of the medium within which the artists are working.

Several friends of mine have experienced whole new surges of creative energy when they fell in love later on in life, after they thought that sexual love was lost to them. Poets Joan and David Watts met at Squaw Valley Writers' Conference, fell in love, and wrote a series called "Epithalamium" to each other. Joan's part of it won her an Individual Artist Fellowship from the Ohio Arts Council.

Poet James Tipton's muse, who is novelist and memoirist Isabel Allende, wrote an introduction to two of his collections of poems, *The Wizard of Is* and *Letters From a Stranger*. Here is what she wrote: "One day, during the summer of 1994, I received a letter from a stranger." Tipton had written to her from the top of the Andes near Machu Picchu after reading her work. He wrote again a few weeks later with a story about an alcoholic woman in a wedding dress scavenged from a garbage can who was arrested making love on the railroad tracks with a stranger from a bar. He offered to find out more. Allende said: "I was hooked, not only by the fascinating mystery of that woman, but mainly by the man who had the intuition to send me that precious gift." She replied, and a correspondence began.

Tipton would send her several poems a week. Allende, whose daughter had just died, said, "I found myself waiting for the mail with a secret anxiety that I did not want to admit even in the silence of my heart." She began to be very interested in the man and his poems; the poems "would go deep down inside my sorrow and swim like small fish." They would bring her "to their soft light…like shadows, like sounds I heard in sleep, like ships that slip unnoticed into the port at night." Finally the poet and the novelist met, more than a year after Tipton began the correspondence. (Allende is married and lives more than a thousand miles from Tipton.) "And thus, one poem at a time, our friendship evolved slowly and the stranger became a dear friend." Tipton's book about their muse-like friendship, *Letters to a Stranger*, won the 1999 Colorado Poetry Book of the Year award.

Muses are virginal, pure, and faithful. The artist longs for the muse, and in the process of longing, creates a song, a play, a poem, a theorem. When the creative person is being visited by the muse, he or she often feels possessed and enters another world, a world of reverie, of be*Mused* silence. Many creators throughout history have claimed that they take dictation from a muse and claim no relationship between their own selves and the selves they create on paper.

Francine Prose, in a 2002 book *Lives of the Muses*, describes the muse/artist relationship of nine couples, such as John Lennon and Yoko Ono, Salvatore Dalí and Gala Dalí, Suzanne Farrell and George Balanchine, and others. Once the muse becomes a wife, the relationship changes, Prose said. Wives take care of the artist's business, manage his life. Once Charis Weston married Edward Weston, her relationship as inspiration for his work ended. Only one of the muses Prose wrote about later became an artist in her own right—photographer Lee Miller.

Jacques Maritain contrasted the Platonic and the Surrealistic views of the inspiration of the Muse. The idea of the Muse, in the Platonic view, is that art is inspired from somewhere outside the intellect, from the world of ideas that transcends the material world—thus, "visitation" of the Muse. The surrealistic view is that inspiration for poetry comes from the Freudian unconscious, from within. One source is outside, in a spiritual realm; the other is inside, in a psychological realm.

It seems that both views are quite common. Creators often speak as if what they write was sent from something within but afar. Inspirations "come." For example, poet Octavio Paz said in an interview with MacAdam that he wrote the first 30 voices of his poem "Sun Stone" "as if someone were silently dictating them to me. They came from far off and from nearby, from within my own chest." In his *Paris Review* interview with Drue Heinz, British Poet Laureate Ted Hughes seemed to think that his poems surfaced from within: "Poems get to the point where they are stronger than you are. They come up from some other depth and they find a place on the page."

Some creators feel as if they are go-betweens, mediums. Some mysterious force impels them, works through their hands, wiggles through them, shoots from them. Stanislav Grof, a transpersonal psychologist who conducted the first LSD experiments, called it the "Promethean impulse." The Greek Titan, Prometheus, stole fire from the gods on Mount Olympus and as a punishment was sentenced to be chained to earth with his liver eaten by vultures. The impulse to steal fire from the gods speaks to inspiration from some outside force.

This type of inspiration also applies in theater. For example, some actors speak of being receptacles for their characters' souls, of being possessed. Brian Bates, a psychologist who worked with actors at the Royal Academy of Dramatic Art in London, quoted actor Dirk Bogarde on receiving a character in the film *Death in Venice*: "I started to walk slowly round and round the room emptying myself of myself...willing [the character] himself to come towards me and slip into the vacuum which I was creating for his reception." Bates commented, "For some actors, possession is not only what they experience, it is what they *seek* to experience.". That acting includes possession stems from the historical role of the traditional actor, who interpreted the gods for the people. Today actors talk about building characters or "getting into" character. They often have pre-acting rituals for entering the state of mind necessary to act. This might include putting on their makeup, meditating, or being alone for a period of time.

Harman and Rheingold describe several such events of transpersonal inspiration. Einstein envisioned the theory of relativity kinesthetically, through his muscles; Tesla saw the design of the alternating current generator in a vision; Gauss could calculate complex formulas instantly; the uneducated mathematical genius, Ramanujan, said that his genius came in dreams from a goddess named Namagiri. Brahms said that the inspiration for his music flowed into him from God, and that he could see them in his mind's eye. The inspirations arrived in perfect form, harmony, and orchestration.

The Inspiration of Nature

The inspiration of nature, of trees, brooks, skies, birds, and other flora and fauna is a well-known venue for breath-taking writing. The poets of the T'Ang Dynasty of eighth-century China influenced countless modern poets with their natural scene setting. Zhang Jiuling began a poem, "A lonely swan from the sea flies"; Li Po wrote: "Your grasses up north are as blue as jade"; Du Fu wrote: "What shall I say of the Great Peak?—The ancient dukedoms are everywhere green." (Translations by Witter Byner.) The English romantics used nature as inspiration and decried the industrial revolution as in Wordsworth's sonnet, "The world is too much with us; late and soon,/Getting and spending, we lay waste our powers;/Little we see in nature that is ours;/We have given our hearts away, a sordid Boon!"

To grow dizzy from contemplation and inhalation of natural glories is so commonplace in the creative process that it almost goes unnoticed. What causes youngsters to want to become scientists, especially biologists? The inspiration of nature. What inspires Sunday painters to stand by the seashore dabbing away? The inspiration of nature. Surely nature inspired the art of Audubon, the books of Roger Tory Peterson, and the works of Jean Sibelius.

Berge de Torne described the inspiration for a Sibelius andante thus:

On a cold day at the end of autumn he went for a walk. The crimson of the setting sun was reflected in the wide surface of the lake outside his villa, and the calm mirror of water was framed by a border of thin, pale gray ice. A huge bird came flying from the north and alighted on the lake. It was a white swan, resting for a while on its long journey to southern climes. As the sun went down the transparent frame of ice gradually approached the solitary bird from either side. Sibelius watched the scene until nightfall. He then went home to compose one of his andantes. (p. 47)

A new field of psychology called ecopsychology has arisen, led by professor, novelist, and social critic Theodore Roszak and others. The earth is personified into a female creature called Gaia, and we are all charged with not harming our Mother Earth by burning forests in the Amazon nor by polluting blue coral in Japan. People should realize and recover their deep connection with the earth. Depth psychologist Stephen Aizenstadt said, "Imagine a world in which carpenter knows beaver, lawyer knows eagle, philosopher knows the silence of the deep night." When people re-establish this essential connection, they will be "compelled to make the journey back to the source in nature that inspires their work" (p. 96). Wuthnow, in *Creativity and Spirituality: The Way of the Artist,* interviewed 100 artists in various genres about their creativity. He found many who receive their inspiration from nature. In fact, many consider nature to be their church. Wuthnow said, "Contemporary artists' views seem particularly influenced by an awareness of the natural environment's fragility" (p. 201).

Inspiration through Substances

The use of substances—alcohol, drugs, herbs—has a long and respectable reputation within the literature on the creative process in writers, artists, and others. Aldous Huxley wrote about the influence of mescaline, Samuel Taylor Coleridge about the influence of opium, Jack Kerouac about amphetamines, Edgar Allen Poe about absinthe, the seventh-century Chinese Zen poet Li Po about wine, Fyodor Dostoevsky about whiskey, Allen Ginsberg about LSD, Michael McClure about mushrooms—peyote—and also about heroin and cocaine.

The list of substances used could go on and on. The altered mental state brought about by substances has been thought to enhance creativity—to a certain extent. The partaker must have enough wits about self to descend (or ascend) into the abyss to reap what is learned there, but also to be able to return and put it aside. The danger of turning from creative messenger to addicted body is great, and many creators have succumbed, especially to the siren song of alcohol. Alan Bold put together an anthology of writers writing about drinking called *Drink to Me Only.* In his introduction, he wrote, "The artist, as explorer of emotions, frequently makes an unsteady odyssey across an ocean of drink.... The danger, of course, is that drinking will become a surrogate for creativity" (p. 13).

However, the use of substances has often taken on a mystical, spiritual aspect in the creative process. Allen Ginsberg had a vision of William Blake. "I had the impression of the entire universe as poetry filled with light and intelligence and communication and signals. Kind of like the top of my head coming off, letting in the rest of the universe connected to my own brain." The sensations and awarenesses continued. Biographer Barry Miles said Ginsberg viewed the initial vision as the most important, "the only really genuine experience I feel I've had" (p. 278).

Ginsberg was quoted by Dan Wakefield in *New York in the Fifties* as saying that the experimentation with mind-altering drugs by his group did not bring destruction to them. "Nobody I know died of an OD on junk, or committed suicide on acid, though some people did get freaked out on amphetamines. The big killer drug was booze...the casualty list of academic poets is enormous" (p. 171).

Psychoanalyst Albert Rothenberg noted that more than half of the U.S. writers who have won the Nobel Prize for Literature had difficulties with alcohol. However, his research showed that making a list of writers who abused alcohol could be matched by a list of writers who did not. He theorized that writers use alcohol after writing in order to forget and to cope with their anxious feelings that arise from going into the creative process. During and after this intense work, writers experience irritability. Some writers experience depression, some behave flamboyantly and eccentrically, some have affairs, some do what everyone does after work in order to relax—shop, play golf, see friends. And some writers drink. Novelist Robert Olen Butler, in a speech at the Art and Soul Conference at Baylor University in 2002, also asserted that the substances are used to relax rather than to inspire.

LSD has also been connected to creative inspiration. Psychoanalyst Stanislav Grof experienced a cosmic change in his orientation when he participated in one of the first LSD experiments. He then conducted experiments on others in his laboratory in Prague. He said, "The research led to a deeper understanding of the human psyche, the enhancement of creativity, and the facilitation of problem solving" (p. 72). Molecular biologist and Nobel Prize-winner Kary Mullis, who was one of the discoverers of polymerase chain reaction (PCR), described his college days at Berkeley studying astrophysics. He said he took LSD every week, and he would go to

Tilden Park and "sit all day thinking about the universe, time going backwards and forward. Some mornings I'd wake up and think I ought to write that out. So I did." Today such talk is not politically correct, as the dangers of addiction and the climate of recovery and co-dependency groups has led everyone to be more cautious about substances.

Inspiration by Others' Creativity, Especially by Works of Art and Music

Many creators are inspired by others' creativity, especially by works of art and music produced by other artists. Writer George Dennison was inspired by seeing the black-and-white paintings of Willem de Kooning just after World War II in 1948. Dennison sat down and looked at them for a whole day. The paintings spoke to him and for him in an unfathomable way. It was as if before seeing them, he had been incomplete, and now, for the first time, his intellectual and spiritual searching was being answered. The strong emotions he felt formed his aesthetic senses.

Art inspires. Music also inspires. Poet Laureate Rita Dove said in an interview with S. T. Smith, "I have a very personal connection to music." She has played the cello since she was a child and says, "music is one of the most intimate pleasures of my life. I think that my musical bent has spilled over into my writing. I love to experiment with the motion of words, and to me, language that doesn't sing in some way isn't valid."

On another note, friendships between artists of different genres abound in biographical literature. Dan Wakefield described the cross-fertilization among artists in Greenwich Village of New York of the 1950s. Likewise, the scene in the 1960s put in close geographic proximity playwright Sam Shepard, songwriters Bob Dylan, Joni Mitchell, and Patti Smith, photographer Robert Mapplethorpe, visual artist Andy Warhol, and many others.

Artist Juan Miró described his neighborhood in Paris on Blomet Street from 1921 to 1927. He said that Blomet Street was a crucial place at a crucial time for him. The street represented friendship and a lofty exchange of ideas and discoveries among a superior group of creative people. Miró and his friends listened to music, talked, drank, and were poor struggling artists together. Their favorite drinks were brandy and water, and Curacao tangerines. The young artists traveled by Metro through the Nord-Sud station between Montparnasse and Montmartre. They also read Rimbaud and Lautreamont, Dostoevsky and Nietzsche. Others he saw often included writer Antonin Artaud, visual artists Jean Dubuffet and Juan Gris, and even surrealists Andre Breton and Paul Eluard.

Pablo Picasso, a fellow Catalonian, came to visit Miró at the Rue Blomet, and he so liked Miró's work that he sent dealers to look at his paintings. Miró frequently visited Ernest Hemingway, who lived nearby and fell in love with Miró's painting, *The Farm*. Hemingway bought it, though he was a poor, starving writer. Miró and Hemingway would often have dinner with James Joyce. Ezra Pound was also part of the group. The cross-inspiration among these famous creators is legendary.

Thinkers and scholars routinely get inspiration from reading the works of others. French philosopher Michel Foucault found inspiration for his work, *The Order of Things*, in the works of Argentine playwright and novelist Jorge Luis Borges, who was making up an incongruous classification of animals from a fictional Chinese encyclopedia. Borges' audacious invention of this reference work inspired Foucault to consider the very nature of taxonomies, which to him were ceremonial categories that did not have life or place. Foucault began to deconstruct the very taxonomies that build our bureaucracies, our institutions, and our societies, and his philosophical works have become must-reading for postmodern thinkers.

In physics, the creation of the Manhattan Project put scientist Neils Bohr, Joseph Carter, Enrico Fermi, Richard Feynman, Hans Bethe, and Robert Oppenheimer, among others, together in a remote location in New Mexico, where they inspired each other to perfect the atomic bomb that was later dropped on Hiroshima and Nagasaki.

Inspiration from Dreams

The other side, the dark side, the night side, is very important to the creative process. Many creators trust their dreams, and dreams have inspired many creative works. Poet Tess Gallagher said, "I began to experience a kind of psychic suffocation which expressed itself in poems that I copied fully composed from my dreams." Her dreams seemed to predict the dissolution of her marriage, and her poems taken from her dreams were witnesses to what was happening inside her.

Dream researcher Stanley Krippner, writing on dreams and creativity in the *Encyclopedia of Creativity*, noted that people who are highly creative often believe in their dreams. Dreams can have secret, esoteric symbols and meaning. Dreams can help them with their inventions and with creating art. Dreams can predict the future. Creative people believe they can program their dreams, try to remember their dreams, and believe that their dreams help them to solve problems.

Robert Louis Stevenson had a dream that later became *The Strange History of Dr. Jekyll and Mr. Hyde*. Country western songwriter Alan Jackson said in his acceptance speech at the 2002 American Country Music Awards ceremony that the song "Where Were You When the World Stopped Turning?" came to him whole in a dream. He said, "I thank God for sending the words and music down to me because I believe I was an instrument for that for whatever reason." Poet and novelist Jim Harrison noted that one-third of one's life is spent in sleep and should not be dismissed. He said that humans have been noticing their dreams since the Pleistocene period, but for the past 20 years, we have been paying more attention to the global economy than to our dreams.

Literary critic M. Stratton, in an article in 2001, conjectured that dreams are parallel to films, a "creative artifact that spins a new perspective, sometimes enlightening, sometimes depicting, other times obscuring a specific issue or dynamic." Film maker Akira Kurosawa crowned his career with his 1991 film "Akira Kurosawa's Dreams" at age 80. Kurosawa created in this film eight of his most significant dreams throughout his life. I particularly loved the one called *The Crows*, in which Kurosawa as a young man steps into the Van Gogh painting *Bridge at Arles* and begins walking, dreamlike, in the landscape as if it were real. Kurosawa was an art student and said that when he would look at an exhibit by any one artist, say Cézanne, or Van Gogh, when he would step outside, the world would look like the paintings.

The Surrealists encouraged creators to use their dreams as inspiration. Freudian psychology had a great influence on the Surrealists. Both Freud and Jung wrote extensively on the significance of dreams. From Freud's belief that dreams are wish fulfillment to Jung's assertion that dreams capture the collective unconscious—the primitive archetypes lost to us in our waking state—these thinkers have sought to explain dreams. Books with dream images abound, purporting to say that a tooth dream is sexual, or a dream of falling reflects one's deep-seated fears. Whether or not this is true, creators don't seem to care. They use dreams' jolly, whimsical, dark, or brooding content for material, delighting in a dream's mysteriousness.

Songwriter Paul Simon, in an interview with Wilkinson, described how words come to him in dreams. Words begin to arrive after the music is mostly formed. They often come in the middle of the night. Once he told

Wilkinson, "I didn't get much sleep last night. The words are starting to come—they woke me up at six. Usually, when the words come in the middle of the night, I think, 'I'll remember that,' but I thought this time it was important to get up and write them down." Simon read a few entries from his notes. "The ocean and the atmosphere, clouds on fire, pay dirt, dancing DNA, wake up, don't sleep, get out of the way. Star quilt. That became 'quilt of stars.' 'If I was a guitar I wouldn't play that song'—didn't use it. 'Sage and sweet grass'—used it. 'Guru in the morning, bored by the afternoon, fool by sunset'—nope."

The Inspiration of Novel Surroundings: Travel

The railway journeys of Paul Theroux and Bruce Chatwin enhance our travel literature. One can imagine them energized by novelty as the windows open to new sight after new sight—scribbling in their notebooks and filing impressions in their brains as the scenery changed. Theroux has been traveling to exotic places for more than 30 years, and he still finds travel exciting and inspirational, as he continues to write interesting travel books.

Travel seems to facilitate the creative process, perhaps because the novelty of sensory experience is inspirational and a sense of naiveté is easy to maintain. Shifting our perspective by going to a new milieu, seeing how others do things differently, sleeping in strange rooms, eating exotic food— all can usher in great creative explosions. Physician Irving Oyle wrote about how his whole perspective on healing and on health was changed by a visit to the Tarahumara Indians in Mexico. Travel changed his whole worldview. "I had been taught in medical school…that all I could do was create the conditions under which healing can take place." In Mexico, he watched the work of an Indian medicine man who saw himself as a channel for cosmic energy through ritual. He saw how people believed they would be healed. He came to appreciate the importance of belief in healing ritual: "It is possible that this inner belief is a vital factor in any healing."

The above examples are some of the major themes when creators speak of inspiration.

Extrinsic Inspiration

Inspiration can also come extrinsically, from a sense of perfectionism, from the need to try again and again in order to make the perfect work. The process is a fluency, a sense of more more more…again again again. Dean Keith Simonton (1988, 1997) called it the "constant probability of success"—that is, once one has received some recognition for a creative work, the inspiration to do more and more continues, and the work gets another twist and another take. Endless elaboration seems possible, as witnessed by the work of comedy writer teams in a sitcom's tenth year, still coming up with new stories about the same characters on the same set.

Imagery

What's the difference between imagery and the imagination as regards the creative process? *Imagination* is a more artistic word and a more complicated process. *Imagery* is a more psychological word. Imagery is the ability to mentally represent imagined or previously perceived objects accurately and vividly. Imagery is an attribute of imagination.

According to Houtz and Patricola in the *Encyclopedia of Creativity*, imagery is not only visual, but also auditory, tactile, olfactory, and gustatory. There are even imagery theorists, mostly psychologists, who do experiments with various types of imagery. Three types of studies of creativity and imagery have been done: (1) biographical and anecdotal studies of creators telling about their personal imagery and how it inspired them; (2) studies which compared people's ability to create imagery and their scores on certain tests of creative potential; and (3) studies about creative imagery and creative productivity.

Guided imagery training goes on in creativity enhancement classes, in schools, and in business and industry. This training attempts to help people learn to manipulate images in their minds. Imagery is essentially spatial and, as such, concrete evidence of the mind's power to construct. Coaches teach athletes to imagine their performances before they compete; they visualize the ski run, the football play, or the course for the marathon and imagine themselves through every part of it. Athletes put on their "game faces" before athletic games and events, the image of the tough, strong, prepared player. Gallwey's *The Inner Game of Tennis* is an example of a book about guided imagery, as is a book by Maureen Murdock appropriately titled *Spinning Inward*. Murdock includes guided imagery exercises such as "Waterfall of White Light," "Mandala," and "Adventure with the Flower Fairy" to enhance children's creativity.

Imagination

Imagination is a mental faculty whereby one can create concepts or representations of objects not immediately present or seen. Imagination involving memory is called "reproductive imagination," and imagination that involves the formation of concepts beyond those derived from external objects is called "productive imagination." Imagination is called, in the OED, "the creative faculty of the mind in its highest aspect; the power of framing new and striking intellectual conceptions; poetic genius." To imagine is to make an image. Steven Spielberg as a child imagined strange and unusual creatures that lived on the other side of a large crack in his bedroom wall. The movie *E. T.* featured a re-creation of one of these.

"Oh, it's just your imagination," we say when our child "sees" a monster under his bed after we put the lights out. "Use your imagination," we tell someone who is stuck in solving a problem. The philosopher Aristotle, however, considered works of the imagination such as poetry, drama, and fiction more true than history because the artist could fabricate truth from the elements of history rather than exhaustively tell all of the facts. The artist is able to tell the truth on a deep level, being able to see the patterns and the overarching themes, using the imagination.

Archetypal psychologist James Hillman, in 1999, said that you don't train the imagination by studying psychology, but by studying film, theater, literature, history, the arts, and law, where practicing imagination is encouraged. "Imagination is one of the great archetypal principles, like love, order, beauty, justice, time." Thus it is beyond us. We cannot order love or make beauty without the help of chance and inspiration, and it is so with imagination. "Fantasies are more like the spirit. They blow where they will, and we are lucky if one comes near enough and lasts long enough to grasp."

Working from the imagination is both stimulating and entertaining. While writing my first novel, I chortled as the funny situations rolled out of my fingers onto the typewriter keyboard. I couldn't believe I was imagining all of this and that it was so pleasurable. After putting in one day writing 10 pages, I couldn't wait to walk, to think, and to imagine what my characters would do tomorrow. Rolling along from situation to situation as an improvising storyteller, I felt what jazz players must feel.

Visual imagination is not the only kind of imagination that creators use. Singer, in the *Encyclopedia of Creativity*, noted that composers imagine works in their "mind's ear," and mechanics imagine problems in their physical, spatial array. Imaginative thought is also called daydreaming, and may be called night dreaming, as well as fantasy. Let's try something gustatory. Picture yourself eating a half lemon. What do you feel in the back of your mouth as you imagine that?

Children's play is the seed ground of adult imagination. Pre-school children engage in make-believe. Story lines begin to develop in children's play as they grow toward kindergarten age. Games with rules follow during the primary years. Then symbolic play continues into adulthood with video games, gambling, amateur theater, or the vicarious enjoyment of stories in books, movies, and on television. The enjoyment of these takes imagination.

Intuition

Intuition. Having a hunch. "Just knowing." A gut feeling. What does this have to do with creativity? Everyone has intuition, but not everyone trusts intuition. Creative people not only trust their intuition, they prefer to use their intuition.

Carl Jung theorized that people prefer either Intuition or Sensing as a way of perceiving and understanding the world. Isabel Myers and her mother Katherine Briggs developed a forced-choice test based on Jung's theory called the *Myers-Briggs Type Indicator*, also known as the MBTI. In the MBTI, test-takers choose responses which indicate preferences such as intuition or sensing, introversion or extraversion, thinking or feeling, and judging or perceiving. Myers and McCaulley later described studies of National Merit Finalists, of gifted seventh-to-ninth-grade males and females, and of creative men and creative women. All preferred to use intuition over sensing. Over the years, I have given the *Myers-Briggs* to more than 800 talented teenagers. Profiles show that the majority of this group overwhelmingly preferred intuition. Though only 25% of the general population prefers intuition to physical sensing, 80% of the talented teenagers I tested have a preference for intuition.

Intuition is not verifiable by scientific or empirical means. Intuition is ambiguous, nebulous, whereas insight (which will be discussed next) is a brilliant flash. Policastro, in the *Encyclopedia of Creativity*, said that "creative intuition may be technically defined as a tacit form of knowledge that broadly constrains the creative search by setting its preliminary scope." She noted that creative people seem to have a sense when they start their creative work of what the end result will be. Biographical information, testing, historical and archival research, and experimental studies have shown that creative people use intuition in doing their work.

Intuition seems to be a personality preference for artists, scientists, and writers. The place of intuition in creating has long been honored. Plato thought that what we intuit was actually remembered from ancient imprints of the ideal, the true. Jung thought that intuition was a message from the collective unconscious of the archetypes of the deep human experience. I will discuss what studies using the MBTI show about creators and intuition in Chapters 6 through 11.

Poet Gary Snyder discussed "wild intuition" and imagination in an interview with Bill Moyers in Moyers' book *The Language of Life.*

I go to meet that blundering, clumsy, beautiful, shy world or poetic, archetypal, wild intuition that's not going to come out into the broad daylight of rational mind but wants to peek in. I never find words right away. Poems for me always begin with images and rhythms, shapes, feelings, forms, dances in the back of my mind. And much of the poem is already dancing itself out before I begin to look around for the words for it.... For me, language comes after imagination. My imagination is pre-linguistic, pre-verbal.

The importance of intuitive perception of the world, of a non-concrete but still tangible apprehension of underlying truth informs the creator's view of life. One is reminded of the Jungian psychological concept of synchronicity, that all coincidence is no coincidence, but a meaningful juxtaposition that can inform, if one can only see with intuitive powers. The mind turns in on itself, often in a meditative, contemplative atmosphere. Some people like to sleep for a few hours and then work in the wee hours of the night when everything is quiet and the mind is fresh from dreams; it is then that intuition may be strongest.

Insight

Insight is defined in Webster's *New World College Dictionary* as "the ability to see and understand clearly the inner nature of things, especially by intuition." Sternberg and Davidson, in the *Encyclopedia of Creativity*, elaborated on this definition, saying that when psychologists talk about intuition, they disdain the mystical associations, as they cannot be scientifically tested. Insight (1) has the appearance of suddenness, (2) requires preparatory hard work, (3) relies on reconceptualization, (4) involves old and new information, and (5) applies to ill-structured problems. Several types of insight have been researched by cognitive psychologists.

Insight, according to cognitive psychologists, involves restructuring the problem so that it can be seen in a different way. However, general verbal insight can be trained without the long training program advocated in 1995 by Sternberg and Davidson, (according to a 2000 study by Ansburg and Dominowski). Insight is important because it is universal, interesting, and many notable creative works have originated from it. We have all experienced the opening of the door of insight. When it happens, we just have to say "Aha! So that's how it works. So that's the answer. So that's what it's all about. So that's what the pattern is." The most famous image of insight is the image of Archimedes rising from the bathtub, saying "Aha!" and running down the street naked after he discovered the principle of the displacement of water. The "Aha!" generally comes after knowing the field really well, and after incubation.

Buckminster Fuller gained insight on the stability of the triangle in kindergarten while building structures from toothpicks and dried peas. The triangle later became the basis for his geodesic dome. George de Mestral, a Swiss inventor, gained insight needed to invent Velcro from burrs sticking to hunting clothes. When we gain insight, we glimpse the basic structure of the problem we are working on, and then we can create a solution. Everyone gets insights, but the process by which people get them remains somewhat mysterious, though cognitive psychologists have been working to make what happens in the brain during the insight process more clear. After receiving an insight, a person often uses imagination, fantasy, and dreaming to work on the insight. This is the period called incubation.

Incubation

The mind is at rest. The body is at rest. You have gone on to something else. The problem is percolating silently through the mind and body. This is incubation. But somewhere, inside, down there below the surface, the dormant problem is arising. A solution is sifting down. I always know when it's time to begin work in earnest on something that I have been incubating. I get a dream in which I am late in getting somewhere. Trains block the crossing. Bridges collapse just as I approach them. Roads wind to nowhere, and I can't get where I have to be. I am late. When I have that dream in its various configurations, I know it's time to begin working on that speech, that article, that poem, that story, that project, that book. My dreams are telling me that the solution is at hand. As I write, then, I spend long periods of time not writing, pacing, resting, reading, walking about in town, incubating the next part, the organization, the outline, the image that arose, the right word for that poem. You probably are the same, though your incubation might be in a different form.

Incubation was one of the steps in Wallas' four-part description of problem solving. Smith and Dodds, in the *Encyclopedia of Creativity*, listed six possible causes for the "incubation effect": (1) conscious work—that is, most problems are not finished all at once, and the person mulls the problem over; (2) recovery from fatigue—that is, the person has spent so much time preparing to solve the problem that they're darn tired; (3) forgetting inappropriate mental sets—that is, the person forgets what doesn't work; (4) remote association—that is, while waiting, the unconscious mind works on putting unlike things together for a solution; (5) opportunistic assimilation—that is, the person experiences helpful ideas and then incorporates them into the problem; and (6) unconscious work—that is, the problem solver isn't aware that he or she is working on a problem, but suddenly, awareness comes and the answer is there.

Time is needed after the problem is posed. Experiments have shown that if people are given a problem and told to solve it right away, they solve it less successfully than if they are given the problem and told to go away and think about it.

People often incubate while driving, sleeping, exercising, even showering. Kary Mullis, a Nobel-Prize winner, told the story about how he came up with PCR (Polymerase chain reaction) while driving:

> *Driving up to Mendocino and thinking about an experiment...I designed a system in my mind.... That was the eureka point.... By putting the triphosphates* [DNA building blocks] *in there myself, I could do this process over and over and amplify the DNA. I slammed on the brakes and stopped by the side of the road to calculate it out.... A couple miles down the road I stopped again. I realized I could use thes...oligonucleotides* [short pieces of DNA] *and get the enzymes to reproduce as big a piece as I wanted to.* (p. 68)

The relaxed drive brought the material to the surface. The Nobel Prize was engaged.

Improvisation and an Attitude of Playfulness

Jazz musician Nachmanovitch, in *Free Play,* also spoke of the creative life as improvisation, or "risky business." He said, "to follow your own course, not patterned on parents, peers, or institutions, involves a delicate balance of tradition and personal freedom, a delicate balance of sticking to your guns and remaining open to change."

The importance of improvisation and an attitude of playfulness cannot be understated. To play your musical instrument without music in front of you is frightening to some who have learned to trust in their reading ability and not in their intuition and musical memory. Think of children making up the game as they go along, lost in imagination, forming teams and sides in a fluid, all-day motion generated by the discourse of the moment. This fluidity, this improvisational forming and re-forming, is something most adults have lost. Games of charades, the game of Pictionary, and other improvisational toys often capture that delicious feeling of glee, joy, and bawdy humor that lends itself to creative expression.

Improvisation seems to be a key part of the creative process. Hayden Carruth stated that his writing process was like playing jazz. He asked, "What happens, subjectively and spiritually, when a musician improvises freely? He transcends the objective world, including the objectively conditioned ego, and becomes a free, undetermined sensibility in communion with others equally free and undetermined." Carruth, a fervent jazz aficionado, said that "my best poems have all been written in states of transcendent concentration and with great speed...I have interfused thematic improvisation and...metrical predictability." His poems are musical; they use meter and rhyme that he disguises within the line so that the reader will not notice. "Jazz gives us a new angle of vision, a new emphasis...in creative intuition."

The poet James Merrill used automatic writing as an improvisational technique: "Writing down whatever came into one's head, giving oneself over to every impulse—reasonable and unreasonable—concrete and abstract...is a means of granting oneself permission to speak from the heart, the depths of one's unconscious, the edges of the language." Other writers work similarly. William Butler Yeats used both his own and his wife's automatic writing as inspiration for work. Poet Octavio Paz also engaged in the practice.

Sawyer, in the *Encyclopedia of Creativity*, focused on theater and jazz. He said that "improvisation is present in all creativity," noting that the stakes are higher in music and theater because the performer cannot revise the work as writers or painters can. He also noted that improvisation in theater and music is almost always collaborative and requires instant communication between people in the improvisation group. Improvisation reveals inner truth. As theater director Peter Brook said, "Those who work in improvisation have the chance to see with frightening clarity how rapidly the boundaries of so-called freedom are reached." When an actor becomes calcified in doing a part, improvisation reveals the point where the lie begins. "If the actor can find and see this moment he can perhaps open himself to a deeper, more creative impulse."

Dance choreographers rely almost universally on improvisation in order to begin to make a dance. Martha Graham would begin to dance, outlining the pattern she wanted, and her dancers would imitate her. Then she would work on fixing the gestures so that the dancers would be moving together.

Theater games, scat singing, doodling, word rivers, and free dancing are all techniques I use in teaching improvisation. Fantasy games with role-playing also encourage improvisation, as do storytelling and joke-telling, which help instigate in the performer a trust that one will land on one's feet when sent out into the jungle.

Other Aspects of the Creative Process

In the studies, biographies, and memoirs I have read, I have noticed several other aspects of the creative process: (1) the need for solitude; (2) creativity rituals; (3) meditation; and (4) creativity as the process of a life.

The Need for Solitude

Psychologist Anthony Storr noted that modern society believes that people are their best selves when they are in human relationships. People who don't have human relationships, who are not married or in love or in a family, are viewed as somehow sick. The communion reached in human relationships has been viewed, ever since Freud, as the highest form of communion.

This is not necessarily the case. People strive for what in the creative process is called the illumination, or the feeling of wholeness, an inner unity. Having a relationship is just one way of attaining this. In creative people's lives, their work is often the most important thing. Others achieve inner peace through their spirituality or religious contemplations, contemplation of nature, art, or music, or through exercise. All of these are usually done alone. Creative people may be solitary, but that doesn't make them neurotic or unhappy.

These experiences that take place when a person is alone need not occur with external stimuli, but there is something transcendental about such experiences. When the person is suddenly alone and able to concentrate, she is able to decipher what may have seemed too puzzling and to unite ideas that may have seemed too different. Not being able to achieve solitude is a huge frustration for many creative people. Virginia Woolf, in her 1954 *Writer's Diary,* wrote:

> *And every time I get into my current of thought I am jerked out of it. We have the Keynes; then Vita came; then Angelica and Eve; then we went to Worthington, then my head begins throbbing—so here I am, not writing—that does not matter; but not thinking, feeling, or seeing—and seizing an afternoon alone as a treasure.*
> (p. 142)

Jung was one psychoanalyst who encouraged solitude, urging his patients to set aside part of each day to go into a reverie of active imagination. This active imagination is similar to what Maslow called "self-actualizing behavior," and it is similar to the creative process. Maslow said that when the creative person is being inspired, he suspends time and seems unconscious of time passing, being so concentrated that the moment is all that is there. Maslow said this ability to become "timeless, selfless, outside of space, of society, of history, is the prerequisite for creativeness."

Solitude induces reverie. The state between sleeping and waking is relaxed, allowing images and ideas to come so that attention can be paid. What is important is a state of passivity and receptivity. Some people achieve this while cooking, cleaning, or sewing alone, walking in the woods, or during a long, boring drive. Virginia Woolf called solitude "real life" and went on to say, "I find it almost incredibly soothing—a fortnight alone." Visual artist Audrey Flack said that working in solitude helps the artist see her destiny. "When you are working, you are alone with yourself. You get in touch with your own destiny. Like entering a dream state, the tendency is to disbelieve that that state has validity. But that is the true reality" (p. 3).

Most of my students are mothers, wives, teachers, busy women who barely have a minute's peace. Their moments of solitude must be stolen early in the morning, late at night, or while commuting to work. It is indeed odd that educators and theorists rarely mention the necessity for solitude in most of their advice on how to be creative. In creativity class, we go on a field trip to a woods, to a cemetery, and to an art museum to meditate on nature, on the dark side, and on beauty. The students are not to talk to anyone, including each other, while we visit these places. These busy teachers/mothers walk alone throughout the day. Their Thoughtlogs often bloom with thanks for a day of this kind of solitude.

Creativity Rituals

Ritual is repetitive practice. How is someone who improvises, who is spontaneous, who is risk-taking, also prone to want ritual when he or she creates? Ritual involves special places, special procedures, special repetitive acts during or before creating. Rituals are sometimes personal. The artist, Marlene Ekola Gerberick, described going to her studio, creating a circle, pacing around the current work she is making, lighting candles, picking up stones and feathers, all the while transporting herself from the world of her outside life to her inner world of creating.

My own creativity ritual is simple. I get up, make coffee, read a poem or two, and come up to my office to work. I work for several hours, pausing to watch the birds outside or to listen to the Amish buggies that clip clop down the street. Then, when my stomach tells me, I go down and have lunch. In the afternoon, I leave the house and go to my office at the university, to the outer world. I teach at night, so I get the mornings to work. Ritual serves to remove the creator from the outer and propel her to the inner. What rituals do you observe when you create?

Some people walk or exercise before creating, and they often get their best ideas while doing it. Some people go for a long drive. Some arrange their rooms or desks a certain way. Some like to work at a certain time of day. The approach to the work is ritualistic, and the work itself could be called, perhaps, the ceremony.

Meditation

Meditation is in. Look at the books on the shelves at your local bookstore. Some have said the past decade and the next are marked by a spiritual need—a need for communion with the self and with others. An ongoing curiosity about eastern religions continues from the 1960s. Writers, artists, and scientists with backgrounds in Christianity and Judaism seem to reject dogma, and they also reject mystical traditions they find in their homegrown religions. They begin to study eastern religions.

An astonishing number of writers, for example, have embraced Buddhism. One suspects that this is because of the attention paid to meditation, to solitude, to the going within oneself of that religious faith. Here is a partial list: Allen Ginsberg, Robert Bly, W. S. Merwin, Anselm Hollo, Anne Waldman, Gary Snyder, Jane Augustine, John Cage, William Heyen, Lucien Stryk, and Philip Whalen. Rock poet Leonard Cohen recently emerged from several years in a Buddhist monastery.

Others have embraced the contemplative life of the Christian monastery—for example, poets Kathleen Norris (who is a minister) and Daniel Berrigan (who is a priest). Norris wrote a book, *Cloister Walk*, on her search for peace through the Benedictines. MacArthur Award "genius" award winner Patricia Hampl wrote a book, *Virgin Time*, about her search for creative and spiritual peace through pilgrimages to Assisi, in Italy, and to various cloisters and holy places.

The vehicles for discovering one's self are breath control, meditational technique, visualization, imagery. Often, the creative work follows the meditation, and the meditation is a preparatory ritual for the creative work.

Several workshops I attended were remarkably similar. The leaders took us through relaxation exercises in which we progressively relaxed our toes, our feet, our legs, and the rest of our bodies, breathing deeply. Then we were mentally placed in a setting, often a beach with the waves crashing, or a forest with the birds singing and the leaves rustling, or the ramparts of a castle looking over the purple plain. Soft synthesizer music or tinkling bells played on a tape recorder controlled by the group leader, and we visualized ourselves in these places.

With 500 other people, I attended a workshop in New York City by Daniel Goleman, whose best-selling book *Emotional Intelligence* took the world by storm, even in places like Taiwan, where it was the best selling book ever. His wife, a psychotherapist, led us through a meditation on being mindful by having us contemplate and slowly taste a raisin. The next day, I attended a labyrinth workshop by Lauren Artress. We walked a canvas replica of the 11-circuit Chartres labyrinth, a concentric circular path, in slow meditative beats.

These group relaxation and visualization techniques help us contemplate our inner selves, discover our inner truths, quiet us to the point where we will pay attention to what is going on inside, calm us, and release us from the pressures of the hustle and bustle. Of course, the popularity of these workshops and techniques is based on truths spiritual people have known for ages. Creative people, mystics, and ascetics of all religions have always known that calm inner solitude is essential for true knowledge. Jesus fasted and prayed for 40 days alone in the wilderness before he led the believers into Jerusalem.

The connection of meditation with the spiritual and with therapy is implicit, and workshop leaders, like therapists, are often viewed as priests or gurus. This investiture of psychology with religious import began with the advent of psychoanalysis. A few years ago, after I won a $5,000 Individual Artist Fellowship in poetry, I used some of the award to attend a workshop on spiritual autobiography given by Dan Wakefield, who wrote his own spiritual autobiography, *Returning*, in the early 1990s. Wakefield said that for his generation of young, creative people in the 1950s, psychotherapy replaced God. He said, "I entered psychoanalysis with the high seriousness of purpose and commitment of any acolyte taking his vows to a rigorous religious order. Like many in my generation, I had already made the intellectual substitution of Freud for God." During Wakefield's workshop, we learned about writing in community and shared how our creativity has been affected by our autobiography.

Research evidence has shown that altered consciousness does aid people not only in divergent thinking, but also in capturing internal essence. Cowger and Torrance trained students in meditation and in relaxation. They found that the meditators had significant gains in heightened consciousness of problems, perceived change, invention, sensory experience, expression of emotion and feeling, synthesis, unusual visualization, internal visualization, humor, and fantasy. Those trained in relaxation had gains in synthesis and unusual visualization. All were pre- and post-tested on the *Torrance Tests of Creative Thinking*; results showed that meditation and relaxation do have some relationship to perceived processes of creativity, at least in their effect on paper and pencil measures. Torrance and Cowger, in 1999, described other studies, especially in Japan, which showed that meditation enhanced creative thinking as measured by the tests.

Creativity as the Process of a Life

Others have viewed the creative process not merely as an altered consciousness, an immense concentration, an attainment of solitude, but as more. That is, we can look at the process of a creative person's life and see how an adult creative producer has lived. Gruber, in *Darwin on Man*, looked at Darwin's life from the psychological perspective to see how lifelong creativity unfolded and developed. He is still writing about Darwin's life, discovering new insights.

We all live lives that could be studied. The creative process is viewed these days as the province of every human being, and not just of the Darwins of the world or of those who make creative products such as music or poems or mathematical formulas, or of those who reach eminence. People's lives are their creative products.

In enhancing people's creativity, teachers sometimes use methods such as visualization, imagery, metaphorization, chanting, and the formulation of affirmations. People hold sacred objects such as quartz crystals and sit beneath pyramids. They go on vision quests and bang drums, chant in tones and dance like dervishes, seeking inner peace and the guidance for living a creative life. Creativity is intertwined with the feeling of awe, of closeness to the essential that results.

Other, less exotic methods such as writing in journals (Julia Cameron, Ira Progoff, and Natalie Goldberg), drawing (Betty Edwards and Peter Jones), crooning and engaging with the Mozart effect (Don Campbell), or dancing (Gabrielle Roth) are also employed in teaching people to be more creative and thus to enhance the process of their lives.

This quest for inner meaning has even made it to our public television stations where, just last month, fund-raising was led by former high school guidance counselor Wayne Dyer, one of the top spiritual teachers and self-help authors of the day. I myself have attended workshops at the Open Center in New York City and at the Omega Institute at Rhinebeck, New York, where I studied and sought the truth of my inner self through various special workshops that featured creative expression—an intensive journal workshop, dream workshops, singing workshops, empowerment workshops, improvisational theater workshops. I was even a visiting lecturer on an ocean cruise called an " Intuition Cruise," where I taught a writing workshop and spoke about enhancing creativity using the ideas in this chapter as an example of various ways people experience the creative process. As I stated in Chapter 1, everyone purports to be an expert on creativity, and the new age thinkers are no exception. Almost all of them have books that tell us how to enhance our creativity.

All of these theories and techniques have common threads and are outgrowths of the humanistic psychology movement and of the work of such humanistic psychologists as Carl Rogers and Abraham Maslow, and of such Gestalt psychologists as Fritz Perls. We are all interested in probing our inner psyches and making our lives our works of art, to reach inner placidness as human beings. Many people react strongly and positively to these experiential exhortations. The talk shows abound with psychology experts who say we must work on ourselves first, and then happiness and fulfillment will follow.

In speaking of creativity as the process of a life, Anthony Storr noted three periods in the process of the creative life. The first is the imitative stage, the period in which the young creative person learns what has been already done and spends a lot of time imitating. The second is where the creative person dispenses with what has already been done and enters upon an assured and masterful period of production in which the need to communicate with a wide public becomes clear. In the third period, the creative person pulls back from the need to communicate and may turn to unconventional forms without rhetoric or posing, continuing an exploration of areas that are not intrapersonal but perhaps are spiritual or universal.

Dabrowski and Piechowski also spoke to lifelong development, of life as a process and not a series of stages. They say higher forms of development are achieved once a person has moved beyond primitive drives, selfishness, feelings of inferiority toward others, to transcendence, self-determination, and "sustained creativity and lucidity of the mind in spite of infirmity of the body." In the Dabrowski theory of emotional development, with reference to the creative person, creativity is manifested in the person's overexcitability, or "enhanced and intensified mental activity distinguished by characteristic forms of expression which are above common and average." It has been said that while most people live with the radio on, creative people have satellite dishes. These are their amplified overexcitabilities.

Another theory of the creative process of a life is that of archetypal psychologist James Hillman. In 1996's *The Soul's Code*, he propounded the myth of the acorn. He spoke of the notion that everyone has a "call" to his or her work in life. A child knows his daimon from the images that he is enamored of and cannot get enough of. This image can be described as compressed potential—an acorn. During early life, if a child is lucky, a mentor arrives who "sees" the child in ways that the parent cannot, for the parent is involved in putting a roof over the child's head and food on the table. The image that is seen by the mentor helps the child to realize his destiny or "call." This image, or guide, is called a "daimon" in Greek mythology, a "guardian angel" in Christian mythology, and a person's "genius" in Roman mythology. Alternatively, the child may discover the acorn in later life by recalling the images that were acted out in childhood. In a review of *The Soul's Code*, Jay Griffiths spoke of his own childhood images:

> *You will remember… bits of your childhood when your Daimon,
> furiously demanding, saw what it needed. For me, what I needed
> was books. I read* War *and* Peace *when I was eight, and pulled the*
> Interpretation of Dreams *off the library shelves before I was ten.
> I read it. It frustrated me till I cried with incomprehension, but I
> had to read it.*

The daimon is perceived through intuition, gut feelings that a person gets as to what path to take. Visual artist Audrey Fleck spoke about the importance of the initial images in the work of the artist. An artist who works hard can make the images she has always known, which are images that come from her own inner truth. These images "triggered an impulse to go into the field of art." Then the artist learns to define art as the world defines it and to make images that will define her as a "professional artist. Finally, with enough courage, discipline, detachment, passion, and resistance," the artist can put the world of art away and "reconnect with your initial impulse—that which you always believed." Now, however, the artist can "blend" the information learned from the world of art with the initial images. Fleck said, "You have now appropriated art. Until that point, art appropriated you" (p. 21).

Hillman's explanation is similar to Feldman's theory of the crystallizing experience that grabs a person and sets him on his path, and it is similar to my concept that certain predictive behaviors are common to each domain of talent. Saying that the acorn theory is neither fatalistic (for a person can refuse the intuition and the insight) nor deterministic (for a person's destiny is not pre-formed), Hillman argues that human creativity thus follows a certain developmental path. The path is formed by the Platonic myth of the daimon, acorn, or call. I have called this the "Thorn" on the Piirto Pyramid of Talent Development. Other names for it are: Genius, Name, Incurable Mad Spot, Sacred La, Divine Spark, Invisible Sun, Configuration of Purpose, Solar Angel, Gift, Cosmic Task, Delight, Leader Within, Archeus, Salt, Sacred Calling, Stone, Inner Fire, Native Star, Vision, Character, and Guiding Image (Reynolds, 2003).

In 1997 and 2002, commenting on the theory of the acorn, fellow creativity instructor at our university, F. C. Reynolds, said that the daimon can be discerned in the life of an individual by considering the etymological difference between the words "talented" and "gifted." A *talent* is like a valuable to be used at the convenience of the owner. There are many people who have a talent for music, but feel free to take it or leave it. However, the root of the Germanic word "gift" includes the concept of poison. Someone gifted is blessed and poisoned all at once. The *gift* is where we experience oceanic consciousness, lose track of time, become so involved in the frenzied doing of our creative passion that time, food, sleep, and place don't matter. The gift is all-consuming, dazzling; the person loves doing it, and when she's not doing, it she's thinking about it, and if she doesn't do it, she becomes ill.

The person may find through a car crash, through therapy, or through some life-altering experience that he should have been a writer, a musician, a scientist. According to Reynolds, this is the daimon interceding to return the individual to his "gift," where the mind is appropriately on fire, full of light and din. When he teaches his Creativity, Inc. course to high school and college students, Reynolds assists the students in finding where the "gift" has been at work in their lives. This might be in where they have been wounded or where they have spent much time as children but have forgotten what caught their hearts. Reynolds asks his students to bring their favorite book from preschool to his classes and to recapture the images that engaged them then.

Creativity and Madness

In the last few years, this aspect of creativity and the creative process has been well researched. Socrates, in Plato's *Phaedrus*, said there are two kinds of madness, the first, "one produced by human infirmity," the second, "a divine release of the soul from the yoke of custom and convention." He further differentiated four kinds of creative madness, or divine inspiration: (1) prophetic, or Apollonic; (2) initiatory, or Dionysian; (3) poetic, governed by the Muses; and (4), the erotic, governed by Aphrodite and Eros. That philosophers in the fifth century B.C. so finely differentiated among types of inspiration shows how long creative people have been suspected of being a little mad.

The methodology of those who study the mental illness of creators has been questioned in 1990 by Rothenberg and in 2002 by Schlesinger, both of whom said that the diagnosis list in the DSM-IV (*Diagnostic and Statistical Manual*), which is used to categorize mental disorders and is referred to by physicians and psychologists for coding for insurance, is confusing, as it includes milder forms of disorders within the same diagnoses as psychotic forms. Schlesinger pointed out, "the highly creative person may well experience natural oscillations in mood and productivity, and periods of intense focus with a free tumbling of excited thoughts," and noted that even the DSM-IV *Manual* "grudgingly" says that persons experiencing certain psychotic disorders may be "creative and productive." Thus, categorizing creativity as a state of mental disorder is out of line. The controversy continues.

Lombroso equated genius with madness in the late nineteenth century. Studies by Jamison and Andreason affirmed the connection of creativity with manic-depressive illness (bipolar disorder). Rothenberg disagreed and said instead that schizophrenia was more closely related to creativity. The Academy Award-winning movie about the mathematician John Nash, *A Beautiful Mind*, romanticized the schizophrenic struggle. The movie seemed to show that schizophrenia both enhanced and hindered Nash's creativity.

In 1995, Ludwig looked at more than 1,000 biographies that had been reviewed in the *New York Times Book Review*. Over half of them were of people in the artistic professions. Depression, anxiety, substance abuse, and psychiatric hospitalizations were more common among these people than in others who had had biographies written about them. A 1996 study by Stack showed that "painters, sculptors, craft artists and printmakers were at higher risk of suicide than musicians, dancers, actors, directors, and authors." These discoveries by researchers confirm old images, as throughout the ages, the word "creative" has been tied to the "losing of mind." The ancient cave paintings of Lascaux, the shamanic trance states of northern tribes, the fear and ridicule of traveling troupes of entertainers all point to the ancient connection of the arts with the strange.

Suicide Among Creators

A consequence of depression and mental illness can be suicide. In 2000 and 2001, Preti and Miotto, in several retrospective studies, looked at 4,564 eminent artists from the nineteenth and twentieth centuries using entries in biographical encyclopedias. The artists were 94% male. Poets and writers were most likely to commit suicide, with women poets having the highest incidence. Painters and architects had a lower than average rate of suicide. The mean age for suicide was 44. Preti and Miotto concluded that "the result is suggestive of a greater prevalence of mental disorders among artists than among the general population."

Preti and Miotto theorized that the reason may be the enormous toll that rejection of their work takes on the artists. "Rejection of personal product is the precipitating antecedent of suicide," they stated. Disease, social upheaval such as the Nazi persecution of Jews, addiction, and mental illness were also thought to be possible causes. Mood shifts are common in some creators, and during the down times, meditation and introspection are common. Preti and Miotto stated that "depressive episodes…give access to 'inner dimensions' of life, allowing considerations of themes linked to guilt, sorrow, and death," which can provide subject matter for creativity. The more solitary creative professions have the higher risk of suicide.

Suicide rates in musicians were found to be lower than for other types of artists. The authors speculated that social status might play a part; in order to become a musician, one must have some financial resources in order to persevere. Suicide rates are lower in privileged social classes. Another reason is that the technical and physical skills required in music and the fact that music performance requires social presence are less congruous with mental disorder than the solitary milieu of creators such as poets and writers.

Arguably, music also serves an emotional purpose that is more widely recognized than literature, or as the authors said, it "requires the elaboration of elements which are ultimately linked to the more profound areas of the mind"; working with sound could perhaps be "working in a realm one step closer to the Self, even to those parts of the Self that are the source of conflict and upset." Musicians might therefore sublimate emotional conflict.

For some, poetry, not music (though the ancient Greeks always had the two together), is closer to the self. The events of September 11, 2001 turned the nation to poetry as solace, as comfort, as Caroline Kennedy said on the Diane Rehm Show, July 5, 2002, on National Public Radio. Our souls need poetry. Poet Ted Hughes said poetry exists on a deep, bottom level:

> *Poetry sales are supposed to rise during a war, aren't they, when people are forced to become aware of what really matters.... [W]e all live on two levels—a top level where we scramble to respond moment by moment to the bombardment of impressions, demands, opportunities. And a bottom level where our last-ditch human values live—the long-term feelings like instinct, the bedrock facts of our character.... [P]oetry is one of the voices of the bottom level.*

Jung said, "The [artistic] vision is not something derived or secondary, and it is not a symptom of something else. It is true symbolic expression—that is, the expression of something existent in its own right, but imperfectly known" (1933, p. 169). Jung thought that the artist was a vehicle, "one who allows art to realize its purposes through him." The artist is not only a private human being, but also "collective man, one who carries and shapes the unconscious, psychic life of mankind." The life of the creator cannot explain the work of the creator: "It is his art that explains the artist, and not the insufficiencies and conflicts of his personal life."

My point of view is similar. Although the life of the artist (creative person) is interesting, the work of art (the creative product) stands on its own; through somewhat mysterious channels, art speaks for all people who find a relationship to it. This is perhaps best explained in people's bonding to popular songs, which are the society's rune songs, or poetry. While the creative process described here is interesting, going through the process does not guarantee that the work itself will be judged creative, worthy, or germane.

Conclusion

Perhaps the suggestions in this chapter on the creative process—that the process is rich, sometimes mysterious, and certainly complicated—will lead to an expanded repertoire on the part of educators seeking to enhance creativity. What we have learned and what we continue to learn about the creative process may, ultimately, help us understand the world, help us understand ourselves, reconcile the humanities and the sciences, help us be more creative, help us make better products, save the world, heal the world, or just design a new dress for the prom. It all depends upon your point of view.

Summary

1. The creative process has engaged the best thinkers of the world from ancient times.

2. The creative process is a concern of scientists as well as humanists. Scientific experimentation has resulted in the demystifying of many popular creative process beliefs.

3. Brewster Ghiselin's essay on the creative process spoke of oceanic consciousness, automaticity, restlessness, aesthetics, trance, hard work, and the concentration of a life.

4. Four core attitudes for creativity are naiveté, self-discipline, risk-taking, and group trust.

5. There are Seven I's of the creative process: Inspiration, Imagery, Imagination, Intuition, Insight, Incubation, and Improvisation.

6. Various types of inspiration are the visitation of the muse, the inspiration of nature, inspiration through substances, inspiration by works of art and music, inspiration from dreams, and the inspiration of novel surroundings.

7. Solitude seems to be a necessary condition during some aspects of the creative process.

8. Creators have personal rituals they undertake when they create.

9. Meditation is commonly used in the creative process.

10. Contemporary psychological and religious thought emphasize that the creative process has universal implications. Creativity is often thought of as the process of a life.

11. In the process of a life, some creators more than others have a tendency toward mental illness and higher rates of suicide.

Part II

How To Enhance Creativity

Chapter 3
Encouraging Creativity: Motivation and Schooling

My life is what I have done, my scientific work; the one is inseparable from the other. The work is the expression of my inner development, for commitment to the contents of the unconscious forms the man and produces his transformations. My works can be regarded as stations along life's way. All my writings may be considered tasks imposed from within; their source was a fateful compulsion. What I wrote were things that assailed me from within myself.
—Carl Jung

How does one become a creative adult? Can creativity be taught? What have we learned about how creative adults become creative? Do we even want more creative people? Where do creativity and the discipline to practice intersect? Whose responsibility is it to encourage creativity? Is it the responsibility of the schools?

Can we stifle creativity? What happens when we stifle creativity? What is the place of trauma in the enhancement of creativity?

In reading the many biographies and accounts of the childhoods of creative people to research this book, I have been both awed and dismayed. Often, the childhoods of creative people had sad or traumatic elements; some of these very creative people experienced literal orphan-hood, while others had seriously dysfunctional and troubled families. This makes it difficult to write a chapter on how to enhance creativity. While writing this book, I often shared the process with my students, as each week they ask me whom I've been reading about and what their childhoods were like. I began joking that when I got to the chapters of this book about teaching and parenting for creativity, I would give just a few words of advice and be done with it. For teachers, these words are the following: Try to be the teacher that the creative child will remember as encouraging, not as discouraging. For parents, these words—only partially tongue-in-cheek— might be: To enhance your child's creativity, get divorced or have some other family trauma.

The jokes fade, but the question remains. Does family trauma automatically yield creative genius? Do not all the biographical reports point to this? Perhaps Alice Miller is right when she notes in *The Untouched Key* that creative people experience trauma in their childhoods, but they also have some warm, encouraging person to be close to, while destructive persons experience trauma in their childhoods without that warm, encouraging person being there. Of course, nowadays it is fashionable to come from a dysfunctional family. Everyone is somehow codependent, addicted, or otherwise messed up. We can all blame our mothers and fathers for our problems. A whole industry is based on psychological healing from childhood trauma. If the ideal family ever did exist, no one these days comes from one. Then why isn't everyone creative?

Many creative people have little or nothing positive to say about their families or their schools, and many creative people certainly have had family lives with early trauma, including frequent moves, death of a parent, sickness, absence of a parent through divorce or substance abuse, or childhood abuse and neglect. You name it, creative people have experienced it during their childhoods.

What Creative Writers Said about their Schooling

A few years ago, I did a survey of published poets and novelists who worked in the old National Endowment for the Arts Poets in the Schools program. These were writers listed in *A Directory of American Poets & Writers* who met certain criteria. To be eligible for listing, a writer must have 12 points of accumulated credits based on previous publications. For example, a published novel is worth 12 points, as is a chapbook or book of poetry. A short story in a journal is worth four points, and a published poem is worth one point. Most of these published authors are still writing—producing novels, poetry, essays, and criticism. And most still chose to list themselves in the 2002 *Directory.*

Here is a sampling of what 25 contemporary American writers had to say about their own childhoods and school experiences in answer to this question: "How did your own experiences as a child in school help or hinder your creativity?" Their responses follow.

Writer 1:   *I was given responsibility and allowed to fail, but I was also allowed to see myself grow and was given recognition. I was also given the sense that there are forces working through us that help us grow and do worthwhile work, and I have ever since believed in these forces.*

Writer 2:   *I was lucky enough to have teachers who told me to get started, praised what I did, and encouraged me to continue. They also insisted I learn much of what is my craft, the skill of using the tools and rules of the trade. My family also, being creative and artistic, kept me encouraged, admonished, and also believing it to be not unusual but ordinary to do such things well. They were often my best critics.*

Writer 3:   *My artistic life is a negative response to the negativity of this world to my well being. I think it is therefore very positive in its energy flow. I've never quit being the daydreaming non-conformist I was at 18.*

Writer 4:   *Hard to remember—I was always full of "chutzpah." I always loved school, even when I had awful teachers, the way Francie, in* A Tree Grows in Brooklyn, *loved the library. You must understand that no creativity can occur in uptight, tense, places. Kids must feel good in themselves. That's the first job.*

Writer 5:   *It is tempting to say that they hindered it. But not all. In my day, when a quick child was finished before the rest of the class he or she was asked to do a report or sometimes write a story. What began as busy work sometimes became the best part of any day. But all too often, the different answer was crushed, the need to question what seemed too pat was seen as insolence, a novel approach or use of materials was disallowed automatically without a trial. An abiding horror from grade one on was the objective test in which no possible answer was really right, and my desperate need to explain why could not be met. Under the pressure, one's creativity soon gets put to figuring out what might have been in the test maker's mind, so one can guess what the test maker expects. The best thing was learning, in high school, to put a textbook in front of me, to look up from time to time with an interested expression as if I were taking notes, while I wrote my stories in class after class and refined them in study hall. Aside from two excellent high school teachers who continually challenged our imaginations and abilities, virtually nothing in my schooling helped much.*

Writer 6:   *We had "dramatics" for 30 minutes each Tuesday, and were required to recite—with prescribed gestures—a poem. God, how dreadful! Art class was a reward if the whole class was good the whole week and if the teacher had a project she liked, and if there were materials (which our parents paid for in September but we never saw except as a handout of one sheet of manila paper at a time), this on Friday afternoon. Music wasn't much more. What helped my creativity was having a place of my own in the attic that even my brothers, even my mother, couldn't invade, where I could even spill ink or paint (not to mention tears) without being punished.*

Writer 7:   *I had the benefit of encouragement by a fine teacher—fine teachers, I should say—my parents, especially my father; and much luck. Most of what gets done in school and most of what gets encouraged in school does not contribute to creativity. When I feel I'm dealing with my own experiences at something like their true value—however those around me and my environment bring this about—I feel capable of doing things. I learned perseverance working in the fields; I learned about persons and nature in those same fields. Having operated a commercial garden and orchard for some 30 years, I've had reasons to cultivate the habit of observation and reflection. Schools have helped in that regard, I think.*

Writer 8:   *As a child in a small town school in a high Colorado valley, my teachers let me express my feelings for the earth, my horse, and how I hated leaving the ranch to come to town. The influence before that was the limited far-from-town library of three books—the Bible, the poetry of Robert Burns, and* The Diseases of Cattle. *The latter book first made me want to write poetry. I came across the words* hemorrhagic septicemia. *When my father pronounced them for me and told me what they meant, I heard the words sing and saw the tragic death of cattle.*

Writer 9:   *Totally terrible; depressing and self-destructive; made me develop a "closet" personality and a disdain for mass society at large.*

Writer 10: *I was a bookworm and read for escape; I was also paranoid and persecuted by other kids through fifth grade or so. After that, I eventually went to a school for gifted children that was better socially—I wasn't so weird. High school was an utter waste, and that was one of the country's supposedly best school systems. My creativity? Growing up outside New York and having access to Manhattan's cultural life was my salvation. Also, sympathetic parents.*

Writer 11: *Even though teachers encouraged us to draw, and even though some of my own paintings and pastel drawings were given special honor and hung in the hall outside the principal's office, I lost all interest in visual art by the fifth grade. Art projects were too structured (so that teachers wouldn't fail, I imagine). But then too, in those days, imagination wasn't much of a priority.*

Writer 12: *Since I was an only child and my parents were divorced, I grew up in a fairly lonely environment. I think this fostered my reading and my work habits. Writing is a lonely profession. So I was prepared.*

Writer 13: *School must have helped—but who knows, finally, where the lyric impulse comes from? Some aestheticians believe the creative impulse begins with an experience bordering on the traumatic. But certainly my reading—which was intense and wide—helped. Otherwise I might believe that schooling plays a very minor part in kindling the creative fires. But I know many poets who never read a book until their late teens who were uniformly poor in school.*

Writer 14:

I had a wonderful language/literature teacher through junior high/high school that offered sheer encouragement. As far as anything in early life helping or hindering my urge and ability to write, experiences as a child at home, certainly, were the far greater factors.

Writer 15:

I got an "F" in conduct in junior high. That helped a lot. I had fun in class. My father was pissed. But I don't mean badness, cruelty, "hoody" behavior. I mean acting up wittily, that glee that shakes up a long school day. My father and I get along fine now, but in those days he must have imagined that I was being mean and foul or something—to get that "F." I was being, simply, irreverent and spontaneous. I was finding my own way to like school while the teacher was going over and over stuff. And I know that's elitism. Some of the kids needed all that drill—and I was in the way with my whispering and chortling. But I kept it up. Irrepressible. A pain. Guilt tormented me when I lay awake thinking how much the teachers resented my ways. Next day I'd do it all again. Well, I was, luckily for me, intellectually quick, and they might have had some way of endorsing that. The "quick" kid is often discriminated against by the necessities of disciplined mass education. Something in me was addicted to rebellion in this matter.

Writer 16:

I would say that most of my school experiences were god-awful. However, I was a very rebellious student and often learned things of value by default. For example, at 13 I was subjected to the first "teaching" of Shakespeare (The Merchant of Venice). I immediately responded to Will S. and realized that the teaching had nothing to do with the poetry. Accordingly, and with full recognition of what I was doing, I read all of Shakespeare on my own. I did not wish to have it spoiled. One old classics master was also an amateur botanist, and he sparked a lifelong interest in me on walks in the woods, which got me out of competitive sports. Probably the most positive of any of my school experiences.

88

Writer 17: *A dual language background and a large dose of ethnicity helped. I was, for the most part, discouraged rather than encouraged by my teachers.*

Writer 18: *For the most part, I was lucky. I ran into several teachers who encouraged me to write as much as I wanted to and rewarded me with kind words. Also, my classmates seemed to enjoy my efforts. God bless them all. In college, however, I was not so lucky. I could not and would not write a standard paper. One idiot actually asked me if I would mind writing a more conventional paper the next time. And I did mind, and that's why I dropped out. I'm getting mad right now just thinking about it—and also this other idiot in teachers college, who took us to visit a classroom—where, by coincidence, this incredible woman was doing a creative writing class. I wrote an essay on whatever it was we were supposed to report from that visit, but I went on to report on the creative writing aspects—and this nut marked me down for going beyond the limits of his assignment. Shame on him. He is the reason I seriously question the creative capacity of anyone who graduates from a teachers college. In fact, my college experience was so bitter, so anti-creative, I have my doubts about anyone who graduates. Period.*

Writer 19: *I remember school as a struggle to slant my paper in the same direction as the right-handed kids. School generally is carefully constructed to eliminate sensitivity, assertion, intelligence, and guts. The question is, if I didn't get the creative impulses from school, where did they come from? Certainly not from middle-class parents. Not from my genes. I think they came from the fact that I was fat, repressed, left out of the social scene. And when you've got that many strikes, you've got to be creative to survive. Creativity, then, was a survival option—and survival is the synonym of public education and of middle class, middle-Ohio parents.*

Writer 20: *I think my experience hindered my creativity in the sense that there was no structured openness. We would write an occasional poem (in rhyme, of course) for a holiday or for some kind of Catholic school competition, but there was no joy or*

89

interest in the process of the poem, only a dogged persistence until a certain result was achieved. There were no "arts" taught, no music, and so I think it might be fair to say that creativity was neglected rather than hindered. Real hindrance and destruction did not begin until college, where no one made any bones about women's inability to create anything but babies.

Writer 21: I certainly go back to moments of childhood often. I think I give a special place to "creative/ epiphany" experiences. I'm not sure any specific "creative projects" were important in their own right. But if you listen and respect someone who fascinates you with the ability to perceive what you can't quite (and I think a creative artist should do this naturally) and offers you an opportunity to pierce the veil of the mysteries, I think this becomes the route to creative experiences of your own. Creative experiences are not planned—that's an opposition of concepts.

Writer 22: I was somewhat self-made. Schools did not hinder or help. They simply functioned. I was the one with the motivation, and it was outside of their sphere.

Writer 23: Creativity was a secondary, perhaps even tertiary, priority in my schooling; hence, even though my creative output was exemplary, it did not truly flower until college. Curriculum designers need to develop creative tracks in the same way that academic and business tracks are defined, to isolate students with creative talent and to model their studies to develop and refine this talent. This is not to say that the minimally creative student should be ignored; every student should be exposed to creative endeavors and encouraged to foster, if not their own creative output, at least an appreciation and understanding of the arts.

Writer 24: My school experiences were hindered, thwarted, denigrated, ignored by insensitive, dull, prejudiced elementary school teachers on the one hand, but freed up, encouraged, praised, and shown off by loving, caring, talented teachers in junior high school on the other.

Writer 25:   *I didn't get help from school until I was in college. I started to write a lot in Latin, where I was bored silly, and to avoid getting bad citizenship marks, I wrote and kept my mouth shut. It was a great place for "reverie." An hour where no one could interrupt me (except to translate an occasional sentence). College classes were even better because in lectures I wouldn't be called on.*

From these comments, one can see that some writers liked school and others hated it; some were openly rebellious and others were sneakily rebellious. Some hated college while others liked it. But they all had a strong reaction to their schooling and praise for good teachers and encouraging parents.

Perhaps the personality traits of creative people were already taking hold; the independence of judgment, the nonconformity, the challenging of authority, the search for truth, the uncompromising verbal intelligence that saw fools for what they were and called them that. Personal attention from teachers, encouragement, and love for the subject matter being taught—all influenced these writers and led them to praise. Writers are probably not much different from other creative people in their reactions to school, though one would suppose writers would get better grades, since so much of school curriculum is verbally oriented.

Motivating Creative Behavior

Should we do nothing special but just continue what we are doing now, and then the truly creative ones will emerge through rebellion? If so, the next generation—our children—should be very creative, since 50% of them are children of divorce.

Strong Emotion as a Motivator

I remember talking with five college-age people who attended select eastern colleges. All had parents who had divorced; as youth, they had all experienced trauma, and the emotional consequences were still clearly evident in their unconventionality. Actually, their dress was conforming, but conforming to current styles of rebelliousness. They wore black, dyed their hair black, green, or red, or had it bleached blond. The young men wore spiked hair and earrings in the proper ear for their preferences. I remember asking, "What will happen when you begin writing your novels?" Their pointed statement in reply was, "We are just beginning to deal with our anger."

A few years have passed, and these youth, now graduated from their colleges, are settling into careers. They have gravitated toward the arts, publishing, theater, music. One, who began as a physics major, switched to music composition and transferred from M.I.T. to a liberal arts school. I have no doubt that emotion played a great part in their career choices, as well as in their motivations to be creative.

Singer/songwriter Christopher wrote a song about the internal war fought by a sensitive young man with an alcoholic father:

My War

My old room
Was a dirty cold room
Many ways to get in
I know every one
To drag us both here.
Someone inside
Is locked there inside.
When we try to ignore him.
Feel him beat against the door.

This is my war
I have fought from every side
I've conquered and I've died
This is my war.
I am the blood on the steel
Chariot and the wheel. Oh.

My old room.
Remember my cold room?
You're dead and gone.
You'll tend to your own
Inside your home
My head of stone
Is a heavy cold stone
Stands between us like a wall
We climb and then we fall
Never really touch at all.

This is my war.

With regard to emotion as a motivator, we parents had already planted seeds for creativity but didn't know it. Even so, it remains important when working with children to try to create an atmosphere that permits relatively free expression of emotion within the structures of school and home. But besides this, what are some specific processes or techniques that may be helpful in enhancing the creative process?

Close Your Eyes

In an early article I wrote, I detailed the creative process I used as an Arts in Education poet in the schools. I described helping students with the creative process through the use of preparation, imagery, and most important, having them simply close their eyes. I talked about the incubation phase of the creative process and how to use it in the schools.

Guided breathing and imagery are also helpful in facilitating a feeling of creativity, though some schools may be nervous about teachers using this technique, fearing it too suggestive or "strange" for the classroom. These kinds of complaints are similar to those heard when individuals complain that the Harry Potter books tout magic and the occult and should therefore not be used in schools.

In my exercise with high school students, I knew I would have to put them in the mood to write if they were to produce any inspirations or random thoughts written down which some teachers call poems. I took some Gestalt training when I was a school counselor, and I have since found the fantasy work in Gestalt helpful to my own writing. This technique combines relaxation and suggestion in order to facilitate what could be called a "creative response" in the participant.

My objective with the students was to have them explore their teenage desire for privacy, for a place to go where they could be alone and be themselves. I talked to them a little about this need, and I read them a few short poems. I used a soft voice and spoke slowly, and with a smile. One of the characteristics of high school students, especially boys, is that they never have pencils or paper and must borrow from the girls, thereby having a chance to flirt a little, and so I made sure, before starting, that they all had pencils and paper; so they knew they were going to be asked to write.

"What a weirdo," one boy said. "I can't think of anything to write about; I just took this class for an easy English credit."

Undaunted, I asked them to close their eyes after I felt they were with me, and I asked them to get into their own private spaces, to forget the presence of their friends, to focus on themselves and on their breathing. I took my time. There were, at first, protests and giggles, but soon they were all quiet and listening to me.

I asked them, after a few moments, to think about their bedrooms at home, to imagine themselves behind a full-length mirror, looking through the mirror into their bedrooms. "How does your room look right now, empty, with no one there? Pretend you are a stranger seeing the room for the first time. What details do you see that will tell you who the person who sleeps in this room really is? It could be the dusty rock collection on top of the dresser, or the dried flowers pinned up on the bulletin board, or the hubcap in the middle of the floor, or the beer can collection on the shelf, or the dirty clothes under the bed." I paced this slowly and then paused, asking them to focus on these details.

Soon I asked them to open their eyes, and in the same soft voice, I asked them to write about their room to show the reader, by use of specific objects, who the owner of that bedroom really is. I gave them about 15 minutes, and I suggested that they write at least 10 lines. The time and space limit helped to focus them, to give their reverie some structure.

I said that I would collect the poems after they were done with this initial draft, and would read them aloud so that the whole group could share; if they were shy about this, they could make up a *nom de plume*. Adolescents are usually very shy about having their work read, while young children clamor for the privilege. Perhaps this speaks to the inculcation within the schools of a fear of spontaneous expression as children grow older.

Then I included in the article some of the poems the recalcitrant teenagers wrote, and I concluded the lesson. Perhaps parents and teachers should pay more attention to allowing daydreams and reverie into the lives of their children. Who ever heard a parent or teacher say, "Go and think awhile.... Go and daydream"? Perhaps we should send them out into the woods to sit under the trees and contemplate. Or perhaps we should give some thought to creating conditions and situations conducive to incubation.

When I think about the structured lives most children these days seem to lead, with lessons in music and tutors for math and sports teams coached and organized by adults, in city leagues and with many rules, I wonder whether children ever get a chance to play freely and experience creative solitude away from the watchful eyes of caretakers. In my book, *A Location in the Upper Peninsula*, I describe the rural neighborhood I lived in, Cleveland Location—the woods and bluffs, the lakes we swam in, the rocks we climbed, the long summer days when we would hear the distant calls of someone's mother at suppertime. We would reluctantly awaken from our imaginative play to re-enter our family and sit at the dining table for dinnertime grace. We would shake off our world of cowgirls and jungle girls, descend from the high rocky bluff, and join the neighborhood boys for a rousing game of Capture the Flag. That imaginative world of childhood play when we would be literally in another mental place, as I look back on it now, seems necessary in shaping the writer I became many years later. When I close my eyes, I can still remember the joyous feeling of freedom.

I wish all children could feel that joy in these days of fearful guarding, when we teach kindergartners about "stranger danger," how to be "street smart," and to shout "This is not my mother!" if they are being kidnapped or to roll under a car if they are being abducted. In my research on creativity and creative people, adult creativity is often shown to be shaped by free imaginative play during childhood. Many inventors, for example, come from rural backgrounds. Being able to play freely without the invading eyes of adults was a gift of our neighborhood to us.

I often assign my students to watch children play. The voices of children at play, shouting and squealing, laughing and arguing, unconscious of adults, need to be heard once again. Sitting on my front porch, I watch the neighborhood girls playing. Their favorite activity is running. Not once do I see them move from one place to another by walking. They are in their own free world. Close your eyes and hear the child you once were.

Escaping and Getting the Giggles

When I was principal of a school in New York City, The Hunter School, I would take my little writing group of talented boys and girls to the Metropolitan Museum of Art for our "poets' lunches," and we would walk down Fifth Avenue to the museum, jotting down details with our newly sharpened pencils as we walked. I remember feeling the bumpy bricks on the Central Park side of the Avenue through the thin soles of my leather shoes. Then we would go to the museum and settle in a room, chosen by one of the kids, and we would each write a poem or two about an object in the room.

Sometimes I invited other writer friends along, sometimes not. But uniformly, by the time we got back to school where I had to resume being a principal again, we were all filled with giggles and a feeling of having escaped to do something special and secret. When my schedule didn't allow time for visiting the museum, the kids would come to my office and bring their lunches, and one of them would tape a sign, "Poets at Work," to my door. While eating our lunches, we would talk, write, and giggle. I certainly felt creative then, and I think the kids did, too. We had fun. Those moments with the kids stand out as high points in my otherwise pressured, over-scheduled days.

The secret feeling of escape, the liberation of release from duty, the relaxed feeling of being able to giggle all contributed to our sense of being creative. We were participating in a safe way of breaking the rules, just for an hour. Teachers and parents can do this with small gestures; I have seen classrooms where children sit on beanbags under worktables during reading—they are quietly escaping momentarily. I have known parents who take each child out alone, without siblings, for their special times together—to fly paper kites or to attend a recital or to share some other "new and different" experience.

Creativity as Spontaneous Adventures

A friend, whose two boys have turned out to be art majors like their mother, said that she encouraged them in their art by springing "adventures" on them when they were little. On a particularly boring Saturday when the boys were lolling around on the living room floor watching cartoons, she would announce: "All right, up! It's time to go have an adventure!" Then, with their sketchbooks, they would all pile into the car and go out to some nearby site to sketch. Afterwards, they would stop off at the restaurant with the best ice cream cones in town to have double dips. Her boys grew up loving these impromptu "adventures" as special opportunities to do art. Of course, their home was also filled with art books, art reproductions, and discussions of the latest show at the Toledo Museum. But again, the motivation for doing their art was as play, not work.

Perhaps we can extrapolate from these stories four hints for enhancing creativity in children. First, from the cold anger shown by college-age youth, it could be that creative production is motivated by deep emotion. Second, creative production even in a school classroom can occur following quiet reverie and closed eyes. Third, children need free time for free imaginative play. Fourth, creative production as escape from the mundane is special, secret, and delicious.

Creativity Is Not Permitted

In 2002, the federal government issued an education program called "No Child Left Behind." In response to this, one school principal in Colorado called his teachers together and made the following statement: "Creativity is not permitted." He then went on to detail how the teachers were to concentrate on teaching students to take multiple choice tests based on state standards. With this kind of attitude from their instructional leader, can you imagine what a dreary, horrible place that school is?

Yet creativity cannot be suppressed for long. What is necessary are some creative ways to subvert such drastic and ill-informed statements. Research on creativity shows that the major factor in creativity is motivation. I know that if I were a teacher in that school or a parent whose child was in that school, hearing a statement even resembling "Creativity is not permitted" would lead me to subversive activity.

Motivation for Creativity

The main cause for creativity is that the creative person wants to be creative, in whatever domain he or she is working—whether it be woodworking in the basement, dancing, acting, drawing, singing, experimenting, computing, inventing, being an entrepreneur, being an athlete, cooking, sewing, building, designing. People who are creative must have motivation.

Six terms used in the field of social psychology are "intrinsic motivation" and "extrinsic motivation"; "field dependence" and "field independence"; and "inner locus of control" and "outer locus of control." People who produce the most creative works have "intrinsic motivation," are "field independent," and have "inner loci of control." To have intrinsic motivation is to proceed in the work for love of the work itself, and not for fame or glory. To have field independence is to proceed with confidence and individuality rather than with wanting to be liked or wanting to please. A person who is field independent sings "Climb Every Mountain." A person who is field dependent sings "Raindrops Keep Falling on My Head." To have an inner locus of control is to do what you do because you need or want to do it, and not because someone else has given you an assignment to do it.

Theresa Amabile, a social psychologist, has done some of the major work on motivation for creativity. Her books reinforce the view that motivation is an important key to creativity. She writes, "This motivation to be creative has been so neglected that you might call it creativity's missing link." In 1989, Amabile came up with a Venn diagram and said that creativity takes place where the following three elements intersect: (1) domain skills; (2) creative thinking and working skills; and (3) intrinsic motivation.

Domain skills are those that are necessary for functioning in the specific area of creativity; for example, a painter needs to know how to paint, and a composer needs to be able to read music. Creative thinking and working skills are those practical habits that we develop as we grow up. Intrinsic motivation is the inner drive necessary for achievement. Beth Hennessey, Amabile's colleague, described their studies on creativity and the enhancement of intrinsic motivation. They found, with a group of undergraduate college students, that the students who did not expect to be evaluated or judged made the more creative art collages.

Amabile and Hennessey also found that young children made more creative art products in a free play situation than in a structured and evaluative situation. They discovered that it is possible to "immunize" students against having their creativity be motivated by extrinsic rather than intrinsic rewards. They found that two 15-minute video tapes of teachers discussing with students the joys of learning, the pleasures of doing creative projects, and the inner feeling of satisfaction gained from doing something well did seem to motivate or inspire 11-year-olds. Hennessey said, "If experimenters, virtual strangers, were able to affect this much attitudinal and behavioral change…think how much more could be done by classroom teachers who build naturalistic discussions about motivation, interest, and playfulness into the school day."

Rewards

To enhance intrinsic motivation, parents and teachers need to rethink how they interact with children. Under what circumstances do we give rewards? Behavioral psychologists advocate token systems as rewards, but cognitive psychologists say these are extrinsic and do not produce the joy for learning that is needed for intrinsic motivation. External rewards do not enhance intrinsic motivation. When the child comes home from school with the report card, what is the parent's response? No matter what the grade is, does the parent say, "What did you learn?" No. More often the parent says, "Only a 'B'? Why didn't you get an 'A'?" Rewards should be given as rewards for quality of performance, for learning and trying, and not just because the child completed the chore.

Dean Keith Simonton, one of the giants of creativity studies, spoke in 1999 of the motivation to create. He said, "Creative people are actively engaged in creating new ideas, and creativity is a purposive activity that assigns meaning to their lives."

People have to want to be creative. Creativity takes a long time and a certain amount of obsession. Rothenberg said that the creator prepares by study and mental readiness: "Creative people want very much—need very much—to create, partly because they have the talent to do so and partly because of strong environmental influences that instill such strong motivation." Environmental influences include those that begin in the family.

We can extrapolate from psychological work on reward. What are the rewards for being creative? Fame is not usually one of them. Musician Mat Callahan said, "I have never found any correlation between money and the effectiveness of the creative process and its results." He went on: "Do I produce a demand for my creative work…do I produce marketable commodities? Maybe. Do I apply my energies to my creative work, regardless? Certainly. Continuously. Why? Because of the satisfaction I derive from the process itself and the pleasure it brings to others."

The most enhancing rewards for creative endeavor are in the pleasure the creator takes in doing the work itself and in achieving the result, not from the pay or the prize. Even painters who don't have galleries, musicians who don't have audiences, writers who aren't published, actors who act in community theater, dancers who dance alone, scientists and mathematicians who spread the table with arcane formulas to solve personally challenging problems, do not stop doing. While some may say that creative people need a killer instinct and need to be so driven that they would do anything for fame, recognition, or validation, continued creative production derives from less cruel motives. The work itself is intrinsically interesting and motivating to the creator.

Summary

1. Although creative adults often experienced childhood trauma, there are other positive ways to enhance creativity in children.

2. Writers have very specific reactions to their schooling and very specific suggestions for how that schooling could be improved.

3. Setting a creative tone and valuing creative expression are both essential in enhancing creativity.

4. Creating a feeling of escape, of adventure, of play and fun are important in enhancing creativity.

5. Creative expression comes from the need to express emotion and from an inner drive.

Chapter 4
How Parents and Teachers Can Enhance Creativity in Children

A basic premise of this book is that we can enhance creativity—that the core attitudes for enhancing creativity can be taught. Let us begin with my 13 suggestions for parents and teachers for enhancing creativity in children.

1. Provide a Private Place for Creative Work to Be Done

For Teachers

In a school, where and how can a child find privacy for doing creative work—writing, drawing, composing, thinking? If you are a teacher of young children, take a look around your room. Reconfigure the room so that you have a loft or a special place where children can go. The early childhood days of classrooms with desks bolted to the floor and lined up in rows are gone. Group desks together to make tables. Push them together to make a circle so that all of the children can see each other at all times. Create a hideout beneath a table or a desk in the back or the front of the room. Pitch a tent in the room. Replace the desks with soft chairs and couches. Use your own creativity to imagine a place where good schoolwork can get done and yet there is a place to read, to think, to draw. Use this place as a reward for good work.

For Parents

In all my years of work in schools, I have done a little informal research on children's private places. "Where do you go when you want to think?" I ask. "Have you ever built yourself a place that is just yours?"

Almost all of the students have, and when I am doing a writing workshop with them, I ask them to describe this place. As a parent, I remember the places my own children built—beneath the staircases, in the garage, in the living room with blankets and pillows. In fact, I published a poem called "Forts" about my own children's search for private places away from adults.

Forts

there's one beneath the basement steps
carpeted with a crib mattress
closed off with a worn out bedspread

there's one in the attic
secret in the junk and jumble
small hollow under caving boxes

there's one in the garage
where this week's neighborhood club
exchanges officers
"No Grils Allowed"

there's one this rainy Sunday
hung from the television
over chair and stool, one quilt's

drooping width to the beanbags
holes shut with towels
corners pegged with books

the cat slips in to visit
reclining brother and sister
covered inside a warm soft roof

whispering and bickering
in the world of the marxes
three stooges

they told me
when I peeked in
I'm too big to fit

Adult creativity is often shaped by free imaginative play during childhood. Many inventors and scientists, for example, come from rural backgrounds. As I mentioned in Chapter 3, being able to play freely without invading eyes of adults was a gift of our neighborhood to me and my friends growing up. We used to play in the woods, imagining ourselves as ladies in long dresses with wicker picnic baskets and checkered tablecloths, languishing in the clearings near the picnic fire pits that lay along the trail. We had the homes and manicured grounds of the mine bosses from the Cleveland Cliffs Iron Company. We used to sneak onto the property and play spy, watching the goings on of these foreign, wealthy families. We took a path through cow fields and cedar swamps to Cedar Lake, where the boys swam naked at the west end of the lake and we girls swam in swimming suits on the north side. We girls had to block our eyes as though wearing blinders as we passed the boys, and a guard boy would lead us by. This was serious play.

Play is the *work* of childhood. If a child must be fearful and is watched over by adults at all times, there is no time for imagination to develop. When I was a school principal, I would watch the children play. The children who always had to ask an adult "Did you see me swing on the bars?" were the children who could not let themselves go into their imaginations and into the freedom of play, and they were the most rigid and most anxious. I'll wager they didn't become creative adults; their need for approval was too great.

If parents and teachers keep in mind that a safe, secret place is a necessity for children's creativity to unfold, then they will be providing much that is valuable in later life. For example, the writer Graham Greene, by any accounts an imaginative adult, used to sneak upstairs to the attic to read alone in a private place. He was reading mysteries and adventures before his family even knew he could read. Then, when he would come back downstairs, he would sit patiently while they read him the primer. At age six, he already had a private place for creative work to be done. Even for large families living in small spaces, an effort must be made so that each child can have privacy for thinking, dreaming, wishing.

2. Provide Materials: Musical Instruments, Sketchbooks, Fabric, Paper, Clay

For Teachers

If the child has talent in a certain area and if the parents do not have the means to develop that talent, the school has a responsibility to try to do so. School materials should be made available to students. Does your classroom have supplies, and are the children encouraged to be creative and free with these supplies? Creative teachers are known for their propensity to gather odd pieces and bits of materials and to recycle them for use in the classroom. Oatmeal cartons, scraps of cloth, milk bottles, discarded containers can all become part of the teacher's supply closet. Old clothes can be put into costume boxes for dramatic play; I know one teacher who haunts auctions and stays until the end when leftovers are sold for a dollar. She has gathered countless treasures this way, and many find their way into her classroom in craft projects, fantasy play, and even science fairs and invention conventions.

For Parents

Yes, it costs something, but those rental payments for the piano, the trumpet, or the saxophone are important. No one started to be creative in adulthood without having some thread for that creativity leading back to childhood. My son, who decided to become a visual artist in college, says he will never sell his trumpet, the one he played for so many years in jazz bands, marching bands, drum and bugle corps, and small combos. Yet he became a visual artist. He had also always kept sketchbooks, and he spent hours alone in his room drawing. He had a good memory for the paintings in the museums our family would visit, and he would enthusiastically discuss them on the way home. He credits his becoming an artist to these early childhood experiences, even though, as his mother, I had predicted that he was more likely to become a musician. The point is that there were opportunities to experiment with both art and music in his childhood environment.

Biographies of creative people often indicate that there were certain *predictive behaviors* in their childhoods. A predictive behavior is one found in retrospective accounts by adults who later became practitioners in the domain. For example, many visual artists were known as the class artist as children. They also practiced a lot on their own. This implies the presence of materials and supplies and the opportunity to use them freely and with curiosity.

3. Encourage and Display the Child's Creative Work, but Avoid Overly Evaluating It

For Teachers

Do you as a teacher know what creative talents your students have, and do you praise them for themselves, or are you in the dark? Many a child has stopped singing or drawing because of a teacher's or other students' sarcastic comments. We all know people—and perhaps we are among them—who, in giving a speech or demonstration, say when illustrating something on the blackboard, "I'm not an artist, but..." They make the drawing anyway, and most often we can tell what it is. The self-deprecating statement reflects on some past-perceived failure in drawing.

Look back at your childhood in school for a moment. Did a teacher or a peer say something to you that made you stop singing, stop drawing, stop writing? Are you that same teacher, making similar negative remarks to children? Remember that your remarks will live forever in those children's minds. As a teacher myself, I have to remind myself constantly that any remark I make will be magnified by my students, and they will take it into themselves. A colleague told me this story the other day. He wrote on a student's paper that she was very talented in mathematics, and then he forgot about the comment. A few years later, this student sent him a card, telling him that she was finishing studies for her Ph.D. and that his comment had given her the inner permission she needed to go to graduate school.

In each of the creativity classes I teach, my graduate and undergraduate students have to do an individual creativity project as a final assignment. "But I'm not creative," my graduate students often say. "I was going to drop the course the first night." One student made a timeline of her project, and for the first step, she spent some time asking friends and acquaintances "How am I creative?" She had no view of herself as being a creative human being. Who had done that to her? I have another friend who was told he couldn't sing, and so he always simply mouthed the words of songs. He wanted to sing. Then he told the choir director at a local church. The choir director, who believed that everyone could sing, challenged my friend to try it. It turned out that my friend was a tenor, though he had always thought he was a baritone. He's been in the choir for 10 years now and recently started singing with a barbershop group. One ill-informed teacher had kept this man from singing for 30 years.

For Parents

So what if it doesn't look like a dog? Do you make comments to your children when they come to you with their attempts to draw a dog, an automobile, a person? I have a theory that many people stop attempting to draw when they view their work and see that it lacks verisimilitude—doesn't look like the object being drawn. The child knows; you don't have to rub it in. Is the refrigerator door an art gallery, covered with your child's work? How about the walls of the child's room? Do you need to have control over your home? So much so that your child can't display creative work? Does it show that your child lives there also? One of my students told a story after reading this precept. She said that she keeps yelling at her youngest child, who won't keep her room to the immaculate standard of the household. She said that her daughter kept running away to the space beneath the porch, and so the mother had made a vow to close off that space next summer. After hearing my suggestions in class, the mother felt tears rising in her throat. She loosened her immaculate standards so the house could become a home for the child as well as for the mother. "I let her begin being a person who lives there, and not just a hotel resident," my student said.

Does your child's practicing of his musical instrument drive you nuts? My sister's violin practice used to do that to me. But she had to practice. That was a rule of the house. She was so rebellious about having to practice both the violin and the piano that our mother finally let her quit the piano after the five years of lessons that were requisite for us young musicians growing up in our home. Now my sister says our mother should have made her take longer, as five years wasn't enough to do the accompanying she wants to do. She has since taken up the mandolin, and her training in violin has helped her master the chords and strings in record time.

When I was a teenager, I was the church organist, and being lazy about my practicing, I would often just go in and wing it. Now I play for groups to sing along, as I never stop, no matter how many mistakes I make. "Creative risk taking," I call it, as I plow on and the crowd gathers behind me, squinting at the words to the show tunes that I am so blithely playing. Some people say you shouldn't force lessons on your children, but I'm the living, grateful example that it didn't hurt me. Although I never had the raw talent or practice discipline to become a professional musician, my piano goes with me whenever I move, and the hours of solitary pleasure it provides as I improvise and sing feed my soul. I play well enough for my own pleasure and those of the people who like to sing "Oldies" behind me.

Among the most musically talented families I know is one that would invite visitors to hear the latest piano or violin piece. When you went to visit Suzanne and John, you heard the children play for you. And they played well! John, a college professor, sat with each child for an hour each night, listening to them practice their music lessons. It provided not only quality time for the children with their father, but also a household atmosphere that said that music was important. Their son quit playing violin in high school, ashamed to let his friends know that he played the violin in concerts throughout the area where they live. His father was hurt and disappointed but philosophical. He said, "He'll come back to it some day, and he'll never go to a concert and be ignorant about the music being played." Parents' support of talents and interests is important if the talent is to develop.

4. Do Your Own Creative Work, and Let the Child See You Doing It

For Teachers

So what if you're a math teacher? Do your students know you are also a cabinetmaker? A painter? A writer? That you sew, or knit, or design boats? The wee bit of humanizing that such personal information gives your students can make a huge difference in their feelings of freedom of expression with you. Try it. When I conduct workshops with teachers, I often ask them to write briefly and then to share how they are creative. I ask them what puts them into a state of "flow," where the activity is so engaging that they lose track of time. Many of them say they aren't creative, but when I push them, it turns out that their creativity comes out in the hobbies they do when they are not teaching school. They are involved in cooking, crafts, building, refinishing of furniture, designing of exercise routines and gardens—all these creative endeavors emerge in these teachers' descriptions as times when they feel creative.

When I give workshops for teachers, I ask them what activities allow them to lose track of time, what activities are challenging enough to entice them, so pleasurable that they can keep doing them for a long time. The teachers mention everything from computer games to running, but what inevitably is said by someone or other is that teaching well also gives them the pleasure of flow. This leads me to think that teaching as a creative activity is undervalued by the curriculum designers who tell teachers that they should teach this for 15 minutes and this for 10 minutes. The postmodern idea that teaching is meandering pleasurably with students in a river of knowledge, where the ideas to be pursued arise from the context of the discussion, supports the idea of teaching as a creative activity. However, the curriculum planners who make teachers hand in detailed behavioral lesson plans and check off detailed task boxes have taken the creativity out of what is essentially an art form, a skilled craft which is raised to the sublime when the teacher is really in there with the kids.

For Parents

Does your house have a special place where the parents (as well as the children) can do their creative work? The writer Lucia Nevai, winner of the prestigious Iowa Short Fiction Award, lived in a small apartment in New York City. When she wrote, she went to her room and puts this sign on the door: "Lucia's writing." The message machine on her telephone had this message. "Lucia's writing. She'll get back to you later. Leave a message." She values her own creativity, and her family values creativity also.

Blocking out time for creativity is especially difficult for women. Loeb called it the "If I haven't dusted the furniture do I have the right to begin carving?" syndrome. We women think that we have to sneak our creative work and not tell anyone that we're doing it. When my children were young, I wrote while they were outside playing or after they went to bed. I would be alone in the living room or in the small office in our home, working on poems, my husband and kids long asleep. It was the only time I had as a working mother to be alone, to be private. But everyone knew I was doing it, as the rejection letters and a few acceptances arrived regularly. Here is a poem I wrote at that time.

Poetmother

the afternoon is calm
silence time to write
the paper is green
like the summer

the mind floats into itself
like distanced birdsong
with images bright
as the kitchen sink
the polished coffee table
slowly right there

the words twist
from the images

and the fingers
take dictation
fast and willing
then the back door slaps

and his feet
in dirty sneakers tramp
and the voice begins

"Mom where are you?
I can't find anyone to play with
Where's the juice?"

(Mom I want)
(Mom I own you)

"You can't catch me!"
and the front door crashes
and a little girl runs
shrieks laughing

through the twisting words
and out again
the back door slams
on my resentment

a child's voice yells
"Bye Mom!"
I sit up and try again
for stillness

Now I write in the morning. For me, such morning writing time is a joyous luxury. The point is that people must make space and time for their creative work.

5. Set a Creative Tone

For Teachers

When I was a school principal, I tried administratively to set the tone of the school as one of valuing creativity. When the long-awaited, six-months-late first copy of my novel arrived from my publisher one afternoon just before an assembly, I was so thrilled to see it that I jumped up and down and shouted, "Yes! Yes!" As the assembly began, one of the teachers announced to the group why I was behaving so strangely. Everyone applauded and laughed. They recognized that I was a struggling writer as well as a principal.

When I left the school a few years later, one of the students in his goodbye speech said that he would remember me because I encouraged the kids to write a lot of poems and stories. Besides hiring professional writers to work with the students through Teachers and Writers Collaborative, I myself wrote for them. Each year, for my Principal's Message in the yearbook, I would tell a story—because Principal's Messages are usually such dull reading for the students. One year, I wrote about the neighborhood characters I remembered from my growing up years, and I exhorted my readers to "read my story, and then write your own story about your own neighborhood characters." In my story, I told them about Mrs. Ollikainen, who made rag rugs and dolls out of hollyhocks; and Old Joe, who had a bull that we used to tease; Mr. Nelson, who yelled for his kids all the time; Brandon, who had a mysterious past and walked all over downtown; and Bulltop, a character who drove old cars into the mine pit. Many of the children subsequently did write about their neighborhoods. It seems important to have someone in authority be a model for the risk-taking involved in creativity.

Many of the teachers in that school likewise set examples of creativity, and it showed in their rooms. The halls were filled with artwork; the bulletin boards were replete with children's efforts. The rooms were filled with learning centers, and every week there was a performance or a class project. Getting detailed behavioral lesson plans from these teachers was virtually impossible. They weren't the types who wrote as an objective: "*The student will* be able to recite the Pledge of Allegiance correctly 75% of the time."

The point I am trying to make here is that the school's *atmosphere* was creative. Talk in the teacher's lounge was often of movies, plays, books and musical performances, with opinions freely given about the latest pan by the local theater critic. These teachers traveled, too, even on their limited teachers' salaries—to Europe, Asia, even Africa. Many had never been to Yellowstone Park, but they had been to the Louvre. They were interesting people, interested in creative things, and it showed in their interactive teaching. When you enter a school, you can tell within 60 seconds what the atmosphere is—and what the administrators and teachers value. Are there stern signs ordering visitors to go immediately to the principal's office, but no directions for how to get there? Are there institutional lockers and gray walls? Is the school more like an army barracks than a joyful place where children learn to value their own creativity and humanity? Just go into any school and see what feelings and messages are conveyed by the walls, including things posted on the walls and in corridors, the signs, the windows, and the mood of the children themselves.

When I was a central office consultant for regional education offices, I had to go into many schools each day. That is when I learned this lesson about tone. The schools I enjoyed coming back to were the ones that conveyed a warm welcome, especially to children and frightened parents, but also even to central office administrators who are used to schools. I remember one school well. There was an actual waiting room near the entrance, with couches, lamps, magazines, and bulletin boards full of children's work. When parents came, they could visit with one other, share the gossip of the day, and feel as if they, too, had a place in the school their children attended.

For Parents

Picture your author, now a grandmother with a five-year-old granddaughter, on her exercise bike with a Mexican sombrero on her head, peddling fast, castanets clacking between her fingers, and loudly singing "La Cucaracha." The granddaughter runs to the kitchen, gets a wooden spoon, and begins hitting the wind chimes that hang from a chandelier in the foyer, jumping up to give the chimes whacks. Grandmother and granddaughter collapse in giggles. Then it's time for the parade. The grandmother sits down at the piano, and her whole family marches around the house. "I want to play the rain stick!" shouts the granddaughter. "No, I get to play the rain stick," says the son-in-law, all 6'4" of him, quite an authority. "Then I get to play a duet with Grandma," says the granddaughter. I move over on the piano bench, and she takes the high notes, pounding out the rhythm to the tune I am now playing on the bass notes. "You're a great grandmother!" says my granddaughter." No I'm not," I say. "I won't be a great grandmother until you have your own children!" She pauses for a moment and then bursts out in laughter. "No. No. I mean you're a GREAT grandmother!" "That's what I said," I respond, repeating. My daughter says, "Oh, Grandma is just being funny." Family fun. A creative tone and atmosphere.

6. Value the Creative Work of Others

For Teachers

Yes, I know you live in some small rural town miles from any *real* cultural life. I know. I grew up there, too. So why, in my hometown of Ishpeming, Michigan, is there a project that has preserved the local history, the accomplishments and experiences of an entire community? Furthermore, why has that research been done by seventh graders? Yes. Called The Red Dust Project, a small junior high school has, since 1975, been collecting oral histories of the local residents and publishing them in an illustrated book. Every summer, when I go back to visit my family, I go to the local newspaper store and buy the latest edition. This project was initiated by a teacher.

I have come to believe that teachers are usually the most stable part of a community. Administrators often leave, and parents are involved only while their children are in school, but the teachers often stay for 20, 25, 30 years. What one teacher and her supportive administrator did was simply teach the children to interview and then to write up the interviews. The children have had their work presented at the Smithsonian Museum and have been featured on national television, all because one teacher had an idea that the creative people—all of the people—in this small mining community should have their words and thoughts preserved. Now, each year, a new theme is chosen, and students volunteer to participate in the project. Teachers in small towns across the land could initiate similar creative projects, even in remote areas where museums and live theater are far away.

For Parents

Is your house filled with books? Do you subscribe to any magazines? Do your children subscribe to any magazines? Do you visit the public library? Does your child have a library card? When was the last time you visited a museum? Attended a live performance of theater or music? You say you live in South Dakota and have two radio stations on the dial, both country western? Photographer James Mackay grew up in Pollock, South

Dakota and ran his family's newspaper there for many years. He is among the most creative people I know. His collection of blues albums taught me almost all I know about that genre of music.

My late friend, poet and novelist Peggy Simpson Curry, grew up miles from any town on a ranch in Wyoming. She was one of the least provincial people I knew. As James Thurber once said, "The most provincial people I ever met were the ones I met in New York City." When we moved to New York where my daughter attended La Guardia High School for the Performing Arts, one of her friends asked if there were drugstores in Ohio. (Yes, that is a true story.)

One day I was stuck in traffic on my way from my apartment in Brooklyn to my work in Manhattan. A radio station was giving away two tickets to a Broadway show. A person from Queens, five miles from Broadway, won them. She said it was her first Broadway show, and she was 40 years old.

Provincialism is a state of mind, not geography.

7. Incorporate Creativity Values into Your Family Mythology

For Parents

What I like to call your family mythology, or your family script, is important. "In our family, we...." "In our family, we value the arts and talk about art." "In our family, we go to college." "In our family, we read books." "In our family, we go to museums." When parents ask me how to get their kids to do certain things, I ask them about their family mythology. In my family, I knew I was going to college from kindergarten, even though my parents were children of Finnish immigrants and neither had been to college. In fact, my parents couldn't speak English when they went to kindergarten. But in our family mythology, we went to college. On my paternal side, 18 of my first cousins went; only two, both female, did not. My younger sisters and I represented only one of very few families in our mining location whose children went to college (we called our neighborhoods *locations*). I wrote about this in my book *A Location in the Upper Peninsula*. In my high school class of 130, a friend and I are the only ones with Ph.D.s. One of our classmates is a dentist, and another has an M.S.W. However, a lot of us got bachelor's degrees and master's degrees—certainly more than was true of our parents' generation.

What family mythology made all of my cousins, my sisters, and me believe that we could go to college? I suspect it had to do with our grandmother, who was educated only through elementary school in Finland. Once, when my father wanted to drop out of high school, his father said that he would have to work harder then, and he put him to shoveling manure all day long (they kept cows and delivered milk before school). My father said that he went back to high school rather than do that hard manual labor, and he graduated. Ten of his 11 brothers and sisters had some education beyond high school, mostly in the trades, but there were two teachers, a dentist, and a nurse in that group of siblings, too.

For Teachers

The motivation of immigrant families is not new, and your family's story may be similar to mine. This story is still happening today with immigrants from other countries. Parents make the difference.

○ Parents who value their children's education so much that they infuse the importance of that education into every aspect of their lives.

○ Parents who actively monitor and supplement what the schools teach their children.

○ Parents, and therefore children, who believe that academic effort and hard work are rewarded with accomplishment.

○ Parents, and therefore students, who support the schools.

○ Parents, and therefore students, who believe in taking the most challenging courses.

One may argue that the increased necessity for both parents to work, as well as the great rise in single-parent families, most of which are headed by overburdened mothers, preclude this parental involvement. But if parents become aware of their great importance in their children's education, and if schools become welcoming places for parents, with planned outreach efforts such as personal telephone calls to share good news and not just bad news, parents might overcome their great fear of school. Schools must remember that parents often retain some of their childhood memories of school. One Wall Street broker parent said, "Even though I've been out of school 20 years, when I go back, I still feel as if I'm without my hall pass and the principal will call me on the carpet."

Looking back on the many biographies that my students and I have studied, the influence of parents on creative people is quite remarkable. The influence of the family mythology upon creativity is similarly noteworthy. As National Book Award winner in poetry, Louise Glück wrote: "My sister and I were encouraged in every gift. If we hummed, we got music lessons. If we skipped, dance. And so on. My mother read to us, then taught us to read very early." In that family, creative pursuits were valued, so much so that as an adult, she remembered her parents' message that creativity is important.

If your students don't have a family mythology that encourages cultural activities such as museums, concerts, or books, then your role is crucial. Field trips are a bother, yes, and busy school administrators often discourage efforts to take students to cultural events, but this should be a priority and a necessity, not a burden. Almost all of my graduate education classes take field trips. Sometimes I'm shocked that some of the teacher/students are visiting the local museums for the very first time! A rule of thumb is that *doing* is better than passive *viewing*.

At the very minimum, each student should have a public library card, and each classroom should have a set of encyclopedias and enough computers with access to the Internet so that there is little wait time. As teachers, you can model for your students that research and learning are part of your everyday life as well. Here is what one writer I studied said about her favorite teachers:

My "creative writing" teacher in high school was certifiably senile; I switched out of the class, an honors one, to a regular English class with a teacher who loved grammar. I hated grammar, but I learned there to love learning and precision with words. Other memorable teachers were so only because they loved what they taught; thus I, who cannot draw a straight line with a ruler, recall the electricity and excitement of geometry class; I have a lot of buried knowledge and continuing fanaticism about Alexander the Great, because of an ex-jock-turned-history-teacher whose love of that period of history sent me to the most obscure and advanced of resources, gave me a knowledge of library sources that has served me since, and gave me an absolute adoration of the whole process of knowledge: from the atmosphere in libraries to love of books for their new bindings and type as well as for their contents. It was not, I emphasize, WHAT these people taught, but HOW that worked the miracles—and I try to remember that every day I go into a classroom.

8. Avoid Reinforcing Sex-Role Stereotypes

For Parents

I'll bet the Marlboro Man and the Sweet Young Thing aren't very creative, for they represent the extremes of masculine and feminine stereotypes. Creative men and women are more androgynous. On a continuum of masculinity vs. femininity, with the *most* masculine and *most* feminine at either end, creative children and adults will be grouped more toward the middle. Humorist and screenwriter Nora Ephron, in her essay "A Few Words about Breasts," described her childhood thus: "I did not feel at all like a girl. I was boyish. I was athletic, ambitious, outspoken, competitive, noisy, rambunctious, I had scabs on my knees, and my socks slid down into my loafers and I could throw a football."

The emphasizing of sex-role stereotypes by parents and teachers makes for rigid, rules-filled environments where boys don't cry and girls don't climb. The enforcement or support of these rules is what stifles creativity. By the age of five, children are strongly identified with their genders, and whatever the family environment, they seem to understand that firefighters are usually boys and ballet dancers are usually girls. The creative home and school environment softens these stereotypes and expectations, and children can come to understand that girls can be firefighters and boys can be ballet dancers.

There is a strong element of homophobia in our society. A teacher once told me that when she noticed that one of her talented students was a great actor, she complimented his parents on their son's talent. The mother then said, "We don't want him to act in any more plays. Actors are homosexual." Perhaps she had forgotten John Wayne. A softening of gender role expectations does not lead to homosexuality, for most people are heterosexual. The presence of gays in many creative fields may represent the attitudes of creative people, who seem more tolerant of differences and more accepting of people whose beliefs and lifestyles differ.

Androgyny is the key word. Or, put another way, creative people seem to have both yin and yang. My colleague John Fraas and I did a small study at our summer honors institute at my university using a personality inventory that indicated that yes, indeed, high school boys in the arts were more tender-minded and more nonconforming than comparison boys, while high school girls in the arts showed no difference in personality from girls not in the arts. Both groups were equally aggressive and assertive. Androgyny in creative youth was supported here.

For Teachers

Many people who are homosexuals, regardless of gender, seem to have always known this about themselves, though some repress the knowledge. A book about how a talented boy discovered his homosexuality is the cult classic *Best Little Boy in the World* by John Reed. The works of prize-winning fiction writer David Leavitt are also instructive in the description of coming to awareness of one's homosexuality. Whether homosexuals are more creative than other people is not known, but it would seem that creative fields are more open to sexual divergence.

The presence of red ribbons on the lapels of entertainment stars at award ceremonies on national and international television is not just a political statement that there should be research on AIDS; it is a personal statement that good friends and colleagues have died, and the wearer is wearing a token in memoriam. One characteristic of creative people is emotionality and empathy, and every red ribbon probably means a friend has died.

But the point is not that there is a risk of homosexuality in being creative; the point is that following rigid sex-role stereotyping limits creativity. In order to succeed in the world of visual arts, for example, a female artist needs to be willing to exhibit what are typically called masculine characteristics. The profession of artist demands an extraordinary commitment in terms of willingness to take rejection, to live in poverty, and to be field independent. Those are typical traits of committed males, but not of committed females, who often choose careers as art educators and not as artists. Girls' problems come when they try to reconcile the stereotypical paradox of the nurturing, recessive, motherly female with that of the unconventional artist. Boys' problems come when they try to reconcile the stereotypical paradox of the six-shootin' muscle-flexing "real" man with that of the sensitive, perceptive, and insightful artist.

There is no evidence that creative people are more often homosexual than people in other fields, such as teaching, politics, the military, or athletics. In the field of fashion, however, recent AIDS deaths of homosexual males have decimated the industry. A corollary question might be whether the field of athletics attracts more lesbians than other entertainment fields. The answer again may probably be in the affirmative. So what?

9. Provide Private Lessons and Special Classes

For Parents

Most schools, unless they are special schools for the arts or sciences, are not going to provide all of what your child needs to truly develop the talents he or she has, and so you must be the one to do so. This means lessons as well as materials. Even if your child plays in the band, the orchestra, jazz band, or string ensemble—if your school is fortunate enough to have such groups—your child also needs private lessons in order to develop musically. This is usually understood in the field of music and dance, but it is less understood in writing, visual arts, and theater. Few children who have talents and desire to learn get private lessons or tutoring in these fields, and this is a terrible shame.

The Development of Talent Project (Bloom, 1985) documented well the sacrifices that parents make for their talented children. Parents are the first and most important influences on their children's talent development. If there are special schools for the arts or sciences in your area, consider them. Students who attend these special schools demonstrate potential in the particular domains they are studying. Students are admitted as a result of their concrete performance on tests and auditions, in portfolios, and with assessment by professionals. A typical eight-period day at the La Guardia High School for the Arts in New York City contains three to four periods of intensive study of a particular art field. For example, an instrumental music student will have music theory, then an ensemble period, and then one or two periods of band or orchestra, in addition to four periods of general academic study. Most schools for the arts have similar curricula. The danger of attending these special schools is that the students may, in developing their special talents, become too narrow. The challenge in special schools is to provide young, developing minds with a general education as well as a special, focused education, and some of the students may regard general education subjects such as literature, mathematics, history, geography, and government as boring, irrelevant, and unnecessary.

Teachers in general education at such special schools often must justify and relate the material being taught so that the students will see a reason to learn it, to remember it. Most students at special schools are so focused on the specific skills they are developing that they would prefer not to have any liberal arts classes at all. They are vocationally minded, and their teachers must be very skillful in order to educate the whole person and not just the creative person.

Talented adolescents are chosen for these schools on the basis of their creative products, not for the successful completion of paper and pencil tests that measure divergent production. While they attend the school, they practice. Talented children who become successful adult professionals study and practice the skills of their field to the point of automaticity. The notion that creativity is separate from what is produced by the talented adolescent, that it springs from exposure to general exercises in fluency, flexibility, brainstorming, and elaboration, without specific nurturing in the field or domain in which the creativity is exhibited, seems not to have influenced, at this time, the curricula of special schools for talented adolescents. Whether such activities would enhance the adolescents' creativity or whether such activities are desirable as curricular options is doubtful.

Actually, the role of parents and specialized teachers in these adolescents' talent development seems more important than whatever structured creativity training they may have had. Parents often nurture and direct their children in the fields in which they themselves have interest and talent. The child is then taught by a teacher who passes on what knowledge he or she can; then that teacher passes the child to another, more masterful, teacher. That is the path of creative adult production. In the very depth of their special training, these talented children are developing automaticity. Parents who don't have proximity to special schools should send their talented students to special summer and Saturday programs and make sure that they have access to private lessons.

For Teachers

The value of mentors is often spoken of in the literature for the talented. Researchers have gone so far as to say that a person will not reach eminence in science without apprenticing himself to a mentor scientist, without studying with the right teacher. Having the right teacher who will have access to the right connections is important.

The classroom teacher and the specialist in talent development education also have a role, and that is to provide the talented child and the parents with information about suitable mentors or other opportunities. While the relationship between mentor and mentee is deeply personal and cannot be legislated or mandated, efforts can be made. Schools must also play a part in the development of talent, helping to find private teachers and mentors for talented children from families without financial resources. Petitioning local clubs and organizations to pay for lessons for a struggling but talented child can best be done by the school (anonymously, of course). A teacher paid for the room and board of one of our students at a summer institute last year. She did it so quietly that I never learned her name, but the child's life was changed by the experience. The Black poet Derek Wolcott, Nobel Prize winner and MacArthur Fellow, in an interview in the "Writers at Work" series in the *Paris Review*, told this story about growing up in the Caribbean country of St. Lucia, where he had the good fortune to come under the influence of the visual artist Harry Simmons. He described Simmons in an interview with Ed Hirsch:

> *Harry taught us. He had paints, he had music in his studio, and he was evidently a good friend of my father's. When he found out that we liked painting, he invited about four or five of us to come up to his studio and sit out on his veranda. He gave us equipment and told us to draw. Now that may seem very ordinary in a city, in another place, but in a very small, poor country like St. Lucia it was extraordinary. He encouraged us to spend our Saturday afternoons painting; he surrounded us with examples of his own painting. Just to let us be there and to have the ambience of his books, his music, his own supervision, and the stillness and dedication that this life meant in that studio was a terrific example. The influence was not so much technical. Of course I picked up a few things from him in terms of technique—how to do a good sky, how to water the paper, how to circle it, how to draw properly and concentrate on it, and all of that. But there were other things apart from the drawing. Mostly, it was the model of the man as a professional artist that was the example.* (p. 271)

Harry Simmons might not have had a teacher's certificate, but he was certainly a mentor and a teacher.

10. Use Hardship to Teach the Child Expression through Metaphor

For Parents

The first and second versions of this book received concerned comments and criticism, because the description of the childhood and the young adulthood of many adult creators seemed to have so many traumatic elements. "Aren't there creative people who are normal?" people asked. "Why have you made the connection between trouble in a person's life and a person's creativity? Can't a person be creative and live in a happy family, have a happy life?" "Well, of course," I answer. It just seems that those whose contributions and achievements, especially those in the arts and in literature, were deemed significant enough to have attracted the attention of a scholarly biographer seemed also to have had some personal trouble along the way. This doesn't mean that if your life is not worthy of attention by a biographer, you can't contribute significantly to the world by your creativity. Look at the lives of scientists. Many, if not most, of them had childhoods with active involvement by both parents, as well as support for study and for projects.

If trouble comes into your life, try to make something of it. Writer and storyteller Marie Vogl Gery told me of her yearlong residency at a junior high school where the mother of one of the boys she worked with committed suicide. This boy demonstrated talent and expressed his feelings through poetry that didn't specifically refer to the suicide, but that permitted him indirectly to defuse his feelings of sorrow, confusion, and sadness.

Release of emotion through the arts is often indirect, thus more therapeutic than therapy itself. There are branches of therapy through the arts called music therapy, art therapy, poetry therapy, and dance therapy—all of which recognize the positive effects that the arts can have when a person has experienced trauma or emotional upheaval. The depth psychologists, the archetypal psychologists, the Jungians, speak of the fire within that is turned into an *image*, a thing *out there*. However, the child should also have a right to privacy. Snooping in private journals, asking for detailed explanations of what may seem to be weird artistic endeavors is against the rules. The expression is itself enough. Remember the life of Christy Brown in the movie *My Left Foot*? His family refused to let him be institutionalized for his profound handicaps and provided him instead with materials, company, support, and a neighborhood full of loving friends.

Singer/songwriter and Berea, Ohio high school teacher Christopher Reynolds has an extracurricular program called Creativity, Inc. He works with selected students in 10 areas that combine their personal experience with the creation of image. In our joint presentations, we have emphasized that much of the creativity curriculum extant focuses on the "springtime" of creativity, but the creative person must visit winter as well. Many speakers about creativity celebrate the joyful "Spring" of creativity, using such words as "enhancing," "unlocking," and "tapping" with images of leaps, flights, openings, growings, and increases. These metaphors are good, useful, and necessary. Creativity is also reflection as to what has occurred, and this is felt in a receptive mode—returning what has been received—versus making brand new things, acting outward, and making things happen. Spring is innovation. Fall is reflection, which is also essential in walking the path of creative development. Christopher and I sing the blues in poetry and song, and our workshop participants have an opportunity to express their own images, and *not* have to share them, but to take them inside and nurture them.

Our sessions explore the Fall and Winter of creativity, which is not a response to a potential to grow, but one that includes loss, depression, and the tragic modes of life. In this way, creativity can be permitted to be somber and to sing the blues, drawn inward toward gravity. This talk has as its theme that creativity and productivity across a lifetime should not only mean optimism and excitement, the idea of constant improvement with no regrets or wrong turns, but that creativity also involves "the dark side," the introvertive, contemplative, intuitive, insightful side in order to round out the whole picture. James Hillman, the archetypal psychologist, has said that depression and loss are essential for creativity.

When the image is created, a personal poem, story, song, painting, theater piece—anything that objectifies the emotion that is churning, the young creator can begin to have some peace. One of the groups that visited Kuwait after the Gulf War was a team of art therapists who asked Kuwaiti children to draw the horror they had seen of invading soldiers breaking down the doors of their homes and being violent with their mothers. The therapeutic value of creative work should not be overlooked. Autotherapy (or self-help, or self-therapy) is one powerful reason for creativity. After all, the word "creativity" itself means "to make."

Biographer Joan Dash differentiated between ordinary auto therapeutic creativity and the creativity of very talented people. Of Edna St.
Vincent Millay, American poet/playwright, she said:

> *If Edna Millay had been only a neurotic woman, death-haunted,*
> *claustrophobic and sexually ambiguous, she might have found*
> *considerable satisfaction as well as worthwhile therapy in what-*
> *ever art form she took up in her spare time.... But she had also*
> *been born with the peculiar genetic equipment that can become*
> *high talent, perhaps even genius, and in her earliest years had*
> *acquired the habit of hard and precise observation of the world*
> *around her, as well as the discipline that leads to transmuting*
> *experience into something more than therapeutic art. Her fears of*
> *death became everyman's fear of death, her longing for love and*
> *her denial of it became the universal cry of the spirit to be part of*
> *something greater than the single self. Just as the poetry tran-*
> *scended her own individual nightmares, so did the poet herself, in*
> *the very act of writing, push back the cage of self to join humanity*
> *at large. (p. 79)*

This question of whether trauma is necessary to creative expression is
debatable. One new study has shed some light on this. Barbara Kerr and
her colleagues studied undergraduate and graduate students who called
themselves creative. She found that they came from homes where the parents were at home a lot and where the parents were in creative occupations.
The families were also larger than the average family. The families were
lively, and the children and adults communicated with respect. Notable was
that these students had one parent whom they called "very creative." These
families are ordinary creative families, without the trauma that seems to be
present in those creators who have had biographies written about them.

An earlier study, in the book *Cradles of Eminence* by Goertzel,
Goertzel, Goertzel, and Hansen, which has recently been updated, looked
at more than 400 twentieth-century eminent persons and found that less
that 15% of them had supportive, warm, and relatively untroubled homes.
They concluded that persons who are comfortable and contented do not
ordinarily become creative.

For Teachers

Try to notice and be sensitive to the personal situations of the children you teach. Ban the term "broken home" from your vocabulary. Don't be under the impression that a child will not be creative because he or she is poor or disheveled. A former student of mine, a bilingual Spanish/English teacher, discovered the creativity of a boy living in extreme poverty because he was always reading. She took photographs of him reading in the bus line, in the lunchroom, in the hallways, in math class, on the playground. She then identified him as having potential writing talent by asking him to write stories, which were extraordinary blends of Mexican and Central American mythological characters. She recommended him to the specialists in talent development education in his district, even though his test scores did not meet the threshold cutoff. Since the boy was from a poor family, the district was glad that she had noticed these behaviors, as their identification procedures did not identify poor children well enough.

11. Discipline and Practice Are Important

For Parents

Talent is only a small part of creativity. Talent is necessary but not sufficient. True realization of creativity comes through hard work. This has been emphasized repeatedly through studies of creative people and their interactions with their domains of creativity. A child gradually realizes that talent is developed through habits of hard work. Bamberger's work on the development of musical talent is important to remember. She said that there are two stages in the development of talent, and that the first stage is the natural stage, where everything seems to come easily; during the second stage, the adolescent learns the formal aspects of the discipline—the talent becomes consciously developed. The world is full of talented people, but fully creative people also do a lot of hard work.

Does that mean you should make your child practice the piano? Use your own judgment. The key is to realize that discipline and practice are important. No creative adult in any field became successful without first having had many fits and starts and having spent many hours in conscious practice. How many times did Edison have to try and fail before he came up with a successful electric light bulb?

For Teachers

Teachers of the talented especially must realize that such children are often overly praised and rewarded just for possessing the talent. Teachers of the artistic disciplines—the visual arts, writing, music, dance, theater— know what it takes to realize that talent, but often, such talented students are not given special help by the school. They are instead thrown in with far less talented students in art, music, math, and science. This would never happen in athletics, where talented students are permitted to advance according to their abilities and compete with people at their own levels of expertise. Accurate and qualified feedback is important in the development of talent, and the child should have access to people who have some expertise. Mentoring is important.

Talented people are often talented in many dimensions, and it is hard for them to choose which field to pursue. Art? Music? Acting? Athletics? Helping talented children to make these choices without closing down options is a challenge. Parents and school counselors can expose these students to options in creative ways. Take the child's interest and help her see which careers would fit well with those interests and abilities. English? Law, journalism, and academic careers are ones an English major might enjoy. Science? Math? Engineering? A student interested in these areas might want to explore medicine, scientific research, or medical engineering. Begin talking about careers while the child is still in elementary and junior high school. Explore summer internships, mentorships, or summer jobs in those areas to give the child a better idea of what the career entails. Another clue for the multi-talented, multi-interested person is to ask, "When do I lose track of time while doing something? When do I enjoy something so much that I am barely conscious of time passing?" This is an indicator that the person may have the interest and the motivation to sustain the long process of study and engagement each career path requires.

Another challenge is not to counter-identify. Often, the teachers of talented students are almost as jealous and anxious as parents are. Such teachers hesitate to lose the student to other, more advanced teachers. A movie I like to show to illustrate this point is *Madame Sousatzka,* which illustrates how a music teacher at a lower level loses her students to teachers at a higher level. When teachers counter-identify, they feel horrible when the student doesn't perform or when the child makes a mistake. They are as narcissistic as the parents described by Miller in *The Drama of the Gifted*

Child, or the parents and coaches described by Tofler and deGeronimo in their book about achievement by proxy.

Not to overly identify with the talented student is particularly difficult when the teaching relationship becomes a coaching relationship. Some teachers can be temperamental and cruel, pushing hard until the students hate the field. A former swimmer once told me that he would never swim again, never go near a pool, because his college coach demanded that he swim seven hours a day in order to improve his time a few seconds. He fears that swimming will never again be a pleasure for him. Miami Gators' quarterback Bobby Sabelhaus's experience with coach Steve Spurrier drove him out of football. In a 2002 interview with sportswriter Baldwin, he said: "Everything I did was wrong. I was used to coaches yelling at me, but they would also sometimes pat you on the back. Not Spurrier. Even when I threw a touchdown pass in practice once, he said to me, 'Are you just stupid or is it a lack of talent?'" Kogan also spoke to this difficulty while describing the idiosyncratic Juilliard teachers.

Tofler and DiGeronimo warn parents against permitting their children to be with instructors who want to achieve by proxy. They say parents should avoid the "Win-at-Any-Cost Instructor," "The Verbal Batterer," and "The Parent Substitute." If their talented child is to spend any amount of time away from home, they also recommend that parents look into the coach's record with regard to harassment or sexual abuse of minors. They cite 30 cases of coaches who were arrested or convicted of sexually abusing children in sports.

12. Allow the Child to be "Odd"; Avoid Emphasizing Socialization at the Expense of Creative Expression

For Parents

So, your daughter didn't get to be Clara and had to settle for being a soldier in The Nutcracker. Or your son didn't get his brilliant short story accepted for publication by that magazine of children's writing. Is this the end of the world? Is it your child's or your own ego that is hurt? Parental narcissism—that is, parents investing so much of themselves in their children's successes and failures that they lose sight of the purpose of the practice—can harm children. In the high-powered world of national children's chess, parents have become so involved in their children's chess tournaments that fathers came to blows, and the chess association finally had to ban parents from the chess arenas at the primary levels.

We all know the phenomenon of the Little League parent. This syndrome is found in the creative world as well. In the arts, these parents are sometimes called stage mothers. Sylvia Rimm, in *The Underachievement Syndrome,* wrote about the necessity for children, especially talented children, to be able to take the second lead in the play or second chair in the band. She said that when children work for their achievements, they learn how to fail and thus appreciate their achievements more.

Other parents either deny that their children have talent, seemingly fearful of what might be the implications for their future development, or they don't see their children's talent as important. Or, like the mother of a talented young actor who told the teacher never to put her son into another play because all actors are weird homosexuals, they see actors as odd.

But the need to get along with others is not paramount in creative people. Most creative people weren't president of the club or queen of the prom or the one voted most likely to succeed. Often, they were odd. For many, high school was the most painful time of their youth, as the pressures for conformity beckoned. Often, too, high school creative youth will band together in what they call nonconformity but will still dress the same as their other nonconformist friends, listening to the same music, reading the same books, and rebelling together. I read in a movie magazine that the *enfants terribles* of the great 1970s movie directors—i.e., Spielberg, Lucas, Bogdanovich, Coppola—were not, in high school, the boys that the pretty blond cheerleaders chose for boyfriends, and they spent a lot of time yearning for these ice goddesses. It was only when their creative talents were realized, years later, that they got to make themselves noticed by their high school dream girls, as Bogdonovich did by casting Cybill Shepherd in *The Last Picture Show.* This is probably why many adult women also love the movie *The Way We Were,* because the odd rebel, Barbara Streisand, got the gorgeous blond hunk, Robert Redford, a scenario that seemed very improbable in real life

For Teachers

The schools often see their major role as that of socializing children to fit into a mold, to become acceptable to the society that the schools serve. Many educators consider socialization to be as important as teaching the children to read, write, and figure, for this is what the "real world" demands. But creative people are often at odds with the world and are prickly, rebellious, and nonconforming. (Note: Often their nonconforming is actually conforming, but conforming to a stereotype of their perception of creative people.) Creative students tend to act out in class, are argumentative, and consciously underachieve—that is, they do well in classes they like, but don't care about classes they don't like or see as irrelevant to their futures.

Often, creative students stereotype their teachers by age and by looks. One summer, I was teaching a fiction writer's workshop to a group of specially selected teenagers from throughout the state of Ohio. One of the young women was quite surly as she looked at me in my middle age, with my conservative haircut, my comfortable but rather rumpled summer clothes. When I mentioned that one of the guest readers I was going to bring in was poet Nick Muska, a good friend of mine who had written a theater piece about Jack Kerouac called *Back to Jack*, this young woman's attitude changed. She was from Toledo, Nick's town, and knew him from the poetry scene in that city. "*You* know Nick Muska?" she said incredulously. "Yes. We've been friends for many years," I said simply. "But I *love* Nick Muska!" she said. And the very next session, she brought in her personal collection of Jack Kerouac's books to show me. She had thought me an old schoolmarm, not cool enough to be a writing teacher from whom she might learn.

Rimm recommended that some creative students may need therapy. They view themselves as *too* different, *too* creative, *too* cool for anything the schools might have to offer. Often, their rebelliousness carries over to the therapist's office as well. One teenage creative writer I know said that she sat in stubborn silence when she was sent to a therapist. Another creative child who was videotaped for a case study by one of my students said that even though her mother made her go to therapy because of her nonconforming behavior, she didn't benefit because she felt so much smarter than the therapist. One of our creative adolescents at a summer institute was taking psychotropic drugs and fell asleep in her morning classes. Her parents insisted that she take them because she had taken to wearing black clothes and black lipstick and they worried about her, so they sent her to a therapist who prescribed the drugs.

Perhaps when considering whether a creative child needs therapy, families and the schools should themselves be willing to undergo therapeutic questioning. The selection of the therapist is also quite important.

Creative people generally understand creative people because they recognize kindred spirits. Sending a creative child to a rigid behavior therapist may not work. Consumers have the right to a free initial interview with a therapist to discuss a treatment plan and determine whether they think they can "connect" with the therapist. Including a teenager in this process might make the teen more amenable to therapy.

13. Use Humor, and Get Creativity Training

For Parents and Teachers

Besides enjoying and being frustrated by a child's sense of humor, we as parents and teachers should monitor our own ways of dealing with creative children. Do we enjoy children? Do we laugh with children (or at them, when appropriate)? Do we have fun with children? In other words, is being with creative children a pleasure? Bryant and Zillman studied the use of humor in the classroom and found that elementary school teachers use more humor than junior high teachers. Junior high teachers most frequently use funny comments, funny stories, and jokes, though male junior high teachers told jokes more often. But the alarming thing is that junior high, high school, and college teachers used hostile and tendentious humor such as ridicule and sarcasm much more often than elementary teachers. In fact, nearly half the humor used by these teachers of older students was sarcastic. Humor used in a hostile manner can be hurtful to children, especially sensitive, gifted and talented children. Sarcasm is not what is wanted here, but rather humor used in gentler ways to create a happier, more relaxed classroom, thus helping students have positive attitudes toward learning. Humor contributes to the development of creative thinking, and one can see why, for non-hostile humor creates the feeling of freedom and play that is necessary for creative thinking.

Get creativity training. If school districts are serious about effectively teaching creative thinking, they must provide the necessary backup training. Many commercial programs are available, and trained people can provide creativity training to school districts. School districts should also provide rigorous instruction in the fields in which the creativity training can be applied. Many opportunities for teaching students to be more creative exist. (See Chapter 13 for a long list of already existent creativity training materials.) Few schools offer special classes in how to be more creative, so the techniques and lessons must be integrated and incorporated into the courses as they are taught. But teachers do teach students to be creative, and every school has experts who can help the student who is creative in some domain to be nurtured in that domain.

Many people do not believe that the school is the place to work to enhance student creativity, and in fact, they doubt whether any such exercises really do train people to be more creative. I am of mixed opinion on this; on the one hand, doing such exercises can make people aware of what goes into creativity, if the exercises are based upon the research about creative people. These would be likened to the drills that athletes practice or the scales that musicians practice or the skills that one seeks to acquire to get automaticity in an area in which one wants to be expert. On the other hand, perhaps such exercises are too abstract to promote transfer.

After all, does practice in risk-taking encourage the risk-taking that creative people must have in doing their creative work, as well as in pursuing their careers? Is risk-taking teachable through a creativity enhancement exercise? If one begins to think about this, one realizes that the "ropes courses" through which many businesses send their employees to build a sense of trust in each other also encourage physical risk-taking as a "safe" rehearsal for "dangerous" life. With these caveats in mind, I have compiled a list of possible activities that teachers could use to construct educational experiences for their students in hopes that they will learn to be more creative. Ultimately, the purpose of such training is to free the inner person through imagery. Colleagues who teach in our program use finger-painting, storytelling, clay, construction paper, singing, and other means to encourage the students to express themselves through metaphor. These are described more fully in Chapter 13. The following suggestions in the Summary work well for parents and teachers. Have fun trying them.

Summary

1. Provide a private place for creative work to be done.

2. Provide materials (e.g., musical instruments, sketchbooks).

3. Encourage and display the child's creative work, but avoid overly evaluating it.

4. Do your own creative work, and let the child see you doing it.

5. Set a creative tone.

6. Value the creative work of others.

7. Incorporate creativity values into your family mythology.

8. Avoid emphasizing sex-role stereotypes.

9. Provide private lessons and special classes.

10. If hardship comes into your life, use it positively to teach the child expression through metaphor.

11. Emphasize that talent is only a small part of creative production, and that discipline and practice are important.

12. Allow the child to be "odd"; avoid emphasizing socialization at the expense of creative expression.

13. Use humor, and get creativity training.

Part III:

Personality and Intellectual Characteristics of Creative People In Various Domains

Chapter 5
The Piirto Pyramid of Talent Development Model

The "Pyramid" is excellent—a compact, eloquent, graphic synthesis.
—Frank Barron

In 1992, after reading almost all of the research extant about talented, gifted, and creative children and adults, I was driving to my newly married daughter's home in Brooklyn, New York. As I sailed along Interstate 80 through the beautiful Pennsylvania countryside, I asked myself over and over again, "What have I learned?" "What have I learned?" My editor at Macmillan had told me that in writing my textbook, I had a choice. I could formulate a theory, or I could just report research. Being somewhat of a risk-taker, I decided to formulate a theory based on what I had read. "What have I learned?" "What have I learned?" What are the common threads of talent development and creativity? The fact that few women had proposed theories of creativity and talent development only made me more determined to take the risk.

That night, in steamy August, sleeping on the newly carpeted, sticky, hot floor of my daughter's apartment on a clammy sleeping bag, I had a dream. "It's personality," the dream told me. "It's personality that affects the most. Not test scores. Personality." This became the base. I got up and, in the middle of the night, sketched a picture of Greek gods and goddesses shooting arrows or darts. The next week, I presented it to my graduate students. The image was confusing, my students said. Then one night I was looking at the designs of perfume bottles in one of the glossy magazines I subscribe to. I saw a perfume bottle that looked like a 3-tiered pyramid.

Having seen the Step Pyramid during a trip to Egypt, I knew this was what I wanted. I sketched the model.

I published my first version of the Piirto Pyramid in 1994. Over the years, it has evolved, thanks to talks and critiques from friends, students, and colleagues. My model of the human and developmental influences on a person is sometimes humorously called the Piiramid of Talent Development (with thanks to Michael Piechowski for the wit). This model has guided my work on talent in domains (Piirto, 1994/1999; 1992/1998, 2002). It is a contextual framework that considers person, process, and product, as well as environmental factors.

Figure 5.1: Pyramid of Talent Development

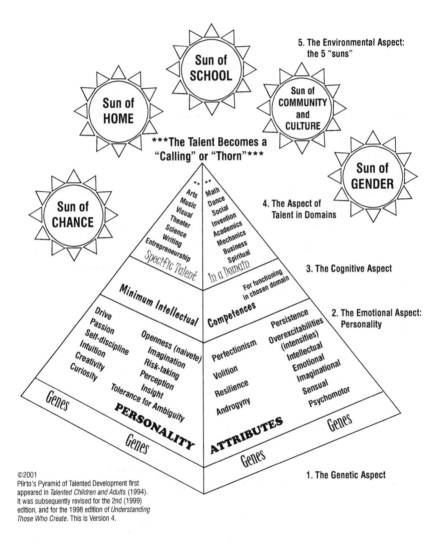

The Pyramid (Piiramid) of Talent Development

1. The Genetic Aspect

All of our traits have a genetic component, which is now being unlocked with the exciting work being done on the human genome. On the Pyramid, this genetic aspect lies beneath. Symbolically, if you think of the pyramids in Egypt, the king and queen's burial chambers lie beneath, far below. So it is with genes. Genetics shows us where we came from and who we are. Children who have been adopted seek their "birth" parents in order to unlock the mystery of their genetics. Family reunions are filled with discussions of who looks like whom and who takes after whom.

At a recent family reunion, I overhead my daughter and my niece comparing their feet. "Your feet are ugly, just like mine." In a photograph I took in a Spanish street, I saw my daughter with her hands on her hips looking one direction and my granddaughter in an identical pose looking the other way. I recalled a photograph of myself in front of the Great Pyramid, with my hands in the same position on my hips. It is a distinct way of standing. Then I pulled out a photograph of my grandmother standing on a porch with—you guessed it—her hands on her hips in the same odd position. I put the photographs together and sent them to my first cousins— "Did any of your mothers put her hands on her hips this way?" We call it the genetic aspect of hands on hips. We laugh, but buried beneath and within us, our genes tell—and determine—certain propensities. Note that I use the term "aspect" with intention here. "Aspect" means "the appearance or interpretation of an idea, problem, etc. as considered from a specific viewpoint." Another definition of "Aspect" is "face."

2. The Emotional Aspect: Personality Attributes

Many studies have emphasized that successful creators in all domains have certain personality attributes in common. These make up the base of the model and are the affective aspects of what a person needs to succeed; they rest on the foundation of genes. Among these attributes are *androgyny, creativity, imagination, insight, introversion, intuition, naiveté or openness to experience, overexcitabilities, passion for work in a domain, perceptiveness, perfectionism, persistence, preference for complexity, resilience, risk-taking, self-discipline, self-efficacy, tolerance for ambiguity,* and *volition or will.*

There is research support for these personality attributes: *androgyny* (Barron, 1968; Csikszentmihalyi, Rathunde, & Whalen, 1993; Piirto &

Fraas, 1995); *creativity* (Renzulli, 1978; Tannenbaum, 1983); *imagination* (Dewey, 1934; Langer, 1957; Plato; Santayana, 1896); *insight* (Davidson, 1992; Sternberg & Davidson, 1985); *introversion* (Myers & McCulley, 1985; Simonton, 1999); *intuition* (Myers & McCaulley, 1985); *naiveté or openness to experience* (Cattell, 1971; Ghiselin, 1952); the presence of *overexcitabilities*, called OEs (Dabrowski, 1964, 1967, 1972; Dabrowski & Piechowski, 1977; Piechowski, 1979; Silverman, 1993); *passion for work in a domain* (Benbow, 1992; Bloom, 1985; Piirto, 1994); *perceptiveness* (Myers & McCaulley, 1985); *perfectionism* (Silverman, 1993); *persistence* (Renzulli, 1978); *preference for complexity* (Barron, 1968, 1995); *resilience* (Jenkins-Friedman, 1992; Block & Kremen, 1996); *risk-taking* (MacKinnon, 1978; Torrance, 1987); *self-discipline* (Renzulli, 1978); *self-efficacy* (Zimmerman, Bandura, & Martinez-Pons, 1992; Sternberg & Lubart, 1992); *tolerance for ambiguity* (Barron, 1968, 1995); and *volition or will* (Corno & Kanfer, 1993; Simonton, 1999). Although these personality traits have recently been consolidated into the so-called "Big Five" (McCrae & Costa, 1999), earlier work on creative people has noted these other traits as listed, and so I include them here.

The personality attributes highlighted above are by no means separate from each other or a comprehensive list, but they show that creative adults have achieved effectiveness partially by force of personality. Talented adults who achieve success possess many of these attributes. Ellen Winner said that personality factors should be looked at when attempting to understand the gifted child. Csikzsentmihalyi, Rathunde, and Whalen said that personality attributes make up the autotelic personality, where "flow" or the ability to tap into optimal experiences keeps one in a state of self-stimulation to do the creative work. Feist showed in a review of literature that "creative people behave consistently over time and situation and in ways that distinguish them from others." However, it is not the cognitive measurement of intellectual aptitude but their personality traits that cause this consistency.

These aspects of personality are present in some way in highly creative people. One could call these the foundation, and one could go farther and say that these may be innate to a certain extent, but at the same time, they can also be developed, encouraged, and directly taught.

What does it mean to have such personality attributes? What is personality, and how does it contribute to effectiveness? Personality is, fortunately or unfortunately, an area in which there are many competing theories. Defined simply as "the set of behavioral or personal characteristics by which an individual is recognizable," with synonyms such as "individuality," "selfhood," "identity," and "individuality," personality theory is sometimes more attributable to belief than to empiricism.

Personality theory can be psychoanalytic (ego psychology, object relations, transpersonal), behavioral or cognitive (quantitative studies using factor analysis such as those of Cattell and Eysenck), or humanistic (using Phenomenology, Existentialism, Gestalt, Humanistic, and Transpersonal theories). Personality is sometimes equated with character, directing how one lives one's life—according to one's personal teachings or values. The personality attributes mentioned here have been determined by empirical studies of creative producers, mostly adults, but in some cases adolescents in special schools. Empirical means that the researchers gave personality tests to the people and also observed them and interviewed them.

Many of the personality attributes from studies used in this book have focused on the *Myers-Briggs Type Indicator*, based on the Jungian theory of personality. Other tests such as the Cattell *16 Personality Factors Questionnaire*, the *Eysenck Inventory*, the *Gough Creative Personality Inventory*, the *California Psychological Inventory*, the *Minnesota Multiphasic Psychological Inventory*, and others have also been used in studies cited here. More recently, personality is being assessed using ways that focus on the so-called "Big Five" factors—extraversion vs. introversion, agreeableness vs. antagonism, conscientiousness vs. undirectedness, neuroticism vs. emotional stability, openness to experience vs. not open to experience. Nevertheless, some researchers, such as Barbara Kerr, who are interested in creativity and personality have told me that they think that these instruments do not differentiate enough within personalities.

3. The Cognitive Aspect

The cognitive dimension in the form of an IQ score has been over-emphasized with regard to creativity. The IQ test is often an abstract, "out there" screen that serves to obfuscate our efforts to discover creative, productive people. IQ is a *minimum* criterion, mortar and paste. A certain level of intellectual ability necessary for functioning in the world, but studies by researchers such as Baird have repeatedly shown that having a really high IQ is not necessary for the realization of most talents. Rather, college graduation seems to be necessary (except for professional athletes, actors, and entertainers), and as Simonton said, most college graduates have above average IQs but not stratospheric IQs. Simonton also listed the IQs necessary for functioning in various domains; theoretical physicists and philosophers need the highest IQs. A reasonable IQ is necessary and helpful for creative production, but for creativity, the IQ is a minor ingredient. Things like motivation—i.e., wanting to create—are more important.

4. Talent in Domains

The talent itself—inborn, innate, and mysterious—should also be developed. Talent is the tip of the Pyramid. Some domains in which talent is realized are: *mathematics, visual arts, music, theater, sciences, writing and literature, business, entrepreneurship, economics, athletics, dance, the spiritual and theological, philosophy, psychology, the interpersonal,* and *education.* They are all quite well-defined academically, and people can go to school to study in any of them. Each school has experts in most of the talent domains that students will enter.

How will educators and individuals know talent areas to be developed? Most talents are recognized through certain *predictive behaviors*—for example, voracious reading for linguistically talented students, and preferring to be class treasurer rather than secretary for mathematically talented students. When a child draws so well that she is designated the class artist, or when he can throw a ball 85 miles per hour, or when a student is accused of cheating on her short story assignment because it sounds so adult, there is obvious talent present and working.

These talents are demonstrated within domains that are socially recognized and valued within the society, and thus they may differ from society to society. For example, hunting ability, i.e., acuity of eye combined with a honed instinct for shooting and a knowledge of animal habitat, is not as valued in western society as is verbal ability—a sensitivity to words and their nuances as expressed through carefully crafted communication written or spoken for a purpose—to persuade or inform. In earlier decades, hunting ability was valued much more than verbal ability. Hunting talent is still inborn in certain children, no matter how much urbanites, divorced from nature and its cruelties, deny that it exists.

In reading for this edition, I was glad to see that Kaufman and Baer are honoring creativity in domains with an edited volume, *Faces of the Muse,* and that creativity in domains is also now prominently featured in the *Encyclopedia of Creativity.*

5. Environmental "Suns"

These four levels together could theoretically be called the individual person. In addition, everyone is influenced by five "suns." These suns may be likened to certain factors in the environment. The three major suns refer to a child's being (1) in a positive and nurturing *home* environment, and (2) in a *community and culture* that conveys values compatible with the educational institution and provides support for the home and the school. The (3) *school* is the third key factor, especially for those children whose other "suns" may have clouds in front of them. Other, smaller suns are (4) the influence of *gender*, for most adult creative producers tend to be androgynous—that is, they show personality attributes of both genders—and (5) what *chance* can provide. The presence or absence of all or several of these suns makes the difference between whether a talent is developed and whether it lies dormant, undeveloped.

Unfortunately, it must be said that it is truly miraculous when a student emerges into adulthood with his or her talent nurtured and developed, because there are so many influences that encroach upon or stifle talent development. We all know or remember people with outstanding talent who did not, or were not able to, use or develop that talent because of circumstances represented by one or more of these "suns." For example, a student whose home life contains serious trauma such as divorce or violence may be so involved in the trauma that the talent cannot be emphasized. In the absence of the home's stability and talent development influence (e.g., lessons, atmosphere for encouragement), the school's and the teacher's or coach's role is to recognize the talent and to encourage lessons, mentors, or special experiences that the parents might have provided had their situation been better. Clouds may hide the various "suns" that shine on the Pyramid, and in that case, the school plays a key role in the child's environment.

As another example, in a diverse society with racist elements, the genes that produce one's race are acted upon environmentally—that is, a person of a certain race may be treated differently in different environments. The school and the community and culture are important in developing or enhancing this genetic inheritance. Retired general and cabinet member Colin Powell has said that he entered the army because he saw the military as the only place in a racist society where he would be treated fairly, where his genetic inheritance would not be subject to discrimination or prejudice, and where he could develop his talents fully.

The Sun of Gender is called environmental, although many gender differences are genetic and innate. The influence on talent development of gender, though, is environmental. Boys and girls may be born with equal talent, but something happens along the way. Few personality attributes show significant gender differences. Except for "Thinking" and "Feeling" on the *Myers-Briggs Type Indicator* (MBTI) and "tender mindedness" on the *16 Personality Factors Questionnaire*, few intelligence or personality test scores show significant gender differences (though boys consistently score higher in spatial ability in mathematics). We should therefore look at how the environment influences the development of talent according to gender. Gender differences according to creative domain of talent will be discussed along the way.

The importance of chance or luck cannot be overemphasized. As a principal at a school in New York City, I received many calls from casting agents and producers wanting to look at our bright children for possible roles in movies, television, and theater. These children had the luck of being born in and living in a center for theatrical activity. I'll warrant that few school principals in Kansas City, say, or in Seattle, Washington get the weekly or even daily calls I got from casting agents.

The influence of chance is evident when a person happens to meet someone who can connect him or her to another person who can help or influence the first person's opportunities to interact with the field or domain. A play was even written about this phenomenon, John Guare's *Six Degrees of Separation*. But the "sun" of chance has clouds over it when a talented adolescent in a rural high school does not get the counseling needed to make a college choice that will enhance a career. For example, in consulting with overseas schools, I noticed that most of the counselors recommended U.S. colleges in the East and in the West. One counselor from the Midwest, who began recommending his own alma mater, a state university in the Midwest, was asked to leave, as too many of the high school students began to apply to this university for their eastern establishment parents' comfort. In this case, the "chance" of a student's college choice was expected to be enhanced by a counselor who knew the Ivy League. And the chance factor can, in fact, sometimes be "improved" by manipulating oneself so that one is placed where opportunities might occur, or in other words, one can be in "the right place at the right time."

Talent Multipotentiality: Feeling the Call, or the "Thorn"

The presence of talent, although absolutely necessary, is not sufficient. Many people have more than one talent and wonder what to do with them. What is the impetus, what is the reason, for one talent becoming dominant—taking over and capturing the passion and commitment of the person who has it? One useful explanation comes from Socrates, who described the *inspiration* of the muse (Plato, *Ion*). Carl Jung described the *passion* that engrosses; Csikszentmihalyi described the process of *flow*. Depth psychologist James Hillman described the presence of the *daimon* in creative lives. All these—inspiration, passion, flow, daimon—give clue as to what talent a person will choose to develop.

Hillman described the talents in a way similar to Plato's and Jung's: "The talent is only a piece of the image; many are born with musical, mathematical, and mechanical talent, but only when the talent serves the fuller image and is carried by its character do we recognize exceptionality." Hillman's idea is similar to the notion of *vocation* or *call*. I would call it inspiration or passion for the domain. Philosophers would call it *soul*. Thus, I have put an asterisk or "thorn" on the pyramid to exemplify that talent is not enough for the realization of a life of commitment. Without going into the classical topics of desire, emotion, wisdom, or soul (Adler, 1952), suffice it to say that the entire picture of talent development ensues when a person is pierced or bothered by a thorn, the daimon that leads to commitment.

Crystallizing Experiences and Catalysts

Feldman was close when he described the *crystallizing experience* in 1982, but the thorn is more than crystallizing; it is fortifying. Much evidence exists that the creative person decides to pursue the development of his or her talent after some catalyst reveals that this is what must happen. It may be winning a contest, or receiving praise, or becoming so pleasantly engrossed in the making and creating that the person realizes that this is what he or she must do, come hell or high water. It may be a depression that is assuaged by making or creating, so much so that the self-healing that happens when one is creative warns the person that he or she must create in order to prevent illness. It may come after a long period of thought and meditation. The creative person recognizes that the thorn is pricking and that the call must be answered. Here is an example. A former student of mine wrote me this letter about answering his call:

Dear Dr. Piirto,

 I am writing to you now in order to ask for your help. I had contact with two of my relatives recently. Each approached me individually and asked what I have planned for the future. I began to tell each of them of my plans to get my master's in public administration. I tried my hardest to explain this career for them, but I felt like a fool. I explained the different aspects and I tried to define it, but I stumbled and faltered. I felt as if I were lying to their faces.... I am accepted into the School of Public Policy and Management [at a Big Ten university].... I plan to start grad school in the fall. I am getting married.... My heart is not in public administration. But I had this great fear/anxiety. If I were to die, at the end of my life, and go to heaven, I fear God's gaze on me. I could imagine Him asking me, "What did you do with the gifts that I gave you?" And I could only show him a shabby degree in public administration. I am at the point now when I have suppressed my desires too much. I want to live entirely for my true talents rather than just using them casually. I have never had enough faith to believe that I could support myself and a family with a job that involves writing.... Jane, I want to write. I want to live inside this inexhaustible gift that God has blessed me with....

Support for the Pyramid Theory

Over the years, my students have done hundreds of biographical studies in the creativity classes I teach. They place the people that they study on a blank Piirto Pyramid. Over and over again they have found that personality attributes outweigh measured intelligence and that certain characteristics apply according to domain of creativity. In 2002, I published a book on creativity in writers called *"My Teeming Brain": Understanding Creative Writers*, and I organized it according to the Piirto Pyramid. I have organized *Understanding Creativity* in the same way. The next few chapters talk about what creativity means, what happens during the creative process, and about creativity in the domains of visual arts, architecture, creative writing, science, mathematics, invention, entrepreneurship, music, theater, dance, and athletics.

Summary

1. The Piirto Pyramid is a contextual framework for creativity that considers person, process, and product, as well as environmental factors.

2. All human traits have a genetic component.

3. Successful creators have several personality attributes in common.

4. Personality attributes are more important than IQ for the realization of talent.

5. Talent appears in various domains. Each domain has its own path to eminence, known well to people who work within the domain.

6. Most talent can be recognized by predictive behaviors in childhood.

7. Environmental factors such as home, community and culture, school, chance, and gender influence creativity and may determine whether talent is developed.

8. The "chance factor" (Sun of Chance) can sometimes be manipulated to help a person be in the right place at the right time.

9. Talent is not enough; one must also experience the "thorn," a passion or calling that leads to commitment.

Chapter 6
Visual Artists and Architects

That which fills my head and my heart must be expressed in drawings or pictures. Drawing becomes more and more a passion with me, and it is a passion just like that of a sailor for the sea.
—Vincent Van Gogh

The stereotypic visual artist, with ragged jeans, dirty fingernails, a beard, and a cape or scuffed leather jacket, prowls the streets. Or an artist in a beret with palette in hand on the banks of the Seine River paints a riverscape of people and boulevards in Paris. How much do these stereotypes reflect the truth?

From ancient times to rather recent times, the artist was regarded as a craftsman, a solid worker who made art, carved friezes, and worked with tools to create useful decorations under the tutelage of a well-known artisan in his workshop. The Bohemian stereotype arose later, a result of the individualizing and personalizing that came out of the romantic era—the late eighteenth and the nineteenth centuries.

The Industrial Revolution changed the perceived role of artists in society. Art became a romantic search for abstract "beauty," and artists were viewed as romantic figures. The ultimate romantic, Gauguin, who came to art late in life, was actually disdained as a "Sunday painter" by the elite artists in France and Belgium. Having come under the influence of Pissarro, Manet, Monet, and Renoir in 1876, Gauguin finally got into his first show in 1880. Manet's statement that "No one is a painter unless he loves painting more than anything else" was a warning and a challenge to Gauguin. Gauguin's *Study of a Nude* in 1881 finally impressed the gatekeepers. Even though he had been a banker for 11 years, was married, and had five children, Gauguin resigned his position at Bertin's banking house and in 1882 gave up his secure living to become a painter. His wife never forgave him, and the family never recovered financially.

From a time when many artists were anonymous—craftsmen under the patronage of the rich—to today when the rebellious artist is an accepted stereotype, the fascination with artists' lives has continued. What have studies of visual artists shown? Is this stereotype true? In this chapter, I will review some of the most important studies of visual artists.

The Goertzel's studies, in 1962 and 1978, were biographical studies of 700 eminent people, among them artists. The subjects of the study had least two books written about their lives. The Goertzels then divided the eminent into four groups—the political, the literary, the artistic, and other. The artistic category included sculptors, painters, actors, composers, film directors, dancers, and performers.

Anne Roe also studied artists who had already achieved. Another well-known study of visual artists is Barron's *The Making of an Artist.* Barron chose students at the San Francisco Art Institute and the Rhode Island School of Design and administered tests of intelligence, personality, and divergent production to them. Getzels and Csikszentmihalyi, in *The Creative Vision,* studied visual arts students at the Art Institute of Chicago. Another study was of accomplished sculptors, conducted by Sloane and Sosniak in connection with Bloom's Development of Talent Research Project at the University of Chicago. Sloane and Sosniak chose 12 men and eight women sculptors who had won either Guggenheim Fellowships or the Rome Award. In 1986, Foley did a study of painters who were also mothers. Others who did biographical studies were Alice Miller in 1990 and Howard Gardner in 1993. These studies will be discussed here.

The themes in these studies will be arranged using the Piirto Pyramid as a framework, beginning with (1) Genes, (2) Personality, (3) Intelligence, and (4) Talent in a Domain and the Thorn. The five environmental suns will then be considered: (1) Sun of Home and Family, (2) Sun of School, (3) Sun of Community and Culture, (4) Sun of Gender, and (5) Sun of Chance.

The Genetic Aspect for Visual Artists

Is the ability to do visual art genetic, or is it environmental (like father, like son)? It's both, of course. The Goertzels wrote, "There are families who paint, families who sculpt, families who act, families who are musical." They cited the families of Calder, Renoir, Wyeth, Picasso, Charles Aznavour, Charles Ives, Georgia O'Keeffe, Edith Piaf, and Maurice Utrillo.

In their study, family backgrounds and emphasis within the family upon a specific creative form did not uphold the common myth of "the lonely, temperamental artist starving alone in a garret." Another artistic family was that of Van Gogh. Vincent served an apprenticeship in his uncle's art gallery, as did his brother Theo. Their sister also seemed to have an interest in art, although Vincent did not believe that she should pursue this interest.

In both the Getzels and Csikszentmihalyi studies, oldest sons were more likely than middle sons to experience success as artists, and that led the authors to say that there may be "a peculiar constellation of experiences that first-born sons undergo, alien especially to middle sons" that leads to a tendency to find the right problems and to be oriented to discovery, as well as to achieving success in art. The Goertzels, and later Simonton (1995), who studied creators in general, not specifically artists, found similar predominance of older children achieving success. However, Sulloway, who also studied various creators, did a study on later-born children, saying that the younger-borns throughout history have been more creative and rebellious. He listed many examples.

Germaine Greer, in her book about female visual artists through the ages, *The Obstacle Race*, said that most women who were visual artists came from artistic dynasties, and if they did receive training in visual art, their work was often not signed. She also said that easel painting has not been a preferred medium for women, and she wondered why easel painting has gained such credibility as being the most prestigious way for doing graphic arts. Greer said, "Daughters were ruled by love and loyalty; they were more highly praised for virtue and sweetness than for their talent, and they devalued their talent accordingly."

Architecture also sometimes runs in families, as shall be seen later in the example of the Saarinens.

The Emotional Aspect: Personalities of Visual Artists

Anne Roe (1975) gave personality tests to adult artists who had achieved. The artists objected to the inferior artistry of the stimulus pictures on the *Thematic Apperception Test* (TAT), and so administering the test was difficult. The creative people often looked askance, were sarcastic and even rebellious about being subjected to pencil and paper analysis.

Barron's *Artists in the Making* was a study of young artists at the San Francisco Art Institute and at the Rhode Island School of Design. Results showed that these artists were not interested in making a good impression on other people and were not as well socialized as other students. They cared little about social conformity, but they had a high need to achieve success independently, on their own. They were more flexible in outlook and less cheerful than others. Both women and men were similar.

On the *Minnesota Multiphasic Psychological Inventory* (MMPI), the art students, both men and women, scored in the "pathological" ranges on all of the scales. This may be an indication of their low need for conformity. They differed from truly psychotic people, though, in that they were far less rigid. Barron described the male artists as "gentleman pirate" types who showed "an independence of thought and unconventionality" which made their experiences and their conclusions unusual. The flair with which they lived their lives may account for the "pirate" description. Perhaps they swaggered when they walked, but they also paid attention to nuance, to detail, and they were open to experience, sensitive to the world around them, and sensually tuned in.

Getzels and Csikszentmihalyi's *The Creative Vision* described a study of 321 sophomore and junior student artists—152 females and 169 males in their early twenties—at the Art Institute of Chicago. The researchers tried to determine what personality characteristics these students had as compared to students who were not studying art. In personality, they found that the artists were aloof, reserved, introspective, serious, and nonconforming to contemporary social values. They had low scores in "superego strength," or conscience. They were unconventional, subjective, intense, and imaginative. Independent, they preferred to make their own decisions, and their self-sufficiency was high. They were both radical and experimental. The stereotype of the unconventional artist seems to have some basis.

Androgyny

The Barron study and the Getzels and Csikszentmihalyi studies showed that, like other creators, artists also showed androgynous personalities. In other words, they were not concerned about whether activities and choices would be considered masculine or feminine. The women artists showed more masculine values than women college students of their age, and the men artists had more feminine personalities than male college students. Thus, both genders have characteristics that have been traditionally associated with the opposite sex. Women were more tough-minded, and men were more tender-minded. The authors expressed this personality characteristic thus: "The psychology of creative men is a feminine psychology by comparison with less creative men; the psychology of creative women is a masculine psychology by comparison with less creative women."

Barron's study, above, found that the women were also not conventional, were flexible, open, showed independence, approached life vigorously, and were sensitive to details. Their patterns were different from the male artists in that they had less flamboyance, seemed more naive, and were more introverted. Remember, that's compared to the male artists. In the world, these women artists, compared with other women, would appear to be adventurous, independent, and very willful.

A case in point might be Frida Kahlo, who, in a psychological case study by Dosamantes-Beaudry, strongly identified with her father. During childhood and adolescence, she tried to be the son he had lost shortly after birth. "She sometimes dressed and behaved in the manner of an arrogant and rebellious adolescent boy," often cross-dressing. Her father thought of her as the intelligent daughter, "the most like me." She did not feel that her mother loved her. Her painting *La Venadita Herida* (*The Little Wounded Deer*) showed her androgyny—the deer has her face, male antlers, and a female body. Among the many affairs she had before and after she married Diego Rivera (who also had many affairs, including one with her sister) were many women.

Pacifism and Androgyny

Barron, in *Creativity and Personal Freedom,* described that highly creative people tended to be pacifists, eschewing violence as a way of expression. He said that "pacifistic tendencies are related to personality development and are found most prominently in persons whose inner life and creativity are more highly developed." Perhaps this explains the passionate antiwar sentiments of many people in the arts. Barron also related these pacifistic tendencies to the androgyny of creative people, saying, "it is still the men and not the women among us who decide to go to war."

Tolerance for Ambiguity and Preference for Complexity

One of the consistent findings throughout all of the studies is that creative people in all domains prefer complexity and asymmetry in design. This came to be called tolerance for ambiguity. Tolerance for ambiguity is listed on many if not most lists of characteristics of creative people. It describes the ability to hold several conflicting ideas in the mind at the same time—in fact, preferring to do so. Psychoanalytic theorist Rothenberg called it "Janusian."

Naiveté

The artists in these studies were not shrewd. Naiveté, in the sense of creativeness, is openness. As discussed in Chapter 2, viewing the world with naiveté is necessary for the creative process. These artists were able to be open to new ways of doing things, to see the old things in new ways. This enabled them to find creative problems to solve. They were not blasé about what they experienced, but rather they opened themselves to questioning with childlike wonder and awe. Some traits that have described this openness are: having an inquiring intellect, being flexible, independent versus subdued, rebellious, imaginative, artistically sensitive, aesthetically sensitive, sensitive, intellectual, curious, having depth of feeling, and having a need for variety. Recently, personality psychologists have consolidated similar personality traits into the "Big Five," and openness is one of them.

A look at the childlike yet sinister wonder with which the artist Maurice Sendak illustrated childhood fears in his children's book *Where the Wild Things Are* is an example of openness or naiveté, as is the dream work of famous modern artists Paul Klée and Joan Miró, and the circus and mobiles of Alexander Calder. Red Grooms, with his fanciful cartoonish urban sculptures, and Jonathan Borofsky, with his sinister silhouettes, also come to mind in their ingenuous ways of looking at urban life.

Ideally, any work of art teaches the perceiver to see old things in new ways. The artist approaches the world with newborn eyes and helps the jaded and blasé audience to see again. This is true in all of the arts, as well as the sciences. Magritte took naiveté to its essence. Gablik (1976) said of him, "For Magritte, paintings worth being painted or looked at have no reducible meaning: they are a meaning." Magritte himself said, "The mind loves the unknown. It loves images whose meaning is unknown, since the meaning of the mind itself is unknown."

Nonconformity

In the majority of the studies, the one personality feature that seemed most related to being a successful artist was that of low self-sentiment, defined as lacking a desire to conform to acceptable social behavior and being unconcerned with social approval. Artists seem to like their independence; they need to experiment, to go beyond what others have done.

Intuition

The *Myers-Briggs Type Indicator* has been used to indicate the Jungian-based types of many occupational groups, including scientists, artists, laborers, writers, and counselors. The creativity studies conducted with the Indicator were done in conjunction with the famous studies done at the Institute for Personality Assessment and Research (IPAR) at Berkeley after World War II. The subjects for the Institute's studies were chosen by peer nomination. Among the types of creative people studied were architects, mathematicians, scientists, and writers.

Simon, in 1979, conducted *Myers-Briggs* testing on 114 professional fine artists. Here are the personality types found in the artists in descending order, from most common to least common.

INFP (Introversion, Intuition, Feeling, Perception)
INFJ (Introversion, Intuition, Feeling, Judging)
ENFP (Extraversion, Intuition, Feeling, Perception)
ENFJ (Extraversion, Intuition, Feeling, Judging)

The presence of the intuition (N) and the feeling (F) types stands out. The artists overwhelmingly preferred intuition as a way of perception. Jung saw that people perceive the world in two ways—by sensing, or by intuiting. The person who uses the intuitive mode prefers to understand the world by the way of the unconscious. Intuitive persons look toward possibilities and may not notice realities. They prefer to make decisions not on what may be seen and heard, but on what may come as a hunch or a sudden insight.

Here is how Myers and McCaulley, in the MBTI *Manual,* describe the INFP, INFJ, and ENFP personalities.

INFP: Full of enthusiasms and loyalties, but seldom talk of these until they know you well. Care about learning, ideas, language, and independent projects of their own. Tend to undertake too much, then somehow get it done. Friendly, but often too absorbed in what they are doing to be sociable. Little concern with possessions and physical surroundings.

INFJ: Succeed by perseverance, originality, and desire to do whatever is needed or wanted. Put their best efforts into their work. Quietly forceful, conscientious, concerned for others. Respected for their firm principles. Likely to be honored and followed for their clear convictions as to how best to serve the common good.

ENFP: Warmly enthusiastic, high-spirited, ingenious, imaginative. Able to do almost anything that interests them. Quick with a solution for any difficulty and ready to help anyone with a problem. Often rely on their ability to improvise instead of preparing in advance. Can usually find compelling reasons for whatever they want.

The *Myers-Briggs Type Indicator* will be discussed more, as much research has been conducted using it. For now, it seems obvious that artists had definite personality type preferences in common. Remember, these are *preferences*. Myers and McCaulley said that "preferences are like handedness; one uses both hands, but reaches first with the preferred hand which is probably more adept." If one is right handed and has broken it, one can write with the left hand, but like Bartleby in the Melville story "Bartelby the Scrivener," one *prefers* not to.

Ambition, Drive

Ambition and drive are necessary for creative production, though they are not always traits that are easy to live with. Picasso is an example. I was at Picasso's posthumous show at the Guggenheim Museum in the mid 1980s. As I turned to look backward, down the architectural coiled spiral walls and floors designed by another modernist, Frank Lloyd Wright, I was struck at how similar these lined-up paintings of grotesque, unsmiling, and deformed women looked. How the aged artist must have hated women to have such an urge to repeat this theme over and over again. Howard Gardner's case study (1993) indicated that Picasso increasingly identified with the Minotaur, the mythical beast, half bull and half man that waited at the center of the labyrinth for the sacrificial maidens.

Gardner wrote, "those who remained involved with Picasso were likely to meet a bitter fate." Picasso's first wife became insane, one mistress hung herself and another had a breakdown, and his second wife committed suicide. The feisty Madame Gilot resisted his destructiveness, and he even came to show some admiration for her, though he was also jealous of her friendship with Matisse, the man he admired most of all. Picasso's horrible treatment of both his women and his men friends showed his cruelty. His Faustian side—which all creators seem to have, according to Gardner—was evident in his ruthless approach to developing his career. All is not rosy when considering the drive and ambition of certain well-known creators.

Interests and Values of Visual Arts Students

Barron found that the art students had interests most closely resembling musicians, artists, authors and journalists, advertising men, and architects. They rejected occupations such as school superintendent, business education teacher, army officer, and other occupations that call for managing people physically and in practical ways. They were highly dedicated to their work and to their beliefs, as well as very independent. They preferred working alone and often lost themselves in their work. They could visualize their emotional lives.

Differences in Values Among Artists According to Specialty

In the Getzels and Csikszentmihalyi study, the fine artists (as opposed to advertising and industrial arts majors) cared less for economic things and cared more for aesthetic things. The advertising arts majors also had higher political values, and art education majors cared more for social issues. Fine arts majors were lowest of the art students in sociability, while the advertising arts majors scored highest. The fine arts majors were the most radical, being more naïve, more imaginative, less conforming, and less conscientious than the other arts students.

The Barron study also found that the students were quite "extreme." Both women and men artists differed from college students in economic, aesthetic, social, and political values, and women artists differed from female college students on theoretical and religious values as well. Getzels and Csikszentmihalyi suggested in their study that art students are committed to their profession in the way that the clergy are committed to their religions. Having little care or concern for money or society's opinions is necessary for people who have careers "in which they only thing they can count on is economic insecurity" and where working alone in a studio constitutes the social milieu.

A more recent study of British artists by Dewey, Steinberg, and Coulson showed that the artists were bothered by loneliness; isolation; the toxicity of paints, dyes, and solvents; backache; the lack of recognition by the media and fellow artists; depression; and artist's block. They wished they had means of having contact with other artists, better knowledge about health risk, and techniques for dealing with melancholy and artist's block, such as meditation and dreaming. They were also often worried about impending deadlines for commissions and exhibitions.

The Cognitive Aspect: Intelligence of Visual Artists

Spatial Intelligence

Howard Gardner, in *Frames of Mind,* made useful differentiations among kinds of intelligence. For example, he identified spatial intelligence as one of his original seven intelligences (he has since revised the theory to include eight intelligences) and stated, "The centrality of spatial thinking in the visual arts is self-evident." Spatial intelligence is the ability to see the world accurately and to make and perceive changes and transformations in the physical world. Vincent Van Gogh, in *Dear Theo,* talked about the importance of spatial visualization, or truly seeing, to an artist. Van Gogh wrote, "It is at bottom fairly true that a painter as man is too much absorbed by what his eyes see, and is not sufficiently master of the rest of his life."

Spatial visualization ability is one area where strong gender differences have been found; male artists generally score higher than female artists in spatial visualization tasks. While Gardner called these "intelligences," others have asserted that they are "talents," and in *Frames of Mind,* Gardner said that if he had called them "talents," people would not have paid so much attention to his theory.

Visual arts-talented children may or may not have high scores on intelligence and achievement tests. They will, perhaps, score high on the spatial portions of ability tests. Visual art talent is made up of figural intelligence in Guilford's terms, and spatial intelligence in Gardner's terms. Guilford said that figural intelligence is "concrete intelligence." The students in the Getzels and Csikszentmihalyi study were similar on IQ tests to college students. However, in visual-spatial perception, the artists outshone regular college students. It is interesting to note, however, that the female artists performed lower in spatial perception tests than the college men, though higher than the college women, while the male artists performed the highest of all.

Gardner said that spatial intelligence is necessary but not sufficient for visual arts achievement. Spatial intelligence is necessary in the sciences and in mathematics as well as in visual arts. The person with spatial intelligence possesses the ability to see imagery. The spatial ability necessary for visual (plastic) arts seems to be a certain "sensitivity to composition" found in both connoisseurs of arts and artists themselves.

While the eight Gardner intelligences are hugely popular as a means to plan curriculum, they are still abstract, focusing on the cognitive, the mind. I prefer to differentiate talents by domains of practice. For example, visual artists need spatial intelligence to do their art, but they also need other intelligences in order to be successful in their domain. Each artist needs interpersonal intelligence to sell the work and logical-mathematical intelligence to plan the work. Sternberg's assertion that intelligence is executive, creative, and practical, seems to be at work when one speaks of how a talented person makes, manages, and functions in order to be effective in the domain of choice.

Use of Tests to Assess Artistic Intelligence or Talent

Interest in the identification of artistic talent began early. In 1926, Florence Goodenough theorized that intelligence can be measured by drawing. In 1939, Norman Meier wrote a monograph on factors in artistic aptitude. Other more recent researchers have been Clark and Zimmerman. Clark, in 1989, published his *Drawing Abilities Test*. His point was that children are identified by behaviors related to the talent. Clark and Zimmerman have also advocated the use of observation, portfolio, nomination, and interviews. They were awarded a Javits grant in the mid-1990s to continue their work in identifying and serving visual arts talent; they called their work Project ARTS.

I subscribe to the belief that the identification of these creative youth should be keyed to the characteristics discussed in this section. The drawing production tests mentioned earlier can also be administered. No particular IQ cutoff score should be required.

Problem-finding

Visual arts intelligence can also be assessed according to the ability to find problems of artistic representation. Thirty-five male college art students were observed by both expert artists and trained psychologists while the students worked. Getzels and Csikszentmihalyi then interviewed the students, asking them how concerned they had been in finding the right arrangement before, during, and after making the drawing. Art teachers, artists, business students, and mathematics students evaluated the students' works for originality and craftsmanship. Five years later, after the students had graduated, about half, or 15 of the young men, were in careers at least peripherally related to art and were still painting; about one-fourth had quit painting, and about one-fourth said they wanted to paint but were not presently doing so.

Other findings were interesting as well. The students who were still working in the domain of art had the highest grades and ratings in their studio courses, though they may not have had good grades in their academic courses. Both parents were likely to be in the professions. They came from higher socioeconomic backgrounds than those who were not successful artists. The authors speculated that a higher socioeconomic status might encourage problem-finding behavior, because if the artists can feel that they have a family to turn to for help if times get tough, or if they know they can succeed in another profession like their parents, they may feel freer to pursue a marginal career. It is also likely that their early environments may have included "more sensory and intellectual stimulation."

This problem-finding study led to many other assessment studies that are still going on. Developmental psychologists have postulated that in the Piagetian way of looking at development, the highest form may not be formal operations, but *post*-formal operations, in which the person, as an adult, finds problems. Runco (1994) concluded that problem finding in artists is "inextricable" from the inner self—that is, the emotional or the affective aspect of the problem is involved to a great degree, and so to separate the emotion from the problem that is found is perhaps impossible. Emotion becomes part of the brush stroke, the color, the style, and the composition. Thus, in paintings by Van Gogh or Kahlo or other artists, emotion is so much a part of the work that viewers can literally "feel" it.

The Domain "Thorn" in Visual Artists

How do visual artists know they want to be visual artists? Often, they have done art for a long time, since early childhood. What does talent in the visual arts domain look like in a child? Two things—early passion for the domain, and talent in the domain—seem to be present, as demonstrated below.

Predictive Behaviors for Visual Arts Talent

Since one cannot produce a work of visual art without that characteristic called talent, it is logical that early talent be recognized and nurtured. Art educator Al Hurwitz noted that certain behavioral and work characteristics are common for visual arts-talented children. He said that "no child, however talented, can reflect all of the characteristics," but conversely, "it is unlikely...that one who lacks all or most of them possesses special talent in art." The following list gives the predictive behaviors of visual arts talent:

1. *Interest*: Interest in visual arts begins early and emerges through drawing.

2. *Precocity*: The young visual artist often moves rapidly through the stages of drawing, just as young musicians move rapidly through the mastery of music. This is called precocious development, and when the child is between nine and 11, he often becomes frustrated with his development, as he begins comparing his efforts with images from mass media. Psychologist of art Ellen Winner said that young talented visual artists demonstrate precocity. They can do three-dimensional contour drawings like those of older children. Their drawings are precocious in these ways: (1) shapes that are recognizable; (2) lines that are fluid and confident; (3) volume and depth; (4) drawing objects in difficult positions; (5) the composition shows dynamic proportion; (6) realism; (7) an ability to master the drawing customs of their own culture; and (8) the ability to tell stories in pictures.

3. *Realistic representation or verisimilitude*: Talented young artists also are able to control their compositions, blending and mixing colors and consciously linking forms and experimenting. Junior and senior high school students will begin to surpass their teachers in realistic representation; they may draw detailed comic strips with narrative structure.

4. *Ability to concentrate*: Another behavioral indication that the young visual artist displays is the ability to concentrate for a long period of time on an artistic problem, as well as a preference for being alone while doing art.

5. *Works on own time*: The child is self-directed and does art on her own, away from the art room.

6. *Draws for emotional reasons*: Hurwitz commented that the visual arts-talented person may not fit the common perception of creative people, especially with regard to the personality aspect of risk

taking, for the talented young person has put in a lot of time and effort to try to master the techniques of visual art and thus is often unwilling to try new genres or media. The child may use art as a retreat, drawing for comfort. The art students in the Getzels and Csikszentmihalyi study said that they would draw when they were lonely.

7. *Fluency:* There is also an indication of fluency in the talented young artist—that is, the child often has more ideas than there is time to enact them. The work has details that other children miss, and the child will often do multiple drawings.

8. *Communication:* The child may use a drawing to illustrate a point, because drawing to the talented young visual artist is like talking or writing to the verbally talented student. Young artists can control their environment better through drawing. They get praise and recognition, so their motivation follows, and their values change as they come to realize that art has more power than merely gaining them acceptance and praise; art has the power to interpret the meaning of life and to help them resolve the problems of life. The "thorn" is born.

9. *Use of detail:* Even in young children, the use of detail in drawings is extraordinary.

10. *Visual and kinesthetic memory:* Their extraordinary visual and kinesthetic memories show up at an early age, and they are able to use such recall in filling three-dimensional space, as when playing with clay.

11. *Use of a wide variety of media:* Talented young artists practice for hours and use a wide variety of media, not just pencil and paper. They are curious about the possibilities of other media and will often do multiple drawings of the same subject using different media.

12. *Improvisation:* They are doodlers, improvising with shapes and lines, seeing patterns that appear from negative space. Hurwitz said, "Art functions as an extended conversation between form and imagination." A study of Monet's early drawings by Stokes noted that "garlands filled the margins of his exercise books." He drew "highly irreverent" sketches of his teachers and gave them to

his classmates. A sketchbook from when he was 16 showed landscapes that were advanced in the techniques of "composition, shading, and simplification," as well as caricatures that showed "exaggeration and condensation."

Both Gardner and Hurwitz also differentiated between visual arts talent and critical sensitivity to the arts, saying that the latter is also a visual perception talent, but that it relies more on verbal ability in its expression. Both said that the lack of critical sensitivity in the general public is due to the lack of arts appreciation study in the schools. As Elliot Eisner, well-known art education professor at Stanford, noted, the training of connoisseurs is essential to the maintenance of a domain, because the critics and the knowledgeable buying public, the museums and the galleries are all necessary for the viability of the visual arts.

In the 1990s, domain appreciation in the form of discipline-based art education, or the Getty plan, was funded by the National Endowment for the Arts "Arts in Education" programs in order to train the necessary art appreciators.

Art appreciation can begin early. Back in the 1940s and 1950s when I was in school, we had "picture studies" every Friday morning in each grade. We would paste, with that salty white goo, a glossy print of a famous work of art onto the upper left hand quarter of our blue wide-lined paper. Then we would write the name of the painting and the artist's dates of birth and death. On the bottom half of the page, we would write a fact or two about the picture and then our own opinion. These "picture studies," led by Mrs. Ostlund, the art coordinator of our Michigan Upper Peninsula small, iron mining town school system, continued from first through eighth grades. My fellow townspeople and I agree that we still remember these pictures when we visit museums. My favorite was the fourth grade Friday when we studied "The Horse Fair," by Rosa Bonheur, which I now visit at New York's Metropolitan Museum several times a year. It was the first time that I, as a girl, realized that a woman could be an artist. This early capture of my passionate interest in a horse painting has led to a published poem, "Women Like Horses," and a song based on that poem by a songwriter, as well as a Chinese scroll of good luck horses that hangs in my living room. Here's the poem:

After the *Kalevala*: *"On the sand he saw the horse, the grass-mane among spruces."* Canto 14

Women Like Horses

we are a group of many women
all naked
galloping up the stream bed
in the mud
in a herd
our breasts swinging
our hair flying
mud splashing
up over
our heels
wild and free
we are going to the end
where the stream meets the dam.
over the dam.
we laugh. we whinny.

Passion for the Domain

Barron commented that art is a vocation and not an occupation—a "sacred calling," and one who heeds the call has a certain character, besides the interest and the talent. "Honesty, at whatever cost, is one of the traits of the artist in his or her art."

The decision to commit their careers to making art—to being artists—came, as one sculptor said, "as a progressive or sequential revelation. It's nothing like a blinding flash. It didn't happen at any one time." When they did decide to commit their lives to making art, they did so "ferociously." For some, that commitment didn't come until seven or eight years after art school. As one said, "Partially it had to do with really floundering around for personal identity as well as artistic identity." The artists who attained success often felt lucky, but some of them said that their luck was a matter of preparation. They had prepared themselves to be ready to take the chances that came into their paths. "I've had this uncanny luck at always being at the right place at the right time with the right people."

The sculptors were still viewed as young artists, even when they had reached 40, and Sloane and Sosniak noted that the sculptors' commitment hadn't flagged and that they still were doing what they wanted to do. One of the sculptors said, "Nobody calls me in the morning and says, 'Hey, it's time to mix that concrete, kid.'...You do it because you want to do it."

Sun of Home in Visual Artists

Feldman and I noted that talent seems to run in families. Actors breed actors (the Fondas, the Redgraves, the Sheens, the Baldwins), professors breed professors (Margaret Mead), racecar drivers breed racecar drivers (the Unsers, the Pettys), athletes breed athletes (the Ripkens, the Roses), artists breed artists (the Wyeths, the Renoirs), writers breed writers (the Cheevers, the Updikes), musicians breed musicians (the Graffmans, the Bachs). The current spate of movies starring the children of movie stars is certainly not a function of heredity, but of proximity of these children to movie making. The fortune of birth has made many of these children the film stars of today. However, the Goertzels found that the artists in their biographical study were more likely to be first- and second-generation immigrants than the others. A family tradition seems helpful, but it is not necessary.

Sloane and Sosniak's interviews with the sculptors found no outstanding demographic patterns. As many were first-borns as were later-borns. As many fathers were professionals as were blue-collar workers. As many mothers worked outside the home as inside the home, and of those who worked outside the home, as many were professionals as were nonprofessionals. As many of the sculptors came from higher socioeconomic levels as from lower and middle socioeconomic levels. Their social lives were normal; as children, they played in the neighborhood with the other kids. Only one of their fathers was a commercial artist, though some of them came from families that went to museums, talked about art, and valued art.

Anne Roe's study of painters included 23 male artists whose average age was 50 and beyond—that is, they were long-time achievers. Fourteen were from the lower middle, middle, and upper middle classes. Their fathers' occupations ranged from farmer, to usher, to brigadier general, to businessman, and 25% of them had fathers in the visual arts. Most of them had gone to art school, but only 12% were college graduates. Their fathers generally disapproved of their choices of professions because being an artist means being poor. Their mothers approved in the sense of wanting their sons to do what they wanted to do. However, the mothers who had suffered the economic deprivations of being themselves wives of artists also disapproved.

In their relationships with their parents, Roe postulated that the artists had "unresolved Oedipal problems." Roe also found that 25% had suffered rejection, social isolation, or had serious childhood illnesses.

Twenty-five percent had lost a sibling or a parent through death. All of the artists were married or had been married from one to four times.

Most of the students in the Getzels and Csikszentmihalyi study were from intact families, conventional in their religious backgrounds. Most chose art as a career between the ages of 14 and 19. More women than men decided on art as a career before age 10. They chose art for self-discovery, self-knowledge, to gain an understanding of others, and to find out what's real and what's not. One young artist said, "I paint because it's necessary…it's something you have to say." Another said, "In other kinds of jobs, you rarely see the outcome of what you have been doing. There was charcoal, paint—but without me nothing would have happened." In other words, they chose art for intrinsic reasons that emphasized inner growth, self-discovery, and expression of feelings, rather than for extrinsic reasons that emphasize fame, recognition, and worldly gain.

Older than other college students, they often attended art school after trying college or after working for a while. The parents of the men disapproved of this decision. One young man said that his father had supported him when he went to college but now considered him a college dropout; the young man had to drive a cab to pay for his study at the Art Institute of Chicago. Barron's study also found that male artists had difficulty in being taken seriously by their families. Research revealed no clear childhood reasons for choosing the visual arts as a career. As Getzels and Csikszentmihalyi stated, "Instead of finding an inevitable destiny springing from a single source," the researchers found "a highly complex formative process—innumerable events slowly building up to a final commitment."

The male artists remembered their mothers as being "warm and close," but remembered their fathers as being "harsh." Their elementary years were remembered as being "bleak," but their high school years were a little better. The artists did not participate in athletics, but their competence was beginning to show, and they designed stage sets, posters, and other art works that talented high school students usually do.

Swiss psychoanalyst Alice Miller did some compelling case studies of artists. In *The Untouched Key,* in 1990, she postulated that the work of visual artists such as Picasso, Kathe Kollwicz, and Chaim Soutine is the result of childhood trauma. Picasso's *Guernica,* one of the most critiqued, lauded, and famous works of the twentieth century, details the beginning of the Spanish Civil War in 1936. Widely viewed as a representation of the cruelties of war, Miller saw in Picasso's painting the realization of repressed childhood trauma.

Studying Picasso's life, reading all of the biographies extant about him, she noted that all of these accounts glossed over his childhood, saying that he came from a happy family where his father was an artist also. Instead, Miller found that at the age of three, Pablo had experienced the consequences of a devastating earthquake. Three days after that earthquake, his first sister was born. His second sister was born shortly before he began school, and Miller postulated that these two births, which may have disrupted Picasso's position in the family, are what caused him to paint such angry portraits of women throughout his life. She said, "The three-year-old Picasso was painfully reminded of the trauma of his own birth by the horrors of the earthquake, the proximity of death, and the birth of his sister."

These blows, however, according to Miller, were compensated for by his warm and happy home life. Picasso came from an indulgent family, and he was permitted to quit school at the age of seven, never properly learning mathematics or reading. This was because he so hated going to school. Miller wrote that these two factors combined—the happy home life and quitting school—made Picasso as creative as he was. She said that if his father had not carried him along and made him feel safe in his strong arms, Picasso could perhaps have become psychotic and, in repressing these childhood traumas, "would have become an upstanding, compulsive functionary in Franco's Spain."

Miller's point is that people respond to childhood trauma with creativity or with destruction. They become creative if there is some warmth in the traumatic environment, and they become destructive if there is no warmth. For example, Hitler's mother stood by and tacitly approved of the beatings he received at the hands of his stepfather; there was no warmth; thus, Hitler became a destructive adult. Miller's attribution of Picasso's creativity to his reaction to an early childhood earthquake and then to the birth of sisters is an example of the psychoanalytic point of view about human behavior—that one incident and one's childhood reaction to it can be the "key" to a person's later behavior and personality.

Sun of School in Visual Artists

Visual artists have a specific path of development in their middle years, and this often takes them to special conservatories of art or to the college of art in the university. Summer programs for young artists at special institutes, as at the University of Indiana at Bloomington, are also important in finding and nurturing young artistic talent. One necessity in the recognition of such talent is the development of a portfolio, in which the art student keeps a collection of work he wants others to see. Like a resume, a portfolio can be planned to fit a particular purpose.

In their study of sculptors, Sloane and Sosniak found that for their elementary school years, the sculptors remembered intense drawing and the emphasis on products, on making the drawings realistic and recognizable representations of what they were drawing. The sculptors didn't remember elementary school art as challenging, or even as art.

During high school, the sculptors began to gain identity and recognition as artists. Some remembered art classes in high school as the class for "flunkies." They were referred to in their yearbooks as "Rembrandt," or "the class artist." The teenagers' work was also commented on positively and displayed. However, this is not a clear trend. Sloane and Sosniak showed that many times, their talent was not recognized in high school; in fact, some of the sculptors took no art in high school. Specialists in the field had not noticed them.

When they graduated from high school, these sculptors typically had no idea about what it took to make art as a professional, and they possessed no portfolios, perhaps no high school art classes on their transcripts, and perhaps no letter of recommendation from art professionals or teachers. But somehow, they stumbled into four-year art degree programs, and three-quarters of them went on to earn Master of Fine Arts degrees. Their serious study of art began in college with a "hazy goal" of doing something in the arts. They had been building, sketching, drawing, molding throughout their adolescent years; these predictive behaviors alone differentiated them and foretold that they would go on to study art. They had been recognized by peers and adults for their competence, and they had gained self-esteem about their talent.

They began to encounter teachers who were also artists, and this had a profound effect on them. They were treated like artists. Their teachers were committed and intense. The young artists acquired peers who were as intense as they were. They learned the language, the vocabulary of art; they learned to function in the competitive climate of art school; they learned what it took to market their work. They learned to be professionals.

Their teachers were professional artists themselves who worked in the field and who had access to a network of other artists and connections to the art world. They took studio master classes. One said, "I mean he was a very important person in the art world. And the fact that he was teaching at that school, it was the spirit of it or something." Another said, "Your teachers were professionals. We went to New York. We saw the shows. I knew what was going on."

As they took courses and studied, the competition and exposure to the other students was intense. Almost all of the sculptors went through a stage of imitating artists, trying to find the essence of what made a Henry Moore or a Jackson Pollock. But the breakthrough to finding their own styles, their own problems, eventually came. One said, "In art you make up your own problems." They drew their problems from what was going on in art at the time. "If on the walls of Fifty-Seventh Street they're hanging abstract expressionist paintings, the [art student] will usually pick up from that point and say, 'Now where do I take Jackson Pollock from here? What do I do next?'" Often, their works became bigger and bigger, more three-dimensional. Most of them were painters before becoming sculptors, probably because art school is very painting-oriented. Some of them shifted to pottery before they shifted to sculpture. The Goertzels found that those in the artistic category were less likely to have gone to college than others who had biographies written about them; as a corollary, the artistic people were not known as being good students in school and were not likely to be omnivorous readers. However, they were more likely to have had special schooling, perhaps because their precocity stood out early.

Sun of Community and Culture in Visual Artists

Going to art school seems to be a common thread for musicians and writers, as well as artists. It is interesting to speculate on how many rock stars met in art school. Victor Bockris, Rolling Stone Keith Richards' biographer, wrote: "Between 1959 and 1962 John Lennon, Ray Davies, Pete Townshend, Jimmy Page, Ron Wood, and David Bowie had just left, were in, or were about to enter British art schools. Almost every school contained at least one of the men who would go on to become the first generation of pop musicians." To Keith Richards, most of the teachers in art school were "drunks, freaks, and potheads who didn't care what the kids did." One of his teachers said that if he had worked as hard on his art as he did on his music, he'd be a successful artist. Perhaps art school is viewed as a place where one can be freer than in regular college.

One of the people Barron interviewed said that when he transferred, after six years of college in the University of California system, to the San Francisco Art Institute, he found that the lack of rules there helped him to excel, and thus he graduated with honors. A poor student academically—because he would test the teachers, and if he didn't like them, he wouldn't work for them—he said people should go to art school just to experience the looseness and the craziness. This freer atmosphere made him feel fulfilled, and he assumed the persona of an artist after graduation. This man made a marginal living as a fisherman and plumber, but he also filled 30 journals with autobiographical writing and artwork, and he helped other people with their creativity. He saw himself as an artist.

Community and Culture for Picasso

Gardner, in his 1993 case study of Picasso, pointed out that a tragic incident, the suicide of Picasso's friend Carlos Casagemas, induced the "blue period" painting *La Vie* in 1903. This was Picasso's "first defining work." Other key paintings followed, including *Les Demoiselles d'Avignon* in 1907, which took the art world by storm. Gardner compared the impact of *Les Demoiselles* to the impact of Stravinsky's *Le Sacre du Printemps*, as both defined the domain for years to come.

Picasso's friendship with Georges Braque initiated cubism, and the Zeitgeist was prepared through the presence of "Nigerian masks...optical illusions in William James's posters...the master Cézanne." Side by side, the two artists remade art history. For several years, they were seldom apart, and rumors of homosexuality abounded. Fame and celebrity came to Picasso, and he began to travel, to live high, to flaunt his adulteries, and to collaborate with artists in other genres. Though his work had always had images of bulls—the bulls of the bullfight ring and the bulls of mythology—in the late 1920s and 1930s, these creatures began to appear even more often in his work.

The bombing of Guernica in 1937 by Franco's German air force shocked the world, as thousands of innocent people were killed. Picasso was inspired to make a huge painting condemning the slaughter. This one work—*Guernica*—was viewed throughout the world as Picasso's defining work. The painting has been called the most important of the twentieth century. Picasso was 55 years old when he painted it, yet he was to work for more than 30 more years, constantly re-inventing himself and his work. But this painting still stands as his masterpiece.

Cross-Fertilization and Cross-Cultural Influences among Artists

Picasso's repeating theme of the Minotaur had a profound influence on a young American artist in New York City in the 1930s. His name was Jackson Pollock. Pollock went to see *Guernica* in 1939 when it came to a gallery in New York as a fund-raiser for refugees from the Spanish Civil War. He went many times and made many sketches. He began to take the sketches to his Jungian analyst and to realize that his own childhood bestiary, of chickens and snakes and coyotes, had a place in his art, despite what his teachers said. Picasso's images gave Pollock permission to work with his own dreams and images. Biographers Naifeh and Smith said that Jackson identified with Picasso's art as revealing Pollock's own unconscious. Picasso, in *Les Demoiselles d'Avignon*, had changed prostitutes into creatures with African masks for faces, and in *Girl Before a Mirror*, he had suggested breasts like vegetables.

Pollock began to make similar transformational creatures. The image that struck him most was the image of the bull, and Pollock was dumbstruck by the coincidence, for "Picasso had fixated on the very same animal that had prowled and terrorized Jackson's unconscious since childhood." Pollock then went beyond Picasso and combined the bull image with images drawn from American Indian lore. The postmodernist was using the modernist, the abstract expressionist was using the expressionist. Such cross-fertilization is common in the development of any domain; in this case, one artist drew from another's images and went on to transform the domain. The visual arts were never the same after Picasso, and the visual arts were never the same after Pollock. And so it goes.

The influence of community and culture upon the development of visual art talent passion is illustrated by another example. Georgia O'Keeffe and her fellow students at the Art Students League often went together to see the latest galleries and shows, and this is how she met Alfred Stieglitz, her future husband, when she was 20 and he was 44. When she came back to New York several years later to study to be a fine arts teacher with Alon Bement at Teachers College, she and her friends continued to be avidly interested in art. In her biography, Robinson detailed the excitement and stimulation in which Georgia O'Keeffe participated in the art world of New York City. She visited museums, went to art shows, and met working artists. One show that influenced her was that of Arthur Dow, who exhibited paintings of a trip to the western United States. His paintings of the Grand Canyon at the Montross Gallery in 1914 drew both Georgia and her new friend, Anita Pollitzer. A new gallery, "291," opened, run by Alfred Stieglitz. O'Keeffe and her friends also visited this avant-garde gallery, and when she was teaching in Columbia, Georgia, she sent her work to Anita, who showed it to Stieglitz. Stieglitz told Anita to write to Georgia and to say, "They're the purest, finest sincerest things that have entered 291 in a long while." Thus, the relationship between Georgia and Alfred, her lover, mentor, future husband, and agent, began.

Cross-Cultural Differences

Certain cross-cultural differences exist as to how to do the visual arts. Howard Gardner, in an article called "Learning Chinese Style," shared his observations about repetition and practice. He noted that young Chinese students are taught calligraphy, repeating over and over certain patterns and figures. The differences between U.S. education and its emphasis on early exploratory activities in art and early Chinese art education are so great that he wondered whether the Chinese children would be able to transfer their training to freehand drawings. So he asked them to draw a portrait of him with their calligraphy brushes. They were able to do so, with several of the 10-year-olds making recognizable portraits. This showed him that the Chinese children, even though they are taught in rigid and formulaic ways, are still able to improvise when asked. He also said that a cross-cultural difference is that art education in China is more performance-oriented than that in the United States.

A response to Gardner's article by Cheng, called "East-West Differences in View on Creativity: Is Howard Gardner Correct? Yes and No," surveyed art teachers in Singapore. Contrary to Gardner's assertion that teachers directly intervene in Chinese culture to the detriment of the flowering of creativity, Cheng found that they did, in fact, permit the students to do independent work, but that they did have a Chinese view of art-making, which was that art is to be beautiful and to unfold in the process of a life.

Sun of Gender in Visual Artists

In their study, Getzels and Csikszentmihalyi chose to follow 35 male fine arts students through the beginnings of their careers, because women fine arts students were less likely to become well-known artists. The high achieving students seemed to become successful by the strength of their personalities rather than by their perceptual or intellectual abilities. All of the high achievers fit the personality extremes described above—they were aloof, had low ego-strength, were introspective, sensitive, imaginative, self-sufficient, and nonconforming. They all had little care for the economic aspects of life.

The most successful artists were oldest sons. Many had not done well academically in high school or college. They chose art because it was not a nine-to-five job. One of the artists had been a stutterer, and his skill in drawing gained him acceptance from peers. One began drawing when a younger sibling was born. Another used drawing as a way to compete with older siblings.

In contrast, the most successful women students were dramatically different. Their teachers viewed them as talented with relationship to their perceptual abilities, while they judged male students as talented on the basis of whether they liked their personalities. The authors evaluated these differences this way: "This may reflect a tacit belief that a male student will develop his aptitudes with time, while a women student who does not have them to begin with will abandon her aspirations and settle for more traditional pursuits."

Biographical Example of Judy Chicago

Judy Chicago has spent years trying to recapture a sense of the value of the art that women have traditionally made. In her biography *Through the Flower*, she described her odyssey through art history and her thrill at discovering that women have always been artists. She wrote, "Much of the work of women possesses a world view, a set of values, and a perception of reality that differs fundamentally from the dominant perspective of our culture." Examples are her exhibit of women creators exemplified through plates, *The Dinner Party*, and her work with *The Birth Project*, honoring the history of women's needlework and weaving. Chicago said, "My images are about struggling out of containment, reaching out and opening up as opposed to masking or veiling." In 2002, *The Dinner Party* finally gained a permanent home at the Brooklyn Museum of Art, 23 years after its debut at the San Francisco Museum of Art in 1979. The length of time from first tour to permanent home might indicate the regard for which feminist art is held.

Foley's Study: Having a Supportive Husband Helps

In 1996, Foley published her 1986 study of 15 painters who were mothers of children ages three months to eight years with regard to their ability to combine mothering and being painters. They exhibited most of the characteristics of all visual artists—passion, commitment, androgyny, and intuition—but as most creative women, they also experienced role conflicts between being a mother and being an artist. In order to do both, they used childcare help in the home or at daycare centers, and they had husbands who were extremely supportive of their careers. The women were artists before they became mothers and so were well launched in their careers, having galleries to represent them and showing regularly in juried exhibits.

In their personalities, they exhibited the same core traits as the artists elsewhere here described, and Foley said, "it cannot be said that women artists' commitment and motivation to becoming artists is any less than men's; rather, it appears to be more a difference in the timing of the commitment." The women artists were passionately committed to their careers and to their families, and Foley quoted one of them thus:

> *Interviewer:* What does it mean to you to be an artist?

> *Artist:* Almost everything! I mean it is I; it's what I actually am. I don't just make art. I am it. I live it out…I mean, my whole life.

Foley found that in her comparison group of mothers who were in professions such as law and business, the conflicts were a little different. While the artist mothers wished that they had time to paint, the mothers in professions wished they had more time with their families. The artist mothers had more flexible schedules, and when their children went to school, they often used the period from 9 AM to 3 PM to do art. The professional mothers were involved in careers with inflexible hours, and the mothers who were in professions had difficulty in meeting all of the demands on them, while the artist mothers had trouble defining the demands. For the artist mothers, the conflict came from having to cope every day with allocating time for each role.

The intrinsic rewards of making paintings made for a certain emotional well-being in the artist mothers, and one of them said, "The most gratifying internal—which is ultimately more important—thing is when I feel like I've answered a question. To me, each painting I do is like plunging into the abyss, and I never know if I'm going to swim out…by swim out of the abyss, of course, I mean solve the visual problems that each painting has."

Here we see that the conflicts that arose with being a mother and an artist didn't diminish the rewards of doing the art. It should be noted that these women were in the middle and higher socioeconomic levels; they did not have to struggle financially, and they had help with the children and supportive spouses. But Foley said that even if they hadn't had the financial wherewithal, they would somehow, somewhere make art "because making art was an integral and vital aspect of their being."

Biographical example of Lee Krasner

A case in point might be the career of the artist Lee Krasner. The Brooklyn-born child of Jewish immigrants, Krasner decided to study art but was rejected from the Washington Irving High School for the Arts in Manhattan. Applying a second time, she was accepted, but she was then told by her art teachers that she had no talent. She didn't listen and went on to the women's school of Cooper Union, where she interested one of her male teachers in her good work. She began to model (as did Georgia O'Keeffe) for spending money and was urged to apply to the National Academy of Design. She hated the conservatism and rigor there and determined to get out early by painting a portrait in *plein air* that the faculty committee would accept. She shocked them when she did a self-portrait with extreme skill.

Most of her teachers called her a nuisance, aggressive, and difficult. She didn't care. She continued to follow her own course and began to have an affair with a fellow student, a Russian immigrant named Igor Pantuhoff. He became a popular portrait painter and also an alcoholic. She transferred to Hans Hoffman's art school, where her portfolio won her a scholarship. Again she attracted the patronage and attention of a few teachers, while with others she retained the reputation of being too pushy. She began to have her work accepted into group shows. Her reputation as a nonconformist and "tough cookie" preceded her wherever she went. Her teachers chose her for her talent and not for her looks, and by the time she met Jackson Pollock, she was a more advanced artist than he. She spent the rest of her life living in the shadow of his growing fame and as his grieving widow, and her work was not much valued until recently. The movie *Pollock* and Marsha Gay Harden's Academy Award-winning portrayal of Krasner vividly illustrate this.

Women's search for connectedness dominates their development during and just after their college years to the detriment of their drive to succeed in their chosen field of creative endeavor. Few, if any, gender differences are found in creativity until after college, when women must decide

173

how they will manage being mothers, wives, and creators. I wrote about this in an article called "Why So Few Creative Women?" in 1991. The double bind hits hard, and this gender difference cuts across all fields and domains. The men creators never seem to wonder how they will manage raising a family and having a career. The women creators always do. That is why many women who reached prominence were childless and even lived alone without a mate.

Self-Promotion

Male artists seem to believe that they must self-promote in order to be recognized. This relates to the major gender difference found in all studies across domains—that is, that males are more aggressive—the old testosterone argument. A study by Blake in 1997 of 420 winners of the Scholastic Art Awards showed this to be true. Self-promotion includes ambition to achieve, self-confidence, perseverance, and drive. While both males and females held a positive opinion of their abilities, were highly competitive, and were willing to go back to the drawing board if they failed, and while most had plans to be artists and had confidence that they would succeed, significant gender differences were found in the area of willingness to do self-promotion. Males had more willingness and more aggressiveness in this area.

Sun of Chance in Visual Artists

Sun of Chance

Tannenbaum pointed out that much of the realization of potential comes from factors that are other than personality or intellectual. Following upon his work, I put the Sun of Chance in my framework for talent development (see the Pyramid in Chapter 5). Luck, for example, plays a large part in the realization of potential. Simonton (1984, 1988) called it being in or putting oneself into *proximity*. For creative people, this involves the very important step of choosing mentors. Luck may also come with the accident of the family into which one is born.

The social context, the luck, the chance, the circumstances in which one finds oneself are extremely important, perhaps equally as important as that mysterious possession called talent—that is, talent is not enough. One must try to improve upon one's chances, upon one's luck, even if one has had the fortune of being born into a talented family. In order for artists to be successful in realizing their creativity, Getzels and Csikszentmihalyi said they need to do four things.

1. Rent or buy a loft so that they can socialize, show their work, and establish a reputation for being a serious artist—that is, they have made the commitment to renting a working space.

2. Be in an art show. A group show is acceptable, but a one-person show sponsored by a private art gallery that represents one's work is preferable.

3. Move to New York City, for no artist is taken seriously as a major fine artist in the United States unless the New York City art scene has validated him or her. (Los Angeles would disagree, and so would other art centers in the United States, but New York City still seems to be *the* place.)

4. Alternatively, relocate to a provincial art center. This is viewed as a less desirable but sometimes necessary option. Taos in the Southwest, or Provincetown in the Northeast are popular choices. Some artists also take the path of getting a Master of Fine Arts degree from a university or art school and then of teaching in the academy while doing their art on the side. Doing this is considered a safety step, and the artist takes the risk of being isolated from the trendsetters of the art world and stagnating.

Actively pursuing these social contexts may go against the personality grain of the creative visual artist, who is an introvert, a loner, an iconoclast, difficult to get along with, and who values aesthetics far more than economics. Getzels and Csikszentmihalyi said that many of the young men, when they moved to be in social proximity to the art world, took two years to get back into the swing of producing art. Their art works changed in character, style, and size. They experienced depressions and frustrations caused by the pressures of establishing themselves in different geographies from where they had begun their art. Several of them had spouses who worked, or they had married rich women. The necessity of having a steady breadwinner, especially if one is not independently wealthy, cannot be overemphasized when looking at the lives of creative artists whose work does not sell. Many of them turn to teaching or to working for arts groups doing short residencies in elementary and secondary schools.

Biographical Example of Georgia O'Keeffe

Georgia O'Keeffe's career path was illustrated in Robinson's biography. She showed that O'Keeffe had strong ties to New York City's "loft culture." O'Keeffe, a native of Sun Prairie, Wisconsin, arrived in New York City after studying for a year at the Art Institute of Chicago and after having taken classes at the University of Virginia with a visiting professor from Teacher's College of Columbia University. This teacher, Alon Bement, propounded the theories of Arthur Wesley Dow. O'Keeffe was taken by the theories and, at the age of 27, came to New York to study with Dow at Columbia in 1914. A year later, she began taking classes at the Art Students League, and as mentioned above, her group of friends began regularly visiting the Alfred Steiglitz gallery called "291." After sending Stieglitz her work, O'Keeffe was granted a one-woman show by Steiglitz.

Although O'Keeffe didn't live in New York City at the time, her connections there were strong, and after her relationship with Steiglitz began, she spent many years in New York City exhibiting at Steiglitz's various galleries before establishing residency in New Mexico. Whether her work would have had its impact without her New York City "loft" and without her "luck" of coming to the attention of Steiglitz cannot be known. Certainly his falling in love with her, moving in with her, and eventually breaking up his marriage, as well as his dedication to the promotion of her work, did not harm O'Keeffe's visibility.

The 1997 exhibit at the Metropolitan Museum of Art called "Steiglitz's O'Keeffe" showed Steiglitz's many photographs of O'Keeffe, including nudes, photographs of her strong hands, and photographs of her looking mysterious behind high-collared coats. Steiglitz was attracted to her mannish wardrobe and nonconformity, and he made arguably his loveliest works of art about her. Even when they lived apart, he in New York and she in New Mexico, they wrote to each other many times a day. Although O'Keeffe wanted to have children, Steiglitz, who was much older than she and who already had a daughter, refused, saying that she would diffuse her attention to her work if they had children. He told her that her work was her child. Thus, she never had to experience the double bind of creative women who become mothers.

Artists continue to make their way to New York City. Andy Warhol came from Pittsburgh. Jackson Pollock came from California and points west. The artist Elizabeth Murray grew up in Illinois in an eccentric family that Murray described in an interview with Deborah Solomon as "unorthodox" and "goofball." She "spent the whole time fantasizing about moving to New York." When she arrived in New York, she rented a loft. She got married, had a son, and did the practical thing that women artists seem to do. Like O'Keeffe, she taught art, trying to do her own work at night. Solomon had her first one-woman show in 1976, and her fame continues to grow within the New York art world. Again, the influence of the loft culture of New York City is evident in the path of her success.

The Sun of Chance may also have clouds in front of it. The artist may have trained, may be excellent, skilled, and talented and still not be successful. Barron in 1995 described a 10-year follow-up study of the artists he studied. He found that most were still working at art, but none, even those who would be called successful, were able to support themselves with their art. They would work part-time or full-time in jobs that paid the rent and put food on the table, but they considered themselves first and foremost artists. Some would go on and off welfare periodically. Among creative activities that they had completed since art school were the writing and publishing of poetry, children's literature, movies, theater, photography, and even pornography. In 2002, Joan Freeman, describing her 27-year follow-up of gifted children in England, in explaining why most of them did not become creative producers in their domains, said, "life is awfully hard." The Sun of Chance often determines whether one succeeds.

Architects

Is the architect an artist or a scientist? A businessman or an aesthete? The answer, of course, is all of the above. Architects are hybrid creators; they combine the characteristics of almost all of the creative types and provide an interesting and spicy addition to the creativity brew.

IPAR (Institute for Personality Assessment Research) also studied architects. Using the system of peer nomination, a group of architects was invited to be interviewed and tested. MacKinnon discussed the results and Barron described follow-up studies and a few typical cases in 1995. Among the architects were Philip Johnson, I. M. Pei, Eliel Saarinen, Louis Kahn, Pietro Belluschi, A. Quincy Jones, and Richard Neutra.

Genetic Aspect in Architects

Some architects had fathers who were architects, for example the Saarinen family, discussed below. There is no evidence, though, that most architects come from families of architects.

Emotional Aspect: Personalities of Architects

Not surprisingly, the architects had personality characteristics similar to both scientists and artists. Independence, intuition, a theoretical orientation, a preference for complexity, originality, and openness to experience or naiveté, and the like were characteristic. These were the top 10 traits of architects according to a trait analysis: (1) originality; (2) aesthetic sensitivity; (3) sense of destiny; (4) responsiveness to ideas; (5) cognitive flexibility; (6) independence; (7) inquiry as a habit of mind; (8) sense of personal identity; (9) intellectual competence; and (10) valuing of intellectual pursuits.

All of the architects were highly creative and respected in their fields. They had a sense of destiny common to most creative producers. MacKinnon said, "With a marked degree of resoluteness and almost inevitably a measure of egotism, the creative person typically considers himself to be destined to do what he is doing, or intends to be doing, with his life." Although many had experienced great frustration and depression, the architects felt that their work was worthy. They had passed through the adolescent period having attained a strong sense of ego identity, even though their adolescences, like those of other creative people, were characterized by confusion and conflict. MacKinnon said that they often had teachers and parents who emphasized a tolerance for ambiguity and kept them open to possibility. Most of them made their decision to become architects after high school, but a few waited until after college.

Among the personality tests that IPAR gave the architects was the *Myers-Briggs Type Indicator*. MacKinnon noted that the architects preferred P (perception). He said, "A preference for the perceptive attitude results in a life that is more open to experience both from within and from without, and characterized by flexibility and spontaneity." They also preferred N (intuition) as a means of viewing possibilities. Likewise, the adult creators studied by psychologists overwhelmingly prefer intuition. MacKinnon said, "In contrast to an estimated 25 percent of the general population who are intuitive, 90 percent of the creative writers, 92 percent of the mathematicians, 93 percent of the research scientists, and 100 percent of the architects are intuitive as measured by this test." The architects were evenly divided in their preference for thinking and feeling.

Other tests were administered as well. In values, the architects most valued aesthetics and the theoretical. They were able to make unusual and odd mental associations, and they preferred complexity. On the *California Psychological Inventory*, they came out as dominant, caring about social status, self-confident, not especially sociable or participating in social activities, outspoken, self-centered, aggressive, unconventional, strongly motivated to achieve, and feminine. Since all of the architects were males, this last characteristic points to androgyny. MacKinnon commented:

> *The evidence is clear: The more creative a person is the more he reveals an openness to his own feelings and emotions, a sensitive intellect and understanding self-awareness, and wide-ranging interests including many which in the American culture are thought of as feminine. In the realm of sexual identification and interests, our creative subjects appear to give more expression to the feminine side of their nature than do less creative persons.* (p. 156)

MacKinnon noted that Jung would say that creative people are not "so completely identified with their masculine *persona* roles as to blind themselves to or to deny expression to the more feminine traits of the *anima*." However, this tendency toward androgyny may have led, in the architects and in other creative people, to "considerable psychic stress and turmoil."

Sun of Chance in Architects

Barron discussed the 20-year follow-up study of the architects in 1995. He noted that some had continued to be successful while others were still struggling to make a living as architects. Most of them thought that architecture had become more of a business due to overwhelming government regulation and rampant rising costs. The architects who survived were often heads of or employed by large firms with sophisticated business methods. They felt that the profession of architect required less artistic creativity than it had in the past.

However, a June 1997 interview by Charlie Rose seemed to differ. This interview was with the Israeli architect who created the Montreal World's Fair Habitat '67, Moshe Safdie. Rose asked Safdie, "When a young architect comes to you for a job, what do you look for?" Safdie replied, "The drawings." He said that the architect's drawings are like a confessional. When you look at the drawings, you have a sense of what the person is about. The second thing Safdie looks for is in the eyes of the young architect—he looks for a sense of social commitment, a commitment to create a better human environment.

Barron asked the architects to evaluate their own creativity. Typical responses to how their creativity shows itself were these:

○ I'm a poet in materials.

○ I let the building express itself.

○ I have a strong feeling for form; I know how to refine, to redo things.

○ I have a strong feeling for color.

○ I am able to incorporate the other arts in my architecture.

○ I can scuttle conventionality and do original work.

○ I am able to achieve complete integration of many facets; I can express a single idea in structure, circulation, and visual form.

○ My structures are free of turmoil and noise.

○ My work represents myself completely.

Barron concluded that "These clearly were people who had a high opinion of themselves and their own importance." The still-successful architects were now in their 60s, and Barron noted that these had begun well; they had come from families with artistic and musical interests, and their parents were often foreign-born. In their childhoods, they had been encouraged to use their imagination in play and had spent much time drawing, reading, hiking, building things, and playing music. They liked to play alone and preferred individual rather than team sports. They felt inferior in childhood, especially physically, and reported doubts about their athletic ability. Their parents were often described as "severe," and their mothers were the dominant parent.

The architects matured late sexually, and they often did not have their first sexual experience until they were in their twenties. All but one had eventually married, and they had an average of three children. However, Barron said, "even in adulthood, many had not achieved sexual intimacy in an enduring relationship," and they said they were not interested in sex as a motive in their lives.

They had selected architecture after considering careers in art or in science. The reason for selecting architecture was to help society, a reason of social commitment. They reported that early on, they had a relationship with an important mentor who inspired them to be architects, often in summer internships or as students of sparkling teachers. The difficulty in finding commissions was their most disappointing early experience. They valued courses in the other arts as well as in visual arts as giving them a broad view of the world. As they progressed in their careers, they continued to value relationships with older architects.

After early careers significant enough to have them be nominated to be studied, those who were disappointed in their careers were described by Barron thus: "embittered, talented people, some with sheer bad luck in their stories, others with foolish mis-reckoning, and still others with little talent after all, though with a love for building and design." Barron noted that some of these unsuccessful talented architects had struggled with family tragedies, alcoholism, and depression. Some of their tests had shown unusually high levels of psychopathology, which led Barron to comment, "The failures usually had manifested the seeds of serious problems of personal adjustment, and they had to expend a lot of their energy in just keeping themselves together."

Dudek and Hall in 1991 conducted the third follow-up study of these same architects. Seventy—or 78%—of the surviving architects responded. They showed five characteristics that helped them be so productive for so long. These were: (1) commitment/drive; (2) high skillfulness/mastery; (3) a continued pleasure in and sensitivity to aesthetics; (4) good business ability; and (5) an ability to delegate responsibility. They continued to work after their age mates had been long retired, and Dudek and Hall commented that their drive to create kept them going. Their work was their life. "The desire to succeed, the image of oneself as a winner, and the joy of doing, the pleasure of being engaged in an activity to which one is totally committed" were the main factors in their continued creativity.

Biographical Example of the Saarinens

In 2002, during an ethnic festival, I attended a lecture at Christ Lutheran Church in Minneapolis, which was designed by architect Eliel Saarinen. The lecture, about the life and career of Saarinen, reinforced the findings over the years that these biographical themes, as demonstrated in the Pyramid, seem to hold up over and over again. Eliel Saarinen grew up in a bourgeois family in Finland and formed an architectural company there with two friends. The group traveled in the company of the Helsinki upper classes, building elegant homes next to each other in elite suburbs.

They designed the Finnish pavilion for the 1900 World's Fair in Paris in Scandinavian national romantic style, and the world began to pay attention. In 1922, Saarinen won second prize for the Chicago Tribune Tower. He spent much of his time designing schools for boys and girls, and for the Academies of the Arts and the Sciences. He also designed an Academy of Architects project to be similar to the German Bauhaus, a consortium of like-minded architects able to work and live in concert with their beliefs about architecture. In 1925, Saarinen, while doing a stint as a visiting professor of architecture at the University of Michigan, was asked by Scripps newspaper mogul George G. Booth to develop the Cranbrook Educational Center at Bloomfield Hills, Michigan, a wealthy northern suburb of Detroit.

The Saarinens, having moved to the U.S., became a family team. As chief architect of the school's buildings, Saarinen was aided by his wife Loja, who designed its carpets and other textiles, and his son Eero, a furniture designer. Young architects from all over came to apprentice there, and they entered design competitions, winning many. Some of Saarinen's students at Cranbrook were Charles and Ray Eames, Florence Schust (later Knoll), and Harry Bertoia. His son Eero also studied there and became his successor. Eero also studied sculpture at the Académie de la Grande Chaumiére in Paris (1929/30) and later architecture at Yale University in New Haven, Connecticut, graduating in 1934.

Eero married a New York art critic, Aline Bernstein, who furthered his career through her contacts. She was the associate art editor and critic at *The New York Times* from 1948 to 1953 and associate art critic from 1954 to 1958. She was divorced with two sons when she interviewed Eero, and attraction gave way to marriage. They had a son, Eames, named for the designer Charles Eames, in December 1954. In 1971, Aline became chief of the NBC's Paris News Bureau—the first woman to become the head of an overseas news bureau.

At Cranbrook, architectural and design students and fellows worked collaboratively on projects steeped in the ideas of the Arts and Crafts movement, touched with the decorative leanings of Art Deco, and a modern style emerged. Eliel Saarinen taught the importance of approaching work with the idea in mind that, "if the form is there, it is of minor importance if we use the hand of man or machine. Both are necessary." Eliel Saarinen was both a friend and a rival of Frank Lloyd Wright, who followed the same ideas with his two Taliesins, one in Wisconsin and the other in Arizona, and the two men contemporaneously formed their U.S. architecture student retreats and training centers.

Under Eero, the Saarinen firm won several prestigious design competitions, for example, the TWA Terminal at Idlewild Airport (now Kennedy) in New York, the Gateway Arch in St. Louis, the Dulles Airport terminal in Chantilly, Virginia, the Kresge Auditorium in Cambridge, Massachusetts, and the John Deere building in Moline, Illinois. Their designs had soaring roofs like wings and often featured high arches. Suspended roofs over the new concept of the departure lounge, and flying and curvilinear shapes became their signature. The Saarinens' contributions to architectural history were many. The vagaries of history, preparation, talent, school, social class, family, community and culture, genes, gender, and chance all played a major part in their success.

Biographical Example of Frank Lloyd Wright

A case example will also illustrate how these characteristics worked in the childhood of one of the United States' most famous architects: Frank Lloyd Wright. In his poetic *Autobiography*, which he revised many times, Wright detailed the experiences that made him a creative, productive adult.

His mother, Anna, was a schoolteacher from an immigrant Welsh Unitarian family that valued education with a capital "E." She found her ideal educated mate in Frank's father, whom she met near their family valley in Wisconsin where he worked for awhile as a circuit rider and music teacher. Wright's father was a dilettante, "tirelessly educating himself, first at Amherst, then to practice medicine, soon found by him to be no genuine science. Then the law, but again—disillusion." The spectre of the ineffectual father seems apparent here. Finally taking up the call to be a Baptist preacher, he moved the family back to the Weymouth, Massachusetts when Frank was three years old.

Anna's loyalties swerved from her husband to her son after Frank was born. Her "extraordinary devotion to the child disconcerted the father," and the father began to recede into the background in her affections, for she "now loved something more, something created out of her own fervor of love and desire. A means to realize her vision" (all quotes from *Autobiography*). They lived in genteel poverty. Frank's father took his consolation from music and would play into the night alone in the empty church on the organ. Frank would have to pump "with all his strength at the lever" and would be "crying bitterly as he did so." But Wright came to love music through these nocturnal experiences.

Meanwhile, Anna became very interested in the Froebel methods of education, which were similar to our present emphasis on manipulatives and concrete experiences for young children; she brought home gifts of blocks and paper in geometric shapes. The young Frank played with them for hours. She had in mind that he was to build buildings, and she hung his room with drawings of English cathedrals. When Frank was 11, his uncle came to take him to the family valley in Spring Green, Wisconsin to work on the farm. (He would later found the first Taliesin there.) Frank worked there every year from April to September, when he would go back home to Madison, Wisconsin to school.

At the farm, Frank protested about the heavy labor, the milking of cows, the chopping of wood. He often ran away but was always brought back. One of his uncles pinched his flabby upper arm and told him that he must work so hard that he would "add tired to tired—and add it again," and Frank saw his physical and mental strength grow. He learned that "work is an adventure that makes strong men and finishes weak ones." He was a dreamy boy, a reader, a lover of music, imagining the time away, and his summers at the family farm, while strengthening him physically, also provided him solitary time, working to the rhythm of machinery, ranging in the woods listening for the tinkle of the bells of the cows he had been sent to find. He said that his uncle would see him go into a trance of dreamy thought and would shout, "Frank, come back! Come back, Frank!" Wright remembered, "One eleven-year-old was turning to inner experience for what he heard, touched, or saw."

Back to school each September in Madison, Wright and a friend who was crippled and mercilessly teased by the other boys formed a comradeship of outsiders. The two boys were odd and didn't fit into the group of other boys. They read, and read together, in secret hideouts, basements, and attics. They developed crushes on the girlfriends of Frank's sister, and they spent a lot of time tinkering and inventing things. They invented a water-velocipede, a catamaran, a cross-gun, bows and arrows, a bobsled, kites, a water wheel, a scroll-saw, and a turning lathe, designing and drawing always. Their real life was lived outside of school. Wright said, "But…of the schooling itself? Not a thing he can remember! A blank! Except colorful experiences that had nothing academic about them."

The two boys were also enterprising, and they formed a printing firm. They began publishing a newspaper in their mid-teens, and Wright again commented that the schooling that was going on simultaneously meant nothing: "But the schooling! Trying to find traces of it in that growing experience ends in finding none. What became of it? Why did it contribute so little to this consciousness-of-existence?" Wright said that even though his memories of school were so negative, school perhaps was not purely harmful:

> *You can't let boys run wild while they are growing. They have to be roped and tied to something so their parents can go about their business. Why not a snubbing post or—school, then? A youth must be slowed up, held in hand. Caged, yes—mortified too. Broken to harness as colts are broken, or there would be nothing left but to make an "artist" of him. Send him to an Art Institute.*
> (Autobiography)

Wright's imaginational intensity was so strong that once he imagined that his mother was going to have a party for him and his friends. He began talking of it to his friends, describing the food and the presents there would be at the party. They believed him and came in their Sunday best. His mother was surprised to see them. But when they said they had come to a party, she looked at Frank, understood, and made a party, even getting Frank's father to play for them on his violin. She went along with her beloved son, even though they were poor. Frank's intensity of imagination was so great that he didn't think he was lying to his friends; he believed his own fantasy. His real life was the life of his imagination.

During the summers, he helped fix and improve the farm machinery, and he recalled that the rhythms of the farm became an opportunity to internally compose music: "All machinery makes some recurrent noise, some clack or beat above the hum that can be made into the rhythm of song movement—a rhythm that is the obvious poetry in the mathematics of this universe." His apprenticeship pumping the organ for his distracted father paid off in his being able to relate the structure of music to the pounding of machinery.

"After one thousand two hundred and sixty todays and tomorrows like those yesterdays" he turned 16 and prepared to enter the University of Wisconsin. The farm experiences left him with "a self-confidence in his own strength called courage" and with a fear of people. He was very shy with girls. "The sight of a girl would send him scampering like a scared young stag." Meanwhile, his father and mother were not getting along. His scholarly father was now teaching himself Sanskrit and was escaping into his music, and their poverty was so overwhelming that his mother would wait to eat what the family had left on their plates. Wright had become so muscular and strong that at age 16, when his father tried to beat him, he held his father down on the floor until the man promised he would beat him no more.

Frank's mother soon asked her husband to leave, and "Father disappeared. Never seen again by his wife and children." He took only his violin and his clothes. The marriage was quietly dissolved, and the family felt great disgrace and shame. Wright felt that his mother had been dealt a great injustice, as divorced women were not usually found in society, especially divorced wives of ministers. She kept working in an engineer's office and kept pushing her son, getting him a job with a civil engineer at the University of Wisconsin. Wright entered college with a plan to study civil engineering. He said that he was glad he was spared architectural schooling at the time and that he instead got a practical education in civil engineering. He continued his voracious reading and dreaming, and he kissed his first girl.

At college, he was still an outsider and never graduated. He left Madison for Chicago, feeling a "sense of shame in accepting the mother's sacrifices for so little in return." During college, he experienced an event that was to haunt his dreams vividly for years afterwards. A new wing on the State capitol building collapsed because of the criminal negligence of the architect. Wright said that the horrible carnage "never entirely left" his consciousness. In Chicago, he began as an apprentice to architect Louis Sullivan, but then broke off to found his own architectural firm in Oak Park.

The achievements of his adulthood are legendary. The 2002 Ken Burns series on Public Television described his three careers, the last one beginning when he was 70. He founded two architecture schools called Taliesin—one in Wisconsin and one in Arizona—that carried on his ideas with scores of young architects. During his last career, he built one-of-a-kind homes—including "Fallingwater" in Pennsylvania—and designed the Guggenheim Museum of Art.

Thus went the childhood and young adulthood of one of the world's greatest architects. He was encouraged to be creative, to dream, to range freely. He had artistic parents who were interested in education. He was provided with music lessons, tools, and books, even though his parents were very poor. His mother suggested architecture to him at an early age and then moved heaven and earth to influence him in that direction. He was engaged in many projects and had a few friends who were interested in the same things. His father was viewed by the son as ineffectual, and the mother was viewed as a major influence in his creativity. In his family mythology, the attainment of an education was emphasized, as well as an ethic of hard work. The family experienced hardship and took it in stride. Wright was not chided for being odd; rather, his family encouraged him. The seeds of his later accomplishment were planted in his early years.

These case studies of well-known architects demonstrate a remarkable consistency in characteristics over their life span. From early to late, they continued to be creative producers.

Summary

1. In genes, artists are often sons and daughters of artists.

2. In personality, visual artists and architects prefer intuition and perception, independence, intellect, passion, persistence, and a rejection of conventional economic values.

3. They excel in spatial intelligence, and in IQ, they are normal but not unusually high.

4. In the Sun of School, their talent for art is often not formally developed until after high school.

5. The Sun of Home indicated that they sometimes experienced childhood trauma, but most did not. Fathers disapproved of their becoming artists, and mothers were nurturing and dominant.

6. The Sun of Community and Culture indicated that they learned from other artists with whom they studied and attended galleries and openings.

7. The Sun of Gender indicated the personality attribute of androgyny and the necessity for artist mothers to modify their own dreams. Gender differences were apparent in spatial ability and treatment by teachers.

8. The Sun of Chance indicated that proximity to a loft culture was necessary in the realization of their promise.

Chapter 7
Creative Writers

A writer is someone born with a gift. An athlete can run. A painter can paint. A writer has a facility with words. A good writer can also think. Isn't that enough to define a writer by?
—Cynthia Ozick

If people only knew what lies at the heart of my novels! What a tumult of desires these carefully written pages conceal! I sometimes have a loathing for the furious cravings that give me no peace except when I am working.
—Julian Green

What leads to someone choosing such a solitary life as the life of the writer? To watch a writer write is, well, as boring as watching a bear hibernate. Joyce Carol Oates said that the writer needs to "verify experience by way of language." Katherine Anne Porter, in her *Paris Review* interview, said, "This thing between me and my writing is the strongest bond I have ever had—stronger than any bond or any engagement with any human being or with any other work I've ever done."

Directory of American Poets and Fiction Writers

Who are the poets and writers of today? A *Directory of American Poets and Fiction Writers* lists names and addresses of contemporary poets and fiction writers. The standard for being included in this *Directory* is rather high. Only those writers who have published at least one novel, or three short stories, or 12 poems in at least three different literary publications, or who have won major literary awards, or any combination of these are included. Only about 7,400 American writers, or .000038% of the citizenry, have met these qualifications. Those who qualify as both poets and fiction writers are even fewer. Approximately 1,100 writers are listed (of which I am one). This is .0000055% of Americans. While the sensational aspects of the lives of poets and writers will always draw attention, these and the others who are writing, alone in their rooms, collecting rejection letters, perform the real story of the creative writer.

I have studied creative writers since 1978, when I presented at a conference a survey of their school experiences. In 1995, I presented a study of themes in the lives of women writers who qualified for listing in the *Directory*. This was published in 1999. Then, in 2002, I looked at the themes in the lives of 80 U.S. women and 80 U.S. men writers in *"My Teeming Brain": Understanding Creative Writers* (2002). I organized the book according to the Piirto Pyramid (see Chapter 5).

The Genetic Aspect: Creative Writers

Whether or not there is a writing gene is not known. Few writers come from families of writers, but some do: Andre Dubus and his son Andre Dubus II; John Cheever and his son and daughter Ben and Susan. Screenwriters and novelists Nora and Delia Ephron are the daughters of Hollywood screenwriters. The Goertzels found that literary people were less likely to come from literary families than were artistic, business, and political people to come from families established in their respective areas.

The Emotional Aspect: Personalities of Creative Writers

The creative writer seems to have certain core personality attributes, present to different degrees: (1) independence/nonconformity; (2) drive/resiliency; (3) courage/risk-taking; (4) androgyny; (5) introversion; (6) intensity or OEs—overexcitabilities; (7) naiveté or an attitude of openness; (8) preference for an intuitive and perceptive way of looking at the world; and (9) energy transmitted into productivity through self-discipline. Personality attributes of writers that may or may not be present in other creative people who practice their creativity in other fields or domains are: (1) ambition/envy; (2) concern with philosophical matters; (3) frankness often expressed in political or social activism; (4) psychopathology;, (5) depression; (6) empathy; and (7) a sense of humor. Some of these will be discussed here. They are discussed in greater detail in *"My Teeming Brain."*

Ambition/Envy

Writers need ambition, as do other creative producers, but that ambition often produces horrible feelings of inadequacy and anxiety as one writer compares him- or herself with other writers. Writer's conferences, unfortunately, can foster low self-regard. They often engender jealousy and anxiety among the participants, who may see each other as rivals. Stratification exists in all professions, not only in writing, and people know on which levels they rest.

While writers obviously need other writers, they are also threatened by other writers. The ambition needed to survive is often accompanied by envy and insecurity in the face of others' success. For example, poet Molly Peacock, in an interview with Friman and Templin, made no apology for her ambition:

> *From when I was a little girl I wanted to be an artist.... I had a drive to get out of that house and that town. That takes ambition, and my ambition is located in that very early desire to succeed.... I think people who don't discuss their ambition contribute to a veil of deception and a mythology that does not serve writers, and certainly not women. Ambition is a fact of anyone's life who aspires to anything.* (p. 41)

Productivity/Self-Discipline

In addition to the need/fear relationships among writers, writers value productivity. As in any creative profession, writers must be productive in order to achieve the "senior" ranks. For example, the prolific John Updike doesn't know how many books he has written. "But do I count just the forty hardcover volumes that the obliging firm of Alfred A. Knopf has published?" To try to count the numbers of books that the author Joyce Carol Oates has written is similarly difficult. Another prolific author is Stephen King, whom *Time Magazine* referred to as King, Inc. We can add to this group Isaac Asimov, Ray Bradbury, May Sarton, and James Michener. Other well-known and well-respected writers have written little. Consider William Styron, who has had a relatively modest output, J. D. Salinger, who has not produced for many years, and Frank Conroy, who has written just a few books.

Concern with Philosophical Matters

Writers are concerned with the meaning of life and with the search for truth and beauty, and furthermore, they are particularly concerned about behaving in an ethically consistent fashion. Supposedly, this is the lofty purpose of literature; thus, a writer's search for truth and beauty is not surprising. This is not to say, however, that literature is written expressly to set forth doctrines or dogma. Rather, the writer uses experience as a search for meaning, and not for meaning itself.

The Aesthetics of It All

Writers take an aesthetic pleasure in the texture of the paper, the placement of the type, the sewing of the binding, the spacing of the headings. Many of the fine small presses are owned and run by writers. Passaro, in an interview with the novelist Don DeLillo, noted DeLillo's love of how sentences are constructed and how words are juxtaposed: "not just how they sound and how they mean, but even what they look like."

Aesthetic pleasure is physical with writers as well. Poetry, especially, is often made into high quality, hand-set, hand-sewn books that provide the eye and the finger with aesthetic pleasure and the brain with poetic delight. These are called "chapbooks," small, beautifully printed books with fewer than 30 pages. Many writers collect rare and fine books, first editions, chapbooks, and "broadsides," which are poems set in the manner of old handbills. I do also, and I love to run my fingers on the embossed leather covers or along the faded yellow pages, smelling the musty print. Even going to a book sale is an aesthetic pleasure, not to mention a financial one. Once, I found John Irving's *Setting Free the Bears*, bought it for 70 cents, came home, and looked it up to find that it was worth several hundred dollars. At an estate sale, I found a first edition of Hemingway's *Death in the Afternoon*, the dust cover still on, with small tears and rips that spoke of years of reading by the now-dead owner. Such discoveries make my day, as the many bookshelves in my house attest.

Independence of Thought: Frankness

Writers may value freedom of expression more than the feelings of others. Barron's 1968 study shows that creative writers are not good cooperators or committee members; they do not have a great need for harmony, nor do they seek easy praise.

Indeed, writers throughout the world have often been the first to be thrown into jail or sent into exile for what they have written and said. Solzhenitsyn and Brodsky were sent to Siberia for what they wrote. The British writer Salman Rushdie was sentenced to death by the Ayatollah of Iran for his novel *Satanic Verses* and had to go into hiding in 1989. The writer's organization, PEN, has a Freedom to Write Committee, a watchdog group concerned about writers throughout the world being persecuted for expressing themselves.

A study by Brower looked at a variety of creators who had spent time in jail. Of his list, most—30—were writers. Then, in descending order, were political prisoners (28), artists (5, including Gauguin and Egon Schiele), moral innovators (4, including Jesus and Ghandi), scientists (3, including Galileo and Lonsdale), stage performers (2, including Mae West and Lenny Bruce), musical composers (1), and miscellaneous (10, including Frank Lloyd Wright and Socrates). Brower said that this is really not very surprising, as creativity is often equated with being different or deviant. Those who create are rebels, contradictors, and they often go against what most people think. Their new ideas are very often met with society's rejection and even repression. At a less lofty level, young creative writers often publish frank, underground newspapers that are the bane of their teachers and school administrators. Sometimes they are rewarded with expulsion hearings or other disciplinary action.

Writers attract the interest of others, probably because of their ability to say what they think. Writers are often frank individuals who need to communicate and who are likely to take risks in doing so. Through psychological testing, Barron's 1968 Institute of Personality Assessment and Research (IPAR) study found that the writers showed a desire to achieve through their work, and not through conformity to a social group. They had presence, they wanted to achieve social status, and they liked themselves.

Psychopathology

Yet creative writers were also notably divergent from the general population. Barron said that writers seem to be psychologically both sicker and healthier when compared with the general population—that is, the writers may have had psychological problems, but they also had inner strength. Barron said that writers are high performers who are proud and distinctive, but they often show their readers and admirers a side of themselves that complains, protests, is emotional, and seeks distancing, withdrawing from the world. "They are clearly effective people who handle themselves with pride and distinctiveness, but the face they turn to the world is sometimes one of pain, often of protest, sometimes of distance and withdrawal, and certainly they are emotional."

Psychoanalysts and psychologists have often stated that writers write because of deep-seated pathologies. Freud, in "Creative Writers and Day-Dreaming," theorized that writers use their personal childhood fantasies. Ernst Kris wrote, in *Psychoanalytic Explorations in Art*, that writers write because of "regression in service of the ego."

Other psychoanalytically-oriented critics have weighed in. Schneiderman proposed that Faulkner wrote because of ego defects, including low self-esteem caused by an overprotective mother and a rejecting father; Lillian Hellmann wrote out of narcissistic "chronic rage" that resulted from "material deprivation"; Tennessee Williams wrote to compensate for his "incestual feelings" toward his mother and sister; Flannery O'Connor wrote out of guilt for getting ill with lupus in her late twenties and being dependent upon her mother during adulthood; John Cheever wrote because of "early withdrawal of parental empathy"; Vladimir Nabokov wrote out of a "longing for his presexual days"; Jorge Luis Borges wrote because of oncoming blindness and his shame after a series of crises in his family's fortunes in Buenos Aires; Samuel Beckett wrote out of a "character disorder marked by extreme rigidity and self-centeredness"; playwright Harold Pinter wrote out of "regression to a past that was as emotionally deprived as is the present." Schneiderman said, "great literary art is a synthesis of technical skill with tremendous fear, rage, or other powerful emotions, and the fundamental character of great writers reveals significant failure along developmental lines, that is, a basic lack of maturity."

Rothenberg, in more than 2,000 hours of interviews for *Creativity and Madness*, including some with award-winning writers, formulated a theory of the Janusian process, as described in Chapter 1. The theory propounds that creative people are able to hold two contradictory ideas in their minds at the same time. A comparison group, similar in success, age, and sex, was also studied. The ability to see the other side of any idea or thought and its creative possibilities is what differentiated the two groups—the creative producers, and those who had no creative products.

Kay Jamison, in a study of 39 British writers and eight artists, found that 38% of them had been treated for affective illness, versus 5% of the normal population. They reported mental problems including hospitalization of their first-degree relatives to a greater extent than in the normal population. Psychiatrists should be cautious in their diagnoses and drug prescriptions; the side effects of commonly prescribed drugs may damage the creative process. Several writers stopped taking lithium because of its deadening effects on their creative thinking.

Depression

Pulitzer Prize-winning author William Styron wrote an op-ed piece for *The New York Times* and later turned it into the book *Darkness Visible*, about the cavalier treatment of the suicide of Primo Levi, the Italian writer. Styron himself had fallen into a deep depression after he stopped drinking, and he was hospitalized for his mental condition. Styron named other writers and artists who had suffered from debilitating depression—Albert Camus, Romain Gary, Jean Seberg, and Randall Jarrell, among others. Styron wrote that Jarrell "almost certainly killed himself" because he was a coward, not out of any moral feebleness, but "because he was afflicted with a depression that was so devastating that he could no longer endure the pain of it." Other artists who suffered depression were poet Hart Crane, painter Vincent Van Gogh, writer Virginia Woolf, abstract expressionist Mark Rothko, photographer Diane Arbus, playwright William Inge, and humorist Art Buchwald. Of the origins of such depression, Styron wrote:

> *When one thinks of these doomed and splendidly creative men and women, one is drawn to contemplate their childhoods, where, to the best of anyone's knowledge, the seeds of the illness take strong root; could any of them have had a hint, then, of the psyche's perishability, its exquisite fragility? And why were they destroyed, while others—similarly stricken—struggled through?* (p. 34)

Styron suffered a relapse in the summer of 2000, and when interviewed, again thanked the mental health community. He said that if suicide can be prevented when a creative person suffers from depression, the depression can usually be cured.

Kay Jamison found that artists, poets, and writers were 35 times more likely to seek treatment for serious mood disorders than the average person, and of these three groups, poets suffered the severest forms of disturbance. Jamison gave diagrams of the genealogies and documented manic-depressive illness (bipolar disorder) in the first-degree relatives of writers Alfred, Lord Tennyson; Henry, Alice, and William James; Herman Melville; Samuel

Taylor Coleridge; Virginia Woolf; Ernest Hemingway; Mary Wollstonecraft and her daughter Mary Shelley; Samuel Johnson; James Boswell; and George Gordon, Lord Byron. Following is a table based on Jamison's research. I added the name of novelist Michael Dorris, who committed suicide at age 52.

Table 7.1: Poets with Depression or Manic-Depression
✺ = Asylum or psychiatric institution; ❖ = Suicide attempt; ☛ = Suicide

✺	Antonin Artaud		John Keats
❖	Charles Baudelaire	☛	Vachel Lindsay
✺, ☛	John Berryman		James Russell Lowell
	William Blake	✺	Robert Lowell
✺	Louise Bogan		Louis MacNiece
	Rupert Brooke	✺, ❖	Osip Mandelstam
	Robert Burns	✺	Edna St. Vincent Millay
	George Gordon, Lord Byron	✺	Boris Pasternak
☛	Paul Celan	☛	Cesare Pavese
☛	Thomas Chatterton	✺, ☛	Sylvia Plath
	Samuel Taylor Coleridge	❖	Edgar Allan Poe
✺	William Collins	✺	Ezra Pound
✺, ❖	William Cowper		Alexander Pushkin
☛	Hart Crane	✺	Theodore Roethke
	Emily Dickinson	✺	Delmore Schwartz
✺	T.S. Eliot	✺, ☛	Anne Sexton
	Anne Finch	❖	Percy Bysshe Shelley
	Oliver Goldsmith	✺, ❖	Sara Teasdale
	Thomas Gray		Alfred, Lord Tennyson
	Gerard Manley Hopkins		Dylan Thomas
✺, ☛	Randall Jarrell		Walt Whitman
	Samuel Johnson		

Table 7.2: Writers with Depression or Manic-Depression
1 = Asylum or psychiatric institution; 2 = Suicide attempt; 3 = Suicide

	Hans Christian Andersen	✹, ❖	William Inge
	Honoré de Balzac		Henry James
	James Barrie		William James
	James Boswell	✹	Charles Lamb
	John Bunyan	✹, ❖	Malcolm Lowry
	Samuel Clemens		Herman Melville
❖	Joseph Conrad	✹, ❖	Eugene O'Neill
	Charles Dickens		Francis Parkman
❖	Isak Dinesen		Mary Shelley
☞	Michael Dorris	✹	Jean Stafford
	Ralph Waldo Emerson		Robert Louis Stevenson
✹	William Faulkner		August Strindberg
✹	F. Scott Fitzgerald		Leo Tolstoy
	Nikolai Gogol		Ivan Turgenev
❖	Maxim Gorky	✹	Tennessee Williams
	Kenneth Grahame	❖	Mary Wollstonecraft
✹, ☞	Ernest Hemingway	✹, ☞	Virginia Woolf
✹, ❖	Hermann Hesse		Emile Zola
	Henrik Ibsen		

Andreason studied 27 male and three female faculty at the University of Iowa Writers' Workshop over a period of 15 years. She compared them with a control group. The average age was 38 years. Bipolar, manic-depressive affective disorder was found in 80% of the writers and in 30% of the comparison group, which itself had a higher than usual incidence of affective disorder. Two-thirds of the writers had sought psychiatric help. Two of the 30 writers committed suicide during the 15 years of the study.

Andreason found that almost half of the members of this study came from creative families, though they may not have been in the writing field. This indicates that there may be a general creativity factor that is genetically transmitted. The verbal intelligence of the faculty members (a verbal IQ of about 125) was no higher than that of the comparison group. Andreason thought that they would be schizophrenic, but instead she found manic depression, and she noted that the writers wrote during the long periods between episodes rather than during the highs and lows characteristic of bipolar disorder.

The self-analysis that creative writing engenders within the artist may be dangerous. John Cheever wrote this: "I must convince myself that writing is not, for a man of my disposition, a self-destructive vocation. I hope and think it is not, but I am not genuinely sure."

The 1991 suicide of the Pulitzer Prize-winning novelist Jerzy Kosinski brought this letter from the playwright Kenneth Brown:

> *Jerzy Kosinski was a friend of mine, hence the enclosed poem. He committed suicide recently by pulling a plastic bag over his head and sitting in a hot tub and suffocating. It was a great shock to me. We used to sit in the saloons late at night and talk about his childhood. The Nazis killed his family when he was about eight years old, and he became a street urchin for a while. Have you read* The Painted Bird? *He adored the SS troops because they were tall and clean and handsome with shiny boots and black uniforms. It haunted him all his life; he had enormous guilt about his success and his survival, worried about having become a Nazi equivalent through his fame and fortune. I tried to reassure him that his work was a weapon against fascism. Alas, what I said was not enough. I guess nothing would have been enough.*

Highly verbal, highly conceptual, highly opinionated, often nonconforming, frank, highly driven writers, it seems, are prone to self-abusive and self-destructive behaviors, even as they are enriching the lives of their readers. But this is not always the case, and there are many writers whose lives are not lived so tragically or who have, as Styron said, "struggled through."

The picture that emerges can perhaps be summarized in the words of E. L. Doctorow, who said in his *Paris Review* interview with Plimpton in 1988:

> *A writer's life is so hazardous that anything he does is bad for him. Anything that happens to him is bad: failure's bad, success is bad; impoverishment is bad, money is very, very bad. Nothing good can happen...except the act of writing itself.*

This statement perhaps illustrates the intrinsic nature of writing talent. The writer does not know what he or she thinks until it's written down.

A Sense of Humor

Humor is essentially verbal talent. Those humorists who are physical humorists, such as Jerry Lewis or the Three Stooges, are actors using their bodies. Actors and dancers, the physically talented, are discussed in Chapter 11.

Humor is developmental and cultural. What we laugh at in our society is not what is laughed at in another society, and if we go to a comedy club in Japan or India, we will probably not laugh; we will miss the point, even if we understand the language, for humor—especially stand-up comedy, written humor, and political cartoons—relies on idioms of the language and culture. When we learn a foreign language, idioms are the most difficult to master.

Many of the most admired humorists in our society have been writers: Mark Twain, James Thurber, E. B. White, Tom Wolfe, Damon Runyon, Groucho Marx, Kurt Vonnegut Jr., Dave Barry, Joseph Heller, Roy Blount Jr., Calvin Trillin, Garrison Keillor, Erma Bombeck, Steve Allen, and Woody Allen are all examples. Comedians who are not writers hire writers.

The Myers-Briggs Type Indicator and Writers

Writers tested with the *Myers-Briggs* were found overwhelmingly to be introverted, intuitive, feeling, and perceptive—INFP. These findings showed them to be similar to artists. Individuals who prefer introversion, intuition, feeling, and perception show inner strength, especially with regard to their personal values, and are reserved. They look for a type of job that provides satisfaction rather than money, where they can be perfectionistic about their work. They are interested in ideas. I administered the *Myers-Briggs Type Indicator* to women writers in my 1995 study. The preference of INFP (Introversion, Intuition, Feeling, Perception) held. However, several of them refused to take the inventory because it is a forced choice instrument; they did not like to be forced to choose (itself an indication of a preference).

The Cognitive Aspect: The Intelligence of Creative Writers

The intelligence of writers is easy to measure by conventional tests because the usual IQ tests have a section on verbal intelligence, utilizing definitions of words, grammar, word analogies, and such. Writers usually score very high on these sections of the IQ tests, but their IQs might not be the highest because they often do not score so high on the sections of the tests that measure mathematical and spatial ability. At IPAR (Institute for Personality Assessment Research), not surprisingly, writers scored high in verbal intelligence. Creative writers scored an average of 156 on the *Terman Concept Mastery Test*. Compare this to 137, scored by the gifted population that Terman observed in his famous longitudinal study. Captains in the Air Force scored 60 on this test, and the general population scored lower than that.

Several intelligence theorists say that intelligence consists of more than verbal, mathematical, and figural elements. Guilford is one of these. He listed semantic intelligence as one of his five "Contents," in his *Structure of the Intellect* (1967). In *Frames of Mind* (1983), Gardner listed linguistic intelligence and called it "the capacity to use language, your native language, and perhaps other languages, to express what's on your mind, and to understand other people."

One of the marks of high intelligence is memory. Writers possess the kind of academic memory that enables them to score high on tests—memory for what they have studied. Visual and verbal memory are often intertwined. Writers also possess memory for emotional events of childhood that the rest of the family has forgotten. In an interview with C. Joyce, novelist Russell Banks spoke about memory: "You have to tap into your remembered emotional experiences.... You have to separate from it. Your memory improves to the degree that you can get somewhat detached from the experiences.... It's painful, but it's clear."

Poet Gerald Stern said, in an interview with Bill Moyers, "the poet's main job might be to preserve memory." He said that our culture doesn't value memory, perhaps for economic reasons—that is, companies advertising products don't want consumers to remember the old objects; they want them to throw them away so that they will constantly want new things. Lack of political memory is also desirable in our society, because if people remember the past, they might resist. He said, "I suspect the very first thing dictators do is to efface memory." In ancient societies, poets and storytellers kept the memories for the people and chanted them down the years around campfires and at ceremonies.

What Is Writing Talent?

Scoring high on a test that measures verbal ability is not sufficient to indicate writing *talent*. Many of the highest scorers on such tests are scientists and philosophers, whose talent with the written word, at least in the creative sense of fiction, poetry, playwriting, or songwriting, might not be there. Creative writers can use figures of speech, can speak plainly, can convey through image the right word, and through rhythm with meaning that moves the reader. What constitutes writing talent is most often a matter of peer judgment—the field itself judges who has the talent. In my study, one finding was that almost all of the writers had won either a National Endowment for the Arts Individual Artist Fellowship or a state arts council award. Prizes such as the Pulitzer, the National Book Award, and the National Book Critics Circle Award are all juried by peers—experts in creative writing. As in any domain, those who are talented are judged by critics/connoisseurs of the domain. The winners may not be those authors who are on the best-seller lists, but they are thrust into prominence by the gatekeepers of the field—fellow creative writers and critics. Each year, I buy the nominated books of poetry, fiction, and nonfiction to keep up with the latest writing style.

Many writers who would not even be considered for these grants and awards attain a large popular following. These writers exist in the realm of the best-seller, but few best-selling authors win respect from literary peers and also attain a popular following, though the Oprah Book Club, during its tenure, did produce crossovers—literary writers who became best-sellers. Jonathan Franzen, the 2002 National Book Award winner, was one. For most literary writers, however, peer recognition is more important than public recognition. The literary world, as is the world of other domains of talent, keeps tabs on those with most talent and elevates them through the review processes of the domain.

Gardner (1983) spoke of the different kinds of writers and asserted that the poet composes in the most difficult of the verbal arts—one that requires the greater verbal or linguistic intelligence. The poet must have these language talents: (1) an ability to sense the several meanings of words; (2) an ability to position the words so that their meanings resonate with words on other lines, or a spatial ability with words; (3) an ability to catch, in an imagistic way, the feelings that made the poet want to make the poem. The novelist wants to "wrest the essence, the real truth" from life. The writer of narratives wants to show the reader what she has experienced or envisioned.

Most literary writers begin to publish through small presses with limited popular appeal. Then, "suddenly," they burst upon the public screen as winners of a major award. Their peers have known about them for years; they have been working for a long time and have been publishing for a long time. Many lie in the wings of literary oblivion, ready with their talents already approved and sealed by their peers through publication in the literary underground. It is only after they have won the big award that their names become household words. "The House that the Book Bought" was the title of an article in the *New York Times* by Leland in October 2002 describing the Provincetown condominium that Pulitzer Prize-winner Michael Cunningham bought with the movie royalties for his book *The Hours*. Cunningham was not a one-book wonder, but had been working and publishing for years before his novel won the coveted Pulitzer Prize.

The Domain "Thorn" in Creative Writers

Why does the writer write? Because one can't not write. Because he has to. It is that simple. The urge and psychological need to write often begins very early, though it can arise at any time. The writing is not for fame, money, or notoriety, but to fulfill a more personal need, the need to find out what one is thinking, the need to put it down so that it can be dealt with, the need to codify emotion. Novelist Dorothy Allison talked about the courage it takes to write:

> *The best fiction comes from the place where the terror hides, the edge of our worst stuff. I believe, absolutely, that if you do not break out in that sweat of fear when you write, then you have not gone far enough. And I know you can fake that courage when you don't think of yourself as courageous—because I have done it.... I know that until I started pushing on my own fears, telling the stories that were hardest for me, writing about exactly the things I was most afraid of and unsure about, I wasn't writing worth a damn.* (Cited in Graff, 1995, p. 42)

Passion for the Domain

"I don't like to write," said an academic colleague. "I like to have written." This is not quite true for most writers, who voluntarily exile themselves to desks and pads, computers and word processors, offices and retreats in order to focus their eyes and thoughts on the written word. Most say they don't know what they think until they write it down. Many would agree with the writer Katherine Anne Porter, who said in an interview with Barbara Thompson that her commitment to writing came from an early passion: "I started out with nothing in the world but a kind of passion, a driving desire. I don't know where it came from, and I don't know why—or why I have been so stubborn about it that nothing could deflect me." Porter kept on writing through all the pains of her life.

The Sun of Home in Creative Writers

What do the childhoods of writers look like? What may predict adult creative writing talent? Here are the themes I found.

Theme 1: Predictive Behavior of Extensive Early Reading

The most common predictive early behavior for writers is their constant reading. All studies, all biographies of writers point this out. For example, the Goertzels found that writers were voracious early readers. Writers often retreat from the world by reading and fantasizing, and when they were young, they didn't need as much companionship as other children. The childhood reading was often indiscriminate and compulsive, and reading was used both to escape and to learn about the world. Parents may or may not have nurtured this early reading, but the writers discovered books at an early age and have not yet lost their interest. This desperate need to read continues into adulthood.

Reading is such an intense pleasure that memories hold the experience as special. Writers seem to remember the names of the books they read. In *How I Grew,* Mary McCarthy spent 14 of the first 28 pages listing and describing books she remembered reading as a child. She remembered them by name, by color, by author, even into her mid-sixties. She listed all of the books in the house, and even remembered an unfinished fairy tale that had been read to her by her father before he died. She searched for that book through all her life. When she described her high school friends, she remembered the books they talked about. When she was permitted to go to the library in her sophomore year, she described herself as a "colt in a big, green pasture."

Scholars also have the predictive behavior of reading. However, for creative writers, the reading is not enough; the emotional need to express themselves through writing also exists.

Theme 2: Predictive Behavior of Early Publication and Interest in Writing

Many of the writers early on published in local poetry and fiction magazines and in children's magazines. They won contests, and some were accused of plagiarism by teachers who couldn't believe they could write so well. This early validation of their writing talent by others served to spur them to further efforts in writing. Novelist and screenwriter Richard Price said that being a writer became a badge of identification in the culture of the school:

Oh, I was writing in elementary school. What happens is that when you're a kid, you know, everybody hates themselves, but they always have this one thing that they feel makes them different.... For me, I could write. I was a precocious writer. For another kid, he was the best athlete.... Everybody's like, "What's the one thing I can hang on to desperately, so I can feel like a member of the human race?"...And for me it was writing. (Garner, 1998)

Poet Ted Hughes had a similar experience. He wrote comic verses for his class at age 11. "I realized that certain things I wrote amused my teacher and my classmates. I began to regard myself as a writer; writing was my specialty." By the age of 14, he was writing long sagas imitating Kipling's poems, and he showed them to his English teacher. She said, "It's real poetry." Hughes said it was "the hammer of a punt gun on an imaginary wildfowling hunt. I immediately pricked up my ears. That moment still seems the crucial one."

Stephen King, in his biography in *Contemporary Authors*, said that:

Guys like me...were duds in high school. Writing has always been it for me. I was just sort of this nerdy kid. I didn't get beat up too much because I was big, played a little football and stuff like that. So mostly I just got this, "King—he's weird. Big glasses. Reads a lot. Big teeth." I've thought about stopping—sometimes it seems to me I could save my life by stopping. Because I'm really compulsive about it. I drive that baby."

Theme 3: Unconventional Families and Family Traumas

Family life is not an idyllic, carefree time in many writers' lives. They often come from unconventional families that were artistically oriented and that used storytelling as a means of communicating, with books and reading as a presence. The families were often laissez-faire in their approach to discipline, though some writers had parents who were quite authoritarian. Among the experiences are orphan-hood, parental disability, neglect, frequent moving, parental alcoholism, suicide of family members, and other extraordinary childhood trauma.

The Goertzels noted that the writers were often ill as children, or handicapped, or homely. "Their photographs as children and adults are less attractive than those of politicians, athletes, and performers." Their childhoods and adult lives were judged to be more "lonely, unhappy, and difficult" than others. On the positive side, they were as children very sensuous, reacting profoundly to visual, olfactory, and tactile sensations. But even this sensitivity worked against them. As small children, they "were intensely responsive to the emotional climate in their homes" and were "acute observers of the family dramas being played out before their eyes."

Novelist and poet Kelly Cherry described her childhood in an unconventional family. Her parents were preoccupied members of a string quartet, consumed by their music, poor, and working at day jobs to make ends meet. She and her sister were neglected, not even taught to brush their teeth until they went to school; they were kids on the loose, kids at large, who were not taught to groom themselves in any way. A neighbor once commented to Cherry's parents that she was a "child of nature," and her mother thought it was funny, not realizing that the neighbor meant it as an insult. Cherry also had the dubious honor of being rejected by the Brownies.

Writers weren't popular. In fact, they often provoked dislike and rejection from peers, adults, and teachers because of their outspokenness. Although peaceful children, they often had to be pushed into doing physical activities or studying subjects they didn't like, such as math or science. Writers also are not joiners of causes, except to contribute (but not to hold office), and are content to be alone much of the time. The Goertzels studies showed that two-thirds of the writers described their childhood home life as unhappy, while less than half of the other eminent people described their early years so. Literary people were also more likely to have alcoholic parents.

Parental Alcoholism

Parental alcoholism is as present for writers as it is with the rest of the world, but perhaps the writers' emotional intensity, coupled with an ability to communicate through words, makes the alcoholism a reason to write. Fiction writer Lee Abbott said, "My mother was a drunk, institutionalized when I was twelve; my father was a drinker." Tess Gallagher described waiting in the car with her mother and three brothers while her father drank in the beer joints. She said, "this car sitting and the stillness it enforced contributed to a patience and curiosity that heightened my ability to see." Her parents often argued over the drinking, which, she said, made her childhood full of terror. This unreliability of mood in the household taught her that "any balance was temporary, that unreasonableness could descend at any minute, thrashing aside everything and everyone in its path. Emotional and physical vulnerability was a constant."

The poet Robert Bly said that it took him years to put the word "stagger" into a poem about his father, whose alcoholism filled him with shame. Poet Frank O'Hara's mother was alcoholic. So was gothic novelist Anne Rice's. It is not known whether writers had more alcoholism in their families than other people, for alcoholism seems to have touched most families. Perhaps the writers' responses to the alcoholic environment were different in quality, and perhaps not; perhaps they responded with greater overexcitability or intensity.

Perhaps I would be remiss, as your author, not to tell my own story here. When the first edition of this book came out, I was interviewed by the book editor of the Columbus *Dispatch*, George F. Myers. I knew him from the writing world of Ohio. I confessed to him that as I was doing the research, I identified with many of the themes I found, and I told him about my own alcoholic father as he told me about his. When the book was featured on the front page of the Sunday Arts section, I went down to the local Dairy Mart to get my copy. There I saw in black and white what I thought I told him off the record:

> *When Jane Piirto began finding commonalities among specific groups of creative people, she was startled by her own conclusions. "I found a lot of my own life in what I found out about writers in general," Piirto said recently. "My father was an alcoholic, and it turns out that a lot of writers had absent or ineffectual fathers, as I did."*

There it was, out there to 100,000 readers or so, our family's secret. My cheeks flamed. My heart pounded. I waited for my mother to return from church 600 miles away, and I called her and read her the paragraph. She paused and said, "Well, it's true."

The off-balanced life that a drunk in the family causes is intimate knowledge to me. The shame, the secrecy, the boiling rage fill my memory. The hours spent waiting on a winter street in an idling car outside the Elks Club where he popped in to have a "snort" with the boys, the shouting and weaving that caused my sister ulcers at age 15, the earplugs that hung over the doorknob upstairs where we would retreat when he railed downstairs, the broken door kicked in rage, the overheard parental fights and ensuing days of silence—all stay in my memory.

There was also the gentle, caring father who wrote me many letters when I was 18 and away at college. One that I have framed says how much he loved me and how I could have the car when I came home for Thanksgiving. He urged me to keep studying and getting good grades.

Psychiatrist Alice Miller wrote that creativity results when there is trauma with warmth present; destructiveness is the result when there is no warmth present. Psychoanalyst Albert Rothenberg said that creativity results from having one parent who was frustrated in a creative endeavor, who was not good enough, or whose creativity was thwarted. As the daughter of an artist mother and an alcoholic father, I found these themes to resonate in me, as well as seeming to be prevalent in the writers I studied.

Search for the Father

The search for the father is a predominant theme for many writers. Poets John Berryman and Stanley Kunitz and fiction writer Ernest Hemingway had fathers who committed suicide. The playwright Arthur Miller noted that many writers have had ineffectual fathers. He said, "It would strike me years later how many male writers had fathers who had actually failed, or whom the sons had perceived as failures." He went on to list William Faulkner, F. Scott Fitzgerald, Ernest Hemingway, Thomas Wolfe, Edgar Allan Poe, John Steinbeck, Herman Melville, Walt Whitman, Anton Chekhov, Nathaniel Hawthorne, August Strindberg, and Fyodor Dostoevsky, and he said, "the list is too long to consign the phenomenon to idiosyncratic accident." Though Miller listed male writers, this is true for female writers as well.

Miller called the American male writers "fatherless men abandoned by a past that they in turn reject, the better to write, not the Great American Novel or Play, but verily the First." Clark Blaise theorized that the writer son wants a reconciliation with his father. "I don't know any man my age who wouldn't want his father back, no matter how deformed their relationship had been." The search for the missing father is not just the search of their sons. Mary Gordon's memoir, *Shadowman: A Daughter's Search for Her Father*, is ample proof that some of the women writers seem to undergo such a search also. Gordon grew up with a belief that her father was a pious Catholic, a misunderstood poet, and a Harvard man who had fallen upon hard times. He was actually an immigrant Jew to Lorain/Cleveland, Ohio who never graduated from high school, the head writer for a hack girlie magazine called *Hot Dog*, a man with false everything, including his false teeth.

Theme 4: Depression and/or Acts such as Use of Alcohol, Drugs, or the Like

This theme has been described in Chapter 2, with reference to the creative process and substances. Let it be said, first, that many writers do not imbibe to excess. When John Irving was interviewed by Ron Hansen for the *Paris Review,* he said, "I'm such an incapable drinker, I'm lucky. If I drink half a bottle of red wine with my dinner, I forget who I had dinner with.... Drunks ramble; so do books by drunks."

Nevertheless, the use of drugs and alcohol is present in the interviews and memoirs of many contemporary writers. Pamela Durban, for instance, stated that after the break-up of her second marriage, "I drank too much, and did all kinds of undignified and destructive things, and started to write poetry." Novelist Laura Kalpakian described similar behavior. "If I couldn't crack up, break down, court madness, sleep with death, flirt with suicide on my own, then there were always drink and drugs to help me." Poet John Ashbery, in an interview with John Tranter, discussed a period when he was seeing a psychoanalyst about his drinking: " I had a tremendous drinking problem, and I would go to somebody's house for dinner and get drunk and leave before dinner was served."

Robert Stone talked about the use of drugs and alcohol. He related this social behavior among artists to the Zeitgeist of the times. "We never could have foreseen back when we were all getting loaded in the '60s that it was going to be in every junior high in America." In an interview with Dwight Garner, he commented, "I mean, we kind of associated ourselves with Joan Miró and Baudelaire in that tradition of Bohemian hashish eating and so forth."

Carolyn See, novelist and member of the National Book Critics Circle, posed the thought that inherited tendencies toward depression precipitate alcoholism and drug use. "What if depressives clan together in a series of genetic secret handshakes, so that depressed men meet depressed women and they breed depressed children and so on, in perpetuity?" See pointed out that those who are depressive often think that they are more intelligent than those around them. "That's why they struggle with scholarly papers on Hemingway, while their happy classmates take engineering classes, and don't even worry about the atom bomb. They pay off their mortgages, invest wisely, coach Little League teams, sing in the choir, and look around for good country clubs."

See continued with the thought that such alcohol and drug use has its historical use in the class struggle. "[T]he people in trailer parks drink, the kids in the slums do crack cocaine, the wannabe rock musicians shoot heroin, the sobbing wife cracks open the Southern Comfort, the mail-order merchant hides his scotch in a desk drawer. Because there was supposed to be more than this. There really was.... Is the American Dream, to put it bluntly, nothing more than a sham and a crock?"

Other behaviors include eating disorders. When Pulitzer Prize-winning poet Louise Glück was 16, she suffered from anorexia: "I realized that I had no control over this behavior at all. And I realized, logically, that to be eighty-five, then eighty, then seventy-five pounds was to be thin; I understood that at some point I was going to die." She also suffered from mental illness and underwent seven years of psychoanalysis. Glück was afraid that the analysis would silence her poetry. At 18, she was so rigid and dependent upon ritual that she could not enroll in college, but her need to write poetry was great, so she enrolled in a poetry seminar. She went on to win many awards.

Kathryn Harrison also struggled with anorexia. She attended the University of Iowa Writers' Workshop and stayed in a shabby rooming house where "Rather than go downstairs or into the horrible basement, I peed in the sink." She found herself "enduring the tenth year of chronically relapsing anorexia." Harrison wrote in secret notebooks about how many calories she ate and how much exercise she did. She said she spent her life "within a deliberate internal architecture assembled to protect and contain."

The Goertzels found that literary people were twice as likely to attempt or to commit suicide than other subjects of biographies. Poet Patricia Goedicke wished for death because of a conviction of womanhood's essential worthlessness. She said, "although I never seriously considered suicide, up until I was about thirty-seven years old, I very frequently longed to die and be rid of the whole business."

Kaufman's study in 2001 showed that female poets were more likely to suffer from mental illness than female fiction writers or than male writers of any type. He called this the "Sylvia Plath effect." Preti, DeBiasi, and Miotto, studying suicides in eminent creators for the past two centuries, found that 2.6% of poets, 2.3% of writers, and 1.8% of playwrights had committed suicide.

Of course, such behavior is immensely personal, and many of the writers in their published interviews and autobiographical essays do not comment on such. They are, after all, alive, and such confession is risky. One writer, in responding to my e-mailed question about the themes in this study, responded affirmatively to this theme, saying, "Yes. I've suffered deep depressions." This had never been spoken of in any of the other material submitted by that writer.

Theme 5: Being in an Occupation Different from their Parents

Although some occupations seem to have the characteristic of passing from parent to child (e.g., the family business, athletics, teaching, and acting), writing does not seem to be such an occupation; less than 5% of the 160 writers had parents who were writers. That is fewer than the percentage of sons and daughters who follow their parents into school teaching or into business. However, several parents were teachers or professors, and writing would seem to be a natural outgrowth of being in a home where the presence of books and encouragement of reading would be present.

The Sun of Community and Culture in Creative Writers

Theme 6: Feeling of Marginalization or Being an Outsider, and a Resulting Need to Have their Group's Story Told

One similarity among African-American, Latino, American Indian, and European-American writers seemed to emerge. The need to have one's own group's stories heard and recognized was a theme in many of the interviews and essays. African-American writers almost unanimously expressed that they were writing in order to be able to portray the real lives of African-Americans, not filtered through White writers' sensibilities, which were often formed by association with their servants.

The Mexican-American novelist Gloria Anzaldúa talked in *Borderlands/La Frontera* about how her culture silenced its women: "The silencing from the outside came from my family and my culture, where you were supposed to be seen but not heard. This was especially true for the girl children." She said, "My brothers could say bad words and I couldn't. They could go out at night, but I wasn't allowed."

The feeling of being a misfit, an outsider, occurred in many of the writers' lives, whatever their ethnicity. Novelist Martin Cruz Smith said, "you have to be an outsider to write." Whether the feeling of not fitting in is more true for writers than for the general population is not known. Whether or not they actually were, the feeling of being a misfit or outsider was present.

Poet Amy Clampitt said, "The happiest times in my childhood were spent in solitude—reading.... Socially, I was a misfit. I didn't know the right things to say to anybody."

An expression of marginalization was sounded in many of the published interviews with writers of all ethnicities. One source of such feeling emanated from religious beliefs. In the *Contemporary Writers* reference series, a large number of the writers listed their religion as Jewish, and although not often spoken out loud, the theme of anti-Semitism sounds in their written works. Poet Adrienne Rich said, "I need to understand how a place on a map is also a place in history within which as a woman, a Jew, a lesbian, a feminist, I am created and trying to create."

Sexual preference also influences writers to write. Paul Monette, whose memoir *Becoming a Man* won the National Book Award, described in excruciating detail his outsider life in elementary school, grammar school, prep school, and during college life at Yale. When he looked into his prep school yearbook and found out that he had been voted as first place "Faculty Magnet," he "felt the sting of ridicule," was "suddenly ashamed to bring my yearbook home or have it signed by anyone. They really didn't like me, the class of '63. My outsider status had now been cut in stone."

Finally, though, perhaps many of the writers would echo what American Indian writer Leslie Marman Silko said to Perry about being an outsider. "Really strong writing springs from such depth of the psyche that there aren't such differences." The quality of the experience shared has authenticity because it has been lived.

Theme 7: Late Career Recognition

Because of the financial precariousness of continuing with writing as a profession, many writers have experienced more than their share of types of jobs. It's amazing to go through the lists of previous occupations in the author blurbs in the end pages of small and large literary journals. Many writers had other career starts before settling on and accepting their emotional need to write. Poet Frank O'Hara worked at the Museum of Modern Art as a curator. Gayle Elen Harvey has been a dental hygienist for years while publishing many poems and winning many contests. Jorge Borges was a librarian in Buenos Aires. Herbert Scott won a poetry prize for his book called *Groceries*, with poems gleaned from his years in management at a chain grocery store. They wrote and wrote while holding these jobs. To make a living from one's creative writing is almost impossible. Most writers become college professors or high school teachers. This necessitates the schooling required to qualify to do so.

The Sun of School in Creative Writers

Theme 8: High Academic Achievement and Many Writing Awards

These writers were bright. Many graduated with honors from high school and were given scholarships and fellowships to pursue their academic careers. Many had risen from humble backgrounds by way of their academic talents. It is evident that the Sun of School was upon them and that teachers had a place in their talent development.

Writers do well in the test-taking and paper-writing tasks that are necessary for academic success and achievement. Science fiction writer Joanna Russ was a Westinghouse Science Award Winner in high school; cult novelist Thomas Pynchon graduated as salutatorian of his high school class in Oyster Point, Long Island, New York and won an award for being the senior with the highest average grade in English. The poet Diane Wakoski was given a scholarship to attend the University of California at Berkeley. Poet and fiction writer Marge Piercy was the first in her family to attend college, receiving a full scholarship to the University of Michigan, and then later, Northwestern University. National Book Award-winner Tim O'Brien graduated summa cum laude from Macalester College.

Many were honor students. MacArthur Award-winner David Foster Wallace graduated summa cum laude from Amherst College; Madison Smart Bell received similar honors from Princeton; Jane Smiley received a Fulbright grant during graduate school at Iowa that led to her writing of a novel about Iceland; John Updike was awarded a full scholarship to Harvard and graduated from there summa cum laude. Erica Jong received a Woodrow Wilson Fellowship while at Barnard, enabling her to write her novel *Fear of Flying*, which shocked the world and heralded the beginning of the 1960s sexual revolution. Maxine Kumin casually described being a "Cliffie" and going over to Harvard to take Russian because she wanted to be able to read Dostoevsky in the original. John Edgar Wideman was a Rhodes scholar; Dana Gioia, who was appointed the Chair of the National Endowment of the Arts in 2002, graduated from Stanford magna cum laude; Tobias Wolff took First Class Honors from Oxford University.

The predictive behavior of high academic achievement in the lives of the writers continued into adulthood, as the writers receive awards for their literary accomplishments. As mentioned before, many writers received an National Endowment for the Arts Individual Artist Fellowship. The ongoing furor over the funding of the National Endowment for the Arts seems unjustified when one looks at how many of these writers, during their years of struggle, had their work supported with fellowships given on the basis of literary merit and not on the basis of need. Such fellowships enabled them to continue to write, and the enrichment and knowledge they have brought to the nation cannot be underestimated.

However, this did not mean that these writers liked school. The Goertzels found that about half hated school, teachers, and the school curricula.

Theme 9: Nurturing of Talents by Both Male and Female Teachers and Mentors

For writers, the Sun of School is often supportive, although this is not the case for people talented in other domains. While the Sun of Home presents emotional challenges, school is often a refuge. The writers were often encouraged by teachers who discovered their talent as writers. These teachers frequently became mentors, and the gender of the mentors was more often male than female. Louise Glück spoke of the scrutiny of her teachers: "One of the rare, irreplaceable gifts of such apprenticeships is this scrutiny; seldom, afterward, is any poem taken with such high seriousness."

National Book Award-winner Bob Shacochis said that he had three fathers, one a writing teacher, "a professor in Missouri…who fathered my passion to be a writer." Colette Inez studied with Jean Star, who "treated her small brood of poets with an affection, tact, and flexibility that appealed to me."

However, a startling lack of helpfulness by teachers is also sometimes mentioned. Jane Smiley, in answer to a questionnaire I sent to women writers, said that "No teachers. None" helped her. Chinua Achebe, the Nigerian who won the Nobel Prize, described in an interview with J. Brooks how he entered a short story contest at the University of London in Inuabe, Nigeria. None of the entries was chosen, but his story was mentioned as having potential. When he asked a professor in the English department what was wrong with it, she told him that the form was wrong. He asked her to teach him about form. She avoided him for a whole term. When she finally was willing to talk with him, she looked at the story and then said, "Actually there's nothing wrong with it." Achebe said, "That was all I learned from the English department about writing short stories. You really have to go out on your own and do it." Research has shown that mentors are often of the same gender and same race as those who are chosen to be mentored. Achebe's story supports this.

Theme 10: Attendance at Prestigious Colleges, Majoring in English Literature but Without Attaining the Ph.D.

Another theme in these successful writers' lives indicates that perhaps the college one attends as an undergraduate or graduate student has some relationship to future success. Meeting professors and writers who can help and to whom the writer can apprentice oneself should be an important facet of college choice.

Half of the men and two-thirds of the women writers had graduate degrees, although the degrees were Master of Arts and Master of Fine Arts. Whereas a number of the writers seem to have begun studies for their Ph.D.s, only 12.5% completed them. This indicates a difference in requirements for eminence in different domains. Talented scientists and mathematicians, for example, must have the Ph.D. in order to do viable and respected research. For writers, this is clearly not the case. For example, novelist and memoir author Isabel Allende attended a Catholic girl's school in Chile but did not attend college. Her eminence is based on her publication of magical realist novels and heart-wrenching memoirs rather than on her educational background. Does the fact that so few completed a doctorate degree indicate that their nonconformity overtook their persistence?

Psychologist Dean Keith Simonton (1995) has indicated that many creative people quit college so that their creativity won't be stifled. Simonton indicated that many writers "tend to detest school, and to do poorly in it besides." He mentioned Stephen Crane, Eugene O'Neill, William Faulkner, and F. Scott Fitzgerald, all of whom "endured scholastic disasters in college" while rigorously educating themselves through their reading. However, I did not find this to be the case in my recent study. All of the writers except Allende had at least a bachelor's degree.

Most writers, especially people from the working class, attended a college near their home, and so the daughter of an auto worker, poet Carolyn Forché, attended Michigan State; the daughter of a lumber worker, Tess Gallagher, attended the University of Washington; the resident of an Indian reservation, Sherman Alexie, attended Washington State at Spokane; and the son of a steel foreman, William Heyen, attended SUNY-Brockport. Though it is difficult for people from the working class to rise to eminence, this seems not to be the case for creative writers, whose verbal intelligence attracts the support of teachers, mentors, and college admissions committees. Marge Piercy said in her essay in Lifshin's anthology: "Going to college was a never-ending education in the finer distinctions of class insult and bias. It kept kicking me in the teeth."

The Sun of Chance in Creative Writers

Theme 11: Residence in New York City at Some Point, Especially among the Most Prominent

An odd fact surfaced—many writers had lived for a time either in or near New York City. Although they had grown up all over the nation (and the world), for some reason New York City figured as a domicile for at least a while. Whether this was to put themselves into proximity with the publishing world or for other reasons is not known.

Stories of New York life abound. Poet Louis Simpson, in his autobiography, described meeting "younger writers...whose attitudes were new to me." One night he gave a party. "There was a thin, sallow young man with staring eyes and a puzzling smile, Allen Ginsberg." With him was "a burly fellow with an all-American face, Jack Kerouac. Another named Neil Cassady." Proximity is key in New York City. Simpson attended poetry readings introduced by Stephen Spender, a British poet who was a friend of W. H. Auden's. He became friends with Ginsberg.

This is but one example of the odd but true fact that more than half of the writers I studied had New York City connections for some period of their lives. Professor of creative writing and poet-in-residence at Michigan State University Diane Wakoski said:

> *The very first day I was in New York City, in spite of having just come from a terrible experience personally, in spite of being in a totally new and different (and to many, intimidating) place, in spite of not having any money at all, or any idea of what the future held, I felt as if I were in the most wonderful place in the world. I loved walking the streets of New York...the possibilities of poetry readings, concerts, so many free things.... I was never to feel otherwise in New York, in spite of having to deal with scams...or the poverty I lived with.* (Contemporary Authors Autobiography Series)

Theme 12: The Accident of Place of Birth and of Ethnicity

Of course, the Sun of Chance shines most clearly with our circumstances of birth. Where, into what family, into what community we are born all influence the trajectory of our lives. Regional writers are only "regional" to those of other regions. The environment in which we are born and in which we grow influences us forever. Poet Gary Snyder, in an interview with Bill Moyers for his book on poets, *The Language of Life*, talked of the influence of the giant evergreens in his childhood and, later, on his calling to be a writer: "Right back of our cow pasture there were stumps twelve feet high and twelve feet across, the giant Douglas fir and western hemlock and western red cedar of Puget Sound, and I played among them as a kid." Snyder grew up on a dairy farm and reminisced about his rural childhood, "I became so tuned in and, in a certain sense, radicalized so early that I like to think that the ghosts of those giant trees were whispering to me as a kid, 'Do something about this.'" When Snyder writes about the Pacific Northwest, he is writing about his Sun of Chance.

Some places of birth and growing up have more cachet than others; New York, of course, leads others for being the coolest place, as witness the myriad books, movies, and television shows set in its boroughs and environs.

The Sun of Gender in Creative Writers

Multitudes of anthologies of the works of women writers continue to be published. I was interested in what I would find when I added the men to my 1999 study of women writers. Were there themes specific to the men and not to the women? What were the gender differences? How does the Sun of Gender shine differently—or the same—upon men and upon women?

The classic stereotype that achieving women were tomboys and that artistic men didn't like sports is borne out a little in the childhoods of the writers. However, no clear trends are evident. Even though male writer and gay activist Paul Monette said he had a "ball problem," even describing himself as "crouching in terror" in the outfield when forced into a game of baseball, other male writers such as John Irving excelled in the sports arena. Irving was a wrestler, coached wrestling, and said he had two loves in his academic life: wrestling and writing. John Edgar Wideman coached basketball after playing for the University of Pennsylvania and achieving a Rhodes scholarship at Oxford University. William Heyen played basketball in college as well, and novelist David Foster Wallace played tennis at a semi-professional level.

None of the women were sports achievers as far as I know. Childhood sports simply did not seem to matter as much to the women as to the men. Yet male poets seemed to love baseball, and many played in adult softball leagues. Whereas discussions with male writers, especially poets, invariably veered to a discussion of baseball teams loved in childhood and the related fan activities, discussions with women writers rarely focused on favorite teams. One wonders whether this would change if the subjects grew up after *Title IX*, the federal legislation that mandated equality in sports opportunities for women within the schools.

Personality traits, extracurricular activities, past accomplishments, and practical, tacit knowledge about how to further one's chances of successful entry into a profession also play a large role in whether a talented student writer will go on to show substantial adult performance. Again, remember that within groups of creative professionals, intelligence test scores are not very different. Instead, those who are most creative and productive have large and constant differences in their *personalities* and in their *drive*.

Theme 13: Conflict with Combining Parenthood and Careers in Writing

Like most women creators and women who have careers, the women writers experienced overlapping interferences in their attempts to combine family life with their creative work. Is it the book or the baby? Pam Durban stated: "Anger must be one of motherhood's best-kept secrets. Everyone talked about the intensity of the love I'd feel for my child, and that is certainly real, but no one said something like this: listen, when you have a child and you want to keep writing, you will be so angry sometimes you will not know which way to turn when what you need collides with what he needs."

Durban expressed what many creative women feel, the pull and tear between needing to do their own work and being there for their children. Durban said, "and everything around you and much of what's inside you is screaming that what your child needs is more important than what you need because you're a MOTHER now, and MOTHERS give up things for their children, up to and including everything, even their own lives." But then Durban stated that her writing creates a space for her to vent. "If I did not write, I would be a terrible vengeful mother."

Rebecca West expressed regrets about her inability to combine having family responsibilities and her writing. "I've always found I've had too many family duties to enable me to write enough. I would have written much better and I would have written much more. Oh, men, whatever they may say, don't really have any barrier between them and their craft, and certainly I had." Of course, fellow British writer Virginia Woolf's assertion that a woman writer needs "a room of her own" and an independent income is famous. So is her question, "What if Shakespeare had a sister?"

South African writer Nadine Gordimer's children understood that when they came home and saw her door closed, they must not bother her and must not turn on the radio loud. "My children don't hold it against me," she said.

Gordimer told Jannika Hurwitt in her *Paris Review* interview, "I see all around me women who are gifted and intelligent and who do have these struggles." These are women who complain that they can't do it all. Gordimer said, "I think writers, artists, are very ruthless, and they have to be. It's unpleasant for other people, but I don't know how else we can manage. Because the world will never make a place for you."

When interviewer Barbara Kevles asked Anne Sexton, "Do the responsibilities of wife and mother interfere with your writing?" Sexton replied, "Well, when my children were younger, they interfered all the time. It was just my stubbornness that let me get through with it at all, because here were these young children saying, 'Momma, Momma,' and there I was getting the images, structuring the poem." As her children have become older, Sexton said, they "creep around the house, saying, 'Shh, Mother is writing a poem.'" Her husband was known to say to her, "I can't stand it any longer, you haven't been with me for days." The poem "Eighteen Days" is about her husband's feelings of neglect. Sexton's daughter Linda wrote about her mother's distance and difficulty in being both a mother and a writer in a book called *Private Acts*.

Stories such as these told by the women writers abound. In none of the interviews of male writers was the question asked: How has being a father affected your career as a writer? If the question isn't asked, the answer isn't volunteered. I e-mailed some male writers just to ask them the question and see what they might say. Here is the response of Howard McCord, poet and novelist and head of the Bowling Green State University MFA program in creative writing: "My writing must come second to my family—to my wife, and to my children." Here is a subject for interviewers of the future.

Theme 14: Societal Gender Expectations Incongruent with their Essential Personalities

Ambivalence about the role they play in society did not start with motherhood for many of these women writers. The women had been equivocal about being female long before they became mothers. Some of them did manage to rise above their earliest negative feelings about their gender and writing, and some even found a great advantage in being a female writer, but most struggled with this identity. The theme of androgyny (that is, not being rigid in sex-role behavior—having characteristics of both men and women) seemed key.

It is unusual for men, even men writers, to stay home with the children. The theme of androgyny is heard in an example of one male writer who does. Writer Jon Katz, a stay-at-home writing father who crowned himself "The Prince of Rides," commented that his daughter's friends thought his constant presence as a car pool driver was odd. "Doesn't your daddy work?" one girl asked. His daughter replied, "He's a writer." Katz said, "Real work was something people dressed up and left home to do; sitting in a basement office clacking away at a keyboard all day didn't qualify."

Laura Kalpakian had such ambivalent feelings about being a woman that she titled an essay about her writing life "My Life as a Boy." She grew up not wanting to be a writer but a heroine, a heroine with strong male qualities, a tomboy. But as an adult, she realized that there is no grownup word for tomboy; girls do not become tom-men or tom-women. She said, "My life as a boy began in earnest when I became a single mother. Since then and in order to fend off poverty, I have had to live like a boy." Kalpakian described the time when one of her ex-husband's colleagues called her an authoress. She said, "An authoress is less than an author. Not quite an author. The term is an emasculating diminutive.... An authoress cannot have dash, even on paper, cannot have spirit, even in print, cannot have virility in ink."

Jane Hill summarized the dilemma of being both a woman and a writer when she said that women writers are different from men writers in their self-expectation to do all things well. She stated the conflict as a need in women to be all things to all people, partly as a societal expectation for women to be thoughtful and nice, and partly as a compulsive drive for perfection. "I have this image of all us writers, successes and wannabes and has-beens, lined up in that receiving line at the gates of art." Hill continued, "I see male writers, ones whose work I admire, wearing clothes that look like they've been slept in, without a gift for the host and hostess, trying to break in line or grumbling about having to wait. I see their thinking that their art itself will be enough." But the women writers "are well-groomed, they haven't got hangovers. They hold flowers or books or boxes of candy as gifts…knowing deep within, that *you* have to do it all. You have to, and the thing most likely to suffer, to get shortchanged, is the thing closest to you." What gets shortchanged is "your rebellion, your testing of the constraints built into your psyche and your schedule."

Theme 15: History of Divorce More Prevalent in Women

The Goertzels observed that more literary people had marriages that ended in divorce than others, and more of the writers never married in the first place.

In my study, I found that the women writers got married, got divorced, and many remarried. Others had two marriages and a divorce, and some had been married three times. At least 85% of the women writers had at least one divorce. This is far higher than the figure given for the population at large, which has been estimated at 40%-50%. However, those who remarried or were in primary relationships without benefit of the legal ceremony wrote and spoke about having supportive mates who encouraged their work. Others were single by choice after having divorced, or they had never married. Several were unmarried but in lesbian relationships.

The men seemed to be more committed husbands than the women are were as wives, as only 29% of the men married more than once, which is much better than the current divorce rate of 50% for the population at large. However, several of those male writers who did divorce seemed to have divorced more than once; Norman Mailer was married six times; Saul Bellow five times; Russell Banks, Gary Snyder, and Robert Olen Butler four times; Sam Hamill, Jay McInerney, Arthur Miller, and Robert Kelly three times; and others, more normally, twice. Robert Olen Butler told me that he didn't have childhood trauma, as he had a smooth and lovely childhood, but that his trauma came in adulthood during his several divorces.

Why would the women writers have divorced almost three times as often as men writers? An easy answer could be that the duties and responsibilities of wifehood and motherhood may be so demanding that the passionate writer can't write regularly and faithfully while fulfilling these duties. Another reason may be that the prickly and frank personalities of these women writers do not lead to the patience or docility that wives are traditionally expected to show. The "last wife syndrome" for famous men goes like this: The last wife is often much younger, and she is the one who must be the executor of the famous man's estate and care for his interests throughout the world. Ernest Hemingway's last wife, Mary, and Pablo Picasso's last wife, Jacqueline Roque, are examples. The "last husband" syndrome isn't mentioned, though several famous women artists took up with much younger men near the end of their lives, and these young men fulfilled the "last wife" duties. Georgia O'Keeffe is one example.

Theme 16: Military Service More Prevalent in Men

One theme surfaced in the biographies and interviews of male writers, and that is the influence of being in the military. None of the women had been in the military, but 30% of the men had. These were mostly the older men of the group, those born in the 1930s and 1940s. The subject matter for such writers as Norman Mailer (*The Naked and the Dead*) and Joseph Heller (*Catch-22*) was World War II; and for Tim O'Brien (*Going After Cacciato*) and Yusef Komunyakaa (*Neon Vernacular*), it was the Vietnam War. Profoundly affected by their military experiences, these authors shared the horrors of war with a public that was hungry for a sensitive portrayal of men at war.

Other military experiences were recounted by Sam Hamill, who described his initiation to the Buddhist religion while stationed in the Pacific, and by Tobias Wolff, who wrote a book of short stories about the Vietnam War. Howard McCord's prose has some roots in the Korean War. Robert Olen Butler won a National Book Award for his short stories about the Vietnamese, a language he learned while an intelligence agent in Vietnam. Yusef Komunyakaa is perhaps the best-known poet to have experienced Vietnam. Wolff, Komunyakaa, and Hamill were from the working class, when entering the military was a rite of passage for young men.

However, most of the male writers in my study do not have military experience, perhaps a tribute to the years of relatively peaceful coexistence that we experienced during the past 20 years. Several of the poets—Robert Bly, Allen Ginsberg, and Galway Kinnell among them—became leaders of the anti-war movement during the 1960s. Norman Mailer, in a *Fresh Air* radio interview in October 2002, said that being a Jewish scholarship student at Harvard was a quite a culture shock, but being an enlisted man in the army was the most profound experience of his young life.

These gender themes show how this Sun of Gender in the talent development path has a great influence on the emergence of the writer into adulthood and career success.

In summary, like visual artists, writers write because they must, and because they have talent, and not just because they think it would be fun to be a writer. The high incidence of depression would seem to be an indication of the intense sensitivity with which creative people apprehend, view, and experience the world. It is as if the senses were tuned louder, stronger, higher, and so the task becomes to communicate the experience of both pain and joy. The creative person's products become consumable commodities for the public, but these very products are the stuff of life for the creative person.

Summary
This is what we know about creative writers:

1. Genetic Aspect: They don't often come from families of writers. There is little evidence that writing ability is inherited.

2. Emotional Aspect: They have personality attributes similar to other creators. They also have some personality attributes that stand alone, especially their frankness and forthrightness about social issues.

3. Cognitive Aspect: They have high verbal intelligence and high conceptual intelligence.

4. Passion for the Domain or "Thorn": They have a need to write and often use writing as self-therapy.

5. Sun of Home: Their families are unconventional. They were early readers and tended to use reading as escape.

6. Sun of School: They were often high academic achievers and have won many prizes, especially scholarships to attend prestigious schools and the National Endowment for the Arts Individual Artist Fellowship.

7. Sun of Community and Culture: They often feel like outsiders.

8. Sun of Chance: Many have lived in or near New York for some period of their lives.

9. Sun of Gender: Women writers seem to have more divorces than men. Men have more military service. Women struggle with the "double bind" of having a career as a writer and being a mother.

Chapter 8
Creative Writers: Children with Extraordinary Writing Talent

Sweet aromas fill the stallion's heart
Eyes of blue, hide of white
Glimmering with its sweat
On the run, under burning sun.
As quick as a shimmering, sunny stream.
Panting wildly, wildly panting
Suede rabbit hops in its way.
—nine-year-old girl

Music...the most amazing thing about music is that you can't
describe the tonal quality of a sound. Before you say anything, make
sure you're not giving me any of that scientific stuff about waveforms,
attacks, decays, sustains, and releases. A sound is relative to the ear,
and those words are relative to an idea a computer showed a bunch
of scientists who don't even know how to carry a tune.
—eleven-year-old boy

This chapter continues the study of writers, but with an emphasis on children. Little work has been done on the juvenilia of eminent writers, and in fact, little work has been done on the quality of youthful creative production in most of the arts. In particular, there appears to have been little analysis or study of what makes children's writing good, with the consequence that much excellent work goes unmarked as such. Parents or teachers may say to a youngster, "Oh, that's a very nice poem!" without knowing or appreciating the aspects of the writing that make it truly remarkable. Hence I believe that writing prodigy occurs more frequently than is commonly thought.

The material presented in this chapter comes from two areas of study. The first is my examination of the writings, partially presented here, of seven children: four were selected from 400 students in a Manhattan school for high IQ children where the mean IQ was 140+, and three were brought to my attention by professional writers, parents, or administrators. From these writers, as well as from many years of observations, I have generated 16 characteristics of quality juvenile writing. Secondly, I have studied childhood biographies of well-known adult writers to determine, if possible, the early situational factors that lead to success as an adult writer.

What exactly is a child prodigy? In *Nature's Gambit*, David Feldman asserted that the youthful talents of child prodigies emerge with the "fortuitous convergence of highly specific individual proclivities with specific environmental receptivity." In other words, a child prodigy gets that way through the extremely lucky combination of a very strong inner impulse toward an activity and an environment that is supportive. For his six case studies, Feldman defined "prodigy" as a child of 10 or younger who produced work on the level of an adult professional. A conflicting definition is proposed by Radford in *Child Prodigies and Exceptional Early Achievers*: prodigies may be older than 10, and their achievements need not have "lasting merit." Radford said, "Indeed, if the work of children is always to be measured against the highest adult standards, there would probably be none who could be called prodigies at all." However, *The Random House Dictionary of English Language* defines a prodigy simply as "a child or young person having extraordinary talent or ability."

For Feldman, with his emphasis on environment and the fortuitous, the prodigy phenomenon is obviously more than just an effect of high IQ or of special neurological makeup, as in the case of idiots savants; rather, prodigies are those who manifest high ability in one specialized field of intellectual development. The three disciplines in which prodigies most frequently occur are mathematics, chess, and music. Most prodigies are found in music and in chess, fewer in mathematics, fewer still in art, and very few in writing. Feldman, who studied only one writing prodigy, asserted that:

For the most part, writing is not a domain where prodigious achievement occurs. Serious child writers are uncommon for at least two reasons. The field itself has few organized supports or strategies for instruction in the craft...[and] child writers may be rare because children normally lack the kind of experience, insight, and understanding that writers are expected to convey in their works. (p. 44)

However, my data conflict with Feldman's; there are more children than Feldman thought who write at an adult level of competence. I have come into contact with such children in the course of my work in the schools, as have many of my colleagues, both writers and teachers. The following poem, which was printed at the beginning of this chapter, was written by a nine-year-old girl enrolled in a school for high-IQ children, but her ability far surpassed those of her peers. She graduated from college and went into retail. One day, she saw a writing contest posted on a bulletin board at a nearby university. She entered and won. She liked getting the prize money, but she did not want the economic uncertainty that a writing career promises, and she stayed in retail, managing a store on the Upper West side. She continues her voracious reading.

Sweet aromas fill the stallion's heart
Eyes of blue, hide of white
Glimmering with its sweat
On the run, under burning sun.
As quick as a shimmering, sunny stream.
Panting wildly, wildly panting
Suede rabbit hops in its way.

This poem illustrates unusual linguistic precociousness in the repetition of consonant and vowel sounds (assonance and consonance), the sophisticated rhythms ("Eyes of blue, hide of white"; "On the run, under burning sun"; "Panting wildly, wildly panting"), the improbable images ("suede"). "Sweet aromas" in the horse's heart creates an initial paradox. It is not known, nor logical, that there would be aromas in a horse's heart. This girl pays no attention to the logic. The second line uses the repetitive device of parallel structure to create a rhythm. The third line sets up a visual image that is answered in line five—"Glimmering" and "shimmering." In the fourth line, the letters r, u, and n, are repeated in various melodic combinations: "run," "under," "burning"; then, "run" is resolved into "sun," which is repeated in the next line in an alliterative phrase, "shimmering, sunny stream." The urgency of the reversed phrases in the fifth line, "Panting wildly, wildly panting," keeps the excitement of the poem. Then, when a suede rabbit hops, we can feel the danger inherent in that ordinary situation. The use of the unusual adjective, "Suede," to describe a rabbit is in no way the usual cliché that people come up with when they refer to rabbits.

Such children's writing tends to show certain qualities. The 16 characteristics of quality juvenile writing that I have generated and which I mentioned above are as follows.

Qualities Found in the Writing of Children Who Display Extraordinary Talent

1. The use of paradox.
2. The use of parallel structure.
3. The use of rhythm.
4. The use of visual imagery.
5. Unusual melodic combinations.
6. Unusual use of figures of speech—alliteration, personification, assonance.
7. Confidence with reverse structure.
8. Unusual adjectives and adverbs.
9. A feeling of movement.
10. Uncanny wisdom.
11. Sophisticated syntax—hyphens, parentheses, appositives.
12. Prose lyricism.
13. Displaying a "natural ear" for language.
14. Sense of humor.
15. Philosophical or moral bent.
16. A willingness to "play" with words.

Following are six haikus. Three are by an adult professional, and three are by a child. Can you tell whose is whose? The young poet was featured on an episode of *Nova* called "Child's Play" in 1984 when she was eight years old and in second grade. The adult professional is Bernard Einbond, a professor of literature who won the Japan Airlines Haiku contest over thousands of entries. His haikus below are taken from *The Coming Indoors and Other Poems*.

Treading glory lane
To see it end in flood
Or go up in flame

At day's end, straying
the ocean's edge, tang
salt on my lips.

In the crowded train,
two women seated apart
who must be sisters.

Delectable crumb—
the quickness of a sparrow—
indignant pigeon.

Tides of the ocean long
serving the moon's every whim of
leaving skeletons.

Words without meaning
Rebel without a cause
Constant paradox.

Let's take a few more examples from children in New York City, Ohio, Michigan, and New Jersey. Some of the writings were sent to me, some I discovered, and some were shown to me by teachers, parents, and professional writers. The children were Caucasian, Asian, Hispanic, and African-American, girls and boys, though mostly girls. However, Feldman asserts that "boys have more frequently been identified as prodigies," most likely for reasons of cultural selection and support.

The next poem, by a six-year-old, was given to me by her mother when I did a workshop in New Jersey. The girl wrote it while riding in a car during a rainstorm.

Ripples of Liquid Caterpillars

Ripples of liquid caterpillars
Roll down my window
They travel slowly
Shedding old transparent skins
How sad
They will not stop long enough
To want to see
Their winged reflections
In the sunshine.

This poignant reflection, with its automatic repetitions of the letters i, l, r, s, t, and o, uses a logic that is also paradoxical. Not that they won't see their "winged reflections," but that they will not "want to see" them. And how did caterpillars turn into butterflies in just the length of a rainstorm? The meditative, almost Buddhist, quality of the poem should also not go unnoticed.

Here is another example by the nine-year-old girl who wrote the haikus.

Star Poem

I am picked up by a star
And flung on to Saturn's turning ring
The star begins to throb
And turns bright red.
All the heavenly bodies turn to fire.
They are rejoicing in the birth of a sunset.
The stars toss me into the sunset.
It is a joy,
It contains all the dreams
People will dream tonight.
A sunset is a dream keeper.

The movement in this poem—the flinging, tossing, turning, throbbing, picking up—is immediately evident. The attributing to the star of an ability to pick someone up is a kind of unusual personification. Usually, children's personification takes the form of animals becoming people. The rings and stars and heavenly bodies and sunsets are all in the skies, and evocative of the dream is being portrayed here. The progression from beginning to end of this work, from being picked up by a star, being flung onto a ring of Saturn, being witness to a sunset being born, and then being tossed into that sunset, which paradoxically keeps the dreams of people, is reminiscent of the wisdom of the psalmists.

The next two examples, given to me by a writer from Teachers and Writers Collaborative in New York City, were written by a junior high school boy from a poverty-stricken area in the South Bronx.

Expression

A comedy of errors,
throughout changing time
you live. Die all in one maze
you run, hide still it all ends
the same. Life is an ever changing
play that blossoms and closes
then dies.
Just a comedy of errors,
Forever a comedy.

Sin-Eater

A clear pure soul of simple logic.
You milk the moment,
Taking a deliberate pace of time.
You don't seem to quit as
You pull the trigger.
He's dead. You're glad. It's
over. You touch him.
Blood smears your fingers.
Running crazy, you feel a sharp pain.
It skips through your mind,
You forget. You're in a war.
You're dead. Simple, isn't it?

Again, these poems show a sense of music and rhythm, of heard phrases turned upon themselves in different contexts, of macabre details (common among junior high boys), perhaps a reflection of the circumstances in which the boy finds himself in his neighborhood. But the talent is evident: the line, "clear pure soul of simple logic," stands out as a measured musical phrase. The use of "a deliberate pace" in reference to time, and not to walking, shows that the writer has absorbed and heard the common language and is able to put it into an artistic context. The echo of "a poor player that struts and frets his hour upon the stage" is heard in the writer's "Life is an ever changing/play that blossoms and closes/then dies." Above all, these poems show a natural ear for language that makes this boy's poetry stand out as exceptional in the context of his classmates, whose poems in the anthology are typical of children's poems.

Here is another example by an eight-year-old girl.

Colorful Wildlife

Colorful wildlife is a beautiful violet sun
covering the earth with warm rays.
Wild sweet music all at once.
It is really Phasiphe.
Love, love all around.
Phasiphe Phasiphe Phasiphe
All Phasiphe

This poem was written spontaneously in response to a jar in the Metropolitan Museum of Art. What stands out about it is the repetition of the word "Phasiphe." The child demonstrates a sense of playfulness with an intriguing word. The willingness to play with words and a joy in pure sound is a mark of all writers, especially poets. This girl early shows such a joy—and a fearlessness. She doesn't know what Phasiphe means, but she is willing to ascribe adjectival powers to the word.

Prose Talent

What about prose? Does extraordinary talent exist among child writers of prose? If so, what are the characteristics of such writing? On my first day on the job as a coordinator for gifted programs, a principal came to me with the following composition and asked that most common question: "Do you think this child is gifted?" I did indeed. This reminiscence was written by an eight-year-old girl from a small rural town in Northwest Ohio.

The Dog Who Stayed With Me

Jimmy, me, and Carol were excited today. It was time to meet under my apple tree. We often, after we met, played in the empty house next door (which was for sale), and brought Teddy to play too. It was one Sunday morning, a chilly one, too. We hardly met that day. But we met inside my house instead of under the frozen, cold apple-tree, pale blue frozen sky, cold icicles of sun falling on us. We were very chilly as we instead went into the empty house with Teddy, who was kept overnight by Carol. "Rudy!" Ma yelled at me, "Get away. Here comes the moving truck. I didn't have time to ask questions. I just ran in to get Teddy if dad meant moving in the empty house. Carol said, "Rudy! Look!" A little setter, just a baby, leaped out of the car (behind the moving truck) and ran to my arms. "Why, hello, there!" Carol said, scratching the setter puppy's red-shining back, "Rudy, ball time!" I chattered my teeth, as another sun-icicle fell on my head. The wind furiously blew, and almost knocked the puppy out of my arms. "Come on, puppy!" and I tried to run without jolting the puppy. But I was so cold I couldn't help it. "Rudalas, come!" Dad yelled, and he saw the puppy. "Bring it in, but hurry!" I flung open the door and put the setter down upstairs in my warm bedroom. I ran downstairs, and the puppy followed. I got some meat scraps and a small, low bowl of milk. I teased him and held out the meat. He didn't need teasing, though. He followed me anyway. "Come on, Caboose." I began to call him Caboose. "Little Red Caboose," I often said. He followed me like a caboose and was fed. I went to bed, and below my bed I heard Caboose lapping up the milk and snapping the meat. I fell asleep at last, for Caboose's lullaby of panting was wonderful. His panting was like a lullaby. Next morning was school. I flung up my coat, and caught it. Last of all, I patted Caboose. But every time I turned my back, he whined. He leaped up and followed me. I didn't even know until I entered the school, for the marble-tile on the halls made Caboose's claws go click, click. When I got to school, Mrs. Dainty, my fourth grade teacher, just about died. "Don't you ever bring pets to school without my permission," she said.

This prose piece by an eight-year-old displays remarkable use of syntax. The phrase, "We often, after we met," shows an understanding of grammatical apposition. The use of parentheses "(which was for sale)" and "(behind the moving truck)" is unusual. The use of the hyphen in the words "apple-tree," "red-shining back," and "marble-tile" is unusual. These words may or may not be hyphenated in common usage, and in fact, their hyphenation suggests that the writer has read prose works where the hyphen, the parenthesis, and the use of apposition is common—perhaps nineteenth-century or early twentieth-century novels? The lyricism of the child—"under the frozen, cold apple-tree, pale blue frozen sky, cold icicles of sun falling on us" and "lullaby of panting"—is adult in quality. Many adult professional writers strive for such lyricism, whereas this child, composing this piece after church and before dinner, effortlessly wrote this way. "I chattered my teeth," again suggests that she knows that teeth chatter, but not that they do so by themselves. The "lapping" and "snapping" of the dog show a sense of parallel structure and prose rhyme.

The next prose piece is mature in subject matter and shows a remarkable sophistication. An entire third grade class of verbally talented students wrote novels, but this nine-year-old girl's stood out. When I asked her for permission to use her story in this book, she assented with reservations—she thought this piece was too childish. I disagreed.

Petrova Polinski

Petrova Polinski was a thirty-seven-year-old Russian immigrant to America. She was poor and depressed. She had black hair and eyes and wasn't really short or tall. There were always rings of weariness from hard work under her eyes. Her situation was like that of a tiny weather beaten rowboat in the middle of a raging storm, far from any help. Her pathetic sighs of self-pity made you feel very sorry for her and her family. Now that she, Petrova Polinski, had actually COME to America, she wished she were back in Russia. Everybody back home had said that in America the streets were paved with gold. Instead they were paved with sweat, hard work, and poverty. She hardly spoke her language and didn't read or write it either. She could only pin her hopes of a better life on her children, of whom there were five. She sighed and then her baby cried. Then she sank into a shabby chair with stuffing protruding from beneath the cover and closed her eyes.

The baby wailed again. Suddenly she jumped up and went over to the cupboard, took out the last crust of bread, threw it at the baby and screamed, "THERE! Now eat it!" She walked back to her chair, sank down and began to reflect on her situation again. Why was it that some people, no matter how hard they worked, never had any money? Why was it that people who never worked were so rich? If He (God) was really there, then why didn't He give them a good life? She was beginning not to believe in Him. It wasn't fair. She never had a moment to rest. And why didn't her husband at least DO something?

Then came the voice of her six-year-old daughter, Olga "Mama, Papa's coming home. Let me help you get dinner. Papa'll be hungry."

This story goes on about Petrova and her family, but already in its first few lines, one can see the maturity of the writer in both style and substance. "Her situation was like that of a tiny weather beaten rowboat in the middle of a raging storm, far from any help. Her pathetic sighs of self pity…." And again, in the narrator's wondering about why some people are poor and some are rich, and why hard work doesn't pay, the nine-year-old author is asking questions great novelists have struggled with, from Tolstoy to Roth. This child's work showed the frankness and concern with moral questions that writers are known for, so it was no surprise when she was chosen to be a child reporter during the 1988 Presidential campaign. I turned on my television one Saturday and saw her on national television addressing Dan Quayle: "You mean that if my father raped me and I got pregnant, you wouldn't let me get an abortion?" Quayle sputtered in amazement. She was also several times a finalist in her city's spelling bee.

There is another characteristic of good literature that is most difficult for children—uncanny wisdom—or even "wisdom." This is the quality that we look for in the literature that we read, and this is the reason that we don't give credence to literature by children. What wisdom can children have? Wisdom is acquired by experience. The subject matter of the poems and stories by children is usually childlike. The plots of the stories are predictable, with space ships for the boys and mysteries for the girls. There are monsters and fantasies. The poems are also about the concerns of the children writing them. Maturity is essential in literary quality. No Nobel Prize for literature will, nor should it, go to a child or even a young adult of prodigious talent. But the talent does exist, and sometimes children display wisdom not won by age, as shown by the excerpts from this essay by an 11-year-old boy who was in my writing group. Extraordinary talent in writing shows itself not only in poetry and fiction, but also in nonfiction. His talent as a writer had been recognized by his teachers since second grade. He is a polymath, also a talented composer and musician. He gave this to me, and when I said I wanted to use it in a talk I was giving, he said he had changed his opinions in the meantime, but I was welcome to use it.

Philosophy

If I could put a Bronx cheer on paper, I would. Philosophy is a fake. It's just a bunch of ordinary people capitalizing words and writing theories about things they know nothing about. Sometimes I make up theories. I spend a lot of time with them and play around with them, but I keep forgetting them and they will never get on paper.

Actually, I do remember one faintly, about the universe as a constantly changing picture God wants to frame in his living room. When everybody in the whole universe is doing the right thing, the picture will stop moving, and God will go and buy a frame, and put it upon his wall. If you find this theory interesting, you are probably the kind of person who sits in his or her room and reads German epic poetry.

Music

The most amazing thing about music is that you can't describe the tonal quality of a sound. Before you say anything, make sure you're not giving me any of that scientific stuff about waveforms, attacks, decays, sustains, and releases. A sound is relative to the ear, and those words are relative to an idea a computer showed a bunch of scientists who don't even know how to carry a tune.

Lyrics

Before I tell you anything, I have to tell you something. From where I see it, there are two kinds of writing. The first is the kind I like, which is in fact writing as if you were speaking. The second kind would be prose or verse following a rigid structure, using fancy words and stuff.

Lyrics are the other kind of writing in its extreme form and in verse. I admire good lyricists because I cannot write verse at all, let alone using fancy words. Good lyrics depend on the type of music they are sung to. For example, if I were commissioned to write lyrics for a country or folk tune, I'd write simple-minded lyrics.

Sometimes wonderful lyrics are ruined by the type of music they are sung to: Here's a song everybody knows: "Row, row, row your boat/Gently down the stream,/Merrily, merrily, merrily, merrily/Life is but a dream." Now take a closer look at these lyrics and absorb what they mean. See what I mean? They are beautiful lyrics. It's the music that makes them corny.

Bugs

Bugs are the most annoying things on the face of this earth. Sometimes I think bugs just spend the winter thinking of gross things they can do to me. Once when I was about 5.33333333 1/3, I was walking near my country house or someplace that had a lot of bugs. Without warning, those disgusting tiny green aphids or gnats or something made a beeline for my eyes and I was rubbing them out for the rest of the week. I used to have brown eyes. I'm not kidding. Since God made more insects than humans in this world, we can conclude that He meant for them to be the dominant species. Therefore, I believe that we should honor the bugs by giving them the entire turnip and spinach crop every year.

These writings show not only wisdom, but humor. A sense of humor is one of the marks of the verbally advanced child.

Predictive Behaviors in Children with Writing Talent

What predictive behaviors do children with such talent have in common? I have surveyed adult, published poets and young, unpublished poets about their youth and have found that: (1) they all read a lot; (2) their parents read to them—a lot; (3) they admired words and expression by words. One nine-year-old girl said that writing "is a sometimes better way to express feelings, than words and actions. It also helps me to think logically." (4) They read early. Research on early readers has shown that they have parents who answered their questions, who spent much time reading to them, and who were readers themselves (Roedell, Jackson, & Robinson, 1980). One of the girls, age nine, said that her mother was now reading Shakespeare with her—"the real stuff and not the watered-down stuff."

I have a hunch that further study of the overexcitabilities by Piechowski and his colleagues will show that writers engage the written word with an intensity that is often interactive, almost physical. One example is a young writer in our study of creative adolescents, who spoke out loud to the characters when reading an exciting book. Another example is from Green's *Diary*, in which he described André Gide reading from Sologub. "His voice reminds one of a bird of prey; it suddenly pounces on a word, swoops off with it, and feasts on it. Then he lowers his book and smiles as though he had really eaten something delicious."

Whether these young writers will become well-known novelists, poets, essayists, is impossible to say. Few well-known child prodigies become adult geniuses. Mozart is an exception. The Sun of Chance plays a large part in the flowering of creativity, as well as in the honoring and rewarding of it. It is precisely because we cannot predict which child will be of great benefit to society as an adult artist that we must nurture the potential of all talented children.

Bloom, in *Developing Talent in Young People*, noted that talented children who become successful adult professionals study their field to the point of "automaticity." Musicians practice, athletes practice, mathematicians practice, chess players practice—all to acquire higher and higher levels of performance that becomes automatic. The notion that prodigy springs full-blown without specific practice in the field is false. Idiot savantism may do so, but not prodigy. However, the practice must soon come from interest, engagement, and motivation on the part of the young talented person. Being forced to practice only works until the practice takes hold. This is true in other fields as well: the tennis champion Andre Agassi's father, a tennis coach, insisted that Agassi serve thousands of balls per day, seven days per week. Tiger Woods began to notice and focus on golf while still in his high chair. His parents then put a golf ball in his crib so he could swat at it, developing hand-eye coordination.

Perhaps writers practice the use of words and thus develop automaticity when they are read to and when they read, as well as when they write. Parents often nurture and direct their children in the fields in which the parents themselves have interest and talent. The talented child is then taught by a teacher, who passes on what knowledge he or she can, and then the teacher passes the child to another, more masterful teacher. That is the path of talent development and of prodigy.

On the other hand, some thinkers such as Chomsky, Jung, Roszak, Hillman, and Bloom have postulated that this early mastery in prodigies is a knowledge of form that has come about through intuition, or through archetypal or innate knowledge, or even through reincarnation. In their adolescent years, spontaneity in young writers often gives way to conformity. But as studies from Galton's *Hereditary Genius* in 1869 up to the present have shown, some writers come from "eminent" families who themselves are erudite, extremely literate, and encouraging, or at least tolerant of the voluminous reading these writers did in childhood. It is also true that some writers came from non-erudite families, and in fact, the Goertzels found that only one adult poet who had had a biography written about him had a parent who was a poet. Allen Ginsberg would have been another; Ginsberg's father was the poet Louis Ginsberg, who was also a high school teacher.

In adolescence, potential writers should acquire the knowledge that they need—being "divergent producers," they now become the necessary "convergent producers." Adolescence is a stage of life that all people, creative or not, talented or not, must go through. In youngsters with writing talent, the compulsive reading usually continues, and the study of literary works becomes more formalized as they approach adulthood. Young adult writers become older adult writers, and their wisdom and experience become part of the literature they create. That is the good thing about literary talent. Precocity or prodigy is not necessary for adult achievement, since most literary achievers continue writing throughout their lives, though precocity or prodigy is often predictive, as the biographies of writers tell us.

Bamberger discussed the development of young musicians. She observed a self-conscious stage, a "midlife crisis" through which young musicians must pass if they are to progress from "early prodigiousness to adult artistry." Many factors may enter in, including a dislike of practice, caring too much what others think, and having too many other activities. Csikszentmihalyi, Rathunde, and Whalen noted in *Talented Teens* that students who continued with their talent areas were often not sexually active, did not have part-time jobs, had a small group of friends with the same interests, and did not mind spending time alone. To pass through the crisis of adolescence also requires a regular return to the pleasurable state of trancelike concentration, or " flow," while doing the work. Since reading is the activity that most people mention as producing flow, young writers may not be at such great risk as students in other domains.

Famous Writers as Children

I do not remember when I could not read.
—Benjamin Franklin

There were books in the study, books in the drawing room, books in the cloakroom, books (two deep) in the great bookcase on the landing, books in a bedroom, books piled as high as my shoulder in the cistern attic, books of all kinds reflecting every transient stage of my parents' interest, books readable and unreadable, books suitable for a child and books most emphatically not. Nothing was forbidden me.
—C. S. Lewis

Will these writing talents become manifest as the children reach adulthood? Working backwards, I asked the question: What were famous writers like as children? What was their interaction with the written word? A look at the juvenilia and early life of a sample of prominent writers, using a biographical approach, is illustrative that many prominent writers wrote and read young.

George Eliot
In *George Eliot's Life as Related in her Letters and Journals* (1903), Cross described Eliot's father as a strong, powerful, middle-aged man, sitting in his leather chair with his six-year-old daughter. "The child turns

over the book with pictures that she wishes her father to explain to her—that perhaps she prefers explaining to him." There was little children's literature in their home, but Mary Ann Evans (George Eliot) recalled "her passionate delight and total absorption in *Aesop's Fables*...the possession of which had opened new worlds to her imagination." When she went to school at age eight, "she read everything she could lay hands on, greatly troubling the soul of her mother by the consumption of candles as well as of eyesight in her bedroom." One book had to be returned before she could read it to the end, and she wrote the rest of the story out for herself. This is one example of the delight that young writers take in the act of reading.

Stephen Crane

Stephen Crane began writing as a journalist at the age of 15, writing legibly and fast because the salary of a compositor depended on speed and legibility. Berryman's 1950 biography, *Stephen Crane*, noted that Crane's mother "encouraged the boy's reading with worthy narratives like the Rev. James Dixon's tour of America," while his sister, a schoolteacher, gave him a more "rakish" book called *Sir Wilfred's Seven Flights*. His sister had a great desire to write, and she encouraged him "from his dissertation at eight on *Little Goodie Brighteyes* she followed his stories and verses with pride for four years." Crane devoured Westerns, war books, the Frank series, and other paperbacks. He led his gang in play based on the stories in the books. He only attended college for one year, and Berryman said that the extent and breadth of his reading has been "understated."

Jane Austen

Jane Austen, unlike most children in Georgian England, grew up in a home that placed no restrictions on reading and no restrictions on the subject matters of conversations. Her earliest writings were parodies and satires, and her satirical slant pervaded all of her work later on. Halperin, in his 1986 biography, *The Life of Jane Austen*, counted that her juvenilia total about 90,000 words and that they were written to amuse her younger brother Charles and her older brother Frank, away in the Navy. The juvenilia illustrate that Austen was, even as a young girl, well read. "Richardson was her favourite novelist, and she knew his works intimately, but she read all the fiction she could get her hands on."

Sinclair Lewis

Sinclair Lewis was the son of a doctor in Minnesota. Shorer's 1961 biography, *Sinclair Lewis,* noted that there were about 300 books in the house, including Scott, Dickens, Goethe, Milton, Beattie, Collins, Gray, and Young. These books "formed the boy's earliest literary preferences and the subjects for his reverie." Lewis graduated from grammar school seventeenth in a class of 18; he was a poor speller and a poor hand writer. During his junior year in high school, he started his diaries. By this time, he was an "omnivorous, unsystematic reader." He opened the diary with a list of books, about 50 of them, that he had read during the summer, including Kipling, Thackeray, George Eliot, Victor Hugo, and "trash," as Schorer called it. He read "continually and often guiltily ("Wasted a lot of time reading tonight" is a kind of refrain in the diary during the high school years).

Dylan Thomas

Fitzgibbon, in his 1965 biography, *The Life of Dylan Thomas,* said that Thomas taught himself to read from comic books. When he was four, his father, a schoolteacher, used to read him Shakespeare. Thomas's mother used to tell her husband not to read Shakespeare to a little child, and the elder Thomas would say, "He'll understand it. It'll be just the same as if I were reading ordinary things." His sister said, "He wrote a poem, a most interesting little poem, about the kitchen sink. And then another about an onion. That kind of thing."

Thomas Wolfe

In the biography, *Thomas Wolfe* (1960), Nowell noted that Wolfe attributed his becoming a writer to a great urge within him, nurtured by his father, who was a stonecutter and who had "great respect and veneration for literature." (Once again, observe the prodigy-producing phenomenon of "highly specific individual proclivities with specific environmental receptivity" described by Feldman.) Wolfe's father had a very good memory, reciting such works as Hamlet's soliloquy, Macbeth, Mark Antony's Funeral Oration, Gray's "Elegy." Wolfe was also a great reader as a child. Between the ages of five and 11, he read every book in the public library of their small town.

Virginia Woolf

Virginia Woolf's literary family is well known. When she was a child of nine, she produced a newspaper called *The Hyde Park Gate News,* illustrated by her sister Vanessa. The two Stephens sisters read books aloud to each other and then reviewed the books in the newspaper; with childlike fascination, they included in their reviews the number of deaths in each story. Their reading material included Thackeray, Richardson, Eliot, and most of the Victorian writers. Virginia was avid for praise from her parents; their "Rather clever, I think," overjoyed her. The children produced this newspaper well into their teenage years. But by then, "the charm and fun of the earlier numbers has evaporated. Occasionally a phrase, a joke, a turn of speech anticipates her adult style; but the general impression is rather flat," according to Bell, in his 1972 *Virginia Woolf*. Bell noted that Virginia changed as she entered adolescence—while she continued to write in order to appeal to adults, she became self-conscious and tried to be safe. Later biographical work by Louise DeSalvo on Woolf revealed that she was being sexually abused by her cousins at this time, so her change in style might also reflect this abuse.

Tennessee Williams

Spoto, in his 1985 biography, *The Kindness of Strangers,* noted that Tennessee Williams' mother read stories, plays, acted out tall tales, recited Scottish and English ballads, told stories about folk heroes such as Annie Oakley and Davy Crockett, and sang hymns to her children. Bible tales were told by neighbors. The Black maid sang spirituals, hymns, and lullabies. Williams soon began making up his own stories. He was small and sickly and teased by the children at school, and solitary reading became his refuge. By the time he was nine, he had read at least two of Dickens' books, some of Scott's Waverly novels, and some Shakespeare. A few years later, his mother bought him a typewriter, and he began to write poems, stories, and articles. His junior high school newspaper published many of these. He also contributed to his high school newspaper and yearbook. His grades were average, but he was already entering literary contests.

The Brontë Family

The Brontë family—Emily, Charlotte, and their less famous brother and sister Quentin and Vanessa—created little books that were written beneath magnifying glasses in an invented language known only to them. These long sagas told tales of fantasy, a genre then, as now, of great interest to children. The Brontës all became adult writers of various degrees of success. Their early interest in books and writing seems typical in the lives of writers, as does their early, intense interest in reading. Radford, in his book on prodigies, discussed the early lives of Alexander Pope, Samuel Johnson, Thomas Chatterton, and Daisy Ashford (who wrote a critically acclaimed novel in 1890 at age nine and stopped producing at 13), and their early interaction with books was also apparent.

Harry Crews

The writer Harry Crews, who grew up in a sharecropper family in abject poverty, also interacted with books, but his book was the Sears Roebuck catalog. He would look at the "Wish Book" and make up stories about the "perfect" people there, telling the stories to his cousin. Crews wrote, in an excerpt from his book *A Childhood* in the 1987 anthology, *American Childhoods*, "fabrication became a way of life," and he described how these stories helped him "understand the way we lived" and form "a defense against it." His imaginative life as a child "was no doubt the first step in a life devoted primarily to men and women and children who never lived anywhere but in my imagination. I have found in them infinitely more order and beauty and satisfaction than I ever have in the people who move about me in the real world."

John Updike and C. S. Lewis

Besides a childhood environment filled with books and words, health factors can affect whether a person becomes a writer. The winner of the Pulitzer Prize for 1990's *Rabbit at Rest*, Updike is a prolific novelist, essayist, reviewer, and poet. He was an only child, the son of a high school teacher (it is noteworthy that many creative adults have been the children of teachers) and a writer mother whose typewriter clacking in the living room. Updike as a child suffered from stuttering and psoriasis. Of the influence of the psoriasis on his writing, Updike said in his 1989 memoir, *Self-Consciousness*:

> *Only psoriasis could have taken a very average little boy, and fur-*
> *thermore, a boy who loved the average, the daily, the safely hidden,*
> *and made him into a prolific, adaptable, ruthless-enough writer.*
> *What was my creativity, my relentless need to produce, but a parody*
> *of my skin's embarrassing overproduction? Was not my thick literary*
> *skin, which shrugged off rejection slips and patronizing reviews by*
> *the sheaf, a superior version of my poor vulnerable own, and my*
> *shamelessness on the page a distraction from my real shame?* (p. 75)

The stuttering made him careful of his spoken words, and so he poured his thoughts out on paper. He called his stuttering "this anxious guilty blockage of the throat," and said that despite the impediment, he has "managed to maneuver several millions of words around it."

C.S. Lewis also suffered from a physical disability that he called "extreme manual clumsiness" in his 1955 memoir, *Surprised by Joy*. He wrote:

> *What drove me to write was the extreme manual clumsiness from which I have always suffered. I attribute it to a physical defect, which my brother and I both inherit from our father; we have only one joint in the thumb. The upper joint (that furthest from the nail) is visible, but it is a mere sham; we cannot bend it. But whatever the cause, nature laid on me from birth an utter incapacity to make anything. With pencil and pen I was handy enough…but with a tool or a bat or a gun, a sleeve link or corkscrew, I have always been unteachable.… It was this that forced me to write. I longed to make things, ships, houses, engines. Many sheets of cardboard and pairs of scissors I spoiled, only to turn from my hopeless failures in tears. As a last resource…I was driven to write stories instead; little dreaming to what a world of happiness I was being admitted. You can do more with a castle in a story than with the best cardboard castle that ever stood on a nursery table.* (p. 12)

Another reason that young writers write was pointed out by Updike. He said that it was the thought of his words in print that motivated him. "To be in print was to be saved." Updike, like most young writers, spent "dreamless endless solitary afternoons" reading nineteenth-century novels, books of humor, and mysteries. He did not recall that his reading interfered with his social or academic life, and he graduated president of his small town Pennsylvania high school class with a scholarship to Harvard, even with the stuttering and the psoriasis. Lewis, also, spent "endless rainy afternoons" reading, taking "volume after volume from the shelves. I had always the same certainty of finding a book that was new to me as a man who walks into a field has of finding a new blade of grass."

Graham Greene

Graham Greene's childhood is a good illustration of the high emotionality and strong imagination that incipient writers show. He liked to be sick, and his biographer Norman Sherry, in the 1989 *The Life of Graham Greene*, revealed: "Minor ailments pleased him for they confined him to bed and brought him a sense of peace, endless time, and a night-light burning in his bedroom, a feeling of security." He had fears of darkness, bats, the footsteps of strangers, drowning, and of touching the feathers of birds. All of these appear in his novels. This "sensitivity toward animate and inanimate nature was apparent when Greene was only four years old."

As a child, Greene stayed a loner, though he grew up in a large family with older brothers, younger sisters, and relatives and servants about; he was secretive and kept these terrors a secret. When he was seven, he discovered that he could read. The book was *Dixon Breet, Detective*. He didn't want anyone to know, and so he went to the attic and read the book in secret. His parents were concerned, because he was a late reader and was unwilling to read basal textbooks with their childish approach to reading. But from then on, Greene read "with absorption and intelligence." He read widely and said that one of the advantages of being the headmaster's son was that during holidays, he could read from the many books in the school library.

Greene said that only in childhood does reading have a "powerful influence on people." He recalled "the missed heartbeat, the appalled glee" he experienced when he first read Dracula: "the memory is salt with the taste of blood, for I had picked my lip while reading and it wouldn't stop bleeding." But he said that reading had other importance apart from providing excitement, fear, and escape. "In childhood all books are books of divination, telling us about the future, and like the fortune-teller who sees a long journey in the cards or death by water they influence the future." Greene expressed his belief that early reading has more influence on conduct than any religious teaching, and he said that the books for children in the early twentieth century (he was born in 1904) not only provided adventure and excitement and the strangeness of foreign lands, they instilled standards of heroism, idealism, courage, and self-sacrifice.

At age 10, he moved from prep school to the junior school and realized that the world was not as he had gathered from his reading. While the loss of innocence and childhood illusions is part of the normal process of maturing, in Greene's case, it would seem to be the abruptness of his awakening to reality that was traumatic—and yet, even at an early age, there was a strangeness about him. As a child, Greene invented a language of his own called the "lollabobble dialect." Schoolmates thought he was "very different and perhaps a bit bonkers."

He early demonstrated a great sympathy for people that would make him weep. He was quoted as saying, "I remember the fear I felt that my mother would read us a story about some children who were sent into a forest by a wicked uncle to be murdered, but the murderer repented and left them to die of exposure and afterwards the birds covered their bodies with leaves. I dreaded the story because I was afraid of weeping." His biographer said that this "imaginative sympathy with the predicaments of others helped to make him a novelist." Even until his death in 1991, he would weep at a sad movie.

Greene shed some light on the life of a young boy who is about to become a world-class writer in an essay in the *Spectator* in 1933:

> *Against the background of visits to grandparents, of examinations and lessons and children's parties, the tragic drama of childhood is played, the attempt to understand what is happening, to cut through adult lies, which are not regarded as lies simply because they are spoken to a child, to piece together the scraps of conversation, the hints through open doors, the clues on dressing-tables, to understand. Your whole future is threatened by these lowered voices, these consultations...the quarrels in the neighboring room, but you are told nothing, you are patted on the head and scolded, kissed and lied to and sent to bed.* (p. 22)

Thus it can be seen from these examples that adult writers can be poor spellers, poor hand writers, and just plain poor. It can also be seen that the childhoods of writers helped form their later passions for words.

To recognize which children have the talent shown here and to nurture that talent is essential. Though family interest and encouragement are essential also, perhaps the identification of potential will encourage the families and schools to supply the environments within which the potential can grow. The necessary library cards, the quiet places in which to write, the supportive and not overly evaluative atmosphere, the reading aloud and discussing of literature together (perhaps the turning off of the TV) can all be encouraged by those who discover young children with the potential shown here.

Summary

1. Young talented writers may appear more often than some researchers have shown.

2. This talent seems to occur in all socioeconomic and ethnic groups.

3. There are at least 16 qualities found in the works of talented young writers.

4. A look at the childhoods of writers who became well known as adults shows that they often were early readers, and they read a lot.

5. Talented children often go through a developmental crisis in adolescence as they move into formal operations.

Chapter 9
Creative Scientists, Mathematicians, Inventors, and Entrepreneurs

I still can't get over it that you can sit at your desk and noodle around with equations and try out ideas and put together physical principles that may or may not be right, and every once in a while, you can say something about the real world. You can predict the result of an experiment, or a new particle, or say something about the forces of nature or about the way the universe evolves—and all out of pure thought.
—Steven Weinberg

There he is, immortalized in many teenage movies—the nerd. His shirt pocket lined with a plastic pen holder, glasses held with an elastic band around the back of his head, his high-water pants and clumsy shoes, his plaid shirt, his floppy leather belt clasped just below his breast, the shock of red hair, and with an earnest gaze through thick glasses, he is a whiz at math or science or computers. But the last thing a teen—even one who is academically talented—wants is to be called is a nerd. Often, such students opt out of the special program for academically talented students just to avoid the stereotype.

The Genetic Aspect in Scientists and Mathematicians

There is some evidence about genetic propensity for science, mathematics, invention, or entrepreneurship. Some children follow in their parents' footsteps. The Darwin family—Erasmus, Sir George Howard,

Francis Galton, Sir Francis Darwin, Sir Horace Darwin, George Galton Darwin, Josiah Wedgewood, and Thomas Wedgewood—are certainly an example. The Huxleys—Sir Andrew Fielding Huxley, who won the Nobel Prize; Sir Julian Huxley, biologist; and Aldous Huxley, a novelist who wrote science fiction, most notably *Brave New World*—is another example.

The Emotional Aspect: Personalities of Scientists and Mathematicians

Fortunately, many of the psychologists who have studied the personalities of creative people have focused on scientists, and many studies have used both tests and a biographical approach. We now know much about the personalities of scientists. The personality attributes on the bottom of the Piirto Pyramid (see Figure 5.1 in Chapter 5) are present in scientists, and they are found in mathematicians, inventors, and entrepreneurs as well. Cattell and Drevdahl, in their research using the *16 Personality Factors Questionnaire* (16 PF), found that creative scientists had personalities similar to artists and writers, with one difference—the scientists had more emotional stability than artists and writers.

Self-Discipline and Productivity

Simonton, in *Scientific Genius*, held that on one personality dimension, all creative scientists are alike. They are devoted to their work; their motivation differentiates them from others. And if someone is devoted to his or her life's work, huge productivity is more likely. Simonton said, "Darwin could claim 119 publications at the close of his career; Einstein 248; and, in psychology, Galton, 227; Binet, 277; James, 307; Freud, 330; and Maslow, 165." Edison may be best known for his incandescent light bulb and phonograph, but all told, he held 1,093 patents—still the record of the United States Patent Office.

However, it would seem that all creative people are devoted to work, not just scientists, as we have seen already with visual artists and writers, and as we shall see with musicians, actors, and dancers. Piechowski once told me that in his view, the idea of scientific productivity as being a mark of genius may be particularly American: "productivity may be a byproduct of genius but is not its fundamental characteristic."

Simonton's data led him to conclude that scientific productivity has an age curve, beginning in the scientists' twenties and reaching its highest point in the late thirties or early forties, then tapering off. Botanists and disease specialists are most productive in their early thirties. Bacteriologists, physiologists, pathologists, and general medical scientists are most productive in their late thirties. Chemists peak in their late twenties.

Mathematicians and physicists peak in their early thirties. Geologists and astronomers reach their peak productivity in their late thirties. If theoretical mathematicians and physicists have not made their contributions by the time they are in their late twenties, will probably never do so. Putting these age constraints on scientists' peaks of productivity is frightening to some people, but Simonton derived these numbers from statistical analyses of the lives of scientists. Individual cases differ. Simonton further wrote that this characteristic of early productivity holds true for other creative people as well, including artists, writers, and musicians. He said that producing early predicts that one will produce later on as well. This is true for all domains of creativity.

Those who begin their productivity early often continue producing. They refuse to acknowledge retirement, and they retain their enthusiasm for scientific research, as well as the publication of their research, much later than less creative scientists. They are more likely to have their careers ended by illness or death than by a lack of ideas. It is often said in the halls of academe that those who publish more also publish the most high-quality papers, just as those who submit the most grant proposals get the most grants. In other words, quantity is needed for success and recognition. Simonton called this the "constant-probability-of-success model," and it also applies to the careers of those in literature and in music. Often, the creator cannot choose which idea, which composition is the best one among all the others being created. But if one continues to produce, something is bound to "hit."

Motivation—Volition

As in any field, one has to want to be creative. You don't solve a problem unless you spend a lot of time on it. Nothing comes easily, and creators in the science and mathematics domains work very hard and have a will to succeed. Picture the scientist or the mathematician obsessed with a problem, distracted and distant while the mind spins around in haunting and tantalizing whorls to find an answer, a path, a road to take that will produce meaning. Family members, friends, and colleagues see the distracted, absent-mindedness of the thinker. Not one problem but many surface and submerge. The daily walk, the silent house, the necessity for solitude in order to think permeate the practice of science and mathematics. But underneath it all is will—volition—motivation to do the work. The concept of the think tank resonates here. The existence of such centers as that at Princeton, where mathematicians and scientists are invited to go just to think, as illustrated in the movie *A Beautiful Mind*, seems ideal.

The Cognitive Aspect: Intelligence of Scientists and Mathematicians

People who are good in mathematics and science have what Gardner calls "logical-mathematical intelligence," one of his eight frames of mind. The development of logical-mathematical intelligence seems to be what Piaget had in mind when he traced childhood development from sensory-motor to pre-operational to concrete to formal operational stages. People who are academically talented in mathematics have certain abilities that seem to make up what Krutetskii, a Russian researcher into mathematical ability, called a "mathematical cast of mind."

Gardner said that these mathematically inclined individuals have: (1) a good memory for mathematics and science, have the ability to solve problems in their heads, and often can intuitively skip steps to come up with the right answers; (2) the ability to perceive a process of mathematical reasoning and to recreate it; (3) the ability to make new problems and solve them. The ability to be creative in mathematics is, Gardner said, the ability to work with rigor and skepticism. Mathematicians don't accept facts that have not been proven step by step in proofs that have been established universally.

Scientists use mathematics as a tool. While mathematicians find joy and fulfillment in the beauty of mathematics for its own sake or the elegance of the proof, scientists find joy and fulfillment in considering the true nature of physical reality. Scientists want to unlock the secrets of nature and are motivated by their beliefs in underlying universal themes or patterns in nature. Theoretical physicist Richard Feynman said that humans' ability to reason is sorely tested when they try to understand how nature works. The scientist must have an ability to work with delicate chicanery and to walk a thin line of logic so that one doesn't make an error in prediction.

Gardner went so far as to say that science is akin to religion, as it involves an array of beliefs that one must adhere to with devoted zealotry. Scientists, equipped with mathematics, observational powers, and technical knowledge, are often motivated by the hope or even mystical conviction that their beliefs will be proven to be right as they perform their experiments on the physical world. These interests emerge when children are quite young, so talent for mathematics and science can be discovered early.

Cognitive Insight in Scientists and Mathematicians

Besides having optimal family, school, community, gender, and chance factors, as well as having the personality attributes and the intellectual abilities, it is necessary for thinkers in these fields to produce insights as part of their creative processes. Studies by psychologists have been collected by Sternberg and Davidson. An essay by Seifert and her colleagues described several types of insight. They called one perspective the "Wizard Merlin" perspective, which described the leaps made by such thinkers as theoretical physicist Richard Feynman. Gleick, in his biography of Feynman, told of how Feynman's process of problem solving was described by his friend Murry Gell-Mann: "You write down the problem. You think very hard. [Gell-Mann shuts his eyes and presses his knuckles periodically to his forehead.] Then you write down the answer."

Another type of insight described by the Seifert group was "The Prepared-Mind" perspective on scientific and mathematical insight. This follows the four steps that Wallas wrote about in 1926. Insight is information processing. First there is the mental preparation. Second is the incubation. Third is the illumination. Fourth is the verification. Insight comes during the first and second phases. It can be helped by study and knowledge. When a person reaches an impasse or comes to a dead end, he or she is forced to consider all possible information stored in memory. During the "down time" of incubation, an accidental stimulus might occur which leads the person to reconsider the path taken.

Descriptions of the incubation phase often use such words as "subconscious," "unconscious," "spontaneous," and "unexpected" to describe the appearance of the insight. Psychological research has begun to show that these insights may not be so unexpected. Even Feynman, the genius-wizard-magician, received his insights as a result of accidental encounters with a previously forgotten aspect of the problem. Gleick described how Feynman gained insight into a complex physics problem after a colleague mentioned that one type of particle rather than another might be crucial to the interaction he was trying to decipher.

Associative Richness

In *Origins of Genius*, Simonton described "associative richness" or, as William James described it, "abrupt cross-cuts and transitions from one idea to another…rarefied abstractions and discriminations…unheard of combination of elements…subtlest associations of analogy" (p. 218). These combine in a "seething cauldron of ideas, where everything is fizzling and bobbling about in a state of bewildering activity…where the unexpected seems only law." These prolific connections have been documented by such tests as the Remote Associates Test and have been noted by many who speak of the creative process.

Cognitive Imagery

The biographical examples of mental visual imagery in scientists have been commonly referred to in the creativity literature. The most common example is Kekulé imagining the structure of benzine from a dream he had of a writhing snake grasping its own tail. Darwin's use of the metaphor of the "tree of life," Poincaré's reference to "dancing" atoms, and other formings of guiding images are also examples. Dreams as inspiration in the creative process often provide such images.

Threshold of Intelligence Needed to Do Science and Mathematics

Why did Einstein and Teller choose science as opposed to mathematics? Is there some disposition of personality toward one or the other? Research reported by Tannenbaum and Bloom has found that young mathematicians and young scientists do differ, but that both need a certain threshold of general intelligence. According to Tannenbaum, "After the scientist's first job, IQ influences positional recognition directly; regardless of first job prestige, educational background, and scholarly performance." Simonton said that people in the physical sciences have the highest IQs, with physics Ph.D.s having IQs of about 140. People in the biological sciences have "somewhat less Olympian minds," and those in the social sciences are even lower in IQ. Simonton said that merely learning what is essential in the physical sciences requires high intelligence. For instance, Einstein's field, theoretical physics, requires more basic intelligence than Freud's field of psychoanalysis.

You may be feeling a little intimidated right about now, whether you know your IQ or not. You may believe that you have been predestined to achieve according to your IQ. But remember that Simonton didn't say which IQ test was used, nor what it measured; also, as we shall see later, the IQ scores of innovative inventors were not always unusually high. IQ tests were made by scientists for scientists. Do not ascribe mystical properties to pencil and paper tests.

Young mathematicians also display their talent early, and in addition to high IQs, they also have high spatial visualization ability and high verbal ability. Krutetskii studied 200 children and found that the able and very able students had six characteristics that surfaced early. These were: (1) the ability to grasp the structure of a problem, separating extraneous information from essential information; (2) the ability to easily find abstract principles within problems; (3) the ability to skip steps in the process of solving problems and still come out with the right answer; (4) the ability to appreciate elegant mathematical solutions; (5) the ability to be flexible and to solve the same problem in many ways; and (6) the ability to remember essential features of problems, even many months later. For the latter, a young mathematician might exclaim in the middle of a solution, "Oh, we had this problem last summer!"

Krutetskii also found that mathematical talent comes in four varieties: the analytic, the geometric, and two types of harmonic abilities. Young mathematicians with analytic talent have strong verbal-logical abilities and weak spatial abilities. Those with geometric talent have strong spatial visualization abilities and weak verbal-logical abilities. Both types of harmonic ability math students have strong verbal, logical, and spatial visualization ability. Krutetskii emphasized that the ability to calculate is not a prerequisite for strong mathematical talent. However, analytic ability is a prerequisite, for mathematics requires the ability to think abstractly.

Young scientists also showed early differences, according to specialty, with biologists preferring hobbies and books related to nature. For example, a plant geneticist I know had his own gardens in his family's backyard from an early age. Young physical scientists often like to work with mechanical toys and gadgets, and young social scientists are often spellbound readers. Tannenbaum said that scientists had "an early and persistent interest in science." Science students were interested in the causes of things, were daydreamers, liked to solve mental puzzles, and liked art that was symbolic and music that had classical structures. They liked to read science books, to build models, and to take walks in nature.

Often solitary, their interests in high school tended to emphasize science clubs, science experiments, and they liked to solve scientific problems.

Science teachers often had great influence on them. Brandwein studied about 1,000 New York City high school science students and found that they had high IQs, were predisposed to like science, and had teachers who inspired them. These teachers themselves were science achievers, active professionals in their learned societies, active also in curriculum writing, and they had hobbies associated with science, such as memberships in hiking clubs or bird-watching societies.

The Domain Thorn: Passion for Science and Mathematics

Predictive behaviors for science and mathematics reveal both the talent for doing the work and the passion to continue doing it. What have psychologists and biographers discovered about creative scientists and mathematicians? While young scientists may be conforming and self-disciplined, they also have been found early on to incorporate their science interest into their play. As children, they had collections of rocks, insects, spiders, and the like; they had a parent, a relative, a family friend, or a teacher who encouraged them and who talked to them about their interests; and they had a sense of wonder about nature and its manifestations. A case in point is the description of early family fun by Jonathan Weiner, a science writer, who told a story about making a computer from Dixie cups with his father and brother. He said, "I still recall our delight as we sat around the kitchen table and watched the Dixie cup computer making better and better moves until by the end of the evening it trounced us every time. (Evenings like this are not for everyone)."

One mother, a student of mine with a son completing his Ph.D. in mathematics, commented that even early on, he was fascinated by numbers. A family photo showed him at the age of three, perched on the fireplace shelf reading the telephone book.

As another example of passion for numbers, at the age of three, a colleague was put on exhibit by his father to his father's friends, counting backwards from 100 by threes. This same young man mastered calculus on his own at age 13 while taking advanced algebra in his Long Island high school. However, at about the same time, he began listening to his father's classical music records, playing certain symphonies over and over again. The mathematics of music began to appeal to his passions more than the mathematics of mathematics, and he became a composer instead of a mathematician. He has the ability to do mathematics, but not the fervor. His ardent love for a domain is for the domain of music. This example illustrates that one must want to do the work; talent is necessary but not sufficient. This individual now feeds his mathematical talent by teaching creative problem solving in our summer institute, using the master's degree in mathematics that he acquired along the way. It serves as anecdotal evidence of what larger studies have found; a passion is born early and is fed by interests related to the passion.

Sun of Home in Scientists and Mathematicians

What about the Sun of Home in scientists' and mathematicians' life paths? Creative scientists and mathematicians seem to have had more stable homes than artists, especially writers. Birth order is also important. First-borns make up more than half of active scientists. (This figure includes only children, who are somewhat different from first-borns.) The reasons for the achievement of only children and first-borns are obvious: the child is exposed to exclusive adult care, whereas subsequent children or close-in-age siblings have to deal with a more complex family environment from the moment of birth. Of the second-borns and other younger siblings, there is more of a chance to achieve scientifically if the birth order is spaced at about five years between children.

Later-born children who have lost an older sibling are also more likely to achieve creatively than those who have intact families. The research on the achievement of first-borns often makes middle children angry, for they achieve also. Sulloway published extensive research on birth order, saying that the last-borns are the rebels, and they are the ones who often do the groundbreaking scientific work. He used Darwin and many other scientists and revolutionaries as his examples.

The Sun of Home in Einstein and Teller

The childhoods of Albert Einstein and scientist Edward Teller were remarkably similar. Einstein was born in 1879 in Germany and grew up there, and Teller, born in 1908, grew up in Hungary. Like Einstein, Teller was thought at first to be mentally slow. Einstein did not speak well until about age six, and Teller did not speak until about age three. However, by the age of four, "The words gushed forth in polysyllables, understandable phrases, complete sentences," according to biographers Blumberg and Panos.

Before age six, Teller showed his precocity in mathematics by putting himself to sleep with multiplication problems, asking himself the number of seconds in a minute, hour, day, week, and year. However, a few years later, he was bored in math class: "His keen interest in mathematics had propelled him into the realm of basic algebra, and he was so far ahead of the class that he seemed apathetic." His grade school teacher ignored him when he tried to answer questions, for Teller was so advanced that the teacher assumed that he was repeating the class and hence knew all of the answers. Similarly, Einstein was demonstrating precocity in mathematics by the age of nine.

Both boys were interested in other subjects as well. Both were readers, Teller especially liking Jules Verne's science fiction. Both began musical instruction at age six; Einstein studied the violin and Teller the piano. Before long, Teller was playing so well that his mother, a talented musician, had hopes that he would become a concert pianist. As a young teen, he would often become "engrossed for hours at time in the sonatas and fugues of Bach, Beethoven, and Mozart." Interestingly, Einstein was roughly the same age, 14, when he discovered the mathematical structure of music through the works of Mozart. And at 14, Teller was plunging into Einstein's book on relativity.

It is an odd fact that there were several other eminent Hungarians who grew up along the same river valley in Hungary at the same time, an era of political unrest. These boys didn't know each other then, and later, when they met, they joked that they must have come from Mars. Other mathematicians and scientists from the same region were these—Eugene Wigner, a 1963 Nobel Laureate; Leo Szilard, who in 1942 with Fermi produced the world's first controlled nuclear reaction; Theodor Von Karmann, an aeronautical engineer; and John Von Neumann, considered one of the finest mathematicians in the world. All of these men as boys came from families that were close, that valued education, and that provided a stimulating intellectual atmosphere in the home.

Both Teller and Einstein had the fortunate influence of a university mentor. Teller's father feared that his love of mathematics would lead him to be a poorly paid and low-status mathematics teacher. However, he contacted a mathematics instructor at the University, Leopold Klug, who appraised Teller's aptitude for mathematics. Klug brought Edward a copy of Euler's *Geometry* and discussed the book with him. After several visits, Klug told Teller's father, "Your son is exceptional." For Edward, the meetings were inspirational, and he began to want to emulate Klug.

Einstein's parents took in a boarder, Max Talmey, a medical student. Talmey called the Einstein home "happy, comfortable, and cheerful" and wrote a book on his impressions of the 12-year-old Einstein. Talmey gave the child Bernstein's books on physical science, Buchner's *Force and Matter*, and Spieker's *Geometry*, a textbook. Talmey said that the young Einstein quickly finished the books and then began studying higher mathematics. "Soon the flight of his mathematical genius was so high that I could no longer follow." Then the two began to discuss philosophy, and Talmey introduced the young Einstein to Kant. "At that time he was still a child, only thirteen years old, yet Kant's works, incomprehensible to ordinary mortals, seemed to be clear to him."

Teller often helped his older sister with her mathematics homework; Einstein did likewise with his younger sister. Both men stayed extremely close to their sisters throughout their lives. Both boys wanted to be physicists, but their fathers were afraid that they wouldn't be able to make a living, and so they were persuaded to enroll in engineering school. Both were from Jewish backgrounds that were not particularly religious. Both fled the Nazis to come to the United States during World War II. And both young men, strong in mathematics, chose to become theoretical physicists.

Niels Bohr and Viktor Weisskopf had similar childhoods. As a child, Weisskopf's mother insisted that he take lessons and participate in musical groups. As a teenager, he was strongly attracted to music, but "in the end, science won." He said, "My father had wanted me to be something practical, like an engineer, but I knew that I wanted to work in physics." Bohr's father was a professor of physiology, and his mother came from a wealthy Jewish family. This highly cultured childhood led him to follow his father's footsteps and become a professor himself.

Three theoretical physicists born in the U.S., Richard Feynman and the Oppenheimer brothers, had similar backgrounds as well: an early interest and precocity in mathematics; the influence of a practical father who spent time with his son discussing science and mathematics; an obsession with the meaning of life in the cosmos; the strong "suns" of family and of school; the connections to important mentors; the early publication of their research; and a continued trajectory toward eminence, as the Zeitgeist needed their contributions and talents because of the world war.

Other Home Factors

According to Anne Roe, the personal problems of young scientists like these include the following: (1) the lack of in-groups, or groups where they will be accepted; (2) the conflict between students' values and family values, if parents and siblings devalue science; (3) the development of verbal abilities in the early grades; and (4) the attitudes of the schools, where teachers often dismiss their "off-the-wall" and non-conforming ideas. These problems are similar to those that any creative young person suffers.

Researchers have found that scientists and mathematicians more often come from stable homes with stronger positive father influences than do other creative types. Another positive benefit is that the parents of the scientific achievers allowed the child to be present when adults were around and to interact with these adults. SMPY and the University of Iowa studies have yielded information about young highly talented math students. Even at age 13, these students resembled adult mathematicians in their values and career interests. The studies showed that they were highly theoretical and had a great interest and much background knowledge about careers in math and science. In high school, they had strength of personality enough to fend off the social challenges caused by their high ability.

Verbally talented students have more trouble and are less popular. The mathematically talented youth are more outgoing, mature, and independent. They come from small families with well-educated parents who are often professionals. Their parents are often older and very child-oriented. Few of the families experience divorce. The family as a whole comes together to support the mathematical or science talent of the precocious child. Toys are often educational, such as building sets, puzzles, and many books.

Sun of School in Scientists and Mathematicians

As they go into high school, these young people often skip grades, and they take the most challenging courses. Their favorite courses are in mathematics and science. Schooling is important for scientists and mathematicians because in order to be recognized later as contributors to their fields within the domains of science and mathematics, they must study to obtain a Ph.D. and go beyond to the post-doctorate level.

The largest numbers of people obtaining Ph.D.s in the U.S. in 2001 were scientists and engineers. Of 40,744 doctoral degrees awarded, engineering accounted for 5,502 (75% males); life sciences had 8,296 (53% males); physical sciences had 5,970 (75% males). The median age for obtaining a Ph.D. in life sciences was 31.8; for physical sciences, it was 30.6. By contrast, the median age for people to obtain Ph.D.s in education was 43.8. To go to school so long requires a conforming demeanor, even though it might hide a rebellious, creative soul.

One strategy for educating talented mathematicians is rapid progression through their coursework. Researchers who have worked with the top 1% of math talent through the Study of Mathematically Precocious Youth, especially Stanley, Benbow, and Lubinski, have advocated acceleration of these talented students (that is, permitting them to take higher level courses or even skip high school). This has been shown to be a strategy that is quite beneficial. The researchers assert that not permitting highly talented math and science students to accelerate at a pace that matches their intellect could be called "educational malpractice."

School behaviors predictive of mathematical talent are that the student may volunteer to collect money, run for treasurer of a club or class, do the statistics for the sports teams, or appear at the door of the math teacher just to talk about a certain intriguing problem. The mathematically talented student may also join the math club. For example, Richard Feynman won statewide awards in mathematics in high school. Challenger Astronaut Judith Resnik appeared in her yearbook from Firestone High School in Akron, Ohio as the only female member of the math club. Her Advanced Placement Calculus teacher saved her papers as models of excellence for other students. She was the valedictorian of her class.

School behaviors that can predict future scientists are similar: they have collections of flora, fauna, baseball cards, and such. Some say such collections indicate the obsessive-compulsive nature necessary to scientific categorization. They like to read, but usually not fiction except for science fiction, and not poetry. They are conformist enough to school rules and policies so that they can do the course-taking necessary to gain college degrees, continuing through the Ph.D. They have a breadth of interests and often know quite a bit about many odd things. They join science clubs.

Vera John-Steiner said that young scientists often have "informal apprenticeships of the mind." These function as a type of mentorship. For example, Einstein hated the discipline of the secondary school and instead turned to reading and thinking and talking with people such as his uncle Jakob, a sound engineer who played algebraic games with his young nephew and who made mathematics fun. Uncle Jakob called x, "a little animal whose name we don't know," according to Clark, Einstein's biographer.

Choice of college is extremely important to potential scientists and mathematicians. If the student attends a college that is not elite, not demanding, that is located in a backwater away from major action, chances are slight that the young scientist will make major achievements in science. This is important, and it illustrates that academic and college counseling for scientifically talented students is essential. How much education is enough for scientific creativity? The attainment of the Ph.D. at a young age is almost *de rigeur*, although many of the scientifically creative made their contributions before they attained their Ph.D.s, including Einstein.

If the student qualifies to get into a highly competitive college and does not go because of finances, counselors should be aware that admission is the important thing and that the finances will follow once admission is achieved. The influence of the right school, the right mentor, the right environment for the nurturing of scientific creativity is crucial, and such placement should be a priority of school counselors, who should help these talented students to seek scholarships at competitive institutions. Many worthy students from rural areas are deterred by the myth that they can't afford a competitive college, but frequently, where there's a will, there's a way. Students who want individual attention as undergraduates could attend a smaller liberal arts institution that specializes in placing its talented science and math students into major graduate schools. This option would get the student instruction and laboratory time from a professor and not a teaching fellow.

Teachers should emphasize inquiry learning rather than rote learning, should encourage independent reading and study, and should recognize the importance of self-instruction. Perhaps the reason that both Einstein and Darwin disclaimed the influence of formal education in their lives was that lecture was the primary method of discourse in German gymnasiums and British public schools. Most creative people speak of their schooling negatively, but they speak of their self-taught learning positively.

Mentors

Subotnik and her colleagues, in studying Westinghouse Science Talent Search winners, found that the mentor is extremely crucial to the full development of scientific talent. To be recognized and selected by a mentor is essential to the young scientist who seeks to compete in the top echelon of scientists. The young scientist must be both deferential and unafraid to challenge the mentor in dialogue and analysis. In science, an apprenticeship, which is a form of role-modeling, is necessary.

For example, Nobel Prize winners have studied under other Nobel Prize winners (and sometimes married their daughters). Doing so enhances the opportunities of winning the prize. Simonton said that the scientist mentor should be about 20 years older, but never less than 10 years older. The mentor should still be in the "intuitive" stage of creativity, not in the "analytic" stage that comes in later years. Instructive as the role model is, however, there is a danger if the student becomes too imitative of the mentor and does not strike out on his or her own.

Sun of Community and Culture in Scientists and Mathematicians

Another social institution has less of an influence than school and family, and that is the religious institution. The role of formal religion in the lives of scientists is often minimal. The least scientists and mathematicians can say is that they don't object to religion, though very few scientists have come from dogmatic, fundamentalist, rules-filled denominations. While most scientists are seeking the meaning of nature in their own disciplines and fields, they often reject or pay minimal lip service to institutionalized religions in order to carry on their scientific inquiries. The intellect of young scientists and mathematicians often rejects easy answers and doctrine. Recent, passionate debates about creationism in various state legislatures have been greeted by scientists and mathematicians with disdain.

Feynman's comment in *The Meaning of It All* illustrates: "I do not believe that the scientist can have the same certainty of faith that very deeply religious people have. The uncertainty that is necessary in order to appreciate nature is not easily correlated with the feeling of certainty in faith, usually associated with deep religious belief" (p. 113).

The Influence of the Zeitgeist

The researchers and thinkers about creativity also postulate that certain times and places are better, historically, for scientific or other creativity. Simonton noted, for example, that great advances in biological knowledge take place the generation after advances in medicine, chemistry, and geology. Politically, a sense of nationalism enhances creative production, while large empires do not. By one generation after the overthrow of an empire, though, scientific creativity is on the upswing. This is because diversity increases the number of ingredients or ideas that go into scientific discovery. However, great upheaval, such as that found in the Middle East or in Africa, with revolts, shootings, rebellions, and terrorist activities, do not produce the climate for scientific innovation.

Some say that the best proof of the power of the Zeitgeist is when multiple inventions happen—when two or more scientists come up with the same invention or creation. Simonton cited the near-simultaneous invention of calculus by Newton and by Leibniz, and the manufacture of oxygen by Priestley and Scheele; Gruber discussed the proposing of the theory of evolution by both Wallace and Darwin. However, in 1999, Simonton noted that if this were true, all of the characteristics, attributes, and situational factors that lead to creative genius and creative production would be false. He explicated a Darwinian theory of creative genius that goes beyond the small units of information, or memes, within the brain, saying that "The Zeitgeist helps provide the necessary conditions." Small units of information combine into new variations of ideas. The ideas are spread about, disseminated, and eventually gain acceptance. "The creative genius does the rest."

Csikszentmihalyi, in 1988, said, "We cannot study creativity by isolating individuals and their works from the social and historical milieu in which their actions are carried out." Gardner, in a 1993 case study of Freud's career as a creative person, argued that Freud's work could not have been done without the milieu of Vienna at that time in history, the early twentieth century. Likewise, the period of the Renaissance in Florence is often cited as being especially fertile for creativity. Simonton argued, though, that in all cases, one of the discoveries is always more completely designed and described than the others that come during the same time period. For instance, many people tried to invent photography, but only one came upon the daguerreotype, scene designer Louis Daguerre, in 1826.

The production of multiples by scientists working separately is often used to suggest that the arts demand a higher level of creativity, for the artistic product cannot be duplicated. Simonton demurred: "Of course, Beethoven's Fifth Symphony was created just once. Yet, by the same token, only Darwin wrote *The Origin of Species* and probably was the only scientist who could have done so." There is only one Michelangelo, and only he could have created the particular ceiling of the Sistine Chapel loved by millions. There was only one Faulkner, and only Faulkner could have created his particular Yoknapatawpha County. There was only one Einstein who could meld the theories of his predecessors into coherence. These works of creativity would not exist if their creators had not existed. Some other works of creativity would have existed. Did the world need a ceiling, a county, four notes that resonated throughout ensuing history? We have these marvelous creations because of the inner visions and even inner needs of their creators.

Creativity in the Sciences as Different from that in the Arts

Weisskopf ruminated on the difference in creativity between the arts and the sciences. "In art it is impossible to separate form from content, whereas it is often pedagogically useful in science." In science, the work of many people contributes to "a single edifice" which is called "the scientific worldview." While art also grows out of cultural and historical trends, art stands alone. Feynman said that the scientific imagination is different from the artistic imagination—that is, in science, we definitely know more than we did 100 years ago. In art, a work produced 100 years ago is as valuable as work produced today. Its value may even be greatly increased. A tendency toward more refinement exists in both art and science. Newton would admit that Einstein advanced his theories. The presence of the power of the idea is crucial. Weisskopf said that in science, more complexity of ideas is needed. "The increased sophistication of art may lead to a wider scope of subject matter and a greater variety of creative forms, but hardly to more powerful forces of artistic expression."

The world needed a polio vaccine, a phonograph, a steam engine, a theory of evolution. The world needed geometry, calculus, and quantum theory and computers. The world needed space travel and will need time travel. Scientific creativity has invented these when they were needed. Buckminster Fuller's timeline of inventions in *Critical Path* is a case in point. He showed the rapid acceleration of inventions and their impingement on world history, using his own life span as an example.

Fuller said that there is a lag of 22 years between an invention and public use of that invention, and that is why we are on a "critical" path. In his last book, *Grunch of Giants*, Fuller advanced the hope that there would be "bloodless socioeconomic reorientation" made between nations by young business people in pinstriped suits, straddling continents while propounding international technological sharing and commerce. He said that the question is: "Can it be successfully accomplished before the only-instinctively-operating fear and ignorance preclude success, by one individual, authorized or unauthorized, pushing the first button of chain-reacting, all-buttons-pushing, atomic, race-irradiated suicide?" (p.90).

We still ask the same question today. The existence of nuclear capabilities in so many countries with histories of instability and revolution comes to mind. Use of the term "weapons of mass destruction" to justify invading other sovereign countries comes to mind. The careless burning of Amazonian forests comes to mind. The smarting eyes and scratchy throat that signal unregulated emissions in cities throughout the world come to mind. The crack in the ozone layer signaling global warning comes to mind. Will the benevolent use of new inventions and discoveries of creative mathematicians and scientists come to the aid of the peoples of the world in time?

Outsiders

Another factor that contributes to scientific creativity is what Simonton called "marginality," one of the meanings of which is to live in two cultures. Significant numbers of creative people have been first- or second-generation immigrants, able to straddle two cultures and thus able to see things in new ways, and not in the old, timeworn ways. Simonton cited as an example the Jews, who are eminent in various fields to an extent that exceeds their percentage in the population. "This prominence holds especially for mathematicians, physicists, chemists, biomedical researchers, economists, lawyers, violin virtuosos, chess champions, and faculty members at prestigious universities."

Another theory for why Jewish culture has produced so many scientists came from Abba Eban in 1955. R. Clark quoted Eban thus: "The Hebrew mind has been obsessed for centuries by a concept of order and harmony in universal design." Eban continued, "The search for laws hitherto unknown which govern cosmic forces; the doctrine of a relative harmony in nature; the idea of a calculable relationship between matter and energy" have all contributed to Jewish interest in science.

Another type of marginality Simonton talked about is professional marginality, or being skilled in two professions. In fact, many contributions to science have been made by people who have switched from one field to another. This would seem to be evidence against "the earlier the better," for when one switches fields, one is older, past one's early bloom, yet switching fields permits people to combine and to see in new ways, perhaps becoming younger mentally.

However, a third type of marginality, geographical marginality—or coming from the provinces, so to speak—seems to operate against creativity rather than for it. Being away from the action does not contribute to either aesthetic or scientific creativity, because such creators have little access to those who are producing and creating or those who can help them along. Simonton urged such creators to hurry to a cultural center, for it is difficult to influence a field from the countryside.

The outsider mentality caused by marginality in religion, in sexual orientation, in race or ethnicity, or in social acceptability because of disabilities or quirks often enables creative people to create at the same time as it causes them social discomfort. This seems odd, but it is true. One sees differently from the outside, from the threshold, and seeing differently, naïvely, is often inspiration for making things new and changing the commonplace from a new point of view.

Sun of Gender in Scientists and Mathematicians

And what about the girl who is a whiz, a creative young scientist or mathematician? She is thought to be so rare that she is not even stereotyped. Brody, reporting on Johns Hopkins University's Study of Mathematically Precocious Youth (see also Stanley and Benbow) showed that those few girls who qualified for radical acceleration, or grade skipping, (the ratio is 20 boys to one girl) had mothers with Ph.D.s who did not work outside the home. She also found that these girls were predominantly Asian. In 1999, Simonton noted that historically, women's chances of becoming eminent in science were less than 1%: "In the annals of science, fewer than 1% of all notables are female. Names like Hypatia, Caroline Herschel, Marie Curie, and Barbara McClintock are but drops in a sea of male scientists."

Helson's Study of Creative Female Mathematicians

The first major study of women mathematicians was Ravenna Helson's, done in connection with the classic IPAR project. Helson compared women mathematicians who were creative and those who were thought not to be creative. She found the creative women to be essentially like other creative people, especially creative writers. They were, however, marginal in the profession of mathematics—that is, they did not hold academic posts but worked at home. Their average age was 41, one-third were Jewish, and foreign cultural influence (European and Canadian) was strong, as it is with male mathematicians. Creative male mathematicians scored 148 on the

Terman Concept Mastery Test. In mechanical reasoning, the creative and comparison women mathematicians did not differ, and they both scored lower than men. The average IQs were similar to those of the men, in the low 130s.

Both groups of women mathematicians often came from families of girls, and the creative women mathematicians had few brothers. Helson said "A number of the women mathematicians seem to have been adopted as the 'son' of an intellectual father." The creative women mathematicians had superior intellect and great perseverance. They were adaptive and sensitive to the new and to the unforeseen. Their temperaments were subdued but still individualistic. They were independent and autonomous, taking pride in their objectivity and rationality while still being able to form associations and think in new ways. They were seen as being dramatic personalities, even "histrionic," and as moody and nonconforming rebels. The creative female mathematicians differed from creative male mathematicians, also. The creative males were higher on social ascendancy, or a desire to rise on the social ladder, as well as intellectual efficiency, or how fast and clearly they could express themselves.

Studies throughout the twentieth century—for example, the Terman studies of high IQ students—have shown that parents rated their boys as having higher ability in mathematics and mechanics and their girls as having higher ability in drama and music. More recent studies at Johns Hopkins University of mathematically talented students showed that parents expected their boys to enter math-related occupations but expected their daughters to enter traditional female occupations and then step out for a while to have children.

Helson theorized that there might be biological or societal causes for the gender differences. Creative women mathematicians and creative women writers were remarkably similar. Interestingly enough, she also found that the creative male writers were more like the creative women mathematicians and women writers than they were like the creative male mathematicians. This led to Helson's describing the creative male mathematicians as people who were socially assured, assertive, and who fit into the group. Helson did further studies and came up with the hypothesis that there are two creative styles: (1) high in ego-assertiveness, or the need to push oneself in the world; and (2) low in ego-assertiveness. Women creators seem to be the latter, while men may be either.

The low ego-assertiveness style does not publish many papers, nor is it productive in the way that Simonton said creators must be. These glaring differences between creative women mathematicians and creative men mathematicians speak to the continuing difficulty of women in achieving in creative fields because of their double bind—the continuing social expectation that they work the second shift at home as well as the first shift at their creative work.

Recent Studies

Unfortunately, as of this writing, as indicated by the recent studies of women in science, little seems to have changed. National Science Foundation reports in 1996 showed that women were 22% of the science and engineering labor force as a whole and 20% of doctoral scientists and engineers in the United States. Women were more than half of sociologists and psychologists, but were only 23% of physicists and 13% of engineers. Of people with bachelor's degrees, 29% of the women but only 1% of the men who were not employed cited family responsibilities as the reason for not working. In university positions, women were 44% of faculty in non-science and engineering fields, but only 24% of science and engineering faculty. Again, more women were in psychology (43%) than in physical science (14%) and engineering (6%).

The SMPY studies have found that by college, about a third of the girls had dropped out of the mathematics and science tracks and no longer aspired to get a Ph.D.—this despite the fact that the girls had better academic records and grades than the boys. The students most likely to be underachievers were boys from families in which both parents had not finished college. The most important variable in this brew was the level of challenge in their high school and college courses. Those who took and succeeded in the most challenging courses were often those who continued in college to take the courses necessary to obtain the Ph.D. and to enter the world of mathematics or science.

A 1996 study by Sandra Hanson called *Lost Talent: Women in the Sciences* utilized sophisticated statistical techniques to analyze large databases. Results showed that although young women and men have similar experiences in the sciences up until tenth grade, the males were more likely to stay in science and continue taking the courses. As mentioned before, course-taking is a necessary behavior in the development of science talent. Home support for science course-taking was higher for the young men, and young women who were taking science courses were twice as likely as men to have a child or to marry within two years after high school.

The women who continued in the science pipeline leading to the Ph.D. were less likely to date than the women who stepped out of the pipeline. Those who continued also had lower self-concepts than the other women. This corresponds with the findings of Csikszentmihalyi, Rathunde, and Whalen, who found that the teenage students who continued to develop their talent in science were less precocious in sexual behavior, tended to date in groups, and liked to work alone on projects. Other evidence that girls may be influenced by the urge for popularity with peers and for acceptance by attractive males—urges which may cause them to downplay their intelligence and eventually drop out from developing their science, mathematical, and other academic talents—was shown by Tomlinson- Keasey and Little when they found that a pursuit of social goals and popularity had a negative effect on the development of intellectual skills.

In two longitudinal studies of very bright women, Westinghouse science award winners and valedictorians from Illinois, Subotnik and Arnold noted that after 10 years, most of the women who had intended to pursue science careers had left science. Their reasons had primarily to do with their love relationships. Subotnik and Arnold noted that research science is not an area where one can drop out for a few years to raise children and then return without going back to school to retrain. Until the culture of science itself changes, the presence of women who must balance childbearing and career pursuits will, no doubt, continue to be problematic.

The consequences for dropping out and picking up a career in science or mathematics (or any creative field) after one has taken care of one's small children may be great. The necessary track record for eminence may not be produced. When I have said this to my female students, they have often said, "Who cares about eminence? I want to be happy and raise my family." Some research indicates that women drop out of their career trajectories happily and voluntarily. Karen Hughes, a top aide to President George W. Bush, decided to leave the fast track in April 2003 and to move back to Texas to spend more time with her family. So did Victoria Clarke, an aide to Secretary of Defense Donald Rumsfeld. Photographs in the news showed her with three small children. Her reason for resigning was partly to spend more time with her family. These two resignations of high profile women illustrate the fact that the constant conflict between raising children and working on a career is common to all women in all domains. There is no research evidence that men experience this conflict of roles.

The age curves necessary for eminence shown by Simonton may be misleading for women, also. Women may be prevented from producing at such young ages by the double bind—that of bearing children and taking most of the responsibility for the household as well as being creatively productive in their career. Women may have a different career pattern, peaking in productivity later than men tend to. In the past, this made them less able to achieve eminence, but today is a new day; people are living longer, and eminence for women may come later, after their family duties are diminished and when they can focus on late careers.

Sun of Chance in Scientists and Mathematicians

A man walked into my office the other day. He is single, the foster father of a gifted and talented teenage boy who was taken away from his drug-addicted mother when the boy was two. The man was doing a field experience as an education student and met the boy and took him in. The boy's IQ is 144; he never does his homework, but at his rural high school, he still gets B's. He has never been academically challenged. The foster father receives no state help in raising the boy. The boy loves math and science and is called "Harry Potter" by his classmates. This teasing causes him to fistfight and to get into trouble. How can the Sun of Chance be made operational in this boy's life?

To help the Sun of Chance gleam, I invited the boy to take a scholarship to our summer honors institute where we have math and science classes (with little homework and no grades) where he will be put into proximity with other highly talented students. We have college and career planning sessions, and students have said that the honors institute has changed their minds and changed their plans. We'll see what happens. The father is looking into transferring the boy to a nearby high school that is more academically challenging, since the local high school says it has no services, no courses, and does not have to serve this child.

Compare this boy to a mathematically and scientifically talented boy who is born into a family without trauma, with both a mother and a father, a family that provides special tutors, that has no financial challenges, that can send the child to expensive and rewarding elite summer programs such as talent searches, that has high schools nearby that offer Advanced Placement courses, a school that is receptive and not obstructive. The Sun of

Home has clouds over it, and the Sun of School must pick up the ball. How much potential creative talent is lost because of circumstances of chance? The Sun of Chance shone when the boy met his foster father.

Serendipity

Simonton noted the place of accident or fortuitous coincidence in the history of discoveries. He mentioned Columbus' discovery of the New World in 1492, Grimaldi's discovery of the interference of light in 1663, Galvani's discovery of animal electricity in 1781, the discovery of ozone by Schonbein in 1839, the invention of dynamite by Nobel in 1866, the discovery of penicillin by Fleming in 1928, and the invention of Velcro by Maestral in 1948. Serendipity can take place when a person has tried and tried to solve a problem but has failed until a universal characteristic becomes apparent, when a chance discovery truly happens, when an unanticipated find occurs, when an entirely different problem is solved, or when someone is tinkering and just seeing what happens.

Biographical Example: Darwin

Darwin's life and work engages writers on creativity. Howard Gruber wrote the seminal psychological study. Gardner used Darwin as one of his case examples in *Creating Minds* to illustrate logical-mathematical intelligence. Simonton's 1999 book on creativity is subtitled *Darwinian Perspectives on Creativity*, and he interspersed biographical tidbits about Darwin's life to illustrate his points. Sulloway's *Born to Rebel*, a study of birth order, also used Darwin as a major example. Psychologists who write on creativity love Darwin!

In *Darwin on Man*, Gruber asserted that the detailed study of one life was necessary to uncover the essence of scientific creativity. Gruber studied the development of Darwin's theory of evolution utilizing Darwin's notebooks of 1837 to 1838, written after his famous voyage to the Galapagos on the *Beagle* in 1831 to 1836. Gruber wrote that scientific creativity takes courage, often painstakingly wrought through turmoil and misfortune. Scientific creativity does not come about through a few moments of insight, but from a long and laborious process of thinking, revising, and reformulating.

Darwin waited until 1859, when he published his *Origin of Species*, to make public his belief that natural selection through the survival of the fittest had operated to transmute species. Alfred Wallace had written

Darwin a letter in 1858 about his field observations in the South Sea islands. This precipitated Darwin's writing, finally, of the book, for Darwin was well aware of the social consequences of coming out with such a theory. Wallace's work caused Darwin to try to act first. Wallace was also influenced by Malthus' work, and the Linnaean Society gave both men credit at the same time for publishing the theory of natural selection. (However, Wallace stopped short of saying that human intelligence had evolved through natural selection.) Gruber called Darwin's delay in publishing his theory, a "grand detour" of 23 years, a delay that was illustrative of the psychological process of creativity in people.

For example, a scientist is taught to use the scientific method, to gather data and to form a hypothesis and to construct an experiment to prove or disprove that hypothesis. Gruber called this view of the scientific process "the rationalist myth" and said that a person who takes hold of one theory or one point of view discovers hypotheses "with difficulty." Darwin's notebooks showed that he worked differently. Gruber said that Darwin's life showed that while the hypothesis was in the air, so to speak, certain events in his life were necessary before the hypothesis could be formed.

Gruber also spoke about a "network of enterprises" contributing to the formulation of a scientific theory, or of any theory. While Darwin was delaying in publishing his *Origin of Species*, he spent eight years studying barnacles, he wrote many articles and papers, he continued to accumulate geological and biological information. He delayed also in publishing *The Descent of Man* in 1871, for he was fully aware that the suggestion that man also had evolved would be explosive, invoking the ire of the church. And so between 1859 and 1871, he published many works, accumulated more evidence, and wrote and thought and spoke on related topics. He lived his life and continued to consider. His theories did not spring instantaneously but came to fruition after many related projects brought them to being—a "network of enterprises."

Gruber concluded that creativity, or creative thought, is the "work of purposeful beings." Those who say that creative thought arises from chance or the Zeitgeist are only partially correct, as are those who say that creative thought arises from unconscious processes and internal, not rational mechanisms such as night dreams and daydreams. While both of these are necessary and important, the scientific creator is "governed by a ruling passion" that informs all of his activities. When Darwin went to the zoo, he found behavior that informed his theory; when he went to the opera, he did the same. Darwin was seeing everything in the context of the theory he was hatching. However, since he was working on this theory over a long period of time, he was able to take such events not as proof of his theory, but as part of the fabric.

A scientist combines personal imagery (for example, Darwin's image of the irregularly branching tree, and the wedge) that has been developed through intense exposure to the natural world with empirical data gathering. This intense imagining and forming of images arises from the unconscious and is personal, informing the creator as much as those who apprehend the image later. The scientist develops his theory as a means to put coherence to the enormous amount of information that is coming in.

Darwin claimed that his schooling was not important, but in looking at his school life, one can see that Darwin had been informally exposed to all that he would later propose as theories. Darwin's grandfather, Erasmus, was also part of his development. The family itself was interested and involved in science. At Cambridge, he had casual conversations and relationships with his friends and his teachers. This was for Darwin, as for all students, a major influence. The educational foundations were laid, and a mentor stepped in. This was Alexander von Humboldt, who had sailed to the Tenebrides and who recommended Darwin as the naturalist on the *Beagle*.

When Darwin took on the post, he was already well prepared by his family milieu and his school interests. Then he undertook the five-year task of taking notes, collecting specimens, and making sketches. Sailing on the Beagle was the logical result of being in proximity, close to the opportunities. Darwin began as a geologist and ended as an evolutionist. During this process, he went through many phases, and he ended up challenging the very beliefs of society about the origins of biological systems. He did not do this through a moment of insight or a rigorous application of the five steps of the scientific process, but through the process of life-long creative production.

However, his talents were not only for scientific observation, but also for creative writing and for fine drawing of specimens. Hark to some of his beautiful descriptive language as published in *The Voyage of the Beagle*, his first book.

> *DARWIN ON FIREFLIES: At these times the fireflies are seen flitting about from hedge to hedge. On a dark night the light can be seen at about two hundred paces distant...the light has been of a well-marked green colour.... I found that this insect emitted the*

most brilliant flashes when irritated: in the intervals, the abdominal rings were obscured. The flash was almost coinstantaneous in the two rings, but it was just perceptible first in the anterior one. The shining matter was fluid and very adhesive: little spots, where the skin had been torn, continued bright with a slight scintillation, whilst the uninjured parts were obscured. When the insect was decapitated the rings remained uninterruptedly bright, but not so brilliant as before: local irritation with a needle always increased the vividness of the light. The rings in one instance retained their luminous property nearly twenty-four hours after the death of the insect. From these facts it would appear probable, that the animal has only the power of concealing or extinguishing the light for short intervals, and that at other times the display is involuntary. (Darwin, 1845/ 1906, p. 29)

Inventors

Donald MacKinnon was head of IPAR. MacKinnon's specialties were the study of inventors and of architects. To be designated an inventor, a man (they were all men) had to have obtained a patent or applied for a patent. MacKinnon made a useful distinction between types of inventors. There are three major types. First are those who are employed by business and industry, working as researchers, who are known as "captive" inventors. This, for example, is my brother-in-law, who is a plant breeder for a seed company. He invented a garden tomato that is a best-seller in Europe and Australia. His company reaps the profits.

Second are those who work on their own, known as "independent" inventors. This latter type may be self-employed as inventors or may invent in their spare time, after working for money at another job. In this, independent inventors are similar to creative people in the arts, who are often unable to find employment or to support themselves with their art. An example is the Amish man a few miles away from me in the countryside who has invented a way of barn-raising that permits huge barns to be built in one day. A third type of inventor is the "basic" inventor, who may not even see himself as an inventor but who creates "truly radical" new things such as telecommunications, printing, or explosives.

Despite Mackinnon's distinctions, IPAR found no basic inventors, and so they studied independent and captive inventors. All of the captive inventors were highly educated, most with Ph.D.s, with fathers who were professionals or semi-professionals, while the independent inventors had fewer professional fathers and more fathers in the skilled trades. Only three of the independent inventors had completed a bachelor's degree, and only half had completed high school.

MacKinnon noted that many of the major inventions in the twentieth century have been made by independent or individual inventors operating without support from industry and without financial backing. These were such things as air conditioning, automatic transmissions, bakelite, the ball-point pen, the catalytic cracking of petroleum, cellophane, chromium plating, cinerama, the cotton picker, the cyclotron, domestic gas refrigeration, electric precipitation, the electron microscope, the gyro-compass, the hardening of liquid fats, the helicopter, insulin, the jet engine, Kodachrome film, magnetic recording, penicillin, the Polaroid camera, power steering, quick freezing, radio, the safety razor, the self-winding wrist watch, streptomycin, the Sulzer loom, titanium, xerography, and the zip fastener. We could add Steve Jobs in his garage inventing the Apple computer, and Bill Gates in his spare time in his early college years inventing the platform called Microsoft.

Nowadays most inventions are of the captive kind—for example, almost all new drugs are invented by people who are already employed by drug companies. Medical journals have a hard time getting independent reviewers for these inventions, since almost all of the reviewers are employed by rival companies, and they cannot be unbiased.

Emotional Aspect: Personalities of Inventors

MacKinnon's group analyzed the two types of inventors according to personality and preference and came up with eight categories. These were men who could be described as the following types: Type I: The Zealot; Type II: The Initiator; Type III: The Diagnostician; Type IV: The Scholar; Type V: The Artificer; Type VI: The Esthetician; Type VII: The Methodologist; and Type VIII: The Independent. The group concluded that the research inventors were mainly Initiators and Diagnosticians, as were the independent inventors. The Initiator was described as having the ability to focus quickly and to generate ideas when a research problem is presented. Other people find him exciting, and he is willing to give time. He is a good team player. The observers described him as "ambitious, well-organized, industrious, a good leader, and efficient." The Diagnostician is a good evaluator, able to diagnose problems and to improvise quick answers when research runs into trouble. He is patient with others when they make mistakes. The observers described him as "forceful and self-assured in manner, and as unselfish and free from self-seeking and narcissistic striving."

Independent inventors, not surprisingly, had high self-confidence and self-esteem and a willingness to troubleshoot and to plunge in. MacKinnon theorized that this personality aggressiveness may have contributed to their low test scores, since they guessed wrong answers as often as right answers. The captive inventors, while less cautious than their colleagues who are employed by industry but who don't invent, were much more cautious in taking the tests and didn't guess as often.

Cognitive Aspect: Inventors

Inventors have spatial intelligence, in Gardner's terms, or figural intelligence, in Guilford's terms. This type of intelligence is the ability to manipulate objects in space, from parallel parking a bus to figuring out gears, levers, and the drawings that accompany children's toys on Christmas Eve. Most job titles in the U.S. government's directory require figural intelligence as opposed to semantic (linguistic) or symbolic intelligence; however, figural intelligence is not as valued as linguistic, or semantic, intelligence (logical-mathematical) in our society.

The inventors were administered the *Terman Concept Mastery Test*, which does not test spatial or figural intelligence. The captive inventors had a mean score of 119, and the independent inventors had a mean score of 51, the lowest among the groups tested. We send the students who have figural or spatial intelligence to vocational school. Silverman, in 2002, published a book on visual-spatial learners. She called it *Upside-Down Brilliance*, and in it, she called such people "technologically brilliant."

Patterns in the Lives of Inventors

Another analysis of inventors was done by the Colangelo team, who studied mechanical inventiveness and inventors. Their group was made up of 34 inventors who held patents and who ranged in age from 44 to 82 years. These inventors had certain patterns in their lives.

In personality, they were driven and motivated. They had few outside hobbies, and they viewed their work as their fun. Their inventions were always on their minds. They were strongly independent, and they were risk-takers in their inventions but "normal" in all other areas—family, religion, politics, dress. For the Sun of Home, they had extremely happy childhoods and came from intact homes, probably because they grew up at a time when divorce was less likely. Ninety-five percent of them viewed their families as very close. During their childhoods, they all had some area to tinker in. They were married, and their wives were very supportive of their work. For the Sun of Community and Culture, they had very strong religious ties. About two-thirds of them came from farming background. They were politically conservative. For the Sun of Chance, many of their inventions came about as ways to cut down on time done in chores. For the Sun of Gender, all of them were males. Female inventors are rare.

While the Colangelo and Kerr study was conducted recently, a look at the inventors in the Inventors Hall of Fame in Akron, Ohio indicates that those who reached this pinnacle are mostly captive inventors working for a university or for a company (except for a few maverick inventors like Steve Wozniak of the 1970s). Here are those inducted in the decade of the 1980s: Scanning Tunneling Microscope: Gerd Karl Binnig of IBM; Computer Peripherals: Mark Dean of IBM; Laser: Gordon Gould of Patlex Corporation; Peripherals: Dennis Moeller of IBM; Prozac: Bryan B. Molloy and Klaus K. Schmiegel of Eli Lilly Pharmaceuticals; Polymerase Chain Reaction: Kary Mullis of Cetus Corporation; Scanning Tunneling Microscope: Heinrich Rohrer of IBM. Kary Mullis also received the Nobel Prize in 1993 for his polymerase chain reaction. The inventors in the Colangelo and Kerr study believed that too much schooling would ruin a person's good ideas. Also, they cautioned young inventors to keep their ideas to themselves for two reasons: to avoid theft, and to avoid society's sometimes dampening effect, for most inventors had difficulties in realizing or selling their ideas. These inventors seem to be similar to the maverick or the independent inventors that MacKinnon studied.

However, the inventors who are elected to the Inventors Hall of Fame have Ph.D.s and work for major corporations. It seems that the captive inventor is the influential inventor of the present. Perhaps not surprisingly, of the 154 inventors in the Inventors Hall of Fame, only six of them are women: Helen Free (Glucose), Rachel Brown (Nystatin), Gertrude Elion (Anti-leukemia drugs), Elizabeth Hazen (Nystatin), Stephanie Kwolek (Kevlar), and Patsy Sherman (Scotchgard).

Entrepreneurs

Of my mental cycles, I devote maybe ten percent to business. Business isn't that complicated. I wouldn't want to put it on my business card. When I read about great scientists like, say, Crick and Watson and how they discovered DNA, I get a lot of pleasure. Stories of business success don't interest me in the same way. Part of my skill is understanding technology and business. So let's just say I'm a technologist.
—Bill Gates

The entrepreneur is stereotyped as ruthless, loving money, loving risk, and taking risk. Studies of entrepreneurs have shown that they do have some characteristics in common.

Emotional Aspect: Personalities of Entrepreneurs

In a study of personality preference of entrepreneurs, Reynierse compared the *Myers-Briggs Type Indicator* preferences of entrepreneurs with those of small business owners, business managers, lower-level managers, and business executives. Results showed that business entrepreneurs and managers are quite different and represent opposing perspectives of their worlds. The following chart summarizes the findings.

Table 9.1: *Myers-Briggs Type Indicator* **Preferences of Entrepreneurs and Managers**
(Summarized in Reynierse, 1997)

Extraversion-Introversion (E-I)	1. Entrepreneurs are more extraverted than managers. 2. Entrepreneurs are more frequently E than managers and small business owners.
Sensing-Intuition (S-N)	1. Entrepreneurs are highly innovative (N), executives more functional (S). 2. Entrepreneurs are more frequently N than managers and small business owners.
Thinking-Feeling (T-F)	1. Entrepreneurs and managers are more frequently T than small business managers. 2. Management at all levels have higher frequencies of T.
Judging-Perceiving (J-P)	1. Management at all levels have higher frequencies of J. 2. Entrepreneurs have higher levels of P.

Reynierse theorized that the P, or perceiving, preference would be found in entrepreneurs, since P's have generally been thought to be innovative and creative. He said, "Although entrepreneurial P managers may be a source of discomfort within bureaucratic J or judging organizations, in a business environment where change is perpetual, and stability and control an illusion, they are probably essential for any organization to remain competitive."

He said that the mindsets of entrepreneurs and managers are often radically different. The entrepreneur "has an external orientation that promotes opportunity recognition (E), tends to be innovative and can detect patterns and shifts (N), and is highly flexible, promoting an action orientation and responsiveness to change (P)." The business managers "Have an inward orientation toward their own practices (I), are particularly attentive to immediate events within their span of control and influence (S), and generally adhere to internal policies, structure, and plans, a commitment that is antagonistic to flexibility, action, and change (J)."

Intuition (N), as with other creative people, seems crucial in the personalities of entrepreneurs as well. Reynierse noted that the frequency of N increases with level of management, with proportionately more N's in higher levels. "[B]oth business entrepreneurs and business executives tend to be visionary N's." That small business owners have more preference for F may reflect their preference for working closely with individuals and caring about them. The sensing-perceiving (SP) combination is very rare, and not much is known about them. Reynierse thought that perhaps this is because these people often hate to take personality tests and do so only when required by their bosses.

Several other studies of entrepreneurs revealed other characteristics. Miner showed four personality types emerge that hold promise for succeeding as an entrepreneur: personal achiever, empathic super salesperson, real manager, and expert idea generator. Psychiatrist Kets de Vries presented a case study of a 44-year-old entrepreneur undergoing psychotherapy. The study gave insight into how an entrepreneur is made. Characteristics included a need for control, a sense of distrust, a desire for applause, and a need to resort to primitive defense mechanisms. The entrepreneur exhibited narcissistic tendencies, was reactive, and had difficulties with self-esteem. de Vries concluded that "running a business appears to not necessarily be a rational process, but more a retrospective rationalizing of decisions." Still another researcher, Roberson-Saunders, found that entrepreneurs are focused and controlled from within, they have a high need for achievement, and they are risk-takers.

When I interviewed California business consultant Jerome Stein, himself the son of an entrepreneur, about entrepreneurs, he said that even in moderately successful entrepreneurs, the maverick quality stands out, as well as the intuitive insight and independence. Stein's father, Sam, noticed a need for frozen hamburger patties, and the family began to make them in their home refrigerator freezer. A frozen food company was born. It was later sold to a conglomerate, and the family retired to California. Wherein lies the creativity of entrepreneurs? Their personality characteristics of risk-taking, their high mathematical intelligence, their obsessiveness and passion for their work, and their ability to see their fields in new ways.

Sun of Gender in Entrepreneurs

Individual entrepreneurs differ, of course, and there are gender differences also. Many male entrepreneurs come from families that are well off—that is, they are used to living well. Their role model for being an entrepreneur is often their own father or another relative they knew well in childhood. They usually have at least some college, usually a bachelor's degree. They are married and have children.

Female entrepreneurs are usually first-borns and from the middle class, and they have often experienced divorce. Langan-Fox and Roth published a study of Australian women entrepreneurs. The women were motivated by a need for power and influence, by their ability to obtain influence and to have power, by resistance to being subordinate, by an internal locus of control, and by a need to achieve. Langan-Fox and Roth thought that there are three psychological types of female entrepreneurs: the need achiever, the pragmatic, and the managerial. A lust for power was highest in the need achiever and the managerial women entrepreneurs.

Brodsky also reported a study on female entrepreneurs as compared to corporate managers. Managers were more trusting and required lower levels of control than the entrepreneurs, who wanted to define their own work situations. Although managers viewed the corporate environment as safe and supportive, entrepreneurs considered it confining.

Sun of Community and Culture in Entrepreneurs

Entrepreneurs across cultures are remarkably the same. A cross-cultural study of entrepreneurs in India and the U.S. was reported by

Stimpson, Narayanan, and Shanthakumar. In the U.S., both male and female entrepreneurs had higher scores on innovation, achievement, and personal control than non-entrepreneurs. Also, female entrepreneurs and non-entrepreneurs both had higher self-confidence scores than their male counterparts. In India, both male and female entrepreneurs scored higher than non-entrepreneurs on personal control.

Roberson-Saunders found that minority entrepreneurs often came from lower- to middle-income backgrounds, and likewise were first-borns and had attended college. Entrepreneurs often chose to go off on their own because they lacked opportunities for advancement at their jobs and they wanted to make more money. When they started their first company, they were about 30 years old. Minority entrepreneurs had more difficulty obtaining initial funding from banks and financial institutions.

Successful African-American entrepreneurs said that racism was their main obstacle and that access to capital was related to racism. They also lacked the role model of a successful father or relative, as most had come from blue-collar backgrounds; this, they felt, was why they began their entrepreneurial careers later than other entrepreneurs.

Biographical Examples: J. Paul Getty, Warren Buffett, and Bill Gates

The lives of J. Paul Getty, Warren Buffett, and Bill Gates have striking similarities. Getty was an oil baron and takeover specialist; Buffett is a financier; Gates owns a software company. They are among the richest men in the world.

For the Sun of Home, all three came from families that already had a comfortable way of life. Getty's father was a wealthy attorney in Minneapolis. Buffett's father was a Congressman and a stockbroker. Gates' mother was a banker, and his father a prominent Seattle lawyer. All three as young boys were discipline problems in school. Getty's parents pulled him out of the local high school and put him into a military academy in Los Angeles. Buffett experienced trauma when the family moved from Omaha to Washington, D.C., and he had a difficult adjustment. When he finally came to permanently live with his parents in Washington, D.C., he paid more attention to his five paper routes and the profit they brought him than to his studies. According to biographers, Manes and Andrews, Gates was a cut-up and bored in his local public school; in seventh grade, his parents placed him in a private boys' school with high academic standards.

All three demonstrated early their ability in mathematics and their affinity for the fields in which they would make their money. Getty described a trip to Indian territory (Oklahoma) in 1903 where his father, George Getty, had to take care of a client's legal problems. The trip introduced the Gettys to the oil frenzy. Getty wrote, "There are men who seem to have an uncanny affinity with oil in its natural state. By some mysterious instinct, they appear to sense its presence even when the pool is thousands of feet below ground." Getty's father had this instinct. In 1904, at the age of 11, the young Getty witnessed his first oil well come in. At the age of 16, he began to work for his father's oil company as a roustabout. He said, "I could expect no preferential treatment because I was the Boss's son." He went to college and worked summers in the oil fields. He spent a year at Oxford University in Great Britain reading political science and economics, thinking he would try for the diplomatic corps.

Getty's father wanted his only child to come into the business and persuaded him to try wildcat oil operating for one year. On a stipend of $100 per month, the young Getty scouted for promising leases. It took a year to find one. The well was built and came in for 700 barrels a day. By the age of 24, Getty was his own millionaire. Of being a millionaire, he said, "Anyone who starts from scratch—even someone like me, who started from scratch but with family wealth behind him—is likely to regard the figure and the label as ultimates, and ends in themselves."

Bill Gates met his future Microsoft partner, Paul Allen, at prep school. The school had connections with an infant computer company, and the boys in the honors mathematics class were invited to play with the computers and to experiment with programming them. The two boys fell in love with computers. Gates straightened up his academic act. He was so quick that he barely needed to study, and he became so obsessed with computer programming that he would sneak out at night and go back to work on programming problems.

Gates displayed the classic characteristics of the underachieving gifted boy who only does the homework in the classes he likes. The private school was good for him. He began to get straight A's and received a perfect 800 on his SAT mathematics test, becoming a National Merit Finalist. He was admitted to Harvard, Princeton, and Yale, and he chose Harvard. He continued working with Allen, who was in college back in Washington, on BASIC programming, learning the other languages as well (COBOL, PASCAL, etc.).

At Harvard, Gates rarely attended class except for the first day, but he would study for the finals and received A's and B's. He illegally used the graduate school computers and amassed great amounts of user time. Harvard considered kicking him out. His activities at Harvard also included a heavy dose of poker playing. He took a leave from Harvard after six semesters to move to Albuquerque to develop the software business with Allen. He never returned.

Buffett's mathematical ability was so keen that he began to buy low and sell high at age six, when he bought a six-pack of Coke for a quarter and sold it for five cents a can. He always had what his biographer Kilpatrick called "an auditor's instinct—the ability to get at the real numbers, not the supposed numbers passed along by others." He skipped a grade in elementary school. His mathematical ability took its form in an interest in finance and the stock market, and he bought his first stocks at age 11. He had been following the stock market, and at the age of eight, he began reading books on investment that his father had around the house. He also began following the horses while in middle school and published a betting sheet, selling it for a quarter.

Buffett's fascination for mathematics and his interest in money bordered on obsessive. In church, he would calculate the longevity of the hymn writers to see if they lived longer than other people. Kanter said that Buffett, even during adolescence, "was a tireless entrepreneur." For example, when he was 14, he invested $1,200 on a 40-acre plot of land in Nebraska and leased it to a tenant farmer. He used the money from his paper routes. In high school, he and a friend set up a pinball machine business. He also worked at a golf course retrieving lost golf balls.

Buffett's grades in junior high were poor, and they improved only when his congressman father threatened to take away his paper routes. He briefly attended the Wharton School of Business, but he transferred back to the University of Nebraska, graduating at age 19. He was rejected for the Harvard Business School and enrolled instead in the Columbia Business School. His academic record there was excellent, and he graduated with a master's degree in economics at age 20. He is a world-class bridge player.

All three young entrepreneurs were readers from a young age and continued to enjoy reading throughout their lives. Getty experienced a real quandary when his father asked him to take over the business, because he valued the time he spent reading about political science and economics. He disdained the "rah-rah" social life and lack of academic rigor at UCLA, but said, "Oxford was, for me, an ideal place to study. The underlying philosophy was that if a student desired an education, he would obtain it without constant, niggling supervision."

Reading was emphasized in the families of these three young men. Gates said, "When I was young, we used to read books over the summer and get little colored bookmarks for each one. There were girls who had read maybe 15 books. I'd read 30. Numbers two through 99 were all girls, and there I was at number one. I also liked taking tests. I happened to be good at it. Certain subjects came easily, like math. And all the science stuff. I would just read the textbooks the first few days of class."

When Buffett would play basketball with his high school friends, he was known for taking a break to go off to the sidelines for a while and read the *Wall Street Journal*. He would then come back into the game. Even now he rarely watches television, saving his time for reading and studying.

All three men were workaholics, driven to compete and to win. Their shrewdness in contract matters, in protecting their interests, and in slyly and ruthlessly beating all competitors is legendary. These adult behaviors were also predicted in childhood—for Getty, in his striving to prove himself to Oklahoma wildcatters even though he was a rich kid, son of the boss; for Buffett, in his willingness to leave a stockbroker position and start his own business in his bedroom, not even telling his investors where their money was being spent, but just to trust him; for Gates, in his reputation, even among his childhood friends, for screaming arguments that lasted for hours, often ending in disdainful putdowns of "stupid" or "dumb" ideas. Gates wants people to stand up to him and argue it out, as that is where the problems are solved.

The need for independence, for control, and for being the boss shows strongly in all three men. All were hands-on managers, setting examples by working long hours and modeling obsessiveness for their employees. While Getty, who is now dead, liked the fast life of cars, yachts, and blondes in his limited free time, both Gates and Buffett seem to have trouble enjoying their billions, living rather modestly with few opulent indulgences. Buffett still lives in his modest neighborhood in Omaha; Gates' large house has many electronic devices, and though he loves fast cars and buys the software rights to great art, he often flies coach.

Getty's interest in art led to his endowment to the Los Angeles Getty Art Museum. Gates has contributed to various charities for children's health and says he plans to give most of his money away when he reaches his fifties. Buffett also plans to give most of his money away, leaving little to his children. Gates said he'll give his children a million dollars, but not a billion. Getty gave up his fast cars and yacht-buying habits and said of himself, "Those who wish to call (or consider) me frugal, parsimonious—or even miserly—are welcome to do so.... I long ago outgrew the neon-lighted suit worn by those who believe they should make a great show of wasting money for no other reason than to demonstrate that they can afford to be wastrels."

The insight and ability to foresee what will be needed is a great part of their personalities. While the computer mavens were building hardware, Gates and Allen saw the need for software for those machines and positioned themselves by legally protecting themselves. While the world was gearing up to exploit fossil fuels for the running of the machines necessary for an industrial society, Getty was scouting for that fuel and protecting his interests through complicated and ruthless maneuvers for control. When the stock market goes down, and everyone sells, Buffett buys low, creating a portfolio of solid, performing stocks. The creativity of the entrepreneur consists of insight, intuition, and sheer guts, combined with canniness and cunning and a deep knowledge of their domain.

Summary

1. In personality, scientists, inventors, and entrepreneurs have similar characteristics to those of other creators, especially in the areas of intuition and perceiving.

2. In passion for the domain, they demonstrate an early aptitude and love for their field. They are motivated less by external concerns than by internal concerns, or the desire to know.

3. Sun of School: Scientists and mathematicians have to obtain a Ph.D., which requires a lengthy period of course-taking before their creative contributions are manifest. Some inventors have Ph.D.s, some don't. Entrepreneurs do not.

4. Sun of Home: Family life is usually stable, with great and positive father influence.

5. Sun of Community and Culture: The influence of the Zeitgeist, the spirit of the times, is viewed variously.

6. Sun of Gender: Not much has changed over the twentieth century for women scientists, mathematicians, and entrepreneurs. Few women are inventors.

7. Sun of Chance: Putting oneself into a position in which chance can be helpful.

8. Inventors are often from rural areas and have conservative backgrounds. They demonstrate their risk-taking through their inventions and not in their lives.

9. Entrepreneurs across races, cultures, and gender seem to have similar personality characteristics.

10. J. Paul Getty, Warren Buffett, and Bill Gates have many similarities in their biographical paths.

Chapter 10

Musicians, Conductors, and Composers

Of music so delicate, soft, and intense
It was felt like an odor within the sense
                    —Shelley

I have always been opposed to background music. How can
one converse about trivialities at a party or even engage in
serious work if, at the same time, the deepest expressions of
life and death, sorrow and elation, fill the room?
                    —Viktor Weisskopf

W hat comes to mind when you picture a musician? Do you see a young boy forced to practice his piano lesson who plays a tape-recording of himself so that he can escape to play baseball? Or a young girl lugging her cello case to school for orchestra rehearsal or down the street for her private lesson? Or a garage band practicing at all hours of the night, waking you up and inspiring you to call the police? Or do you see young Van Cliburn wowing them in Moscow, making the evening news?

Whatever you see, it is probably an image that includes practice. Musicians practice. They take private lessons. They play alone. They play in groups. Even if they are in school groups, choirs, bands, or orchestras, they must take private lessons in order to further themselves in their music. Schools have the responsibility to identify students who are musically gifted, as well as the responsibility to serve them in music programs, but no child who has musical talent will proceed very far unless he or she has private teachers.

The power of music to move us—of whatever level of complexity, whether sung or played—cannot be disputed. Few people have not experienced moist eyes when hearing some tune or another. I once wrote a newspaper column on what makes us spontaneously weep, and most people whom I asked said that they got emotionally choked up or got tears in their eyes upon hearing children sing, hearing an old love song, singing the national anthem, or singing a favorite hymn. Music is all around us—in our supermarkets, in elevators, in our cars as we impatiently push the select buttons to find music that we want to hear. We are often stuck in the musical era in which we grew up—thus the popularity of oldies stations and television channels. We wallow in nostalgia, choose certain music to help us relax, to help us feel happy, to help us reminisce about lost love. We buy CDs and subscribe to cable channels which have many choices of music.

When a young person chooses music or any of the arts as a career, it is often with the knowledge that our society does not really support its young artists. In some ways, young creative artists are less valued in our society than young scientists and mathematicians. A career in music is not as prestigious nor as respected as a career in medicine or law, and parents will usually tell their aspiring musician son or daughter to make sure that he or she has something to fall back on.

The arts, all of them, are necessary for human well-being. The pleasure and knowledge of ourselves that we get from the arts cannot be duplicated in any other human enterprise. A person who does not get pleasure from the arts has an impoverished soul. The arts feed our spirituality, speak to our humanness and our universal similarity, and bridge continents and languages. Unfortunately, the arts are often the first programs to be cut in schools because they are viewed as extraneous to the school experience. Yet when children remember what they learned in school, it is often what they learned in an "arts" experience—projects they did, concerts they sang in, plays they were in, athletic performances they gave in sports, editorials they wrote for the school newspaper.

What is musical talent? Haroutounian discussed talent as musical aptitude, as musical intelligence, as performance, as creativity, and as giftedness. She said that musical aptitude is an ability to listen to sound with care and discrimination. Talent development in music takes certain developmental paths. Whether the musician is to play classical music or popular music, the paths have certain commonalities. Haroutounian said that talent in music is actualized in physical performance. The musically talented person mixes innate capabilities to perceive sound with the bodily capability of being able to interpret music through physical performance. The only type of musical talent not realized through performance is that of the connoisseur, the critic, who is often a writer with strong musical sensitivity to the subtleties of various renditions and genres.

Musical talent has several basic foundations, according to Haroutounian:

1. Musical awareness and discrimination.
2. Perceptual awareness of sound.
3. Rhythmic sense.
4. Sense of pitch.
5. Creative interpretation.
6. Meta-perception.
7. Dynamic of performance.
8. Motivation and commitment.

The Genetic Aspect in Musicians

We don't know whether there is a music gene or music genes. Yet meet a professional musician, and you will most likely find a family of amateur musicians—or at least a family that attends musical events. Music is in the household air. "Music is in our blood," say many families.

Biographies of classical musicians often reveal the musical interest and talent of the parents that spilled over to the children. Mozart's father is an example. The Mendelssohn family is another. The Bach family, another. And so on. And then we have the popular musicians: the Dylans—Bob and his son Jakob, of The Wallflowers; the Simons—Paul and his son Harper, a guitarist in a British band; and Greg Allman's son Elijah Blue. However, this anecdotal evidence is not enough to say that there are genes for music. Haroutounian commented on whether musical talent is more nature or nurture, saying that to attribute talent to nature is, at this time, merely theoretical. She said that the environment—taking lessons early and having parents who create a musical atmosphere—is most important in the talent development of musical prodigies. She was talking about prodigies, but the same is probably true of non-prodigy musicians as well.

The Emotional Aspect: Personality Attributes in Musicians

Kemp's Studies

Many studies of the personality attributes of musicians were conducted by Anthony Kemp using the Cattell instrument, the *16 Personality Factors Questionnaire*. Kemp did many studies of several hundred performers, composers, and student teachers in Great Britain. Secondary school musicians were found to be more intelligent, dominant, conscientious, individualistic, self-sufficient, and controlled than non-musicians. They were also less emotionally stable, less happy-go-lucky, and less outgoing than non-musicians. The more talented musicians attending conservatories were less outgoing and less adventurous than the secondary school musicians. The more talented musicians were also more excitable, individualistic, and apprehensive. This might indicate more sensitivity in the more talented musicians.

Adult professional musicians were more outgoing, intelligent, individualistic, imaginative, forthright, and self-sufficient than other musicians. Male musicians were less emotionally stable, more suspicious, and more radical than male non-musicians. Perhaps this is because professional musicians have had to weather great competition from peers, always checking to see who might be gaining on them, and they also need great personal drive and passion for their music. Women professional music performers were more dominant and more "tense" than comparison females. Again, drive and passion are needed for success in musical performance, and the women would need to be more like men performers than like other females.

Kemp also did a study of music teachers and performers. Musicians who were studying to be teachers were more extraverted and outgoing and less sensitive to criticism than those who wanted to be performers. The music teachers were also more conforming. Kemp thought that the "rich, colorful and imaginative inner mental life" of musicians "renders them self-sufficient and detached from others." Teaching may be the right choice for musicians for whom performance is too demanding.

Composers differed from performers and teachers. Kemp compared student composers with music students who did not compose. He also compared members of the Composers Guild of Great Britain with professional musicians who did not compose. Male professional and student composers were found to be more aloof, dominant, sensitive, controlled, imaginative, and self-sufficient. The only difference between the students and the professionals was that the professionals had higher IQs. Female professional composers were also dominant and self-sufficient. Composers were the most extreme in all the personality factors.

Other Personality Studies

Wubbenhorst did a study of personality and androgyny of students studying to be music educators and performers. He used the *Myers-Briggs Type Indicator* (MBTI) and the *Bem Sex Role Inventory* (BSRI). Both groups preferred ENFJ (Extraversion, Intuition, Feeling, Judging). Again we see that these musicians were similar to other creative people studied, in that they prefer intuition (N). Both groups also turned out to be psychologically androgynous on the BSRI. Someone who is androgynous is flexible in being able to be both feminine and masculine. This flexibility may be viewed as an enhancement or an advantage both in the classroom and on the performance stage.

Buttsworth and Smith studied personalities of Australian keyboard, string, woodwind, and brass players, as well as singers. The musicians were more emotionally stable, sensitive, and conservative. Male musicians were more sensitive and shrewd than female counterparts. Brass players were more suspicious, imaginative, apprehensive, and radical than singers, and more extroverted and less anxious and creative than string players. Keyboard players were more warmhearted, emotionally stable, and shrewd than the others, perhaps because they had to be so adaptable to changing roles of soloist, accompanist, or ensemble player. Singers were more distrustful, imaginative, anxious, and extreme than the instrumental musicians.

The study uncovered some resentment among section players. The string players viewed the brass section as alcoholic, loud, and rowdy, while the brass viewed the strings as effete, oversensitive, and conceited. The authors theorized that brass players more often play solo parts than members of a string section, and the aggressiveness shown may be necessary for solo performers. How players and instruments are matched remains a matter of conjecture; do the personalities of the players determine the instrument they play, or do their personalities change as they get more experience playing in the instrumental section?

Dyce and O'Connor published a study of the personality characteristics of 150 popular rock and country bass players, guitarists, and drummers.

Popular performers tended to be significantly more extraverted, arrogant, and dominant when compared to university students, and more neurotic than the rest of the population. The authors hypothesized that the neuroticism might be caused by these musicians' nomadic lifestyle and employment instability. Neuroticism might also be necessary for conveying passion when performing music. The popular musicians also showed more openness to experience in the realm of fantasy, and they seemed to be more imaginative than the general population.

Another study of 72 rock musicians by Gillespie and Myors showed similar personality attributes. Neuroticism and openness were high, and agreeableness and conscientiousness were low. Excitement-seeking and positive emotions were high; trust, straightforwardness, and compliance were low. Conscientiousness was low. Achievement striving was average. It did not matter which musical instrument, which type of rock music, how long they had been rock musicians, how well they played, nor how commercially successful they were. The authors said, "The research suggests that rock musicians share a common core of traits."

Personality Attribute of Introversion/Shyness

Shyness is a heritable quality of temperament and personality that is often present in creative people. Many creators, including composers, prefer introversion. Shyness is related to introversion, and it is also an aspect of neuroticism. Sulloway thought that shy people were introverts who were quite anxious when strangers are present. Sulloway related shyness to birth order, saying that shyness is more common to later-borns, who were often taunted and criticized by older siblings.

However, shyness may occur no matter what one's birth position in the family. For musicians, perhaps shyness can be overcome by the playing of music—by speaking in another language, the language of music, using another code for communication. Jenny Boyd, a former model and wife of Mick Fleetwood of Fleetwood Mac, earned a Ph.D. in psychology and began to write on creativity in musicians in her book *Musicians in Tune*, which is based on 75 interviews of rock and popular musicians. She described how her husband courted her when they were teenagers. Mick Fleetwood was quite shy, and having a normal conversation was painful for him. He would telephone her, she said, and after they had greeted each other, he would lay the telephone next to his drum and begin to play, sometimes for as long as three-quarters of an hour. The anxiety and tension shy people feel can be assuaged through creating, through making something through metaphor, whether musical, artistic, poetic, or physical.

Personalities of Conductors

The profession of conductor requires certain skills and attributes. Among these are a deep knowledge of music and the social skills for being able to be perceived as a leader. Polkow quoted well-known conductor George Solti, who said that a conductor needs to be intelligent and to have a sense of intuition about what the players are feeling and thinking from moment to moment. Solti said that determination and drive are key personality characteristics that conductors need. Single-mindedness and ambition help the conductor to endure and to prevail through roadblocks. Conducting must be the only goal. Lebrecht said that exceptional conductors must have a keen ear, the determination to get their own way, high organizational ability, unswerving ambition, forceful intelligence, the ability to find the artistic core in a score, force of personality which will motivate musicians, physical and mental fitness, and the ability to interpret a score and convey it to the musicians and audience.

Conductors often discover that their talents on their musical instruments are not enough to propel them to the top levels of instrumental performance and that their conducting talents are greater than their musical talents. Renowned conductor Dennis Russell Davies, born in Toledo, Ohio, was a fine pianist; he studied at Juilliard. However, when he realized that he wasn't going to win major competitions (e.g., the Moscow Tchaikovsky Competition and the like), he turned to conducting.

In fact, the conductor often has to bear the resentment of both the musicians who play the music and the composers who write it. Composer Igor Stravinsky likened conductors to politicians and diplomats; he said that the nature of the position of the conductor demands that he be very good at many things, but being a great player is not one of them. Above all, Stravinsky said, the conductor must be able to get along with the wealthy female supporters of classical music, who don't worry about his musical aptitude, but about how politically successful he is able to be.

Because so much of the work of conductors is repetitive, Stravinsky thought that they may often become indifferent to music. The social and organizational talents of the conductor often take precedence, for the conductor must get to know prominent, wealthy, and influential people and persuade them to support and further the interests of the orchestra.

Solti said that the conductor must always remember that music is an abstract and theoretical art, and the conductor must have such force of personality that he "can take his abstract image of the musical score and put it above other people's." The conductor Herbert Blomstedt, in an interview with Wagar, said that the conductor must have "psychic energy" in order to convey the composer's intent.

Few conductors are also composers. Esa Pekka-Salonen of Los Angeles is the only conductor of a major American orchestra who is also an active composer. Salonen told D. P. Stearns in an interview that when he heard one of his compositions performed on the radio, he reacted like a composer, berating the conductor for not understanding the piece. His wife reminded him that composers were doing the same to him, and he realized that the profession of conductor carried a great responsibility to the intent of the composer. Ewen said that the conductor's ability to interpret must awaken the audience from lethargy and daydreaming so that they can experience the spirituality of great music. The conductor is a cross between a high priest and a chief executive.

Thus we have seen that musicians differ in personality depending upon whether they are performers, conductors, or composers. However, intelligence, sensitivity, strong intuition, motivation, determination, and self-discipline seem to be present in all.

The Cognitive Aspect in Musicians

Musical intelligence, another of Howard Gardner's eight "frames of mind," is characterized by acute hearing ability, or audition, as well as the ability to understand the organization of rhythms. Many have likened musical intelligence to mathematical intelligence, but Gardner pointed out that this ignores the emotional impact of music and the musically talented person's ability to evoke emotion. Most of us listen to music because of the wordless emotion that wells up within us.

Gardner also noted that musical illiteracy is acceptable in our society, and that little training in music beyond basic singing and reading of notes in elementary school happens. It is perfectly acceptable for people to be musically illiterate, perhaps because of the lowly place of music education in contemporary culture. An aside here might be appropriate. Isn't it interesting that music is such an important part of teen culture, and yet music is not taught to everyone in school? Boom boxes, car radios turned up high, the phenomenal popularity of *American Idol* stars, the admiration of rock and pop stars—all form a big part of teen culture, but many students go through high school without any music classes.

Musical intelligence is apparent very early, even at ages one or two. Spontaneous singing, chanting, creating sounds with instruments, imitating songs, remembering songs heard, interest in playing the piano—all are signs of musical intelligence.

Standardized Tests

Schools should never use IQ tests as a screen for identifying musical talent. If a paper and pencil type of test is desired, schools should use the musical aptitude measures that have been validated over the years. These can be used to identify talent in youth from musically deprived families where the school is the only agency that identifies the child. These are such tests as the Seashore Measures, the Gordon Measures of Music Audiation and others similar. Checklists such as The Musical Characteristics Scale from the Scales for Rating the Behavioral Characteristics of Superior Students are also available. Items such as "easily remembers melodies and can produce them accurately" and "is sensitive to background noises, to chords that accompany a melody" are included on this list.

Recently, a coordinator of programs for the talented wanted to change his district's identification procedures to reflect the Multiple Intelligences (MI) approach. He asked me what tests he should use to identify musical talent. I sang a note and asked him to sing the same note. He could not match my pitch. "You can't get into my choir," I said. I tell this to illustrate that musical talent is most truly found by looking *directly* at the intelligence, not by filtering the assessment through linguistic or logical-mathematical paper and pencil tests.

IQ Intelligence of Musicians

How intelligent are musicians? Kemp found that in comparison with other undergraduates, the IQs of college musicians were slightly higher. These data suggested that music students were capable of entering other professions, but they chose music because they wanted it. Kemp also said that many adult musicians use their intelligence to leave music for more lucrative professions. In fact, there is a basic assumption in schools that music students tend to be smart. When the band director addressed parents of fifth graders at my son's school, he said that an advantage of playing in the band is that a child's peers are the kids who are often on the honor roll.

When people ask me how to get their children through middle and high school intact, I often tell them to get their children into the band; the entire school schedule often revolves around scheduling the music periods, so their schedule will be such that the kids will be in classes with good students. A high school band director told me that the grade point average of students in all his bands is 3.2 on a 4.0 scale. Whether bright students join music groups because they are good at it or whether they join music groups because their parents make them is not known. Regardless of whether they score higher on IQ tests because they have studied music from a young age when their brains were developing or for some other reason, it is well known that a high IQ is positively related to having high grades.

Musical performers and conductors need a phenomenal memory for music. Within a year after his debut in London, Esa Pekka-Salonen had memorized 30 symphonies! Some conductors have photographic memories and study the musical scores with grave intent. Others conduct without the scores in front of them, having memorized entire compositions.

Talent in the Domain: The Thorn

Emotion is an important component of music composition and performance. When Simonton (1995) studied 10 of the most famous composers, examining the aesthetic merit of their compositions, he found that the most artistically original music was composed when they were in most pain, facing hard life challenges such as family deaths, job insecurities, moving, troubles in their marriages, legal problems, and political upheavals in their countries. The composers' life circumstances and emotional stresses influenced their melodies. They turned to music to heal themselves, just as other creators turn to their domains. The work in making music heals.

Conductors are transported by both the music and by the conducting. Conductor Herbert Blomstedt described to Stearns a state of great elation after a concert and said that he was always enthusiastic about making music. Esa-Pekka Salonen, in an interview with A. Ross, said that when he studies the scores of the great composers, he feels joyful and euphoric.

Again and again we see in the anecdotal comments of musicians the great pleasure and passion they have for their music. Composers, performers, and conductors have at least one thread in common. They love music. Music arouses great emotions within their souls.

The Sun of Home in Musicians

Musical talent often shows up early, and if a family has a keyboard instrument, the musically talented child will probably be picking out tunes at a young age. Michael Howe and his colleagues found that childhood spontaneous singing was observed earlier in those who later became the most accomplished young musicians. The age at which parent and child first listened to music together tended to be lower, and they were more likely than the others to have had a keyboard instrument in their home from an early age.

The pattern of the family giving up many things for the sake of the musical talent of the child is quite common. Young musicians must practice before school, after school, on weekends. Understandably, the conflicts of the necessity for practice and the demand to live a normal life are difficult for young musicians and may contribute to the them giving up music during adolescence. John-Steiner noted that Burt Bacharach said that he gave up music from ages 12 to 16, but his mother's encouragement and his early, rigorous training made him come back to composing and playing.

The Development of Expertise

Much of the current research on music psychology examines how deliberate practice works in developing musical talent. Ericsson, Persson, and colleagues have even asserted that there may be no such thing as raw talent, but that enough practice will make anyone good enough to compete at the highest levels. Others, such as Williamon and Valentine, said that the quality of practice is more important. In the research on the development of expertise, in whatever field, practice is deemed to be essential. Again, as mentioned earlier, the person learns the task to the point of automaticity. There is some evidence that such attention to practice by musicians is a key to success. In a study of 257 young musicians ages eight to 18, Sloboda and colleagues found a strong relationship between musical achievement and the amount of formal practice. High achievers had more consistent patterns of practice and practiced their technique in the morning. The researchers concluded that formal practice seems to be a major determinant of musical achievement.

Sosniak studied 21 concert pianists who had received international recognition in piano competitions. Mostly only or older children from middle-class families, 80% of them had professional or white-collar parents. Half were urban, and half came from small and middle-sized towns.

Their families appreciated music, and music was in the home, though their parents may or may not have played an instrument. All of their families thought that music lessons were a good thing for children to have. This made the families of these future concert pianists almost indistinguishable from the normal families. In many ways, it was habits of practice that explained the achievements of these young pianists.

The early years are important for developing habits of motivation, discipline, and self-concept in young pianists. Their aspirations to become pianists have a foundation in the family commitment to the playing of the piano as worthwhile and valuable, and in the family's physical, financial, and psychological support of that commitment.

In stage two, during adolescence, the playing of the piano becomes the playing of *music,* with the piano as the instrument for the music. Aesthetic appreciation begins. Lessons and practice become an ingrained habit, and young, talented musicians spend about 20 hours a week in lessons and practice. Their teachers must be dedicated and must challenge them. The students begin to make decisions focused on music rather than on other choices. Families may make long-distance moves to be near the best learning environment. The whole family is affected by the budding career of the young pianist. Perhaps other children in the family are negatively affected by this intense commitment of the family's time, monetary resources, and change in lifestyle. The student gradually moves into the world of music from the world of the family, and the teacher becomes more important. The competition of peers for motivating the music and for providing the student with feedback as to his or her worth as a pianist also becomes more important.

Whether or not a young pianist becomes a professional pianist depends on his or her assessment of the competition. Condoleezza Rice, the U.S. Assistant to the President for National Security Affairs, Secretary of Defense, asked her parents for piano lessons when she was three. She began to perform at various functions. When she was around 10, she got bored with piano and wanted to quit. In an interview with Leman for *The New Yorker,* she said, "My mother said, 'You're not old enough or good enough to make that decision. When you are old enough and good enough, then you can quit, but not now.' And I'm really glad she didn't let me quit." At the age of 15, Rice attended a music camp and realized that she would not be good enough to become a concert pianist. Still, she says, "I was good enough to play just about anything that I wanted to, and that's why even today it's a great avocation." Her stable home and her early practice instilled in her a love of music and a dedication to self-discipline.

The Sun of Home in rock and popular musicians is often less stable, less supportive in terms of lessons, less tolerant of practice, and less full of encouragement than the homes of classical musicians. Resilience is the key personality attribute for many of these musicians. Intelligence and drive are also keys. They may have had unhappy childhoods; they may succumb to addictions to sex, alcohol, or drugs, they may have suffered abuse and may be abusive. For example, Courtney Love moved from living with her parents to foster homes; she was put into reform school; she attended boarding schools; she moved often, with one parent in New Zealand and one in the U.S.; and she was a teenage striptease artist. It was a rough road to success for her. The same is true for LL Cool J, whose father shot and wounded his mother and grandfather. There are many accounts of Michael Jackson's tough, and in many ways, abusive, childhood.

The shelves in bookstores are full of rock biographies and autobiographies that give a flavor of the childhoods of these musicians. Go to a bookstore and pick up one of these biographies, flip through it, and see the pain that many of these rock singers have endured. Many rock musicians' children also have had troubled childhoods, indicating that the pain continues through generations. Mackenzie Phillips, daughter of the Mamas and the Papas' John and Michelle Phillips, recalls the time she was seduced by Mick Jagger when she was 18. Jagger told her he had been waiting to seduce her since she was 10 years old. Kurt Cobain's best-selling private notebooks indicate a life of both existential struggle and the sensitivity of a poet. He died of an overdose.

The Sun of School in Musicians

Choosing a Career in Music

It takes a special breed of person to face the stiff competition that a career in music necessitates throughout one's professional life. A career in music means that one must audition, practice, take lessons from ever more advanced teachers—only to receive what is often a shockingly low salary. Like creative writers who take jobs in university writing departments and visual artists who teach in art, musicians often become music teachers in order to support themselves. Hence many performers moonlight during the day as typists or underwriters or waiters, while school music teachers often gig in orchestras or bands at night.

Many of us know musicians of many trades by day (including teaching) whose weekend nights end at 3:00 AM after the bars close. Their families barely see them, but the supplementary salary helps them stay in a profession that feeds the soul more efficiently than it does the body. In addition, the classically trained musician must take any job that comes along, must audition for faraway symphonies and obscure chamber groups. A friend of mine plays the flute in a symphony orchestra in underdeveloped Latin America. Young and fresh out of music school, she could find work in music only with this faraway symphony.

Perhaps all of this indicates that we have trained too many musicians. Perhaps our conservatories and music departments are turning out students who are unemployable. But perhaps the real problem is a lack of appreciation and employment for highly-trained musicians, because as a society, we are musically illiterate. A quick flip through the radio stations in any urban or rural area will illustrate the types of music and musicians our society supports. Depending on geography, rock 'n' roll, golden oldies, soft rock, hard rock, top 40, or country music of several varieties will be prevalent. The lower end of the dial will have perhaps one jazz station and one classical or public radio station that plays the chestnuts of classical music. Little new classical music hits the airways. Nor does much innovative music of any genre. As listeners, we are untrained, even lazy, and unable to appreciate what countless fine musicians would like to play for us. Nevertheless, we have many young people and adults talented in music. Some make it their hobby and something else their career.

Bamberger said that young musically talented children go through something similar to a "midlife crisis" in their adolescent years. Young, musically talented children approach music holistically, using many strategies quite naturally. The crisis occurs when the child comes to consciousness, becomes more self-critical and reflective about music. This time is a "period of serious cognitive reorganization." Bamberger said, "there can be neither a return to imitation and the unreflective, spontaneous 'intuitions' of childhood, nor a simple 'fix-up'." She said that the mid-life crisis is a process of reorganizing, during which the child learns to analyze and synthesize musical knowledge.

Pianist Lorin Hollander is a case in point. He was a child prodigy whose father was a violinist. When Hollander was three, his father handed him a violin, but Lorin rebelled and smashed it "coldly and empirically." He then began to play only the notes on the piano that were the notes his father couldn't reach on his violin, like the F below middle C. He gave his first concert in kindergarten for a pageant called "Circus," and when he was 11, he played his first concert in Carnegie Hall. He later noted that because of these events, he had experienced several deep and profound personality changes that even affected his nervous system.

Sosniak's study found that being a student of a master teacher means more than just taking lessons; it means adopting a style, a sense of musical repertoire, and a raising in standards of musicianship and performance. The master teachers expect discipline and commitment. They expect the students to practice at least four and as many as seven hours per day between lessons. Because master teachers often travel and tour, lessons may last longer than an hour and be as infrequent as three weeks or a month apart. Master teachers do not tolerate excuses or sloppy preparation. Music students thus move from the world where their parents sacrifice and coddle to the coldly competitive world of music professionals. Having closed their other options of study, they select music conservatories or schools where their teachers are located.

As a final step in talent development, the teachers then themselves become lesser gods to the mature young musicians. Teachers become more like coaches, as the students begin to pursue their own careers, aggressively seeking the correct venues, contests, and awards in order to enhance their visibility as musicians. Many continue to take lessons, as well as give lessons.

Finding a master teacher and being accepted as a student by this teacher are crucial steps in the development of adult musical talent. Such teachers don't advertise for students, operating instead within informal networks of lesser teachers. I often use the movie *Madame Sousatzka* in my classes as a classic illustration of this pattern of talent development in musicians and in other top youthful performers. Madame Sousatzka, a middle-level piano teacher, struggled to keep her prize pupils, who moved on to other teachers when they felt ready. The movie explores the teacher's emotional difficulties and those of her students as they made their transitions.

Mentors, teachers, and other supporters are crucial to musical development. The cellist Pablo Casals was grateful throughout his life to his mother for her devotion to his musical talent; she was instrumental in his attending music school in Barcelona, far away from the tiny Spanish village where the family lived. Composer and conductor Leonard Bernstein studied with

Serge Koussevitzsky, Fritz Reiner, Heinrich Gebhard, Isabella Vengerova, and Aaron Copland. Teachers are so important in the musical world that program notes often list the teacher with whom the performer studied.

The successful conductor and composer, like the successful scientist, depends largely upon mentors. Rudolf said that conductors need older mentors who will initiate them into the requirements of the conductor's world. He noted that the initial success of a conductor is seldom because of publicity, but instead results from internal communication within the profession about who is up and coming. For example, Wagar noted that Dennis Russell Davies, when he was a piano major at the Juilliard School, met Luciano Berio, and "through Luciano I got to meet some very important musicians and composers."

Life at Juilliard

Judith Kogan, in a memoir called *Nothing but the Best: The Struggle for Perfection at the Juilliard School*, described the education of the world's finest young musicians who study at New York City's Juilliard School at Lincoln Center. Juilliard students believe that they are the elite young players of the world. They and the Juilliard administration both "seem to think that students at any other conservatory (except, maybe, the Curtis Institute of Music in Philadelphia) couldn't get into Juilliard and therefore can't play." Kogan continues:

> *Juilliard is the universe where the world starts and stops. Its window sealed, Juilliard is cut off from the world even physically. The tie that binds is music, and the force that creates order is ability. Some invisible hand ranks people. Ability loosely corresponds to technical proficiency. In some ways, the focus on ability blinds people to music itself. In some ways, music is appreciated not as something beautiful but as a tool of commerce. Professional motivation is more important than artistic, the glamour of personality more important than the art of music. (p. 24)*

The 750 talented musicians fought for the 84 practice rooms, where they practiced eight, 10 hours a day, confining their social lives "to those who do the same thing at the same level of proficiency." Students at Juilliard knew each other by the instruments they played, by how well they played the instruments, and by their teachers. They practiced, practiced, practiced until practice became such an internally motivated part of them that it resembled eating and breathing—except that practice was instilled after they were able to walk, and they ate and breathed from birth. Some even practiced their scales while reading their homework.

Kogan noted that practice makes students feel secure. If one practices something 40 times, one feels more secure than if one practices something 30 times. The practice becomes a way of avoiding the real world; through constant practice, students can avoid the stress of living in New York City, the pain of being an adolescent and a young adult, the agony of having one's ego battered, the instability of a profession in music, and even the daily self-evaluation when one can sound beautiful one day and horrible the next. If the students leave the practice room for a bathroom break, they may come back and find that another obsessive practicer has taken over the room.

After the competitions, the rivalries, the hours in the cafeteria, the required ear training and chorus classes, and the egos of the temperamental teachers, the students from Juilliard graduated and found that those who were their rivals were now their friends, for they had all come through, and now they only had to put "Juilliard" on their resumes in order to have people take notice.

Kogan said that few of these musicians have careers as soloists. Some get into orchestras, and some even become principals in orchestra sections. Some become teachers, some become freelancers. Some leave music. Some get to the pinnacles of success and then become jaded. Some move into different careers and find happiness and contentment. The real world demands a new kind of commitment, and the enormous discipline that has been imbued into the recent graduate will carry over into all aspects of life. However, Kogan noted that commitment must be something the musician has chosen, because if the commitment is seen as sacrifice or martyrdom, then the person will end up being bitter.

Despite her frank description of the demands of a profession in music, Kogan, who herself ended up in another profession, found that the ultimate discovery in a talented musician's life is a personal, even spiritual one. The musician ultimately discovers the basic and simple truth: the love of music. It was all worth it for the music.

The Sun of Community and Culture in Musicians

There are cross-cultural differences in attitudes toward musical talent and creativity. In Japan, for example, talent is not thought of as arising in a child; rather, talent is trained. Suzuki, in *Nurtured by Love*, advocated that musical talent could be trained from early infancy in a system of talent education called the Suzuki Method. He wasn't interested in definitions of talent, claiming that any child who learns to speak can learn music. Repetition of the correct, as in learning a foreign language, is necessary. He saw ability as being hard, personal work that necessitates repeating and repeating the correct until it becomes internalized.

Tone-deaf children are not hopeless, either, as is commonly thought in the United States. Suzuki said that if children who are tone-deaf, when singing the scale, usually sing the note *fa* a little high, then a new *fa* has to be taught to them. If 5,000 times they have heard that note wrong, they must hear the right *fa* 6,000 or 7,000 times. The children listen to the correct interval between *mi* and *fa* many thousands of times, and then the right *fa* is imbued into their natural listening and they can produce the right *fa*. The result is that they are no longer tone deaf. It takes six or seven months to achieve this with a six-year-old child.

With the Suzuki Method, a parent, usually the mother, works closely with the child in the acquisition of the rudimentary musical skills necessary for playing the violin. (Suzuki instruction on piano and cello is also available.) In one application of the technique, mothers of infants are first taught to play one piece on a tiny violin that is sized to the child. The child listens to recordings of the piece but does not play at first; training begins when the child asks for the violin. The first song is a set of variations on "Twinkle, Twinkle Little Star." This, it is to be emphasized, is a training method, and it follows the philosophy that musical intelligence can be taught. Asian education utilizes drill and practice to the point of mastery, and Westerners often wonder whether such education creates automatons or maestros.

However, the path to musical creativity may not be as cut and dried or age-related as stated here. Cross-cultural anomalies exist. Take the case of master sitar player Ravi Shankar. Shankar was from a theatrical family from Benares, India that began to tour the world and ended up being headquartered in Paris. Shankar early demonstrated talent in acting and in dancing, and as his family toured, he got used to the partying, the accolades, and the four-star hotels. He began to fool with the sitar, but he had no teacher, and so he copied, watched, and played by ear. In 1935, one of the greatest musicians of India came to be a soloist with the family group. Shankar was mesmerized. The man did not look unusual, but he had an inner flame that glowed like a volcano. The man was only with them for 10 ½ months, but Shankar's life course was transformed.

Shankar was viewed as being talented in poetry, dance, music, and painting, and everyone told him that everything he did was wonderful. This strange man, this teacher, was the first to tell Shankar that he lacked focus, that he was a gadfly, a butterfly, a jack-of-all-trades, a floater. To be good, he had to do one thing well and right. He said that he would teach Shankar if Shankar would leave the family touring company and everything else and come to study with him. Shankar thought about this for more than a year, but he finally went back to India at the age of 18. He stayed with his teacher (or guru) for more than seven years, living next to him in a very old house that had pests, snakes, insects, and wolves howling through the night. He suffered, but he also learned. Shankar went on to become one of the great masters of the sitar.

Shankar's method of composing influenced the contemporary composer Philip Glass, who met Shankar while studying with Nadia Boulanger, a famous teacher in Paris. Glass described their collaboration when the two worked together on the score of a movie. Shankar would come to the composing sessions, drink tea, tune his sitar, ask Glass to play the string drone, the tamboura, and then Shankar would sing the music to Glass and Glass would notate it. "If the piece was, say, three minutes long, he would first sing the entire three-minute flute part, then the entire three-minute violin part, and so on." Shankar's knowledge of the raga was so engrained that he could spontaneously compose after a period of meditation, calming, and praying.

The Indian tradition of music education which Shankar experienced teaches the musician to improvise. Indian classical musicians are improvisational musicians, creating the music spontaneously, creating as they go along. In fact, the term *raga* implies improvisation. The training emphasizes learning the raga from the guru. The musician follows a format, but it is really an ingrained structure. Indian classical musicians don't point to an A or B in the score. The structure imposes order, but they play what naturally comes out; sometimes the improvisational section is long, sometimes short. All in the ensemble work together in communication, automatically reacting to each other from their years of playing and training. Before a performance, Shankar washes, puts on clean clothes, meditates, and prays. Then he tunes his instrument, and while sitting cross-legged in the ancient position of Indian classical music, the music comes into his head and then out of his fingers, and he plays the first note, which fuses into the *raga*. He does not think about what note or notes he's playing. He compares the raga to a human being, to making love; he says the raga amalgamates with him and that he and the music become one.

Glass said that Shankar's way of music-making profoundly affected him. When Glass would try to transcribe the music that Shankar was singing to him, he would put in bar lines. Shankar would tell him that all the notes were equal, and so finally Glass took out the bar lines altogether. When he did this, he saw what Shankar meant. The music was more like a pulse or rhythm, and not groupings of eighth notes. Then Glass finally saw and understood that, indeed, all of the notes were equal. His contact with Indian music opened up for him his own new musical language. Shankar's daughter Anoushka (a genetic factor influencing the environment) is now a world-class sitar player as well. This is very unusual, as few world-renowned sitar players are women. This story illustrates not only the cross-cultural difference in classical music, but also the necessity in some societies for a student to apprentice him- or herself to a master teacher and to sacrifice, study, and learn. It also illustrates that music is a world language, and that creators from one culture often learn from creators from other cultures.

As in visual artists (Picasso's use of the bull influencing Jackson Pollock's use of the bull) and in writers (Ezra Pound's translation of Japanese Zen poets influencing contemporary poets like Robert Bly and James Wright) and in scientists (advances in quantum mechanics in Switzerland influencing theoretical physicists in the United States), musicians also learn from peers from other cultures. One culture can influence another, as talented composers and musicians communicate in the code of music, which is universal to those who want to learn. Paul Simon, in an article by Wilkinson, described his burning interest in South African music after hearing the group Lady Black Mambazo. This led to the collaborative album *Graceland*. Later, *Graceland* led to *The Rhythm of the Saints*, partly made in Brazil, after Simon had become convinced that an understanding of rhythm was essential for where his work would go next.

Hanging around with musical friends is also important. Pianist Gary Graffman, in his memoir *I Really Should Be Practicing*, said that his best friends were always musicians. As high school students, they would go down to the jazz clubs in Greenwich Village or meet at each other's houses and play for each other. Biographies are rife with the cross-fertilization between artists of the same genre and those of others. One of my favorite images is from the movie *Impromptu*. Novelist George Sand (played by Judy Davis) is lying under the piano of Chopin (played by Hugh Grant) listening rapturously to him while he plays. They are spending a month at an estate outside of Paris. In the film, artist Eugene Delacroix, writer Alfred DeMusset, composer Franz Liszt, and their various mistresses also joined the fun.

Synergy

Of course, community and culture are most obvious in the necessity among musicians for collaboration, playing together, communicating together, and being part of a musical group. When musicians play, they reach a state of synergy, in which they feel outside of time. Even though music is structured in time (even improvisational music), the musicians, while playing together, are carried on a wave of energy and group communication through the music. The whole that they create is greater than the individual parts that they are playing. Playing becomes effortless, the sense of self as being separate from the experience and the group disappears, and the experience seems to take on a life of its own.

Statistical Output of Composers

Simonton said in 1995 that the composers he studied tended to compose their best-known melodies between their thirty-third and forty-third years, peaking in production of famous tunes at about age 39. However, their most melodically original works appeared later, for the influence of the Zeitgeist or historical milieu (community and culture) upon their works tended to diminish as composers aged. In their older years, they felt more free to go against the temperature of the times, and they created their most original works after age 56. Bach's "Art of the Fugue" and the music Beethoven composed in his Third Period (the last five piano sonatas, the *Missa Solemnis*, and the Ninth Symphony among others) are examples.

Simonton also pointed out that longevity pays off in long-lasting fame. Those who become most famous had the longest careers, were the most prolific, and were born a long time ago. Like scientists, composers who attained the most eminence tended to begin their productivity earlier, to produce more, and to have long careers. Within those long careers, however, quality of life had a direct influence on quality of composition. That is, those who kept their health longer were able to keep composing.

However, the Sun of Community and Culture shines differently on the longevity of different types of musicians. A study by Patalano of 168 famous jazz musicians and 100 famous classical musicians showed that the jazz musicians died at an average age of 57.2, and classical musicians at age 73.3. Factors such as the use of drugs and alcohol, working conditions in the bars and clubs where jazz is played, the fact that jazz is more accepted abroad as an art form than it is in the United States, and marital and family problems caused by a lifestyle that requires the musician to be on the road contributed to the shorter life span of the jazz musicians.

Influence of Folk Culture

National cultures such as folk music, jazz, and ethnic music influence the music of composers. The Finnish composer Sibelius wrote at the time when the great language shift came, when there was a movement to overthrow the official Swedish language and replace it with the vernacular Finnish. The tone poem "Finlandia," within the larger work of the same name, is a folk tune. Bela Bartok's work is another example, as is the work of Aaron Copland. The derivative nature of much creative work is evident in the work of musicians, as it is in the work of other artists. Much creative work is elaboration, or extending, and much is "piggybacking," in the words of creativity training. The musical composer masters the structures and the forms necessary in order to be able to put them aside or to use them with variation.

Folk music has not only influenced classical musicians, it has influenced popular musicians as well, as do social movements. In Jenny Boyd's book, rock musician Bonnie Raitt described going to a Quaker summer camp where the camp counselors played the music of the Kingston Trio; the Weavers; Peter, Paul, and Mary; Joan Baez; and Bob Dylan. Then blues music began to influence her, and she began to spend her allowance on records by the Beatles and Muddy Waters. Boyd also described Paul Kanter and Jefferson Airplane, who entered the 1960s after the white-bread 1950s and who were middle class and privileged, at least compared to the other people in the world. They went to college and just drifted, as they had no idea what they wanted to do. Then, in 1961, 1962, and 1963, a lot of people began to make music and to join social movements such as the Anti-Vietnam Peace Movement and the Civil Rights movement. The music reflected the social concerns. Folk singers such as Pete Seeger and Joan Baez began to influence the youth with a feeling of social consciousness. The music of the Civil Rights movement, with Black people and White people holding hands and swaying to the gospel sounds of "We Shall Overcome," filled the print and broadcast media.

The Influence of African-Americans on Contemporary Music

The research on talent development does not often include the major contribution of the United States to world music—that is, the influence of African-American music. That contribution was developed in a completely different way from the way of formal training described above. In fact, Haskins noted that the influence of African-Americans on world music has been an influence of the poor, the disenfranchised, the untaught, and the untutored. When Africans were brought forcefully as slaves through the middle passage to the United States, they communicated with each other by way of drums and chants until the plantation owners banned the use of drums. They developed ways to subvert this ruling, and one of these was to tap their heels on the floor in certain rhythms. As the Africans were Christianized, their churches became a source of music through singing that used a call and response similar to that used on ships by the Irish and British sailors and in the fields by the laborers and the foremen. They also brought with them, besides the drums, the banjo and the bones, traditional African musical instruments.

Most Americans know and understand the great contribution of rhythm and blues, spirituals, soul music, and jazz to their national musical culture. Haskins said that it is traditional in many societies that the popular and eloquent music that speaks to everyone comes from the lower classes, and that it was the lot of the Africans who were brought here to provide that music to the United States people. The same is true in Argentina, where the tango is the national music. The tango arose from the urban working classes, from the hordes of immigrants, mostly men from Italy and Spain, who came and worked to send money back to the Old Country. Lonely and mournful, they spent much time in bodegas and in rooming houses where they played their bandonleons and guitars and danced with each other while waiting their turn with the prostitutes.

Thus, the creativity of uneducated musicians takes place in the form of popular music. Black musicians were thought by the elite White classical musicians not to be able to achieve competence in classical forms, and this prejudice prevented them even studying classical music. Those who did achieve competence were not permitted to sing or play in orchestras or in solo concerts. This continued even into 1939, when the Daughters of the American Revolution did not permit Marian Anderson, a well-known contralto, to sing at Constitution Hall in Washington, D.C. Eleanor Roosevelt made arrangements for her to sing on the steps of the Lincoln Memorial instead. The historic performance is hailed as a breakthrough for African-American artists. Female Black opera singers such as Leontyne Price and Jessye Norman were the exception rather than the rule. Sarah Vaughn was found weeping in her dressing room after singing for a state dinner at the White House. When asked why, she said she had come to Washington, D.C. 20 years ago and couldn't find a hotel room. Now she was singing in the White House. She was weeping from joy after years of great frustration.

The music that African-American popular musicians brought to the world was within the world's collective unconscious, according to Boyd. She quoted B. B. King as saying that the blues and the feelings it brings are at the core of most popular music. King said, "When I sing blues today I still get some of the spiritual feeling; it's a thin line between blues and gospel…and the roots of all music that I hear, especially in the Western world, seem to fit into the music that I play. So if I border the line of rock, or soul, country, or any other kind of music, I can incorporate it into the blues because there's a place there" (p. 121).

To illustrate the mammoth influence and role that African-American musicians have played in the world of music, here is a partial list of Black musicians who made American music unique.

- ○ Buddy Bolden (1868-1931), New Orleans jazz
- ○ Scott Joplin (1868-1917), Ragtime composer
- ○ W. C. Handy (1873-1958), Blues
- ○ James Reese Europe (1881-1919), 369th Infantry Band
- ○ Jelly Roll Morton (1885-1941), New Orleans, Chicago jazz
- ○ Ma Rainey (1886-1939), Classic blues singer
- ○ William Grant Still (1895-1970), Composer
- ○ Duke Ellington (1899-1974), Swing, jazz composer
- ○ Louis Armstrong (1900-1971), Jazz trumpeter
- ○ Mahalia Jackson (1911-1972), Spirituals
- ○ Billie Holiday (1915-1959), Jazz singer
- ○ Nat "King" Cole (1919-1965), Ballads, jazz
- ○ Charlie "Yardbird" Parker (1920-1955), Be bop
- ○ Miles Davis (1926-), Trumpet player, cool jazz
- ○ Bo Diddley (1928-), Rhythm and blues
- ○ Ray Charles (1929-), Soul
- ○ Quincy Jones (1933-), Composer
- ○ James Brown (1934-), Soul

○ Smokey Robinson (1940-), Motown
○ Aretha Franklin (1942-), Church soul
○ Stevie Wonder (1950-), Composer, singer
○ The Marsalis brothers—Wynton and Brandon, Composers, conductors

This list could go on and on. What about Bessie Smith, Chuck Berry, Art Tatum, Dizzy Gillespie, Erroll Garner, Billie Eckstine, Jimi Hendrix, The Supremes, Wilson Pickett, Bob Marley, Harry Belafonte, Bobby McFerrin, and Muddy Waters, for example? Would Elvis Presley have made such an impact without having been influenced by Bo Diddley and Chuck Berry? The Rolling Stones and the Beatles?

Rap musicians have a great contemporary influence as well. Teddy Pendergrass commented that rap speaks to the contemporary African American youth and that rap to these youth is a very serious form of art. Rap star Ice-T said that he began to create rap music in order to help his friends, to tell them what he saw. He thought it would be too depressing, but when he recorded *Six in the Morning*, people responded by buying his records. Irish singer Sinead O'Connor commented that hip-hop music is the most powerful and honest form of music because it brings people together with the many messages within the rhythms, drumbeats, and lyrics

Only two of the seminal figures on the list above had a rigorous formal education in music: Wynton Marsalis attended Juilliard, and William Grant Still attended Oberlin. Still later directed the NBC Symphony Orchestra, on radio, where it was not widely known that the conductor was Black, for there would have been repercussions. The Marsalis family is an example of a prototypical musical family, with all of the children playing instruments under the influence of their jazz musician father. However, the process of becoming a musician always entails practice and the influence of other musicians.

The evidence of discrimination and prejudice in the lives of African-American musicians is everywhere. For example, after the Civil War, it was thought that Blacks, especially Black men, were not capable of reading music.

Smokey Robinson, the Motown singer and composer, commented that the music industry was racist, saying it was not fair that his songs had to hit the top of the Black charts before being permitted to cross over to the White charts. In his autobiography, he said that he had symbolically

313

worked his way up from the back of the bus. In speaking about Black artists' influence, he noted that Black artists have changed, adapted, intensified, and spoken for American culture, especially in music.

Rap music, extremely popular among young people in both the cities and the suburbs, has had its influence on attitudes. One study by Johnson and colleagues showed that violent rap lyrics and performances have contributed to the stereotyping of young Black rap musicians as being more violent. The White and Black college students also stereotyped young Black rap performers as less intelligent. Rapper Sean (P. Diddy) Combs, for example, attended a prep school and then attended Howard University. He is the owner of a very successful upscale fashion company, but his image as a rapper portrays him as being "down and out" and prone to violence. This illustrates the influence of socioeconomic and cultural values on the perception of creativity.

The Sun of Gender in Musicians

The poverty-ridden childhood of jazz singer Ella Fitzgerald, her winning of a competition at The Apollo Theater in New York, and her not getting a job with a Harlem band because the leader thought she was too ugly to be a band singer are examples of home, chance, and gender in the life of one of America's premier vocalists. At the age of 15, Ella Fitzgerald, a good student with a memory that could retain lyrics and facts, left her abusive stepfather in Yonkers and moved to a cousin's in Harlem, where she worked as a lookout for a brothel and was sent to the New York Training School. She went truant and became a street performer. Nicholson's biography of her said that Chick Webb, her first bandleader, thought she was too big, didn't know how to dress, and didn't know how to talk to people. Webb thought that she was ugly, and he didn't want her to sing for his band. The "lookism," as Mary Pipher calls it, that is rife in society affected Ella Fitzgerald early. It also affected Janis Joplin, who, while at the University of Texas, was nominated to be "Ugliest Man on Campus." Friedman, in her biography of Joplin, described Joplin's arrival in San Francisco to audition for Big Brother and the Holding Company: Janis was plain, plump, and had a bad complexion. She wore jeans and masculine shirts. She had her hair in a ponytail or on top of her head in a bun and when her hair would fall down, it stuck out all over in disarray.

Physical beauty is important, even in the world of classical music. Anna Sophie Mutter's sexy album covers help sell her albums perhaps as much as her stunning playing of the violin. One commentary in the online magazine *FanFair* said, "When does a violin on a bare shoulder make such a beautiful sound? It is no exaggeration to say that Anne Sophie Mutter makes listening to difficult music easy and indeed quite pleasurable. Could it be partly attributable to the visual dimension she brings to the concert stage?" A reference to her weight included: "As she shed off the baby fat, she metamorphosed into a glamorous virtuoso who made a statement with her music of course, but also with her trademark strapless gown."

A study by Wapnick and colleagues showed that indeed, attractiveness matters for violin performers. More attractive violinists received higher musical performance ratings than less attractive ones.

The biography of cellist Jacqueline DuPré, as written by her sister Hilary and brother Piers, noted that many of the reviews of her work focused on her good looks and not on her playing. "It's not over until the fat lady sings," is a comment about the bodies of certain female opera singers. Who has ever heard similar sarcasm directed at the corpulent tenors who sing with them? "It's not over until Pavarotti sings?" "It's not over until Reuben of *American Idol* sings?"

Why Are There So Few Women Composers?

In an interview by Rosner and Abt, Aaron Copland discussed creativity in composing. Copland spoke of music being a language that expresses emotions at all times, but the composer only becomes aware that he is feeling such an emotion when he begins singing or playing a sad song, for example, and he wonders then why he is feeling sad. The lack of awareness in the mind of the composer about his feelings seems to create an abstractness. A person cannot compose when he is too depressed, because creating art is a positive statement, and the composer has to feel that he is accomplishing something.

If a composer composes when he is depressed, he then becomes elated so that he can express his depression. A composer might also compose to get rid of repressed anger. To create a chord that is fortissimo and dissonant is an expression of anger. Copland wondered why women have not become great composers, even though they have been great singers, pianists, string players, and musical interpreters. He said that perhaps women's inability to think abstractly is the reason, as music is shapeless, formless, and has no logical content.

Women in music, except for the necessary sopranos, mezzo-sopranos, and contraltos, seem to have been relegated to the same place as Blacks. Even those who were rigorously trained became helpmates and muses. Alma Mahler, wife of Gustav Mahler, is an example. She was classically trained in turn-of-the-century Vienna, a prime time for creativity. She was a serious composer and studied with other composers there. But Monson, her biographer, called her a "muse," an inspiration to male creatives. In his biography of Alma Mahler, Monson asserted that she was born too soon. If she had been born in the twentieth century, she could have been a major composer or conductor, but because she was born in the nineteenth century, she became a woman who devoted her life and her talents to brilliant and talented men who she thought were geniuses. After Gustav Mahler died, Alma married Walter Gropius, who founded the Bauhaus, and later she married Franz Werfel, a writer. She also had long affairs with the composer Alexander von Zemlinsky, Arnold Schoenberg's teacher; with Ossip Gabrilowitsch, a pianist; and with Oscar Kokoschka, the artist.

Are creative women musicians only good for being helpmates and muses? The last male bastion in music seems to be conducting—there are few Sarah Caldwells—but today, women composers can be found. Copland probably would have been surprised that the Pulitzer Prize for music composition in 1991 was won by a woman composer, Shulamit Ran, who won for her *Symphony*. Ran is a professor at the University of Chicago, and she said of her music that it is a reflection of life as she, the composer, interprets it. She wants her music to speak equally to the mind and heart.

Biographical Example of Marilyn Shrude

Marilyn Shrude, a Distinguished Artist, Professor of Music, and founder and former Director of the Mid-American Center for Contemporary Music at Bowling Green State University in Ohio, is another successful composer. Born in 1946, she has a doctorate in music from Northwestern University and is in mid-career. She has composed music for large and small ensembles, and her music has been performed in almost every state in the U.S. Performances of her music have also taken place in Korea, Switzerland, Germany, the Soviet Union, Canada, Belgium, the Netherlands, France, Japan, Taiwan, Poland, Spain, Austria, and Australia.

Shrude has received two Individual Artist Fellowships from the Ohio Arts Council and is a former board member with the International Alliance for Women in Music. In 1998, she was the first woman to receive the

Cleveland Arts Prize in music. She has received a Kennedy Center Freid-
heim Award, been named a Woman of Achievement by Women in the
Communications Industry (WICI), received two ASCAP/Chamber Music
America Awards for Adventuresome Programming, and an Ohioan Award
for contributions to the cultural life of Ohio. In 1997, she received an
Academy Award in Music from the American Academy of Arts and Letters.
In 2000, she received a Rockefeller Foundation Fellowship to the Bellagio
Center in Italy, and in 2002, a MacDowell Colony Fellowship. The citation
from the American Academy said that Marilyn Shrude's music is:

> *...imaginative, poetic, at times gentle, at other times powerful.*
> *With few notes, she can write a universe of beautiful sounds that*
> *soon cascade into harmonies of grandiose gesture, such as in the*
> Saxophone Concerto. *Her colorful instrumentation enhances all*
> *her ideas, and the elegant scores immediately give images of her*
> *wonderful conceptions, melodic lines, counterpoint, and fresh*
> *sonorities. All these devices come from a refined, sophisticated ear.*
> *Her works are perfectly constructed, genuine, and at all times*
> *musical.*

In my interview with her in 2002, Marilyn described how she grew
up in an ethnic Catholic Polish and Lebanese family in Chicago and
entered a convent as a high school student of 15. She had always composed
music, though it wasn't particularly valued or noticed. Her career as a
composer began formally during her graduate work at Northwestern University, when she took a course in composition. She was the only woman in
the composition class at the time, the early seventies.

Shrude's middle and late adolescence were times of concentrated
effort in music. She took lessons, and since she was in a convent and had
decided to become a music teacher, she had intensive study—more intensive than if she had been in a regular high school with all its distractions.
She practiced and also spent a lot of time singing. She had been playing the
organ for Masses since the age of 11. The simultaneous and intensive training in religion and music led her to doubt her talent, because humility was
required of a religious girl, and she could never think that her work was
good. When she emerged from the convent, she had to work through many
feelings so that she could accept her talent. Though many of her teachers
and mentors were supportive, the years in the convent had given her a weak

self-concept. Composing was not encouraged because it was vain, and women were not to be proud.

Shrude said, "I always had the urge to write music, and did so since the age of ten; I did it on my own, mostly for school programs. People knew I did it, but it was never encouraged. They rarely looked at it. I had very little professional feedback on it whatsoever." She taught music in a high school for a few years after she left the convent. Then she decided to quit teaching and went to graduate school at Northwestern, where she met her husband-to-be, saxophonist John Sampen.

She was in residency at Northwestern for one year while she got her master's degree, and then she went back to teaching school. She and John Sampen married and moved to Kansas, where Marilyn found herself without a composition teacher. The years in Kansas were spent teaching herself composition by listening to contemporary works. She views this as an exploratory period during which she was gaining literacy, trying out ideas, imitating. She sometimes studied with a good friend on the faculty of the university where her husband was teaching, but she was essentially teaching herself. The couple returned to Northwestern to pursue doctorates. When she got back to Northwestern, she found that her relationship with her mentor on the composition faculty had changed. She had grown. She was not as needful as she had been. She began to strike out on her own.

Shrude talked about the necessity for a composer to know people who perform music. Many of the strides she had made as a composer were as a result of having good performers to write for. The main struggle, she said, is one of time, for she and John have two children.

Like Copland and Ran, Shrude expresses her emotions through her compositions. Even when she has started a composition ostensibly to solve a technical problem, she finds later that the music essentially turns out to have expressed something she was struggling with emotionally. I think most creative artists would agree that their art is an expression of their emotions.

Most of Shrude's pieces are narratives, even though the story is not apparent. The form of "A Window Always Open on the Sea," composed early in 1990, is shaped by lines from a poem by Michael Mott. Mott and his wife were neighbors and good friends of Shrude and Sampen when Michael's wife was dying of cancer. Shrude's father had recently died, and Shrude's sister-in-law was dying of cancer. This piece turned out to be "a working out of all these deaths." She dated the piece the day her sister-in-law died. For Shrude, composing is the expression of emotions, no matter how the piece starts out.

Shrude doesn't compose on a computer or on a piano, but at her table. She tries things on the piano, but "you get to a point where you know how things work. I can hear the sounds in my head." She works in the lengthiest blocks of time she can get. Like most artists in whatever genre, she composes "because I have to." She often uses the poetic texts of others in her compositions. Howard McCord's "Arctic Desert" (1979) was one; "Lines from Tennyson" (1984) and "I Wandered Lonely as a Cloud" (1989) were others.

Works by Shrude include: "Psalms for David" (1983); "Genesis: Notes to the Unborn" (1975); "Four Meditations; To a Mother and her Firstborn" (1975); "Solidarnosc" (1982); "Drifting Over a Red Place" (1982); "Interior Spaces" (1987); "Renewing the Myth" (1988); and "Amish" (1989), the theme music for the nationally-syndicated PBS series *Cooking from Quilt Country, Cooking from the Heartland, Marcia Adams' Kitchen.* "A Gift of Memories" (1992) was based on Wordsworth's poetry and was written on commission from the Cleveland Chamber Symphony at the death of her mother. "Concerto for Alto Saxophone and Wind Ensemble" (1994); "Notturno: In Memoriam Toru Takemitsu" (1996); "Eight Bagatelles" (1997); "Chant" (1998); "Transparent Eyes" (2000); "Portraits" (2001); and "Memories of a Place" (2002).

Shrude composes mainly on commission. She rarely submits her pieces to competitions or blindly to publishing houses. She has a network of fellow musicians all over the country. "I know a lot of people all over and they're helpful. They sometimes give you favors that you don't even expect." As co-director of the New Music & Art Festival in Bowling Green, Ohio, she oversees the audition process for the 500 submissions that the Festival attracts from all over the world. Twenty compositions are chosen for performance. Shrude agrees that it can be difficult and costly for composers, especially for younger people, to have their work performed well. Often, a composer must find some performers, hire them, and organize a studio performance. A good tape can be worthwhile for opening doors to festivals, contests, and the like.

Marilyn Shrude is a mother as well as a composer, and being a mother has put her on a different timeline than other composers. Like the artist mothers in Foley's study, Shrude has had to make modifications in order to combine parenting with composing. The value of having a supportive husband cannot be underestimated, for she stated that the children "have always come first. We've done pretty well at trying to accommodate each others' schedules, even with young children, though it's been difficult."

Whether having children has stymied her career doesn't matter to Shrude. "Having children who are now young adults has been a new and enjoyable phase of the parenting process." She can't imagine not having children. "I love having children. It's so enriching. If I didn't have children I'd be more reclusive. I wouldn't have to schedule myself to cook, to take them places. When I'm alone, I let my duties go and don't seek out social contacts." Letting go of one's children when they become young adults, she said, is one of the most difficult aspects of parenting. "Growing into a relationship which is no longer parent/child has its own set of difficulties, but the rewards are great." She has never thought that she would have been better off without children, nor has she been resentful because of the demands of motherhood interfering with her creative work.

When asked whether improvisation is more or less creative than composing, Shrude said that many improvisational artists can "speak but not read and write. To be able to read the music and to write it down is to know the full language of music. Music is a language. Some people read and some people write and some people do all of it."

Shrude considers herself competitive but not obsessed. There are things that she might try for but doesn't. Like most creators, one of her pleasures as a composer is to receive recognition from peers. To be performed by a major orchestra such as the Chicago Symphony or the New York Philharmonic is always a goal.

Shrude is in the middle of her career and does not exhibit the anxiety or drive observed in most composers. Perhaps the balance she has achieved comes as a result of being a mother. The serenity with which she views her life and her accomplishments seems to reflect an aspect of the creative female personality that hasn't been explored in research.

Foley's study showed that the artist mothers, while they were often in a frenzy trying to get everything done, felt enormous serenity in doing their work. Foley contrasted the artists with professional women who worked in law, medicine, and business and found that the artists, perhaps because they were able to express their emotions through their art, seemed to have less emotional stress. In fact, their emotional stress came from having their responsibilities as mothers interfere with their emotional need to work in their art. One of the artist-mothers was not able to work for 10 months because of a complicated pregnancy, and she said, "Honestly, I'm sort of tearing my hair out about not having painted for that length of time." One of the professional mothers spoke of "going nuts" when she was at home with her children for too long, and of escaping into her workplace where the demands were predictable and appointed. The professionals had been high academic achievers, and they felt accomplishment in achieving a product, a sale, or a contract. By contrast, the artists valued the "process" of painting, which provided "escape and relief of tension and the return of mental tranquility."

Women Conductors

Women conductors are rare. Perhaps this has to do with a perception of dominance. The conductor must be able to inspire the often-recalcitrant musicians by taking charge. Adult men may not want a woman to take charge over them. More women seem to be conductors of junior orchestras, children's orchestras, and young people's ensembles than they are of high level symphonies. This may indicate an extension of the old belief that women are more nurturing than men.

Recent Research

Recent research on gender issues among musicians has included research on female rock performers and classical performers. Stremikis found that female professional musicians are exceptionally self-directed, impelled to make music, nonconforming, and begin preparing for careers in music when they are very young. They come from families that are musical, and there is some evidence that they have no brothers, or if so, they are much younger brothers.

The Sun of Chance in Musicians

On the importance of chance and seizing the chance when it comes, several conductors emphasized that often, as in the case of Esa-Pekka Salonen, conductor of the Los Angeles Philharmonic Orchestra, and of Leonard Bernstein, late conductor of the New York Philharmonic Orchestra, the opportunity, if not taken, may not come again. Salonen's chance came in London when he was very young. He essentially experienced the understudy phenomenon, stepping in and conducting when Michael Tilson Thomas got sick. When the word passed that a 25-year-old Finn would, with five days notice, conduct the Mahler Third, the world's leading classical music managers and record producers flew to London, for the orchestra was taking a serious risk of a kind that had all but vanished from the music business. Salonen had stepped in at a concert in Gothenberg and had caught the attention of a London agent by sight-reading Luciano Berio's work. The London concert likewise went well; Lebrecht described him as directing the six-movement, 90-minute symphony "without turning a hair or missing a tempo change."

The same thing happened for Leonard Bernstein. On November 14, 1943, Bernstein made his debut as a conductor for the New York Philharmonic at Carnegie Hall in New York City. This was Bernstein's "big break" and a major turning point in his career. He got this break because he was substituting for another conductor, Bruno Walter, who had fallen ill. Both of these conductors got their big break through being at the right time in the right place and being ready to step in.

Wagar quoted Catherine Comet, one of the few women conductors, who said:

> ...*a conductor has to study and be ready for the chances, because everybody does get chances. The chances are never at the perfect time, but the conductor just has to be ready when they come. And they often come.*

Solti said, similarly, that struggling conductors must be confident that someday someone will give them a chance, and when it comes, the young conductors must be prepared. They must go and bother people for the chance. Solti said that is how he got started. He got experience wherever and whenever he could get it. He was confident that talent is noticed, but that the talented must be prepared when the chance comes.

The Creative Process in Music: Improvisation and Creativity

Chance also includes improvisation. You may be asking why all of this describes the development of talent and not of creativity. Isn't creativity more loose, more free? All of the studies and memoirs seem to describe practice, competition, and striving in an effort to learn how to use the musical instrument. How is this creativity? Many musicians and devoted listeners would insist that the instrumentalist who has mastered the technique—so that the soul of the music can come through—is as creative as the person who puts the notes down on the page, just as the actor would insist that he is as creative as the playwright. However, without entering into the debate over who is more creative, we will now take a look at composers and improvisers who do sit with the blank page at the piano, and who do put notes on the page, and who do go through what we have conventionally called the creative process.

The difference between improvisation and composing can be illustrated through scenes from the life of composer and conductor André Previn. He has done it all. He's been a successful composer of scores for movies, he was a successful jazz pianist with his own trio, he has been a songwriter, and he has risen in the ranks of orchestral conductors to conduct world-class orchestras. Born in Berlin in 1929, Previn was the son of an enthusiastic amateur musician who took his son to concerts. Previn felt pure joy at the age of five in hearing a symphony, and from then on, he pursued music as a career. In Bookspan and Yodkey's biography *André Previn*, Previn said of his childhood, "I think we musicians have always had rather selfish childhoods. The luxury of having a unilateral talent, which makes one's future life inevitable, is wonderful, but it also makes you selfish." He said that he was insular and had a narrow perspective. "I myself was always so concerned with being a musician, with becoming a good musician, with becoming a better musician, with learning this and with learning that, that even my areas of amusement and leisure time, even my play time seemed to be connected inevitably with music." He said he never even looked at what was happening in the world at large.

Previn was so classically trained that he couldn't improvise. Early in his life, fleeing Hitler, his family moved to Los Angeles, where Previn came under the influence of American pop culture, especially jazz. At 14, he heard a scratchy recording of "Sweet Lorraine" by blind Black piano player Art Tatum. He "just fell apart. It was unbelievable." Previn then scoured the stores for the song "Sweet Lorraine" and found that it was just a "pleasant, folksy little tune." Wondering where all of the notes had come from, it dawned on him that Tatum himself had added them to the arrangement. "He'd taken that puerile thirty-two-bar melody and made ingenious music out of it." Previn became fascinated. He found a recording of the Tatum version of the song, and by painstakingly playing it over and over, he began to "notate each song from the record, note by note," using up several packs of needles.

The process was a long and a painstaking one, for Tatum's playing
was crammed with fistfulls of notes and harmonic changes that

might look like mistakes on paper if you hadn't heard them first. Here was a musical magician whose illusions remain to this day something of a mystery to his fellows. No less a jazz pianist than Oscar Peterson...tells of being stunned by his first hearing of a Tatum record; Peterson at first refused to believe anything but that he'd heard two pianists and a bass player, not just one man on one piano. (p. 103)

Previn finally finished notating the music, and he had page after page of it; sometimes just a few bars would take over one full page of notation as he listened to Tatum. Then he began to practice the music, "like you'd learn a composition of Mozart's." He said he didn't understand how jazz worked. He thought that reading notated music was how to do it. He finally learned Tatum's songs and would practice them for hours. Then he realized that jazz was about improvisation, making things up. He said, "A jazz player had to be his own composer and play not premeditatively, but make up his music on the spot. Improvisation. *That's* what jazz was all about" (p.104).

In a study of improvisation in Indian music (the *raga*, as mentioned above), in flamenco, in Baroque music, in organ music, in rock, and in jazz, guitarist and author Derek Bailey noted that classical training acts against the ability to improvise because of the attitude that it instilled into classical musicians against making mistakes in the notated texts. Conductors would call the notion of asking orchestras to improvise unthinkable. Modern composers have tried to go beyond this by creating music that is not so set, so prescribed that the instrumentalist must follow each note by each note.

Davis interviewed Anthony Pay, a clarinetist who commented that the reason that classical musicians have trouble improvising comes down to a basic difference in approaches to music. Symphony orchestra and chamber musicians are trying to discover what the composers meant when they put down the music. Improvisational players, such as jazz musicians, are trying to discover what is within themselves. They can bend notes in improvisation. Pay thought that improvisation was "unknown poetry in which I can progress. In playing written, precisely notated music I'm not actually progressing" (p. 69).

Rock 'n' roll musicians also improvise. Phil Collins described to Jenny Boyd how the band Genesis would compose its songs. When the band would enter the studio, the members would often have written nothing for the group because they were all solo artists as well, and they saved their compositions for their own albums. "We go in and just turn everything on and start playing, and we improvise and improvise for days until something works." Collins would tape everything, and the group would listen back.

Someone would say, "That sounds interesting. What happened there?" To write songs by such a process, the group needed to be uninhibited, to trust the others, and to go out and take risks. The others can't mind if someone starts to sing out of tune, trying to reach a note in a melody that hasn't been written yet. "We all know we've got to let our trousers down without worrying about it." Such a process of trust, improvisation, and "chemistry" can happen only in certain bands. "And that's what makes the band great, at least the experience of doing that. It's very enjoyable because you're creating something out of nothing," Collins said (p. 251).

Paul Simon's creative process is also improvisational, according to an article by Wilkinson in *The New Yorker*. He seldom "gets" songs in their entirety, as he did with "Still Crazy After All These Years," which "arrived" when he was in the shower. (Note the terms "gets" and "arrived," which have to do with an external inspiration.) A song usually takes him about three months to write. In the early 2000s, Simon experienced a dry period of more than a year and a half.

Simon has a musical memory for many of the songs he heard as a child from the dim radio station from England that played early rock 'n' roll. His melodies begin with a few notes, a short phrase, which he works into longer lines, records, and plays over and over. Melodies also evolve with his talented band members, who are "very intelligent"—they need "no charts, every musician remembers his parts," and they are multinational. Simon called his band so good that they are "like driving a really expensive race car: if you have the touch it responds, and if you don't, it goes everywhere."

Jenny Boyd, in *Musicians in Tune,* said that session drummer Peter Erskine commented that nowadays young jazz musicians are taught to repeat common notes or phrases, "get them under their fingers, so when they're improvising, they're really just recycling a lot of scales they've played before many, many times." When jazz guitarist John Abercrombie taught these young people, he would take a tune and play it in half-notes so that the young musicians would not be able to play what their muscle memory in their fingers knew. "You have to be very creative then because every note has to be a good choice." Keith Strickland of the B-52s described improvisation as being similar to children's play. "Being in touch with the child in you is part of the whole creative process. I don't feel that I write songs as much as I make them up; it's playing the way you do in your childhood." He said that a musician has to be very open and nonjudgmental when doing this. "We do that as a band; we go through the improvisational process; we jam, allowing anything to happen" (p. 81).

New age jazz saxophone player Paul Horn spoke to Boyd about improvising as having a peak experience. "When I started to improvise, I found I could get up and play music, with thoughts coming, and these thoughts could be translated into musical terms." He would hear with his inner ear and this sound would connect down his arms into his fingers. "Intellectually, by the time you've even thought about it, you're eight beats later." Horn said that playing jazz is very fulfilling because the musician never gets bored. "It comes out different every time." He said that the energy in improvising is "a spiritual thing" because the musician can transcend the intellect and get into the here and now. "Jazz comes as close as you can to the spiritual" (p. 160).

Composer Charles Ives grew up as the son of a music teacher and bandleader. His memory was filled with church songs, community songs, patriotic songs. He and his father would compose together for church choirs and community bands. Often, the amateur players and singers would be out of tune. Ives composed tunes where the singers would sing in one key and the accompanist would play in another. In his biography of Ives, Swafford noted that even as a teenager, Ives would go against conventional composition techniques into improvisation. Ives' searching imagination would poke at musical conventions and rules in fresh ways. As a teenage organist in Danbury, Connecticut, Ives performed many pieces, for example, *Variations on "America,"* as improvisations before writing them down.

Is formal study of the medium or achieving a basic level of expertise in the medium necessary for truly creative products to be produced? The British aesthetician Robert Abbs would say yes, even though the ears of the world's jazz lovers would disagree. Abbs believed that only people who are trained in their fields can be receptive to the ideas that come to them and can transform these ideas into useable symbols. In *A is for Aesthetic,* Abbs wrote that:

> ...so-called accidents from the unconscious were really from the minds of people who were already working on a composition problem. Their high level of training in musical composition led them

to create chords they could hear in their minds, such as the E-flat major chord. Only people who were masters in the style of composition of their own culture could solve such problems.

Abbs's comments imply that there is some music that is of a higher form than other music and that "true" originality comes in creating classical music. Others would assert that "true" creativity comes in having no notes in front of you, only a melody in your head, and in being able to transform that melody into jazz, folk, pop, rap, or rock. The improvisational musician Stephen Nachmanovitch, began his book *Free Play* with these words:

I am a musician. One of the things I love best is to give totally improvised solo concerts on violin and viola. There is something energizing and challenging about being one-to-one with the audience and creating a piece of work that has both the freshness of the fleeting moment, and when everything is working the structural tautness and symmetry of a living organism. It can be a remarkable and often moving experience in direct communication. (p. 4)

The artist, no matter what genre he works in, uses his art as an expression of emotion, and when he is deprived of that expression, he feels conflict and tension. Jenny Boyd quoted jazz drummer Robin Horn, who said that when he hasn't practiced for a week, "I start to become a real uptight son of a bitch." He said that the music has to come out. "It has to be satisfied and nurtured. I have a really strong inner drive. It's like an inner voice that nags at me. When I've finished playing, after about an hour, I feel a thousand times better." Ultimately, for these players, composers, conductors, and performers, making music is about passion, a love of the medium, and a natural proclivity to express emotion through music.

Summary

1. The development of musical talent takes much practice, work, and hard training.

2. The Genetic Aspect: Though many generations of certain families enter the domain of music, it is thought that the nature-nurture influence is more nurture than nature.

3. Emotional Aspect: Musicians are similar in personality to other creative people, with slight variations among types of musicians. Composers and conductors had the most extreme personalities.

4. Passion for the Domain: Musicians want and need to use music as a form of expression.

5. Sun of Home: The whole family is affected in the development of great musical talent. The family may move to better teachers, and siblings may be affected by the emphasis on developing one child's talent.

6. Sun of School: Young, talented musicians often undergo a "midlife" crisis in adolescence as they move from natural expression to learning the structure and mechanics of music.

7. Sun of Community and Culture: There are cross-cultural differences in talent development. Asians, for example, emphasize repetition, drill, and training, while Americans emphasize inspiration and improvisation.

8. African-Americans have produced a music heritage that has affected popular music and jazz worldwide.

9. Sun of Chance: The musician must first be prepared. Then, opportunity must be seized when it comes. Chance is also improvisation.

10. Sun of Gender: Women composers exist. Women conductors exist. Women musicians find that their appearance matters.

11. Creative process: Improvisation and formal composition require different skills; there is controversy about which is more creative.

Chapter 11

Physical Performers: Actors, Dancers, and Athletes

*The qualities above all necessary to a great actor: in my view
he must have a great deal of judgment. He must have in
himself an unmoved and disinterested onlooker.*
        —Diderot

*I know a woman, lovely in her bones,
When small birds sighed, she would sigh back at them;
Ah, when she moved, she moved more ways than one.*
        —Theodore Roethke

I don't remember a time when I wasn't moving.
        —Judith Jamison

She is so dramatic about everything. Even the least bit of criticism will send her into a tirade of histrionics. She talks to her dolls a lot and makes up elaborate scenarios taking place in distant lands, where she takes all the parts. And her brother! He can't stop moving. He can't sit still. Teachers get angry and may even call him hyperactive. They say he has a lot of energy. When the chorus sings, he moves to the music, even in church.

    Children like this are incipient actors, dancers, or athletes. As such, they are interpreters, like music performers. I posed a question in the previous chapter in regard to these performers: Are choreographers and playwrights the truly creative ones, and are actors and dancers merely tools of the words and patterns? Let's investigate.

Think back for a week. Can you count the actors you have watched perform? If you have watched an hour of commercial television, you have seen approximately 14 minutes of commercials, each one featuring actors. In each dramatic show, you watched actors. If you went to a store, the salesperson was probably performing for you. (Perhaps they didn't *really* like you that much.)

Did you watch professional sports where someone spiked a ball or lay moaning on the court after a foul? They were giving a performance for the crowd. Did you watch a political speech? Acting again. Did you teach this week? Were you truly so intensely involved with the students as you pretended to be?

Did you tell someone a story, or did someone tell you a story? Chances are, role-playing was part of your week as you heard or told stories: "And then he said...and then she.... Can you believe it?" Even though you might not have gone to the theater this week, you saw acting or performed yourself.

Acting is everywhere, for in its basic definition, acting is pretending. One self pretends it is another self. This pretense is socially desired and approved of by all concerned. If we were our raw selves and did not act instead of act out, the world would be ruled by emotion, and social convention would take a back seat. Athletes and sales representatives are as much performers as actors and musicians. In most schools, each team of athletes receives special equipment, special coaches, and in some places, elaborate stadiums and arenas where they can show their stuff. Yet few athletes play beyond high school except in community leagues.

While athletes are often admired and treated by their schools as special, actors have reputations as being unconventional, of not conforming to classroom expectations or school rules. It is not easy to love a classroom actor. The biographies of many actors reveal that they were class clowns, cut-ups, rebels, or outsiders as children and young adults in their schools, and they were sometimes seen as problem students by their teachers. Besides that, everyone knows that formally trained actors have trouble finding jobs, so why develop those talents? But these students get laughs from fellow students. They want to continue.

The creative process in these physical domains of acting, dancing, and athletics does not differ from the descriptions of those in other domains. The presence of imagery, imagination, and a dreamlike state is often described by people in these career fields. For example, actor Joseph

Chaikin said, "Most of the creative work is done in that dream life between thinking and fantasy, and requires sometimes that the actor rest, and let the image move itself in his mind." An electricity passes between the audience and the performer. Actor Lynne Fontaine said, "When I am on a stage, I am the focus of thousands of eyes and it gives me strength. I feel that something, some energy, is flowing from the audience into me. I actually feel stronger because of these waves."

The communal feeling aroused by a performance is addictive, and people, both performers and audiences, return again and again for the energy that is generated. In 2002, I attended a performance of *Metamorphosis* on Broadway. Taking place mostly in water, the element of life and of the unconscious, the play retells Greek and Roman myths in a compelling and emotional way. At the end, the audience rose to applaud, tears streaming down our cheeks. We were energized, experiencing a sense of bonding. As we stood, one of the actors stopped his bow, quieted our applause, and began to speak to us about contributing to a charity related to medical care for aging actors and for actors with AIDS. We had already spent $75.00 for our tickets, $25.00 for parking, and if we had lunch, another $25.00 or $30.00! But because of our warm feelings generated by the art, we gave more. The actors stood by the exits with baskets and gifts for contributions.

The baskets overflowed with $20 bills. I myself contributed $40 for a signed poster of the cast. Now the magic is gone, the generosity is over, and I look at that poster, knowing I will never hang it on my wall, knowing that I was caught in the holy moment of theater, the shamanic moment of healing, the Aristotelian moment of fear and pity. It happens not only in theater; performance in athletics creates this sort of energy as well. Who has not stood to shout and scream with glee and affirmation when the team scores? The experience of being in the crowd is as transforming as that of being the performer.

Actors

We are mesmerized and mentally transported, whether we attend an athletic, theatrical, or dance performance. If so, why does society have such an ambiguous attitude toward actors and acting? On the one hand, a famous actor is venerated and paid millions of dollars to do a blockbuster action film; on the other hand, the actor is thought to be somewhat frivolous, weird, and outside of the norm. The "theater crowd" in high school and college is often its own group, distinct and separate from other academic achievers and from other social groups.

This ambiguous attitude has historical foundations. The traveling companies that went from town to town in the early days of this country were welcomed as a diversion from the everyday and as carrying the news of the outside world, but they were also looked at suspiciously as having lower morals. We do not remember the names of the characters our favorite actors played in their roles; we remember that the movie or play starred Al Pacino or Tom Cruise, but not the characters that they played. Yet Marlon Brando has been quoted by Richard Schickel as saying that he thinks acting as a profession is not worthy of a man. Even while he devalued his profession, Brando collected the money given him for acting.

The actor, the sacred icon—Marilyn Monroe, Brad Pitt, Julia Roberts—carries a shining weight of awe that could even approach worship. The actor is a shaman, muse, magician, wizard, healer. The similarity in architecture of churches and theaters is also worth noting. This connection of the theater with the divine has existed for centuries, and though this is not the time nor place to discuss the topic at length, we should not leave the topic of the actor without mentioning this strange power of creation and feelings of awe and wonder that actors seem to work within the hearts of their audience. Also worth pondering are the fan clubs, with the doppelganger-like phenomena of "fandom," and then the darker side of such astonishing adoration, the existence of the stalker-fan so enthralled with the celebrity that the actor must have bodyguards and live behind iron gates. What basic need in such cases does adoration of the actor fulfill?

The Genetic Aspect: Actors

Although theatrical children often come from theatrical families, such as the Redgraves, the Fondas, the Bernhardts, the Sheens, the Burtons, and the phenomenally successful Culkin children, it is also interesting to note that many of the New York City parents who refused to let their children audition for casting agents are people from the theater and film industries. "I have seen what can happen to child actors," one said.

The Emotional Aspect: Personalities of Actors

Unlike visual artists, actors—for all the value we accrue to them by paying a few of them millions in salaries and by writing about their loves and lives in popular magazines and gossip columns—have attracted little scientific curiosity as to their personality characteristics. A few psychometric studies do exist. In the *Myers-Briggs Type Indicator* technical manual, a sample of 62 actors was found to be among the top five professional groups that preferred ENFJ (Extraversion, Intuition, Feeling, and Judgment). Also showing this same configuration were clergy, home economists, priests and monks, and health teachers, as well as writers, artists, entertainers, and agents.

The ENFJ personality is thought to combine intuition with extraversion; they are change agents, they have broad interests, and they like new relationships and new patterns. FJ's prefer to use feeling in the behavior they outwardly show, and as would be necessary for actors, they are very observant, especially about the needs of people. They are "expressive leaders" and "spend energy in making people happy and in bringing harmony into relationships."

Another study, by Buchanan and Bandy, was of psychodramatists. Successful psychodrama applicants were found to prefer ENFP (Extraversion, Intuition, Feeling, and Perceiving); they were innovative people who were not conservative. Nine out of 10 certified psychodramatists preferred intuition (N), and only one-fourth of psychodramatists were introverts.

The actor who performs acting as either manipulation or as an art must probe human nature in order to pretend. Intuition is necessary. Such pretense is based on close observation of humankind and its physicality, as well as people's outward expression of inward conditions.

The actor leads a precarious existence in the realm of ego, with rejection almost inevitable. The personality attribute of resilience is essential, as is a tolerance of ambiguity. The actor constructs portraits of characters from observation cycled through self, and so, as psychiatrist Brian Bates noted, actors are probably both the most extraverted and most introverted of all artists. They must strip down to their essence and project to their audience. "To act is to risk, and takes courage."

Actors, Dancers, Athletes: Cognitive Aspect

Of Gardner's "frames" of intelligence, bodily-kinesthetic intelligence is what actors, dancers, and athletes exhibit. Actors and dancers display spatial intelligence also, but the personal intelligences—interpersonal intelligence and intrapersonal intelligence—are what enable them to interpret the world through their bodily actions. Athletes are performers also. Consider the dramatic stamping of the foot and throwing of the tennis racket after a referee's call—the athlete is performing for the crowd. Bodily-kinesthetic intelligence is "skilled use of the body" that has evolved in humans over millions of years.

Westerners too often divorce the mental from the physical and speak of the body as separate from the soul or the heart. Recent thought reconciles the two, as people are urged to try body-mind forms of exercise like yoga and Tai Chi, and research shows that physical activity is positively related to better health and longevity.

All forms of performance are called "play." The term "play" is used in theater to indicate the script the actors perform, in athletics to indicate a special move that is rehearsed over and over again by the person or team, in music to indicate the physical interaction of the body with the instrument. All play is serious, though in our society, we use the term to indicate a lack of seriousness: "Stop playing and come in and do your homework." "Want to play stick ball?" "Do you play bridge?" "I just want to play on my vacation; I'm burned out." "What made you use that play in the game, coach?" "Teach me how to play the guitar."

Play involves movement. "The chess *play*er made a brilliant *move* and beat his opponent." "'*Move! Move!*' the coach shouted to his players during practice." "He made a *move* on her at the party." In order to perform the required *move*ment, the *play*er's body must often be changed permanently or temporarily. The ballet dancer must turn her feet. The football player must bulk up. The actor must diet and exercise to maintain the physical ideal for the ingénue or leading man. The center of balance within the body must be broken down and then rebuilt.

Performers in the arts and athletes are similar. Both need original endowments of great physical talent, and they both depend on health professionals to keep them in physical shape for their performances. Both athletes and artists "play," "train," "exercise," "drill," "practice," "compete," and study with "coaches." Both are called "players." Both have mentors who exert phenomenal influence on them. Both must be able to work with groups and must understand teamwork. Both athletes and performers show their mettle in competitive situations. Performing in competitions is their reason for being.

Performers must also have good memories. This is not required of creators to the degree that it is required of performers. Creators might have good long-term memory for digits or words, but performers have what is called *active memory*. While memorizing has lost its emphasis in most of education, performers must know how to memorize, for as John Sloan

Allen said, "who but a performer has to memorize anything like the score of a symphony or a concerto, the choreography of a ballet, or the role of Hamlet?" The performer begins with the work, and the license to embellish or to improvise is a limited license, because the original work is always there, and straying too far from it negates it.

To put the work into active memory, the performer must practice in order to acquire automaticity. Arduous practice and rehearsal are required. Intense concentration is required. Musicians respond intuitively to sounds, actors to emotional innuendo, dancers and athletes to spatial patterns. They may thus become preoccupied with the "how to," with the practicality of technique, and they may become quite narrow in their orientation to the world. That is the challenge of the educator of performers. If one doubts the physicality necessary for performing, look at the fingers of the pianist surely hitting the right note with great rapidity and accuracy. Look at the ballet or modern dancer leaping or spinning and then landing on the right mark. Look at the calm rib breathing of the actor delivering a Shakespeare soliloquy. How the body should be used is proscribed according to the field in which the performer works.

Passion for the Domain: The Thorn

Like other creative people, actors, dancers, and athletes are obsessed with their work. "What else would I do?" is the watch cry for the passion. "I just want to keep working," Laura Linley said in an interview with Gurewitsch. "It's true what they say. You have to love the work; you have to love acting more than you love success. Or it can really damage you."

However, in movie acting, "the look" is so important that passion for the domain is subsumed to the desire to make money. Many contract actors from the old MGM studios, such as Ava Gardner, were hired only for their looks and not for their passion to act.

Creative Process in Acting

Jill Nemiro studied the creative process in acting. She found three stages: the preparation phase, the rehearsal phase, and the performance phase. Within the preparation stage, she found that the actors relied on their academic training and their observation of other performers and of people in general. Within the rehearsal stage, five activities were predominant: identification with the character, use of personal substitutions, finding the objectives of the character, creating the character physically, and figuring out what the other characters think of the character. Within the performance stage, five activities were also present. These were that the actor focused on what had happened just prior to the situation or on what the character wants, adjusting to the other actors, awareness of and playing to the audience, maintaining energy during the performance, and looking for ways to improve the performance, especially during long runs.

Social influences that interfere with the actor's creativity are poor direction, feeling interchangeable, knowing that a critic in the audience is seeking to evaluate negatively, acting for monetary reward, lack of trust in the ensemble and/or in the director, and feeling as if one is acting alone, that the others are wooden. Another challenge for actors during the creative process is that they not take on the character's persona. Actors found the creative process cathartic, and they avoided playing certain roles because they would experience emotions that would be painful or too personal. Actors felt tired and drained emotionally when they performed certain roles.

In sum, the actor's person and process are complex and difficult.

The Sun of Home in Actors

What do biographies show about the childhoods of people who became actors as adults? They often show that the actors had childhood turmoil such as moving often (John Wayne, Marlon Brando, Wally Cox), the death or abandonment of a parent (James Dean, Steve Allen), parental alcoholism (Greta Garbo, Carol Channing, Richard Burton, Joan Crawford), poverty (Marilyn Monroe, Jim Carrey), and bohemianism (Robert Mitchum, Robert Downey, Jr., Johnny Depp). We do not know whether actors experienced more turmoil than other artists, such as writers, but chances are that if you pick up a biography of an actor, you will find an unconventional childhood. Jack Nicholson, for example, grew up thinking his grandmother was his mother, while his real mother, a dancer who give birth to Jack without being married to his father, lived far across the country with her husband and other children. Such deception laid the foundation for the later duplicity practiced by the actor.

Such unconventionality goes across ethnic groups. Navarro commented on George Lopez's childhood.

> *Fathers? George Lopez never met his. The guy left when Mr. Lopez was an infant and was never heard from again. Birthdays? Mr. Lopez never celebrated one while growing up in the San*

> *Fernando Valley. He was raised by a grandmother whose own life of hardship, he said, left her ill equipped to express love or joy, much less indulge in frivolities like parties. To top it off, Mr. Lopez was endowed with what he describes as a large, lumpy head, the kind that turns schoolmates into sadistic teasers. "And I was the darkest kid in the neighborhood," Mr. Lopez added. "I got called a lot of names." In short, he had no choice but to grow up to be a comedian.* (Navarro, p. E1)

Brian Bates said that actors, when they are young, often adopt the role of humorist to cope with taunts and teasing. Actors' stories of their youths often have in common "the experience of being an 'outsider', being different or struggling to belong. And while it would be facile to accept them as representative accounts of the actors' childhoods, it is striking that they have such a similar theme" (p. 18). The "outsider" role could be imposed from without or within; the actors could have been conscious rebels, such as Marlon Brando or Jack Nicholson, or they could have been painfully shy and rejected by peers, as were Meryl Streep and Dustin Hoffman. The young actor may turn to acting as a way of healing old hurts. The opportunity to play a role may be a chance to create metaphors for situations that are too raw to explore outright. Often, these metaphors are healing or insightful for the viewers as well. The arts as self-therapy can function in metaphorical healing ways.

Actors have always had an ambiguous regard. Fathers don't typically want their daughters to marry an actor. In this, as well as in other societies, actors are considered marginal, somewhat feared, somewhat ridiculed. Actors are somehow not to be trusted; they are considered loose, promiscuous, and they live on the margins of society. Historically, women actors were considered prostitutes and the men considered thieves. Madame Mao Tse Tung was an actor in Shanghai before she met Mao; she had been married several times, she had many lovers, and she hung around with disreputable people, according to the Party line. She had to disavow her acting past in order to assume the role of first lady.

Coming from a family that emphasizes creativity is also important. Kevin Bacon said in an interview with Pogrebin of his family, with its urban planner father and teacher mother, "In our family, creative expression was put on a pedestal in such an extreme way. A piece of paper, a costume box, an instrument. 'Get together and put on a play.' 'Don't sit around the house.' 'Make something, create something.'"

An odd coincidence surfaced in reading biographies of actors. Older sisters seem to have played a large part in actors' decisions to enter the profession. Older sisters of such actors as Robert Mitchum, Ava Gardner, Marlon Brando, Kevin Bacon, and dancer Jerome Robbins provided a window into the theatrical world, as well as couches to sleep on when younger siblings moved to New York or California to audition.

Consider the "stage mother" phenomenon. Many parents impose upon their children their own desire for fame and fortune by submitting them to tryouts and auditions. Judy Garland's mother is an example; she permitted her daughter to take amphetamines and depressants in order to meet movie schedules, according to Edwards' biography. Patty Duke's adoptive parents are another example. After committing her birth mother to an institution, they adopted her and changed her name from Anna to Patty in order to conform to studio wishes. Both Garland and Duke suffered from serious mental health issues later in life. Academy Award-winner Jennifer Connolly, a former child model, in an interview with Kennedy, said, "My mom and I would go into the city after school on auditions. It wasn't my idea, but I didn't totally hate it. But I wouldn't let my son do it. There's a lot of pressure on kids. It was definitely a strain on me, but then again it was great in a way, because I wound up figuring out what I wanted to do in life."

Most often, the child actor does not become the adult actor. Early promise or even achievement is not enough in the acting profession. Other factors, most often chance, intervene.

The Sun of School in Actors

Predictive Behaviors for Acting

Kough identified characteristics that may mark acting talent in elementary school. The following is "Kough's List of Characteristics of Dramatic Talent in Young Children."

1. Readily shifts into the role of another character.

2. Shows interest in dramatic activities.

3. Uses voice to reflect changes of idea and mood.

4. Understands and portrays the conflict in a situation when given the opportunity to act out a dramatic event.

5. Communicates feelings by means of facial expressions, gestures, and bodily movements.

6. Enjoys evoking emotional responses from listeners.

7. Shows unusual ability to dramatize feelings and experiences.

8. Moves a dramatic situation to a climax and brings it to a well-timed conclusion when telling a story.

9. Gets a good deal of satisfaction and happiness from play-acting or dramatizing.

10. Writes original plays or makes up plays from stories.

11. Can imitate others. Mimics people and animals.

Renzulli and his colleagues also made a "Dramatics Characteristics Scale" in his *Scales for Rating the Behavioral Characteristics of Superior Students*. It contains 10 characteristics such as "Volunteers to participate in classroom plays or skits," and "Handles body with ease and poise for his particular age," or "Is able to evoke an emotional response from listeners—can get people to laugh, to frown, to feel tense, etc." These items are tallied on a Likert Scale, with a weighted total. (Note: Weighting totals may not be desirable, because they indicate the "amount" of characteristics a student has, and no one knows how many of these characteristics predict for adult acting talent.) The scale may help teachers become aware of these characteristics, however.

Checklists like this target talents in a specific domain, and schools should routinely try to notice such talents because they can encourage students to develop the talents through opportunities in theater, speech, performance, and acting. However, in reality, acting talent is often not the first reason a child is cast. Peter Brook said that a flicker, a tiny movement of authenticity, is often present instinctually in young actors. Child actors "can give subtle and complex incarnations that are the despair of those who have evolved their skill over the years." Later on, the child actors "build up their barriers to themselves" and find that touching the essential is difficult if not impossible. Take, for example, the many child actors whose acting careers were virtually over when they grew up. An example would be Margaret O'Brien. Another would be Shirley Temple.

This would seem to relate to Bamberger's developmental theory of music talent fulfillment and the presence of the "midlife crisis" in adolescent performers, as discussed in Chapter 10.

The Look

Talent is preceded by how the youngster looks. As I mentioned in Chapter 5 when discussing the Sun of Chance at the Hunter College Elementary School in New York, because the students had high IQs and were talkative and verbal, casting agents would often call and request to see them in order to invite them to audition for theater, film, and television roles. I would show the agents around. They would peek into classrooms and point, and say, "That one." I would give them the names of the children's parents. The "look" came first; then the assessment of acting talent followed. Similarly, acting talent in musical theater is often subsumed to singing talent. The best singers, not the best actors, often get the best role, although at the top levels, both singing and acting talent must be present. Such prior emphases—on looks and on musical talents—may lead a talented actor to despair.

Allen noted that performers are often impatient with a liberal arts education because they are so concerned with the practice necessary to do the performance, they do not see the relevance of having to learn about literature, mathematics, or science. Perhaps this is why the biographies of so many actors, dancers, and athletes show that they have a large dropout rate, mostly from college. Some, like Kevin Bacon, did not attend college. Others, like Kate Burton, graduated with another major, then later decided to go to graduate school to study acting. No clear pattern exists.

One can become an actor without formal schooling, unlike creators in other areas such as science and mathematics, where a Ph.D. is required; or in writing, where most writers have studied English literature on the college level; or in classical music, where attending a conservatory and taking many years of ever-higher level lessons is the norm. Even though there are more than 80 master's degree programs, 300-plus bachelor's degree programs, and several hundred non-degree conservatory programs, many actors do not finish school.

Mainstream educators of the talented are often required to identify performers, but they leave their training up to experts in the domains. One main difference between performing artists and creative artists is that whatever their innate talent, most performers depend equally on teachable skills.

Schools for the performing arts owe their existence to this need for expert training.

Acting is comprised of both mental and physical artistry. Like singers, actors are dependent upon their "instruments"—their voices and their bodies—but unlike singers, their material is other people, rather than notes on a page. Marlon Brando, in his autobiography, described sitting in a phone booth on the Lower East Side of Manhattan, studying the people approaching as if to memorize their gaits and expressions.

Stanislavski, one of the founders of the Moscow Art Theater, described his training as an actor in turn-of-the-century Moscow in *An Actor Prepares*. His tenets of acting came to be known as the Stanislavski Method, later shortened to "The Method" when Lee Strasberg began his Actors Theater in New York City. Stanislavski detailed the processes by which acting is made an art, and in these processes, one can see the great influence of psychoanalysis on the acting profession. The processes include: the use of the subconscious; attention to all movements, even those as simple as sitting down on a chair; the use of the imagination applied to the playwright's words; concentration so deep that the actor is unaware of the audience; observing how people act in real life; rigorous physical training, such as muscle relaxation and conditioning; breaking a piece into its units and its objectives; and using a process of inner probing into the psyche. Stanislavski said that the actor must use emotion memory—recapturing within oneself feelings that one has had—in order to interpret the character at hand. The actor plays herself, but "in an infinite variety of combinations…which have been smelted in the furnace" of the emotion memory. The actor communes with the inner self and with the other actors on stage. This is a deep connection, almost spiritual

The actor adapts to each circumstance so that manipulation of the situation can take place. For example, an actor who wants to get the part of a bully will not appear reserved or shy, or the actor in a situation where she must attract the attention of her mother across the street will project her voice, even though her mother is not really across the street but just across the stage.

Stanislavski said that the most important element is inner motive. Actors must have an inner motive to play the bodily and spiritual instrument that she has developed of herself. The emotions, the will, and the intellect of the character being portrayed must be balanced. The actor must then create an "unbroken line" between the audience and the stage.

Stanislavski called this the "inner creative state." In all works that he performs, the actor must always look for the super-objective that the work
projects. How to get inspiration was described this way:

> *Therefore put your thought on what arouses your inner motive*
> *forces, what makes for your inner creative mood. Think of your*
> *super-objective and the through line of action that leads up to it.*
> *In short, have in your mind everything that can be consciously*
> *controlled and that will lead you to the subconscious. That is the*
> *best possible preparation for inspiration.* (p. 292)

That, to the Moscow Art Theater, was the summary of creativity in
acting. As it was later interpreted by the New York Method acting studios,
Stanislavski's Method became the ultimate expression of the true, inner self.
By the 1950s, Method acting, with its dictate that to be a true artist, one had to
suffer and to bare one's soul, had become a great influence on many actors.
Marlon Brando's portrayal of Stanley Kowalski in Tennessee Williams' *A
Streetcar Named Desire* became to many the epitome of the achievement of
the Method actor.

Conflicts arose between Method actors and traditional actors. Here's
a telling but apocryphal story about Sir Laurence Olivier and Dustin
Hoffman filming *Marathon Man*. Hoffman stayed up all night, running
himself into exhaustion in preparation for the shoot the next day, immers-
ing himself in the actual physical experience of the character. The day after
the shoot, Hoffman collapsed exhausted in a chair, bleary-eyed and rub-
bery-muscled. Olivier came over to him and said, "You know, there's an
easier way. It's called acting." Marlon Brando, Dustin Hoffman, Robert
DeNiro, and Meryl Streep are all reputed to search for the emotional reality
of the character in their preparation for their roles. Actors like Cary Grant
and Laurence Olivier relied on technique and training.

During the 1950s, one of the most revered acting teachers in Hollywood was Jeff Corey. McGilligan described Corey as "an actor's actor" who
had been blacklisted for left-wing political activities. So Corey began to
teach acting. Among his students in the early 1950s were Carol Burnett,
Gary Cooper, and James Dean. The imaginative and physical exercises
Corey created helped the actors for many years. For example, the actors
were asked to do a physical task, and then while doing it, would have to sing
a Gershwin song or recite a monologue from an Arthur Miller play.
McGilligan said, "This taught students not to complicate a role with

'psychological gyrations,' making the point that a physical lie begets a psychological lie." The students would focus on an art reproduction or a piece of antique furniture and then do free associations from their reflections. Corey would have them take a famous scene from a well-known play and re-do the scene in another time, place, and context. This taught students to deal with the subject matter of scenes "obliquely." Corey had studied with the Group Theater, with Yiddish actor Jules Dassin, and with Russian-born actor Michael Chekhov. In his classes, the young actors did not do film scenes, but they would rehearse classic scenes from literature and the Bible. Corey would advise his students to "make the bizarre choice. Be unpredictable. Go for laughter where someone else would think tears. Interrupt yourself with a sudden, inexplicable rage."

In summary, the actor's schooling helps him to create the emotional and nonverbal responses for audiences through the skills that the actor has been studying in order to portray human behavior, gestures, personalities. The actor's body, observational powers, memory of emotions, and prior experiences all enter into the creativity that is expressed when the actor acts.

Actors, Dancers, Athletes: The Sun of Community and Culture

The ensemble—or team—is paramount in these areas of acting, dancing, and athletics. Even when the performer performs alone, the solo performance is part of a team score, as in ice-skating, diving, or track. Solo dancers or solo actors are supported by large behind-the-scenes companies that do everything from set design to lighting and costumes—all essential in the production of the performance. Athletes have trainers, caddies, equipment boys, groundskeepers, and other behind-the-scenes workers. Collaboration is the hallmark of the creativity here. While individuals are themselves creative in their various domains of costume, lighting, set design, directing, accompanying, and such, the performance as a whole is collaborative, with each individual subsuming his or her creativity and putting it to the good of the whole performance. Actor Kevin Bacon spoke of the energy of working in an ensemble. He loves live theater and also has a rock band, both of which provide an energy that working in movies cannot. In an interview with Pogrebin, he said, "Being in front of an audience is an essential part of the creative performer's life. Movies don't give me butterflies. They don't put me on the edge. You have to have some kind of danger. Rock 'n' roll is a very naked place to be. I love that. I need that."

Contrasting movies with live performance, he said, "Movies are an isolated medium. You're taught to look out for No. 1—yourself. Rarely do you encounter something that's really my concept of what an ensemble is."

Famous Ensembles in Theater

Before the Actors Theater, there was the Group Theater in the 1930s in New York City. The Group Theater modified the Stanislavski system. Besides emphasis on the actor's self-awareness and preparation in his craft, the Group Theater brought together the whole company. One of its founders, Stella Adler, said, "This theater demanded a basic understanding of a complex artistic principle; that all people connected with this theater, the actor, designer, playwright, director, etc., had, of necessity, to arrive at a single point of view, which the theme of the play also expressed."

Again, the influence of the new fad of psychoanalysis can be seen, in that the actor was viewed as having personal problems that the whole group could help solve. As the actor got immersed in the whole process of the theater, he was sometimes reeducated. By 1934, the Group Theater had modified Stanislavski's system to emphasize the actor's clarity of actions rather than the actor's inner life. Adler said, "Now, emphasis was put on the circumstances of the play."

The Group Theater was built on the idea of "ensemble"—that is, no one actor was more important than another, but all were essential cogs in the machine, parts of the whole, members of the collective. This idea coincided with the worldwide rise of socialism as a political system. The presence, at this time, of the left wing attraction to communism is evident in the theories of the Group Theater; they felt that the whole company must live together in a commune-like existence. In fact, many of them were later blacklisted during the infamous McCarthy hearings of the House UnAmerican Activities Committee in the 1950s. Actors blacklisted included: Edward G. Robinson, Zero Mostel, Leo Penn (the father of Sean and Chris Penn), Will Geer, Burgess Meredith, Paul Robeson, and Lee Grant.

By the 1960s, Judith Malina and Julian Beck had founded The Living Theater. Malina and Beck modified the purpose of the theater to include dramatic social consciousness. They believed that theater transformed the participants as well as the audience, and many of the plays were staged with students, factory workers, school children, and other non-actors, as well as the members of the company. The actor's technique was subsumed to the social message of the play. The public outcry after this group produced Kenneth Brown's *The Brig* in 1963, a raw and disturbing portrait of life in Marine Corps prisons, may have contributed to social changes in brigs in the Marines.

Actors in The Living Theater spoke of being changed utterly by their work there. The emotional impact of the plays was often so strong that the audience joined the actors in protest, marching out of the theater with them. The lines between stage and audience became blurred. In one play performed in Italy and Brazil, where Malina and Beck were in prison for three months, an actor was hung from a parrot perch and electric shock applied. Malpede, in *Women in Theatre* said of *The Brig* production, "the scene is a brutally naturalistic moment in an otherwise imagistic play; Judith says it is meant to wake us from our trance and make us face the reality of daily torture in prisons throughout the world." Malina saw the actor's art as showing the audience that he really believes what he's saying in order that they listen very carefully "to see whether they are in accord with it."

Peter Brook and Paul Scofield founded the Theater of Cruelty. In 1987, I was privileged to sit through all 12 hours of their *Mahabarata* at the Brooklyn Academy of Music, and in my journal the next day, I wrote this: "I woke up this morning to dreams of Ganesh and the mythological characters of Hinduism; they became so real to me yesterday at the production. I was talking with the Elephant King and rooting for Vishnu. I have not been so moved by a production since I saw Sam Shepard's *Buried Child* at the Pittsburgh Public Theater years ago." The *Mahabarata* is a sacred book of Hinduism, and the play is about the interplay of the gods of Hinduism, a rendering of ancient myth. In 1991, Brook released a shortened movie of the *Mahabarata*, only six hours long.

That spring I went again to the Brooklyn Academy of Music to see Brook's production of Chekhov's *The Cherry Orchard*, and I wrote, "I sat three feet from where Academy Award-winner Linda Hunt entered, and saw her gather herself for her entrance. She focused her attention, took a deep breath, closed her eyes into a squint, opened them wide, and burst onto the stage. I shivered as the doors closed in the final scene. We, the audience, were locked in. We sat sadly and breathlessly. We could hear the axes chop, chop, chop their way to progress. The genius of the playwright, the genius of the director, the genius of the actor all came together last night."

The Theater of Cruelty emphasizes improvisation and the collective lives of the actors in company. Brook's company for the *Mahabarata* included actors of many ethnicities. In writing about the art of acting,

Brook said that the other arts permit one to step back and gaze at the creative product. This is not possible in acting. The painter can step back from the canvas and use other senses to regard his work. While the pianist is playing, his ear can be detached and can hear what his fingers are playing. Acting is not so. Acting is unique because the actor "has to use the treacherous, changeable, and mysterious material of himself as his medium." The actor has to be "completely involved while distanced—detached without detachment. He must be sincere, he must be insincere: he must practice how to be insincere with sincerity and how to lie truthfully" (p. 428).

Brook also criticized the Method actor. He said that the Method actor can only be spontaneous and base his actions on observation. For Brook, this means that the Method actor cannot draw on "any deep creativity." The creativity of acting comes from improvisation, where the actor can come up against "his own barriers, to the point where in place of a new-found truth he normally substitutes a lie." Creativity in acting comes through rehearsals in which improvisational exercises are faithfully done. The really creative actor comes to the opening night in terror, because during the rehearsals, he has only been exploring partial aspects of the character he is playing. Even at the last rehearsal, the creative actor will be willing, if necessary, to "discard the hardened shells of his work" in order to come to a resolution. The creative actor will undergo "the trauma of appearing in front of an audience, naked and unprepared."

Brook continues his contribution to theatrical community and culture. His acting companies are multi-ethnic, and no one plays a role because of the supposed color of the character's skin. A couple of years ago, I was able to see his *Hamlet* and to reunite as an audience member with several of his ensemble members whom I remembered fondly from that pinnacle experience of the *Mahabarata*.

The Sun of Gender in Actors

The age-old gender difference for creators has been the double bind of women maintaining or continuing their creative careers while at the same time being mothers. As mentioned in previous chapters, this has not seemed as much a problem for fathers. An illustration is Anne Bancroft, who in an interview with Marks noted that she had gaps in her stage and movie careers. "I just knew I had a life, and I didn't want to go away from it for too long." With one son with Mel Brooks, Bancroft said that she didn't need to do parts that she wasn't crazy about. "I didn't need the money, and I wasn't interested in the popularity." She wouldn't ask her young son to let her move from Hollywood to New York to do plays. "You make a choice— the price being I didn't work as much as I might have."

Another gender issue has been mentioned with regard to the issue of women having to be thin and beautiful and young in order to be perform- ers. Actress Camryn Manheim, upon winning an Emmy, held it in the air and shouted, "Let's hear it for the fat girls!" Manheim, who studied acting in New York, was repeatedly told she had to lose weight in order to be an actress. She once lost 100 pounds using amphetamines but within four months had put the weight back on again. Even though she is called a spokesperson, Manheim said in an interview with Weintraub, "I'm the only fat, younger actress right now. People know my name; they know Kathy Bates' name. That's about it. Can people open up their hearts and minds to see alternative definitions of beauty? I don't know."

The paucity of roles for older women actresses is also a gender issue. Remember 50-year-old Michael Douglas making love to 25-year-old Gwyneth Paltrow, who played his wife in *A Perfect Murder*? Can you picture a 50-year-old Meryl Streep making love on screen to a 25-year-old hus- band—perhaps someone like Josh Hartnett? We have gotten used to seeing older men with younger women, but not the opposite. As female actors get old, their chances for roles diminish; this is also true for male actors, but not as much.

The Sun of Chance in Actors

The Sun of Chance in actors' lives is paramount. The actor's inher- ited physical characteristics, being in the right place at the right time, connections—all are important. Jane Fonda does not exercise much any- more, but she still stays slim and beautiful. "Good genes," she explained. Whether—or where—one has studied is not so important. Beauty, or "the look," as mentioned above, even in the case of children, is important. Sophia Loren's breasts, from the age of 14 on, were such a lure to the eyes that her biographer, Harris, wrote, "Sophia was no longer an ugly duckling. She still had thick lips and a big nose, but male admirers were too likely to be fascinated by her chest to notice." At age 15, having dinner with fellow models, she attracted the eye of Carlo Ponti. He, though married, began an affair with her, and her career was launched in movies he produced.

Ava Gardner, visiting New York City at age 16, walked across a night- club floor and the band director came over and asked her whether she could sing, as he needed a female singer. She couldn't. But that beauty continued to attract the eyes of powerful men who helped her throughout her film career. Beauty was a burden to her as well; she was told by directors such as John Huston, when she asked him for character direction, just to stand still and be beautiful. No need to act.

Robert Mitchum's sister tricked him into attending an audition at the Santa Barbara community theater. He considered acting too sissy, although he played well and his photographic memory helped him with the lines. It was not until he showed up at RKO's B-cowboy movie sets, and not until he had two children, that he accepted that he could act and that acting in movies was something a real man could do. Everyone liked his looks. He always said he acted for the money. In his early years, he quit school to become a hobo, and he was a beach bum when he did his first theatre piece. He was attractive to women, and he would call his wife, Dorothy, to come and get him when things got too close.

Dancers and Athletes

Almost every little girl wants to be a dancer at some time in her life. She imagines herself as Isadora Duncan being rebellious and so very artistic, in her bare feet, swinging her scarves around, or as Pavlova, Margot Fonteyn, Suzanne Farrell, or Moira Shearer in *The Red Shoes*, dancing a *pas de deux* with Nureyev, Diaghilev, Nijinsky, or Jacques D'Amboise. Or she imagines herself the daughter of Shirley MacLaine in *The Turning Point*, having a romance with Baryshnikov. If her body doesn't meet the ballet standard, she may imagine herself a modern dancer, one of the kids of *The Chorus Line*, or hoofing it with Fred Astaire in an old black and white movie, gliding in a frothy white dress as Ginger Rogers, or Cyd Charisse, or as the *Flashdance* heroine, coming up the hard way from welder to dancer.

The career of the ballet dancer is brief, a flame ignited before adolescence at the age of eight or nine and extinguished in her twenties or thirties, when, if she has had any success at all, she goes back home to the Midwest and opens a ballet school in her hometown to teach hopeful children with the same dreams she had. Of course, there have been exceptions, such as Martha Graham, who didn't dance until she was in her twenties. Modern dancers seem to have longer professional lives than classical ballet dancers. Some continue dancing through their forties and into their fifties.

The creativity of dance is a creativity of the body in motion to the sound of music. Dance is the province, not only of the highly trained ballet dancer, but of the folk dancer, the tribal dancer, the dancer as ritualist from time immemorial. Whirling dervishes danced themselves into trances of ecstasy. All primitive cultures used dance in religious ceremonies. Dance, movement to music, induces ritualistic behavior and, coupled with substances such as alcohol or peyote, bestows a feeling of well-being and of communion with other dancers. Ballroom dancing, disco dancing, rock 'n' roll and hip-hop dancing, slow dancing, jitterbug, the frug, the twist, the mashed potato, the slam dance, the tango, and the waltz have been practiced by people in our culture as a means of entertainment. Dance is an immensely pleasurable form of creativity, both in the watching and in the doing.

It is also painful. Professional dancers are notorious for having injuries, and dance aficionados know the disappointment of coming to a performance and finding a substitute because the featured artist was injured. Readers of dance criticism are just as likely as readers of the sports pages to be regaled with litanies of pulled ligaments, twisted shoulders, overworked knees.

The Aesthetics of Dance

What are the aesthetics of dance? H'Doubler said that the dancer uses bodily tension and disciplined movement to communicate meaning. The dancer is always distant from that meaning, removed, using her body as a tool. The dancer, however, must be inspired by emotion and, through concentration on her body, convey that emotion to the audience. H'Doubler said "thus dance may be considered a neural projection of inner thought and feeling into movement, rhythm being the mold through which the creative life flows in giving its meaning form."

Walter Terry called dance an art of danger—in which we as spectators participate vicariously. The aesthetic of dance is kinesthetic, and we "journey with the dancer along the paths of adventure created by the choreographer." The philosopher Susanne Langer called dance a phenomenological art, an art that exists in the moment that is apprehended in the moment. Dance provides an illusion of force through the skill of the dancer, who uses her body to implicitly provide that force. Even more than the actor, who has voice and speech, the dancer must rely on gesture, extension, and physical being to tell a story. The music is the framework, but the dancer is the frame.

The ballet, begun in the sixteenth century, is the most formal form of dance in the western world. The dancer needs a classic body, a certain shape of neck and curve of the arch of the foot. The dancer must not be too tall or too short, though those limits are being currently stretched. In 1988, Peter Martins defended his use of the short dancer Gen Hogiuchi, who was criticized by dance critic Arlene Croce for being offensively diminutive.

Throughout ballet's history, Russian ballet became the standard for other countries' ballet. In the United States, the New York City Ballet, founded by George Balanchine, preserved the Russian standard, while the American Ballet Theater, under Michel Fokine, began to drift from that standard, according to Agnes de Mille in *America Dances.*

The American Ballet Theater incorporated the techniques of the modern, or Martha Graham, style of dance. De Mille said, "The ballet dancer now on occasion droops and convulses, falls to the floor, spins on a nonvertical or changing spiral axis, beats and jumps off beat." Balanchine, who danced with Diaghilev's company before it closed in the 1920s, was asked by two young Harvard graduates, Lincoln Kirstein and Edward Warburg, to start an American ballet in the Russian style. Balanchine preserved Russian classical ballet but gave it an American flavor. Among his many accomplishments, Balanchine choreographed the works of his fellow Russian, the composer Igor Stravinsky.

While the more avant-garde modern dance draws upon the rigid ballet training of its dancers, it is choreographed to music that is less formal than typical ballet music. Agnes de Mille's use of roping and riding in Oklahoma and of fantasy and dream in Carousel, Twyla Tharp's variations on Sinatra's music, Pina Bausch's abstractions of dance hall behavior, Pilobolus' athletic and not ascetic geometries of gymnastics done to rock 'n' roll, Mark Morris' explorations of form and space done to the music of the Violent Femmes, Merce Cunningham's silent and still interpretations of John Cage's four minutes of silence—all of these have extended dance from the classical standard, yet all have been created by dancers who began in classical training.

Again in our consideration of creativity we come to the word "training." Or "practice." This is the key element in all considerations of the creative product. The development of expertise is predicated on practice, and there is some evidence that the amount of practice affects the attainment of the artist or athlete. Talent, according to some, is not necessary. The product is shaped by practice. The dancer practices to the point of automaticity. The product of the actor is a role. The product of the dancer is a role. The product of the musician is the performance of a piece. The role, in order to be enacted with perfection, demands that the person enacting be trained.

Dance is an ephemeral art, and many dances have not been written down. The Lee Theodore American Dance Machine Company has as its aim the reconstruction of the dances of the American theater, the dances of such choreographers as Jerome Robbins and Bob Fosse. They go to the people who did the dances originally and ask them to remember what they did, and then they write the dances down. Theodore said, in Gruen's *People Who Dance* in 1988, "On one number alone, there might be five or six of them, because what happens is that one person will come in and remember the first sixteen bars, and the next person will remember what happened afterwards, and so on, down the line." Of the dances that have been written down, many of the choreographers' notes are indecipherable, or the dance was changed so much in performance that the choreographer's notes are useless. This, to me, illustrates the nonliterary quality of dance and the lack of interest many dancers have in the written word. Dancers prefer moving over the static drudgery of documentation.

Personality Attributes: The Emotional Aspect in Dancers and Athletes

Personality Studies of Dancers

Dancers' personalities are a little different from those of visual artists, creative writers, musicians, scientists, and actors. They resemble athletes more than any other creative people, except for their tendency to have low self-esteem. Low self-concept was confirmed in a study by Bakker. Two groups of young dancers, ages 11 to 12 and 15 to 16, were compared with control groups, and the results showed that though the leisure activities of the dancers and non-dancers differed only slightly, the dancers had less favorable attitudes in physical self-esteem and self-concept, especially in the older group.

Barron published a study in 1972 of students at a dance school. They had already experienced years of rigorous professional training, had "made the cut," so to speak, in being encouraged to continue to study dance and to fulfill their aspirations. They were flexible, spontaneous, and had "a lot of steam." They had high standards for themselves and their work, and they expected their teachers to set such standards. The most respected teachers were those who had solid knowledge and background in dance, teachers who loved teaching and the dance, teachers who were interested in the students and who interacted with them, but who were still very strict, perfectionistic, and demanding.

Emotion and Personality in Athletes

A study of personality attributes of Olympic athletes by Dieffenbach and Moffett showed that they possess: "(1) The ability to cope with and control anxiety; (2) confidence; (3) mental toughness/resiliency; (4) sport intelligence; (5) the ability to focus and block distractions; (6) competitiveness; (7) a hard-work ethic; (8) the ability to set and achieve goals; (9) coachability; (10) high levels of dispositional hope; (11) optimism; and (12), adaptive perfectionism."

Gifted and Tolerated

The reason that personality difficulties in athletes may not be as well known as those in writers or actors may have to do with a halo effect. Anderson, Denson, Brewer, and Van Raalte indicated in a study of personality and mood disorders among athletes that their aberrations are often tolerated by the public and by their institutions because they are so talented. If they come to practice late, they are barely chastised. If they get into trouble with the law, fines are paid. The two most common personality disorders among athletes are narcissism—a state of excessive self-admiration—and antisocial personality disorder. In the latter disorder, the athlete has a history of behavior that violates the rights of others. Of the antisocial athlete, the authors described a typical case:

> *A male football athlete has been arrested for vandalizing another athlete's car. The incident occurred in a parking lot at a local tavern and seemed connected to an argument over a female. There were several witnesses and an arrest occurred soon after the incident. The athlete had been drinking. This is not the first time the athlete has blown up. He once threw his roommate's tape deck out a fifth floor window because he did not like the rap music. There is also a long history of scrapes with the law such as petty larceny and drug possession while in high school. Hot-tempered incidents in the locker room have occurred and there are hints of continued substance use. Again, as with the narcissist, he is gifted and tolerated.... At the hearing, the victim agrees not to press charges if the athlete agrees to pay for all the damages.*

Mood Disorders

Mood disorders also occur in athletes. It has been estimated that about 5%-6% of athletes suffer from depression, which is similar to that in the regular population. Depression is diagnosed by one or more of these symptoms: eating irregularities, insomnia or sleeping too much, fatigue and low energy, low self-esteem, poor concentration, and feelings of hopelessness. Anderson and colleagues indicated that the depression has usually gone on for at least 22 months within a two-year period. Some athletes also display the "manic" or "elated" end, acting wild and crazy, being the life of the party, cajoling their friends into fast driving, picking up fast women, and acting heedlessly. Athletes usually "underutilize mental health services" because they don't want to admit weakness and want to maintain autonomy. They fear being teased and ridiculed by teammates.

Positive Deviance

Hughes and Coakley wrote that the personalities of athletes are affected by the very expectations for players of their sports. They called this positive deviance. "When athletes use the 'sport ethic'—which emphasizes sacrifice for *The Game*, seeking distinction, taking risks, and challenging limits—as an exclusive guide for their behavior, sport and sport participation become especially vulnerable to corruption," such as the use of chemical muscle enhancers and retaining social control in situations off the game field.

Mental Toughness

Mental toughness has been researched as a personality attribute of talented athletes. Jones, Hanton, and Connaughton asked, what, really, is mental toughness? In an interview study, they found several factors with general and specific dimensions, such as self-belief, desire/motivation, dealing with pressure and anxiety, focus that is performance-related, focus that is lifestyle-related, and pain/hardship factors. A synonym for mental toughness is resilience.

The Domain Thorn: Dance and Athletics

Carlos Agosta, Cuban ballet star for The American Ballet, said that when he was 13, "I realized I could touch people with ballet." His father entered him into the state ballet school in Havana when he was nine years old in order to keep him out of trouble, according to Kisselgoff. He wanted to be a soccer player and skipped his lessons. Then his father transferred him to another school, and he saw a performance by the National Ballet of Cuba. His teachers were also important in encouraging him. "Something clicked," he said. "When I danced, I wanted to show who I am inside. I still do. We are all different individuals."

An Isadora Duncan dancer named Tamara influenced two Martha Graham dancers. Pearl Lang, in an interview with New York Times dance critic Jennifer Dunning, said, "I saw this girl come between two lines from way back, skipping with each knee up to her chin. She skipped to the front of the stage and opened her arms, and there was a gasp. It was like the sun flooded the whole of Orchestra Hall, a very large house." Jane Dudley, at a performance of the same troupe at Carnegie Hall, noticed the same thing. "That was it. Her name was Tamara. I don't know anything else about her." This dual crystallizing moment illustrates the need to expose children to the arts from an early age.

Dance students in Barron's study, when asked the question "Why dance?" expressed that dance gave them a feeling of joy and elation and an uplifting release of emotions. They liked that they could use their bodies for self-expression, that they had honed their bodies to such responsiveness that they could express complex emotions with small movements. They also liked to dance because their dancing gave pleasure to others. Dance was closely connected with emotion. "The purpose of art in general and dance in particular was to provide forms for the expression of universal principles of life, oneself, spirituality, that would allow the artist to share his experiences with others, enriching their lives as well as his own."

Biographical studies of athletes reveal the same. In his memoir, Derek Jeter said, "Baseball drove me. It pushed me." Hakeem Olajuwon, when he discovered basketball after playing soccer and team handball for his high school in Nigeria, said simply, "I was in love with basketball. I couldn't wait for school to be over so I could run right over to the Stadium." While playing the sport, athletes feel that they are their true selves, and they often continue to play throughout their lives on amateur teams. One baseball player who was on the fast track was injured in college. His dreams were shattered. His adult life is spent playing on four different softball teams, on two of which he is a "ringer," pretending he is a truck driver for the local newspaper so he can play first base on their team, and pretending he is a paralegal for the bar association so that he can play on their team. He's one of the most talented softball players in his city as his passion for playing continues.

Sun of Home in Dancers and Athletes

For dancers, the Sun of Home includes parents who were willing to pay for lessons and the intense training necessary. The necessity sometimes to move the whole family in order to find the perfect coach (as in tennis, ice skating, and gymnastics) requires a family with the means and the will to do so. In some instances, the mother moves with the child, and the father stays home to make the living to enable this.

Families do not always support or encourage development of the talent. Disapproval by fathers of their sons' choice of dance haunts biographical accounts of male dancers. Even in the old Soviet Union, with its premier dance troupes and world-class training facilities, the father of Rudolph Nureyev did not want him to become a dancer. Nureyev, however, later sought asylum in the West and became one of the most famous ballet dancers ever. Percival's biography told about how Nureyev's father had said that dance "was fit only for idlers.... [H]e should concentrate on his schoolwork, do well in his examinations, qualify for further studies, make something of his life."

Athletic talent is more often supported. The "family mythology" as described in Chapter 5 is the Sun of Home. Some families want their children to become athletes and enter them into children's sports, such as T-Ball, Little League, hockey, football, soccer, and basketball. The family members attend all of the children's matches. Family talk centers on the last game, the next game, how the high school team is doing, how the regional professional team is doing, and the family attends sports matches much as the families of musicians attend concerts and the families of writers read books. The family mythology reads, "In our family, we go to games, think sports are important, put our money into expensive sports equipment, drive long distances to their games, as they qualify for higher-level competition.

Golfer Arnold Palmer's father, himself a golf course maintenance man, put a golf club in Arnold's hands when Arnold was barely three years old. Tiger Woods' father did it even earlier. Baseball star Derek Jeter said, "I could talk about my parents for a year and still not be able to thank them enough for helping me fulfill my dreams." Parental support is necessary, helpful, and even critical.

Sun of School in Dancers and Athletes

A good dance class was described by the dancers in the Barron study as "demanding, arduous, and challenging," leaving the dancer with fatigue, exhilaration, and a sense of accomplishment from having a "thorough workout," increasing body strength and skill. Good dance students were those who were self-critical about their dance, students who were able to work hard, long, and with great perfectionistic demands on their abilities. Discipline was a trait that the dance students admired in each other.

Physical factors affected their dance; when they were tired or sick, their dancing was less resonant. The dancers said that their extensions were not as high, their limbs didn't respond to their minds, and they were more prone to injury, with the result that they experienced "an overall loss in creativity, bounce, and eagerness" in their dancing. Tension in their outside lives also affected their dance, and they often experienced "deficits in control and concentration." However, several of the dancers said that dancing, even when fatigued or under tension, created a release of these and a feeling of well-being after the dance class. Barron said that the young dancers were very intrinsically motivated and viewed dance as necessary to their existence.

A study by Zakrajsek and colleagues comparing the learning styles of dancers and physical education majors found that there were no significant differences between the two groups and that both preferred to learn in concrete ways. There were also no gender differences in the way they preferred to learn.

Aspiring athletes attend sports camps and special schools for various sports. Hour after hour is spent shooting hoops, keeping a soccer ball in the air, practicing plays and moves. Practice, practice, practice—to the point of automaticity—is again the necessity.

Sun of Community and Culture in Dancers and Athletes

The nature of the ensemble, the team, the corps contains rules, both stated and implicit. If one is not a "team player," in that cliché of business and sport, one will suffer, and so will the team. Each team or ensemble has its own culture, as indicated in the discussion of the various theater ensembles above. One must look for a "good fit."

Sun of Gender in Dancers and Athletes

Gender differences in dancers revealed that the female dancers were open, generous, energetic, and quite excitable, while male dancers were even more so. Barron said of the male dancer, "he is much like his female counterpart, though more complicated, conflicted, and flamboyant." Male dancers were more "impulsive," more likely to "show-off," and their humor sometimes had a "hostile quality," while their external behavior was "mischievous, rebellious, zany, frank, flirtatious, and pleasure-seeking." They were also good-looking. Both male and female dancers were quite ambitious. They both described themselves as "determined, ambitious, and capable," with a need to succeed.

Female dancers tended to be concrete or dependent learners, needing personalized feedback, and they preferring to work with others. They were not interested in self-directed learning through printed materials or books. This would seem to indicate that teachers of dance and of physical education should modify their teaching styles to include concrete experiences rather than lecture.

Androgyny in Athletes

Several studies have shown that male and female athletes at elite levels (on national teams) are remarkably similar in personality. They have high achievement motivation, high tolerance for pain, are highly competitive, and are able to train with great intensity. A study by Anshel and Porter of elite Australian swimmers indicated that there were more similarities than differences between genders. While the males were more willing to sacrifice their recreation time to practice, especially after a disappointing performance, the females also trained extremely hard.

Wittig and Schurr said, "successful female athletes tend to be more assertive, dominant, self-sufficient, independent, aggressive, and achievement oriented, and to have average to low emotionality." They resemble the average successful male athlete. A study by Craig Wrisberg and his colleagues used the *Bem Sex Role Inventory* (BSRI). Sex role orientations among female athletes showed higher femininity scores for females who performed in individual sports and more androgyny in females who performed in team sports. Male athletes showed no differences between team and individual sports.

The androgyny may come with some cost. Sex role identity was investigated in female athletes by Diane Wetzig. Findings showed that female athletes seemed to be more susceptible to alcoholism than other women. Wetzig said, "Some addictive women favor an overtly masculine manner. On the surface they exhibit agentic traits of assertion, independence, and achievement. Under this veneer, however, lie feminine needs for dependency and affiliation." The female athletes she studied (only 30 of them) fell into this category and thus may be more at risk for substance abuse than the regular population. Wetzig said, "The rigors and requirements of competition" pose an additional danger to these females, and "mood altering chemicals initially symbolize the magical key enabling an athlete to be physically and emotionally primed at a moment's notice."

Sun of Chance in Dancers and Athletes

Being in the right place and being prepared to be plucked from the crowd of those auditioning is illustrated in many of the anecdotes. In addition, the "luck" of having the right physical makeup for the dance or sport cannot be underestimated. All young boys want to be professional football players or basketball players. Most grow up without the physical features needed. The same is true for classical dance. Who can predict that one's turn of instep, one's throat length, one's percent of body fat, one's height—all heritable—would prevent one from becoming the premier ballerina?

Biographical Example of Suzanne Farrell

Suzanne Farrell was the premier ballerina for Balanchine's New York City Ballet from the mid-1960s to the mid-1980s. Her work was called by Mark Morris "perpetually astonishing." He said, "I learn things just by watching Suzanne Farrell dance.... She has a spontaneity that I can't believe; I can't believe she can pull it off all the time. She dances with the speed of thought."

Farrell was born and raised in Cincinnati in a family of women. Her grandmother was divorced, her aunts were divorced, and her mother divorced her father. Farrell described life with her two older sisters as that of a daring tomboy, living in a small four-room house. For play, they would walk the beams and pipes of the construction site of a nearby subdivision being built. She had, like most active girls, a childhood of scrapes and bruises, of scabs on knees and elbows, but this was the childhood of a girl slated to become one of America's premier ballerinas.

Suzanne and her sisters studied dance at the Cincinnati Conservatory. Her mother was good at getting her daughters scholarships, and so the girls went to school at Ursuline Academy near the Conservatory so that they could get to their lessons easily. The three girls shared a bedroom, and one of their favorite games was called "Ballet." One would be the Teacher, one would be the Mother, and Suzanne would be the Student.

What she liked about her early ballet lessons were the acrobatics they did for the first 15 minutes and the tap dancing for the last 15 minutes. Farrell said that early on, she "loved the way the clicks and the rhythms overtook my body and made it move." The only reading she remembered doing while she was growing up was looking at picture books of ballet that she found in the Cincinnati Public Library. She also had a girlfriend who was as obsessed about dance as she. The two girls would call each other up on the phone and give each other combinations to do, writing them down in the dark, using flashlights: "Glissade, jeté, glissade, jeté, pirouette…and then we'd both put the receiver down and get up and slide, jump, slide, jump, turn before reconvening on the phone to discuss the difficulties and changes necessary."

School was not her favorite activity, and she said, "I wasn't stupid, but I had a hard time sitting still in class and was always being reprimanded for fidgeting. Nonphysical concentration was simply boring." Suzanne's talent was apparent early on. She was chosen to be Clara in the *Nutcracker*.

Farrell was discovered in Cincinnati by a Balanchine scout, the ballerina Diana Adams, who had been sent by the New York City Ballet throughout the country after the Ballet received a Ford Foundation grant. Adams spotted Suzanne, advising her that if she ever got to New York, she should audition. That was enough for Suzanne's mother, and within weeks, in July of 1960, the family moved to New York City. Diana Adams had told Balanchine that Suzanne had one flat foot, injured when a horse had kicked it. During the audition, Balanchine examined the foot, pressing it hard to test for resilience. When Suzanne's foot successfully passed the test, Balanchine arranged a scholarship for her to study with the company. She attended two high schools, but her dance schedule at the New York City Ballet was so strenuous and the tour schedules so demanding that she never did graduate from high school.

While she credited her mother for the opportunity to go to New York City, Suzanne said that her mother, a nurse, was not a stage mother. She had made lessons available to the girls, but she didn't watch the classes, and she never stayed outside the room commenting on their progress with the other mothers. Her mother had to work, and "She had been lonely as a child, and perhaps she knew that if you have the arts in your life you will never be lonely. I have often been alone, but I have never felt lonely when I was dancing, even dancing by myself." Her father was absent and never came to the sisters' recitals. Farrell said, "It mattered to me that he didn't seem to care."

Within two years after the family arrived in New York, Balanchine, then in his sixties, was making ballets for the 18-year-old Suzanne, sending her love poems, and treating her as a real ballerina. He had been married several times to several ballerinas and was still married, but young Suzanne became his latest muse. They would take long walks next to the Seine, talking, when the Ballet played in Paris. By 1964, Suzanne had danced 16 new ballets. This progress was unusual, and she said she "skipped through the natural hierarchy of the profession" because "Balanchine felt there wasn't time." Years later, in a 1997 television documentary, Farrell stated that she loved Balanchine and he loved her, but that was not the important thing. What was important was that Balanchine was the foremost choreographer of the world, and he felt that she could do the dances that he created better than anyone else. She said, "He obviously had already chosen to commit himself to me, and he had plans, serious plans, for what he might do with me."

Meanwhile, Farrell was also being courted by another dancer in the company, Paul Meija, and in 1969, when she was 23, they married. Her mother was so upset that she stopped speaking to Suzanne, and Balanchine was so upset that he dropped her and her new husband from the New York City Ballet. "I was now a Balanchine dancer without Balanchine," Farrell said. Occasionally, she was asked to guest-star with such companies as the National Ballet of Canada, and finally, she and Paul were asked to join the Ballet of the Twentieth Century in Brussels, Belgium. The company, more avant-garde than Balanchine's company, did more world touring than the New York City Ballet, and Farrell got rave reviews.

In 1975, she wrote to Balanchine, asking to dance with him again, and he took her back—but not her husband. In 1977, the Company performed on the Corporation for Public Broadcasting "Dance in America" series. Farrell said about the filming of her dancing that the results were not representative of either her dancing or of the ballets, for the editing and splicing took their toll, and the immediacy of the performance was lost as "videotape seemed to spread an even sheen over the nuances of any movement." This again illustrates the transitory nature of dance, of choreography, of the creativity that goes into the performance.

Farrell, like many creative people, suffered a deep depression just when everything seemed to be going well. "I couldn't understand why I was so depressed at such a wonderful time in my life—I had come back to the company, I was dancing, and Mr. B. was making new ballets." Creative people of all types have been prone to depression.

Mikhail Baryshnikov joined the company in 1979, but Farrell didn't work with him because of the great difference in their heights. Balanchine had suffered heart attacks. Her husband Paul was in Chicago working with one of Balanchine's five ex-wives, Maria Tallchief, choreographing for the Chicago City Ballet. Balanchine died in 1983. By 1985, when she was 40, Farrell had developed a hip problem that prevented her from rehearsing for the long hours necessary. The hip degeneration continued. "I could find no relief. I could hear clicking and grinding inside my hip where the cartilage was completely gone. Bone was gnawing bone, and I was visibly limping. In 1987, a hip operation, a plastic hip, and a reunion with her father after 30 years followed. She performed again in 1988. Her last performance was on November 26, 1989, with Peter Martin. She then retired to teach at her school in the Adirondacks and to teach as a guest with other ballets.

Farrell's life as a ballet dancer was typical of that of many other great dancers. The concentration and dedication necessary must come early. The biography of any dancer reads like a medical report, at times, as well as a list of dances performed and people met. But the physical repercussions to the bodies of dancers are always present.

Biographical Example of Arnold Palmer

Arnold Palmer was born in 1929 in Latrobe, Pennsylvania to a golf course groundskeeper and his wife, a bookkeeper. Palmer said that one of his earliest memories was of his father putting his hands around a golf club when he was three years old. His father showed him the Vardon grip and told him to hit the ball hard. He never wavered. Later, he would receive advice about his "homemade golf swing," but his father had told him never to let anybody change his swing: "Anytime I ever got in trouble with my swing, lost the feel or touch in a shot, it was usually because I became enamored of some popular teacher's ideas about the 'mechanics' of the golf swing, and gave their advice a try, often really screwing myself up for a time."

Palmer experienced the feeling of being an outsider, a boy of lower class, son of the help at the country club where his father became the pro. He spoke at his high school class's fiftieth reunion: "To them, I was simply 'Arnie'

Palmer, the skinny, golf-crazy son of Deke and Doris Palmer, the boy who would grow up and do well enough to buy the club where once upon a time he was permitted on the course only before the members arrived in the morning, or after they had gone home in the evening." The family experienced its challenges, including a time when his father physically beat him when, as a 16-year-old, he protested his father picking on his mother while drunk.

While Palmer was not a good student in school, he was a good athlete, winning many junior tournaments. He received a scholarship to Wake Forest University. He flirted with the idea of studying law or business, especially business, so that he could get a well paying job and play amateur golf. He had a dream of turning professional but told no one. He won several Southern Conference championships and went to the NCAA finals. When his best friend died in an auto accident, he lost his sense of purpose for a time, and staying in school seemed pointless, so he enlisted in the U.S. Coast Guard, which asked him to build a golf course. He went on to build 250 more. Eventually he was transferred to Cleveland, Ohio, and he began to play golf for money. He tried to make the cut at the U.S. Open but was a few strokes short. He went back to Wake Forest University, where he was named interim golf coach and played a lot of golf, but he didn't attend classes. He was a few credits short and did not graduate.

What he called the turning point of his life came when he won the U.S. Amateur in 1954. He then went on to win 61 tour victories and seven major championships. After getting married to Winnie, he and his wife followed the PGA tour. He would practice with discipline, before and after each match, and he continued this habit throughout his career. He began to make money. Children arrived, first Peggy and then Amy.

He became a pioneer in sports marketing and acquired wealth beyond the wildest dreams of a working class boy from Pennsylvania. He got sponsorships, including one for L & M cigarettes. (He smoked two packs a day, but then in 1970, after his sponsorship was over, he kicked the habit.) He also endorsed Munsingwear and Haggar clothes, and one of the iconic television images of the 1960s is of Arnold Palmer in his Sansabelt slacks. Wilson Sporting Goods also sponsored him. He designed the Arnold Palmer golf clubs and began Arnold Palmer Enterprises. A franchise chain of 110 Arnold Palmer Dry Cleaning Centers opened.

Among other offers I politely declined were a line of houseboats, a revolutionary manure dispenser, a golfer's vacation club, countless children's toys, a brand of walking sticks, an endless procession of personal exercise gizmos, several brands of liquor, French cologne, more offshore golf resorts than I care to remember, fallout shelters, orange groves, an African safari, apartment houses, and a one-act play that hoped to make it to Broadway called What Is the Verdict? (Palmer, 1999, p. 164)

Palmer continues to live in his hometown of Latrobe, and his respect for the game endures. Whether one's talent is enough for the game–no matter what the game—is a constant theme in sports biographies and memoirs. Palmer said, "Golf is the most democratic game on earth, a pastime of the people that grants no special privileges and pays no mind to whether a man is a hotel doorman or a corporate CEO. It punishes and exalts us all with splendid equal opportunity."

Physical Repercussions of Dance and Athletics

Dancers' and athletes' lives are constantly filled with practice. Along with that practice comes an ethic of self-denial. Researchers have found that dancers and athletes suffer not only from physical injuries, but also from physical maladies, among them eating disorders, trouble with menstrual periods, and wounded self-concepts.

The rigorous demands on the body along with the continuous pressures to meet the body standard of ballet often produce eating disorders in young dancers. In one study of 45 dancers and 44 non-dancers, Braisted, Mellin, Gong, and Irwin found that adolescent ballet dancers exhibited the characteristics of anorexia nervosa significantly more often than did the non-dancers. These characteristics were: being underweight, a distorted body image, amenorrhea (absence of menstrual periods), and binge eating. The dancers also used frequent strategies to reduce their weight, such as fasting and purging. They also used vitamin C more and were not prone to eat carbohydrates.

Lowenkopf and Vincent, in a study of 55 female student ballet dancers, found that most of them weighed significantly below national norms and had the eating and hyperactivity patterns of people with anorexia nervosa. The girls were obsessed with food and weight. They also experienced delayed menstruation, were likely to be virgins, and did not date.

Their "bizarre eating habits" were reinforced by the dance world in which they were immersed. Their concern with their dancing ability went along with their rejection of their body images.

Dancers, figure skaters, and swimmers were studied by Brooks-Gunn, Burrow, and Warren. This study confirmed the earlier studies, showing that dancers and skaters were leaner and lighter than swimmers, they were more likely to have delayed menarche, and they had more negative eating habits than swimmers. Suzanne Farrell insisted that Balanchine did not encourage the symptoms of anorexia in his dancers, but Buckle's biography indicated that Balanchine would often speak to his dancers about being light, easy to lift, and thin.

Farrell spoke about "the endless diet" and said that the object of her diet was not to overcome obesity, but "to attain the ideal shape for a dancer." Farrell herself failed to recognize that she was pregnant because she was so used to the irregularity of her menstrual periods. "I was having a miscarriage, but I didn't know it because I didn't know I was pregnant. Like many dancers, I had irregular cycles, and skipping a month or two had never been cause for alarm." Kirkland suggested her later addiction to cocaine was related to her obsession with her weight.

In a study of 345 adolescent female dancers and non-dancers that looked at time of maturation, Brooks-Gunn and Warren found that more dancers were late to mature—i.e., they reached menarche after 14 years. These female dancers weighed less, were leaner, and had higher oral control scores and lower diet scores than the girls who matured on time—11 ½ to 14 years. Dancers who matured on time had higher psychopathology, perfection, and bulimia scores than the late maturers. They also had lower body image scores.

Brooks-Gunn, Warren, and Hamilton surveyed 55 adult dancers in four dance companies in the U.S. and Western Europe. They found that 56% of these adult dancers had delayed menarche (age 14 or later), and 19% of these had not had a menstrual period for the preceding five months. One-third of these dancers self-reported that they had had eating difficulties resembling anorexia nervosa or bulimia. The researchers found that amenorrhea and eating problems were related, and that 50% of the dancers who reported anorexia nervosa also were not having menstrual periods. The dancers were dieting at the time, and this was found to be significantly related to their amenorrhea.

Eating disorders occur among certain groups of athletes as well. A study by Stoutjesdyk and Jevne indicated that different groups of athletes may be at different risks of eating disorders. Trent Petrie looked at female collegiate gymnasts. He classified them as normal/ non-disordered eaters, exercisers, bingers, dieter/restricters, sub-threshold bulimics, or bulimics. Only one-fifth of the women athletes had normal eating habits. Three-fifths had intermediate eating disorders. The wish to lose weight, low self-esteem, and a great desire to meet society's standard of female attractiveness were the reasons for the eating disorders. However, Taub and Blinde published a study about eating disorders and weight control in adolescent female athletes and performance squad members that had produced different results. They found that these girls did not have any more eating disorders than other girls, and that about 7%-10% of all teenage girls may begin the habit of disordered eating.

Eating disorders in athletes seem to be a problem that results from the emotional and psychological demands of their sport. Sherman and Thompson thought that the problem, though "well known," is best treated by psychologists who have experience with the sport. Wrestling, swimming, track, and gymnastics are sports in which eating disorders are common.

Besides these eating and menstrual disorders, dancers and athletes are also prone to permanent physical injury. Common dance conditions, according to Arnheim, include ingrown nails and other great toe injuries from being *en pointe*, stress, compression and friction injuries, calluses, metatarsal arch, and other foot injuries. Strains, sprains, dislocations, and fractures are also prevalent.

Assessing the Creativity of Dancers, Athletes, and Actors

The results of the training of dancers, athletes, and actors, the training of their talent into the end result, creativity, is seen in the audience's reaction—being moved, suffering, laughing, ooohing and aahhhing, or the critics rejoicing or grousing. When a friend and I saw Dustin Hoffman in *Death of a Salesman*, we left the theater speechless, went to a restaurant speechless, and sat there speechless. Hoffman defined the role for us, for all time, and we were so struck that we were unable to discuss how he had moved us. That is the result of the actor's art. When Pavlova performed the Dying Swan, crowds all over the world cheered and cried. When young Tiger Woods won the U.S. Open, the beauty of his performance changed the standards of world-class golf. Are actors, athletes, and dancers creators? Yes, of course. Can we find their talent early? Yes.

Barry Oreck, over the years, has developed a Talent Assessment Profile (TAP) that identifies talented students through observation. Developed in the schools of Brooklyn, New York, the profile assesses talent in dance, theater, visual arts, and music. This program shows promise for assessment of poor and disadvantaged students because it does not require that they have had lessons, nor that the Sun of Home be the major influence in the development of talent. Consensual agreement between teaching artists and teachers is gained through a process of audition and call-back. Skills that are looked at in dance are physical control, coordination and agility, spatial awareness, observation and recall, and rhythm. Skills that are looked for in theater are physical awareness, focus/commitment, and collaboration. After students are identified, targeted training is provided, including advanced instruction.

I jokingly asked some basketball coaches once what paper and pencil test they use to find basketball players for their high school teams. They laughed and said, "Can he run? Can he shoot? Can he dribble? Is he tall?" We should evaluate performers by means that look directly at the tasks they have to do while performing. Like baseball scouts who sit in the bleachers at minor league games, we should attend performances, and do the myriads of practical, useful, and time-consuming things that experts have been doing for years in order to determine which of the young actors, athletes, and dancers have potential. The talent can be developed if the possessor of the talent has the drive to do so. Talent development is a partnership between the talented and the field.

Creativity in dancers has to do with gesture. Agnes de Mille, in her biography of Martha Graham, contrasted the gestures of actors and dancers. The actor mimics "exactly with a full awareness of all the overtones and significances." However, the dancer "explodes the gesture to its components and reassembles them into a symbol that has connotations of what lies around and behind the fact, while the implications of rhythm and spatial design add further comment" (p. 144).

Recent research has focused on several aspects of creativity in athletes, including the "flow" experience while performing the sport and the use of imagery in preparing for the performance. Jackson, Thomas, Marsh, and Smethurst found that athletes in Australia who had high self-concept and high psychological skills experienced flow during athletic performance.

Murphy and Martin researched the use of imagery and stated that many, if not most, athletes in high stakes situations use imagery nowadays to "feel the shot" or to "see the shot" before making it. Imagery training programs are offered by sports psychologists such as Gould. In fact, Abma and colleagues found that highly confident athletes used imagery more successfully than minimally confident athletes.

This chapter has focused on physical performers, those whose bodies are their instruments.

Summary

1. Dancers, athletes, and actors are similar to other creative people in that they master complicated tasks in order to do their work.

2. Genetic Aspect: Families of actors are more common than in other domains of talent. Dancers do not seem to come from families of dancers, at least not in the United States.

3. Emotional Aspect: Personality attributes for physical performers are similar to those of other creators.

4. Sun of Home: Actors seem to come from homes that are unconventional and emotionally challenging. Dancers and athletes, because of the early training necessary, come from more stable homes than do actors.

5. Sun of Community and Culture: The ensemble is key and necessary in all three domains—acting, dancing, and athletics. As in other domains, cross-fertilization occurs.

6. Sun of School: Actors study, but usually in college or adulthood, while athletes and dancers must begin special training during childhood. Dancers and athletes often experience permanent physical injuries.

7. Sun of Chance: How one looks is extremely important in acting and in dancing. One's body type matters also in athletics. Chance also operates in getting the "big break."

8. Sun of Gender: In acting, older or overweight women actors do not work as much as young, slim actors. Male dancers are often stereotyped, as are female athletes.

9. There are no paper and pencil tests that will identify talented physical performers. They are identified by consensual assessment.

Several months have passed since Katherine Miller attended the state conference on gifted and talented education. She has been so busy that she hasn't had time to think about what creativity is or about what the creative process is. She has 60 fourth, fifth, and sixth graders who come to her for five hours per week for enrichment through the gifted and talented program. She has obtained several levels of the basic textbooks, and the superhighway between her school and the regional office that serves her school district has grooves from her car wheels as she goes back and forth with materials from the media center. She has coached a team for the Odyssey of the Mind competitions, and her students have joined the Math Olympiad team and the Academic Challenge team. These kids are something.

Even though she has spent every weekend preparing for the next week and hardly sees Brad at all, she feels on fire. She's working with kids who really want to learn. Then, one morning, she finds a note in her mailbox from the regional coordinator, who oversees 79 other schools in the district. The note says it's time to begin selection of kids for the fourth-grade gifted and talented program next year. Has she given the creativity test and checklist to the third grade teachers yet? "What test? What checklist?" Katherine wonders out loud.

The principal overhears her as he passes on his way to the coffeepot. "You have to identify kids for next year. Just call the regional office and ask how to do it. There are special tests. But don't ask me what. Testing was never my strong point." Katherine makes the call. The regional coordinator is out. They play phone tag for several days. Then there's another note. "What test are you planning to use? Half of them are using the Renzulli, and half are using the Torrance. Let me know, and I'll drop them off for you."

"Don't counselors give these tests? Isn't that their job?" Katherine asks the principal.

"Our elementary counselor serves four buildings," he said. "And we need her for the other end students—the slower learners. Read the directions and give the test—or the checklist if you prefer. What did you learn when you went to that workshop? Didn't you tell us at the teacher's meeting that you attended a lot of sessions on creativity? What did they say?"

Katherine goes back to her handouts and notes from the convention. She hasn't had time to do much with them. There, among her handouts of dots, arrows, and charts, are her notes from one of the sessions, "How to Choose a Creativity Test—If You Really Must."

"Why can't I just look at what the child does?" Katherine asked everyone. "I guess I can tell whether or not something or someone is creative, can't I?"

"Oh really?" an art teacher asked. "Do you know when a child is creative in art?"

"Well, maybe not," Katherine answered. "But if I'm in doubt, I can just ask you, can't I?"

But then she thought. "Well, that's art talent—the potential to be creative in art, and not just being creative. And aren't I supposed to just find those kids who are just creative and not creative in something?"

You may be tempted to skip this section, especially if you have a fear of numbers, or testing, but try to read it. What Katherine is about to learn is important, especially since testing is now a major part of every child's life, and especially since important decisions about children are made as the result of their taking tests.

Chapter 12
Creativity Assessment

If creative behavior were determined by heredity, there would be little that parents could do to increase it. There is compelling evidence that this is not true. How a young child's creative behavior is treated by parents and other important people in his life seems to make "all the difference."

—E. Paul Torrance

If one turns to the literature of creativity research and asks the simple questions: What is being measured? What is creativity? One soon realizes that the entire research enterprise moves on very thin ice.

—Mihalyi Csikszentmihalyi

Mrs. Larson, the third-grade teacher, gets the test from the specialist in talent development education, Katherine Miller. It is a paper and pencil test, and the directions are simple. Mrs. Larson makes sure her third graders all have sharpened pencils, scratch paper, that they can hear her and that she can see all of them. "All right, boys and girls," she says. "Today we are going to test your creativity. Listen carefully. I am going to read you some directions, and you will do some tasks according to my directions. Are you all listening?"

Bobby, the class clown who brings Calvin and Hobbes cartoons each day to share with her, is restless. He can't seem to sit still. Bobby, like Hobbes, has an imaginary playmate, only his is a boy, just his age. Bobby is an only child and is lonesome at home because his mother and father are divorced. He carries his key on a string around his neck and spends two hours locked in his house after school until his mother comes home from her job at the telephone company.

"Boys and girls, listen now. Here are a group of squiggles. We are going to do some drawing." Mrs. Larson follows the directions and points to the squiggles on the page, making sure that all of the children have their eyes on her. "Bobby, are you watching? Bobby, I want your eyes on me," she says kindly, walking over to him and putting down the pencil that he has clutched in his hand, making doodles on the squiggles already. "Bobby, you have to wait until I say 'Begin.'" She finishes the directions, which say something about making the squiggles into whatever they want to make them into, anything is okay, and then she says, "Begin."

Bobby has lost interest in making the squiggles into something different and so proceeds to make them into letters of the alphabet, some cursive and some printed. In the first box, he begins to sketch his imaginary playmate. But now the time is up. Mrs. Larson goes on to the next part. "Now you are going to write a story about one of these. The story must begin with these words, but you can end it any way you want. 'Let's pretend' are the words. Begin your story with 'Let's pretend.'"

All of the children begin their stories dutifully, clutching their pencils and laboriously forming the letters into slow cursive shapes, proud of their cursive writing. They have studied the Writing Process, and Mrs. Larson is pleased with their daily work. But this is a test. This is different. Bobby begins to write about a television show he saw last night, when his mother was passed out from the marijuana she had smoked with her boyfriend. He begins, "Let's pretend I got high on marijuana." He has trouble spelling the word, crosses it out, and writes "grass." Then he realizes that this is not right, and he crosses out the whole story except for the first two words, "Let's pretend." Bobby has a whole notebook of stories at home; he writes while he sits in front of the television watching soap operas and children's shows. In one of his stories, a third-grade boy chosen for a quiz show wows them all by throwing a tomato into the face of a bigger boy. The third-grade boy becomes known as "Ketchup" to millions of adoring fans, and he prompts a whole new way of dealing with bullies.

In another story Bobby wrote, he and his imaginary friend, Tony, sneak into a neighbor's basement to spy on him because the neighbor looks like someone from a foreign land. The neighbor carries a cane and wears a pointed beard and sunglasses; Bobby and Tony believe that he carries secret maps rolled up in the cane. Bobby wonders whether he can write any of those stories, but it's too late.

"Time," Mrs. Larson says. "Now, let's go on and do something different." She is reading from the manual that Katherine Miller has given her. "Let's turn to this page, boys and girls," and she shows a page that has on it many numbers. "Let's see how creative you can be with numbers." The directions are a little confusing for the students. Perhaps they should add, and perhaps they should subtract. "How many ways can you think of to get to 43?" the directions say. Just as Bobby is figuring out that 43 is made up of no prime numbers, Mrs. Larson says, "Time." Bobby's father is an engineer, and sometimes, when Bobby is over there and his father isn't complaining about what a horrible person Bobby's mother is, he does math with Bobby. He taught Bobby about prime numbers last week.

Bobby looks over at the girl next to him and the boy across from him and sees that they have both filled in all of the blanks with numbers such as 42 + 1, and 44 - 1. All of the blanks! In fact, all of the squiggles are made into interesting drawings on the boy's paper, and all of the lines for the story are filled up with neat penmanship on the girl's paper. All Bobby has done is get confused, and just when he got an idea, Mrs. Larson called "time."

The above scenario illustrates some of the difficulties with creativity testing. The test will probably be scored according to set scoring rules, and the test scorer will have been trained. Each test is made up of several subtests in which students draw, look at numbers, do mental reversals, do free writing, and the like. Each subtest is timed. Each subtest is scored for several aspects of divergent production—fluency, flexibility, elaboration, originality, and the like. Among the first scores that Bobby will get will be that of fluency. Fluency means "how many," and Bobby will score adequately on the first test because he did use all the squiggles to make letters of the alphabet. On the second score for this test, though, Bobby's slow motor skills will hamper him, and even though the test is normed with other third grade boys who have similar motor developmental problems, perhaps Bobby's slowness has to do with a sense of quality as well as speed. On the third score for this test, Bobby's fluency score will be low because he took too much time thinking of the problem and didn't write down the obvious and easy answers that his two friends did. No matter that Bobby's thoughts were about prime numbers, there is no way that the creativity test can judge that. So the students with the greatest fluency scores will ultimately get the higher scores.

Another way that divergent production tests are scored is for flexibility, or the variety of different ideas that the test taker had. In the first test, Bobby had only two ideas, even though he used all of the squiggles. Letters of the alphabet is one idea. On the second test, Bobby's hesitancy, which resulted in changing his mind about what to write, was his downfall, and he will stand with a low score in both fluency and flexibility. He gets no points for crossing out or censoring himself. And again, he'll get nothing for the numbers test.

While Bobby is probably too young to even be tested with a creativity test, such tests are in wide use in the schools, and for very good reasons. They are easy to use, and they seem to be objective—that is, they don't discriminate against Bobby because he lives in a single parent home or because he has a mother who smokes marijuana. Still, Bobby didn't do very well on the test.

Katherine Miller wants to be sure that youngsters like Bobby aren't missed, so she gives the teachers a checklist to use as well. She has chosen one recommended by the State Department of Education—clearly, then, the best checklist available. She has even done her homework and has looked the checklist up in the latest *Mental Measurements Yearbook*, where it is reviewed and is said by the reviewer to be the best creativity checklist available. The checklist format uses a Likert Scale, where the teacher has to consider the child as she knows him and then check "sometimes," "always," "never," or points in between. Does the child exhibit curiosity? Does he have a sense of humor? Does he ask questions?

The checklist doesn't ask whether the child can write, sing, dance, draw, do science experiments, or think of new mathematical ideas, because this is simply a checklist to see whether Bobby has some of the characteristics that can lead to being a creative adult. Why the checklist doesn't ask such obvious questions is strange, isn't it? These domain questions are not there because "experts" have led educators to believe that creativity exists as a separate kind of mental behavior—separate from the ability to dance, sing, write, or draw. The experts have led the school to believe that such a thing as "creative potential" exists and that it can be discovered if only the teachers will fill out a checklist. The assumption is that if Bobby is talented in creative thinking, he does not need to be able to dance, sing, write, act, draw, do science experiments, or think of mathematical ideas.

At first, Mrs. Larson didn't even get a checklist for Bobby because his school ability index (falsely called an IQ by many school people), extrapolated from the *Iowa Test of Basic Skills* taken last year when her students were in second grade, came out to be 113. The rules in Katherine's state for the talent development education program specify that those students who are identified as creative by a creativity checklist must have IQs of 118 minus the standard error of measurement, and since Bobby is one point below that, he won't be placed in the program. Everyone in the school knows that you have to give the kids 4's on each of the items of the Likert Scale of the checklist or else they won't get into the program. So Mrs. Larson asks for a checklist for Bobby. She knows that Bobby takes unusual books out of the school library. Last week he took out *Moby Dick*. The librarian was amazed, and she told Bobby's teacher. "Why did you take out *Moby Dick*, Bobby?" Mrs. Larson asked. She herself has never been able to get through it. "Isn't it just a little hard?" "Well, I like whales," Bobby said. "Let me know when you finish it," Mrs. Larson said. The teachers had a laugh in the teacher's lounge on that one.

But Mrs. Larson has a suspicion about Bobby from the *Moby Dick* incident and tells Katherine Miller about it. Katherine calls the regional coordinator of the programs for the talented. "My hands are tied," the coordinator says. "We've got parents calling and wanting their kids in the program for the outstandingly talented, and we've got no room. All the kids have IQs over 130 from last year's Iowa test, and we just don't have any room. Besides, his IQ isn't high enough, and what's to say that a kid who wants to read *Moby Dick* is outstandingly talented in creative thinking? Have you heard from his mother?"

Unfortunately, no one, not the coordinator, nor the teacher of the special program for the talented, nor the classroom teacher had thought to give Bobby's mother a checklist. And Bobby's mother, unfortunately, was too busy to come to parent-teacher conferences last Wednesday night. Bobby brought the announcement home, and the letter of invitation from the principal arrived in the mail a few weeks ago, but she's had so much to do at work these days, selling that new line, that when she gets home at 6:00 PM, she just wants to relax and not go out again to Bobby's school. Besides, if something was wrong, the school would let her know, wouldn't they? She adores Bobby. He is her only child. He gets lonely, she's sure, but he never complains. You should see his notebook! Now he's doing sketches along with his stories, and they have to set a place at the table for his imaginary friend, Tony, when they eat supper together. Of course, they rarely eat together because of their schedules. Bobby's mother usually just brings home hamburgers or stops for pizza. When she had to work so late last Wednesday, Bobby just opened a can of Chef Boyardee, put it in a microwave dish, zapped it, and ate that.

The school didn't give Bobby's father a checklist either. Bobby's dad wrote and called the school, asking when the parent's night was, but he can't seem to get put on the mailing list, even though the school says both parents of divorced children should be involved and get notices. He gets a little angry and calls the principal. How the heck can he get involved if he doesn't get the announcement, he wants to know. And when he calls Bobby's mother, they just get into the old recriminations about custody.

Bobby feels pulled between his parents and wants to please them both. He does like school, though. School is fun. Last week he told a joke and the rest of the kids laughed. It was when Mrs. Larson had her back turned, writing the day's schedule on the board. Bobby rolled his eyes up and sat back, his heels hitting the floor, and said, "Oh, my God! She's got a tail!" and everyone laughed. He has started writing more jokes in his notebook.

Back in high school, Bobby's mother used to sing with a rock 'n' roll band, and everybody said she had a good voice. She has a great collection of tapes and CDs, and sometimes Bobby plays them while he is waiting for her to get home from work. He has asked her for music lessons, and she said she'll think about it. He wants to play the guitar, or maybe the drums. She did buy him a keyboard and a book of chords, and surprisingly, he found the notes easy to learn. He has learned the B-flat scale. The music teacher at school notices that he has a good ear and sets him up for a small solo for the Halloween program. Bobby asks his mother to come, but she forgets.

Mrs. Larson wants to spend a little more time to think about Bobby, but in the meantime, she quickly fills out a checklist for Christine, the adorable little girl who starred in the *Nutcracker* last Christmas, who has the most cunning little smile and devilish speed climbing to the top of the jungle gym out on the playground. Christine's mother is active on the advisory committee for the program for the academically talented and has helped in the classroom with birthdays. Mrs. Larson gives the girl all 4's, even though Christine is already in the program for the outstandingly talented under the "academically talented in specific ability" guideline. The girl is a fantastic reader and even better in the writing process.

Does Mrs. Larson know enough about Bobby's secret life to fill out the checklist? Well, it's October, and she's only known him since September, and while he's certainly a sweet boy, she notices that he comes to school with a strange smell on him, sort of like tobacco, a stale smell. Often his hair isn't combed, his jeans are rumpled—and he only wears one pair of jeans each week. The flaps on his shoes are always loose, and he has an annoying habit of zipping the Velcro back and forth while she is reading to the students aloud. He gets so involved in the story that he doesn't know he's doing it. Finally, last week, she told him to take his shoes off during story time. Bobby's reading level is fine, but he's not in the top group because he has no patience for prefixes. He tries, but for now he's just a whole word reader and not a phonics person. Mrs. Larson, while she believes in the Whole Language approach and while she's attended several workshops on it, is still a firm believer that phonics is the way to teach reading. New fads come and new fads go, but Mrs. Larson knows that phonics teaching is the best way, and no one can change her.

Is Bobby a child outstandingly talented in creative thinking? The tests didn't work in his case, and we'll see about the creativity checklist. His behavior at home is a predictor, but who knows about that? His mother doesn't even know the full extent of his creative activities. His slowness in timed tests and his lack of flexibility in doing the timed tests both operated against him. Perhaps his tumultuous home life and his retreat into secret notebooks, sketch books, music, and isolated thought operate best for him. But even if Bobby had done well on the timed creativity test, could the test really predict whether or not he will be a creatively productive adult?

Testing for Creativity

Why assess or measure creativity? Can such a thing even be done? Donald Treffinger gave seven reasons why schools attempt to do so: (1) to recognize individual strengths so that students can do well; (2) to go beyond IQ and achievement testing; (3) to give schools, charged with practical concerns, some basic data so that they can compare their students with norms; (4) to include creativity information in the basic profiles of students; (5) to help teachers discover their own creative talents; (6) to advance the research about nurturing and developing behavior that is creative; and (7) to take away the mystery from the consideration of creativity.

Two Schools of Thought

Two vying schools of thought exist on the value of testing for creativity—though, more accurately, such tests should be called divergent production tests and not creativity tests. The aspects of divergent production, defined by

Guilford, were described earlier in Chapter 3. They include fluency, flexibility, elaboration, and the like. Scott Isaksen said, "there is mounting evidence that creativity can be assessed systematically and scientifically." Bonnie Cramond says that assessing with such divergent production tests as the *Torrance Tests of Creative Thinking* (TTCT) is valid, reliable, and comprehensive. Mary Meeker has said the same with the Structure of Intellect Creative Thinking Test (SOI). The practice of testing for divergent production cognition has continued out of a concern for inclusiveness. Mary Meeker told me, "We have to start somewhere, don't we?" Bonnie Cramond defended the use of divergent production tests by saying, "why not use any and all methods available to ascertain where children's strengths lie?"

Some cognitive psychologists insist that creativity testing has little value. Robert Sternberg of Yale noted, "such tests [psychometric tests of creativity] capture at best only the most trivial aspects of creativity" (1988, p. 35). Howard Gardner of Harvard also commented, saying that "the measures on which they have relied in their studies have almost all been brief tasks—learning word lists, mastery of a maze—which can be surmounted in a matter of minutes (and which are even more rapidly forgotten)" (1982, p. 59). James Borland of Columbia Teacher's College, said in an article, "There are reasons to consider the basic issue as to the extent of the realm of divergent production," and he noted that the Educational Testing Service had dropped tests for spontaneous flexibility and originality from their battery called Factor-Referenced Cognitive Tests.

It appears that there are two major groups of theorists—one group which has spent the last 40 or 50 years trying to develop tests that have validity and reliability, and another group which insists that creativity is a process that is explainable by noticing how creative people think. In the latter group is David Perkins, who called for the inclusion of *motivation* in the assessment of creativity. After all, what are people creating for? Why does the writer write, the painter paint, the inventor invent, the scientist experiment? Perkins thinks that the creativity testing advocates may be off base: "Whereas testing for creativity typically emphasizes flexibility, fluency, and similar indices, values and patterns of deployment seem to offer the best predictors of creativity" (1981, p. 142).

In other words, a student like Bobby has motivation to do creative activities on his own at home. His mother values his creativity. He does many types of creative activities, none of which were adequately represented when he was tested for flexibility and fluency.

Amidst all this controversy about assessment and definition is the bewildered educator responsible for teaching students who are outstandingly talented, whose state department may have a requirement that students with creative thinking potential be identified through using creativity tests or checklists as well as authentic portfolios. The busy educator often does not have the time nor the propensity to wade through the research evidence, and the research itself is often done by the people who can benefit most from showing that their own tests and checklists have validity and reliability. Here are some guidelines that may help when considering tests and procedures that are supposed to be measures of creativity.

Validity

The most important issue for any test, of course, is its validity. Validity is best described as the test's truthfulness—that is, does the test measure what it says it will measure? There are three basic kinds of validity: (1) content/construct validity; (2) criterion validity; and (3) concurrent validity.

Content/Construct Validity

Content or construct validity determines whether the test has measured what it says it measured. To determine whether a creativity test if valid, you must look at what it measures, i.e., its content. But that can be quite difficult when one is trying to validate an amorphous concept like creativity. Creativity is called a "construct," which means that it is an unobservable phenomenon that helps to explain a person's behavior, but because it is not directly observable, it also means that such a "construct" is not directly measurable. Instead, you must measure behaviors that you think are expressions or manifestations of that construct. Csikszentmihalyi has concluded that creativity is such an important construct that it should be considered more than just a construct; it should be thought of as a collection of constructs that constitute a domain in itself, which means that it is a "symbolic system that has a set of rules for representing thought and action."

Confusion about the construct and the domain, and even about the definition, abounds. The lack of a universal definition for creativity—and the complexity of what is creativity—is *the* major problem in developing a valid test or measure. Some researchers use one aspect of creativity—for example, divergent production of figural units, or free drawing within circles and squares—and then conclude that people who were pre-tested and post-tested on that one test were improved in "creativity." That is certainly overly simplistic. Divergent production is not creativity, and creativity is not only divergent production. That is where consideration of the content of what is measured comes in. In various studies, the research subjects may well have scored well in that one area being tested, but creativity is clearly too complex to be measured by a simple five-minute test, or even by an hour-long test.

People using tests that are called "creativity" tests should look carefully at both the structure and content of the test. Is filling in blanks or drawing within boxes "creativity"? Even if the tests are called "divergent production" tests, does the divergent production, simply by implication, translate itself to creativity? Some state education system guidelines apparently make such a naïve assumption because they require that a divergent production test be given in order to assess creative potential.

Donald Treffinger, in commenting on the difficulties in ascertaining validity of specific creativity measurements, said that construct validity should be concerned with creativity testing as a total field, and not as an individual test. "Construct validity refers…to the total pattern of research evidence that supports an instrument." He concluded, "although there are still many isolated, fragmented studies…there have also been some promising signs of progress in validating several specific creativity assessment procedures." Those who disagree might say that no battery, no matter how widely it is conceived, can measure the creativity construct.

The subject of assessing creativity is a difficult one, and in the final analysis, the practitioner must trust in the authorities, because wading through the contradictory evidence of the various studies is a monumental task. Many school districts do not have a director of testing or a tests and measurement specialist, and even if they do, this person might be swayed by the charming personalities of speakers who go from conference to conference, propounding one system of creativity assessment over another.

A related issue having to do with construct validity is whether or not creativity stands separately from intelligence (which is another construct). Gary Davis asserted that having high intelligence certainly enhances one's creativity, because the intelligent person's mind is so full that many options surface when he or she is called on to be divergent. Having a high IQ may be a benefit in functioning in the world, but having a high IQ is not absolutely necessary for creativity. Since creativity is realized in different fields and domains, developed talent in a specific domain *is* necessary for creativity—but that developed talent does not necessarily imply high intellect. Divergent production researchers continue to look at the possible existence of a threshold of intelligence—that is, whether there is a magic IQ number below which a person is no longer creative. More is said below about the so-called Threshold Theory.

Validity and reliability are difficult to assess when trying to measure creativity by testing. Most tests try to measure only one small aspect of creativity—divergent production. The very construct of creativity is not easily defined and may or may not be related in some ways to other constructs, such as the construct of intelligence. Do we know what intelligence means? Its definition has been changing over the years and will probably continue to change, just as, perhaps, the definitions of creativity may change.

Criterion or Predictive Validity

Criterion, or predictive, validity refers to how much the test scores can predict one's performance in other related areas, especially one's performance later on in life. Does a high score on a creativity test given in elementary school, for example, predict that a person will be a true creative achiever when she is an adult, or even when she is in high school?

Of course, the predictive validity is of the most practical importance. Why should we even test students on such instruments if the tests don't show something about how the person is going to be as an adult?

What does the research tell us? Unfortunately, the answers are mixed. Test developers such as Torrance have spent a lifetime testing students, following them up, trying to find out whether their scores on such tests have predictive validity.

Optimally, predictive validity studies would be independently done by someone other than the person who devised the test in order to ensure that there is no unwitting "experimenter bias." In real life, however, the test-maker typically must take the responsibility for proving the validity, and proving predictive validity takes many years. The researcher must keep up with or locate people who took the test in early years, then must control for other life variables, and also must provide a similar comparison group that did not take the test. The issue of possible bias by a researcher toward the instrument that is being validated is a real one, for who wants to spend a lifetime working on a test and doing studies on its validity, only to report that the results were not what were planned? Partners in validation studies are often graduate students seeking degrees, beholden to the professor whose test they are trying to validate. While independent reviewers and researchers do some of the validation work, much of it is done by the test-makers, who may design studies that reflect their drive to prove that their test works.

Not all of the problems have to do with possible researcher bias. Even follow-up studies done by expert teams have demonstrated the difficulties in ascertaining the predictive validity of tests of creativity. Here is an example from one of the Torrance studies. Torrance, in a 1993 article on the predictive validity of his tests, reported on a follow-up 30 years after his participants took the test as high school seniors, and he described two of the students who had scored only moderately high as "Beyonders"—that is, their achievements were far beyond what their test scores would have predicted. Both had made substantial creative accomplishments, one in medicine and the other in anthropology. Torrance concluded that there were more forces operating in these two lives than simply those reflected in their test scores. He wrote of these former average-scoring students: "Forces, such as love of one's work, persistence, purpose in life, love of challenge, diversity of experience, high energy level, a sense of mission…are dominating over creative ability, intelligence, and high school achievement." Perhaps it is not possible to validate such instruments for suitable predictability, at least with regard to an individual student as compared with group results.

A somewhat more optimistic picture was found by Milgram and Hong, who assessed the predictive validity of the Tel-Aviv Creativity Test, a measure of ideational fluency. They found that the creative thinking scores of high school seniors showed a relationship to the amount of their adult leisure activities 17 years later. In other words, creative thinking is related to actual physical activities and hobbies in which people participate. This could be interpreted to mean that people are creative in *something*, and not just cognitively creative in their ability to generate many answers (fluency) or to think of alternatives (flexibility).

They also found that a checklist about extracurricular activities given to these seniors was related to the adult vocations 17 years later. They suggested that future identification procedures could increase predictive accuracy by including some assessment of what students do in their leisure time—that is, the activities that students participate in when they are young predict what they will participate in later on. An extracurricular interest in high school theater may predict an adult interest in community theater or to the formal study of theater. A childhood interest in collecting nature samples may lead to an adult interest in doing science. A childhood interest in reading and writing poems may lead to an adult interest in reading and writing poems.

The Threshold Theory

A related validity issue is whether people who are creative need to be highly intelligent, at least as measured by IQ tests. Must a person have an IQ test before his or her creativity can be measured? Is there a specific IQ threshold that creative people must cross? Runco and Albert have specifically challenged the Threshold Theory—that one needs above-average intelligence in order to be creative—and state that it is incorrect. In their opinion, statements that one must have above-average intelligence in order to show a good score on a creativity test are false. Runco and Albert said, "For now, it appears that the traditional view of the threshold of intelligence necessary for creativity is at least partly a psychometric artifact." By psychometric artifact, they mean that the results were due to characteristics of the tests being used rather than to real differences among people.

For example, some of the studies done on creativity and its relationship to intelligence have used IQs derived from ability tests, such as the *Stanford Binet Intelligence Test*. Other studies have used IQs derived from achievement tests, such as the *California Achievement Test* (that is, the researchers derived a "school-based index" to estimate IQ). The *Stanford Binet Intelligence Test* and the *California Achievement Test* are mistakenly thought by some persons to measure the same things, but they don't. An intelligence test such as the *Stanford Binet Intelligence Test* purports to measure general intellectual ability in computation, verbal, and spatial realms. An achievement test such as the *California Achievement Test* claims to measure actual knowledge in reading, mathematics, science, and social science. Even though the tests measured different things—one measuring verbal, computational, and spatial ability; the other measuring gained knowledge or achievement—several researchers conducted experiments on creativity using them interchangeably, thereby creating a psychometric artifact. Davis also criticized the threshold studies. He commented on the Runco and Albert study by pointing out that "The threshold idea probably cannot be evaluated fairly merely with divergent thinking tests and fifth-grade children."

Whether one must have a certain threshold of intelligence before being deemed creative is an issue that can perhaps be relegated to the esoteric discussions of those who study testing. Most people would say that people certainly can be creative without having an above-average IQ score. We don't even know the IQs of many creative people such as racecar drivers, inventors, Broadway singers, dancers, athletes, visual artists, and the like, and we don't care. We just enjoy and appreciate what they have created.

Concurrent Validity Of Creativity Tests

Concurrent validity examines whether a test correlates with other measures of the same construct—for example, whether it measures what real creative people in the field actually do.

Morse and Khatena, in 1989, published a study showing how the *Something About Myself* and the *What Kind of Person Are You?* inventories were related to an index of life accomplishments. They gave a biographical inventory to conference leaders attending the annual Creative Problem Solving Institute to ascertain their creative productivity as adults by using by a point system over eight categories: (1) job/vocation; (2) interests; (3) leadership; (4) membership in the Creative Education Foundation; (5) artistic endeavors and accomplishments in an artistic field; (6) musical accomplishment; (7) miscellaneous accomplishment, or accomplishment in any field of the performing arts other than visual arts or music; and (8) creative production, or products other than visual arts, music, or performing arts.

Let us critique this study. Only the last four of these categories, for one point each, had anything to do with creative production. Yet (1) job/vocation—the number of different positions the person had held, (2) the number of subgroups within the Creative Education Foundation that the person belonged to, and (3) leadership—the managerial positions that the person had held—all had a possibility of *three* points each. For example, a writer who has published many well-reviewed novels would only get one point, in category 8. Likewise a ground-breaking scientist or mathematician would only receive one point. But someone who had joined many special interest groups—an activity creative people are not known for—would receive three points.

The adult creative producers in this study had accomplishments higher than the norm of the Khatena and Torrance technical manual, and the *Something About Myself* questionnaire items were related moderately to biographical information. The authors concluded, rather weakly, that this study provided concurrent validity for their questionnaire. This is an illustration of an attempt to establish concurrent validity.

Confused? Don't be afraid to admit it. The experiments discussed above demonstrate the complexity of research into creativity testing. Many eminent researchers are spending their professional lives trying to help us make sense of things. Many smart people are trying to figure out how to make tests that sample the complex domain of creativity, but do so in ways that ensure that there are no gender differences, ethnic differences, or socio-economic differences shown in the results. They try to validate the tests on large, representative samples, and to use research samples that resemble those who will take the tests. They try to determine which items to include and which to throw out in order to make the test fair to all who take it. Test development is a very expensive process, and it is not always done well.

Regrettably, because of the pressures of time and expense, many test-makers will release their tests for commercial adoption without the validation studies necessary for the consumer to be able to trust in the results. Of course, that causes more problems. We have the problem of schools making decisions based on tests that are, themselves, based on contradictory research. The result is that often, school leaders end up choosing the research that seems to support their already-held points of view and then justifying decisions by saying that they are "research-based." There is a long-standing cry in the education profession for the research to be translated to solid practice, and maybe someday it will happen; but for now, two carriage horses called inertia and practicality are the main pullers of practice.

The validity studies of divergent production tests have been weak or mixed. The tests have been slowly changing to reflect real world problems that students experience rather than artificial ones such as name all the uses you can think of for a brick. Perhaps new approaches will have more demonstrable validity. However, this will be difficult because of problems establishing the reliability of measures of creativity.

Reliability

Three interrelated types of reliability must be considered by persons who use creativity testing. These are: (1) stability, (2) equivalence, and (3) internal consistency. Is the test stable? If a person takes the test one day and then takes the test later the same day, will the results be relatively the same? The best way to ensure this is to administer equivalent alternative forms of the test, and that is why most standardized tests have a Form A or Form B. The ideal is that the person taking Form A will score the same on Form B and thus assure that the score in each case is equivalent and therefore stable and consistent.

However, in the field of creativity, testing this is very difficult because of the very nature of what is being measured. An analogue would be to compare the reliability involved in scoring a multiple-choice test with the reliability in scoring a divergent production test. It is easy to mark a multiple-choice test. But in an open-ended format with no right answers, it is very difficult to make items equivalent. Is asking a person to list unusual uses for a ball equivalent to asking a person to list unusual uses for a bat?

Another way to establish equivalence is to split the test in half and see whether the scores from each half are about the same, using odds and evens or other ways of splitting the test. Does the test have internal consistency? This is called split-half reliability. Again, this is difficult in testing for creativity because of the difficulties in ascertaining equivalence.

Typically, researchers attempt to increase the reliability of tests by administering them in a standardized way, by using objective scoring measures, by having item difficulties that are equal, by having the test measure only one aspect of creativity, and by increasing the number of items on the test. But all of these are inherently difficult when one is attempting to measure creativity. For example, administering the tests in a standardized way and scoring them objectively is particularly difficult for divergent production tests. Mrs. Larson followed the directions printed on her direction sheet, as she should have done, even though her "standardized" administration of the test left Bobby confused and behind.

Reliability in Administering Tests

Lissitz and Willhoft found that the *Torrance Tests* were highly sensitive to how the directions were given. They said, "The degree to which test takers feel restricted or encouraged may well have a critical effect on their performance." They gave different directions to four groups: one group was administered the test in the standard way, a second was told to be "practical and reasonable," a third was told to list as many ideas as possible, and a fourth group was told to include "unusual, weird, or illogical" ideas. After finding that such differences in giving directions changed the results, they cautioned other researchers that "studies using the *Torrance Tests* should be viewed with extreme caution." More importantly, schools should remember that they are using the tests for making decisions about students' lives, their educational futures. Children often receive differential treatment because of their scores on these tests.

Runco similarly found that telling two groups of students, gifted" and "non-gifted" (non-gifted here means they did not have high IQs), to "be original" as part of the test directions increased their fluency (i.e., the number of responses they gave). Since fluency is always a large proportion of the total scores given in such divergent production tests, increasing the fluency raises the child's test scores. But if some test givers tell the students to be original and some do not, the test scores will be changed and will not be comparable.

Reliability in Scoring

Scoring measures of creativity is also a problem. Scoring is not merely marking which multiple choice questions the student answered correctly or incorrectly. The responses are as varied as the people taking the test, but in the scoring, they will be artificially codified into classes so that the scorer, with training, can recognize certain patterns. For example, a response is called original if it only occurs once or twice in a group of 30 people. The scorer must remember who has done what and how many times it has occurred. I have received and given extensive training in one particular form of divergent production testing and have scored thousands of divergent production tests. Yet there is still an inconsistency in my scoring, especially for humor or the macabre. My mood may be different from day to day, or my understanding of the assignments that the students have recently had may not be clear.

In one instance, I scored a group of stories for a divergent production test. Most of them ended with a moral. If a story ended with a moral, a child received a higher score, according to the directions. It turned out that the students had been writing fables for two weeks. If I had come one month later or one month earlier to test them and to score their responses, the morals at the ends of the stories would not have been as frequent, their scores would not have been so high, and the decisions that were ultimately made on the basis of those scores may have been different.

In scoring such open-ended, vague, and ambiguously interpretable responses, it is better to have several people score the same tests independently—that is, to be inter-raters. If they come up with similar scores, their scoring is called reliable. The scoring is said to have high inter-rater reliability. Another way to score such difficult tests is holistic scoring. Several people score the same test, and the scores are averaged, throwing out the highest and the lowest scores. Such tests as the Advanced Placement essay tests and other composition tests are scored this way.

As these examples illustrate, scoring the tests presents difficulties of over-rating and under-rating the test information, or of giving the same student high scores but for substantially different reasons. Independent researchers such as the Halpins, Rosenthal, DeMers, Stilwell, Graybeal, Zins, Wakefield, and Baer have all found that training issues, scoring issues, and consistency issues plague the divergent production testing enterprise. Apparently, even if scorers are highly trained, there still will be differences that affect the final scores in the areas of originality, say, or in elaboration. If a district does not have highly trained raters, sending divergent production tests in to be hand-scored by the publisher is probably the best idea. A school district trying to save money and having local people score the tests should factor in the dollar value of the local scorers' time and the cost of properly training local people.

Often, the district will find that sending the tests to be scored will save money. Many new revisions of standardized tests use essays now, and these are scored by "hired guns." Interestingly, one person who took a part-time job scoring essay tests reported being urged to score an average of 300 essays in 4 hours, and the company, a major testing firm, had only one person score each essay. "Oh, the exposé I could write about the new testing practices if I hadn't signed a waiver swearing confidentiality," this person said. Just because the testing company is large and famous does not mean it uses ethical scoring practices.

Heausler and Thompson noted that since the same set of responses is scored several different ways with the scorers looking for different aspects of divergent production during each scoring, there is not enough differentiation among the ways each scorer looks at the same test (a subtest is scored for fluency, then for flexibility, then for elaboration, then for originality). They said that people who use the *Torrance Tests of Creative Thinking* should be "cautious" in thinking that the subscales derived from the scoring "provide meaningfully different information." All of the divergent production tests I know of are scored by looking at the same material several different ways. We must take caution and note that the reliability is thus made questionable. Lack of reliability is always a major handicap for demonstrating validity.

Studies of Significant Results

It is overly simple to state that a measure or a test is reliable or valid. Absolutely perfect measures do not exist, and one cannot say that a test is either valid or it is not. Instead, you must figure out *how* reliable or *how* valid that measure is and determine whether the reliability or validity is sufficient that it should be considered significant.

In particular, you need to evaluate whether the results are statistically significant. If the results regarding a test are "significant," people in the schools decide to pay attention. But "significance" is the play territory of college professors of statistics. Many of the studies of creativity testing that report "significance" are correlational attempts to demonstrate concurrent validity. The researchers compare one test with another to see whether the tests are "significantly" related. If the tests are related—more than would be expected by chance—the results are "significant." But such a correlation can obfuscate a more important question that few researchers consider—namely whether the tests are in fact measuring creativity, and whether they have construct validity. Other studies likewise may demonstrate statistical significance that does not have practical meaning for the user. For example, researchers often will try to isolate the factors being measured on the tests. If the researchers find that the factors are, indeed, separate, and isolatable, the results are "significant." These studies are theoretical, and they are necessary—but they're not very helpful to the practitioner.

If the results of a study are significant, what does that really mean? For example, Torrance, in 1987, reviewed 142 studies that investigated methods used to teach students to think creatively. For 103 of those studies, significance was determined by using the *Torrance Tests of Creative Thinking* as an indicator that students became more creative. Students were tested with the *Torrance Tests* before receiving teaching in creative thinking, and they then were tested after they had received the teaching. Their scores on the tests improved. (Note: This is a common experimental fallacy, since why wouldn't the scores improve if something had been taught to students? If one group of students receives instruction in French and another group does not, and if both receive pre- and post-testing in French, wouldn't the group who had received instruction in French probably get better scores on a French test?) However, if the measure used to determine whether students are more creative or not has, itself, questionable validity and reliability, how can one say that students became more creative? Torrance said he would "strongly favor" using "more real-life criteria" such as creative products, but he also stated that those who used his test were using the best measure available.

A Flawed Study of Creative Adolescents

To interpret statistical significance, one must always consider the design of the overall research study. For example, I did a study of 50 creative adolescents who attended a summer institute for 15 intensive days where they wrote and performed operas and participated in creative writing and printmaking. When the students arrived, I pre-tested them with the SOI Test of Creative Thinking (Meeker and Meeker, 1975), a test derived from the Guilford tests of divergent production. I administered DFU, Divergent Production of Figural Units, and also DMU, Divergent Production of Semantic Units.

The day the creative adolescents left, I post-tested them with the same two tests. When I scored the DMU and DFU tests and applied tests of significance to the results, I found that the students had improved to a significant degree in fluency. The significance was $p<.001$ for the girls— about as significant as you can get. However that doesn't mean that the results are meaningful in terms of understanding creativity; it merely means that the results are not due to chance on this particular measure. The boys and the faculty also improved in fluency to the significance of $p<.05$, or a 95% likelihood that the results were not by chance. The students who made transformational drawings on the pre-test did so on the post-test, and no other students did so. The two weeks of intensive creative work did nothing for their transformational ability on paper in drawing.

But what do those results really mean? Can I measure what the summer institute meant to 50 teenagers who wrote, thought, created, made, composed music, performed, and talked until 4:00 am, driving their resident assistants crazy with their creativity and humor, by giving them 10 minutes of two divergent production tests? What does a significant difference in fluency really mean? That these students became more creative? That the faculty became more creative as a group? One would certainly hope so, for the state granted us $40,000 to do that, but one would also have trouble believing that putting down a few more items on a five-minute test would actually prove it.

My small research study, in truth, doesn't show much at all, even though when I presented the results at the state talent development education conference, people were impressed that I had found "significant" changes, and on the surface it appeared to be a result of the training in "creativity skills." About two-thirds of the students did indeed attend a one-hour class daily where fluency, flexibility, elaboration, and originality were taught separately from the other processes they were learning. However, a control group who did not receive the training in "creativity skills" improved in flexibility, fluency, and originality just as much as those who took creativity training—that is, both groups improved, but there were no differences between those who participated in the formal creativity training and those who did not take the creativity training class. They were a small control group. So my "significant" results aren't significant at all, and even if they were, you shouldn't be very impressed that the students and faculty became more fluent. I suspect that the troubles with this study are quite common. My question is, so what? So what if there was an increase in fluency, flexibility, or originality?

The Normal Curve Assumption

Another issue with testing creativity is the assumption that the scores obtained fall on a normal curve, with 68% in the middle and 16% on either end. Though one can construct a normal curve to portray scores from any test, the underlying assumption is that there really *is* a normal curve of creativity. This assumption is an important issue when talking about creativity testing, for it assumes that the person taking the test has "more" creativity when he gets a higher score and "less" creativity when he gets a lower score. This is nonsense. We do not know enough about creativity. Creativity is such an amorphous construct that one cannot say someone has "more" creativity than someone else, at least not in the abstract.

When speaking about the creative person, we can say that the person is creative *in* something or creative *at* something. We should never say that someone has *more* creativity or *less* creativity. But if you use a paper and pencil test and obtain a score, you'll be tempted to admit the highest scorers to the school program. To establish a cutoff score and to say that everyone who scores above the such-and-such percentile gets into the creative thinking program is what many school districts do. The assumption that people fall on a normal curve of creative thinking is operational here. People fall on a normal curve on most tests, and the score on that measure is just an indication of how people did on *that test*. The real question becomes whether or not the test is a true measure of creative thinking.

Often, the person who is most fluent or gives the most answers on a test of creativity will get a high score. If the test is measuring writing fluency, the person who spews out a lot of words will get a higher score than the careful, reticent, accurate poet who writes a few, but well-taken, words. In fact, in divergent production testing, it seems the fluent always win. However, even with these concerns, some educational psychologists who are experts in creativity seem to think that the tests should still be given. Davis, in his 1997 article, thought that creativity testing was all right and said "Creativity tests and inventories are useful when scores are combined with other information—perhaps scores on a second test or teachers' ratings—in order to make reliable judgments."

My position is slightly different. I would not use divergent production tests at all, but would instead rely on consensual assessment of creative products and on a student's motivation to create. I would also not use an IQ cutoff (as in the Threshold Theory). I would not identify children for creative thinking ability, but would enfold the creativity assessment into domain-based assessment. Then why have I written this chapter, you may ask? I have written it because many people still believe that creative thinking ability exists as adult potential in young children, and I wanted to address several concerns about such beliefs.

Using Personality Questionnaires in Creativity Assessment

Beginning with the Institute of Personality Assessment and Research and their many studies into the personality attributes of creators, personality assessment is a part of creativity assessment. Several commonly used personality assessment instruments have a creativity scale, for example, the *Adjective Personality* questionnaire and the *16 Personality Factors Questionnaire*. In Chapters 6, 7, 9, 10, and 11, I noted that studies of creators using the *Myers-Briggs Type Indicator* indicated that intuition (N) preference seems to be part of the creative personality. I have been especially interested in personality assessment during my own research because of the prominent place of personality attributes on the Piirto Pyramid of Talent Development.

Overexcitabilities Questionnaire from the Dabrowski Theory

Research we conducted into personality attributes of creative individuals during our summer institutes seems more promising than the research we did that found significant changes in fluency and flexibility. The work of Piechowski and his colleagues on Dabrowski's theory of overexcitabilities poses new questions about giftedness and creativity, and we wanted to do some exploring of this with our creative adolescents. This was research into understanding what creative adolescents are all about. We were interested in the intriguing possibility that creative adolescents have certain patterns of "overexcitabilities."

Dabrowski's theory of emotional development has been explained by such authors as Piechowski, Silverman, and Falk. They defined an over-excitability as "enhanced and intensified mental activity distinguished by characteristic forms of expression which are above common and average." These forms of expression can be in one or more of five areas: (1) psycho-motor, (2) sensual, (3) intellectual, (4) imaginational, and (5) emotional. Dabrowski supposed that creative individuals often have temperaments with a predisposition to emotional, imaginational, and intellectual inten-sity, or overexcitability.

According to Piechowski, *emotional overexcitability* might show itself as intense feeling, inhibition, fear, anxiety, depressive moods, memory of emo-tions, attachments to places, people, and animals, empathy, self-judgment, and feelings of inadequacy and inferiority. *Imaginational overexcitability* manifests itself in inventiveness, vivid visualization, dream recall, use of metaphor, an interest in fairy tales and magical tales, poetry, drama, and having imagi-nary playmates. *Intellectual overexcitability* shows itself as curiosity, thirst for knowledge and analysis, a preoccupation with logic, the ability to intuitively integrate and synthesize seemingly unlike and disparate ideas, and the capacity for sustained intellectual effort. *Sensual overexcitability* shows itself in a love of physical comfort, in tasting, seeing, smelling, touching, hearing, in overeating, sexual indulgence, buying sprees, and sartorial pleasures. *Psychomotor overexcitability* shows itself in a surplus of physical energy, rapid speech, acting out, compulsive talking, nervous habits such as nail-biting, workaholism, and/or needing always to be moving.

Unfortunately, our results, as of 2000, showed that the adolescents who attended the summer institutes for gifted and talented students were no different from a comparison group of adolescents who attended a vocational high school, except that our summer institute adolescents scored higher in intellectual overexcitability. There were no differences in imaginational or emotional over-excitability. What the *Overexcitability Questionnaire* does yield is some qualitative insight into the young people's thoughts about themselves and their lives.

Here is the *Overexcitability Questionnaire* (Piechowski & Cunning-ham, 1985), used with permission, with sample answers from 21 adolescents who studied musical theater, art, or writing.

Table 12.1: Overexcitability Questionnaire Responses of Talented Adolescents, along with their MBTI Type Preferences

1. Do you ever feel really high, ecstatic, or incredibly happy? Describe your feelings.

   When I'm talking to someone who really understands and relates to me, because many people cannot do that. I like to talk when I get to talk about <u>real</u> things: life, feelings, and <u>writing</u>. I become very hyper and talkative and I can really just feel the words and thoughts rushing out of my gut and I feel like I'm really here, and really attached to the world. Also, when I write something and I really like it, and am praised by someone I really respect about it, it makes me feel really accomplished and that I want to work harder. Female, age 15. MBTI type: INFP.

2. What has been your experience of the most intense pleasure?

   Hearing Mozart's Symphony No. 38 for the first time. Male, age 16. MBTI type: INTP.

3. What are your special daydreams and fantasies?

   I sometimes like to dream about a world in which we can truly be ourselves. There is no hate, there is no rejection. We can be who we really are. Then reality whops me in the face and I realize what a fantasy a world like that would be. Male, age 17. MBTI type: INFP.

4. What kinds of things get your mind going?

   Sad things get my mind turning because I start looking for a way to make it better. I like to discover new things. I like to know everything about everything. I can't stand not knowing about anything. I love to find answers to everything. Sometimes I might look at a simple thing and think of a hundred questions. I can think up 50 questions about a rock that I just kind of wait to discover the answer. I LOVE ANSWERS. I could live on an encyclopedia. Most of the time I do read them. I wonder about everything. Female, age 15. MBTI type: ISFJ.

5. When do you feel the most energy, and what do you do with it?

   I feel the most energy when I'm in a good mood, usually at night. I get a tremendous second wind and practically bounce off the walls. Sometimes I use it to draw, but I like to use it with contemporary or abstract painting more. I use a lot of it by going out or partying at home or just talking to my friends who know me well. Female, age 15. MBTI type: ENTP.

Table 12.1: *Overexcitability Questionnaire* **Responses of Talented Adolescents, along with their MBTI Type Preferences**

6. In what manner do you observe and analyze others?

    I ignore what is visible and concentrate on what is hidden inside. I also try to observe what their analysis of me is. Male, age 16. MBTI type: INTP.

7. How do you act when you get excited?

    A panorama of positive ideas fills my mind. Sometimes I feel faint. Male, age 16. MBTI type: INTJ.

8. How precisely can you visualize events, real or imaginary?

    I can do it great! I see everything as clearly as a window that has just been cleaned. Female, age 15. MBTI type: INFP.

9. What do you like to concentrate on the most?

    What do you mean? I'm the most confusing person in the world and I don't understand half your questions. You need to be more specific; many words have more than one meaning, like "dreams." Thinking, I concentrate on everything. Writing, I concentrate on everything. Academically, English and speech. Physically, creating a better body. Female, age 16. MBTI type: INTP.

10. What kind of physical activity (or inactivity) gives you the most satisfaction?

    Running because it is a solitary sport, and I can clear my mind. Female, age 16. MBTI type: INTP.

11. Is tasting something very special to you? Describe in what way it is special.

    Tasting as in feeling. Tasting the moment (I'm not trying to keep going off on tangents like this; it sounds really stupid but this is what I'm thinking of first). I wrote a poem once about licking the sides of someone's word and another about someone drinking up me. I like that image because that is what it is, and many times I'm tasting depression and indifference like now. Female, age 15. MBTI type: ENFP.

12. Do you ever catch yourself seeing, hearing, or imagining things that aren't really there? Give examples.

    I often think I hear someone call my name—sometimes when I'm alone, or sometimes when I'm with others. Female, age 16. MBTI type: INFP.

Table 12.1: *Overexcitability Questionnaire* **Responses of Talented Adolescents, along with their MBTI Type Preferences**

13. Do you ever think about your own thinking? Describe.

Yes, in my journal I write all of the time about how strange it is for me to ask all of these questions of myself such as why I do things, etc. Most people, it seems, don't do that (or just don't show it and I'm not sure that I show it either). I sometimes think life would be easier if I just accepted things and didn't worry about it or question it. " Female, age 16. MBTI type: INTP.

14. When do you feel the greatest urge to do something? Explain.

When someone tells me I can't. I strongly believe that there's nothing I can't do if I try. Female, age 16. MBTI type: ENFJ.

15. Does it ever appear to you that the things around you may have a life of their own, and that plants, animals, and all things in nature have their own feelings? Give examples.

Yes. For example, in creative writing I've written "Monstrous black clouds casting a mask across the delicate blue sky"; "Compelling the grass to cover within themselves"; "Flowers are closed up, mourning"; "Wind sings out its funeral chant." Female, age 15. MBTI type: ENFP.

16. If you come across a difficult idea or concept, how does it become clear to you? Describe what goes on in your head in this case.

My brain starts to organize different parts of the idea into different drawers, looks at all its parts individually, and then as a whole, spins it around on the tip of my fingers, and eventually understands the idea enough so it becomes clear. Male, age 17. MBTI type: INFP.

17. Are you poetically inclined? If so, give an example of what comes to mind when you are in a poetic mood.

I am a poet. I think of a form or idea. Then I allow my feelings to write the rest. Example: After reading a poem in which the line "oblong rectangles" appeared, I wrote the poem "4-sided triangles" about apparently unsolvable ideas. " Male, age 16. MBTI type: INTP.

18. How often do you carry on arguments in your head? About what sorts of subjects are these arguments?

Yes. I have arguments and discussions with myself all of the time about anything and everything. Male, age 15. MBTI type: INFP.

Table 12.1: *Overexcitability Questionnaire* **Responses of Talented Adolescents, along with their MBTI Type Preferences**

19. If you ask yourself "Who am I?" what is the answer?

I am myself. I change for no one and I accept completely what I am. Male, age 16. MBTI type: INFP.

20. When you read a book, what attracts your attention the most?

The intense parts. Male, age 16. MBTI type: INFP.

21. Describe what you do when you are just fooling around.

I go out and drive in my car in the night and turn out my lights and watch the lightning bugs. Little diamonds among the shrubbery. Female, age 16. MBTI type: ENFJ.

We also added another question that is not on the Overexcitability Questionnaire: *22. In what ways do your dreams influence you?* Most of the students felt that their dreams were quite important in generating ideas, having them think about the meaning of life, and in being predictive or explanatory of events in their lives.

We found, in interviewing the students, that they had often had imaginary playmates. Thus, I was amused to read in articles by Gary Davis that "Two virtually flawless biographical predictors of adult creativity" seem to be the presence of imaginary playmates and involvement in the theater. Since our students were studying theater, the presence of their many imaginary playmates seems to give some credibility to Davis's assertion. Here is a typical answer.

Interviewer: Did you ever have an imaginary playmate?

Yeah. I had a guy named John Hutchins. I didn't have any brothers or sisters, and my mother and father worked overtime, and so there was basically just me—me and my animals. I felt really dumb talking to the cat on the porch. But now that I think about it, talking to nobody that wasn't there isn't better than talking to a cat. So I was by myself all the time, so I invented this guy named John, and before we moved, we had this really big house. And there's a little corner in the dining room and right by it was a walk-in closet. And right there was where John lived, and he would come out and sit at my little table with me when I got my punishment. And he would protect me from everything and stuff. And I really believed in him. He wasn't imaginary to me. He was real. There was John. John was talking to me. And I thought he was naked, so my dad had to give him some pajamas and everything. And my mom had to wash the pajamas all the time, and he was John. John sat there at dinner with me, and John ate my liver for me. John didn't come up and get the liver, no he didn't. John ate my liver and stuff. There was really a John to me.

He was in my life until I was about nine or ten, when we were getting ready to move because I didn't like my step-dad, and I still don't like him. He still comes around, and I still hate him. I guess I don't hate him, but I don't like him very much. And I couldn't tell my mom because she loved him, and when you love somebody they don't do anything wrong. But he was wrong, because he was drunk all the time. He took my money and stuff. So I sat there and told John, and John was like my psychologist. I would tell him how I felt.

Our experience with administering this questionnaire was that we were able to understand those who create a little better after we administered it. Our interviews with the students revealed more about the young creative person than any creativity test or checklist could.

The Myers-Briggs Type Indicator

I included the *Myers-Briggs Type Indicator* preferences in the response in the table above to illustrate that we found that both the faculty and the students overwhelmingly preferred. intuition (N) over sensing (S). They overwhelmingly turned out to prefer NFP (intuition over sensing, feeling over thinking, perception over judging), introversion and extraversion being equally divided. Again, this was not a surprise, but a confirmation that these adolescents were like those studied by Myers and McCaulley for the *Myers-Briggs Manual* (1985) and were also like adult creative people in all domains, as noted by the studies I cited in Chapters 6, 7, 8, 9, 10, and 11.

Lysy and Piechowski thought that the *Myers-Briggs* preference for intuition was similar to the possibility for developmental potential in the Dabrowski theory's levels of development. Since personal growth is a path into the unknown, "perhaps it is a bit easier for those with strong intuition, who are more comfortable with the unseen, with future possibilities, to follow this course than for those whose intuition is not as well developed," they said. People who prefer S (sensing) trust the concrete, that which can be touched and seen. Inner searching produces gut feelings of "I just know it," and the person who trusts intuition trusts the gut. Lysy and Piechowski said, "The inner search, then, for an as yet unmanifest self may well be a process more congenial to the individual with strong intuition."

These differences in preferences may explain the difficulty creative students, who often prefer intuition, seem to have in elementary school. Add the fact that many elementary teachers also prefer judging, and the majority of the creative and intuitive students prefer perception, and you have a basic incompatibility in preference that may lead to misunderstanding on the part of the teachers and a feeling of rejection for the way one thinks on the part of the students. In *The Developing Child*, Elizabeth Murphy spoke to these differences by suggesting that teachers with one preference should offer choice to their students in terms of assignments and that they be flexible in terms of requirements—that is, an open-ended assignment on an area of interest may satisfy the teacher's requirement for the student to demonstrate that she knows the matters at hand just as thoroughly as 20 worksheets drilling the student in skills she already has demonstrated that she knows by completing the first few items correctly.

Creativity Checklists

Several checklists exist for assessing creative behaviors. I was on a committee for the State of Ohio that chose appropriate selection instruments for creative thinking identification of gifted students. Ohio is one of the few states that requires identification of creative thinking. Another is Georgia. In my opinion, the creativity category of giftedness should be dropped because of the lack of availability of valid and reliable instruments and because the existence of creativity in adulthood cannot be reliably predicted in childhood. Ohio requires an IQ cutoff of about 115 (the Threshold Theory, discussed above) and a checklist or test.

Our committee found no creativity tests and only two checklists suitable. One is the Creativity Scale in the *Scales for Rating the Behavioral Characteristics of Superior Students* (Renzulli, Smith, White, Callahan, & Hartman, 1997). This is the best of several checklists available. The other was the Creativity Scale from the *Gifted and Talented Evaluation Scales* (GATES) (Gilliam, Carpenter, & Christensen, 1996). Both checklists use a

Likert Scale to rate individual students in several areas, and they are filled out by professional educators knowledgeable about the child being assessed. Using a Likert Scale means filling out whether the behavior occurs always, sometimes, or never on a five-point range. Such behaviors as being curious, always asking questions, making new things, intellectual playfulness, imagination, and others are within the items.

Other checklists are the *Group Inventory for Finding Talent* (GIFT) and the *Group Inventory for Finding Interest* (GIFI), which are administered to students themselves and then scored. Developed by creativity researchers Gary B. Davis and Sylvia Rimm, they are viewed as adequate, but they have not been re-normed within the last 10 years and thus were viewed by our committee as not meeting the criteria of having been updated recently.

Promising Practices in Creativity Assessment

Using checklists filled out by students themselves is entirely different from using behavior checklists filled out by teachers in the school system, supposedly showing that the student possesses certain researched characteristics and thus is potentially creative. Selection for programs by means of personality instruments should certainly not be done, but it is beyond me why selection by relatively invalid and unreliable checklists is permitted in schools. The problem of assessing young students is a universal one. It bothers me that such checklists can be used, tallied, totaled, and that weighted scores can be added up on matrices to make decisions about young students' lives. That school districts state the false promise of "objectivity" in using such matrices to combine unlike, unrelated, and unreliable data concerns me even more.

Most school personnel, though they have had required courses in testing and assessment, feel uncomfortable with deciding which tests to use. That is why many states have lists of recommended tests and committees such as the one I mentioned above. At least then, schools and school programs can be confident that the assessment measures they are using have been screened by disinterested and independent experts.

Performance Assessment

The assessment of actual student products as a way of identifying creativity is gaining advocates. Baer said that performance assessments—that is, asking experts to look at student products—seem to have promise in assessing creativity. Hennessey and Amabile, in a series of studies described by Hennessey, recommended storytelling assessment to identify verbal creativity. The mammoth fallout and interest in the Gardner Multiple Intelligence (MI) theory and the ensuing large research grants have yielded much that is useful in assessing creative products. Books by Lazear, the Campbells, and Armstrong offer much advice about how to assess by looking directly at the intelligence instead of filtering it through the linguistic and the logical-mathematical.

Morrison and Dungan recommended that looking at student performance at school contests is both a practical and a do-able assessment opportunity. This has the advantage of comparison with others outside of the small realm of the current classroom situation. The highly trained judges who are present at regional music, science, mathematics, art, writing, and sports contests bring to the task a wide background in assessment of similar products. Baer, in 1994, noted that expert evaluation is the way creativity is assessed in real life and that this can be replicated in schools by having panels of experts in the domain look at what the students have made. Clearly, there are many ways to assess creativity other than paper and pencil tests.

The assessment of creative potential has many pitfalls, but careful, thorough, and informed people can sidestep these pitfalls with proper attention. One major criticism of this kind of "authentic" assessment is that it is not validated across the state, the country, or internationally, and what is called "highly creative" in one setting may not have a relationship to what the rest of the world views as creative. Relying upon "experts" in one school system may not produce the specialist or authoritative judgment that the student would compete with on a wider playing field.

Let us use the students in our summer institute as an example. They learned, in a minimal way, how to write the libretto of an opera. They participated in that frustrating, lengthy, mind-filling creative process. They sat for hours at the piano in practice rooms composing. They acted, made costumes, wrote the story, rehearsed, collaborated, and sweated. Their journals showed us that their attitudes changed and the products they produced were novel; they were original; the products had never existed before. The students did the actual work, participated in the actual process, and did not just do abstract exercises twice removed from the process. Their work was *authentic*.

The point is this. We have a mystical belief in tests. But if we would just sit back and look at the tests we have given and stop investing them with such magical powers, we would realize that the tests—which are brief samples of behavior—show little if anything, and cannot do even that in five or 10 minutes of testing. The students increased in creativity all right, but measuring their increase in terms of two 10-minute tests was ludicrous. Yet because of accountability constraints, this is what educators are often asked to do.

Let us take another example. Say there is a boy who can throw a ball from center field to home plate with great and accurate force. Observation would dictate that he would probably do well as a center fielder. Is there any need to give him a paper and pencil test to see whether he has spatial ability?

A better indicator of the enhanced creativity of these adolescents was in the observational or portfolio assessment we ended up with. We looked at what they had made during the institute that had not existed prior to the institute: many poems, short stories, prints, four amateur but earnest operas, all shown on a videotape we put together. These products were not judged or graded in any way, for the emphasis was on the creative process and not on the *quality* of their products. An assessment of *quality* should come after many more poems, stories, operas, and prints are practiced. However, our instructors were themselves "masters" in their fields; they were composers, actors, writers, and artists who could have assessed the products if necessary.

Another type of authentic assessment could be a "creativity portfolio" that a student would assemble throughout the year(s). This portfolio could hold a sampling of products—sketchbooks, journals, concerts, plays, games, camps attended, and other such records. Whether or not the student actually demonstrates specific talent in a domain that is great enough to be developed through the process of training expertise, the student would have a record of creative thoughts and projects and would not be able to say, as so many adults of my acquaintance do, "I'm not creative." Memory of creative times could be awakened and recalled with pleasure and nostalgia. Picture it. Each adult would no longer be able to say, "I'm not creative," for the proof would be there in this authentic portfolio of experiences gathered while maturing.

Talent Assessment Profile

Domain-based assessment of talent contains some relationship to creativity. As discussed in Chapter 11, Oreck's Talent Assessment Profile (TAP), is a promising practice of identification. The advantages of this assessment are that it trains teachers and teaching artists to observe research-based characteristics of the various arts, it includes targeted training, and it is eminently fair, as no previous lessons are required for young students to be assessed. The process that Oreck has developed is being tested nationally in several Javits grants. These are federal grants given for research in the education of the gifted and talented.

Oreck's assessment process also includes assessment of the child's creativity while dancing, acting, performing music, or doing visual arts. The criteria include: (1) expressiveness, (2) improvisation, (3) imagination, and (4) compositional originality. For expressiveness, the key concepts are these: responds with sensitivity, performs with energy and intensity, is fully involved, and communicates feelings. For improvisation, the key concepts are these: responds spontaneously, uses focus to create reality, shows the details, and gives surprising or unusual answers. For imagination, the key concepts listed are as follows: offers ideas, comes up with original or unusual suggestions, finds multiple solutions, makes the situation "real," solves problems, sees the whole picture, invents dramatic situations, and has a sense of effective timing. For composition originality, the key concepts are: improvises spontaneously, takes risks, makes surprising or unusual statements, creates in original ways, makes up songs.

When Katherine Miller was hired to teach outstandingly talented students, she had no idea that she would be asked to give creativity tests and checklists, nor did she have a suitable background for deciding what tests to give, why she should give them, or how to interpret the scores once she obtained them. I hope the information in this chapter will help teachers like Katherine when it comes to assessment of creativity. You are now finished with the most difficult chapter of this book. Congratulations!

Summary

1. Teachers are often not well trained in administering creativity tests and checklists.

2. School districts should understand the research base that went into a particular checklist or creativity test.

3. Sometimes the research is confusing since validity and reliability can be defined in different ways.

4. Predictive validity of creativity tests, creativity training, and creativity checklists are most difficult to establish because the tasks on the tests have little relationship to real life creativity.

5. Scoring is difficult on creativity tests because the scoring requires subjective judgment and scorers must be trained.

6. When reading about results of studies that claim that the treatment made the group "more creative," check whether that meant more fluent, flexible, etc. and judge the results accordingly.

7. There is no normal curve of creativity.

8. Behavioral checklists used to make decisions about students' lives are problematic.

9. Creativity test results used to make decisions about students' lives are problematic.

Chapter 13
Creativity Training

The challenge I see before us in the study of creativity...must be to find a coordinating simplicity. This means using our data differently, making connections among sciences and points of view, finding a common language, advancing to more comprehensive theories. Quite realistically, at least $100 million have gone into research on creativity.

—Frank Barron

The effort to enhance people's creativity takes place in many industrial, business, school, and psychological settings. It is called "creativity training." This section looks at a few of the most frequently used methods.

Transfer is the purpose of all education. Transfer means that what one learns is applicable to real-life or to another field. For example, what is the transfer of algebra? Some people say that there is no transfer; they say it is useless to study algebra. Others say that algebra teaches one to think logically. As with algebra, transfer is the main problem in discussions of both creative and critical thinking. If a person practices separate skills—for example, being fluent or being flexible—then in what situations can the student draw on those skills? In math, when one learns to add and subtract, those skills transfer when that person balances a checkbook. But in creativity training, if a student learns to put down more answers in a short amount of time, where does that skill transfer or later benefit the student in real life? What do the people who undergo creativity training gain? What do we expect them to gain? Creativity training should be subject to the question, "Does it transfer to real life?"

Divergent Production Training

Guilford listed *fluency, flexibility, elaboration, originality,* and *transformation* as aspects of divergent production. He also listed *synthesis* and *analysis,* as well as *evaluation,* some of which appear in Bloom's Taxonomy of Educational Objectives (knowledge, comprehension, application, synthesis, analysis, and evaluation). In an attempt to develop these six to eight key aspects, many creativity enhancement programs use divergent production training.

For example, the Odyssey of the Mind program has an activity that students do called the "Spontaneous Problems." Students are grouped in teams of seven. Five of them enter a room and sit around a table. There are two judges present. The students are given a topic, they think for a couple of minutes, and then they begin to brainstorm possible items, attributes, or issues that fit that topic. They are judged on how many responses they come up with (fluency), how many different categories of responses they have (flexibility), and how rare their responses are (originality). The team with the most points wins. The judging is done swiftly and arbitrarily, though the judges receive training beforehand.

Following is an exercise I use in my teaching to help students internalize the types of divergent production. The first three steps of this exercise are similar to those practiced by teams in the Odyssey of the Mind.

A lesson in *divergent production* that I often use to illustrate fluency, flexibility, originality, elaboration, and transformation is to have the students brainstorm—say, on the topic of birds.

Table 13.1: An Exercise in Divergent Production

Fluency	"Brainstorm birds," I say after dividing them into groups of four or five. (The word "brainstorm" has made its way into the popular lexicon, and few people know its Guilfordian origins as explicated at the State College of Buffalo Creativity Studies Program.) The rules of brainstorming are that the participants must go as fast as they can listing ideas as they come to the mind, with a recorder writing them down. There is to be no judging of answers as in, "That's a really stupid idea," or "No, that doesn't fit," or even "Will you explain that please?" The students make a long list of whatever they come up with.
Flexibility	To illustrate flexibility, ask the students to look at the list and see how many different categories their answers fall into. There may be *athletic teams* with the nicknames of birds—for example, the St. Louis Cardinals or the Baltimore Orioles. There may be *musical groups* named after birds, such as "The Birds," or *movies* named after birds, such as "The Crow." There may be *species* of birds, like robin, bluebird, owl, nightingale. There may be *food made from the flesh* of birds, as in turkey for Thanksgiving, turkey stuffing, chicken cacciatore, pheasant under glass. There may be *idiomatic sayings* using birds, such as "Don't put all your eggs in one basket" or "A bird in the hand equals two in the bush."
Originality	To illustrate originality, or rarity, ask the students to look at their lists again and see which items they think are most original, most rare. They may have the name of a famous professional basketball player, "Larry Bird," or the name of a flower, "Bird of Paradise." If the unusual item does not appear in the lists of the other members in class, we call it original.
Elaboration	To illustrate elaboration, ask the students to take drawing paper and draw one of the most interesting items on their list. Each student individually draws something interesting. I ask them to draw it in some detail and to invest the drawing with individuality.
Transformation	To illustrate transformation as a collaborative assignment in divergent production, I ask the students to exchange drawings and to work on each other's drawings, changing them into a different drawing.

This simple exercise teaches the students the terminology and has them experience what divergent production actually is—in a rather trivial exercise, but in one that is fun and that quickly illustrates the terms and their application to divergent production.

Creativity Training in College Courses

A few colleges offer courses in creativity. McDonough and McDonough found that of 1,504 colleges, 76.5% offered such courses. These creativity courses are taught by diverse faculty in engineering, art, education, psychology, music, and philosophy. A conference for professors of creativity courses is offered every summer in Midland, Michigan at the Northwoods Institute. There, the professors share ideas and try out each others' favorite methods for enhancing creativity. Often, students from their creativity classes come and demonstrate what they have learned. One group of engineering students from the General Motors Institute gave a demonstration on how they thought of various uses for industrial sludge. Another group of students from a liberal arts college in the south demonstrated multi-media presentations that they had done in response to their assignment, "Come to class with no clothes on." Students arrived in cardboard boxes, in tin cans, and encased in rubber tires. They had to exercise their creativity in order to answer this clever professor's assignment.

Creativity Studies Project

In 1967, Alex F. Osborn undertook a massive effort to teach in such a way so as to enhance the creative abilities of college students. Osborn developed the brainstorming technique and the Creative Problem Solving process (CPS), and he was the director of an advertising agency in New York City. His successor, Sidney J. Parnes, founded the Center for Studies in Creativity at the college. The focus of the center was the art of problem solving, and now there is an emphasis on problem finding as well. Students at the center learned the Creative Problem Solving process, combining convergent production with divergent production. They also utilized the intelligence theory of the Structure of the Intellect, in consultation with J. P. Guilford.

Parnes, in 1987, reported an evaluation of the program. After two years, post-tests showed that the students in the experimental group scored significantly better on creative problem solving than did the control group.

The students in the experimental group also did exercises in Noller's *Creative Action Book*. Results indicated that there were significant differences in students' scores.

Most interesting, though, is who dropped out of the creativity studies program. Parnes and Noller found that the students most likely to drop out were students with arts interests who had initially thought that the creativity studies project would feed those interests. Most of these students were females, and those who dropped out were interested in music, entertainment, modeling, art, interior decorating, and journalism. Those who stayed in were interested in practical arts and services such as recreation leadership, mechanical careers, social service, sports, religious activities, and office practice. Parnes said, "Those lower in self-control and higher on 'manic' tendencies (impulsivity, spontaneity, etc.) seemed to seek the quick answer, the novel experience, and when it no longer appeared to be novel and exciting, they tended to drop out of the picture." The dropouts did not like working in the workbooks, and did not like the structure of the program, but they did like the brainstorming and the game-like atmosphere.

Those in education who use the Creative Problem Solving model and similar workbooks and materials must remember that Osborn, whose *Applied Imagination* started it all, was interested in increasing the creativity of *business* people. Parnes said that those who dropped out of the creativity studies program were those who might have "limited value in an organization." From an organization's viewpoint, people who are creative are people who contribute to the profitability of that organization. They are looking for a reward, usually monetary, for their creativity.

The ones who stayed in the creativity studies program got better and better on Guilford's tests measuring evaluation ability. Again, the predictive validity of these tests is a question, though it would seem reasonable, especially to those who work in the area of thinking skills, that training in evaluation would help in real-life situations requiring evaluation.

As your author, an artist and not a business person, I have to admit that I nod off when I read creativity training books and programs. Perhaps I would also have been one who would have dropped out of the Creative Studies Program. It does seem that the people who dropped out had more interests that were similar to mine—music, entertainment, the arts. I don't know—they may have felt that they were creative enough already. I know that I would rather act in a play, go to choir practice, or write a poem or work on my novel than fill in a workbook to enhance my creativity. I would rather go to our Sunday afternoon writer's group and bring a new poem for my friends and me to discuss. Perhaps the value of creativity training books is that they help people who do not consider themselves to be creative to dip one toe into the stream.

A few years ago, I was glad to see that I wasn't alone in feeling weird when asked to do workbook exercises and follow step-by-step "processes" to make me more creative. I had company from another writer, Susan Els, a graduate student trying to write a creative thesis for a degree in education. She had tried all of the techniques that she had been taught in her graduate programs, but when none worked, she made up her own and wrote her thesis on her own creative process as a poet and a writer. It became a book titled *Into the Deep: A Writer's Look at Creativity.*

To their credit, Isaksen, Puccio, Treffinger, and the other researchers at the Buffalo Creativity Studies program took the studies about who dropped out of their program seriously and began to look more closely at the personality preferences of the people who entered both their undergraduate and graduate creativity studies programs. They began to do research on how people with various personality preferences function and contribute to corporations and organizations. This research is currently being published in scholarly journals.

Creativity Training in the Schools

Various people have asserted that creativity can be trained in young people and in adults. These believers have manufactured programs and exercises in divergent production to encourage people to improve their flexibility, fluency, originality, and their ability to elaborate and to make transformations. Many of these programs can be used by teachers to teach and by individuals to enhance their own sense of being creative. Torrance (1987) found that the six most common types of creativity training are these: (1) teaching specific creative problem solving skills; (2) direct teaching of problem solving and pattern recognition; (3) using guided fantasy and imagery; (4) using thematic fantasy; (5) using creative writing; (6) using Quality Circles for quality control. (Quality Circles originated in Japan, and some educators have taken on the strategy and use it in their classrooms). These types of training are structured and prescriptive in that they consist of directions and exercises that are published and used. Here is a partial description of some of these programs or systems.

Table 13.2: A Sampling of Creativity Training Programs

Divergent Production Testing

These tests and the pros and cons of their usage are described in Chapter 12. The practice of testing for divergent production cognition has continued out of a concern for inclusiveness. The problem of "false negatives," or elimination of those who are really creative because they scored low on such tests, is one of the main difficulties. The inclusion of those who score high but who have no creative products or other indicators is a plus, as the high score indicates that these students are able to function divergently. In 1993, Runco stated that "divergent production tests are very useful estimates of the potential for creative thought."

Creative Problem Solving (CPS)

This is the granddaddy of all creativity training, and it is a foundation or basis for such programs as Future Problem Solving and Odyssey of the Mind. People work in groups and solve a "mess" through divergent and convergent processes such as "problem finding" and "solution finding," "criteria setting," and finally focusing on the one best answer. Treffinger, Isaksen, Feldhusen, and colleagues have produced many training materials. So has Doris Shallcross. Each summer, an international creativity conference is held in Buffalo. Thousands of people attend.

Gordon's Synectics

Synectics is putting unlike things together to form a new object or thing. It is a popular teaching approach in textbooks about models of classroom instruction and creativity.

Meeker's Divergent Production Exercises

These exercises are found in the *Sourcebooks*. There are basic and advanced levels that contain exercises in all of Guilford's divergent production factors.

Torrance's Programs

Several programs, workbooks, and the like are available at the Torrance Center for Creativity at the University of Georgia, many of them developed by his graduate students and colleagues over the years. A typical book, developed after Torrance wrote extension exercises for a Ginn textbook series, is *Incubation Teaching: Getting Beyond the Aha!* by Torrance and Safter. Another is *Making the Creative Leap Beyond*, which was published in 1999 and which updated *The Search for Satori and Creativity*.

Taylor's Talents Unlimited

Taylor identified nine talent totem poles: academic, productive thinking, communicating, forecasting, decision-making, planning and designing,

Table 13.2: A Sampling of Creativity Training Programs

implementing, human relations, and discerning opportunities. This program was validated by the National Diffusion Network and is widely used in schools.

Williams's *Ideas for Thinking and Feeling*

Williams created exercises following the Guilford divergent production aspects.

Samples' Metaphorization

Samples suggested ways to help people form metaphors, noting that almost all theory making in science is metaphoric.

Eberle's Work

Eberle wrote exercises in creative visualization. He also invented the term SCAMPER as a code for teaching creative thinking (Substitute, Combine, Adapt, Modify, Put to other uses, Eliminate, Rearrange).

Future Problem Solving

This international competition is based on the Osborn-Parnes model of Creative Problem Solving. Students do research and propose solutions for world and community problems. There are various levels for participation, from primary to high school ages.

Odyssey of the Mind (OM) Competitions

Odyssey of the Mind is an international competitive program in which teams of students invent and create according to certain problems that all have been given.

Edwards' *Drawing on the Right Side of the Brain*

This technique uses upside-down drawing in order for people to form the ability to see holistically and not form brain codes.

Rico's *Writing the Natural Way*

Rico pioneered the now widespread use of "webbing" to generate ideas and organizational structure. Computer software exists to help in this process.

Invention Competitions

These are commercially run by various groups, including Invention Museums.

deBono's coRT *Lateral Thinking*

Lateral thinking is a packaged program used in thousands of schools internationally. Six "thinking hats" are taught.

Table 13.2: A Sampling of Creativity Training Programs

Davis' *Creativity Is Forever*
The Davis program emphasizes the affective as well as the cognitive aspects of creativity enhancement.

Bagley's and Hess's *Guided Imagery*
This popular book has many guided imagery scripts that are useful in all curricular areas.

Crabbe's and Betts' *Creating More Creative People*
These are books written for the Future Problem Solving program, with an emphasis on developing more creative people by means of creativity training.

Cameron's *The Artist's Way*
This 12-step program by a creative writer combines "morning pages" with meditative techniques. It includes 12 weeks of exercises about "Recovering," such as Recovering a Sense of Connection, Recovering a Sense of Autonomy, and Recovering a Sense of Faith. This program speaks to the mid-1990s obsession with dysfunction.

Goldberg's Creativity Exercises
This series of exercises helps creative writers break through their blocks to writing including using such techniques as "writing practice" and writing in public. This extremely popular program for writers has applications for other fields, just as Edwards' drawing program does.

UCONN Confratute
An annual summer conference called Confratute held at the University of Connecticut has a creativity strand. Hundreds of teachers attend and learn how to differentiate their curricula and infuse aspects of creativity into their daily work. The work of Renzulli, Reis, and colleagues is published by Creative Learning Press and is the most widely adopted plan used by schools.

Project Vanguard
This is a 30-hour teacher-training project in providing creativity training for teachers so that they may be able to adequately identify students with creative potential. Teachers receive training in morphological analysis, synectics, metaphors, analogies, visualization, attribute listing, what if's, inferring, random input, forced input, criteria finding, and the creative problem solving process.

Table 13.2: A Sampling of Creativity Training Programs

Reynolds' Creativity, Inc.
This is a high school extracurricular creativity program utilizing affective techniques and art enhancement exercises to help students probe into their inner selves in order to reach their truly creative cores. It has the advantage of cutting to the emotional as a way of reaching the creative. We have used this program at our summer institutes for talented teens. The students respond very positively.

Creativity: *Schools of Curious Delight*
Elaine Starko, a professor of elementary education and a specialist in gifted education, has written a book that tells teachers how to infuse creativity into lessons in the elementary school. Many of her suggestions are valuable and helpful, especially to beginning teachers.

There are many other programs, and the person who wants to infuse creativity training into the curriculum or teach it separately would do well to look around. As one of my graduate students said, it seems as if there's a new catalog of creative thinking materials in the mail every week.

Many reading series and math series include such exercises in the teachers' manuals. Companies such as Good Apple, Zephyr, Synectics, Creative Learning Press, and Royal Fireworks Press specialize in publishing books that help teachers to train divergent thinking and other aspects of creativity. Training in divergent thinking includes such open-ended activities as brainstorming, making up stories, thinking of new and unusual uses for objects, and forcing relationships between unlike objects. In divergent thinking, there are no wrong answers (unless you are scoring a divergent thinking test, and there, it is always the fluent who get the highest scores), whereas in convergent thinking, there are right—and wrong—answers. Most school learning is concerned with convergent thinking, though one of the influences of the field of creativity training is that more divergent thinking is being taught.

What are the results of such training programs? Torrance in 1987 listed the real-life results of creativity training in elementary and secondary schools as the following: (1) increased satisfaction; (2) evidence that academic achievement is not affected by creative performance; (3) writing more creatively in different genres—one student even wrote a novel; (4) growth in personality and the acquisition of a healthy self concept;

(5) improvement in attitudes toward mathematics; and (6) an openness to pursuing creative choices.

A hard-nosed pessimist might wonder whether the creativity training was justified for such tenuous results. But attitudinal and conceptual changes are difficult to measure, though they are vastly important in the formation of the necessary intrinsic motivation one needs to produce creative products. Creativity demands emotional risk-taking. To make and to show what one has made is at base an emotional decision, and as such, the affective must be valued in any training of creativity. Trust within the group and between members of the group and its leader must be established before any training can be undertaken. Perhaps "training" is not the right word—perhaps we could call it creativity "experiencing" or creativity "simulation," as the students and the instructor undertake a journey together.

Creativity Training as Differentiation for the Talented

Special education programs often use creativity training as a means of differentiating the curriculum. Differentiation is the main way of justifying education for the talented. Years ago, I heard the rationale for using creativity training from a famous speaker at a conference. She said that students with high IQs are rigid and like structure, and that they are uncomfortable when they are asked to do something that doesn't have a right answer. They are not risk-takers. Thus, they should be taught to be creative by having training in divergent thinking.

I am not at all sure that students with high IQs are rigid and like structure; in my work with high-IQ students at a school for the gifted in New York City, I found that students' personalities cannot be generalized. They are individuals, kids, humans—some are rigid, and some are flexible. IQs do not presuppose rigidity or flexibility. However, this rationale is still heard as the justification for giving creativity training to students with high IQs. Saying that high-IQ kids are rigid is not justification for using divergent production training in special programs. If some students receive creativity training, then *all* students should receive creativity training.

The science of creativity training is not yet so perfected as to say that some students would benefit more than others. Likewise, on the undergraduate or graduate level, anyone who wants creativity training should receive it. There are few empirical studies as to the value of such training; that research is yet to be completed. There is nothing in the training of fluency, flexibility, elaboration, and originality that justifies it as the special province of classes for high-IQ students. The fun, laughter, easy atmosphere, charged climate, and productivity that result from creativity training should be available to all students.

Creativity Training Is Fun

Let's just admit it. Whether or not creativity training is even the province of the schools, creativity training enrichment is fun. Doing the exercises produces laughter, humor, good feelings, and cohesiveness in a group. Even though I don't like to read the workbooks, I, like most people, love being in a group and doing the training exercises. I remember once teaching a group of teachers the Creative Problem Solving process. It was a dank November afternoon in Michigan. No one wanted to be at this required after-school in-service. It was the week of the annual Ohio State-Michigan football game. Thus, our "mess" for the initial problem solving exercise was, "In what ways can we get tickets to the Ohio State-Michigan game?" By the end of our session, we were laughing, feeling good, and we had invented a way to get tickets to the game. I still remember how we creatively changed the size of the football field in order to add more seats to the stadium.

Teachers Get More Empathy with Creativity Training

Students are not the only ones who should receive creativity training. Teachers need it also. McDonnell and LeCapitaine in 1985 showed that teachers who received 40 hours of group creativity training at Synectics, Inc. in Massachusetts had statistically significant increases in empathy in comparison with a control group. The teachers also reported that the training helped them in being more open with their students, in listening intently to student responses and ideas, in reinforcing students, and in allowing students to experiment more. The teachers in my graduate education classes would probably agree, as we often spend the evening laughing and being outrageous as we try out various creativity activities.

Following is a description of the college course I have developed at my university for undergraduate interdisciplinary studies students and for graduate students who are teachers. First offered in 1992, when the first edition of this book came out, it has been modified over the years with the help of adjunct professors F. Christopher Reynolds and Jennifer Allen. I have created most of the activities myself, or I have combined aspects of other activities I found appealing. I hope you will use them and adapt them for your own purposes as well. Please note that the activities listed on Table 13.3 will be explained in more depth throughout the rest of this chapter.

Table 13.3: A Creativity Course

Theme	Activities
Core Attitudes	Risk-Taking (The Princess and the Pea) Naiveté (The Raisin Meditation) Self-Discipline (Thoughtlogs) Group Trust (Red and Yellow Wounds) Feeding Back (Recognizing Others' Works)
Six of the I's	1. Imagery (A Guided Journey) 2. Imagination (Fingerpainting, Clay, Poetry, Fiction) 3. Intuition (Psychic Intuition, Dreams) 4. Insight (Grasping the Gestalt, Aha, Zen Sketching) 5. Inspiration (Visitation of the Muse) 6. Incubation (*See Meditation*)
The Seventh I—Improvisation	Jazz, Theater, Word Rivers, Writing Practice, Creative Movement, Rhythm and Drumming, Scat Singing, Doodling, Joke Telling
Meditation	Meditate on Beauty (15 Minutes Before a Work of Art) Meditate on the Dark Side (An Image of Your Own Dark Side, A Visit to a Cemetery) Meditate on God (A Sacred Text) Meditate on Nature (I Am a Naturalist, "This Is the Day Which the Lord Hath Made")
Synaesthesia	Mixing It Up—Seeing, Hearing, Smelling, Tasting, Touching
Exercise	A Walk, A Run, Aerobics, Games, Dance
Exploring Passion in a Domain	Noticing "Flow"
Conversation and Friendship	A Creativity Salon
Visiting and Appreciating (Field Trips)	Bookstore/Library, Museum, Concert, Play, Movie, Reading or Lecture, Place (Travel)
Individual Creativity Project – Show how you used all core attitudes toward creativity.	

It has been my experience that in many situations, creativity training exercises are not taught for transfer—the students do not know why they are doing the exercise and what its purpose is. It's my belief that no educational activity should take place without students knowing why it is taking place. Students of algebra ask, "What is the use of this unless one plans to go into mathematics?" In many ways, taking a creativity course might be like taking algebra. What is the earthly use of it unless one is going to try strategies taught in the course within the domains in which they want to be creative? On the other hand, athletes practice dribbling, throwing, and hitting; dancers practice steps and jumps; and pianists practice scales. Perhaps the exercises that follow can be viewed as scales, as practice.

Many of the creativity training programs widely used in schools emphasize divergent production—fluency, flexibility, elaboration, and the like. I call them "linear." In the creativity course I teach, we have developed some methods of creative production that could be called "less linear." They are based on what creative people have actually said about their creative processes (see Chapter 2).

Core Attitudes for Creativity Enhancement

Core Attitude of Self-Discipline

Every creative person who makes a contribution to his or her field has self-discipline. They do the work. They practice, practice, practice. (Remember the musicians at Juilliard in Chapter 10?) They do their work with regularity. Habits of work define their days, whether or not they are on vacation. In order to emphasize the extreme importance of doing the work, I have my students keep a Thoughtlog.

Thoughtlogs

Students in all of my creativity classes (as well as my qualitative research classes) keep a Thoughtlog. I got the idea from Gabrielle Rico when she sent me her syllabus for the creativity courses she teaches at California State University. A Thoughtlog is a record of one's creative thoughts. The purpose is to emphasize self-discipline, to establish the habit of putting it down. Students work in these each day. Evaluation is done by just placing a checkmark or a sticker at the end, noting that the student has done the work. As an instructor, I do not comment on the entries, as the purpose is self-discipline and not dialogue with the instructor. Rather, I count the entries and give a point a day, seven days per week, for each week of the semester. If I were to comment, students would not feel free to make the Thoughtlog their own creative thoughts, but would try to please me. The Thoughtlog is not a journal and does not have to be written—thoughts or ideas can be depicted in sketches or collages. The Thoughtlog is the heart of the self-discipline core attitude part of the course. Here are the directions I put in my syllabus.

Directions for Thoughtlogs

Materials: Sketchbook, pen, pencil, and pastels, colored pencils, or paints, other.

1. Write (or sketch or paste or make a collage) in your Thoughtlog each day for about 10 minutes using automatic writing (just put your pen on the paper and write), conscious sketching, copying (quotations or visuals).

2. In addition, as you read the assignments, you might want to have your Thoughtlog nearby so that you can make comments or write down thoughts that occur to you as you do the assignment.

3. Also, keep a log of the progress of your projects (the creativity exercise assignment, the biographical study, your creative project).

4. Please don't make the Thoughtlog a diary of your every thought about your love life or your work frustrations, though these are certainly an important part of creativity; try to make it a spontaneous *record of your awareness of your own and others' creativity.*

Suggestions: Mention something you have done that is creative, a movie you've seen that is creative, a book you've read that is creative, a comment you overheard, a joke, a poem, etc. You are not required to write; you may make diagrams, draw, paste things in, etc. Just work in your Thoughtlog each day.

Cultivating Risk-Taking

To be creative, a particular core attitude must be acquired—that of risk-taking. Risk-taking is a personality attribute that creative people show. When someone is teaching students about risk-taking, the goal is to have them experience this *in their bodies* and associate this with the personality attribute so that they will remember, when placed in a situation in which their creative selves are asked to take risks, that risk-taking is often beneficial to the development of creativity. It is important to teach this in a safe environment—jumping off the ledge of the building or swimming against the current of a raging river should not be how students are taught about risk-taking.

One exercise I have often used to teach risk-taking is based on the research that shows that most people have a fear of speaking and singing in public. I close the door of the classroom and ask how many people like to speak or sing in public. Few answer. For those, I have another exercise. Meanwhile, I ask those who are afraid to speak in public to take the risk of doing so by sharing a poem or a section of their Thoughtlogs with the whole class or by standing on a chair and singing a song they know. I tell class members to applaud and smile, being careful not to condemn or ridicule the people's risk-taking. The whole class shares in a spirit of caring.

What people will or will not take risks about is usually very personal. I ask people to write down several risks that would be personally difficult for them to do. This exercise is called "The Princess and the Pea." I ask those who do not view singing or speaking in public as a risk to think what *would* be a risk for them. For example, people who are plump or who do not meet the beauty standard put forth by the mass media may have a fear of appearing in public in a bathing suit. I ask them whether they will do this for the class—whether they will come to class some day with a bathing suit under their clothes and sit for a few minutes in the class wearing only that, just to experience physically the process of risk-taking. Or will they call someone with whom they have a conflict and tell the person assertively what they've wanted to say but have so far not dared? Will they take a chance?

I then ask them to fold the sheet of paper into a small wad and put it somewhere on their bodies—in their shoes, in their coin purses, in their pockets, to pat it, to feel its presence there, reminding them to practice risk-taking—and to promise that they will try to do some risk-taking with one or two of the items on the list. These are private, and no one shares, but during the semester in class, we ask people if they are working on their risks, and they may respond if they want to.

Cultivating Naiveté

A third key attitude of mind is the cultivation of naiveté. Again, one thing creative people do is see their domain—and perhaps the world—anew, as if they are seeing it for the first time. This habit of naiveté is automatically present when the creative person works. This is why travel is so creative. When we travel to a strange place, we are forced to put away our old preconceptions and to view the place with young eyes, as we are seeing it, literally, for the first time. How to have students cultivate this habit of mind? I have tried different means.

Sometimes, in the autumn, I stop at the fruit stand and bring in an apple for each student. I pass the apples out and have them study the apples for a few minutes. Then I collect the apples and put them in a bowl. I have the students come over, find their original apples, and then go back and write a few sentences about the unique characteristics of their own apple and why they would recognize it anywhere. Before the exercise, students saw a bowl of apples; now they just see one apple; this forces them to pay attention and to see all apples anew—that each apple is different, unique.

I once took a workshop on emotional intelligence from Daniel Goleman and his wife Tara Bennett Goleman. They led our large group of people in something called the raisin meditation. We breathed deeply, calmed ourselves, and then slowly tasted the raisin. I stole this exercise, which was for mindfulness, according to the Golemans, as an illustration of naiveté, seeing the old as if it were new. My students say they will never taste a raisin the same way again.

The key is for the creative person to pay attention to the field where the talent lies and the passion is. This means not only keeping up on the people who are working at the edge, but cultivating habits of mind that focus one on paying attention. People are always amazed that I know so many authors and the works they have written; this is second nature to me; I am a writer and I have trained myself to notice who is doing what in my field. Paying attention is also important in that one's sense of proportion and distance are also formed by what one focuses on.

In other exercises, I try to have the students look at a loved one as if that loved one were a stranger, or look into the mirror so long at themselves that they see themselves as if they are now a stranger, and then step back, still staring at the mirror, and describe themselves objectively. "I see a face that is quite round, with three double chins, and a mouth that has dry parchment-like lines in the corners. I see a nose that is broad, with ovoid nostrils somewhat large. The nose indents right to the inner brow, between the eyes, so that it looks as if the person has no bridge to the nose." Etc.

Group Trust

Group trust was also discussed in Chapter 2. In creativity class, we try to create an atmosphere of acceptance where people are encouraged to trust each other. One way we do this is to share stories. An exercise that is based upon one often done in group process exercises is one we call Red and Yellow Wounds. People pair up with strips of red and yellow crepe paper. They face each other and tell each other a story about a time when their body was hurt (we are all full of scars, and each scar has a story). Then they tell each other about a time when someone shone the sun of approval and trust on them. They tie a red tie around the wound and a yellow tie around the place of sunshine. We do this exercise at the beginning of a semester so that the students and professors have a common ground of memory by which to begin their journey into creativity.

Another evening we tell stories, stories that our families told about what it was like when we were little, or where we took vacations, or myths that our families tell when they get together. The possibilities for storytelling are endless. And each story creates good feeling among the people in the group, which leads to still more group trust.

In establishing group trust, the way in which we give each other feedback is extremely important. As an exercise in feeding back, students fingerpaint (fingerpainting does not need skill; everyone sort of starts on an even plane) and construct images from clay. I learned about using fingerpaints and clay from F. Christopher Reynolds, who uses them in his Creativity, Inc. classes. Now, I use fingerpainting in almost all of my classes as a way of crystallizing imagery. Reynolds has people fingerpaint their essential selves. I have students fingerpaint images specific to what we are working on. We have also use clay in the creativity classes, another practice adapted from Reynolds' Creativity, Inc. Students build sculptures during the class. Reynolds has his students use a metaphor of earth—"What matters?"—with the double meaning of earth as matter. I may have my students construct an image of their daimon, or of the self they were when they were 10 years old, or of love. Then we do the feeding back.

Feeding back is not evaluative. It does not say, "I like it," "I don't like it," or "It's awesome," "It's beautiful!" Instead, feeding back begins with a walkabout, an art show of people quietly and respectfully circling the room. Then the image is displayed at the front of the room, and the person who constructed the image remains while the rest of the people speak to him or her in a sentence that begins with the words "I see...." "Everything is there," we tell the students, "if only we will see it. You will receive insights into your work (and self) that you did not know you were putting into the work if you listen to the feeding back." This is done carefully and tenderly, with no evaluation, but just description or association. Other possible responses are these: "It reminds me of...," "I want to make a work of art to respond to your work of art," "While I was looking at this, something just popped into my mind"; or most profound of all, being rendered silent by the power of the work.

These core attitudes begin the course, and students work to cultivate them. Then, throughout the course, they work on the "Seven I's."

The Seven I's

The "Seven I's" are essential to the realization of creativity: these are *imagery, imagination, intuition, insight, inspiration, improvisation,* and *incubation.* I discussed these briefly in Chapter 2 on the creative process. Here are the ways we work with them in our course on creativity.

Imagery

Much has been written and said about imagery as a way of accessing the creative in oneself. Imagery is related to imagination, with both referring to pictures and perhaps using the inner eye to see or portray scenes that do not exist materially. Athletes are asked to create mental images of themselves as they do their sports—the ritual is by now so commonplace that it even has a name: putting on one's *game face* after creating a mental image of oneself doing the tasks required. *Imagination* is a more loaded word; a person *uses* the imagination to create new or fanciful scenes, images, or objects. *Imagery,* on the other hand, are the pictures that one sees in the mind's eye within the whole scene created by the imagination. Recently, *imagination* has had connections with *vision,* giving a futuristic turn to the process.

Guided Imagery

Guided imagery is done by having the students close their eyes, relax, and listen to your voice as you guide them on a journey. This is popularly used in the classroom setting by teachers who want the students to "see" a certain setting or place. Suppose the class is studying the Winter War in Finland. The teacher would ask the students to picture a fall day in a certain landscape: "You are in a military automobile going back to the front. The road is rough, and you bounce around. Four others are with you, two in front, and two in back. You are also in back near the right window. These are your friends, and you have gone through many battles with them. You have lost many comrades along the way. As you smoke your cigarette, you are looking out at ruins. Smoke rises from burnt farmhouses and barns. You pass people pulling carts or sitting on top of trucks. You are headed east and they are headed west. They have burned their own farms so that the Russian invaders will not find provisions. Farther and farther your car goes, and still you are not with your outfit. Then you turn into the woods onto a rutted lane, and there emerges from the side of the road a man with a white cover over his uniform, carrying skis. It is your staff sergeant. He hails you. You are back to the front lines. You do not know whether you will ever see home again."

In this guided imagery, the teacher has placed the students into the action through their ability to create visual images. This requires creative imagination and memory. Many lessons in guided imagery are given in creativity training books such as those by Begley and Hess

Imagination

Think about the imagination for a while. Then think about *your* imagination. Come up with some memories of when you used your imagination. Draw or write about these memories, or create a new imaginative piece. It can be a story, something visual, something concrete, something written. Now recall how you felt when you were going along in your imagination. Here's an example:

When my sister was very young, I was in college, as I was 16 years older than she was. I used to tell her stories beginning with an object in the room that she would pick. "Pick an object," I would say. Then I would improvise a story as I went along. I had no idea where the story was going to go next; I just went from one thing to another. Then, when I wrote my novel of fantasy, *The Three-Week Trance Diet*, I had a memory of the stories I had told my sister, and I just kept going along. It was as if I were dreaming but constructing the dream through my fingertips on the keyboard. That is what I feel when I am completely in my imagination.

For an exercise in imagination, I have students write a plot that they have never heard of before. They pick a slip of paper from a hat that has a date, then another slip of paper that has a place. They work in teams of two and write a story in that time and location.

Intuition

The training of intuition has also been debated. Can one improve one's intuition, or do some have it and some not? I believe that all people have intuition. Intuition is "just knowing," and it is connected with what is called the "sixth sense." We have sayings that talk about "a woman's intuition" or "intuitive knowing." This means that there is necessarily little, if any, concrete evidence for a decision. Many creative people have written about the place of intuition in their creativity.

Psychic Intuition

Henry Reed taught us this exercise at the Conference for Creativity in Colleges and Universities. The students choose a partner. Before they begin, they take a piece of paper and write down something that they have been thinking of, something that has been bothering them, something that they have been mulling over in their mind. They try to formulate that something into an image. Then they fold the paper and put it away. With their partners, they face each other on chairs with their knees touching. They may also touch hands if they wish. One person is the "sender," and one is the "receiver." They close their eyes. The "sender" concentrates on transmitting the image and the thought connected to that image to the "receiver." They are to breathe deeply, focus on each other's mind, and try to send the image through the knees or fingertips. This is to be done slowly, with attention. After awhile, they switch roles and repeat the process. After a period of time, they open their eyes and discuss. The discussion should proceed with one receiver saying what was experienced, and then the other. Amazingly, especially with undergraduate students, images are both received and sent with some regularity.

What does this have to do with being creative? Trust in the "under" self, the psychic self, is mentioned by many creative persons. For examples, see the biographies of William Butler Yeats, the poet, and of Albert Einstein, the theoretical physicist. Practice in being aware of one's intuitive, psychic self can't hurt.

Dreams and Intuition

This is another exercise taught to professors of creativity courses by Henry Reed. Again, students choose a partner. They sit quietly, and one tells the other about a dream. The partner will listen with attention and then ask the first student to choose an image from his dream. If he cannot choose one, the partner will choose. Then they act out the image. They become the image. They associate to the image. What does the image remind them of? What associations do they have with it? They switch roles. Now the second student tells a dream to the first, and so forth. This exercise is based on Jung's "active imagination." Johnson defined active imagination thus: "It consists of going to the images that rise up in one's imagination and making a dialogue with them. It involves an encounter with the images." The dreamer speaks to the images, has a conversation with them, and also re-enters the action. This is a symbolic experience and is often deeply powerful. It is not recommended for young children, but it is very effective with teenagers and young adults.

What does all this have to do with creativity? The importance of dreams to creative people has been well documented. Note the paintings of Paul Klée, the poems of William Blake or Samuel T. Coleridge, and the story of the scientist Friedrich August Kekulé, who saw the benzene ring in his dreams. We spend at least one-third of our lives sleeping, and a substantial portion of that time dreaming, yet often people will say, "I don't remember my dreams." This technique of active imagination will help the student remember the dreams and encounter the images. The week before one does this exercise, the Thoughtlog assignment should be to "pay attention to your dreams."

Insight

Grasping the Gestalt

The Zen sketching exercise below deals with grasping the gestalt, or the whole, of a scene and rapidly putting it down in drawing. Grasping the gestalt can also be rehearsed in other ways. (1) For one week, every time you enter a room, try to sum up what has happened before you arrived and what will happen after you leave. What do the people's faces show? What do you observe in body language, in voice tone? You should describe one of these scenes in your Thoughtlog. (2) Look at a book of paintings. Choose one that hits you or entices you. What has happened just before this scene? What is going to happen afterwards? (3) Take a postcard of a painting. (I use a collection of postcards that I have bought at various art museums and galleries throughout my travels.) Tear a piece of paper the size of the postcard, fold it in half, and fold it in half again. Tear out one of the quarters, put the paper over the postcard, and describe the open section. Then turn the paper so that each quarter is open to a different section. Finally, take the paper off and see how each section has made its part of the whole, the gestalt. Put the paper back on and move it from section to section, and then take it back and see the whole. What is the difference between the part and the whole? Discussion of the insight that this exercise provides should follow.

Aha!

The moment of insight is often described as the moment when one says "Aha!" I ask the students, "Think back on your life and describe a moment when you experienced an Aha!" Yes, you have experienced this. It may have been when you first understood how to work a problem, when you found the answer to some difficult aspect of a project you were doing, or when you centered on the topic of the speech you were going to give. Close your eyes and think of your favorite quiet place. What were the circumstances of your receiving that "Aha"? Describe the physical setting and the mental setting when this "Aha" arrived. Do this with other "Aha's" you had. Is there any commonality? For example, I receive many of my "Aha's" while driving on long trips.

Zen Sketching

I took a course in this type of sketching based on the work of Frederick Francks, *The Zen of Seeing: Seeing Drawing as Meditation.* This exercise, based on techniques used in art schools, teaches about rapidity of observation, while the previous exercise taught about closeness of observation. Both are aspects of the creative process. In this exercise, you have a sketchbook, a pen or pencil, and an eye. Sit down in front of a scene and, while viewing the scene, rapidly and surely sketch the major lines within a very few moments. Often this can be done without looking at the paper. Some art teachers do it in the dark, flashing a slide for a few moments while the students try to put the major aspects of the scene into a few well-chosen lines.

Zen sketching helps one get a quick overview of the major points of the subject—and again, while this is useful for artists, it is also useful for creative people. "Just what *is* the problem here?" one might ask when surveying a morass of detail. "What *are* the main points to observe?" "What is the system?" Such training in seeing helps one be reminded that most problems that require creativity are dense and difficult and not easy to formulate. People who use the Creative Problem Solving model (CPS) call it the "mess," and it is what is generated around and about a topic. Zen sketching provides a physical way to deal with the "mess." Here is foliage. Here is a barn. Here is a river. Here are clouds in the sky. Here is a clothesline. What is the problem? What do I focus on? Quickly, now. Quickly.

Recently, on a trip to Arnhem Land, an aboriginal national park in the Northern Territories of Australia, our guide pointed out a native hunter creeping through the reeds near a billabong (river channel) far away, sneaking up on mandarin geese. The hunter was too far away to photograph, and the aborigines do not like people to photograph them, but I have a sketch of him in my Thoughtlog, scrawled from a bouncing four-wheel drive safari vehicle, and this rough image will feed my poems and memories.

What does the conscious attention to insight have to do with creativity? The person who receives an insight is already engaged in the creative process. Insight helps one move on to a solution to the present problem—and to related problems. Many insights are not received (note the passive tense here) through conscious work, but through a physical process in the individual to produce insight. While I work on my poems and fiction, I trust that what comes next will appear to me as I write; nothing is decided before I put pen to paper, fingers to keys. I trust the process of sitting down and just doing it daily. I know that the thoughts will come as I am doing the process.

Inspiration

"I can't get inspired," says the student who has a boring assignment. "I was inspired," says the gleeful sharer of a newly made creative product. Inspiration is thought to be god-sent or derived from mind-searching. Inspiration is thus tied to interest in people's minds. And what interest is more charged than a personal interest? Inspiration often arises through being attracted to someone or something. Interest yields attraction and desire, and then, perhaps, inspiration. Inspiration can take many forms, among them the erotic (or the visitation of the muse), the spiritual, the natural, the intellectual.

Inspiration of Love: Visitation of the Muse

A popularly held conception originating centuries ago and common in many cultures was that the creative person went into a sort of trance while creating. This trance was caused by the visitation of the muse, as discussed in Chapter 2. One of these muses was Erato, the muse of love poerty in classical mythology. The longing for connection is beneath the idea of the visitation of the muse.

Think about your own life. When did you make something in response to a sexual feeling or a feeling of response to a person? I've asked the following focus question of my students in creativity classes: Describe a time when you or someone you know were inspired to create by love—the Visitation of the Muse. Answers have been delightful—young men described feats of physical bravery; women recalled baking cookies and special treats for boyfriends. Paying attention to the reasons for creating has been enlightening to many. I bring to class red envelopes, creamy stationery, a candle, and the directions for writing a sonnet for this lesson. We write love poems based on the Elizabethan sonnet form. According to symbologists, as described in Brown's novel *The DaVinci Code*, the sonnet, with its meter of iambic pentameter, has an ancient connection to soul matters. My students write the poem carefully in black ink on the heavy stationery, seal it in a red envelope with dripping wax, and save it to give to their loved one. I read "How Do I Love Thee" by Elizabeth Barrett Browning, "What Lips My Lips Have Kissed" by Edna St. Vincent Millay, and other love poems to them before we begin.

Out of this assignment has also come the negative impulse—that is, the visitation of the bad or evil muse, the "I'll show *you*" reason for creating. This has been shown to be very powerful also. Many have experienced the shadow side of love, the dark side of love, through divorce, betrayal, and disappointments with their love lives. Creative works also come from this aspect of the inspiration of Erato.

The Inspiration of Nature: I Am a Naturalist

Nature is, of course, a supreme inspiration for creativity—from Wordsworth's "Tintern Abbey" ("getting and spending we lay waste our powers/little we see in nature that is ours") to Jacques Cousteau's voyages to the bottom of the sea, and from the soulful music of Sibelius to the icicle-inspired glass designs of Iitala, nature has been profoundly inspiring to many, if not most, creative people. How does one simulate this experience, this reverence for nature? Again, the mind-set of naiveté is important. I like to do a simple exercise. I gather from my yard twigs and branches, from the beach smooth stones, and from the woods flowers and seeds, one for each person who is in class. I gather drawing paper, graph paper, and a variety of colored pencils, pens, and crayons. Before beginning the exercise, I pull out my copy of *A Naturalist's Voyage of the Beagle*, the young Darwin's classic 1839 account of the three-year long exploration of the British ship *Beagle* to South American and New Zealand waters. I copy a page with a drawing and begin to read one of my favorite passages, and we talk about Darwin's gift for nature description and for doing botanical drawings.

"Imagine!" I say. "This was a man in his early twenties, seeing these insects, these birds, these fossils, these rocks, trees, and flowers for the first time." Then I ask the students to do their own botanical drawing and to spend a little time writing a descriptive paragraph after the style of Darwin about their object. This exercise emphasizes naiveté, as well, seeing the commonplace as if it is new. Then we have a show of works. I also use this to illustrate Gardner's eighth intelligence, the naturalist intelligence. Other classic works could be used as well—for example, the works of Roger Tory Peterson, Sigurd Olson, or John James Audubon. Use your own favorite nature writer and illustrator.

Another exercise we do is to take a field trip to a nature preserve. People walk about the preserve with their Thoughtlogs, with sketching materials, cameras, or collectors' bags (if collecting leaves and twigs is permitted), and the only rule is that they may not talk to anyone. They spend an hour or so in the beautiful woods, and when we return and gather in a circle on the lawn, everyone is calm, quiet, transformed, and in the creativity zone.

The Inspiration of Nature: This Is the Day which the Lord Hath Made

People live fragmented and busy lives, especially my graduate students who are also teachers and parents. This exercise is similar to the field trip, but we don't take a trip afar. I wait for a lovely day, and then at the beginning of the period, I write on the board the words of the psalm, "This is the day which the Lord hath made; Let us rejoice and be glad in it." I send them outside with their Thoughtlogs with these directions: "Go out into the campus and walk, sit, watch, write, draw. But be by yourself. Do not communicate with anyone else. Come back in an hour." When we get back, we are in an "alpha" state—that is, relaxed, refreshed, and alert to our surroundings, having been creative or ready to be creative. One autumn day, I strolled around the grounds and observed a young rock musician sprawled on a picnic table. He was a little late coming in after the hour, but he explained in his Thoughtlog, "I got the best song!"

The Inspiration of the Intellectual: This Takes the Top of My Head Off!

Nothing inspires smart people so much as intellectual challenge. This is one misunderstanding that others sometimes have about academically talented students. They think that those who are academically talented don't like to study difficult books and ideas. Each summer for many years, I have directed a summer honors institute for talented teenagers. These teens actually choose to come and do in-depth study of philosophy, psychology, toxicology, microbiology, physics, mathematics, and the like. The lunch tables and dormitories breathe with their talk and their delight in finding others of like mind. Within a few days, the atmosphere of the institute is charged with intellectual fervor. How we design a creativity enhancement exercise to duplicate the sense of delight, awe, and creativity of these young people is a challenge.

Who is your "book friend," the person with whom you talk about the books you love? Who is the person who has most challenged your thinking? What do you do when you don't know the answer? These are some of the discussion topics we use. Sandi Willmore, one of the assistant directors at our institute, started a Dead Poets Society. The students gather late at night and go to a dark corner of campus with a single candle. There, they talk about ideas. Jennifer Allen, who followed Sandi as assistant director, has carried on this practice. "I just loved Dead Poets Society last night when we talked about the meaning of life," say the students in their morning journals.

Improvisation

Improvisation is an important part of creative production. Nachmanovitch called it "free play" in his book of the same name. Most creators do not lay down an outline or a plan and then execute it in linear function: "1," "2," "3," or "A," "B," "C." Improvisation should be viewed as fun, as play. Many improvisational activities that students have brought to the class have left us in paroxysms of laughter and gaiety. Here are some areas in which one can improvise. Note that much improvisation leads to a good feeling. Talk about the impact of humor on creativity.

Jazz

Play a jazz composition based on a familiar melody. Now play or sing a common children's song, the simpler the better. "Row, Row, Row Your Boat" is fine. Improvise on the melody. Talk about the feeling of going beyond the written notes.

Theater

Get two volunteers for an improvisational theater exercise. One is the desk clerk and one is the person who wants a room. Conduct a conversation in which each person can only ask questions. Switch. Conduct a conversation where each person can only make statements. Switch. Conduct a conversation where one person can only ask questions and the other person can only make statements.

Many theater games exist. Look some of these up and try them. Laughter abounds. Creativity is at home with improvisational theater.

Word Rivers and Writing Practice

Put your pen to paper and do not take it up. Write whatever comes to your mind for the next 10 minutes. Begin with "I have this pen in my hand."

Creative Movement

Play some music that is free-form. The CD of the Bulgarian Women's Choir is good, for the songs are strange and exotic. Listen to the music and begin moving your arms in response. Now add your legs. Add your body. Try the floor, the mid-level position, the high-level position. Have fun. No one is watching you. I have a friend who teaches creative movement, and each semester I make arrangements to use the wooden floored gymnasium of a school nearby. After we get to class, I lead the students over to the gymnasium. I say nothing else, since one year the males in the class all cut class because they didn't want to "dance." In the gymnasium, my friend leads us in an hour of creative movement. Everyone loves it, and it loosens us up to be able to talk freely and to relate to each other in ways we weren't able to do before. In creative movement, no step is wrong; it is not rigid, and one doesn't need to be able to count or imitate.

Another idea is to use one of the tapes of Gabrielle Roth. I use the one called *Wave*. This is music in which people move to abstract concepts. Again, it takes about a half hour, and there are no wrong steps. It's improvisational.

Rhythm and Drumming

Gather a series of items that can make noise: pots, pans, sticks, tubs, bells, whistles, and the like. Play a video of the group "Stomp" or of a drumming group. With some friends, create a musical piece that utilizes rhythm and drumming. Present it to other friends or family members.

Scat Singing

Play a recording of the scat singing of Ella Fitzgerald or Mel Tormé. Sing along with them. Doobie doobie doo.

Doodling

Read aloud a story to others. The requirement is that they must doodle while they are listening. Anything is okay. Now ask them to doodle every time they are listening to something for the next week. Tell them about how President Kennedy's doodles during important security meetings sold for big sums of money. Tell them to fill the margins of their notes with doodles, or if they are too fastidious and like neat notes, take a separate sheet of paper and doodle. While doodling, breathe deeply, listen, and let what comes out come out. This can also be done while listening to music.

Joke Telling

Lighten up. Humor is a definite part of the creative process. Developmental and cultural, humor is so idiosyncratic that at different ages and in different lands, we laugh at different jokes, though slapstick humor seems to be universal. When we learn a foreign language, the language's idioms are most difficult to master and to understand, because many idiomatic expressions are rooted in that language's sense of humor. Improvise by joke-telling. Sit around and tell funny stories. After everyone has told a joke, talk about the effect it has had on the group feeling. Joke telling and humor increase the confidence for risk-taking, a core attitude in creativity.

Incubation: The Seventh "I"—Meditation

Meditation has long been known to work on quieting the mind and body, and to make one receptive to the inner speech that facilitates creativity. Many creative people have meditation programs, as discussed in Chapter 4. Instead of being the hard-drinking, substance-abusing, stereotypical wild artists, many creative people have plumbed their inner selves with disciplined sitting in meditation. In class, we often begin exercises with counting our breaths and deep breathing. Each class begins with a song of gathering, often from the CD that F. C. Reynolds (Christopher) put together for the course, *Creativity: The Pyramid and the Suns.* Students listen while their eyes are closed and their breaths are deep.

Incubation, the Seventh "I," comes from meditation. The idea, the insight, the image, what has been imagined, the inspiration, the "thing" needs to rest awhile. It needs to incubate, to take form from the void. Meditation helps.

Meditate on Beauty

Aesthetic appreciation is a strong reason for creating; the creator wants to create beauty as a response to the appreciation of beauty. Mathematicians talk about the elegance of the proof; scientists talk about the beauty of the universe; visual artists admire the form, line, and use of space of great creators in their fields; musicians speak with awe of how listening to a favored composer speaks to their own creativity. The beautiful is a direct arrow to the creative heart.

Among the activities that bring this aspect of the creative process to the fore is a field trip to a nearby art museum. The assignment is this: Walk around the museum alone with your Thoughtlog for an hour or so. Do not speak to anyone. Look at the works of art. When you come upon a work of art that interests you, stop in front of it and spend about 10 minutes there, meditating upon it, staring at it, writing about it, sketching it, letting it get into your soul. When the class meets again, we will have an art show where we will walk around the museum and we will be our own docents. Everyone will show the rest of us the work of art that moved him or her.

To begin the exercise and to put students into the mood of the contemplation of art, we read from a handout "Ode to a Grecian Urn" by John Keats, "Musee de Beaux Arts" by W. H. Auden, "What is Beauty" sections of "Helen" by Christopher Marlowe, and "My Last Duchess" by Robert Browning.

This activity is very moving to all. A trip with graduate students and classroom teachers to the Cleveland Art Museum took us all over the museum during the art show, as students pointed out beautiful works from a pre-Gutenberg Bible, to a medieval tapestry, to an art installation in the avant garde show in the gallery.

Meditate on the Dark Side

Many creative works are produced as a result of trauma and disappointment. Similar to the "I'll show you!" muse, meditating on the dark side has produced such classic works as Elie Weisel's life work as witness to the Holocaust, most of the war art works, the graffiti art that is found in urban ghettos, the poetry of pain and desolation by such writers as Baudelaire in *Les Fleurs du Mal,* and the soaring octaves of the last movement of Sibelius' Fifth Symphony which recall the end of World War I. When one starts thinking about it, the list seems endless. The assignment is this: Study a creative work inspired by the dark side. Now, with pastels, paints, crayons, pen and ink, create an image of your own darkness. This should not be written about but should be abstract, a drawing, a mathematical formula, a musical tune without words. Take this image with you in your mind for a week. Do not share it with anyone. Hold it in your heart and meditate upon it.

Another exercise is to take a field trip to a cemetery. Several cemeteries near our campus have graves from soldiers from the Revolutionary War to the Gulf War. I read four or five poems about the dark side: Randall Jarrell's "Death of the Ball Turret Gunner," Theodore Roethke's "In a Dark Time," Allan Tate's "Ode to the Confederate Dead," Langston Hughes' "Island," Rilke's "Autumn," Oscar Wilde's "In Reading Gaol by Reading Town," my own poem "Srebreniça." Then students go and walk throughout the graveyard, pausing to reflect on the dark side of life. This exercise, again, takes about an hour. We meet, sit in a circle on the grass, and share thoughts before we leave.

Meditate on Spirituality

The spiritual is also a powerful impetus for creativity. Many works of creative power are dedicated to the spiritual and inspired by it. This also can be a negative or a positive impetus. We have Dylan Thomas' poem about death: "Rail, rail against the dying of the night." We have Job shaking his fist at God. We have in the last works of Matisse the chapel he created for an order of nuns, a celebration of enlightenment and awe before the spiritual power of his creator. Again, as in the last exercise, the meditation on the dark side, think about your idea of the spiritual. Create an image. Do not write about it, do not put it into words, but put it into a metaphor or an image. Do not tell anyone. Carry this image around with you for a week.

Other Organic, Less-Linear Creativity Exercises

Creativity Rituals

The focus question that I ask to have students pay attention to this aspect of the creative process is this: "Interview two people and ask them what rituals they observe while creating. What rituals do you observe while creating, if any? Write the results in your Thoughtlog." One of the most common answers given in these interviews is that some people need solitude or must create conditions of solitude. This result is contrary to many of the activities in the creativity training literature, which emphasize group activities, group fun, group brainstorming, group interaction.

Cultivating Solitude

This leads to another question of the students in creativity classes: "How do you achieve solitude for creativity?" The answers are varied, but many students go walking or jogging; others get up early or stay up late so that their family or roommates are asleep. Achieving solitude in a crowd is also common, and some people go to a restaurant and write in their journals alone, as Goldberg suggests in *Writing Down the Bones*, or they take themselves mentally to a lonely beach or hilltop when they are in a class. Driving alone on a safe highway is also popular; many people get inspirations while in this situation.

Creating Ideal Conditions

The need in creative people to create under ideal conditions was discussed in Chapter 4.

I ask students in their biographical studies to describe the conditions under which the subject of their study created. We discuss the need for artists' colonies and retreat centers, and the new phenomenon that people can stay at home and work by computer in order to achieve the solitude necessary to be creative. We talk about the practice of such companies as Microsoft, IBM, Honeywell, and others of having play areas, relaxed dress codes, and flexible work hours for the newest inventors. The reduction of teaching loads for faculty members at major universities to allow them to write and do research is another example of the institutionalization of support for conditions that support the creative process. Then I ask my students to draw, write, or talk about what would be their own ideal conditions for creativity, and then, within the next week, to act on that as far as they are able. Does having these conditions inspire you to create, motivate you to create? Virginia Woolf called it *"A Room of One's Own."*

Background Music

For one class period, I assign students to bring in and to share the music that they like to listen to when they create. Each shares a cut from a CD, and everyone discusses. This leads to some liveliness, as some people say they couldn't stand to listen to that stuff while they are creating, and others assert that this is the only music that works. The discussion often gets around to the idiosyncratic influence of music on people; everyone likes his or her own music. We even judge others by the music they like. This leads to wondering about what would happen in a school if every teacher were to bring in music that inspires him or her and share it with students during transitions in class? The students would be exposed to many more types of music than is now available on their AM/FM radios.

Synesthesia

This is the combination of senses or the utilizing of one sense for another. A recording engineer asks the band that he is recording to taste the sound they want. Is it sweet? Is it bitter? In order to do this, it is good to practice using the senses one by one before trying to combine them. A good video to view here or a book to read is Diane Ackerman's *A Natural History of the Senses*. In working with creative writers, I often show excerpts from this series because novice writers are apt to be too general and not concrete enough, and sensory information is crucial in conveying emotion and truth. Students practice synesthesia in their Thoughtlogs.

Seeing

Visualization is an important preparatory phase in creating anything. Visualization is creating mental pictures. Spend a little time thinking about your ideal home. Close your eyes and walk up to it. Walk around it. Draw it. Make a diagram of a favorite room. The purpose is to see with your mind's eye. Seeing is a little different from visualization; on your way home, really "see" something you've not paid attention to before—the fire extinguisher, the fence, the doorknob. Someone creative designed it, you know.

Hearing

You can "visualize" with your ears also. Hear a song you know with your mind's ear. Hum it out loud. Now hear a sound that is grating to you, perhaps fingernails on a blackboard. Pay attention to what happens inside of you as you hear these sounds. Discuss.

Smelling

They say the sense of smell is so strong in humans that we judge people by their smells, and we are erotically attracted by smell. Perhaps that's why there's such a market in perfumes. Smell a smell with your mind's nose. First smell a repellent smell. Note what happens in your body. Now smell a smell of food that appeals to you. Note what happens in your body. Now smell a smell of a person you have been favorably impressed by. Discuss the importance of smell memory to your creativity. Look at advertisements; how do they suggest aroma?

Taste

I might say, "Taste something with your mind's tongue. Remember one of the best meals you have eaten. Lick it. Crunch it. Let it roll around in your mouth. Pause. Now imagine you are eating a lemon. Pause." Etc.

Here is a gourmet banquet to try. I bring taste samples to class of something sweet, sour, bitter, and salty. I give the students a paper plate of each and have them slowly savor, writing down their impressions. We end the gourmet feast with a wonderful chocolate treat. Afterwards, the students draw or write their reactions.

Touch

Massage the shoulders of a person you know, and have that person massage your shoulders. Then exchange shoulder massages with a different person. Enjoy the touch of the massage. What sensations does it bring?

Make several bags and fill them with various fabrics that have different textures—silk, wool, real fur, fake fur, cotton, polyester, and the like. Close your eyes. Feel the fabric and texture. Write down what you think it is.

Remember with your mind's fingers a special touch that someone has given you or that you have given someone. What emotions arise in you on remembering this? Write in your Thoughtlog.

Cultivation of Synchronicity

Many accounts of creativity have asserted that coincidence and chance led to the putting together of the creative work. Some psychologists, physicists, and spiritual people have asserted that nothing is by chance, that all coincidence is meaningful. In their book *Synchronicity: Science, Myth, and the Trickster*, Combs and Holland assert, "There are two things I have come to believe implicitly about the world we live in. One is that nothing occurring in it is independent of any other thing; the other is that nothing that occurs is entirely random and prey to chance." The recent explication of the notion of chaos is an example; the fluttering of a butterfly wing in one part of the world can lead to a storm in another part of the world.

As a person cultivating your own creativity, spend a week or so paying attention to synchronicity. Synchronistic events often happen while traveling. The person sitting next to you on the plane may be the great nephew of your best friend's sister and may have a job opportunity where you can show your true creative self. Synchronistic events often happen during times of transition, when you are living on the boundaries between one state and another. They are often presaged in waking or sleeping dreams. Often, when they happen, you feel a sense of great emotion and even of destiny.

Do a small research project. Ask three people you know what place coincidence and chance have played in their creative lives. Do they feel it was truly accidental that these things happened? Write the results in your Thoughtlog.

Exercise

A fact well known by now is that one enters into what could be called an altered state after a certain amount of aerobic exercise. My students and I have tried this out by playing a vigorous aerobic tape and doing it for 30 minutes. Then we lie on the floor and rest, paying attention to what our minds feel. We swear that we feel lighter, more creative, and more alert. The endorphins have kicked in, and we have achieved the "runner's high." Many accounts exist about how creative problems are solved while exercising. The experience even becomes addictive—that is, people sometimes find that they need to exercise in order to think clearly

Solitary exercise seems to be more conducive to creative problem solving, though some people assert that a fast game of basketball or tennis can do it also. Not so many people believe that baseball or football is conducive to creative problem solving, but it's possible. Discuss the effect of exercise in your Thoughtlog. Do you feel more or less creative after exercising? What were your thoughts while exercising?

Passion: Stepping into the River of the Domain

No one ever sustained creative activity without a passion for the field. Once the passion has been identified, experts are available who can help the person who wants to work in that field. The notion of expertise and its acquisition is being rigorously researched and debated by scholars. The question of mentoring comes in as well, for novices proceed through the stages to the acquisition of expertise as a result of being taught and being mentored. Apprenticeship is the key word here. What is your passion? What is the field or domain in which you wish to create? What are the processes for getting to a level where you will be taken seriously? Is it more schooling? A degree? An award? Hanging around with experts? All of the above? Think about this, and do some research as to what the top creators in the field in which you have passion have done to get there.

Flow

"Flow" is a state of "optimal experience," according to Mihalyi Csikszentmihalyi, who coined the word. Spend some time reviewing the activities in which you indulge. Which ones put you into a state of flow? Where do you lose track of time when doing the activity? Flow is achieved when you are challenged enough to keep doing the task and when you are successful enough to feel good about your work. Examine your "flow" states. Many ordinary people mention gardening, shopping, cooking, reading, working on the computer, working on collections, exercising. People with talents in an area often go into a state of flow when working in that area—singing, drawing, writing, inventing, building, composing. Whatever puts a person into a state of flow, it is a surety that the person return to it. Identifying this is a key to identifying passion. Stepping into the river means placing oneself into that field or domain, surrounding oneself by experts and enthusiasts in the field, gaining knowledge of the field, and proceeding to expertise in the field.

Conversation: A Salon

Pick a topic of conversation and invite people over to talk about it. That is what we do at the Second Friday Salon at my house. People bring works of creativity that they or others have made. All that is required is the will, the idea, and some interesting people. These days, some say that conversation has gone away as more people eat meals in front of the television set. Of course, one can always meet a friend for dinner and for talk at a restaurant. I simulate this in class. We pick a topic of conversation and have everyone prepare something to talk about or show having to do with that topic. We imagine the class as a think tank, an organization that has people informed on a subject working on, doing research on, and thinking about a topic—and getting paid for it.

What does this have to do with creativity? The presence of thinkers who make a person encounter ideas never before encountered or revisit ideas previously thought finished can do nothing but stimulate the creative juices. The famous salons of Paris where artists, writers, musicians, and thinkers met to associate with each other are an example. Create one in your own setting.

A Visit

Make a visit while shopping or doing your mundane life errands to places that contain much that will feed the creative spirit. These places are everywhere.

A Bookstore or Library

Visit a bookstore or a library. Go to the cultural events of either. I have to confess that I am hopelessly addicted to books. A visit to the bookstore where my Sunday New York *Times* is waiting for me often means that I don't get out without having spent money on books I think I need to have.

Is there a group called "Book Addicts Anonymous"? Almost all of the books and articles referenced in this book are in my personal library. Yes. I confess.

The public library is a haven. Check out the events that it holds each month. Go to a book talk or a children's reading marathon.

A Museum

Museums are sacred places, places where the muse is in residence, where one can see the created and inspired works of others. Whether it's the natural history museum or the museum of the local hero, museums are sacred places. One can see it in the silent awe of the visitors. The most odd realization of this is at the Rock 'n' Roll Hall of Fame, where one ascends to the very top of the building, up carpeted stairs lit by small lights, to the gallery where the inductees are. The noise becomes noticeably dimmer and dimmer until everyone is silent as they stroll around looking at the exhibits of the rock 'n' roll hall members. It is eerie.

There are two rules for museums: (1) Don't feel duty bound to see everything; spend only an hour or two so you don't feel overwhelmed. (2) Start taking students and children early so these sacred places are part of their growing up culture.

Appreciate the Creative Work of Others

My students must attend one live performance. It can be a concert, a set by a bar band, a dance or music recital, a poetry reading—anything that shows what other artists are trying to do. Lectures also count, if they're by scientists or people talking about their own research and work, presenting their passions. Write about it in your Thoughtlog, focusing on the creativity of the performers. When I assigned teachers to do this, I was surprised that many of them had never attended a concert of classical music and did not know the etiquette of such a concert. They wrote in their Thoughtlogs about their surprise at the number of bows, the silence about the performers, and the numbers being played. They were waiting for an announcer. This made me think that this assignment is absolutely necessary for people who teach our children, especially our musically talented children.

A Play

Attend one professional stage performance. Not community theater, not university theater, but a performance by professionals, equity actors, or performers. The difference is often palpable. Note what is different in a professional performance from the amateur performances in your community.

A Foreign Movie

Rent or attend a cinema showing of an award-winning foreign film, with or without subtitles, dubbed or in the original language. Read up on the filmmaker. Usually, a film that has no Hollywood production staff will yield insights into the culture of the film and the filmmaker. Creativity abounds in film. I recommend *Il Postino* (*The Postman,* an Italian film about the poet Neruda) and *Bring on the Rain* (a Macedonian film about the war in the Balkans). Discuss the film in your Thoughtlog. I heard on NPR the other morning that foreign films are less popular than ever in the United States. What a shame. Give yourself a treat.

A Reading

As a poet and writer, going to literary readings is for me like going to church. I love to listen to literature being read aloud. I am often disappointed when I share this passion with my students, who rarely have attended such readings. Thus this assignment: Attend one reading by a literary figure during the course. If possible, read some of the works of this person before attending the reading. Discuss in your Thoughtlog.

A Lecture or Demonstration

Go to a lecture or demonstration by a business, science, mathematics, or political figure. How is this person creative? What did this person do to get up there on the stage telling the audience what he or she thinks?

A Place (Travel)

Take a trip. Keep a journal. Take pictures. Invite your friends over to see them. All of this will contribute to your creativity—if not now, then later as you recall the trip in the tranquility of your home. Take a trip to a local tourist attraction you haven't visited (and who has visited all of the tourist attractions near to home?). View it with the eyes of naiveté, new eyes, and make a poem, story, or work of art about it. It is a fact that many people who live in New York City have never been to the Statue of Liberty, and many people who live in Arizona have never visited the Grand Canyon. Take a trip—a day trip.

Other

If a student does all of these exercises in the course of a semester, or 15 weeks, he or she is well on the way to a life-change. From practicing creativity core attitudes, to working with the Seven I's, to creating rituals, spaces, and works; from visiting museums to attending poetry readings and foreign film showings; from looking within to expressing passion; this course in creativity has sought to emphasize what real creators do. Whether you are a person who wants to be more creative or a teacher helping others to be more creative, take the above exercises as illustrations of concepts. The concepts are important, not necessarily the specific exercises. Make up your own. Be creative.

Many other activities can speak to the "less linear" aspect of the creative process. The teacher is only limited by his or her imagination. Teaching itself is a very creative profession, and part of the creativity is thinking up how best to teach one's subject. Again, the teacher should be flexible and should let the students lead in these; many of the best ideas have come from students. Classes of teachers should create their own creativity enhancement exercises along these lines and should share them with their fellows, making enough copies for each person to use.

Individual Creativity Project

All of the activities above are just little tools, and a course using them should culminate in a major, extended individual creativity project by each student demonstrating his or her own creativity in some area or another. No kits, no reflections of the season curriculum are permitted. Students must truly "make" their own project. Here are some of the individual creativity projects that students have presented:

- an autobiographical video ("My Creative Self").
- performance of an original song.
- performance of an original radio play.
- design and modeling of an original dress for a sorority formal.
- a plan for an advertising campaign.
- a synchronized swimming routine.
- a rock band audio tape.
- a photographic exhibit.
- an exhibit of original art works.
- a reading of an original short story.
- an autobiographical multimedia presentation.
- a translation into English of some Chinese poetry.
- an original dance routine.
- designs of costumes for a play.
- original poetry.

○ a business plan for a new business.

○ a music video.

○ philosophical musings about the meaning of life.

○ display and demonstration of a particularly creative Thoughtlog.

Students then make a presentation of the individual creative project, with a handout for the audience. By this time, enough has been said about the direct teaching to enhance creativity, and it is time for the students to step out on their own.

Summary

1. Transfer is the purpose of all education, including creativity training.

2. Creativity training has grown substantially in the schools, in industry, and in public workshops in recent years. Many programs are available.

3. Creativity training, while fun, is not sufficient as a curriculum for talent development education.

4. All students should have an opportunity for creativity training.

5. Teachers can benefit from creativity training.

6. Alternative methods of creativity assessment, such as storytelling and performance assessment on aspects of already existing talent domains, look promising.

Appendix A
Creativity Theory

The Need for Theory

The question of what creativity is has many answers. Theories seek to explain what and why. A theory is a framework explaining the relationships among factors that pertain to creativity. Depending on a theoretician's predilection, field of expertise, and sense of self, the answer differs. The impetus for theorizing about creativity may come from a person's thinking about his or her own creativity. There are several basic species of creativity theory. Among them are philosophic theory, psychological theory, psychoanalytic theory, and domain-specific theory.

Those who write psychoanalytic theory are mainly psychoanalysts, and their reason for theorizing about creativity is to probe the psyche of the creative person, looking for the key incidents or events that led to the creative person being as he or she is. There are also some psychoanalysts, therapists, and physicians who belong to a group called "Creativity and Madness." They meet regularly in various locations such as Vienna, Amsterdam, or New York City to discuss the lives of creative people who had mental difficulties. I have been on several of their tours, where I spoke on the creative process and on creative writers.

As stated in Chapter 1, psychological theorists also want to probe the psyche, but to find out what happens in the mind of the person creating (cognitive psychologists) or to make the perfect test for creativity in order to be able to predict who will be creative (psychometrists), and to discover the traits of the creative person and the aspects of the creative process. Humanistic psychologists are not so much interested in a creative product as they are in enhancing the creative potential in every human being. Information-processing theorists want to probe the brain of the creative person in order to find out what dendrons flash with what speed so that the creative person's processing can be replicated, perhaps artificially, with computers.

Philosophers are among the most interesting creativity theorists. They want to assess the meaning of creativity, especially as it relates to certain philosophical problems. Philosophers called existentialists seek to explore the meaning of freedom. Philosophers called estheticians seek to explore the meaning of beauty.

The domain-specific theorists, or artist/scientist theorists, want to explain what it is that happens when they are "creative," and their accounts are likewise fascinating to read. It is when they formulate a theory—that is, when they generalize for all artists, scientists, inventors, or mathematicians—that their accounts get a little questionable.

A look at a basic book, *The Creativity Question* (1976), edited by one of the major psychoanalytic theorists, Alfred Rothenberg, and one of the major philosophic theorists, CarlHausman, gives a clue about the diversity of theories. Another interesting book that summarizes theories is the psychoanalyst Arieti's *Creativity: The Magic Synthesis* (1976). Sternberg, who seems to be the editor of editors, edited a 1988 book summarizing creativity theories in cognitive psychology called *The Nature of Creativity* (1988). Rothenberg took issue with the title of this book in a comment in *The Creativity Research Journal*, saying that the psychologists were falsely implying that they knew the "nature" of creativity and that most of the theorists writing in this book were just recycling their old ideas. Mark Runco edited a book on creativity theory in 1990. He and Pritzker also edited a new *Encyclopedia of Creativity* (1999). Gardner (1993) and Csikszentmihalyi (1996) have elaborated on earlier theories of creativity in best-selling books. The continual visitation by thinkers in the sciences, social sciences, and arts regarding the concept of creativity illustrates again the proprietary feelings that creativity incites.

The following list gives a brief summary of some of the major theories on creativity and their proponents. Some of these ideas were implicitly stated and not fully developed, and some were explicitly developed as full-blown theories of creativity. I have merely mentioned a few of these thinkers, and I have inadequately summarized their thoughts as if I were writing a movie blurb for *TV Guide*. This is not to give them short shrift, but to provide an overview of the deep morass one surveys when one begins to study creativity.

Many of these thinkers have written, studied, summarized, and agonized over what creativity truly is. They have spent much of their professional lifetimes thinking about creativity, and their work is appreciated by us novices. You may have some objections as to which categories I placed people in; for example, I placed Hofstadter in the philosophical category, and Huxley into the domain-specific category. These categories are broad outlines.

Philosophic Theorists

Kant (1778): Genius, or creativity, is found in the arts but not in science. There is a necessary interplay of the faculties of imagination and understanding in the production of art.

Bergson (1907): Creativity is the result of intuition when all precedents are absent.

Croce (1909): Creativity in art is the expression of intuitive pre-cognition.

Collingwood (1938): In creative people, imagination is the synthesizing activity that occurs before discursive or relational thought.

Maritain (1953): Human creativity can be traced to the power of the divine through poetic insight and mystical illumination.

Langer (1957): Creativity is found where the abstract apparition of a form produces a symbolic emotional reaction in the perceiver.

Blanshard (1964): What the creator creates is an end that results from inner necessity. The subconscious is present in invention.

Hausman (1964): Creativity is spontaneous, non-rational, and produces true novelty.

Hofstadter (1985): "The crux of creativity is the ability to manufacture variations on a theme."

Psychologists

Galton (1869): Special talent or genius in diverse areas is inherited.

Thorndike (1911): Relevant experience is essential to creative problem solving.

Wallas (1926): The creative process takes place in four specific phases occurring in a fairly regular sequence, including a phase of incubation in which creative work occurs outside of consciousness.

Rossman (1931): There are seven steps to the creative process. These are similar to Wallas'.

Guilford (1950, 1967): "Divergent production," an intellectual factor, is present in the creative response. The divergent producer provides alternate solutions to open-ended problems.

Osborn (1953): There are seven stages in the creative process. These evolved to the Creative Problem-Solving process.

Stein (1953): There are three stages in the creative process.

Rogers (1954): The creative individual has an openness to experience, an internal locus of evaluation, and the ability to toy with elements and concepts

Watson (1958): Creative problem solving comes because of transfer. Similar old problem solutions are generalized to the new solution.

Taylor (1959): Creativity exists at five different levels.

Gordon (1961): Previous theories of creativity were elitist and stressed inspiration and genius. Everyone can be creative. Making metaphors is the creative process.

Mednick (1962): Remote associations are combined to form creations by contiguity, serendipity, and mediation.

Vygotsky (1962): Creative imagination is developmental, requiring the collaboration of concept formation.

Roe (1963): The creative process is separate from the final product. It happens in most people and is not unique only to those who produce superior final products.

Dabrowski (1964) and **Piechowski** (1989): Creativity is talent in a specific field, exemplified by intense emotional, imaginational, intellectual, sensual, and/or psychomotor overexcitability, or intensity.

Wallach and Kogan (1965): Creativity can be differentiated from IQ or g-factor intelligence.

Torrance (1966, 1979): Certain aspects of creativity can be tested, especially divergent thinking.

Barron (1968, 1972, 1994): Creative people have the paradoxical presence of high degrees of ego strength along with psychopathologic qualities. Creativity can only be understood through the metaphor of ecology; it is so pervasive and environmentally diverse.

Maslow (1968): Creativity is in everyone, and many of the people who created tangible achievements were not self-actualized. He differentiated "special talent creativeness" from "self actualizing creativeness."

Bogen and Bogen (1969): Creativity results from the coordinated function of the repropositional mind and the appositional mind. The connecting structure between right and left cerebral hemispheres is the seat of creativity.

Skinner (1971): Creativity is a result of natural selection over evolved time.

Gowan (1972): The creative individual develops as a result of certain childhood experiences.

Krippner and Murphy (1973): The capacity for extrasensory perception, telepathy, precognition, clairvoyance, and psychokinesis are very necessary for creativity.

Gruber (1974, 1988): Creativity is an evolving system; key phases of this system are insights, metaphors, the transformation of experience, and organization of purpose.

Getzels and Csikszentmihalyi (1976): Creativity comes about in problem finding and not in problem solving.

MacKinnon (1978): Creative people have certain personality attributes that are different from those of noncreative people.

Renzulli (1978): Creativity is a necessary component of gifted behavior, along with above-average intelligence and task commitment.

Willings (1980): Creative people have defensive, productive, adaptive, elaborative, or developmental personalities.

Perkins (1981/1988): Creativity is inevitable invention produced by people with certain personality attitudes using tactics of selection, planning, and abstracting.

Feldman (1982, 1988, 1994): Creativity is the developmental transformation of insight into novelty that makes a product that changes the field.

Amabile (1983): Creative people have certain personality traits, such as intrinsic motivation, which can be temporarily affected by external interference.

Tannenbaum (1983): Creativity is necessary for giftedness and is integrated into all five aspects of what makes giftedness.

Brown (1986): Transpersonal psychology helps to understand creativity through exploring higher states of awareness.

Weisberg (1986): This anti-theorist systematically dismantled what he called the "myths of creativity," stating that creativity is incremental—that is, grounded in the work of those who came before.

Langley and Jones (1988): Creativity involves reasoning by analogy and qualitative mental models.

Schank (1988): The creative person can program him- or herself to ask the right questions.

Sternberg and Lubart (1988/1992): Creativity is derived from an investment of personality attributes, problem definition, insight, flexibility, intrinsic and extrinsic reward, and a certain legislative or executive style.

Gardner (1993): Creativity is the work of a person who habitually solves problems, makes products, or finds new questions in a domain in a way that is at first considered new but that eventually becomes accepted in the culture.

Piirto (1994): Creativity is in the personality, the process, and the product within a domain in interaction with genetic influences and with optimal environmental influences of home, school, community and culture, gender, and chance. Creativity is a basic human instinct to make new.

Simonton (1995; 1999): Creativity comes about through the chance-configuration theory, which postulates that social factors interact with personality factors to produce genius. Creativity is a form of leadership. The more works a creator produces, the more the chance of influencing the domain and of assuming leadership in the domain. Darwinian evolutionary theory speaks to creativity.

Csikszentmihalyi (1996): "Creativity is any act, idea, or product that changes an existing domain, or that transforms an existing domain into a new one." Creativity is the interaction of a person working with the symbols of a domain or field at a certain time in history. Thus it is an internal systems model.

Runco (1997): Productivity is necessary for creativity but not for giftedness.

Sternberg, Kaufman, and Pretz (2002): Creative contributions are similar to a model of propulsion. They differ not only in their amounts, but also in the kinds of creativity they represent. Kinds of creativity are replication, redefinition, forward incrementation, integration, reinitiation, and the like.

Psychoanalytic Theorists

Lombroso (1895): Creative genius is related to insanity; he differentiated between ordinary insanity and the insanity associated with genius.

Freud (1908): Fantasy is essential in the production of literary works. Such fantasy is primarily a manifestation of preconscious thoughts and feelings. The unconscious also has a role in creation.

Jung (1923): Creativity is located in autonomous complexes which unearth the Collective Unconscious. These have a determining effect on consciousness in creation. The Collective Unconscious accounts for an audience's favorable response to a creation. The creative act can never be explained.

Lee (1940): Artistic creation is the result of symbolically compensating for disabilities.

Kris (1952): "Regression in the service of the ego" or ego-controlled regression is the specific means whereby preconscious and unconscious material appear in the creator's consciousness.

Kubie (1958): Preconscious processes produce creations.

Schactel (1959): Allocentric perception, or openness to the world, is necessary for creativity to take place. This is characteristic of the most mature stage of human perceptual development.

Rank (1960): An artist type is distinct from the neurotic type. The artist type overcomes fear of death by an act of will directed toward immortality. Male creativity is developed by jealousy of female ability to bear children.

May (1975): Creativity takes courage in making form from chaos.

Arieti (1976): Creativity is a primitive magic synthesis performed by gifted people.

Rothenberg (1979, 1990): Janusian thinking is involved in creation. This is the capacity to conceive and utilize two or more opposite or contradictory ideas, concepts, or images simultaneously. After this comes homospatial thinking, the capacity to merge the unlike ideas.

Miller (1990): Creative production is a result of childhood trauma where warmth was present.

Jamison (1994): Creative people have more psychopathology, especially manic-depression, than others.

Hillman (1996): Every person possesses a daimon of creativity which influences how life is lived. This daimon is like an acorn, coiled and ready to grow under encouraging conditions.

Domain-Specific Theories

Coleridge (1817): An active and constructive imagination is necessary for poetic creativity.

Poe (1846): Logic and deliberately controlled techniques are important in the creative process.

Morgan (1933): Predictability is perhaps not necessary for scientific creation.

Cannon (1945): Creativity is an extraconscious process rather than an unconscious one, with no necessary determining effect upon consciousness. Hunches are important in certain phases of the scientific approach.

Huxley (1963): The use of psychedelic drugs can enhance creativity.

Koestler (1964): Bicosiation—the combination of two consistent but habitually incompatible frames of reference—is meant to account for creations in all areas: culture, societies, nature, individuals.

Ehrenzweig (1967): The role of the unconscious in artistic creation follows a specific process called "unconscious dedifferentiation."

Findlay and Lumsden (1988): Creativity is evolutionary. Creative products and people have evolved through a mutational process.

Appendix B
Focus Questions

Chapter 1

Making Sense of Creativity

1. Do a small research study. Ask three people for their definitions of creativity. Then ask them whether they think some people have more ability to be creative than other people. Report your findings.

2. Do a small research study. Ask three teachers how they teach students to be more creative. Report your findings.

3. Can creativity be tested? Why or why not?

4. Give four examples of how you would teach divergent production: fluency, flexibility, novelty/originality, or elaboration.

5. Discuss the concepts of *quantity and quality* as reasons for teaching people to be creative.

6. Discuss how *nationalistic emphasis* relates to creativity enhancement.

7. Can a person be creative without a creative product? Discuss.

8. Can a person be creative without outstanding talent? Discuss.

9. Discuss the notion of freedom with relationship to creativity.

10. In order to be truly creative, must a person have mastered the field in which the creativity is demonstrated? Discuss.

11. Make a work of art—a song, poem, story, visual work, etc.—that illustrates the definition of creativity.

Chapter 2

The Creative Process

1. Describe a time when you or someone you know was inspired to create by love ("the Visitation of the Muse").

2. Describe a time when you or someone you know was in a state of "semitrance" or "flow" while creating.

3. Discuss Wallas' steps in the creative process—(1) preparation; (2) incubation; (3) illumination; (4) verification—with relation to your or a friend's creativeness.

4. What do you think Ghiselin meant by "oceanic consciousness" while creating?

5. What is the place of *automaticity* in the creative process?

6. Make an image of your own creative process (song, story, poem, visual art, model).

7. Discuss the aesthetics of a certain field or domain of creativity with which you are familiar. What beauty do the practitioners strive for and appreciate?

8. Interview two people and ask them what rituals they observe while creating. What rituals do you observe while creating, if any?

9. Take one of the seven I's. How would you teach someone about it?

10. Look at the core attitudes. Explain how you would teach someone about them.

11. Discuss your background and experience with right brain and left brain theories of the nature of creativity. Do you think this explanation for creativeness is adequate?

12. Discuss the role of substances (alcohol, drugs, hormones after exercise, etc.) in the creative process.

13. Discuss solitude as opposed to loneliness, and the place of each in the creative process.

14. What connections do you see between spirituality and creativity?

Chapter 3

Encouraging Creativity: Motivation and Schooling

1. What do you think about Alice Miller's statement that creative people experience trauma in their childhoods, but that they also have some warm person with whom to be close?

2. Compare and contrast your school experiences with those of the contemporary American writers discussed in the chapter.

3. Tell a story about how you or someone you know acquired intrinsic motivation to be creative.

4. How is extrinsic motivation also important in creativity?

5. Discuss a time when great emotion helped you to be more creative.

6. Discuss how childhood play shaped the creativity of you or someone you know.

7. Make a work of art—a song, poem, story, visual work, etc.—that illustrates motivation.

Chapter 4

How Parents and Teachers Can Enhance Creativity in Creativity

1. Discuss three of the items on the list in the chapter with regard to your own development or to the development of someone you know.

2. How do you as a teacher nurture creativity? Do any items on the list apply?

3. How do you as a parent nurture creativity? Do any items on the list apply?

4. Make a work of art—a song, poem, story, visual work, etc.—that illustrates one or more of these suggestions.

Chapter 5

The Piirto Pyramid of Talent Development Model

1. Critique the model described in this chapter.

2. Make an image of the theoretical material in this chapter—poem, song, drawing, story, play, etc.

Chapter 6

Visual Artists and Architects

1. Discuss the romantic view of the easel painter/visual artist.

2. Why is spatial intelligence important for the visual artist and architect?

3. Do some research on gender differences in spatial ability. What did you find?

4. Discuss a child you know who has the reputation of being "class artist." Do his/her characteristics fit Hurwitz's observations?

5. Why do male visual artists who decide to go into fine arts often have difficulty when they announce their career choice to their families and friends?

6. Why do many women choose to become art educators rather than fine artists?

7. Discuss the concept of *problem finding* as compared with *problem solving*.

8. Ruminate on the concept of the "loft culture" and the visual artist.

9. Discuss your own *Myers-Briggs Type Indicator* preferences with relationship to those found in studies of visual artists and architects.

10. Interview an architect about his/her career. Note similarities and differences to what the chapter says.

11. Make an image of some concept in this chapter—poem, song, story, visual presentation, etc.

Chapter 7

Creative Writers

1. Discuss why people choose creative writing as a profession.

2. What are some differences between writers in different genres? What are some similarities?

3. Look up some information about your favorite novelist. How does this person compare with the research findings in this chapter?

4. Look up some information about your favorite poet. How does this person compare with the research findings in this chapter?

5. Interview a creative writer—nonfiction, fiction, playwright, screenwriter, or poet. Discuss your findings.

6. Look up the writers in your state in the *Directory of American Poets and Fiction Writers*. Make some observations.

7. Look up all the works of a famous writer. Are you surprised at his/her productivity? Discuss the concept of productivity with regard to creativity.

8. Discuss depression with regard to writers. Add information not in the text.

9. Why is humor an aspect of verbal intelligence?

10. Make an image of some concept in this chapter—poem, song, story, visual presentation, sculpture, etc.

Chapter 8

Creative Writers: Children with Extraordinary Writing Talent

1. Look up the juvenilia of a writer you admire. Make some comments.

2. Try a writing exercise with your students or with a class. See whether you can recognize a talented writer with the lists given in the chapter.

3. Survey your students or your friends for their reading habits. Make some comments about those whom you discover to be omnivorous readers. Are they writers also?

4. Make some comments about the children's work shown in this chapter.

5. Discuss the concept of overexcitabilities, or intensities, as it relates to young talented creators.

6. Look up the childhood of a writer you admire. Was there a developmental crisis? Make some comments.

7. Compare your own childhood reading and writing with that of the children discussed here.

8. Take the work of a child writer you know and analyze it using the characteristics listed in the chapter.

9. Make an image—poem, song, story, play, visual, sculptural, etc.— of a concept in this chapter.

Chapter 9

Creative Scientists, Mathematicians, Inventors, and Entrepreneurs

1. In considering the patterns in the lives of creative scientists, mathematicians, and inventors, which patterns seem to you to be the most surprising? Explain.

2. Which seem to you to be most expectable? Explain.

3. Interview a scientist, mathematician, inventor, or entrepreneur. Relate the patterns in the chapter to the life of a person in a biography you have read.

4. The aesthetic appreciation of any domain by the person doing work in the domain seems to be its most salient feature. Describe your aesthetic appreciation of science or mathematics.

5. Why are scientists likened to religious people in their mysticism?

6. Describe your own experience as a science student or mathematics student in relation to the patterns of creative lives in science.

7. A characteristic of inventors is their propensity to tinker. Why should tinkering lead to inventing?

8. If you were to invent something, what would you invent?

9. If you were to start a business, what business would you start?

10. Discuss gender with regard to science, math, invention, or entrepreneurialism.

11. Make an image of some concept in this chapter—mathematical, scientific, literary, visual arts, musical, etc.

Chapter 10

Musicians, Composers, and Conductors

1. What is the difference between musical creativity and musical ability?

2. What is the difference between musical intelligence and performing ability?

3. Discuss Copland's statement that women can't be composers because they have difficulty thinking abstractly.

4. Why is it important in musical development that the family have some history in musical appreciation, performance, or amateur participation?

5. Do you believe that a person can become a musician without family involvement in the development of the talent? Give examples. Explain.

6. Interview a musician, conductor, or composer with regard to the findings in this chapter.

7. Discuss your own musical past and why you stopped.

8. Why are people so picky about their music?

9. Why do people often become arrested in their musical appreciation development with the music that was popular when they were young?

10. List and briefly discuss five ways a person can be creative musically.

11. Look at the childhood of a favorite rock star or popular musician. How is it different from and how is it similar to the childhoods of classical musicians?

12. Make an image of a concept in this chapter—musical, scientific, mathematical, visual, literary, etc.

Chapter 11

Physical Performers: Actors, Dancers, and Athletes

1. Why do people forget the name of the character a movie actor played and describe the performance as a "Meryl Streep movie" or a "Robert de Niro movie?" What does this have to do with the actor as shaman?

2. Explain why actors need interpersonal and intrapersonal intelligence.

3. Explain why actors need bodily-kinesthetic intelligence.

4. Look at the biography of a favorite actor (note that this means females, too). What were his/her formative influences or predictive behaviors?

5. Why have actors historically been "outsiders"?

6. True or false: A dancer must be very thin. Discuss.

7. Dancers and athletes have a tendency to retire with permanent injuries, just as football players do. Discuss injuries from dance or athletics with reference to yourself or someone you know.

8. Why is dance so gender-stereotyped as being more suitable for women, and football gender-stereotyped as being more suitable for men?

9. Interview a dancer, actor, or athlete. What were his/her formative influences?

10. How are athletes creative?

11. Make an image of some concept in this chapter—game, dance, song, poem, story, play, visual or sculptural presentation, etc.

Chapters 12 & 13

Creativity Assessment and Creativity Training

1. Can creativity be tested? Why or why not?

2. Discuss the importance of validity in creativity testing.

3. Discuss reliability and testing for creativity. Who cares?

4. Discuss your experience of administering standardized tests. Was the administration reliable?

5. Do people fall on a normal curve of creativity? When? How?

6. Critique the Dabrowski Overexcitability Questionnaire (OEQ).

7. Discuss your experience with any of the creativity training packages.

8. Why should all students (not just the academically talented students) receive creativity training?

9. Why should all teachers receive creativity training?

10. Interview three teachers (perhaps in music, literature, theater, athletics) about how they teach students to be more creative.

11. Make up a creativity assessment instrument.

References

Abbott, L. K. (1992). The true story of why I do what I do. In E. Shelnutt (Ed.), *My poor elephant* (pp. 209-216). Atlanta, GA: Longstreet Press.

Abbs, R. (1989). *A is for aesthetic.* New York: Falmer Press.

Abell, A. (1946). *Talks with the great composers.* Garmisch-Partenkirchen, Germany: G. E. Schroeder-Verlag.

Abma, C., Fry, M., Li, Y., & Relyea, G. (2002). Differences in imagery content and imagery ability between high and low confident track and field athletes. *Journal of Applied Sport Psychology, 14*(2), 67-75.

Adler, M. (1952). *The great ideas: A syntopticon of* Great Books of the Western World. Chicago: The Encyclopaedia Britannica.

Adler, S. (1970). In T. Cole & H. Chinoy (Eds.). *Actors on acting* (pp. 601-605). New York: Crown.

Aizenstat, S. (1995). Jungian psychology and the world unconscious. In T. Roszak, M. E. Gomes, & A. D. Kanner (Eds.), *Ecopsychology: Restoring the earth and healing the mind* (pp. 92-100). San Francisco: Sierra Club Books.

Albert, R. (1975). Toward a behavioral definition of genius. *American Psychologist, 30*, 140-151.

Allen, J. S. (1992). Educating performers. *The American Scholar, 61*(2), 197-209.

Amabile, T. M. (1983). *The social psychology of creativity.* New York: Springer-Verlag.

Amabile, T. M. (1989). *Growing up creative: Nurturing a lifetime of creativity.* New York: Crown.

Amabile, T. M. (1996). *Creativity in context: Update to* The Social Psychology of Creativity. Boulder, CO: Westwood Press.

Anderson, M. B., Denson, E. L. Brewer, B. W., & Van Raalte, J. L. (1994). Disorders of personality and mood in athletes: Recognition and referral. *Applied Sport Psychology, 6*, 168-184.

Andreason, N. (1987). Creativity and mental illness: Prevalence rates in writers and their first degree relatives. *American Journal of Psychiatry, 144,* 1288-1292.

Andreason, N., & Canter, A. (1974). The creative writer: Psychiatric symptoms and family history. *Comprehensive Psychiatry, 14,* 123-131.

Ansburg, P. I., & Dominowski, R. L. (2000). Promoting insightful problem solving. *Journal of Creative Behavior, 34*(1), 30-60.

Anshel, M. H., & Porter, A. (1996). Self-regulatory characteristics of competitive swimmers as a function of skill level and gender. *Journal of Sport Behavior, 19*(2), 91-110.

Anzaldúa, G. (1999). *Borderlands/La Frontera: The new mestiza* (2nd ed.). San Francisco: Aunt Lute Books.

Arieti, S. (1976). *Creativity: The magic synthesis.* New York: Basic.

Armstrong, T. (1995). *Multiple intelligences in the classroom.* Arlington, VA: Association for Supervision and Curriculum Development.

Arnheim, D. (1975). *Dance injuries: Their prevention and care.* St. Louis, MO: C. V. Mosby.

Artress, L. (1995). *Walking the sacred path: Rediscovering the labyrinth as a spiritual tool.* New York: Riverhead Books.

Baer, J. (1991). Generality of creativity across performance domains. *Creativity Research Journal, 4*(1), 234-243.

Baer, J. (1993/1994). Why you shouldn't trust creativity tests. *Educational Leadership, 51*(4), 80-83.

Baer, J. (1994). Performance assessments of creativity: Do they have long-term stability? *Roeper Review, 17*(1), 7-11.

Baer, J. (1999). Domains of creativity. In M. Runco & S. Pritzker (Eds.), *Encyclopedia of creativity, Vol. 1* (pp. 591-596). San Diego, CA: Academic Press.

Bagley, M., & Hess, K. (1983). *200 ways of using imagery in the classroom.* New York: Trillium.

Bailey, D. (1991). *Improvisation: Its nature and practice in music.* New York: Da Capo Press.

Baird, L. L. (1985). Do grades and tests predict adult accomplishment? *Research in Higher Education, 23*(1), 3-85.

Bakker, F. (1988). Personality differences between young dancers and nondancers. *Personality and Individual Differences, 9,* 121-131.

Bamberger, J. (1986). Cognitive issues in the development of musically gifted children. In R. J. Sternberg & J. Davidson (Eds.), *Conceptions of giftedness* (pp. 388-415). New York: Cambridge.

Barron, F. (1968). *Creativity and personal freedom.* New York: Van Nostrand.

Barron, F. (1972). *Artists in the making.* New York: Seminar Press.

Barron, F. (1995). *No rootless flower: An ecology of creativity.* Cresskill, NJ: Hampton Press.

Barron, F., Montuori, A., & Barron, A. (Eds.). (1997). *Creators on creating: Awakening and cultivating the imaginative mind.* Los Angeles: Jeremy P. Tarcher/Putnam.

Bates, B. (1987). *The way of the actor.* Boston: Shambhala.

Bell, Q. (1972). *Virginia Woolf: A biography.* New York: Harcourt Brace Jovanovich.

Benbow, C. (1992). Mathematical talent: Its nature and consequences. In N. Colangelo, S. Assouline, & D. Ambroson (Eds.), *Talent development: Proceedings from the 1991 Henry B. and Jocelyn Wallace National Research Symposium on Talent Development* (pp. 99-123). Unionville, NY: Trillium Press.

Benbow, C., & Lubinski, D. (1995). Optimal development of talent: Respond educationally to individual differences in personality. *The Educational Forum, 59*(4), 381-392.

Bergson, H. (1976). The possible and the real. In A. E. Rothenberg & C. Hausman (Eds.), *The creativity question* (M. Andison, Trans.) (pp. 292-295). Durham, NC: Duke University Press. (Original translation published 1946)

Berryman, J. (1950). *Stephen Crane.* New York: William Sloane Associates.

Blaise, C. (1993). *I had a father: A post-modern autobiography.* Reading, MA: Addison-Wesley Publishing Company.

Blake, P. L. (1997). Similarities and gender differences in personality attributes of talented adolescent visual artists. *Dissertation Abstracts International Section A: Humanities & Social Sciences.* Vol. 57(7-A), 2810.

Blanshard, B. (1976). The teleology of the creative act. In A. Rothenberg & C. Hausman, (Eds.), *The creativity question* (pp. 97-103). Durham, NC: Duke University Press. (Original work published 1964)

Block, J., & Kremen, A. M. (1996). IQ and ego-resiliency: Conceptual and empirical connections and separateness. *Journal of Personality and Social Psychology, 70*(2), 349-351.

Bloom, B. (Ed.). (1985). *The development of talent in young people.* New York: Ballantine.

Bloom, B. (1986). The hands and feet of genius. *Educational Leadership, 43,* 70-77.

Blumberg, S. A., & Panos, L. G. (1990). *Edward Teller: Giant of the golden age of physics.* New York: Macmillan.

Bogen, J., & Bogen, G. (1969). The other side of the brain III: The corpus callosum and creativity. *Bulletin of the Los Angeles Neurological Societies, 34.* Los Angeles: Los Angeles Society of Neurology and Psychiatry.

Bold, A. (Ed.). (1982). *Drink to me only: The prose (and cons) of drinking.* London: Robin Clark.

Bookspan, M., & Yodkey, R. (1981). *Andre Previn: A biography.* New York: Doubleday.

Borland, J. (1986). A note on the existence of certain divergent-production abilities. *Journal for the Education of the Gifted, 9,* 239-251.

Boyd, J. (with Warren, H. G.). (1992). *Musicians in tune: Seventy-five contemporary musicians discuss the creative process.* New York: Simon & Schuster.

Braisted, J., Mellin, L., Gong, E., & Irwin, C. (1985). The adolescent ballet dancer: Nutritional practices and characteristics associated with anorexia nervosa. *Journal of Adolescent Health Care, 6,* 371-376.

Brando, M. (1994). *Songs my mother taught me: The autobiography of Marlon Brando.* New York: Random House.

Brodsky, M. A. (1993). Successful female corporate managers and entrepreneurs: Similarities and differences. *Group & Organization Management, 18*(3) 366-378.

Brody, L. (1989, Nov.). *Characteristics of extremely mathematically talented females.* Paper presented at National Association for Gifted Children Conference, Cincinnati, OH.

Brook, P. (1989). The act of possession. In T. Cole & H. Chinoy (Eds.), *Actors on acting* (pp. 223-229). New York: Crown.

Brooks, J. (1994). Interview with Chinua Achebe. *Paris Review, 136,* 142-166.

Brooks-Gunn, J., Burrow, C., & Warren, M. (1988). Attitudes toward eating and body weight in different groups of female adolescent athletes. *International Journal of Eating Disorders, 7, 749-757.*

Brooks-Gunn, J., & Warren, M. (1985). The effects of delayed menarche in different contexts: Dance and nondance students. *Journal of Youth and Adolescence, 14,* 285-300.

Brooks-Gunn, J., Warren, M., & Hamilton, L. (1987).The relation of eating problems and amenorrhea in ballet dancers. *Medicine and Science in Sports and Exercise, 19*(1), 41-44.

Brower, R. (1999). Dangerous minds: Eminently creative people who spent time in jail. *Creativity Research Journal, 12*(1), 3-13.

Brown, F., & McDonald, J. (1997). *Growing up southern: How the south shapes its writers.* Greenville, SC: Blue Ridge Publishing.

Brown, M. (1988, Aug). *Transpersonal psychology: Exploring the frontiers in human resource development.* Paper presented at the Annual Meeting of the American Psychological Association, Atlanta, GA.

Bryant, J., & Zillman, D. (1989). Using humor to promote learning in the classroom. In P. McGhee (Ed.), *Humor and children's development* (pp. 49-78). Binghamton, NY: Haworth Press.

Buchanan, B. G. (2001). Creativity at the metalevel: AAAI-2000 presidential address. *AI Magazine, 22*(3), 13-45, 47-57.

Buchanan, D., & Bandy, C. (1984). Jungian typology of 37 prospective psychodramatists: Myers-Briggs Type Indicator analysis of applicants for psychodrama training. *Psychological Reports, 55,* 599-606.

Buckle, R. (1988). *George Balanchine, ballet master.* New York: Random House.

Bulfinch, T. (1855). *Bulfinch's mythology: The age of fable.* Boston: S. W. Tilton.

Buttsworth, L. M., & Smith, G. A. (1995). Personality of Australian performing musicians by gender and by instrument. *Personality & Individual Differences, 18*(5), 595-603.

Byner, W. (Trans.). *300 Tang poems.* Retrieved from http://etext.lib.virginia.edu/chinese/frame.htm

Callahan, M. (1997). Creation myth. In F. Barron, A. Montuori, & A. Barron (Eds.), *Creators on creating* (pp. 216-221). Los Angeles: Jeremy T. Tarcher/Putnam.

Cameron, J. (1992). *The artist's way: A spiritual path to higher creativity.* Los Angeles: Jeremy Tarcher.

Campbell, D. T. (1960). Blind variation and selective retention in creative thought as in other knowledge processes. *Psychological Review, 67,* 380-400.

Campbell, D. (1997). *The Mozart effect: Tapping the power of music to heal the body, strengthen the mind, and unlock the creative spirit.* New York: Avon.

Campbell, J. (1968). *The masks of god: Creative mythology.* New York: Viking.

Campbell, L., Campbell, B., & Dickinson, D. (1992). *Teaching and learning through multiple intelligences.* Stanwood, WA: New Directions for Learning.

Cannon, W. (1945). *The role of hunches: The way of an investigator.* New York: W. W. Norton.

Carruth, H. (1983). The formal idea of jazz. In S. Berg (Ed.), *In praise of what persists* (pp.33-44). New York: Harper & Row.

Cattell, R., & Cattell, M. C. (1969). *Handbook for the High School Personality Questionnaire (HSPQ).* Champaign, IL: Institute for Personality and Ability Testing.

Chaikin, J. (1969). The context of performance. In T. Cole & H. K. Chinoy (Eds.), *Actors on acting* (pp. 665-667). New York: Crown Publishers.

Cheever, J. (1991, January 28). Diaries. *The New Yorker*, 50-57.

Cheng, S. K. (1999). East-west difference in views on creativity: Is Howard Gardner correct? Yes and no. *Journal of Creative Behavior, 33*(2), 112-121.

Cherry, K. (1989). Why the figure of Christ keeps turning up in my work. In E. Shelnutt (Ed.), *The confidence woman: 26 female writers at work* (pp. 27-41). Marietta, GA: Longstreet Press.

Chicago, J. (1977). *Through the flower: My struggle as a woman artist.* New York: Anchor Books.

Christopher. (1997). *Released from the past.* Recording on compact disc. Berea, OH: Shirtless Records.

Christopher. (2000). *Creation: The pyramid and the suns.* Recording on compact disc. Berea, OH: Shirtless Records.

Christopher (2002). *The new heavens and the new earth.* Recording on compact disc. Berea, OH: Shirtless Records.

Citino, D. (1990). *The house of memory.* Columbus, OH: Ohio State University Press.

Clark, G., & Zimmerman, E. (1983, November). Identifying artistically talented students. *School Arts*, 23-31.

Clark, G., & Zimmerman, E. (1984). *Educating artistically talented students.* Syracuse, NY: Syracuse University Press.

Clark, G., & Zimmerman, E. (1986). A framework for educating artistically talented students based on Feldman's and Clark and Zimmerman's models. *Studies in Art Education, 27*(3), 115-122.

Clark, G., & Zimmerman, E. (1987). Tending the special spark: Accelerated and enriched curricula for highly talented art students. *Roeper Review, 105*(1), 10-16.

Clark, R. (1971). *Einstein: The life and times.* New York: World Publishing.

Cobain, K. (2002). *Journals.* New York: Riverhead Press.

Colangelo, N., Kerr, B., Huesman, R., Hallowell, K., & Gaeth, J. (1992). The development of a scale to identify mechanical inventiveness. *Talent development: Proceedings from the Henry B. and Jocelyn Wallace National Research Symposium on Talent Development* (233-239). Unionville, NY: Trillium Press.

Coleridge, S. T. (1817). *Biographia literaria, I.* London: Rest Fenner.

Colin, R., & Amabile, T. (1999). Motivation/Drive. In M. Runco & S. Pritzker (Eds.), *Encyclopedia of creativity, Vol. 2.* San Diego, CA: Academic Press.

Collingwood, R. (1976). Consciousness and attention in art. In A. Rothenberg & C. Hausman (Eds.), *The creativity question* (pp. 334-343). Durham, NC: Duke University Press. (Original work published 1938)

Contemporary Authors Autobiography Series. (Ongoing). Detroit: Dale Research.

Contemporary Authors New Revised. (Ongoing). Detroit: Dale Research..

Cowger, H., & Torrance, E. P. (1982). Further examination of the quality of changes in creative functioning resulting from meditation (Zazen) training. *Creative Child and Adult Quarterly, 7,* 211-217.

Crabbe, A., & Betts, G. (1990). *Creating more creative people II.* Greely, CO: Autonomous Learner Press.

Crews, H. (1987). From a childhood: The biography of a place. In D. McCullough (Ed.), *American childhoods* (pp. 327-344). Boston: Little, Brown.

Croce, A. (1990, Oct. 15). Angel. *The New Yorker,* 124-127.

Croce, B. (1976). Intuition and expression in art. In A. Rothenberg & C. Hausman (Eds.), *The creativity question* (pp. 327-333). Durham, NC: Duke University Press. (Original work published 1909)

Cross, J. W. (1903). *George Eliot's life as related in her letters and journals.* New York and London: Abbey.

Csikszentmihalyi, M. (1990). *Flow.* New York: Cambridge.

Csikszentmihalyi, M. (1993). *The evolving self: A psychology for the third millennium.* New York: HarperCollins.

Csikszentmihalyi, M. (1995). *Creativity.* New York: HarperCollins.

Csikszentmihalyi, M. (1999). Implications of a systems perspective for the study of creativity. In R. J. Sternberg (Ed.), *Handbook of creativity* (pp. 313-337). New York: Cambridge University Press.

Csikszentmihalyi, M., Rathunde, K., & Whalen, C. (1993). *Talented teenagers: The roots of success and failure.* New York: Cambridge University Press.

Dabrowski, K. (1965). *Personality shaping through positive disintegration.* Boston: Little Brown.

Dabrowski, K., & Piechowski, M. M. (1977). *Theory of levels of emotional development.* Oceanside, NY: Dabor.

Dash, J. (1973). *A life of one's own: Three gifted women and the men they married.* New York: Harper & Row.

Davis, G. A. (1989). Testing for creative potential. *Contemporary Educational Psychology, 14,* 257-274.

Davis, G. A. (2000). *Creativity is forever* (4th ed.). Cross Plains, WI: Badger Press.

Davis, G. A., & Rimm, S. G. (1980). *Group inventory for finding interests II.* Watertown, WI: Educational Assessment Service.

Davis, G. A., & Rimm, S. B. (1982). Group inventory for finding interests (GIFFI) I and II: Instruments for identifying creative potential in the junior and senior high school. *Journal of Creative Behavior, 16,* 50-57.

de Törne, B. (1937). *Sibelius: A close-up*. Boston: Houghton Mifflin Company.

deBono, E. (1970). *Lateral thinking*. New York: Harper Colophon.

deBono, E. (1978). *CoRT thinking lesson series*. Blanford Forum, Dorset, UK: Direct Education Services.

deBono, E. (1992). *Serious creativity: Using the power of lateral thinking to create new ideas*. New York: HarperCollins.

deMille, A. (1980). *America dances*. New York: Macmillan.

deMille, A. (1991). *Martha: The life and work of Martha Graham*. New York: Random House.

DeSalvo, L. (1989). *Virginia Woolf: The impact of childhood sexual abuse on her life and work*. London: Women's Press.

Dennison, G. (1983). In praise of what persists. In S. Berg (Ed.), *In praise of what persists* (pp. 69-92). New York: Harper & Row.

Dewey, A., Steinberg, H., & Coulson, M. (1998). Conditions in which British artists achieve their best work. *Creativity Research Journal, 11*(4), 275-282.

Dieffenbach, K., & Moffett, A. (2002). Psychological characteristics and their development in Olympic champions. *Journal of Applied Sport Psychology, 14*(3), 172-204.

Directory of American Poets and Fiction Writers. (2000-2001). New York: Poets & Writers, Inc.

Dosasmantes-Beaudry, I. (2001). Frida Kahlo: Self-other representation and self healing through art. *The Arts in Psychotherapy, 28*, 5-17.

Du Pré, H., & Du Pré, P. (1997). *Hillary and Jackie*. New York: Ballantine Books.

Dudek, S., & Hall, W. (1991). Personality consistency: Eminent architects 25 years later. *Creativity Research Journal, 4*, 213-231.

Duke, P., & Turan, K. (1987). *Call me Anna*. New York: Bantam.

Dunning, J. (2001, Sept. 16). Still paying heed to Graham's cry. *New York Times Online*. Retrieved from www.New York Times.com

Durban, P. (1991). Layers. In E. Shelnutt (Ed.), *The confidence woman: 26 female writers at work* (pp. 7-26). Marietta, GA: Longstreet Press.

Dyce, J. A., & O'Connor, B. P. (1994). The personalities of popular musicians. *Psychology of Music, 22*(2) 168-173.

Eberle, B. (1982). *Visual thinking*. Buffalo: D.O.K.

Edwards, A. (1975). *Judy Garland*. New York: Simon & Schuster.

Edwards, B. (1979). *Drawing on the right side of the brain*. Los Angeles: Tarcher.

Ehrenzweig, A. (1976). Unconscious scanning and dedifferentiation in artistic perception. In A. Rothenberg & C. Hausman (Eds.), *The creativity question* (pp. 149-152). Durham, NC: Duke University Press. (Original work published 1967)

Einbond, B. (1979). *The coming indoors and other poems.* Tokyo: Charles E. Tuttle.

Eisner, E. (1999). *The enlightened eye* (2nd ed.). Columbus, OH: Prentice Hall.

Elliott, M. (2001). Breakthrough thinking. *IIE Solutions, 33*(10), 22-25.

Els, S. M. (1994). *Into the deep: A writer's look at creativity.* Portsmouth, MA: Heinemann.

Encyclopedia of Creativity (2 vols.). (1999). San Diego, CA: Academic Press.

Ephron, N. (1983). A few words about breasts. In M. Richler (Ed.), *The best of modern humor* (pp. 467-475). New York: Knopf.

Ericsson, K. A. (1996). *The road to excellence: The acquisition of expert performance in the arts and sciences, sports, and games.* Mahwah, NJ: Erlbaum.

Ericsson, K. A., & Lehmann, A. C. (1999). Expertise. In M. Runco & S. R. Pritzker (Eds.), *Encyclopedia of creativity, Vol. 1* (pp. 695-707). San Diego, CA: Academic Press.

Estés, C. P. (1991). *The creative fire: Myths and stories about the cycles of creativity.* Audiotapes. Jungian Storyteller Series.

Estés, C. P. (1992). *Women who run with the wolves: Myths and stories of the wild woman archetype.* New York: Ballantine Books.

Ewen, D. (1968). *The man with the baton: The story of conductors and their orchestras.* Freeport, NY: Book for Libraries Press.

Eysenck, H. J. (1993). Creativity and personality: Suggestions for a theory. *Psychological Inquiry, 4,* 147-178

Farrell, S. (1990). *Holding on to the air.* New York: Summit.

Feist, G. H. (1999). Influence of personality on artistic and scientific creativity. In R. J. Sternberg (Ed.), *Handbook of creativity* (pp. 273-296). New York: Cambridge University Press.

Feldhusen, J., & Clinkenbeard, P. (1986). Creativity instructional materials: A review of research. *Journal of Creative Behavior, 20,* 176-188.

Feldhusen, J. F., & Treffinger, D. J. (1985). *Creative thinking and problem solving in gifted education.* Dubuque, IA: Kendall/Hunt.

Feldman, D. H. (1982). A developmental framework for research with gifted children. In D. Feldman (Ed.), *New directions for child development: Developmental approaches to giftedness and creativity (pp. 31-46).* San Francisco: Jossey-Bass.

Feldman, D. H. (with Goldsmith, L.). (1986). *Nature's gambit: Child prodigies and the development of human potential.* New York: Basic.

Feldman, D. H. (1988). Dreams, insights, and transformations. In R. J. Sternberg (Ed.), *The nature of creativity* (pp. 271-297). New York: Cambridge.

Feldman, D. H. (1990, November). *Universal to unique: Developmental domains of giftedness.* Paper presented at National Association for Gifted Children Conference, Little Rock, AR.

Feldman, D. H. (1999). The development of creativity. In R. J. Sternberg (Ed.), *Handbook of creativity* (pp. 169-187). New York: Cambridge University Press.

Feldman, D. H. (2003, in press). The creation of multiple intelligences theory: A study in high level thinking. In V. John-Steiner & K. Sawyer (Eds.), *Development and creativity.* New York: Oxford University Press.

Feldman, D. H., Csikszentmihalyi, M., & Gardner, H. (1994). *Changing the world: A framework for the study of creativity.* Westport, CT: Praeger.

Feldman, D. H., & Piirto, J. (2002). Parenting talented children. In M. Bornstein (Ed.), *Handbook of parenting, 2ᵈ ed.* (pp. 195-219). Hillside, NJ: Erlbaum.

Feynman, R. P. (1998). *The meaning of it all: Thoughts of a citizen-scientist.* Reading, MA: Perseus Books.

Findlay, C., & Lumsden, C. (1988). *The creative mind.* London: Academic Press.

Fitzgibbon, C. (1965). *The life of Dylan Thomas.* Boston: Little, Brown.

Flack, A. (1986). *Art & soul.* New York: E. P. Dutton.

Foley, P. (1986). *The dual role experience of artist mothers.* Unpublished doctoral dissertation. Northwestern University, IL.

Foley, P. (1996). Artist mothers. *Advanced Development, 7,* 2-23.

Fontaine, L. (1969). Thoughts on acting. In T. Cole & H. K. Chinoy (Eds.), *Actors on acting* (pp. 610-612). New York: Crown Publisher.

Foucault, M. (1996). The order of things. In F. Barron, A. Montuori, & A. Barron (Eds.), *Creators on creating: Awakening and cultivating the imaginative mind* (pp. 108-112). Los Angeles: Jeremy P. Tarcher/ Putnam.

Freeman, J. (2002, October). *Twenty-seven year follow up of gifted youth.* Paper presented at European Council for High Ability Conference, Rhodes, Greece.

Freud, S. (1976). Creative writers and daydreaming. In A. Rothenberg & C. Hausman, (Eds.), *The creativity question* (pp. 48-52). Durham, NC: Duke University Press. (Original work published 1908)

Friedman, M. (1973). *Buried alive: The biography of Janis Joplin.* New York: William Morrow & Company.

Friman, A., & Templin, C. (1994). An interview with Molly Peacock. *Poets & Writers Magazine, 22*(1), 23-31.

Fuller, B. (1981). *Critical path.* New York: St. Martin's.

Fuller, B. (1983). *Grunch of giants.* New York: St. Martin's.

Gablik, S. (1976). *Magritte*. New York: New York Graphic Society.

Gablik, S. (1991). *The re-enchantment of art*. London: Thames and Hudson.

Gallagher, T. (1983). My father's love letters. In S. Berg (Ed.), *In praise of what persists* (pp.109-124). New York: Harper & Row.

Gallwey, T. (1997). *The inner game of tennis*. New York: Random House.

Galton, F. (1976). Genius as inherited. In A. Rothenberg & C. Hausman, (Eds.), *The creativity question* (pp. 42-47). Durham, NC: Duke University Press. (Original work published 1869)

Gardner, A. (1990). *Ava Gardner: My story*. New York: Bantam.

Gardner, H. (1982). *Art, mind, and brain*. New York: Basic.

Gardner, H. (1983). *Frames of mind*. New York: Basic.

Gardner, H. (1988). Creative lives and creative works: A synthetic scientific approach. In R. J. Sternberg (Ed.), *The nature of creativity* (pp. 298-321). New York: Cambridge University Press.

Gardner, H. (1989, December). Learning Chinese style. *Psychology Today*, 54-56.

Gardner, H. (1993). *Creating Minds: An anatomy of creativity seen through the lives of Freud, Einstein, Picasso, Stravinsky, Eliot, Graham, and Gandhi*. New York: Basic Books.

Gardner, H. (with Laskin, E.). (1995). *Leading minds: An anatomy of leadership*. New York: Basic Books.

Gardner, H. (1997). *Extraordinary minds: Portraits of exceptional individuals and an examination of our extraordinariness*. New York: Basic Books.

Garner, D. (1997). The apostle of the strung-out: Interview with Robert Stone. *Salon Magazine*. Retrieved from www.salon.com/april97/ stone4704.html

Garner, D. (1998). The resurrection man: Interview with Richard Price. *Salon Magazine*. Retrieved from www.salon.com/book/intl/ 1998/05/cov_si_13int.html

Gawain, S. (1978). *Creative visualization*. New York: Bantam.

Getty, J. P. (1976). *The autobiography of J. Paul Getty*. New York: Prentice Hall.

Getzels, J. (1987). Creativity, intelligence, and problem finding: Retrospect and prospect. In S. Isaksen (Ed.), *Frontiers of creativity research* (pp. 88-102). Buffalo, NY: Bearly, Ltd.

Getzels, J., & Csikszentmihalyi, M. (1976). *The creative vision: A longitudinal study of problem finding in art*. New York: Wiley.

Getzels, J., & Jackson, P. (1962) *Creativity and intelligence: Explorations with gifted students*. New York: Wiley.

Ghiselin, B. (Ed.). (1952). *The creative process*. New York: Mentor.

Gillespie, W., & Myors, B. (2000). Personality of rock musicians. *Psychology of Music, 28*(2), 154-165.

Gilliam, J. E., Carpenter, B. O., & Christensen, J. R. (1996). *Gifted and talented education scales.* Austin, TX: Pro-Ed.

Glass, P. (1987). *Music by Philip Glass.* New York: Harper & Row.

Gleick, J. (1992). *Genius: The life and science of Richard Feynman.* New York: Vintage.

Glover, J. S., Ronning, R. R., & Reynolds, C. R. (1989). *Handbook of creativity.* New York: Plenum.

Glück, L. (1991). The education of the poet. In E. Shelnutt (Ed.), *The confidence woman: 26 female writers at work* (pp. 133-148). Marietta, GA: Longstreet Press.

Goedicke, P. (1991). Entering the garden. In E. Shelnutt (Ed.), *The confidence woman: 26 female writers at work* (73-98). Marietta, GA: Longstreet Press.

Goertzel, V., & Goertzel, M. G. (1962). *Cradles of eminence.* Boston: Little, Brown.

Goertzel, V., Goertzel, M. G., & Goertzel, T. (1978). *Three hundred eminent personalities: A psychosocial analysis of the famous.* San Francisco: Jossey-Bass.

Goertzel, V., Goertzel, M., Goertzel, T., & Hansen, A. (2004). *Cradles of eminence: Childhoods of more than four hundred famous men and women, 2nd edition.* Scottsdale, AZ: Great Potential Press.

Goldberg, N. (1986). *Writing down the bones.* New York: Quality Paperbacks.

Goleman, D. (1995). *Emotional intelligence.* New York: Bantam.

Goodenough, F. L. (1926). *Measurement of intelligence by drawings.* Yonkers-on-Hudson, NY: World Book Company.

Gordon, M. (1996). *Shadowman: A daughter's search for her father.* New York: Random House.

Gordon, W. (1961). *Synectics: The development of creative capacity.* New York: Harper & Row.

Gould, D., Damarjian, N., & Greenleaf, C. (2002). Imagery training for peak performance. In J. Van Raalte & B. Brewer (Eds.), *Exploring sport and exercise psychology* (2nd ed.). (pp. 49-74). Washington, DC: American Psychological Association.

Gough, H. G. (1952). *Adjective Check List.* Palo Alto, CA: Consulting Psychologists Press.

Gough, H. G. (1979). A creative personality scale for the Adjective Check List. *Journal of Personality and Social Psychology, 37,* 1398-1405.

Gough, H. G., & Heilbrun, A. B. (1983). *The Adjective Check List Manual.* Palo Alto, CA: Consulting Psychologists Press.

Graff, E. J. (1995). Novelist out of Carolina. *Poets & Writers Magazine, 23*(1), 40-49.

Graffman, G. (1981). *I really should be practicing.* New York: Bantam.

Graves, R. (1948). *The white goddess.* New York: Farrar, Straus, and Giroux,

Green, J. (1961). *Diary: 1928-1957.* New York: Carroll & Graf.

Greenacre, P. (1957). The childhood of the artist. *Psychoanalytic Study of the Child, 12,* 47-72.

Greer, G. (1979). *The obstacle race: The fortunes of women painters and their work.* New York: Farrar Straus Giroux.

Gregg, L. (1984, Fall). Taken by each thing. *Paris Review, 93,* 170.

Griffiths, J. (1998). Review of *The Soul's Code: Resurgence, 184.* Retrieved on June 14, 2003 from http://resurgence.gn.apc.org/184/ griffiths184br.htm

Grof, S. (with Bennett, H. Z.). (1993). *The holotropic mind.* San Francisco: Harper SanFrancisco.

Gruber, H. (1982). *Darwin on man* (2nd ed.). Chicago: University of Chicago Press.

Gruber, H. (2001). Creative work: The case of Charles Darwin. *American Psychologist, 56*(4), 346-349.

Gruber, H., & Davis, S. (1988). Inching our way up Mount Olympus: The evolving-systems approach to creative thinking. In R. J. Sternberg (Ed.), *The nature of creativity: Contemporary psychological perspectives* (pp. 243-270). New York: Cambridge University Press.

Gruber, H., & Wallace, D. B. (1999). The case study method and evolving systems approach for understanding unique creative people at work. In R. J. Sternberg (Ed.), *Handbook of creativity* (pp. 93-114). New York: Cambridge University Press.

Gruen, J. (1988). *People who dance.* Princeton, NJ: Princeton Book Co.

Guilford, J. P. (1950). Creativity. *American Psychologist, 5,* 444-454.

Guilford, J. P. (1967). *The nature of human intelligence.* New York: McGraw-Hill.

Guilford, J. P. (1970). Traits of creativity. In P. E. Vernon (Ed.), *Creativity* (p. 167). London Harmondsworth: Penguin.

Guilford, J. P. (1988). Some changes in the Structure-of-Intellect model. *Educational and Psychological Measurement, 48,* 1-6.

Gurewitsch, M. (2002, March 3). A star stays faithful to her first love, the stage. *New York Times Online.* Retrieved from New York Times.com

H'Doubler, M. (1968). *Dance: A creative art experience.* Madison, WI: The University of Wisconsin Press.

Halperin, J. (1986). *The life of Jane Austen.* Baltimore: Johns Hopkins.

Halpin, G., & Halpin, G. (1973). The effect of motivation on creative thinking abilities. *Journal of Creative Behavior, 7,* 51-53.

Hampl, P. (1992). *Virgin time: In search of the contemplative life.* New York: Ballantine.

Hansen, R. (1986). Interview with John Irving. In G. Plimpton (Ed.), *Writers at work: The Paris Review interviews* (8th series) (pp. 413-441). New York: Penguin Books.

Hanson, L., & Hanson, E. (1954). *Noble savage: The life of Paul Gauguin.* New York: Random House.

Hanson, S. L. (1996). *Lost talent: Women in the sciences.* Philadelphia: Temple University Press.

Harman, W., & Rheingold, H. (1984). *Higher creativity: Liberating the unconscious for breakthrough insights.* New York: Houghton Mifflin.

Haroutounian, J. (2002). *Kindling the spark: Recognizing and developing musical talent.* New York: Oxford.

Harris, W. G. (1998). *Sophia Loren: A biography.* New York: Simon & Schuster.

Harrison, J. (1991). *Just before dark: Collected nonfiction.* New York: Houghton Mifflin.

Harrison, K. (1997). *The kiss.* New York: Random House.

Haskins, J. (1987). *Black music in America: A history through its people.* New York: Crowell.

Hausman, C. (1976). Creativity and rationality. In A. Rothenberg & C. Hausman, (Eds.), *The creativity question* (pp. 343-351). Durham, NC: Duke University Press. (Original work published 1964)

Heausler, N., & Thompson, B. (1988). Structure of the Torrance Tests of Creative Thinking. *Educational and Psychological Measurement, 48,* 463-468.

Heinz, D. (1995). An interview with Ted Hughes: The art of poetry LXXI. *The Paris Review, 134,* 54-94.

Helson, R. (1983). Creative mathematicians. In R. Albert (Ed.), *Genius and eminence: The social psychology of creativity and exceptional achievement* (pp. 211-230). London: Pergamon Press.

Helson, R. (1999). A longitudinal study of creative personality in women. *Creativity Research Journal, 2*(2), 89-102.

Hennessey, B. A. (1997). Teaching for creative development: A social psychological approach. In N. Colangelo & G. A. Davis (Eds.), *Handbook of gifted education, 2nd ed.* (pp. 282-291). Needham Hights, MA: Allyn & Bacon.

Hennessey, B. A. (1999). Intrinsic motivation, affect, and creativity. In S. Russ (Ed.), *Affect, creative experience, and psychological adjustment.* Philadelphia: Taylor & Francis.

Hennessey, B. A. (2000). Rewards and creativity. In C. Sansone & J. Harackiewicz (Eds.), *Intrinsic and extrinsic motivation: The search for optimal motivation and performance* (pp. 55-78). San Diego, CA: Academic Press, Inc.

Hennessey, B. A., & Amabile, T. M. (1988). Storytelling as a means of assessing creativity. *Journal of Creative Behavior, 22*, 235-247.

Hennessey, B. A., & Amabile, T. M. (1999). Consensual assessment. In M. Runco & S. Pritzker (Eds.), *Encyclopedia of creativity, Vol. 1* (pp. 347-359). San Diego, CA: Academic Press.

Hill, J. (1991). Writing against the wind: Being all things to all people and the arrogance of the female stance. In E. Shelnutt (Ed.), *The confidence woman: 26 female writers at work* (pp. 372-392). Marietta, GA: Longstreet Press.

Hillman, J. (1996). *The soul's code: In search of character and calling.* New York: Random House.

Hillman, J. (1999). *The force of character and the lasting life.* New York: Random House.

Hirsch, E. (1985). Interview with Derek Walcott. In G. Plimpton (Ed.), *Writers at work: The Paris Review interviews* (pp. 265-298). New York: Penguin Books.

Hocevar, D. (1980). Intelligence, divergent thinking, and creativity. *Intelligence, 4*, 25-40.

Hofstadter, D. (1985). *Metamagical themas.* New York: Basic.

Hollander, L. (1987). Music, the creative process, and the path of enlightenment. *Roeper Review, 10*(1) 28-32.

Hosmer, R. (1993). The art of poetry: Interview with Amy Clampitt. *The Paris Review, 126*, 76-109.

Houtz, J. C., & Patricola, C. (1999). Imagery. In M. Runco & S. Pritzer (Eds.), *The Encyclopedia of Creativity, II.* (pp. 1-11). San Diego, CA: Academic Press.

Howe, M. J., Davidson, J. W., Moore, D. G., & Sloboda, J. A. (1995). Are there early childhood signs of musical ability? *Psychology of Music, 23*(2) 162-176.

Hughes, R., & Coakley, J. (2001). Positive deviance among athletes: The implications of overconformity to the sport ethic. In A. Yiannakis & M. J. Melnick (Eds.), *Contemporary issues in sociology of sport* (pp. 361-374). Champaign, IL: Human Kinetics.

Hurwitt, J. (1980). An interview with Nadine Gordimer. In G. Plimpton (Ed.), *Women writers at work: The Paris Review interviews* (pp. 225-261). New York: Penguin Books.

Hurwitz, A. (1983). *The gifted and talented in art: A guide to program planning.* Worcester, MA: Davis.

Huxley, A. (1963). *The doors of perception.* New York: Harper & Row.

Inez, C. (1991). The journey of an exiled daughter. In E. Shelnutt (Ed.), *The confidence woman: 26 female writers at work* (pp. 281-306). Marietta, GA: Longstreet Press.

Isaksen, S. (Ed.). (1987). *Frontiers of creativity research: Beyond the basics.* Buffalo, NY: Bearly, Ltd.

Isaksen, S. G., Puccio, G. J., & Treffinger, D. J. (1993). An ecological approach to creativity research: Profiling for creative problem solving. *Journal of Creative Behavior, 27*(3), 149-170.

Jackson, S. A., Thomas, P. R., Marsh, H. W., & Smethurst, C. J. (2001). Relationships between flow, self-concept, psychological skills, and performance. *Journal of Applied Sport Psychology, 13*(2), 129-153.

James, W. (1880). Great men, great thoughts, and the environment. *Atlantic Monthly, 46,* 441-459.

Jamison, J. (with Kaplan, H.). (1993). *Dancing spirit: An autobiography.* New York: Doubleday.

Jamison, K. (1993). *Touched with fire: Manic depressive illness and the artistic temperament.* New York: The Free Press.

Jamison, K. (1995). *An unquiet mind: A memoir of moods and madness.* New York: Vintage Books.

Jamison, K. (1995, February). Manic-depressive illness and creativity. *Scientific American,* 62-67.

Jarvie, I. (1981). The rationality of creativity. In D. Dutton & M. Krausz (Eds.), *The concept of creativity in science and art* (pp. 109-128). The Hague: Martinus Mijhoff.

Jenkins-Friedman, R. (1992). Zorba's conundrum: Evaluative aspects of self-concept in talented individuals. *Quest, 3*(1), 1-7.

Jenkins-Friedman, R., & Tollefson, N. (1992). Resiliency in cognition and motivation: Its applicability to giftedness. In N. Colangelo, S. Assouline, & D. Ambroson (Eds.), *Talent development: Proceedings from the 1991 Henry B. and Jocelyn Wallace National Research Symposium on Talent Development* (pp. 325-333). Unionville, NY: Trillium Press.

Jeter, D. (with Curry, J.). (2000). *The life you imagine: Life lessons for achieving your dreams.* New York: Crown Publishers.

John-Steiner, V. (1985). *Notebooks of the mind: Explorations of thinking.* New York: Harper & Row.

Johnson, G. (1998). *Invisible writer: A biography of Joyce Carol Oates.* New York: Dutton.

Johnson, J. D., Trawalter, S., & Dovidio, J. (2000). Converging interracial consequences of exposure to violent rap music on stereotypical attributions of Blacks. *Journal of Experimental Social Psychology, 36*(3), 233-251.

Jones, G., Hanton, S., & Connaughton, D. (2002). What is this thing called mental toughness? An investigation of elite sport performers. *Journal of Applied Sport Psychology, 14*(3), 205-218.

Joyce, C. (1998). Interview with Russell Banks. *Salon Magazine*. Retrieved from www.salon.com/books/int/1998/01 /cov_si_05int3.html

Jung, C. G. (1933). *Modern man in search of a soul*. New York: Harcourt Brace.

Jung, C. G. (1965). *Memories, dreams, reflections*. New York: Vintage.

Jung, C. G. (1976). On the relation of analytical psychology to poetic art. In A. Rothenberg & C. Hausman (Eds.), *The creativity question* (pp. 120-126). Durham, NC: Duke University Press. (Original work published 1923)

Kalpakian, L. (1991). My life as a boy. In E. Shelnutt (Ed.), *The confidence woman: 26 female writers at work* (pp. 43-58). Marietta, GA: Longstreet Press.

Kaltsounis, B. & Honeywell, L. (1980). Instruments useful in studying creative behavior and creative talent. Part IV. Non-commercially available instruments. *Journal of Creative Behavior, 5,* 117-126.

Kant, I. (1952). Genius gives the rules. In A. Rothenberg & C. Hausman (Eds.), *The creativity question* (pp. 37-41). Durham, NC: Duke University Press. (Original work published 1790)

Kanter, L. (1999, August 31). Warren Buffett. *Salon Magazine*. Retrieved from www.salon.com/people/bc/1999/08/31/buffett/index1.html

Karnes, F., Chauvin, J., & Trant, T. (1985). Comparison of personality profiles for intellectually gifted students and students outstanding in the fine and performing arts.

Katz, J. (1999). Driving. In C. B. Kline (Ed.), *Room to grow: Twenty-two writers encounter the pleasures and paradoxes of raising young children* (pp. 177-184). New York: Golden Books.

Kaufman, J. C. (2001). The Sylvia Plath effect: Mental illness in eminent creative writers. *Journal of Creative Behavior, 35*(1), 37-50.

Kaufman, J. C., & Baer, J. (Eds.). (In press). *Faces of the muse.*

Keane, G., & Shaughnessy, M. F. (2002). An interview with Robert J. Sternberg about educational psychology: The current "state of the art." *Educational Psychology Review, 14*(3), 313-330.

Kemp, A. E. (1981a). The personality structure of the musician I: Identifying a profile of traits for the performer. *Psychology of Music, 9,* 3-14.

Kemp, A. E. (1981b). The personality structure of the musician II: Identifying a profile of traits for the composer. *Psychology of Music, 9,* 67-75.

Kemp, A. E. (1982a). The personality structure of the musician III: The significance of sex difference. *Psychology of Music, 10,* 48-58.

Kemp, A. E. (1982b). Personality traits of successful music teachers. *Psychology of Music,* Special Issue, 72-73.

Kemp, A. E. (1996). *The musical temperament: Psychology and personality of musicians.* New York: Oxford University Press.

Kennedy, D. (2001, Nov. 4). Working actors: Ever more familiar, but still hard to get to know. *New York Times Online.* Retrieved from NewYorkTimes.com

Kerr, B., Gottfried, M., Chopp, C., & Cohn, S. (2001). *The happy family studies: Exploring the origins of creative lives.* Barbara Kerr website. Arizona State University.

Kets de Vries, M. (1996). The anatomy of the entrepreneur: Clinical observations. *Human Relations, 49*(7) 853-883.

Kevles, B. (1968). Interview with Anne Sexton. In G. Plimpton (Ed.), *Women writers at work: The Paris Review interviews* (pp. 263-290). New York: Viking.

Khatena, J., & Torrance, E. P. (1973). *Norms-technical manual: Thinking creatively with sounds and words.* Lexington, MA: Personnel Press/Ginn.

Kilpatrick, A. (1996). *Of permanent value: The story of Warren Buffett.* Birmingham, AL: APKE.

Kisselgoff, A. (2002, June 13). In the ranks of the idols. *New York Times.* Retrieved from http://query.nytimes.com/search/article_printpage.html

Kizer, C. (1990). A muse. In L. Lifshin (Ed.), *Lips unsealed* (pp. 26-32). Santa Barbara, CA: Capra.

Klein, E. (1967). *A comprehensive etymological dictionary of the English language.* New York: Elsevier.

Kletke, M. G. (2001). Creativity in the organization: The role of individual creative problem solving and computer support. *International Journal of Human-Computer Studies, 55*(3), 217-237.

Koestler, A. (1964). *The act of creation.* New York: Macmillan.

Kogan, J. (1987). *Nothing but the best: The struggle for perfection at the Juilliard School.* New York: Random House.

Kough, J. (1961). *Practical programs for the gifted.* Chicago: Science Research Associates.

Kozinn, A. (1991, April 11). Shulamit Ran and the Pulitzer Prize. *New York Times,* p. B4.

Krippner, S. (1999). Dreams and creativity. In M. Runco & S. Pritzker (Eds.), *Encyclopedia of creativity, Vol. 1* (pp. 597-606). San Diego, CA: Academic Press.

Krippner, S. & Murphy, G. (1973). Humanistic psychology and parapsychology. *Journal of Humanistic Psychology, 13*(4), 2-24.

Kris, E. (1952). *Psychoanalytic explorations in art.* New York: International Universities.

Kris, E. (1976). On preconscious mental processes. In A. Rothenberg & C. Hausman (Eds.), *The creativity question* (pp. 135-142). Durham, NC: Duke University Press. (Original work published 1952)

Krutetskii, V. (1976). *The psychology of mathematical abilities in schoolchildren.* In J. Wirszup & J. Kirkpatrick (Eds.) (Trans. J. Teller). Chicago: University of Chicago Press. (Original work published 1968)

Kubie, L. S. (1958). *Neurotic distortion of the creative process.* Lawrence, KS: University of Kansas Press.

Langan-Fox, J., & Roth, S. (1995). Achievement motivation and female entrepreneurs. *Journal of Occupational & Organizational Psychology, 68*(3), 209-218.

Langer, S. K. (1953). *Feeling and form.* New York: Charles Scribner's Sons.

Langer, S. K. (1957). *Problems of art.* New York: Charles Scribner's Sons.

Langley, P., & Jones, R. (1988). A computational model of scientific insight. In R. J. Sternberg (Ed.), *The nature of creativity* (pp. 177-201). New York: Cambridge University Press.

Lawrence, G. (2001). *Dance with demons: The life of Jerome Robbins.* New York: Putnam.

Lazear, D. (1994). *Multiple intelligence approaches to assessment: Solving the assessment conundrum.* Phoenix, AZ: Zephyr Press.

Lebrecht, N. (1991). *The maestro myth: Great conductors in pursuit of power.* New York: Birch Lane Press.

Lee, H. (1940). A theory concerning free creation in the inventive arts. *Psychiatry, 3.* The William Alanson White Psychiatric Foundation, Inc.

Leland, J. (2002, October 24). The house that the book bought. *New York Times,* F1.

Leman, N. (2002, October 14 & 21). Without a doubt: Has Condoleezza Rice changed George W. Bush, or has he changed her? *The New Yorker,* 164-174.

Leonard, L. (1989). *Witness to the fire: Creativity and the evil of addiction.* Boston: Shambhala.

Lewis, C. S. (1955). *Surprised by joy: The shape of my early life.* New York: Harcourt, Brace, Jovanovich.

Lifshin, L. (Ed.). (1990). *Lips unsealed: Confidences from contemporary woman writers.* Santa Barbara, CA: Capra Press.

Lissitz, R., & Willhoft, J. (1985). A methodological study of the Torrance Tests of Creativity. *Journal of Educational Measurement, 22,* 1-11.

Loeb, K. (1975). Our women artist/teachers need our help: On changing language, finding cultural heritage, and building self image. *Art Education, 18,* 10.

Lombroso, C. (1895). *The man of genius.* London: Charles Scribner's Sons.

London, P. (1989). *No more secondhand art.* Boston: Shambhala.

Lowenkopf, E., & Vincent, L. (1982). The student ballet dancer and anorexia. *Hillside Journal of Clinical Psychiatry, 5,* 53-64.

Lozanov, G. (1978). *Suggestology and outlines of suggestopedia (psychic studies).* New York: Gordon & Breach.

Ludwig, A. (1995). *The price of greatness: Resolving the creativity and madness controversy.* New York: Guilford.

Lysy, K. Z., & Piechowski, M. M. (1983). Personal growth: An empirical study using Jungian and Dabrowskian measures. *Genetic Psychology Monographs, 108,* 267-320.

MacAdam, A. (1991). Interview with Octavio Paz. *Paris Review, 119,* 82-123.

MacKinnon, D. (1962). The nature and nurture of creative talent. *American Psychologist 17,* 484-495.

MacKinnon, D. (1978). *In search of human effectiveness: Identifying and developing creativity.* Buffalo, NY: Bearly, Ltd.

Madigan, C., & Elwood, A. (1984). *Brainstorms and thunderbolts: How creative genius works.* New York: Macmillan.

Malina, J. (1983). In K. Malpede (Ed.), *Women in theatre* (pp.196-217). New York: Limelight.

Manes, S., & Andrews, P. (1993). *Gates: How Microsoft's mogul reinvented an industry—and made himself the richest man in America.* New York: Doubleday.

Maritain, J. (1953). *Creative intuition in art and poetry.* Trustees of the National Gallery of Art, Washington, D.C. The A. W. Mellon Lectures in the Fine Arts. Bollingen series XXXV. Princeton, NJ: Princeton University Press.

Marks, P. (2002, Feb. 17). Anne Bancroft finds her own way back. *New York Times Online.* Retrieved from NewYorkTimes.com

Martindale, C. (1999). Genetics. In M. Runco & S. Pritzer (Eds.), *Encyclopedia of creativity, Vol. 1. (pp. 767-771).*

Maslow, A. (1968). *Creativity in self-actualizing people. Toward a psychology of being.* New York: Van Nostrand Reinhold Company.

May, R. (1975). *The courage to create.* New York: Bantam.

McCarthy, M. (1987). *How I grew.* New York: Harcourt Brace Jovanovich.

McClure, M. (1966). *Meat science essays.* San Francisco: City Lights Books.

McCrae, R. R., & Costa, P. T. (1999). A five-factor theory of personality. In L. A. Pervin & O. P. John (Eds.), *Handbook of personality theory and research, 2ⁿᵈ ed.* (pp. 139-153). San Diego, CA: Academic Press.

McDonnell, D., & LeCapitaine, J. (1985). *The effects of group creativity training on teachers' empathy and interactions with students.* ERIC ED294858.

McDonough, P., & McDonough, B. (1987). A survey of American colleges and universities on the conducting of formal courses in creativity. *Journal of Creative Behavior, 21,* 271-282.

McFadzean, E. (1999). Creativity in MS/OR: Choosing the appropriate technique. *Interfaces, 29*(5), 110-122.

McGilligan, P. (1994). *Jack's life: A biography of Jack Nicholson.* New York: W. W. Norton.

Mednick, S. (1962). The associative basis of the creative process. *Psychological Review,* 220-232. Washington, DC: American Psychological Association.

Meeker, M. (1973). *Divergent production sourcebook.* Vida, OR: SOI Institute.

Meeker, M., & Meeker, R. (1975). *Structure of Intellect Learning Abilities Test— Examiner's manual.* El Segundo, CA: SOI Institute.

Mellow, J. R. (1974). *Charmed circle: Gertrude Stein & company.* New York: Praeger.

Merrill, J. (1992). Permission to speak. In E. Shelnutt (Ed.), *My poor elephant: 27 male writers at work* (pp. 83-100). Atlanta, GA: Longstreet Press.

Miklus, S. (1989, April). Forum. *Omni,* 16.

Miles, B. (1989). *Ginsberg.* New York: Simon & Schuster.

Millar, G. W. (2001). *The Torrance kids at mid-life: Selected case studies of creative behavior.* Westport, CT: Ablex.

Miller, A. (1981). *Drama of the gifted child.* New York: Doubleday.

Miller, A. (1987). *Timebends.* New York: Harper & Row.

Miller, A. (1990). *The untouched key: Tracing childhood trauma in creativity and destructiveness.* New York: Doubleday.

Miner, J. B. (1997). The expanded horizon for achieving entrepreneurial success. *Organizational Dynamics, 25*(3), 54-67.

Miró, J. (1992). *Selected writings and interviews.* Margit Rowell (Ed.). New York: DeCapo Press.

Modern Mutter: Modern Music. Retrieved on November 24, 2002 from www.ffaire.com/mutter/mutter5.html

Monette, P. (1993). *Becoming a man: Half a life story.* San Francisco: HarperSan Francisco.

Monson, K. (1983). *Alma Mahler: Musto genius.* Boston: Houghton Mifflin.

Montuori, A., & Purser, R. E. (Eds.) (1999). *Social creativity, Vol. I.* Cresskill, NJ: Hampton Press.

Morgan, C. (1933). *The emergence of novelty.* London: Williams & Norgate.

Morgan, D. L., Morgan, R. K., & Toth, J. M. (1992). Variation and selection: The evolutionary analogy and the convergence of cognitive and behavioral psychology. *The Behavior Analyst, 15,* 129-138.

Morrison, M., & Dungan, R. (1992). *The identification of creative thinking ability: A multifactored approach.* Columbus, OH: Ohio Department of Education, Gifted Education Research and Demonstration Project.

Moustakas, C. (1967). *Creativity and conformity.* New York: Van Nostrand.

Moyers, B. (1995). *The language of life: A festival of poets.* New York: Doubleday.

Mullis, K. (1997). The screwdriver. In F. Barron, A. Montuori, & A. Barron (Eds.), *Creators on creating* (pp. 68-73). Los Angeles: Jeremy P. Tarcher/ Putnam.

Murdock, M. (1987). *Spinning inward: Using guided imagery with children for learning, creativity, and relaxation.* Boston: Shambhala.

Murphy, E. (1995). *The developing child.* Gainesville, FL: Center for the Application of Psychological Type.

Murphy, S. M., & Martin, K. A. (2002). The use of imagery in sport. In T. S. Horn (Ed.), *Advances in sport psychology (2nd ed.)* (pp. 405-439). Champaign, IL: Human Kinetics.

Myers, I. B., & McCaulley, M. H. (1985). *Manual: A guide to the development and use of the Myers-Briggs Type Indicator.* Palo Alto, CA: Consulting Psychologists Press.

Myers, S. A. (1983). The Wilson-Barber Inventory of Childhood Memories and Imaginings: Children's form and norms for 1337 children and adolescents. *Journal of Mental Imagery, 7*(3) 83-94.

Nachmanovitch, S. (1990). *Free play: Improvisation in life and art.* Los Angeles: Tarcher.

Naifeh, S., & Smith, G. W. (1989). *Jackson Pollock: An American saga.* New York: Clarkson Potter.

National Science Foundation. (1996). *Women, minorities, and persons with disabilities in science.* Retrieved on June 18, 2003. from www.nsf.gov/sbe/srs/ nsf96311/wmch1.htm

Navarre, J. Piirto (1978). *A study of creativity in poets.* Paper presented at National Association for Gifted Children Conference, Houston, TX.

Navarre, J. Piirto (1979). Incubation as fostering the creative process. *Gifted Child Quarterly, 23,* 792-800.

Navarro, M. (2002, November 27). A life so sad he had to be funny; George Lopez mines a rich vein of gloom with an all-Latino sitcom. *New York Times*, E1, 5.

Nemiro, J. (1999). Acting. In M. Runco & S. R. Pritzker (Eds.), *Encyclopedia of creativity, Vol. I* (pp. 1-8). San Diego, CA: Academic Press.

Nicholson, S. (1996). *Ella Fitzgerald: A biography*. London: Indigo.

Nickerson, R. S. (1999). Enhancing creativity. In R. J. Sternberg (Ed.), *Handbook of creativity* (pp. 392-430). New York: Oxford University Press.

Nixon, L. (1996). Factors predispositional of creativity and mysticism: A comparative study of Charles Darwin and Thérèse of Lisieux. *Advanced Development, 7*, 81-100.

Noller, R. B., Parnes, S. J., & Biondi, A. M. (1976). *Creative actionbook*. New York: Scribners.

Norris, K. (2000). *The cloister walk*. New York: Lion Publishing.

Nowell, E. (1960). *Thomas Wolfe: A biography*. New York: Doubleday & Co.

Oates, J. C. (1988). *(Woman) writer: Occasions and opportunities*. New York: Dutton.

Olajuwon, H. (with Knobler, P.). (1996). *Living the dream: My life and basketball*. Boston: Little, Brown.

Olivier, L. (1967). In H. Burton (Ed.), *Great acting* (pp. 23-32). New York: Hill & Wang. Reprinted in T. Cole & H. Chinoy (Eds.), (1970), *Actors on acting* (pp. 410-417). New York: Crown.

Oreck, B. (1996). *Arts Connection. Talent beyond words*. Report to the United States Department of Education, Office of Education Research and Improvement (#R206A00148).

Oreck, B., & Baum, S. (1994). Talent beyond words: Identifying and developing potential through music and dance in economically disadvantaged, bilingual and handicapped children. In C. M. Callahan, C. A. Tomlinson, & P. M. Pizzat (Eds.), *Contexts for promise: Noteworthy practices and innovations in the identification of gifted students* (pp. 119-144). Charlottesville, VA: National Research Center on the Gifted and Talented at the University of Virginia.

Oreck, B., Owen, S., & Baum, S. (2003, April). *Validity, reliability, and equity issues in an observational Talent Assessment Process in the performing arts*. Paper presented at the Annual Meeting of the American Educational Research Association, Chicago.

Ornstein, R. E. (1993). *The roots of the self*. San Francisco: HarperSan Francisco.

Osborn, A. F. (1963). *Applied imagination*. New York: Scribners.

Ostrander, S. (1979). *Superlearning*. New York: Delacourte.

Oxford English Dictionary, 2nd ed. (1989). Oxford: Clarendon Press.

Oyle, I. (1997). Odyssey. In F. Barron, A. Montuori, & A. Barron (Eds.), *Creators on creating: Awakening and cultivating the imaginative mind* (pp. 150-156). Los Angeles: Jeremy Tarcher/Putnam.

Palmer, A. (with Dodson, J.). (1999). *A golfer's life.* New York: Ballantine.

Panter, B. (Ed.). (1996). *Creativity and madness.* Pasadena, CA: American Medical Education Institute.

Parnes, S. (1967). *Creative behavior guidebook.* New York: Scribners.

Parnes, S. (1981). *The magic of your mind.* Buffalo, NY: Creative Education Foundation.

Parnes, S. (1987). The Creativity Studies Project. In S. Isaksen (Ed.), *Frontiers of creativity research: Beyond the basics* (pp. 1456-1488). Buffalo, NY: Bearly, Ltd.

Passaro, V. (1991, May 19). Dangerous Don DeLillo. *The New York Times Magazine,* 34-38, 76.

Patalano, F. (2000). Psychosocial stressors and the short life spans of legendary jazz musicians. *Perceptual & Motor Skills, 90*(2), 435-436.

Percival, J. (1975). *Nureyev.* New York: Popular Library.

Perkins, D. (1981). *The mind's best work.* Boston: Harvard University Press.

Perkins, D. (1988). The possibility of invention. In R. J. Sternberg (Ed.), *The nature of creativity* (pp. 362-386). New York: Cambridge.

Perry, D. (1993). *Backtalk: Women writers speak out.* New Brunswick, NJ: Rutgers University Press.

Persson, R. (2000). Survival of the fittest or most talented? Deconstructing the myth of the musical maestro. *Journal of Secondary Gifted Education, 12*(1), 25-38.

Petrie, T. A. (1993). Disordered eating in female collegiate gymnasts: Prevalence and personality/attitudinal correlates. *Journal of Sport & Exercise Psychology, 15*(4), 424-436.

Pfeiffer, J. E. (1982). *The creative explosion: An inquiry into the origins of art and religion.* New York: Harper & Row.

Piechowski, M. M., & Cunningham, K. (1985a). Patterns of overexcitability in a group of artists. *Journal of Creative Behavior, 19*(3), 153-174.

Piechowski, M. M., Silverman, L., & Falk, F. (1985). Comparison of intellectually and artistically gifted on five dimensions of mental functioning. *Perceptual and Motor Skills, 60,* 539-549.

Piirto, J. (1985). *The three-week trance diet.* Columbus, OH: Carpenter Press.

Piirto, J. (1987). *The existence of writing prodigy.* Paper presented at the National Association for Gifted Children Conference, New Orleans, LA.

Piirto, J. (1989a). Does writing prodigy exist? *Creativity Research Journal*, *2*, 134-135.

Piirto, J. (1989b, May/June). Linguistic prodigy: Does it exist? *Gifted Children Monthly*, 1-2.

Piirto, J. (1990). Profiles of creative adolescents. *Understanding Our Gifted*, *2*, 1.

Piirto, J. (1990, March). *Creative adolescents at a Governor's Institute*. Paper presented at the Ohio Association For Gifted Children Conference, Columbus, OH.

Piirto, J. (1991a). Encouraging creativity in adolescents. In J. Genshaft & M. Bireley (Eds.), *Understanding the gifted adolescent* (pp. 104-122). New York: Teachers College Press.

Piirto, J. (1991b). Why are there so few? (Creative women: visual artists, mathematicians, musicians). *Roeper Review*, *13*(3), 142-147.

Piirto, J. (1992). The existence of writing prodigy: Children with extraordinary writing talent. In N. Colangelo, S. G. Assouline, & D. Ambroson (Eds.), *Talent development: Proceedings of the 1991 Henry B. and Jocelyn Wallace National Research Symposium on Talent Development* (387-388). Unionville, NY: Trillium Press.

Piirto, J. (1994a). A few thoughts about actors. *Spotlight: Newsletter of the Visual and Performing Arts Division of the National Association for Gifted Children*, *4*(1), 2-5.

Piirto, J. (1994b). *Talented children and adults: Their development and education*. New York: Macmillan.

Piirto, J. (1995a). Deeper and broader: The Pyramid of Talent Development in the context of the giftedness construct. *Educational Forum*, *59*(4), 363-371.

Piirto, J. (1995b). *A location in the Upper Peninsula: Poems, stories, essays*. New Brighton, MN: Sampo Publishing.

Piirto, J. (1995c). Predictive behaviors and crystallizing experiences in male college student artists. *Spotlight: Newsletter of the National Association for Gifted Children Visual and Performing Arts Special Interest Group*, 1, 4.

Piirto, J. (1995d). The Pyramid of Talent Development in the context of the giftedness construct. In *Talent Development*. Proceedings of the European Council for High Ability Conference. University of Nijmegen, The Netherlands.

Piirto, J. (1995e). *Themes in the lives of female creative writers at midlife*. Paper presented at the 1995 Henry B. and Jocelyn Wallace National Research Symposium on Talent Development. Iowa City, IA.

Piirto, J. (1996a). *Between the memory and the experience*. Ashland, OH: Sisu Press.

Piirto, J. (1996b). Why does a writer write? Because. *Advanced Development*, *7*, 39-59.

Piirto, J. (1996c). Women like horses. *Forkroads, 2,* 25.

Piirto, J. (1998a). *Feeling boys and thinking girls: Talented adolescents and their teachers.* Presesnted at the proceedings of the CAPT Conference, Orlando, FL.

Piirto, J. (1998b.) Themes in the lives of contemporary U.S. women creative writers at midlife. *Roeper Review, 21*(1), 60-70.

Piirto, J. (1998c). *Understanding those who create, 2nd ed.* Scottsdale, AZ: Gifted Psychology Press.

Piirto, J. (1999a). A different approach to creativity enhancement. *Tempo, XIX,* 3, 1,

Piirto, J. (1999b). Implications of postmodern curriculum theory for the education of the talented. *Journal for the Education of the Gifted, 22*(4), 386-406.

Piirto, J. (1999c). A survey of psychological studies of creativity. In A. Fishkin, B. Cramond, & P. Olszewski-Kubilius (Eds.), *Investigating creativity in youth.* Cresskill, NJ: Hampton Press.

Piirto, J. (1999, Spring). Asynchrony and the gifted. *Understanding Our Gifted, 11*(3), 12-15.

Piirto, J. (1999, November). Metaphor and image in counseling the talented. *Spotlight: Newsletter of the Arts Division of the National Association for Gifted Children,* 6-7.

Piirto, J. (2000a). How parents and teachers can enhance creativity in children. In M. D. Gold & C. R. Harris (Eds.), *Fostering creativity in children, K-8: Theory and practice* (pp. 49-68). Needham Heights, MA: Allyn & Bacon.

Piirto, J. (2000b). Questions for the education of the gifted and talented. In D. Montgomery (Ed.), *Able underachievers.* London: Whurr Publishers, Ltd.

Piirto, J. (2001). *Journeys to sacred places: Poems.* Ashland, OH: Sisu Press.

Piirto, J. (2001, Spring). Themes in the lives of adult creative writers. *Tempo, XXI,* 2, 4, ff.

Piirto, J. (2001, Winter). The Piirto Pyramid of Talent Development: A conceptual framework. *GCT.*

Piirto, J. (2002). *"My teeming brain": Understanding creative writers.* Cresskill, NJ: Hampton Press.

Piirto, J., Beach, L., Rogers, R., Cassone, G., & Fraas, J. (2000, November). *A comparison of talented teenagers and vocational school teenagers using the Overexcitabilities Questionnaire.* Paper presented at National Association for Gifted Children Conference, Atlanta, Georgia.

Piirto, J., & Fraas, J. (1995). Androgyny in the personalities of talented teenagers. *Journal of Secondary Gifted Education, 2,* 93-102.

Pipher, M. (1995). *Reviving Ophelia.* New York: Ballantine.

Plato. *Dialogues.* In R. Hutchins (Ed.), *Great books of the western world, Vol. 7.* Chicago: University of Chicago Press.

Plato. *The republic.* In R. Ulrich (Ed.), (1954). *Three thousand years of educational wisdom: Selections from great documents* (pp. 31-62). (Trans. P. Shorey). Cambridge, MA: Harvard University Press.

Plimpton. G. (Ed.). (1988). *Writers at work* (8th series). New York: Penguin.

Plimpton, G. (Ed.). (1989). *Women writers at work.* New York: Penguin.

Plsek, P. E. (2000). Creative thinking for surprising quality. *Quality Progress, 33*(5), 67-73.

Poe, E. (1846, April.) The philosophy of composition. *Graham's Magazine of Literature and Art, 28,* 4, 163-164.

Pogrebin, R. (2002, February 3). Out onstage alone, making monologues exciting: A father himself, he's touched by the poetry of fatherhood. *New York Times Online.* Retrieved from NewYorkTimes.com

Policastro, E. (1999). Intuition. In M. Runco & S. Pritzker (Eds.), *Encyclopedia of creativity, Vol. 2* (pp. 89-93). San Diego, CA: Academic Press.

Polkow, D. (1988). Solti speaks: A rare and candid conversation with the Maestro (Part I). *Journal of the Conductors' Guild, 9*(1), 2-15.

Preti, A., deBiasi, F., & Miotto, P. (2001). Musical creativity and suicide. *Psychological Reports, 89,* 719-727.

Preti, A., & Miotto, P. (1999). Suicide among eminent artists. *Psychological Reports, 84,* 291-301.

Project Vanguard: A manual for the identification of creatively gifted students. (1991). Ohio Department of Special Education.

Prose, F. (2002). *The lives of the muses.* New York: HarperCollins.

Radford, J. (1990). *Child prodigies and exceptional early achievers.* New York: Macmillan/ The Free Press.

Random House Dictionary of the English Language, 2nd ed. (1988). New York: Random House.

Rank, O. (1960). *Art and artist.* New York: Knopf.

Razik, T. (1970). Psychometric measurement of creativity. In P. Vernon (Ed.), *Creativity* (pp. 147-156). Harmondsworth: Penguin.

Redgrave, M. (1946). The Stanislavsky myth. *New Theatre, 3,* 16-18. Reprinted in T. Cole & H. Chinoy (Eds.), (1970). *Actors on acting* (pp. 403-408). New York: Crown.

Reed, H. (1985). *Getting help from your dreams.* Virginia Beach, VA: Inner Vision.

Reese, W. (1980). *Dictionary of philosophy and religion: Eastern and western thought.* New Jersey: Humanities Press.

Renzulli, J. (1978). What makes giftedness? Re-examining a definition. *Phi Delta Kappan, 60,* 180-184, 261.

Renzulli, J., Smith, L. H., White, A. J., Callahan, C. M., & Hartman, R. K. (1997). *Scales for rating the behavioral characteristics of superior students.* Mansfield Center, CT: Creative Learning Press.

Reynierse, J. H. (1997). An MBTI model of entrepreneurism and bureaucracy: The psychological types of business entrepreneurs compared to business managers and executives. *Journal of Psychological Type, 40,* 3-19.

Reynolds, F. C. (1990). Mentoring artistic adolescents through expressive therapy. *Clearing House, 64,* 83-86.

Reynolds, F. C. (1997). *Reifying creativity during the adolescent passage.* Paper presented at Ashland University Ohio Summer Institute, July 13, 1997, Ashland, OH.

Reynolds, F. C. (2003, March 28). *Following the call: Wide awake and walking: Creativity and the daimon.* Paper presented at Christopher Urrealist Teach-in, Café Ah-Roma, Berea, OH.

Reynolds, F. C., & Piirto, J.(2002). *Depth psychology and giftedness: Bringing soul to the field of talent development and giftedness.* Paper presented at the National Association for Gifted Children 49th Annual Meeting, Denver, CO.

Rich, A. (1986). *Blood, bread, and poetry: Selected prose.* New York: W. W. Norton.

Rico, G. (1983). *Writing the natural way: Using right brain techniques to release your expressive powers.* Los Angeles: Jeremy Tarcher.

Rico, G. (1991). *Pain and possibility: Writing your way through personal crisis.* Los Angeles: Jeremy Tarcher.

Rimm, S. B. (1986). *Underachievement syndrome: Causes and cures.* Watertown, WI: Apple Publishing Co.

Roberson-Saunders, P. (2001). Minority and female entrepreneurship. In G. Libecap (Ed.), *Entrepreneurial inputs and outcomes: New studies of entrepreneurship in the United States (Advances in the study of entrepreneurship, innovation and economic growth)* (pp. 223-280). Oxford, UK: Elsevier Science, Ltd. (JAI Press).

Robinson, R. (1989). *Georgia O'Keeffe: A life.* New York: Harper & Row.

Robinson, S., & Ritz, D. (1989). *Smokey: Inside my life.* New York: McGraw Hill.

Roe, A. (1952). *The making of a scientist.* New York: Dodd, Mead.

Roe, A. (1963). Psychological approaches to creativity in the sciences. In M. Coler & H. Hughes (Eds.), *Essays on creativity in the sciences.* New York: New York University Press.

Roe, A. (1975). Painters and painting. In C. Taylor & J. Getzels (Eds.), *Perspectives in creativity* (pp. 157-172). Chicago: Aldine.

Roedell, W., Jackson, N., & Robinson, H. (1980). *Gifted young children.* New York: Teachers College Press.

Rogers, C. (1954). Toward a theory of creativity. *ETC: A Review of General Semantics, 11*, 250-258. New York: International Society of General Semantics.

Rogers, C. (1976). Toward a theory of creativity. In A. Rothenberg & C. Hausman (Eds.), *The creativity question* (pp. 296-305). Durham, NC: Duke University Press.

Root-Bernstein, R. S. (1987). Tools of thought: Designing an integrated curriculum for lifelong learners. *Roeper Review, 10*(1), 17-21.

Rosen, C. L. (1985). Review of Creative Activity Packet. In Buros Institute of Mental Measurements, *The Ninth Mental Measurements Yearbook* (Vol. I, pp. 411-412). Lincoln, NE: The University of Nebraska Press.

Rosenthal, A., DeMers, S. T., Stilwell, W., Graybeal, S., & Zins, J. (1983). Comparison of interrater reliability on the Torrance Tests of Creative Thinking for gifted and nongifted students. *Psychology in the Schools, 20*, 35-40.

Rosner, S., & Abt, L. (Eds.). (1970). *The creative experience.* New York: Grossman.

Ross, A. (1994, Nov. 27). Salonen, becoming the next Bernstein? *New York Times, 144*, Sect. 2, 1.

Roth, G. (1992). *The wave.* Videotape. Boston: Shambhala.

Rothenberg, A. (1979). *The emerging goddess: The creative process in art, science, and other fields.* Chicago: University of Chicago Press.

Rothenberg, A. (1990). *Creativity and madness.* Baltimore: Johns Hopkins Press.

Rothenberg, A., & Hausman, C. (Eds.). (1976). *The creativity question.* Durham, NC: Duke University Press.

Rothenberg, A., & Hausman, C. (1988). A comment on the nature of creativity. *Creativity Research Journal, 1*, 123-124.

Rudolf, M. (1987). The conductor's dilemma: The hazards of being judged. *Journal of the Conductors' Guild, 8*(4), 98-106.

Rugg, H. (1963). *Imagination.* New York: Harper & Row.

Runco, M. (1987). The generality of creative performance in gifted and nongifted children. *Gifted Child Quarterly, 31*, 121-125.

Runco, M. (Ed.) (1990a). *Divergent production.* Norwood, NJ: Ablex.

Runco, M. (Ed.) (1990b). *Theories of creativity.* Norwood, NJ: Ablex.

Runco, M. (Ed.) (1994). *Problem finding, problem solving and creativity.* Norwood, NJ: Ablex.

Runco, M., & Albert, R. (1986). The threshold theory regarding creativity and intelligence: An empirical test with gifted and nongifted children. *The Creative Child and Adult Quarterly, 11*, 212-218.

Runco, M., & Pritzker, S. (Eds.). (1999). *Encyclopedia of creativity* (2 vols). San Diego, CA: Academic Press.

Sagarin, S. K., & Gruber, H. (1999). Ensemble of metaphor. In M. Runco & S. Pritzker (Eds.), *Encyclopedia of creativity, Vol. 1* (pp. 677-681). San Diego, CA: Academic Press.

Samples, B. (1976). *The metaphoric mind.* Reading, MA: Addison-Wesley.

Santayana, G. (1896). *The sense of beauty: Being the outline of aesthetic theory.* New York: Dover Publications.

Sarton, M. (1973). *Journal of a solitude.* New York: W. W. Norton.

Sawyer, R. K. (1999). Improvisation. In M. Runco & S. Pritzker (Eds.), *Encyclopedia of creativity, Vol. 2* (pp. 31-38). San Diego, CA: Academic Press.

Scales for Rating the Behavioral Characteristics of Superior Students. (1997). Mansfield Center, CT: Creative Learning Press, Inc.

Schactel, E. (1959). *On the development of affect, perception, attention, and memory.* New York: Basic Books, Inc.

Schank, R. (1988). *The creative attitude.* New York: Macmillan.

Schechner, R. (1985). *Between theater and anthropology.* Philadelphia: University of Pennsylvania Press.

Schickel, R. (1986). *Intimate strangers: The culture of celebrity.* New York: Fromm.

Schlesinger, J. (2002). "Issues in creativity and madness part one: Ancient questions, modern answers. *Ethical Human Sciences and Services, 4*(1), 73-76.

Schorer, M. (1961). *Sinclair Lewis.* New York: Random House.

Schneiderman, L. (1988). *The literary mind: Portraits in pain and creativity.* New York: Insight.

See, C. (1993). *Dreaming: Hard luck and good times in America.* New York: Random House.

Seifert, C. M., Meyer, D. E., Davidson, N., Patalano, A. L., & Yaniv, I. (1995). Demystification of cognitive insight: Opportunistic assimilation and the prepared-mind perspective. In R. J. Sternberg & J. Davidson (Eds.), *The nature of insight* (pp. 65-124). Cambridge, MA: The MIT Press.

Seligman, M. (2002). Positive psychology, positive prevention, and positive therapy. In C. R. Snyder & S. J. Lopez (Eds.), *Handbook of positive psychology* (pp. 3-11). New York: Oxford University Press.

Server, L. (2001). *Robert Mitchum: "Baby, I don't care."* New York: St. Martin's Press.

Shachochis, B. (1995). Breathing space. In N. Baldwin & D. Olsen (Eds.), *The writing life: A collection of essays and interviews with National Book Award winners* (pp. 117-136). New York: Random House.

Shales, T., & Miller, J. A. (2002). *Live from New York.* Boston: Little, Brown.

Shallcross, D. J. (1985). *Teaching creative behavior: How to evoke creativity in children of all ages.* Buffalo, NY: Bearly, Ltd.

Sherman, R., & Thompson, R. (2001). Athletes and disordered eating: Four major issues for the professional psychologist. *Professional Psychology: Research & Practice, 32*(1), 27-33.

Sherry, N. (1989). *The life of Graham Greene, I.* New York: Viking.

Silverman, L. K. (Ed.). (1993). *Counseling the gifted and talented.* Denver, CO: Love Publishing.

Silverman, L. K. (2002). *Upside-down brilliance: The visual-spatial learner.* Denver, CO: DeLeon Publishing.

Simonton, D. K. (1975). Age and literary creativity: A cross-cultural and trans-historical survey. *Journal of Cross-Cultural Psychology, 6,* 259-277.

Simonton, D. K. (1984). *Genius, creativity, and leadership.* Cambridge, MA. Harvard University Press.

Simonton, D. K. (1986). Biographical typicality, eminence and achievement styles. *Journal of Creative Behavior, 20*(1), 17-18.

Simonton, D. K. (1988). *Scientific genius: A psychology of science.* New York: Cambridge University Press.

Simonton, D. K. (1995). *Greatness: Who makes history and why.* New York: The Guilford Press.

Simonton, D. K. (1997). Creative productivity: A predictive and explanatory model of career trajectories and landmarks. *Psychological Review, 104*(1), 66-89.

Simonton, D.K. (1999a). Creativity and genius. In L. A. Pervin & O. P. John (Eds.), *Handbook of personality: Theory and research* (pp. 629-652). New York: The Guilford Press.

Simonton, D. K. (1999b). *Origins of genius: Darwinian perspectives on creativity.* New York: Oxford University Press.

Simonton, D. K. (1999c). Talent and its development: An emergenic and epigenetic model. *Psychological Review, 106*(3), 435-457.

Simonton, D. K. (2002). Creativity. In C. R. Snyder & S. J. Lopez (Eds.), *Handbook of positive psychology* (pp. 189-201). London: Oxford University Press.

Simpson, L. (1972). *North of Jamaica.* New York: Harper & Row.

Singer, J. (1999). Imagination. In M. Runco & S. Pritzker (Eds.), *Encyclopedia of creativity, Vol. 2* (pp. 13-25). San Diego, CA: Academic Press.

Skinner, B. F. (1971). *Beyond freedom and dignity.* New York: Knopf.

Sloane, K. D., & Sosniak, L. A. (1985). The development of accomplished sculptors. In B. Bloom (Ed.), *Developing talent in young people* (pp. 90-138). New York: Ballantine.

Sloboda, J. A., Davidson, J. W., Howe, M. A., & Moore, D. G. (1996). The role of practice in the development of performing musicians. *British Journal of Psychology, 87*(2), 287-309.

Smith, S. I. (1994, March/April). Interview with Poet Laureate Rita Dove. *Poets & Writers Magazine,* 28-35.

Smith, S. M., & Dodds, R. A. (1999). Incubation. In M. Runco & S. Pritzker (Eds.), *Encyclopedia of creativity, Vol. 2* (pp. 39-43). San Diego, CA: Academic Press.

Solomon, D. (1991, March 31). Elizabeth Murray: Celebrating paint. *New York Times Magazine,* 20-25, 40, 46.

Sosniak, L. (1985). Learning to be a concert pianist. In B. Bloom (Ed.), *Developing talent in young people* (pp. 19-66). New York: Ballantine.

Spolin, V. (1963). *Improvisation for the theatre.* Evanston, IL: Northwestern University Press.

Spoto, D. (1985). *The kindness of strangers: The life of Tennessee Williams.* Boston: Little, Brown.

Stack, S. (1996). Gender and suicide risk among artists: A multivariate analysis. *Suicide & Life Threatening Behavior, 26,* 374-379.

Stanislavski, S. (1935/1964). *An actor prepares.* New York: Routledge.

Stanley, J., & Benbow, C. (1986). Youths who reason exceptionally well mathematically. In R. J. Sternberg & J. Davidson (Eds.), *Conceptions of giftedness* (pp. 361-387). New York: Cambridge University Press.

Stanton, D. (1991). An interview with John Irving. *Poets and Writers, 19*(3), 15-21.

Starko, E. (2001). *Creativity: Schools of curious delight* (2nd ed.). Mahwah, NJ: Longman.

Stearns, D. P. (1993, January). Interview with Salonen. *Stereo Review, 5*(8), 61.

Stein, M. (1953). Creativity and culture. *Journal of Psychology, 36,* 311-322.

Stein, M. (1986). *Gifted, talented, and creative young people: A guide to theory, teaching, and research.* New York: Garland Reference Company.

Sternberg, R. J. (1985). *Beyond IQ: A triarchic theory of human intelligence.* New York: Cambridge University Press.

Sternberg, R. J. (Ed.). (1988a). *The nature of creativity.* New York: Cambridge.

Sternberg, R. J. (1988b). *The triarchic mind: A new theory of human intelligence.* New York: Viking.

Sternberg, R. J. (Ed.). (1999). *Handbook of creativity.* New York: Cambridge University Press.

Sternberg, R. J., & Davidson, J. (Eds.). (1995). *The nature of insight.* Cambridge, MA: The MIT Press.

Sternberg, R. J., & Davidson, J. (1999). Insight. In M. Runco & S. Pritzker (Eds.), *Encyclopedia of creativity, Vol. 2* (pp. 57-69). San Diego, CA: Academic Press.

Sternberg, R. J., & Grigorenko, E. (2000). *Teaching for successful intelligence.* Columbus, OH: Prentice Hall.

Sternberg, R. J., Kaufman, J. C., & Pretz, J. (2001). The propulsion model of creative contributions applied to the arts and letters. *Journal of Creative Behavior, 35*(2), 75-101.

Sternberg, R. J., Kaufman, J. C., & Pretz, J. (2002). *The creativity conundrum: A propulsion model of kinds of creative contributions.* Philadelphia: Psychology Press.

Sternberg, R. J., & Lubart, T. I. (1991). An investment theory of creativity and its development. *Human Development, 34,* 1-31.

Sternberg, R. J., & Lubart, T. I. (1995). *Defying the crowd: Cultivating creativity in a culture of conformity.* New York: The Free Press.

Sternberg, R. J., & Lubart, T. I. (1999). The concept of creativity: Prospects and paradigms. In R. J. Sternberg (Ed.), *Handbook of creativity* (pp. 3-9). New York: Cambridge University Press.

Stimpson, D. V., Narayanan, S., & Shanthakumar, D. K. (1993). Attitudinal characteristics of male and female entrepreneurs in the United States and India. *Psychological Studies, 38*(2) 64-68.

Stokes, P. D. (2001). Variability, constraints, and creativity. *American Psychologist, 56*(4), 355-359.

Stone, I. (Ed.). (1937). *Dear Theo.* New York: Doubleday.

Storr, A. (1988). *Solitude: A return to the self.* New York: The Free Press.

Stoutjesdyk, D., & Jevne, R. (1993). Eating disorders among high performance athletes. *Journal of Youth and Adolescence, 22*(3) 271-282.

Stratton, M. (2001). Akira Kurosawa's dreams: Creating an unconscious autobiography. *The Arts in Psychotherapy, 28,* 103-108.

Stravinsky, I. (1990). On conductors and conducting. *Journal of the Conductors' Guild, 11*(1 & 2), 9-18.

Stravinsky, I. (1997). Poetics of music. In F. Barron, A. Montuori, & A. Barron (Eds.), *Creators on creating: Awakening and cultivating the imaginative mind* (pp. 189-194). Los Angeles: Jeremy Tarcher/ Putnam.

Stremikis, B. A. (2002). The personal characteristics and environmental circumstances of successful women musicians. *Creativity Research Journal, 14*(1), 85-92.

Styron, W. (1990). *Darkness visible: A memoir of madness.* New York: Random House.

Subotnik, R. F., & Arnold, K. (1996). Success and sacrifice: The costs of talent fulfillment for women in science. In Arnold, K. D., Subotnik, R. F., & Noble, K. D. (Eds.), *Remarkable women: Perspectives on female talent development* (pp. 263-280). Cresskill, NJ: Hampton Press, Inc.

Subotnik, R. F., Duschl, R. A., & Selmon, E. H. (1993). Retention and attrition of science talent: A longitudinal study of Westinghouse Science Talent Search winners. *International Journal of Science Education, 15*, 61-72.

Subotnik, R. F., & Steiner, C. L. (1994). Adult manifestations of adolescent talent in science: A longitudinal study of 1983 Westinghouse Science Talent Search winners. In R. F. Subotnik & K. D. Arnold (Eds.), *Beyond Terman: Contemporary longitudinal studies of giftedness and talent* (pp. 52-76). Norwood, NJ: Ablex.

Sulloway, F. (1996). *Born to rebel: Birth order, family dynamics, and creative lives.* New York: Pantheon Books.

Suzuki, S. (1983). *Nurtured by love: The classic approach to talent education.* Smithtown, NY: Exposition Press.

Swafford, J. (1996). *Charles Ives: A life with music.* New York: W. W. Norton.

Tannenbaum, A. (1983). *Gifted children: Psychological and educational perspectives.* New York: Macmillan.

Taub, D. E., & Blinde, E. M. (1994). Disordered eating and weight control among adolescent female athletes and performance squad members. *Journal of Adolescent Research, 9*(4) 483-97.

Taylor, C. W. (1969). The highest talent potentials of man. *Gifted Child Quarterly, 13,* 9-30.

Taylor, I. (1959). The nature of the creative process. In P. Smith (Ed.), *Creativity: An examination of the creative process* (pp. 51-82.). New York: Hastings House.

Taylor, L. (1970). The quality most necessary. In T. Cole & H. K. Chinoy, *Actors on acting* (pp. 596-600). New York: Crown Publishers.

Terry, W. (1971). *Dance in America.* New York: Harper & Row.

Thompson, B. (1963). Interview with Katherine Anne Porter. In G. Plimpton (Ed.), *Women writers at work: The Paris Review interviews* (pp. 45-69). New York: Penguin.

Thorndike, E. (19ll). *Animal intelligence.* New York: Macmillan.

Tipton, J. (1995). *The wizard of is.* Denver, CO: Bread & Butter Press.

Tipton, J. (1998). *Letters from a stranger.* Crested Butte, CO: Conundrum Press.

Tofler, I., & DiGeronimo, T. F. (2000). *Keeping your kids out front without kicking them from behind: How to nurture high-achieving athletes, scholars, and performing artists.* San Francisco: Jossey-Bass.

Tomlinson-Keasey, C., & Little, T. (1990). Predicting educational attainment, occupational achievement, intellectual skill, and personal adjustment among gifted men and women. *Journal of Educational Psychology, 82*(1), 442-455.

Torrance, E. P. (1966). *Torrance tests of creative thinking: Norms-technical manual.* Princeton, NJ: Personnel Press.

Torrance, E. P. (1974). *Torrance tests of creative thinking: Norms and technical manual.* Lexington, MA: Personnel Press/Ginn-Xerox.

Torrance, E. P. (1979). *The search for satori and creativity.* Buffalo, NY: Bearly, Ltd.

Torrance, E. P. (1987a). Recent trends in teaching children and adults to teach creatively. In S. Isaksen. (Ed.), *Frontiers of creativity research: Beyond the basics* (pp. 204-215). Buffalo, NY: Bearly, Ltd.

Torrance, E. P. (1987b). Teaching for creativity. In S. Isaksen, (Ed.), *Frontiers of creativity research: Beyond the basics* (pp. 190-215). Buffalo, NY: Bearly, Ltd.

Torrance, E. P. (2002). *The manifesto: A guide to developing a creative career.* Westport, CT: Ablex Publishing.

Torrance, E. P., Bruch, C., & Torrance, J. P. (1978). Interscholastic futuristic problem solving. *Journal of Creative Behavior, 10,* 117-125.

Torrance, E. P., & Goff, K. (1989). A quiet revolution. *Journal of Creative Behavior, 23,* 112-118.

Torrance, E. P., & Myers, R. E. (1970). *Creative learning and teaching.* New York: Dodd-Mead.

Torrance, E. P., & Safter, H. T. (1989). The long range predictive validity of the Just Suppose Test. *Journal of Creative Behavior, 23,* 219-223.

Torrance, E. P., & Safter, H. T. (1999). *Making the creative leap beyond.* Buffalo, NY: Creative Education Foundation Press.

Tranter, J. (1986). Interview with John Ashbery, New York City, 20 April 1985. *Scripsi, 4*(1).

Treffinger, D.(1987). Research on creativity assessment. In S. Isaksen (Ed.), *Frontiers of creativity research: Beyond the basics* (pp. 103-119). Buffalo, NY: Bearly, Ltd.

Updike, J. (1989). *Self-consciousness: Memoirs.* New York: Knopf.

Van Gogh, V. (1937). *Dear Theo.* I. Stone (Ed.). New York: Doubleday.

Van Gogh, V. (Letters). Retrieved on June 15, 2003 from www.artmuseum.net/vangogh/ catalog

Vernon, P. E. (1986). Creativity. In R. Harré & R. Lamb (Eds.), *The dictionary of developmental and educational psychology* (pp. 44-46). Cambridge, MA: The MIT Press.

von Oech, R. (1983). *A whack on the side of the head.* New York: Warner.

von Oech, R. (1986). *A kick in the seat of the pants.* New York: Harper & Row.

Vygotsky, L. (1962). *Thought and language.* Boston: MIT Press.

Wagar, J. (1991). *Conductors in conversation: Fifteen contemporary conductors discuss their lives and profession.* Boston: G. K. Hill.

Wakefield, D. (1991). *Returning.* New York: Houghton Mifflin.

Wakefield, D. (1995). *New York in the 50's.* New York: Houghton Mifflin.

Wallach, M. (1971). *The creativity-intelligence distinction.* New York: General Learning Press.

Wallach, M., & Kogan, N. (1965). *Modes of thinking in young children: A study of the creativity-intelligence distinction.* New York: Holt, Rinehart, & Winston, Inc.

Wallas, G. (1926). *The art of thought.* New York: Harcourt Brace Jovanovich.

Wapnick, J., Mazza, J. K., & Darrow, A. (1998). Effects of performer attractiveness, stage behavior, and dress on violin performance evaluation. *Journal of Research in Music Education, 46*(4), 510-521.

Ward, T. B. (2001). Creative cognition, conceptual combination, and the creative writing of Stephen R. Donaldson. *American Psychologist, 56*(4), 350-354.

Ward, T. B., Smith, S. M., & Finke, R. A. (1999). Creative cognition. In R. J. Sternberg (Ed.), *Handbook of creativity* (pp. 189-212). New York: Cambridge University Press.

Warner, M. (1981). Interview with Rebecca West. In G. Plimpton (Ed.), *Women writers at work: The Paris Review interviews* (pp. 71-105). New York: Penguin.

Watson, J. (1958). *Behaviorism.* Chicago: University of Chicago Press.

Weiner, J. (1990). *The next one hundred years: Shaping the fate of our living earth.* New York: Bantam.

Weintraub, G. (2001, April 22). A step forward in a campaign for the fat girls. *New York Times Online.* Retrieved from NewYorkTimes.com

Weisberg, R. (1986). *Creativity: Genius and other myths.* New York: W. H. Freeman.

Weisberg, R. (1999). Creativity and knowledge: A challenge to theories. In R. J. Sternberg (Ed.), *Handbook of creativity* (pp. 226-249). New York: Cambridge University Press.

Weisskopf, V. (1990). *The joy of insight: Passions of a physicist.* New York: Basic Books.

Weisskopf, V., Joelson, E., & Eliseo, T. (1961). An experimental study of the effectiveness of brainstorming. *Journal of Applied Psychology, 45*, 45-49.

Weissman, P. (1967). Theoretical considerations of ego regression and ego functions in creativity. *Psychoanalytic Quarterly, 36,* 37-50.

Welsh, G. S. (1975). *Creativity and intelligence: A personality approach.* Chapel Hill, NC: Institute for Research in Social Science.

Wertheimer, M. (1959). *Productive thinking.* New York: Harper & Row.

Wetzig, D. L. (1990). Sex-role conflict in female athletes: A possible marker for alcoholism. *Journal of Alcohol and Drug Education, 35*(3), 45-53.

Wilkinson, A. (2002, November 25). The gift: Paul Simon's search for the next song. *The New Yorker,* 64-75.

Williams, F. (1970). *Classroom ideas for encouraging thinking and feeling.* Buffalo, NY: D.O.K.

Williamson, A., & Valentine, E. (2000). Quantity and quality of musical practice as predictors of performance quality. *British Journal of Psychology, 91*(3), 353-376.

Winner, E. (1996). *Gifted children.* New York: Basic Books.

Wittig, A. F., & Shurr, K. T. (1994). Psychological characteristics of women volleyball players: Relationships with injuries, rehabilitation, and team success. *Personality and Social Psychology Bulletin, 20*(3), 322-330.

Wolff, T. (1989). *This boy's life: A memoir.* New York: Atlantic Monthly Press.

Woody, R. (1999). The musician's personality. *Creativity Research Journal, 12*(4), 241-250.

Woolf, V. (1929). *A room of one's own.* London: Oxford University.

Woolf, V. (1954). *A writer's diary.* New York: Harcourt Brace Jovanovich.

Wright, F. L. (1932/1977). *An autobiography.* New York: Horizon Press.

Wrisberg, C. A. (1988). Sex role orientations of male and female collegiate athletes from selected individual and team sports. *Sex Roles: A Journal of Research, 19*(1-2), 81-90.

Wubbenhorst, T. M. (1994). Personality characteristics of music educators and performers. *Psychology of Music, 22*(1), Special Issue: Assessment in music, 63-74.

Wuthnow, R. (2001). *Creative spirituality: The way of the artist.* Berkeley, CA: University of California Press.

Zakrajsek, D. B., Johnson, R. I., & Walker, D. B. (1984). Comparison of learning styles between physical education and dance majors. *Perceptual and Motor Skills, 58,* 583-588.

Zimmerman, B. J., Bandura, A., & Martinez-Pons, M. (1992). Self-motivation for academic attainment: The role of self-efficacy beliefs and personal goal setting. *American Educational Research Journal, 29*(3), 329-339.

Zuckerman, H. (1977). *The scientific elite.* New York: Free Press.

Index

About the Author

JANE PIIRTO is Trustees' Professor in the School of Education at Ashland University in Ashland, Ohio, where she is the Director of Talent Development Education. She is a native of the Upper Peninsula of Michigan and has her undergraduate degree in English from Northern Michigan University. She has an M.A. in English from Kent State University, an M.Ed. in counseling from South Dakota State University, and a Ph.D. in school leadership from Bowling Green State University.

She has been a high school teacher, a counselor, a college instructor of humanities, a coordinator of programs for the talented, Principal of the Hunter College Elementary School, and an artist in the schools in Michigan, South Dakota, Ohio, and New York City. She has served as a consultant and speaker in Europe, the Near East, Southern Asia, South America, and throughout the United States. She has been a Visiting Professor at the University of Georgia.

Her *Understanding Those Who Create* has been translated into Chinese. She has published over a hundred poems, short stories, and articles, and thirteen books and chapbooks, among them *Talented Children and Adults* (2 editions), *Understanding Those Who Create* (2 editions), *"My Teeming Brain" Understanding Creative Writers*, *Luovuus, A Location in the Upper Peninsula* (collected poems, stories, and essays), *The Three-Week Trance Diet* (novel), *mamamama*, *Postcards from the Upper Peninsula*, *Between the Memory and the Experience*, *Silent Midnight Snow Comes Down*, *Journeys to Sacred Places* (poetry chapbooks).

She has received two Individual Artist Fellowships—one in fiction and one in poetry—from the Ohio Arts Council, and a grant from the Fulbright-Hays Foundation.

She has two grown children and a granddaughter.